Mercer Commentary on the Bible

Volume 7

Acts and Pauline Writings

Mercer University Press

Mercer Dictionary of the Bible
July 1990; 5th and corrected printing July 1997

Mercer Dictionary of the Bible Course Syllabi
July 1990

Mercer Commentary on the Bible
November 1994

Cover illustration: *The Apostle Paul in Prison*, by Rembrandt Harmensz van Rijn (1606–1669). Staatsgalerie, Stuttgart. Oil on wood panel, 28¼×23¾ in.

Mercer Commentary on the Bible

Volume 7

Acts and
Pauline Writings

GENERAL EDITORS
Watson E. Mills, Richard F. Wilson

ASSOCIATE EDITORS
Roger A. Bullard, Walter Harrelson, Edgar V. McKnight

MERCER UNIVERSITY PRESS EDITOR
Edmon L. Rowell, Jr.

WITH MEMBERS OF THE
National Association of Baptist Professors of Religion

MERCER UNIVERSITY PRESS
March 1997

ISBN 0-86554-512-X   MUP/P139

Mercer Commentary on the Bible: Acts and Pauline Writings
Volume 7 of an 8-volume perfect-bound reissue of
the *Mercer Commentary on the Bible* (©1995).
Copyright ©1997
Mercer University Press, Macon GA 31210-3960

The paper used in this publication meets the minimum requirements
of the American National Standard for Information Sciences—
Permanence of Paper for Printed Library Materials, ANSI Z39.48-1984.

Library of Congress Cataloging-in-Publication Data

Mercer commentary on the Bible.
Volume 7. Acts and Pauline Writings /
general editors, Watson E. Mills and Richard F. Wilson;
associate editors, Walter Harrelson . . . [et al.].
lxxx+292 (=372) pp. 6x9" (15x23cm.).
1. Bible—commentaries. I. Mills, Watson Early. II. Mercer University Press.
III. National Association of Baptist Professors of Religion.

CIP data available from the Library of Congress.

Contents

Commentaries (from the *Mercer Commentary on the Bible*)

Preface

This volume includes the commentaries on the Acts of the Apostles and the "Pauline" writings (Romans–Philemon, that is, including those of uncertain authorship) from the *Mercer Commentary on the Bible* (MCB) plus several appropriate articles from the *Mercer Dictionary of the Bible* (MDB). This MCB/MDB fascicle is for use in the classroom and for any other setting where study focuses on the Acts and Pauline writings and where a convenient introduction text is desired. This is number 7 in the series of MCB/MDB portions or fascicles.

1. Pentateuch/Torah (Genesis–Deuteronomy)   Isbn 0-86554-506-5 P133
2. History of Israel (Joshua–Esther)   Isbn 0-86554-507-3 P134
3. (Wisdom) Writings (Job–Song of Songs)   Isbn 0-86554-508-1 P135
4. Prophets (Isaiah–Malachi)   Isbn 0-86554-509-X P136
5. Deuterocanonicals/Apocrypha   Isbn 0-86554-510-3 P137
6. Gospels (Matthew–John)   Isbn 0-86554-511-1 P138
7. Acts and Pauline Writings (Acts–Philemon)Isbn 0-86554-512-X P139
8. Epistles and Revelation (Hebrews–Revelation) Isbn 0-86554-513-8 P140

That these divisions—and their titles—are arbitrary is obvious. These divisions originate in the classroom as convenient and provisionally appropriate blocks of text for focused study during a semester- or quarter-long course of study. Other divisions are possible, perhaps even desirable (combining Acts with the Gospels, for example, rather than with Paul), but the present divisions seem appropriate for most users.

Regarding the use of this and other MCB/MDB portions, please note the following.

A bracketed, flush-right entry at the head of each MDB article and MCB commentary indicates the original page number(s): for example, "Acts [MCB 1083-1122]"; "Justification [MDB 483-84]." The text of both MDB and MCB is essentially that of the original, differing only in format; that is, the text is here redesigned to fit a 6x9-inch page (the page size of both MDB and MCB is 7x10 inches). In addition, however, we have taken advantage of the opportunity of this fascicle reprint to make some corrections and (minor) revisions.

References to other MDB articles are indicated by small caps: for example, WE-SECTIONS on p. 2 of the Acts commentary and ACHAIAH on p. 42 refer to the articles on We-Sections and Achaiah in MDB. In addition, the "See also" sections at the end of the MDB articles indicate other articles that are appropriate for further study. (MDB has introductory articles for every book of the Bible, including those routinely referred to as apocryphal and/or deuterocanonical. Yet these articles are *not* reprinted here, and MCB does *not* include small-caps references to these MDB introduction articles unless reference is made to a specific statement in the article. It is assumed the reader is aware of these MDB introductory articles and will refer to them as needed.)

Notice that small caps are used also for B.C.E. and C.E., for certain texts and versions (LXX, KJV, NRSV), and for the tetragrammaton YHWH.

For abbreviations, see the lists in either MDB or MCB. Regarding the editors and contributors, please see both MDB and MCB. The *Course Syllabi* handbook has a complete listing of MDB articles (pp. 73-80). MDB includes a complete listing of articles arranged by contributor (pp. 989-93).

We intend that these texts be available, appropriate, and helpful for Bible students both in and out of the classroom and indeed for anyone seeking guidance in uncovering the abundant wealth of the Scriptures. Your critical response to these and other texts from Mercer University Press is most welcome and encouraged.

March 1997   *Edmon L. Rowell, Jr.*
Macon, Georgia USA   Mercer University Press

Introduction

Of Apostles and Others in the Early Church

Apostle/Apostleship [MDB 47-48]

•**Apostle/Apostleship.** *Apostle* (a transliteration of the Gk. ἀπόστολος) appears in the NT with the general meaning of "messenger" and as the specific designation of the twelve disciples of JESUS. In historical usage, the specific identification of *apostles* and THE TWELVE has prevailed.

Jesus called twelve disciples who served as the nucleus of his missionary ministry. They were the primary witnesses of his life, teachings, death, and resurrection. The number twelve was so important that a replacement was sought when Judas killed himself. (Matthias replaced Judas [Acts 1:26], but does not thereafter figure in Christian history.) As indicated in Acts 15, the Twelve were very important leaders in the Jerusalem church.

A brief concordance review reveals that the two NT writers who speak most of apostles are LUKE and PAUL. It also is noticeable that in Paul's writings persons other than the Twelve are called apostles. In one passage (1 Cor 15:5ff.) Paul spoke of the Twelve and of "all the apostles" (v 7). Evidently, when Paul wrote his letters, the term had not yet been identified specifically with the Twelve. For example, Paul included the obscure Andronicus and Junia among the apostles (Rom 16:7). He spoke of Epaphroditus as the *apostle* from Philippi (Phil 2:25), but most English translations rightly translate the term here as "messenger."

Antecedents to NT Apostles. The apostle is "one sent" on a mission (ἀποσ-τέλλειν = "to send"). In Greek literature prior to the NT the word appeared often and meant *messenger, delegate, envoy,* or *ambassador.* It even designated a fleet, an expedition, or an admiral. Itinerant teachers and proclaimers were called apostles, but the term did not designate religious teachers prior to the NT.

Numerous scholars have sought to interpret the apostles of the NT against the background of a certain type of Hebrew messenger or agent. Harnack in particular interpreted the NT apostolate in light of the Hebrew institution of agents representing persons of authority. Most of the Hebrew information on Jewish "apostles" comes not from pre-Christian but post-Christian literature. These messengers may be related to the general use of apostle in the NT, but we must look to the NT itself for an understanding of apostleship.

The Apostle Paul. Paul's preferred identification of himself was the term *apostle* (see the beginning of his letters to Rome, Corinth, Galatia, Ephesus, Colossae,

Timothy, and Titus). Paul could not have used the title for himself if the term had already been limited to the Twelve.

The challenge to Paul's authority came to focus on his claim of apostleship (1 Cor 9; Gal 1). Paul defended his apostleship in terms of his call and commission from God and from the Lord Jesus Christ.

Paul's defense of his apostleship appears specifically in Galatians and rather clearly in Romans and 1-2 Corinthians. Paul's understanding of his apostleship reflects an almost total dependence on the Hebrew prophetic consciousness and very little dependence on those who had been apostles before him (Gal 1 and 2).

The Hebrew PROPHET was conscious of (1) a call from God, (2) a mission for God, and (3) a message to proclaim (Robinson). Paul's discussion of his own apostolic call, mission, and message is strikingly similar to that of the Hebrew prophet. He even states his own call by quoting Jeremiah (Gal 1:15; cf. Jer 1:4-5). In short, Paul contended that God had called him to his apostleship to the Gentiles, and had given him a mission that focused on the proclamation of the gospel.

Paul's experience on the Damascus Road entitled him to list himself as one of the witnesses of the resurrection of Jesus (1 Cor 15:8). This is almost certainly the basis also of his claim that his gospel is genuine (Gal 1).

The other apostles certainly included the Twelve who were leaders in Jerusalem. But Paul also recognized a larger or more general group of apostles (1 Cor 15:7) and specific individuals such as Andronicus, Junia, and Epaphroditus who were not among the Twelve.

The Twelve Apostles. While the writers of the Gospels most often spoke of Jesus' closest disciples as *the Twelve,* or *the disciples,* or *the twelve disciples,* they also spoke of *the twelve apostles* and *the apostles* (Matt 10:2; Mark 3:14; Luke 6:13). It is probable that Paul's popularization of the term in his letters—which were written and circulated earlier than the Gospels—led to the identification of the Twelve as *the* apostles.

In his Gospel and in Acts, Luke used the term thirty-four times. Paul (omitting the Pastorals) used the term twenty-eight times. These two writers thus are the primary witnesses for understanding the concept. Luke clearly identified the apostles as that special group of twelve who were Jesus' disciples from the time of Jesus' baptism and witnesses of the resurrection (Luke 6:13; Acts 1:22).

In the Book of Acts, the apostles held a special place in the early church because of their previous relationship with Jesus. They appear to be a council in the Jerusalem Conference (Acts 15), but strangely are not mentioned after Acts 16:4.

The apostles of the NT were the primary witnesses of Jesus and gospel events. Their authority was related to that witness. The NT writings were later selected or canonized because they were "apostolic," either written by an apostle of bearing apostolic authority because of the association of the writer with an apostle (Mark with Peter, Luke with Paul). Such apostolicity was the guarantee of the writings' reliability.

Apostleship. The traditional understanding of apostles is that they are the twelve disciples chosen by Jesus with Matthias replacing Judas, and somehow including Paul whose inclusion is never satisfactorily explained. (Some speculate that Paul instead of Matthias was the choice of the Holy Spirit.)

The role of the apostles was that of being the primary witnesses (WITNESS) of Jesus' life, teaching, death, and resurrection—the gospel. They testify to its truthfulness. As such, they were important in the formation of the NT. As primary witnesses they were irreplaceable. Other terms designate later ministers. Contemporary attempts to reestablish the office do not enjoy great acceptance.

The authority of the apostles derives from their firsthand knowledge of Jesus, the true authority for Christian faith.

See also CHURCH; DISCIPLE/DISCIPLESHIP; JESUS; PAUL; PROPHET; THE TWELVE.

Bibliography. H. F. Camperhausen, "Der Urchristliche Apostelbegriff," ST 1 (1947): 95-130; C. H. Dodd, *The Apostolic Preaching and Its Development*; F. Gavin, "Shaliach and Apostolos," ATR 9 (1927): 250-59; A. Harnack, *The Mission and Expansion of Christianity in the First Three Centuries*; K. Kirk, ed., *The Apostolic Ministry*; H. Knight, *The Hebrew Prophetic Consciousness*; T. W. Manson, *The Church's Ministry*; H. Mosbech, "Apostolos in the New Testament," ST 2 (1948): 166-200; J. Munch, "Paul, the Apostles, and the Twelve," ST 3 (1949): 96-110; K. H. Rengstorf, ἀποστέλλω, κτλ., TDNT; H. W. Robinson, *The Religious Ideas of the Old Testament*; H. Vogelstein, "The Development of the Apostolate in Judaism and Its Transformation in Christianity," HUCA 2 (1925): 99-123.

—MORRIS ASHCRAFT

Church [MDB 150-53]

•Church. "Church" is the English translation of Gk. *ekklēsia* which means "assembly" or "gathering." In the NT, the word *ekklēsia* is never used to refer to a building or to a denomination. It always refers to a group of people, either local congregations, all believers in a locality, or the whole people of God.

The significance of the NT word *ekklēsia* comes from its earlier use in the Greek translation of the OT (the LXX) to refer to the people of God. In the LXX, *ekklēsia* is used ordinarily to translate the Heb. *qâhâl*, "assembly." The Hebrew and Greek words were themselves of no religious significance. They became religiously significant when qualified by the words "God," "Lord," "Most High," etc. Thus, the "assembly of the Lord" (Deut 23:2ff.) and the "assembly of the faithful" (Ps 149:1). The actual character of the *ekklēsia* (as the people of God) is, therefore, not indicated by the word as such; it rather takes its character from the Lord who summons the people to himself, and by the quality of the interest and commitment of those who compose this "assembly" or "congregation."

In its most comprehensive meaning, the church is the whole company of those, in all times and places, who unite themselves, in loyalty and obedience, to God's activity in the world. The church is *the people of God*, the people who acknowledge God's rule as king and father, those whom he has made peculiarly his own through grace, who have trustingly responded to his judgment and goodness and made themselves free servants of his will. Various metaphors or images are more important for indicating the quality or character of the church than is the word *ek-klēsia* itself. Just as ISRAEL, the church has been called "out of Egypt" and brought into full inheritance of the COVENANT promises. Its members function as one body (the instrument for Christ's continuing self-expression in the world); they are the vineyard God tends, the flock he shepherds, the temple he visits, the household of those who are brothers and sisters because they are made sons and daughters of their Father in heaven. They are a "colony of heaven," a fellowship of the divine spirit, a paradigm on earth of the heavenly Kingdom—an approximation in history to the eschatological summation of all things.

Three of these ideas have been treated as most potent both biblically and theologically in the Christian tradition. These are church as: (1) the congregation of the faithful; (2) the BODY OF CHRIST; and (3) the fellowship of the HOLY SPIRIT.

The Congregation of the Faithful. The people of God are gathered (from the world and unto God) either locally (Acts 8:1), or regionally (Acts 9:31; Gal 1:22). They also are regarded generally as the whole of those through whom God now manifests his many-sided wisdom (Eph 3:10). They are gathered in the name of Jesus Christ for the worship and service of God. Remembering its roots in Israel, this "congregation" of God in Christ (while not excluding Israel nor taking Israel's place: Moltmann) may claim the promises and blessings and calling that belong also to Israel as the covenant people (Heb 8:8-10). Thus, in the NT, descriptions of the church's life will make reference to the twelve tribes of Israel (Matt 19:28; Luke 22:30), or to the true CIRCUMCISION (Rom 2:29), or to the descent (even of faithful Gentiles) from Abraham (Gal 3:29). Throughout the NT, the church is perceived, also, as a pilgrim and sojourning people—like Israel in Egypt (Heb 11:26; 1 Pet 1:17). This NT people's central rite of worship, the Eucharist, is a redefinition and renewal of the feast of Passover and possibly of the Jewish *Haburah,* a more or less formal meal among devout companions (cf. 1 Cor 10; Mark 6:30-44; Luke 22:1-30). The fact of this community, as an organ through which God is ruling, evokes memories and sentiments associated with the throne of David (Isa 9:7; Luke 1:32-33; Acts 2:30; Col 1:13): Messiah shall reign, and the faithful shall gather at his great feast (Luke 16:23) and reign with him (2 Tim 2:12; Rev 11:15; 22:5).

These people are *one people* on the basis of their common faith in God through Christ. This oneness of faith is not the same as uniformity of doctrine. If the early Christians are one in their commitment to Christ, they certainly are diverse in their ways of understanding the reality and mystery that Christ was and is. All confess faith in Jesus Christ as Lord, but the Christological perspectives which interpret this basic confession are varied indeed (cf. the Christological understanding, e.g., of Luke with John, or of Colossians with Hebrews).

The church, then, is a renewed Israel brought to its fulfillment (as Christians saw the matter) in the great redemption of Jesus as the Christ. This is their identity: God's people in Christ, Messiah's people. They function in history as a priestly people (Exod 19:3-6; 1 Pet 2:5; Rev 5:10), representing God to the peoples and the peoples to God. They embody faith as trustful obedience, and are in one sense stewards of faith. They embody faith as faithfulness, loyalty, moral commitment—not faith as approved beliefs about God. They are stewards of faith, not as its custodian or *magister*, but as its servants, its witnesses, its interpreters. Their aim, essentially ethical in its sense and direction, is to have among themselves the mind that was also in Christ Jesus (Phil 2:5-8).

This perspective on church as the company of God's faithful people is supported by the whole NT. Jesus' earliest message of the Kingdom is a call to a trusting of life to God as king (Mark 1:15). The apostolic preaching in Jerusalem, in the earliest phase, treated faith as decisive at every point: faith was seen as the means (and, in that sense, as the condition) for entry into the heritage of God's children (Acts 3:16; 4:32; 16:31). John's Gospel even defines the *work* of God as "believing in Jesus whom God has sent" (John 6:29).

It is, however, in Paul that emphasis upon *faith,* as constitutive of the church and as the only proper corollary to revelation and redemption, is given strongest expression. This is the emphasis especially in Galatians and Romans. In Paul, FAITH is given precedence over law (LAW IN THE NT), as in connection with the covenant with Abraham. This giving of precedence to faith over law leads Paul into a full doctrine of the church as those justified by faith—that is the whole of God's people who are put right with God on the basis of faithful obedience (loyal trust) towards God in terms of Jesus Christ. This justification (and clearly the apostle means justification *sola fide*) brings peace (the cessation of our resistance to God through satisfaction with our own righteousness); it gives access to grace, and a joyful hope; it builds firm character in the freedom and power to the Holy Spirit (Rom 5:1-5). In short, all the blessings of the "divine society" come to us through faith.

Looking at this side of the church's reality, it can be said that the "faithful people of God" are constituted solely on the basis of the divine calling, divine promise, and divine guidance as these are responded to in trustful obedience. In short, *the church is constituted by the Word of God as answered by faith.* (I take BAPTISM to be primarily a "visible *word* of God," and a "confession of *faith*.") This society of faith rests on the ancient promise, is nurtured on the continuing Presence, and moves with God through history towards a divine goal. An illustration of the importance of images for conveying the idea of church is the fact that, while the word "church" is absent from Rom 1–15 (appearing only in chap. 16, in the greetings and blessings), the whole letter is as much a statement on the church and the church's life in the world as it is on justification by faith.

The Body of Christ. This important Pauline image presents the church as those who have been incorporated into Christ. Commonly, the outward sign of this incorporation, its symbol, and (in one sense) its seal, is baptism. We are baptized *into Christ* (Rom 6:3). Beyond the suggestiveness intrinsic to this metaphor, another idea is especially important for the determination of its meaning: the Hebrew understanding of corporate personality. The individual (who, also in the NT, is never treated as an end in himself or herself) participates *as a member* in "the body of sin," "the old self," the self in "slavery to sin," and as captive to "the body of death" (Rom

6:6; 7:24; 8:10). We arrive in the world as members of a human race which knows guilt, shame, moral apathy, alienation, and "lawlessness." We are affected by this fact from our first breath until our last. We participate, willy-nilly, in the losses and blessings of the human race. It is this race Christ died to redeem. The race is redeemed! The continued existence of the race is its opportunity to learn what that redemption means and to realize it as a way of life in the world.

But just as we participate as members in the body's sin and loss, so do we live in Christ with all the redeemed. By God's grace we are made *members of his body*; we are "in Christ." Sin, and death which is its issue, no longer hold dominion over us (Rom 8). Christ's life is now given expression even in our mortal body (2 Cor 4:1-12).

One of the most potent of ethical motifs appears in this metaphor of the Apostle. For, we are not only members of Christ and called to share in those virtues and values which God has put forward in him, we are also members one of another—a concrete social organism in which each member has a proper place and value (1 Cor 12:12-27), and upon whom has come an *agapē* equally liberating and compelling (1 Cor 13). Thus each is free; but all are interdependent or mutually obligated.

The life of the body is grounded in the transcendent, but it is exercised in the world. Paul sees the life of the body as a vital, mutual, continuing process whose proximate end is maturity in the graces (Phil 4:8-9), valor in the moral struggle (Eph 6:10-20), and whose final end is glorification and eternal life with him in whom we are given this great salvation (1 Cor 15:51-53), this cosmic freedom (Rom 8:18-21).

This is the vital, mutual, continuing process by which the church becomes what in the design of God it is. There are affinities here, especially for two other metaphors: (1) the vine, emphasizing the location of the church's root in Christ and the production of her fruits through continued association of the branches with the vine (John 15:1-11); and (2) the temple or building, in which we are being built into a "spiritual house," to function as a holy priesthood, to offer "spiritual sacrifices" acceptable to God in Christ—in short, the church as a place of organic life ("*living* stones"), of celebration ("spiritual sacrifices"), of proclamation ("declaring the mighty deeds"), and divine approval ("now you are God's people," 1 Pet 2:4-10).

Such metaphors—that of the body plus these used to extend its meaning—disclose a corporate life in which God's people, Christ's body, is held together in a common life "over which Christ rules, and through which a new creation emerges, a new humanity in Christ" (Minear). Paul coins a phrase with which to characterize this *koinōnia* or communion of life: being "in Christ" (Gal 2:20) and so built into one another through the receiving and sharing of *agapē*.

Here is the ground of the church's unity: Christ is not divided, and those who are "in Christ" are united in Christ—they form his body as *members,* they were baptized *in his name* (1 Cor 1:13). Party spirit, faction, overconfidence in one's own understanding of the gospel—all divide and threaten Christ's body. The Eucharist (1 Cor 10, 11), as the sign of this unity, is a sharing in *one* loaf and *one* cup. Done in faith, in a state of *agapē* with one's neighbor, it is participation (*koinōnia*; Vulgate *participatio*) in the life and redemptive self-giving (the body and blood) of Christ.

The members of this body enter freely (voluntarily, i.e., out of an act of their own volition) into this corporate relationship. But this is an opting for membership in the body; it is not the creation of it. Faithful people volunteer, but the "body of Christ" is only in a secondary sense a "voluntary association of baptized believers." Primarily, it is a living organism whose existence does not depend on the vote of even baptized believers. We have a voice in whether we will be members of the body: we have no voice in whether there is such a body of Christ. For this body has its reality and takes its character not from its members but from its head. Jesus Christ alone is the source of the "sanctification" of this body (Eph 5:26), the truth on which it is built up (Eph 4:15), the moral power by which its members are brought to obedience (Col 2:10), are equipped for ministry and brought to maturity (Eph 4:12-14), and to a unified life in Christ and with each other (Eph 4).

The church as body, then, is the model of Christ's continuing self-expression in the world. This is why the church is sometimes described as "the continuation of the incarnation." I believe it might more helpfully be called (with T. W. Manson) the "extension of our Lord's Messianic ministry."

The Fellowship of the Holy Spirit. Lesslie Newbigin and Jürgen Moltmann have done well to stress this Spirit-dimension of the church's reality. Newbigin has seen the "givenness" of the reality of the church as body as its *organic* (Catholic) dimension; the "given" message, responded to in faith, as the *evangelical* (Protestant) principle, and the emphasis upon church as the community of the "given" Spirit he labels the *Pentecostal* principle. No doctrine of church can be fully a NT doctrine which ascribes small weight to this. The church as "community of the Spirit" exists, to be sure, as those who confess a *common* faith (Eph 4:4-6), it exists as those who know a *common* life in the body of Christ; and it should be noted that the word for "fellowship" (*koinōnia*) means life lived *in common*. But as a *common faith* does not mean unanimity in the understanding of faith, so the common life of the body leaves room for individual members (individual roles and functions). We are "saints," not clones. This *koinōnia* of the Spirit gives prominence to singular experiences, to the freedom of faith and life, to the unpredictable dimensions of faith acting in situations where no "preapproved" guidelines exist. As much as it is anything else at all, the church is "where the Holy Spirit [is] recognizably present with power" (Newbigin). It exists where lives are actually changed, are turned from their condition into their possibility. Little attention is given here to either order or creed. Emphasis falls on the presence, the power, the purpose of God the Spirit (Acts 2, 4, 10). It is this given Spirit who makes us belong to Christ (Rom 8:9); this Spirit is the power and sign of our obedience (Acts 5:32); and this Spirit is the title-deed of our final inheritance (Eph 1:14).

If, however, the Spirit works in members in ways unique to each, in the broadest and deepest sense the Holy Spirit is the *Spirit of the body* (in a quite exact sense, the *esprit de corps*). The NT makes room for spontaneity, for singularity, for the individual member—it is not an encouragement to individualism. The Spirit is given to us as members of the body, to us as those who confess authentic faith with our lives. "Winging it alone," "freelance evangelism," and "untested private revelations" are very difficult to square with a biblically oriented faith. It is the reality and activity of the Holy Spirit that identify the church, and such things that violate the common life and the common faith of Christians also violate the church as the fellowship of God's Spirit.

At the same time, neither does confession, correct doctrine, rightly observing the sacraments, or maintaining membership in an organized church make one a Christian. This is the result alone of God's Holy Spirit bringing us into *living* relationship with Jesus as Savior and Lord. This makes for at least a "semisectarian" potential in the church in its fullness. This is dangerous but nothing is fatal to the church's life if exercized in *agapē*. The reality of the church, the mission of the church, and the hope of the church are guaranteed only in the giving, receiving, and sharing of *agapē*. All the potential one-sidedness of individual spiritual experience is contained within this wholeness.

To conclude: the church is a result of the divine calling (election), is sustained by the divine presence (grace), works with the divine purpose(s) in history (calling), and moves towards the far-off distant goal of creation and the new creation (consummation). The most decisive sign of its "churchliness" appears in terms of its mission in and to the world. "The Church exists by mission as fire exists by burning" (Brunner). It must not simply *have missionaries*; the church must *be mission*. For the church is the servant of God's Word in Christ (Barth); or witness to the New Being (Tillich); or the community whose purpose is the increase of love of God and Neighbor (H. R. Niebuhr); or the embodiment of what the Christian hopes is present as an unrecognized reality even outside organized Christianity (Rahner); or it is that worshiping community which, through faith, receives God's act of justification of sinners as the truth about ourselves and also as hope for the whole world (Wainwright).

Christ loved this church and gave himself up for us all (Eph 5:25). We are related to each other in terms of our relationship to Christ and his church; failure of consideration and kindness towards any one of us is, therefore, to "despise the church of God" (1 Cor 11:22).

See also BAPTISM; BODY OF CHRIST; CIRCUMCISION; COVENANT; FELLOWSHIP; HOLY SPIRIT; ISRAEL; KINGDOM OF GOD; LORD'S SUPPER.

Bibliography. M. Barth, *Israel and the Church;* R. N. Flew, *Jesus and His Church;* J. M. Gustafson, *The Church as Moral Decision Maker;* E. G. Hinson, *The Integrity of the Church;* F. J. A. Hort, *The Christian Ecclesia;* G. Johnston, *The Doctrine of the Church in the New Testament;* T. W. Manson, *The Church's Ministry;* P. Minear, *Images of the Church in the NT;* J. Moltmann, *The Church in the Power of the Spirit;* J. L. Newbigin, *The Household of God;* H. R. Niebuhr, *The Purpose of the Church and Its Ministry;* E. A. Payne, *The Fellowship of Believers;* K. L. Schmidt, *The Church;* L. S. Thornton, *The Common Life in the Body of Christ.*

—THERON D. PRICE

Epistle/Letter   [MDB 258]

•**Epistle/Letter.** Epistles and letters are written messages sent to individuals or groups of people separated from their authors by distance or special circumstances. In antiquity letter writing was a well-established mode of communication and assumed many forms ranging from simple personal addresses to elaborate literary masterpieces. Epicurus, Seneca, and Cicero used the epistolary medium for discourse on moral, ethical, and philosophical questions.

In the early church the letter became the most prominent means of elaborating on matters of theology and Christian conduct. Out of twenty-seven canonical NT works, twenty-one are letters, and two of the remaining ones (Acts and Revelation) contain letters. The practice of writing letters was widely continued in primitive Christianity by bishops and influential church leaders such as Clement of Rome, Polycarp, and Ignatius. Thus there came into existence a new epistolary genre called encyclical letters which were meant to convey doctrinal decisions affecting the whole church.

Adolf Deissmann distinguished between *letter* and *epistle*. Letters, he suggested, are a private, nonliterary means of communication whereas epistles are artistic compositions intended for public dissemination. According to such a definition, Paul's writings were not meant to be literary compositions but simple letters which were not intended for large audiences. Yet many of Paul's letters, even the very personal Letter to Philemon, were in fact written to be shared with the larger community. Most modern scholars refer to NT written communications as *letters* rather than *epistles*. In contrast to KJV (where "epistle" occurs fifteen times), for example, recent versions (RSV, NRSV, NIV, etc.) always translate as "letter."

NT letters, however, have been elevated by the early church to a level of spiritual eminence which places them in a unique category eluding traditional definitions. Their permanent use in the church as inspired texts gives them a quality and a meaning never shared with other epistolary documents.

The NT contains several different types of letters. There are GENERAL LETTERS (written to churches) and pastoral letters (PASTORAL EPISTLES) (written to individuals). The General Letters of Paul tend to deal with larger doctrinal issues affecting the community as a whole. The Pastoral Letters (1-2 Timothy, Titus), whose authorship is often contested, belong to the second generation of Christians. They take the form of private communications to Paul's associates. Early Christians regarded the Catholic Letters (James, 1-2 Peter, 1-2-3 John, Jude) as universal and more complete in their teaching. They are encyclical in character, and are often contrasted to Paul's more personal and more local letters. Hebrews is often considered a letter but would qualify more as a treatise containing a long, sustained argument in favor of the preeminence of Christianity over Judaism.

NT writers could certainly not foresee that their letters would be collected into a body of canonical literature. Paul's open discussions of scandals and misconduct suggest he meant to keep a large portion of his writings private. At the same time,

the direct nature of the letters attests to their reliability and makes them indispens-
able for an appreciation of the apostolic age. It is thus understandable that the early
church elevated them to the dignity of canonical status.

See also GENERAL LETTERS; LETTERS/INSCRIPTIONS; PASTORAL EPISTLES; PAUL; WRITING
SYSTEMS.

Bibliography. A. Deissmann, *Light from the Ancient East*; W. G. Doty, *Letters in Primitive Christianity*; S. K. Stowers, *Letter Writing in Greco-Roman Antiquity*.

—PAUL CIHOLAS

Faith   [MDB 289-92]

•Faith. "Faith" and related words (believe, faithful, faithfulness) are widely used in
the NT. While such words are rare in the Hebrew Bible, the concept of faith is there
important also, especially for understanding the development of the idea in the NT.
The serious student appreciates the range of meanings that attach to the term for,
and are included in the concept of, faith in the Bible. Appreciating this rich variety
means not imposing any single understanding on the diverse biblical materials and
the varying perspectives of faith contained therein.

Hebrew Bible and Judaism. No Hebrew noun means "faith." The word usually
expressing the idea comes from a root (אמן) which can carry the meaning of being
firm, faithful, reliable. While the moral character of the one having faith may be
part of true faith in God in the Hebrew Bible, the Hebrew term simply means being
certain about something or someone, a conclusion supported by the fact that the
term is used in a variety of contexts both religious (e.g., Exod 4:1, 5, 9, 31; Ps
78:22; Job 9:16) and nonreligious (e.g., 1 Sam 27:12; 1 Kgs 10:7; Job 15:22) where
the reliability of the believer is not an issue. Other "faith" words include a verb
usually translated "trust" (e.g., Ps 78:22), and a noun which does translate to "firmness" or "faithfulness" but can also be used in both religious and nonreligious
contexts (e.g., Hab 2:4; 2 Kgs 22:7).

The meager vocabulary is consistent with the fact that the Hebrew mind tended
to think concretely, in contrast with the Greek mind which tended toward abstract
conceptual definitions. Moving from a consideration of vocabulary to a more general
understanding of the concept of religious faith in ancient Israel, one finds that faith
is thoroughly theistic and expressed concretely in stories. That is, faith is illustrated
through stories about model individuals and the whole people of God responding
positively in OBEDIENCE to God's acts of salvation in history on their behalf. God
alone is always and absolutely faithful; the people's faithfulness is often contrasted
with their faithless disobedience.

The patriarchal narratives and the story of the Exodus-Sinai event stand as the
primary pentateuchal expressions of the faithfulness of God and the faith and
faithlessness of the people. Regardless of their historicity—a question continually
debated—these stories were written much later than the events they allegedly
describe, and reflect to a degree Israel's later monotheism and covenant relationship

to the one God, a relationship entailing both the privilege of being God's people and the responsibility of conforming to God's will.

The first significant extended narrative about faith and faithlessness is the Abraham cycle of stories (cf., e.g., Gen 12:1-5; 12:10–13:1; 15:1-21; 16:1-4a; 22:1-19), the themes of which are continued through the Isaac, Jacob, and Joseph stories (Gen 12–50). While these narratives focus on individuals, the faith embedded there is reflective of the communal faith of the people of God rather than the individualistically oriented faith later popular in the Christian religion, in part as a result of Greek influence. God's greatest act of salvation is found in the story of the EXODUS and the related stories of God giving the Law at Sinai and leading the people to the promised land (Exodus-Deuteronomy).

In addition to trust and obedience, Israel's faith included WORSHIP. By Solomon's time (ca. 961–922 B.C.E. Israel was in the process of developing an extensive priestly and sacrificial system which was read back into the stories about the giving of the Law at Sinai. Beginning at least in the eighth century, many of the prophets whose writings found their way into the canon preached against Israel's worship when that "worship" degenerated into hypocritical ceremony devoid of ethical content. Among the prophets, Isaiah speaks more specifically of faith as trust in God in the face of the threat of foreign invasion (e.g., Isa 7:1-9; 28:16; 36-37). Atypically, Deutero-Isaiah (Isa 40–55), along with some Psalms, focuses faith in the direction of the individual.

Postexilic Jewish understanding of faith developed in at least two major directions. First, the element of obedience, always an important component but never the sum total of Israel's faith, moved to center stage. Faith was increasingly understood as keeping TORAH, which included observing the Sabbath and other holy days and, as possible, maintaining the sacrificial system, ideally at the Jerusalem Temple. In part, this move was an attempt to find security in the context of political and cultural uncertainty and the attendant threat to the integrity of Judaism as a people and as a religion. This development continued at least through the beginning of the Christian religion, and can be documented in some of the later books of the Hebrew Bible (e.g., Ezra, Nehemiah), in the Apocrypha, and in the Pseudepigrapha. The rabbis provided authoritative interpretation of the Torah and application of its precepts to every aspect of daily life; their pronouncements on the Torah and on past rabbinic pronouncements were eventually written down in the Mishnah, Talmuds, and other collections. The rabbis equated faith in God and obedience to the Torah, understood as including both the written (Pentateuch) and oral (rabbinic teaching) Torah. After 70 C.E., when the Romans destroyed the Temple, the sacrificial and priestly aspects of Jewish faith disappeared and Judaism became essentially rabbinic Judaism.

Apocalyptic was a second, very powerful expression of faith, especially during times of persecution. Here faith found release in the people's conviction that their faithful God would certainly and decisively intervene soon to crush the oppressors and restore the fortunes of God's people (e.g., Daniel; noncanonical *1 Enoch*, *2 Esdras*).

There were significant exceptions to these trends, as in the more mystical approach of the Hellenistic Jew Philo of Alexandria (20 B.C.E.–49 C.E.), but the thrust was toward an understanding that was practical and legal and/or apocalyptic and away from the earlier, more generalized response to God's saving acts in history.

Classical and Hellenistic Greek Usage. Primary words used by early Christianity to convey the various meanings being discussed were all built from the same stem. These words are the noun "faith" (πίστις), the verb "believe" (πιστεύω), and the adjective (πιστός), which is translated "faithful" or "trustworthy" in the passive sense and "believing" or "trusting" in the active sense. "Unbelief" and "unfaithfulness" were conveyed by adding negative prefixes.

In classical Greek, faith meant trust or confidence in, with the object being a wide variety of persons or things. The idea of being certain about something could also be present. Obedience, though not common, could be stressed where the object of faith was a person. In the passive form the word could refer to a thing (e.g., pledge, guarantee, proof) or person (e.g., husband, wife, someone in a contract) as being worthy of trust. The faith word-group was occasionally used with reference to the divine, but often another word for "believe" (νομίζω), rare in the NT, was used in such cases.

In the Hellenistic period, closer to early Christianity, the faith word-group was used in explicitly religious ways. To believe in the gods embraced theoretical conviction as well as piety, sometimes mystically conceived. As religious propaganda, the terms were widely used by various missionary movements, such as mystery cults. Faith in the Isis-Osiris divinities, for example, resulted in mystical union with the gods and eternal life. Nonreligious use continued, as with the Stoics where the meaning leaned toward reliability, faithfulness, and harmony, but with reference to oneself and one's moral destiny in the cosmos, not to deity.

It is difficult to generalize; however, it seems that intellectual and individualistic tendencies are more prominent in the Greek context, while obedient and communal tendencies are more prominent in the Jewish.

Jesus and the Synoptic Gospels. Among NT scholars the question of Jesus' understanding of faith has produced more ink than answers. The issue is complicated since the primary sources for the JESUS of history, namely, the synoptic Gospels, were written from about 65 to 90 C.E., that is, some 30–60 years after the Christ-event, and reflect to some degree the developing theology of the church rather than the life and teachings of the historical Jesus. The earliest NT writings, those of Paul, which date in the 50s and 60s, provide practically no information about the historical Jesus. In the Synoptics faith plays a minor role, especially when compared to the Pauline and Johannine writings. The noun "faith" and the verb "believe" occur only eleven times in Mark, the earliest Gospel, and, concerning faith, neither Matthew nor Luke add significantly to their source Mark.

Despite the lateness of the sources and the minimal number of references, scholars have probed for the historical Jesus' notion of faith. The most fruitful investigations have concentrated on the synoptic miracle stories where the terms for faith are most common. Scholars once dismissed these stories as later legendary additions to authentic Jesus material. However, form-critical examinations strongly suggest that in his day Jesus was viewed as healer and exorcist, though careful scholars refrain from making judgments about the true nature of the sicknesses and possessions.

Faith plays a crucial role in the MIRACLES, especially the healings, with "Your faith has made you well" being the usual statement found (e.g., Mark 5:34-36 ‖ Matt 9:22 ‖ Luke 8:48-50; Mark 6:5-6 ‖ Matt 13:58; Mark 10:52 ‖ Luke 18:42; Matt 8:13; 9:28-29; 15:28; Luke 7:9, 50; 17:19). Attention is called to the importance of faith in other MIRACLE STORIES in other ways (e.g., Mark 4:40 ‖ Luke 8:25; Matt 8:23-27; 14:31). Matthew sometimes redacts his source by adding his version of the faith statement (Matt 8:13; 9:29; 15:28) and sometimes he connects faith and understanding (e.g., 16:5-12). The Q saying about the miraculous power of faith is important, even faith as small as the tiny mustard seed (Matt 17:20 ‖ Luke 17:6; cf. Mark 11:22-24 ‖ Matt 21:21-22; 1 Cor 13:2; and the Gnostic GosThom 48, 106). Faith is mentioned in connection with the forgiveness of sins (Mark 2:5 ‖ Matt 9:2 ‖ Luke 5:20; Luke 7:50).

It is, then, the incredible power of faith to effect miracles that is emphasized in Jesus' teaching. Noticeably absent is faith directed at Jesus to achieve salvation, traditionally understood. Only twice (Matt 18:6; 27:42) is reference made to having faith in Jesus (Mark 16:16 is not in the best manuscripts, and Mark 9:42—sometimes translated "believe in me"—is also questionable on textual grounds) and in both instances Matthew has added prepositions (me, him) to Mark's version (Mark 9:42; 15:32).

The role of faith in miracles is highlighted when the Jesus exorcism-miracle tradition is compared with similar stories current in Jesus' day. Many details in the Synoptics are paralleled in Hellenistic and Jewish literature; the one thing absent is faith. Because the understanding of faith in the Jesus material is dissimilar to that in Hellenism, Judaism, and (as will be shown) the early church, it is likely that the role assigned to faith in the Synoptics derives from the historical Jesus.

Finally, the main theme of Jesus' teaching was an apocalyptic notion, the KINGDOM OF GOD. Exorcisms and miracles were manifestations of the Kingdom which was being, or soon would be, established. Faith is not mentioned explicitly with reference to the Kingdom of God, and while speculation about Jesus' faith is precarious, perhaps it can safely be said that for Jesus faith in or on God involved trust that God was acting or would act on behalf of the people, and Jesus so challenged his hearers to have similar trust in God's power and providence. This apocalyptic dimension of his ministry, of which the exorcism-healing tradition was a part, sets Jesus firmly in the Jewish tradition and its conception of faith.

Primitive Christianity and Paul. While attempts have been made to reconstruct the theology of the church in the first ten to fifteen years after Jesus, Paul's letters, the first of which probably date from the early 50s, constitute the primary early witness to the developing theology of primitive Christianity. Set in the context of other critical Pauline themes, faith is, roughly, the appropriate human response to God's graceful salvific act in Christ, a response in which one accepts God's righteousness offered in Christ rather than attempting to earn it through vain self-effort. In Paul's theological scheme of things, all persons are separated from God because of sin (Rom 3:23), a reality evidenced among Jews by their having not kept the Law perfectly (e.g., Gal 5:2-3; Rom 2:17-25) and among Gentiles by their having not responded positively to the revelation of God in nature (Rom 1:18-23) and conscience (Rom 2:14-16).

The solution to the sin problem—righteousness—is an act of grace on God's part since it is God's righteousness freely offered in Christ. "Justification," Paul's primary word for this salvific process, is itself a version of the word for righteousness and can be translated "make righteous." In any case, salvation is, at least initially, a movement from God to persons rather than vice versa (Rom 1:16-17); so it is God's grace rather than human works of the Law (Gal 2:16; 5:4). The Law reveals sin (Gal 3:23-24; Rom 3:20) but it cannot produce righteousness. The human response to God's offer is to accept the gift (Rom 5:17), to believe on or in Christ (Gal 2:16; cf. Rom 10:9), and to confess Jesus' lordship (Rom 10:9-10). Faith, necessary initially, continues to be essential to the Christian experience (e.g., Gal 4:1-5:1; 5:6, 13-15; Rom 6:5-11).

Some (e.g., Rudolf Bultmann) view faith as the basic grid for understanding Paul's whole theology, but caution is advisable because all of Paul's books were letters written to specific audiences and to address specific issues. In the above summary of Paul's thought all the references about faith derive from two books (Galatians and Romans). By viewing Paul's teaching in light of concrete historical circumstances, his emphasis on faith as opposed to works is understandable, especially the formulations in Galatians. Paul was primarily a church organizer and one of his most troubling problems was with Judaizers—Jewish Christians attempting to convince Gentile Christians the latter had to keep the works of the Jewish Law, namely, circumcision and dietary prescriptions. In retrospect, this critical issue conceivably could have determined whether Christianity developed as a separate religion or remained a Jewish sect. From a geographical and chronological perspective, the centrality of faith over works of the Law reflects the movement of Christianity deeper into the Hellenistic world and away from its Jewish base.

Paul disagreed with the Judaizers and argued vigorously—in Galatians and Romans—that only faith was required of Jew and Gentile. Clearly Paul felt strongly about this, a fact evidenced by the anger exhibited in the Galatian letter. There he claims that the interpretation came directly through a revelation of Christ (1:12); twice damns the Judaizers (1:8, 9); and, lest anyone question the intensity of his anger, says he hopes the knife the Judaizers are using for circumcision slips (5:12).

The centrality of saving faith in Galatians and Romans and the depth of feeling exhibited in the former are testimonies to the importance of faith to Paul. On the other hand, the subject of faith rarely appears in his other letters (although the term "the believing ones" is found often). So it is safe to say faith was important, but because Paul did not write a comprehensive and systematic theology, the extent of faith's importance in his total thought is debatable.

Regarding a related issue, Paul sometimes (e.g., Gal 3:22; Rom 3:22) uses "faith" in a Greek form that can legitimately be translated either "faith in Christ" or "the faith of Christ." Most scholars think the former translation is the meaning intended, but some argue for the second which, by referring to Christ as a model of faith, perhaps mitigates against overemphasizing human faith.

The significant shift from Jesus to the post-Easter theology of the church should be underscored. Faith in Jesus was limited to a role in the exorcism-miracle tradition; Paul and his brand of primitive Christianity moved faith in Jesus to the center of one's relationship with God. To use a well-worn but apt phrase, Jesus proclaimed the Kingdom of God; the church proclaimed faith in Jesus.

Johannine Literature. Consistent with his preference for verbs over nouns, in John the verb "believe" (in various forms and usually referring to salvific faith) comes to the fore (107 times; only thirty-four times in all three Synoptics); the noun "faith," very common in the Synoptics and Paul, is absent from John.

Concerning faith, the Fourth Gospel reflects more the developed thinking of the early church than it does that of Jesus. To put it another way, faith in John is more like that in Paul than in the Synoptics, though there are certain distinctive Johannine usages. The form "believe in" or "on," found occasionally in other NT books (eight times), is clearly a favorite (thirty-nine times), and reflects John's stress on the believer's personal trust, active commitment, and total reliance. It is a uniquely Christian idiom; with the possible exception of the Dead Sea Scrolls, this use has no parallels outside Christian literature. The object of "believe in" is usually Christ (thirty-one times, e.g., 3:15-18a; cf 1:12; 3:18b; 14:1).

While the personal dimension, which some relate to possible mystical tendencies in John, is prominent, belief understood more as intellectual assent is also present. One "believes *that*" Jesus is the Christ, the Son of God (11:27), was sent by God (11:42), and is the "I am" (13:19). Although not synonyms, believing and knowing are closely related (e.g., 6:69; 16:30; 17:8; 21-23). Not present in John is the Gnostic notion of two classes of people: persons of faith and a higher class of persons of knowledge.

Compared to the Synoptics, in John the most distinctive use of faith relates to miracles, which John usually calls "signs." In the Synoptics, the miracles—usually called "power acts," a term not found in John—show forth the inbreaking Kingdom of God and are generally performed in response to faith. John has no exorcisms and the seven miracles recorded serve to authenticate the person and mission of Jesus (20:31) and symbolize aspects of John's theology (e.g., 6:1-15; 22-71; 9:1-41; 11:1-57). In other words, in the Synoptics, faith produces miracles; in John, miracles evoke faith. Up to four levels of belief have been identified. Some refuse to see signs and refuse to believe (e.g., 11:47); some see signs but misinterpret Jesus as a wonder-worker only (e.g., 2:23–3:5; 7:3-7); some perceive the true meaning of signs and believe (e.g., 4:53-54; 9:38); and some believe without the aid of signs (e.g., 20:29).

So, in the context of John's "high" Christology, saving faith is understood as believing in Jesus as, or believing that Jesus is, God, the eternal Logos. Consistent with Paul, the object of faith is Christ, though John (at least explicitly) pays little or no attention to the antithesis between faith and works of the Law.

Other NT Writings. As the church moved further away from its vibrant early experience of what it understood to be the risen Lord, and worked to define itself over against "heretical" teaching, perhaps it was inevitable that faith would increasingly be understood, especially in the later documents, as correct doctrine (e.g., Col 1:23; 2:7; 1 Tim 1:10, 19; 4:1; Jude 3). James, in a famous passage always compared with Paul, claims that faith without works is dead (2:14-22), but in this apparent contradiction with Paul, James uses faith to mean mere intellectual assent to doctrines.

For the author of Hebrews, faith is that awareness of the ideal world, including God, that enables one to stand true in the face of persecution (e.g., 3:14; 11:1). Heroes of the Jewish tradition are models of faith (11:1-40). Although reference is made to Jesus as a model of faith (12:1-2), there is very little in the book that is specifically "Christian." Noteworthy in Hebrews is the closest thing in the Bible to a definition of faith: "faith is the assurance of things hoped for, the conviction of things not seen" (11:1 RSV, NRSV).

In all of these other NT writings the Christological orientation of Paul and John falls away.

See also ESCHATOLOGY IN THE NT; ESCHATOLOGY IN THE OT; EXODUS; GALATIANS, LETTER TO THE; GOD; GRACE; HOPE IN THE NT; HOPE IN THE OT; JESUS; KINGDOM OF GOD; LAW IN THE NT; LAW IN THE OT; LOVE IN THE NT; LOVE IN THE OT; MIRACLE STORY; MIRACLES; OBEDIENCE; PAUL; RIGHTEOUSNESS IN THE NT; RIGHTEOUSNESS IN THE OT; ROMANS, LETTER TO THE; SALVATION IN THE NT; SALVATION IN THE OT; SIGNS AND WONDERS; TORAH; WORSHIP IN THE NT; WORSHIP IN THE OT.

Bibliography. J. Barr, *The Semantics of Biblical Language*; H. W. Bartsch, "The Concept of Faith in Paul's Letter to the Romans," BR 13 (1968): 41-53; M. A. Beavis, "Mark's Teaching on Faith," BTB 16/4 (Oct 1986): 139-42; R. E. Brown, *The Gospel according to John*; R. Bultmann, *Theology of the New Testament*; C. H. Dodd, *The Bible and the Greeks* and *The Interpretation of the Fourth Gospel*; W. Eichrodt, *Theology of the Old Testament*; V. P. Furnish, *Theology and Ethics in Paul*; H. J. Hermisson and E. Lohse, *Faith*; A. J. Hultgren, "The *Pistis Christou* Formulation in Paul," NovT 22/3 (Jul 1980): 248-63; J. Jeremias, *New Testament Theology: The Proclamation of Jesus*; W. Kramer, *Christ, Lord, Son of God*; G. E. Ladd, *A Theology of the New Testament*; N. Perrin, *Rediscovering the Teachings of Jesus*; D. E. H. Whiteley, *The Theology of St. Paul*; S. K. Williams, "Again *Pistis Christou*," CBQ 49/3 (July 1987): 431-47.

—CALVIN MERCER, JR.

Faith and Faithlessness   [MDB 292-93]

•**Faith and Faithlessness.** FAITH is loyalty to God. It is a COVENANT relation based upon belief in the faithfulness of God. God's faithfulness is one of the five greatest attributes of God mentioned in the OT (Exod 34:6). It is therefore always in the background of all teachings about the faithfulness required of humans in relation to God and of all teachings about faithlessness.

Faithlessness is the opposite of faithfulness, and is treated explicitly and implicitly as such throughout the Bible. Deut 32:20 describes a perverse generation as faithless, and this belief promoted the great reformation in the time of Josiah (ca. 640–609 B.C.E. The most influential proclamation of covenant fidelity was in the dialogue of Habakkuk with the Lord of the covenant. Faithlessness as well as faithfulness are involved. In answer to Habakkuk's complaint that God used wicked Babylon to punish his righteous people (1:12-2:1), the Lord declares: "Behold, he whose soul in not upright in him shall fail, but the righteous shall live by his faithfulness" (2:4 RSV). The RSV, NRSV, and NIV use the word "faith" instead of "faithfulness" (which they place in a note). But the "faithfulness" is nearer the meaning of the original and is critical for understanding why this was so important for the covenant people at Qumran and in the three classical quotations of the passage in the NT (Gal 3:11; Rom 1:17ff.; Heb 2:4).

This essay focuses on key passages that deal directly and indirectly with the relationship between faith (faithfulness) and faithlessness.

Faith and Faithlessness in Paul. At the very heart of the Pauline canon is the citation of Hab 2:4 in Gal 3:11. In this letter, the call for the faithfulness of the believer is critical to understanding what has come to be called "justification by faith." It would be better to speak of "righteousness as faithfulness." Believers who become unfaithful are accused of "deserting him who called you in the grace of Christ and turning to a different gospel" (1:6). Those who had received the spirit by "the hearing of faith" were now about to end "with the flesh" (3:1-5). Abraham is typical of all "men of faith who are the sons of Abraham" (3:7). The ethical implication of Paul's view of righteousness as faithfulness is "faith working through love" (5:6). One can "submit again to a yoke of slavery," be "severed from Christ," and "fall out of grace."

Paul's Letter to the Romans makes Hab 2:4 the theme of his gospel as he declares: "For I am not ashamed of the gospel; it is the power of God for salvation to every one who has faith, to the Jew first and also to the Greek. For in it the righteousness of God is revealed through faith for faith; as it is written, 'He who through faith is righteous shall live [NRSV: The one who is righteous will live by faith]' " (1:16-17). Faith as obedience (cf. 1:5; 16:26) is central in all parts of this most important writing on faith. Israel was broken off as branches of a vine because of unbelief; Gentiles were grafted in because of belief. Gentile believers, too, can be broken off if they do not continue to believe and Israel can be grafted in again if they come to believe (11:17-24). A classic expression of the degrees of faith is found in 12:1-6. Weak believers may stumble and fall by becoming unbelievers (14:13-23). Paul did not hesitate to use the term "law of faith" (3:27) as well as the word of faith (10:8). When Luther added *allein* ("alone") to his German translation of Rom 3:28 as "faith *alone*" he put Paul in opposition to James. This was an unfortunate error.

Faith and Unbelief in Hebrews. The use of "full assurance" (πληροφορία) in Heb 10:22 belongs to the important teaching of faith as a pilgrimage from childhood to maturity (5:11-6:3) and from promise to complete fulfillment in the way of faith (11:13-16, 32-40). The Exodus model out of Egypt into the promised land dominates the life of faith: it is not enough to cross the Red Sea unless spiritual life continues from oasis to oasis into the promised land of full salvation.

The five exhortations against APOSTASY in Hebrews (2:1-5; 3:7-4:11; 15:11-6:20; 10:19-39; 12:1-29) are most instructive for the understanding of faith. The second exhortation clearly considers apostasy or falling away the same as unbelief and disobedience. The fifth exhortation in Hebrews, which concludes with a comment on Hab 2:2-4, calls the righteous to live by faith. Hebrews clearly distinguishes two types of believers: those who shrink back and are "destroyed" and "those who have faith and keep their souls" (10:39).

Faith and Works in James. The discussion on faith and works in Jas 2:14-26 has been called the "theological core" of James. James seems to be concerned about an early antignosticism, that is, the teaching that one could be saved by faith that was not manifested in works of love. James raised the question, "Can this faith save him" (2:15). His answer is, "So faith by itself, if it has no works is dead" (2:17). Abraham did indeed believe the promise of the Lord in Genesis 15:6, but "faith was completed by works," when, in obedience to the Lord, he was willing to offer his son Isaac in sacrifice (Gen 22:1-14). To make sure his reader does not assume that Abraham's faith without works merited salvation, he calls on the testimony of Rahab the harlot who received Israel's messengers. He concludes and repeats "for as the body apart from the spirit is dead, so faith apart from works is dead" (2:26). Much that claims James contradicts Paul has confused the works of love with the works of ceremonial law, but Paul's ethical teaching in Gal 5:6 says much the same as James: "For in Jesus Christ neither circumcision nor uncircumcision is of any avail, but faith working through love."

Faith and Growth in Grace in Second Peter and Jude. The whole of 2 Peter is a polemic against false teachers "who will secretly bring in destructive heresies, even denying the master who bought them, bringing upon themselves swift destruction" (2:1). After many OT examples and some vivid illustrations, the diaspora of believers are warned about the danger of apostasy in which "the last state has become worse for them than the first" (2:20). The conclusion states the theme of 2 Peter: "You therefore, beloved, knowing this beforehand, beware lest you be carried away with the error of lawless men and lose your own stability. But grow in the grace and knowledge of our Lord and Savior Jesus Christ" (3:17-18).

Those who "never fall" are those who grow in grace, supplementing faith with virtue, knowledge, self-control, steadfastness, godliness, brotherly affection, and love. He who lacks these supplements goes "blind and shortsighted and has forgotten that he was cleansed from his old sins" (2 Pet 1:9).

Jude has perhaps been used by 2 Peter too, and the whole question that calls for believers "to contend for the faith which was once for all delivered to the saints" (3) is greatly illuminated by the contrast of apostate persons (3-16) with those who continue in "the faith" of apostolic Christianity (17-23). There are those "who pervert the grace of our God into lasciviousness and deny our only Master and Lord, Jesus Christ." These apostates are "twice dead," dead before they were believers and dead again in apostasy (12), but those who build themselves up in "the most holy faith" keep themselves in "the love of God" and live in the hope of eternal life (20-21) are secure in their salvation. Again the "theological virtues" are the stages in salvation for the spiritually mature. It is promised that the mature believers will be kept from falling by the power of God (24ff.). This teaching is "the faith."

Faith and Perseverance. For Paul, the whole of the Christian life is a walk by faith (2 Cor 5:7) therefore, mature faith increases (2 Cor 10:15). The challenge to the Corinthians was: "examine yourselves, to see whether you are holding to your faith. Test yourselves. Do you not realize that Jesus Christ is in you—unless indeed you failed to meet the test. I hope that you will find out that we have not failed" (2 Cor 13:5-6). The very same word meaning "castaway" or "disqualified" is used by Paul when he speaks of his own spiritual discipline (1 Cor 9:27).

In most of the NT there is movement from faith as personal trust to faith as a summary of beliefs. This is most obvious in the Pauline canon. By the time of the Pastoral Epistles, "faith" is usually "*the* faith." If there is a corrective to the use of the faith as a noun in the Pastoral Epistles and elsewhere, it is surely found in the Johannine canon. Not once does the Gospel of John use faith as a noun: it is always the verb "I believe," not the noun "belief" or "faith." Belief is always a process that must be continued as the mark of the true disciple of Jesus. Only once do the Johannine Epistles use the noun "belief" (1 John 5:4). The Book of Revelation does use the noun four times (2:13, 19; 13:10; 14:12), but the NASB preserves the idea of personal obedience with a translation: "Here is the perseverance of the saints who keep the commandments of God and their faith in Jesus" (14:12).

See also APOSTASY; COVENANT; FAITH.

—DALE MOODY

Flesh and Spirit [MCB 302-303]

•**Flesh and Spirit.** *Flesh* and *spirit* translate Heb. and Gk. words that are used in the Bible with both literal and figurative meanings. *Flesh* is never used of God in the Bible, but is applied both to human beings and to animals. In a literal sense, *flesh* refers to the flesh of people (Job 2:5; 1 Cor 15:39) and of animals (Lev 4:11; Isa 22:13; 1 Cor 15:39). In reference to people, *flesh* may refer specifically to the foreskin (Gen 17:11) or the male sexual organ (Ezek 16:26; 23:20), or it may refer to the whole body (Prov 4:22; Col 2:1). *Flesh* also connotes relationship to other people (Gen 37:27; Lev 18:6; Rom 11:14).

Flesh has an important nonliteral meaning of human life itself as weak, especially in contrast to God. Job asks God, "Hast thou eyes of flesh? Dost thou see as man sees?" (Job 10:4). Ps 78:38-39 says that God restrained his anger against the Israelite people because "he remembered that they were but flesh."

Spirit refers to the vital power of living people, that which gives life to the body (Ezek 37:1-14; Luke 8:55). Removal of the spirit causes death (Gen 6:3). Num 16:22 and 27:16 call God the "God of the spirits of all flesh."

When *flesh* and *spirit* are used together they refer to the whole personality, the material or outer aspect and the immaterial or inner aspect. In 2 Cor 7:1 Paul writes, "Let us cleanse ourselves from every defilement of body (flesh) and spirit;" and in Col 2:5 he says, "For though I am absent in body (flesh), yet I am present with you in spirit." Here the spirit refers to one's insight, feeling, and will—one's inner life.

Flesh and *spirit* are also in contrast to one another in several passages where flesh is closely connected to sin, and spirit to that divine power from God that produces all divine existence. John 3:6 declares, "That which is born of the flesh is flesh, and that which is born of the Spirit is spirit." Paul declares that attempts to please God in the flesh are not acceptable to God, but rather worship by means of his Spirit (Phil 3:3). Elsewhere Paul relates the spirit to faith and freedom and the flesh to Law and slavery. In Gal 3:3, he asks "Having begun with the Spirit, are you now ending with the flesh?" (see also Gal 5:17; 6:8).

In the NT the apostle Paul gives an ethical sense to flesh. People, as flesh, are contrasted with Spirit and are sinful. They cannot please God without the help of the Spirit. Rom 8 is the classic text in which Paul contrasts life "in the flesh" and life "in the Spirit." Verse 8 says "those who are in the flesh cannot please God." Verse 9 is evidence that to be "in the flesh" is equivalent to not having God's Spirit dwelling in one. *Flesh* in this sense refers to the whole person in his or her distance from God, the attempt to live one's life independently of God. When Paul says in Rom 7:18, "I know that nothing good dwells within me, that is, in my flesh," he is not referring to the physical body. *Flesh* here has the ethical sense of his unregenerate nature. Gal 5:19-21 lists the "works of the flesh." Only five of the fifteen are basically sensual (fornication, impurity, licentiousness, drunkenness, and carousing); the other ten are idolatry, sorcery, enmities, strife, jealousy, anger, quarrels, dissensions, factions, envy.

Just as *flesh* can refer to the total person apart from God, so *spirit* may describe the total person in relation to God. In benedictions such as Phlm 25 ("the grace of the Lord Jesus Christ be with your *spirit*") and 2 Tim 4:22 ("the Lord be with your *spirit*"), one's *spirit* is one's self.

Because the apostle Paul uses *flesh* in both a literal sense and an ethical sense, it is sometimes difficult to know which is intended. In 1 Cor 5, writing concerning a man who is having sex with his stepmother, Paul says, "Deliver this man to Satan for the destruction of the flesh, that his spirit may be saved in the day of the Lord Jesus" (5:5). Some interpreters and translators understood flesh here to be the physical body: TEV—"for his body to be destroyed so that his spirit may be saved"; NJB—"to be destroyed as far as natural life is concerned, so that on the Day of the Lord his spirit may be saved"; AT (Goodspeed)—"for his physical destruction, in order that his spirit may be saved on the Day of the Lord." Others understand flesh here in the ethical sense of one's unregenerate nature: NIV—"So that the sinful nature may be destroyed and his spirit saved on the day of the Lord"; Barclay— "This you must do so that this salutory and painful discipline may mortify this man's fleshly desires, so that on the day of the Lord his spirit may be saved."

See also FLESH; HOLY SPIRIT; HUMAN BEING; SPIRIT IN THE OT.

Bibliography. F. Stagg, *New Testament Theology*; H. W. Wolff, *Anthropology of the Old Testament*.

—ROGER L. OMANSON

Gentile/Gentiles in the New Testament [MDB 324-25]

•Gentile/Gentiles in the New Testament. [jen'tɪl] In English versions of the NT, "Gentiles" usually translates a Gk. word (ἔθνη) that normally is rendered "nations." This Gk. word comes from the LXX and translates Heb. words meaning "nations" or "peoples." The singular form may refer to a particular nation, and one of the Heb. words in the singular (עַם) is used to refer to Israel as the people or nation of God *par excellence*. The plural of another word (גּוֹיִם) generally designates other peoples with a depreciative nuance. The English word "Gentile" comes from the Latin adj. *gentilis*, which describes a person belonging to a *gens* ("clan" or "nation"). In English Bibles, it appears almost exclusively in the plural "Gentiles," i.e., "nations" or "foreigners" (*gentes*, pl. of *gens*).

OT usage is reflected directly in the NT. "The nations" or "Gentiles" (ἔθνη) may designate simply the ethnic distinction between Jews and non-Jews; just as the singular (ἔθνος) is sometimes used for the Jews as the Jewish "nation" (Luke 7:5; John 11:48-52; Acts 10:22). In some contexts "heathen" or "pagans" better captures the intention than "nations" or "Gentiles." This holds where "evil passions" are likened to the ways of "the Gentiles (ἔθνη) which know not God" (1 Thess 4:5, KJV), rendered "heathen" in some versions. This parallels the OT, "the nations (גּוֹיִם) that know thee not" (Jer 10:25). More than ethnic distinction is probably implied in passages dealing with incest (1 Cor 5:1), idolatry (1 Cor 12:2), and anxiety over things (Matt 6:32) perceived as pagan.

Paul sometimes uses "Greeks" and "Gentiles" interchangeably (Gal 3:28); but "Greeks" could imply cultural distinction, as in "Greeks and barbarians" (Rom 1:14) or a basic difference in religious mind-set: "For Jews demand signs and Greeks seek wisdom" (1 Cor 1:22).

Non-Jewish Christians are yet termed "Gentiles" when simply distinguished from Jews or Jewish Christians, as in "the churches of the Gentiles" (Rom 16:4).

This usage appears in Paul's rebuke of Peter, who, before the coming of some of "the circumcision" to Antioch, was "eating with Gentiles," i.e., uncircumcised, non-Jewish Christians (Gal 2:12). However, non-Jewish Christians may also be perceived as having a new identity "in Christ," now being neither "Jew" nor "Greek" (i.e., Gentile). In this view, the distinction between "Jew" and "Gentile" is transcended in the creation of a new community "in Christ" (2 Cor 5:16-17; cf. 1 Cor 12:2).

Paul rejected the idea that "all those who are descended from Israel" were really "Israel" (Rom 9:6). "Israel" stood for persons who had entered into covenant relationship with God, not merely the natural descendants of Abraham. Paul distinguished between a Jew outwardly and a Jew inwardly, as between circumcision "in flesh" and "in heart" (Rom 2:28-29; Col 2:11; Eph 2:11). Thus "in Christ," there is "neither Jew nor Greek, there is neither slave nor free, there is neither male nor female" (Gal 3:28). In Eph 2:14-22, Christ is our peace, having destroyed the wall of separation, the cultic "law of commandments and ordinances," creating of the two "one new humanity."

Although the cleavage between Jew and Gentile is overcome in Christ, a continuity with Israel holds. These two ideas appear side-by-side in Galatians: "For neither circumcision counts for anything, nor uncircumcision, but a new creation. Peace and mercy be upon all who walk by this rule, upon the Israel of God" (6:15-16). Although "new Israel" or "true Israel" may capture the idea, there has never been but one "Israel of God," those entering into covenant relationship with him, whether Jew or Gentile. Historically, Jews have been "near" and Gentiles "afar off" (Eph 2:12-13), but neither is "the Israel of God" except through Abraham's kind of faith (Rom 4:16-18). This concept of Christians, Jew and Gentile, as the real "Israel" appears variously in the NT (cf. 1 Pet 2:9-10; Jas 1:1).

According to the Gospels, Jesus' attention to non-Jews was limited, his focus being upon "the lost sheep of the house of Israel" (Matt 15:24). However, by practice and teaching, Jesus undercut all arbitrary and secondary tests for identifying the people of God. He began with his own Jewish people and heritage, but what he did there had far-reaching implications for Jews and Gentiles. Jesus rejected the cultic distinction between "clean" and "unclean," making the test not what enters the mouth but what comes from the heart (Mark 7:15-23). Eventually his followers came to see that this applies to persons, not just foods (Acts 10:9-16). Jesus rejected the codes which excluded such as the lame, the leper, the blind, the deaf, and a woman with an issue of blood (cf. Lev 15:19-20; 21:18-24; Deut 23:1-6). He went out of his way to affirm these. He scandalized piety by eating with "publicans and sinners" (Luke 15:1). He affirmed as his family anyone doing the will of his Father (Mark 3:35). What was offered the Jews first was intended for Gentiles also (Matt 28:19; Acts 1:8; Rom 1:16).

What began as a Jewish community soon included non-Jews. Next, the movement grew from predominantly Jewish to predominantly Gentile, and then almost exclusively Gentile. Inherent in the gospel is openness to all who will hear it. The Jewish struggle for national survival against the Roman Empire made acute the issue of including uncircumcised Gentiles in the fellowship of Jewish Christians who yet were worshipping in the synagogues. Much of this struggle is traced in Acts and Paul's Letters. It was chiefly this issue that caused the parting of Judaism and Christianity, synagogue and church, within the first century. Significantly, in the final book of the NT, when Christians were opposed by the same Roman Empire, the "eternal Gospel" is to be proclaimed to "every nation and tribe and tongue and people" (Rev 14:6). Anyone who thirsts may "take the water of life without price" (22:17).

See also GENTILE/GENTILES IN THE OT; JEWS.
Bibliography. G. Dix, *Jew and Greek, A Study in the Primitive Church*; J. Jervell, *Luke and the People of God: A New Look at Luke-Acts;* G. D. Kilpatrick, "The Gentile Mission in Mark and Mark 13:9-11," *Studies in the Gospels,* ed. by D. E. Nineham; K. L. Schmidt, ἔθνος, ἐθνικός, TDNT; S. G. Wilson, *The Gentiles and the Gentile Mission in Luke-Acts.*

—FRANK STAGG

Grace   [MDB 347]

•**Grace.** Grace is the sheer, self-giving love of God toward suffering and sinful humanity. It has no cause outside the love of God himself; it is not dependent on any merit or worth in the recipient. The Hebrew root of the word translated "grace" (חָנַן) means to "bend down to," suggesting a loving parent bending over a suffering child, or a good Samaritan bending over a wounded man on the Jericho Road.

Because it stresses both the divine initiative and human helplessness, grace is a dominant term in the entire sweep of the biblical history of God's activity. It characterizes God's deliverance of his people from Egypt, his provision for them in the wilderness, the establishment of his COVENANT with them, the continuing FORGIVENESS of their sins, and the renewal of the covenant with them. Although it was first and foremost a term for the nature of God's loving care for his creatures, it became a major term for the biblical understanding of human salvation. The biblical use of the idea of grace can be summarized under two headings: the nature of God and the way of salvation.

The Nature of God. The English word "grace" is related to two OT words, one with the literal meaning "to bend down to" (חָנַן) and another which may be translated "loving kindness" or "steadfast love" (חֶסֶד). The first stresses that all loving concern originates with God and that it is in no way dependent on the action, attitude, or intrinsic worth of the recipient. Even the word "love" in most languages can have a self-gratifying dimension to it. Grace defines God's love in utterly self-giving terms. It is as certain as the being of God, and it is not affected by anything outside the divine nature.

The long experience of the biblical people with the faithfulness of God in the covenant relationship gave rise to the second term. God's grace was not called forth by the obedience of his people, and their faithlessness did not threaten the destruction of the grace of God. However, they learned that grace often took the form of severe discipline, because God's care for them involved punishment, forgiveness, and restoration to relationship. Paul learned the background of this great biblical term from this steadfast grace of God through all kinds of adversity in the experience of Israel. It made it possible to accept the divine "No" to his prayer for removal of his "thorn in the flesh" because he knew from the biblical testimony and his own experience that, indeed, God's "grace was sufficient" for him (2 Cor 12:9).

The Way of Salvation. "Grace" became one of the biggest words in the vocabulary of salvation because of these same two elements: stress upon the divine initiative and affirmation of the divine faithfulness to the relationship.

Like the biblical concept of "election" the doctrine of saving grace has always been plagued by the logical effort to separate the divine choice from the human response. Calvin's doctrine of "irresistible grace" has dominated some reformed theologies to the point that the human being is a passive recipient of election to eternal life or reprobation to eternal damnation, without any opportunity whatever for choice or response. Paul understood the inseparable character of gift and acceptance in the wonderful grace of God: "For by grace you have been saved through faith" (Eph 2:8). Exactly because grace is God's gift, unmerited and unearned by the believer, it must be accepted freely by the recipient. If it were in any way coercive or forced, it would deny the very nature of grace. This paradoxical tension in the saving grace of God has called forth the most lyrical and ecstatic expressions of praise on the part of believers from biblical days to the present time. It gives us some of the greatest passages in the epistles of Paul; it gives us the classic testimony of John Bunyan, *Grace Abounding to the Chief of Sinners*, and the beloved hymn of the converted slave-runner John Newton, "Amazing Grace." Exactly because it is the purest expression of God's redemptive love in the life of the believer, it is beyond logical analysis.

Christian theologians have cataloged the ways of grace in the salvation of humankind, even though they have not been able to define it adequately. They have stressed "prevenient grace," the loving care of God expressed to human beings through nature, through believing parents or teachers, and through all the means of society and environment by which one may be led to respond to God. This emphasizes the biblical concept of the divine initiative and the sheer unmerited favor of God, since no one can pick his parents or his place to be born and can only be thankful for those gifts that prepared the way for a willing response to divine grace.

Other theologians have stressed "effectual grace," thus balancing the divine initiative with the human response by which grace becomes effective in the life of the believer. Yet, even here, biblical writers and centuries of Christian testimony have affirmed the work of God in the faith response of the believer, so that believers cannot "take credit" for their faith, nor say that God saved them because they believed. The paradox might be stated in this way: human beings cannot take credit for believing in God, yet they are entirely responsible if they reject the grace of God. By the grace of God one is enabled to believe; by one's own choice the grace of God is rejected.

The steadfast love dimension of God's grace is illustrated in the theologian's use of the term "habitual grace." Because God was faithful and steadfast in the covenant relationship, a habitual pattern of trust and growing faithfulness could be engendered in the people. A final description of the "state of grace" in many biblical theologies is drawn from the experience of the covenant people in the Bible. They live in the confident assurance that they have been loved and claimed by God for his very own, and they do not have to be preoccupied with a frantic search for certainty and spiritual security. Rather, they are freed for joyful service in the fellowship of God to a world in desperate need of someone to "bend down to" and to help the suffering, dying, and spiritually destitute.

See also COVENANT; FORGIVENESS/PARDON; GIFTS OF THE SPIRIT; LOVE IN THE NT; LOVE IN THE OT; MERCY; PROMISE.

Bibliography. J. Daane, *A Theology of Grace*; H. D. Gray, *The Christian Doctrine of Grace*; O. Hardman, *The Christian Doctrine of Grace*; C. R. Smith, *The Bible Doctrine of Grace*.

—WAYNE E. WARD

Hellenistic World   [MDB 368-72]

•**Hellenistic World.** *The Political Situation* (see PLATES 1, 18). The victorious campaign the Macedonian King ALEXANDER the Great waged against the vast Persian empire beginning in 334 B.C.E. radically changed the ancient Mediterranean world and the Middle East, both politically and culturally. After Alexander died prematurely in 323 B.C.E., his successors fought among themselves for many years. Several successfully carved out manageable domains from the territories conquered by Alexander and founded rival dynastic kingdoms. The more important founders of Hellenistic kingdoms include Ptolemy (whose dynasty controlled Egypt and, until 200 B.C.E., Palestine), Seleucus (the territories between Syria and India), Antigonus (Macedonia), and Lysimachus (Thrace and Armenia).

Meanwhile by 201 B.C.E., Rome had gained complete military control of the western Mediterranean with the conquest of Carthage in North Africa following the First and Second Punic wars (264-241 B.C.E. and 220-201 B.C.E.). Rome continued to expand eastward. In a series of three Macedonian wars (214-205, 200-196, and 148-146 B.C.E.), Rome turned Macedonia and Greece into Roman provinces, and gradually absorbed all the other major and minor Hellenistic kingdoms. The last to fall was Ptolemaic Egypt which was won by the Romans under Octavian (who later became Emperor Augustus) in the battle of Actium, on the coast of western Greece, in 31 B.C.E. against Antony and Cleopatra. After the annexation of Egypt, the last of the independent Hellenistic kingdoms, the Mediterranean Sea became, for all practical purposes, a Roman lake. Octavian's victory at Actium and the resultant conquest of Egypt marked the final transitional stage between the Roman republic and the ROMAN EMPIRE, inaugurating a new age of relative peace and prospertiy, called the *Pax Romana*, which lasted for nearly two centuries.

The Roman period began in 31 B.C.E. and lasted until Rome fell in 476 B.C.E. The eastern half of the empire, with its capital at Constantinople (or Byzantium), survived until it fell to the Turks in 1453. The division of the empire occurred formally in 394 when Valentinian was made emperor of the West, and Valens of the East.

The practical Romans absorbed much of Greek civilization and culture, to which they contributed organizational skill, military might, and political know-how. The entire period from Alexander to the deposition of the last Roman emperor is called the Hellenistic period, a term first applied in 1836 by the German ancient historian J. G. Droysen to the period following Alexander the Great. Though Droysen erroneously understood the term "Hellenists" in Acts 6:1 to refer to orientalized Greeks, he correctly regarded the blending or syncretism of Greek and Oriental culture as characteristic of this period.

Hellenistic Culture. Though the ancient world was politically and economically controlled by Rome after 31 B.C.E. Hellenistic culture dominated the ancient world from ca. 300 B.C.E. to ca. 300 C.E. (i.e., from the death of Alexander the Great in 323 B.C.E. to the conversion of Constantine in 312 C.E.). The Roman empire encompassed many native cultures, each vitally concerned with the preservation of its own identity and traditions. The dominance and attractiveness of Hellenistic culture throughout the Mediterranean world proved irresistible to many intellectuals who were natives of one or another of the numerous cultures that had become subject first to the Macedonians, then to their successors and finally to the Romans.

Alexander and his successors consciously used Hellenistic culture as a tool for unifying and pacifying subject peoples. Various segments of conquered populations responded in different ways to political and cultural domination by foreigners. Hellenistic culture proved irresistible to some native members of the upper classes, typically including intellectuals, bureaucrats, religious functionaries, and aristocrats. In contrast to this largely urban minority, resistance to Hellenism was strongest among rural lower classes. Native intellectuals such as Manetho of Egypt, Berossus of Babylon (both early third century B.C.E.), and Flavius JOSEPHUS the Jewish historian (late first century C.E.), attempted to defend their native traditions in response to the smothering influences of Hellenism by writing propagandistic historical accounts in Greek emphasizing both the priority and superiority of their respective native cultures.

Palestinian JUDAISM came into direct and permanent contact with Hellenistic culture when Alexander subjected Palestine in 332 B.C.E. on his way to liberate Egypt from the Persians. During the entire third century B.C.E. Palestine was under the political control of the benign Ptolemies. The Seleucids, who wrested Palestine from the Ptolemies at the battle of Panion (200 B.C.E.), pursued a more aggressive policy of Hellenization which incited the Maccabean rebellion in 167 B.C.E. Jews, like many other nativistic cultures, had an ambivalent attitude toward Hellenism. They assimilated some aspects of Hellenistic culture more easily than others. The GREEK LANGUAGE, Greek literary and rhetorical forms, Greek styles in art and architecture, and even Greek names were readily adopted. Yet other aspects of Hellenistic culture were more controversial and even repugnant to Jews with a traditional orientation: religious practices, athletic traditions, forms of entertainment, and styles of clothing. While accepted by some liberal members of the upper class including the temple priesthood in Jerusalem, these controversial aspects of Hellenistic culture often met with stiff resistance, even to the extent of armed revolt, on the part of the common people. A type of religious protest literature, called apocalypses, flourished in early Judaism as well as in other native cultures dominated by the Greeks and the Romans.

Hellenistic Language. Philip II of Macedon (who ruled from 359 to 336 B.C.E.) used Attic Greek as the official language of his court and of his diplomatic correspondence. Under his son Alexander (356–323 B.C.E.), Koine ("common") Greek, a popularized form of imperial Attic, became the language of art, science, and literature as well as of administration and commerce throughout the Hellenistic world. The Greek language of the late Hellenistic period can conveniently be divided into two major types, literary and nonliterary Koine. Koine Greek (in contrast to specific dialects like Doric, Aeolic, Ionic, or Attic), was a simplified blend of features from Attic and Ionic Greek (dialects of Athens and western Anatolia).

On the basis of the widespread division of Hellenistic Greek into literary and nonliterary Koine, two categories of literature were proposed by late-nineteenth-century German scholars, *Hochliteratur* ("cultivated literature") produced by and for the educated upper classes of the Greco-Roman world, *Kleinliteratur* ("popular literature"), of which the early Christian literature collectively known as the NT was a prime example. Actually, these categories are ideal types at opposite ends of a complex spectrum of linguistic and literary styles. Recognition of this fact makes it feasible to trace continuities between the patterns and structures of the highest and lowest educational levels. Several scholars have argued for a third kind of Hellenistic Greek between the two extremes of nonliterary and literary Koine. Though there is some disagreement about its exact character, "popular literary Greek" is an appropriate designation of this mediating type of Greek which Lars Ryebeck has labeled *Fachprosa,* "professional" or "technical prose." As the written language of people with some education, it occurs in technical and scientific treatises, in popular philosophical literature, in some of the more literary papyri, and in the the the NT.

Art and Architecture. The idealism of classical Greek art was gradually transformed during the Hellenistic period into an increasing preference for realism. The emphasis on a more realistic imitation of nature in painting and sculpture determined the subjects selected. Alongside mature men and women, a greater interest is reflected in old age, childhood, and deformity, and to the artistic representation of such emotions as pleasure and pain, and such states as sleep and death. Important developments in sculpture took place during the early Hellenistic period, primarily because of the practice of showing municipal gratitude to benefactors by erecting statues of them in public places. Several artistic styles can be differentiated, each emanating from a major intellectual and cultural center. (1) The Alexandrian style consisted of an impressionistic development of the ideas of Praxiteles of Athens (mid-fourth century B.C.E.), combined with a realistic depiction of the grotesque. (2)

The Pergamene style followed the mixed tradition of Scopas (fourth century B.C.E.) and Praxiteles, and is represented by sculptures on the great altar of Zeus from Pergamon depicting the battle between gods and giants. (3) The Rhodian style followed the athletic tradition of Lysippus of Sicyon (late fourth century B.C.E.), and his pupil Chares of Lindos. Rhodes became a major center for bronze casting, while the other centers preferred marble. A typical representative of Rhodian sculpture is the Winged Victory of Samothrace. The creative period of Hellenistic sculpture essentially ended in 146 B.C.E. with the Roman conquest of Greece. Thereafter the Roman demand for enormous quantities of Greek sculpture led to large-scale copying of older works, and Greece became a center for statue manufacturing.

The many new cities founded by Alexander and his successors led to a blossoming of Hellenistic architecture, building, and town planning. By the beginnning of the fifth century B.C.E. the physical requirements of Greek cities included an acropolis, walls, an agora, a theater, a gymnasium, and temples. Some Hellenistic architectural features include the preference for the Corinthian order with its baroque features (rather than the Doric or Ionic orders), the preference for rectilinear rather than curvilinear forms, and the creative use of interior space. There was, in addition, an emphasis on the facade and a tendency to view a building within the setting of other buildings rather than as an isolated work of art (a characteristic of the classical period).

Literature. Both Hellenism and Judaism preserved cultural traditions and ideals of the past through approved collections of classical literature. Works written many centuries before the Christian era (such as Homer and the Hebrew Bible) continued to exert far-reaching influences. While Greek literary classics exerted a broad influence on Hellenistic and Roman culture, in Judaism biblical literature was particularly influential. Yet both cultures were traditional in that cultural and religious values of the present were regarded as anchored in the paradigmatic past as mediated by approved literature. Literature produced from the second through the fourth centuries C.E. was also oriented to the past, since the traditional character of both Hellenism and Judaism ensured the preservation of earlier literary genres, forms, and styles in later literary activity. Throughout Greek history there was a tendency to single out the most accomplished authors of various literary genres (the most important of which were epic, lyric, and dramatic poetry).

Much of this scholarly activity centered at the museum of Alexandria (founded by Ptolemy I) which boasted a great library founded by Ptolemy II (when destroyed by fire in 47 B.C.E. it contained about 700,000 books). Aristophanes of Byzantium (ca. 257–180 B.C.E.), a famous grammarian and librarian at the Alexandrian museum, apparently drew up lists of selected or approved authors (cf. Quintillian 1.4.3; 10.154-59). Since the late eighteenth century, classical scholars have used the term Alexandrian canon for the catalog of more than eighty classical authors, which included five epic poets, ten orators, nine lyric poets, five tragic poets, and so on. The Alexandrian canon had both positive and negative effects on ancient literature. The works of approved authors were read in schools and by the educated, they were copied, recopied and commented upon, and thus preserved for posterity. The works of unapproved authors, however, were neglected and eventually lost. Hellenistic literary culture regarded the works of approved authors as models worthy of emulation. An orator who wanted to describe a contemporary battle turned to Herodotus, Thucydides, and Xenophon for their descriptions.

The *Iliad* and *Odyssey* had an enormous influence on Hellenistic and Roman culture, not only on the art, literature, and philosophy of the educated, but also on the common people. Homer has been called "the Bible of the Greeks." This religious analogy is appropriate since both the *Odyssey* and the *Iliad* claimed to be products of the divine inspiration of the Muse, and the author himself was often called "the divine Homer." Homer was central to the educational system, and at the primary level exercises in writing and reading were based on Homeric texts and large portions were memorized. This was reinforced by frequent public recitals of and lectures on the Homeric epics. In religion, Homer provided the Greeks with basic conceptions of the gods of the Olympian pantheon. With regard to private religious practices, oracles were derived from Homeric texts, and Homeric verses were used on magical amulets. Since the purpose of education was character formation, Homer became the primary source for moral and political guidance. Homer was also regarded as a practical guide in the areas of rhetoric, warfare, and housekeeping. The Greeks thought that virtually every rhetorical and literary genre was anticipated by Homer. According to Menander Rhetor (third century C.E.), in his discussion of the many subtypes of epideictic oratory, "It is necessary to elaborate on the starting points received from the poet [i.e., Homer], after understanding the basic scheme the poet has transmitted to us."

From the late first century through the third century, there was a widespread nostalgia for the past among both Greeks and Romans. This archaism, which was particularly characteristic of the programmatic rhetorical movement called the Second Sophistic, took several forms. Widespread attempts to imitate the language and literary style of the Attic prose writers of the classical period (450–330 B.C.E.) is called linguistic Atticism. The preference for literature written in Attic or Atticistic Greek contributed to the neglect and eventual loss of most Hellenistic literature from the late fourth century B.C.E. through the late first century C.E. Thematic archaism was also prevalent. Greek historians focused on the period of Alexander or earlier, and in so doing both neglected and depreciated the events of the more recent past. Orators declaimed on themes from the classical past, such as "Athens the greatest city," and "Alexander the greatest Greek." Archaism was both the cause and result of emphasizing literary models of the classical past. Dissatisfaction with the political and cultural realities of the present was another contributing factor which encouraged both linguistic and thematic archaism.

Native intellectuals in states subject to the Greeks, and then the Romans, used the Greek language and literary genres to explain the history and traditions of their cultures to the Greeks as well as to themselves. The Babylonian priest Berossus wrote a history of Babylon entitled *Babyloniaka* (early third century B.C.E.), dedicated to Antiochus I, in which he interpreted Babylonian history and traditions for the Greek world. Similarly, Manetho, an Egyptian high priest from Heliopolis and a contemporary of Berossus, did the same for Egyptian history in *Egyptiaka,* a history of Egypt written in Greek dedicated to Ptolemy II. In Rome, one of the first historians was Q. Fabius Pictor (late third century B.C.E.) who wrote his *Histories* in Greek to communicate Roman policies and institutions to the Hellenistic world.

Jewish Hellenistic literature, written primarily in Greek using Hellenistic literary forms and traditions, is the best-preserved Hellenized nativistic literature from the Greco-Roman period. The history of early Jewish literature reflects the increasing domination of Hellenistic literary culture. The penetration of Hellenistic culture into Palestine from the late fourth century B.C.E. on makes it difficult to determine whether particular Jewish writings arose in Palestine or the Diaspora. The SEPTUAGINT, a translation of the Jewish scriptures from Hebrew to Greek during the early third century B.C.E. in Alexandria for Greeks as well as for diaspora Jews, is one important indicator of the impact of Hellenization upon Judaism.

Religion and Philosophy. The political and cultural unity imposed on increasingly larger segments of the ancient Mediterranean world and the Near East, first by the Greeks and then by the Romans, resulted in a period of great creativity in the areas of both religion and philosophy. Previously isolated ethnic traditions came into contact with one other and affected each other in a variety of ways. Religion for the ancients was not an isolatable component of culture but an integral feature which permeated life and thought generally. Cults in the Hellenistic world tended to focus on myth and ritual to the virtual exclusion of theology and ethics. Further, all of the great religious traditions had centers both in their ancestral homeland as well as in a diaspora population of immigrants who worshipped native deities in foreign lands.

Several distinctive forms of religion and religious traditions flourished in the Hellenistic world, including (1) ruler cults, (2) state cults, and (3) MYSTERY RELIGIONS. The ruler cults, which first developed in the Hellenistic kingdoms, provided a religious and political framework for the various national groups united under regional Greek monarchies, and eventually the Roman empire. The Ionian cities of western Anatolia had proclaimed the divinity of Alexander when he liberated them during his campaign against the Persians. Of the mainland Greeks, however, only the league of Corinth voted divine honors to Alexander (324 B.C.E.). Later the Athenians voted divine honors to Antigonus and Demetrius Poliorketes in 307 B.C.E. By 270 B.C.E. Ptolemy II Philadelphus had founded a cult celebrating the divinity of both his wife Arsinoe and himself. The deification of rulers was a grateful municipal response to individuals of great merit. Rome adapted features of the Hellenistic ruler cults to the needs of an enormous empire. Julius Caesar was posthumously deified in 42 B.C.E. Thereafter living emperors took the title *divi filius* ("son of god") referring to their imperial dynastic predecessors (thereby legitimating their own rule), and deceased emperors thought worthy of the honor were enrolled with the gods of Rome by an act of the senate. The imperial cult, particularly strong in such eastern provinces as Asia, became a way for provincial expression of loyalty and patriotism.

The traditional state cults of the Greek and Roman cities continued to flourish but were weakened by the subjugation of the *polis* ("city-state"), first to leagues and then to empires. Since the primary function of state cults had been to ensure national prosperity by promoting peace with the gods, the subjugation of cities to larger political units meant that the quest for prosperity had to be pursued at a higher level, such as the ruler cults.

The growing concern of individuals for their own welfare and salvation encouraged the proliferation of MYSTERY RELIGIONS. The Greek terms *mysterion* and *mystes* mean "secret ritual" and "initiant." Mystery cults, then, are essentially voluntary associations of people who have experienced a secret ritual initiation thought to guarantee prosperity in this life and happiness in the life to come. The Eleusinian mysteries, centering in the worship of Demeter and Persephone, is the oldest known Greek mystery religion. Many oriental cults moved westward with native immigrants and were transformed into mystery cults. Among the more prominent of these are the cults of Isis and Osiris, Cybele and Attis, and Aphrodite and Adonis.

Numerous philosophical schools and traditions, many of which originally centered in Athens, flourished in major urban centers throughout the ancient Mediterranean world during the Hellenistic period. While Greek philosophy in the classical period tended to focus on three main divisions of logic, physics, and ethics, during the Hellenistic period the quest for the *summum bonum* ("the greatest good") resulted in a growing emphasis on ethics. The major philosophical traditions of the Hellenistic world all sought legitimation by tracing their traditions back to Socrates (469–399 B.C.E.). The major competing schools of Hellenistic philosophy include Platonists, Aristotelians, EPICUREANS, CYNICS, STOICS, and Skeptics.

See also ALEXANDER; CYNICS; EPICUREANS; GREEK LANGUAGE; MACCABEES; MYSTERY RELIGIONS; ROMAN EMPIRE.

Bibliography. E. L. Bowie, "Greeks and Their Past in the Second Sophistic," *Studies in Ancient Society,* ed. M. I. Finley; J. B. Bury et al., *The Hellenistic Age*; G. Dickens, *Hellenistic Sculpture*; D. R. Dudley, *A History of Cynicism from Diogenes to the 6th Cent. A.D.*; S. K. Eddy, *The King is Dead: Studies in the Near Eastern Resistance to Hellenism (334–31 B.C.)*; J. Ferguson, *The Heritage of Hellenism* and *The Religions of the Roman Empire*; F. C. Grant, *Roman Hellenism and the New Testament*; R. M. Grant, *Gods and the One God*; E. S. Gruen, *The Hellenistic World and the Coming of Rome*; M. Hadas, *Hellenistic Culture*; A. A. Long, *Hellenistic Philosophy: Stoics, Epicureans, Skeptics*; A. J. Malherbe, *Moral Exhortation, a Greco-Roman Sourcebook*; A. Momigliano, *Alien Wisdom: The Limits of Hellenization*; A. D. Nock, *Conversion: The Old and the New in Religion from Alexander the Great to Augustine of Hippo*; F. E. Peters, *The Harvest of Hellenism: A History of the Near East from Alexander the Great to the Triumph of Christianity*; P. Petit, *Pax Romana*; J. H. Randall, Jr., *Hellenistic Ways of Deliverance and the Making of the Christian Synthesis*; J. M. Rist, *Stoic Philosophy*; W. W. Tarn, *Hellenistic Civilisation*; F. W. Walbank et al., eds., "The Hellenistic World," CAH, 7/1; F. W. Walbank, *The Helenistic World*.

—DAVID E. AUNE

Holy Spirit   [MDB 384-85]

•**Holy Spirit.** *The Old Testament.* Although pervasive in the NT (90 times), the term "Holy Spirit" appears only three times in the OT (Ps 51:11; Isa 63:10, 11). This term brings together two OT ideas originally independent of one another: "holiness" and "spirit." The two ideas were not only distinct but pointed in opposite directions. Holiness pointed to God's otherness and separation from all else, and spirit pointed to God's dynamic action in relation to his created world. Thus, initially, holiness implied the transcendence of God; the Spirit of God implied his immanence. Only as each idea developed in the OT were they eventually brought together in the term "Holy Spirit."

The *holy* as first perceived was something separated or withdrawn from ordinary life. The holiness of God was something mysterious, powerful, awesome, withdrawn, and not directly approachable. From the idea of the holiness of God came that of holy places, times, rites, offerings, and persons qualified to perform holy rites and make holy offerings to a holy God. This idea of holiness originally had no moral or ethical reference, but these ideas emerged and became emphatic in the prophets (e.g., Amos 2:7; Isa 6:1-5; Hab 1:12-13; 3:3; Hos 11:8-12).

Possibly the earliest reference in the OT to Yahweh as the holy God appears in the story of the Ark of the Covenant, where God slew seventy men because they "looked into the ark of the LORD [Yahweh]" (1 Sam 6:19). The question was posed, "Who is able to stand before the LORD, this holy God?" (v 20). In this perception of God as holy, he is complete otherness and unapproachable in his majesty and power.

With this idea of holiness, God may be approached only through holy rites, with holy offerings at holy places (shrines, altars, temples), at holy times (seasons, days, hours), by holy men (cultic priests, male only). The architecture of the Temple in Jerusalem reflected this perception of holiness, with its Holy of Holies representing the presence of God, to be entered by the high priest alone, once a year with the ATONEMENT offering. A graduated sense of holiness was likewise reflected in the divisions of the Temple: outer court open to Gentiles and animals, the court for Jewish women, the court for Jewish men, the Holy Place for Jewish priests, and finally the curtained-off Holy of Holies (cf. Matt 27:51).

The idea of *spirit* had its own independent development in the OT. The Hebrew word for spirit stood for *wind* or *breath* and then for spirit within God or human beings, and even in "the living creatures" (Ezek 1:20-21; 10:17). The word "spirit" appears more than 240 times in the OT (Heb. רוּחַ *ruah*, which "spirit" translates, more than 370 times), and "the Spirit of God" or "Spirit of the Lord" is pervasive. In OT usage, the Spirit of God may imply his presence—"Whither shall I go from the Spirit? Or whither shall I flee from thy presence?" (Ps 139:7)—or his dynamic action (Gen 6:3; Judg 14:6, 19; Joel 2:28-29). In early usage it was restrictively the dynamic power of God, but the term came to serve also the idea of God's revelatory and redemptive activity, as implied in "Not by might, nor by power, but by my

Spirit, says the LORD of hosts" (Zech 4:6). The more comprehensive work of the Spirit is seen in Isa 11:2-3: "And the Spirit of the Lord shall rest upon him, the spirit of wisdom and understanding, the spirit of counsel and might, the spirit of knowledge and the fear of the Lord." The Spirit of God is the source of human life in its physical, intellectual, and moral aspects (e.g., Job 32:8; 33:4; 34:14ff.; Ps 104:30; Isa 11:2; Zech 4:6).

In the OT, "the Spirit of God" does not imply a person separate from God. In Ps 139:7, Spirit is a synonym for God (cf. Isa 31:3). In Gen 1:1ff., there is an interchange between "God" and "the Spirit of God": "In the beginning God created the heavens and the earth . . . and the Spirit of God was moving over the face of the waters. . . . And God said, 'Let there be light!' . . . " The Spirit of God is God acting in the created world. The "Spirit of God," "his Spirit," "thy Spirit," and "Holy Spirit" are all references to God himself, with no implication of plurality or division. Such usage does not undercut monotheism, foundational to OT theology: "Hear, O Israel: The Lord our God is one Lord" (Deut 6:4). The Holy Spirit is not a separate person within deity.

Significantly, in the three occurrences of "Holy Spirit" in the OT, the concern is for moral behavior and not separation. This seemingly appears in Isa 63:10: "But they rebelled and grieved his holy Spirit." Ps 51 is explicit, concerned throughout with cleansing from sin and renewal of "a new and right spirit within" along with the prayer, "Cast me not away from thy presence, and take not thy *holy Spirit* from me" (v 11).

Both in direct linkage with God and in strong moral reference, this OT usage of Holy Spirit anticipates the more pervasive NT usage. Thus two originally independent ideas, *holiness* as the otherness and separation of God from ordinary life (transcendence) and *spirit* as God's action in his world (immanence), are brought together.

The ultimate expression of the creative tension between God's transcendence and immanence appears in Jesus Christ, "the Word became flesh" (John 1:1, 14).

The New Testament. The term "the Holy Spirit" (but almost always "Holy Ghost" in KJV) appears at least ninety times in the NT, and the idea is even more prevalent through interchanging terms: *the Spirit, the Spirit of God, the Spirit of the Lord, the Spirit of Christ, the Spirit of JESUS,* and *the Holy Spirit.* In English, "Holy Ghost" and "Holy Spirit" render the same Greek term. "Holy Spirit" appears throughout the NT. It is most prominent in the Lucan writings, thirteen times in his Gospel and forty-three times in Acts. (When all terms for "the Spirit" are considered, the Lucan emphasis is less distinctive.)

In the NT, the Holy Spirit represents the presence of God, active and powerful in revealing, convicting of sin, judging, guiding, empowering, comforting, enlightening, teaching, restraining, and otherwise. Every step in the Christian life may be attributed to the work of the Holy Spirit, from conversion (John 3:6) to such maturity as reflects "the fruit of the Spirit" (Gal 5:22).

The Holy Spirit is personal in the NT, but not a person separate from God. The oneness of God is as firm in the NT as in the OT. Jesus himself affirmed the oneness of God, building the love commandment upon Deut 6:4 (Mark 12:29-30). The oneness of God is explicit in Paul and other NT writers (Rom 3:30; 1 Cor 8:6; Gal 3:20; Eph 4:6; 1 Tim 1:17; Jas 2:19; Jude 25; John 17:3). The Holy Spirit is not a third God nor one-third of God. The Holy Spirit is God himself, present and active within his world. Significantly, "Spirit of God," "Spirit of Christ," and "Christ" are interchanged in Rom 8:9-11.

The coming of the Holy Spirit upon the disciples on the day of Pentecost is pivotal in Acts, and this is to be given its full significance for the intention of Acts: the disciples spoke in tongues, in such a way that each person understood in that one's native language; about 3,000 persons were saved; the church was united in FELLOWSHIP; they were moved to generosity in giving to the poor; and they were fearless in the face of opposition (Acts 2-4). Breaking through the language barrier on the day of Pentecost foreshadowed the crossing of greater barriers separating Jews from non-Jews. Luke shows the overcoming of such barriers to be the work of the Holy Spirit. Tongues at Corinth later were the opposite: unintelligible to all but the initiated, divisive within the church, and repelling outsiders (1 Cor 12-14).

The Holy Spirit did not first come at Pentecost. The Holy Spirit is prominent in the Gospel of Luke, characterizing the piety of some devout Jews before the birth of Jesus (Luke 1-2). John the Baptist was filled with the Holy Spirit while yet in his mother's womb (1:15). The Holy Spirit came upon the virgin Mary (1:35). Elizabeth was filled with the Holy Spirit (1:41) as was Zechariah (1:67). The Holy Spirit was upon Simeon, and he came "in the Spirit" into the Temple (2:25-27). The Holy Spirit came upon Jesus at his baptism (Mark 1:10; and par.). Jesus gave assurance that the heavenly Father will "give the Holy Spirit to those who ask him" (Luke 11:13), with no implication that the gift was not immediately available or dependent upon BAPTISM or laying on of apostles' hands. Thus, both OT and NT witness to the presence of the Holy Spirit before Pentecost. The new at Pentecost was the completed work of Jesus, culminating in his death and resurrection. This was the mighty plus with which now the Holy Spirit continued the work of God begun in creation (Gen 1).

"Baptized with the Holy Spirit" (Acts 1:5), for the Holy Spirit to "come upon" someone (Acts 1:8), and to be "filled with the Holy Spirit" (Acts 2:4) are interchangeable. These are stylistic differences, not theological distinctions. Luke employs the identical terms for Elizabeth, Zecharia, and Simeon as for the disciples at Pentecost. No single pattern appears in the NT as to the sequence of baptism, laying on of hands, or the presence of apostles for the coming of the Holy Spirit upon a person. The Holy Spirit comes upon anyone with the faith to ask (Luke 11:13).

In the Gospel of John, the Holy Spirit is known also as the Paraclete (ADVOCATE/PARACLETE), one called alongside as comforter or counselor (14:16). He is also "the Spirit of truth" (14:17; 15:26; 16:13), reminding Jesus' followers of the things Jesus had spoken (14:26), bearing witness to Christ (15:26), and guiding

Jesus' disciples in further truth (16:13). The Holy Spirit convicts the world of sin, righteousness, and judgment (16:8-11). He is the spirit of truth, opposite to the spirit of error (1 John 4:6). Essentially, the Holy Spirit is the continuing divine presence which became incarnate in Jesus Christ. Thus, the followers of Jesus are not left orphans by the physical withdrawal of Christ. Before his ascension, Jesus promised: "I will not leave you desolate; I will come to you" (John 14:18). The Holy Spirit is the continuing divine presence, known in Jesus as one who could be physically seen, heard, and touched (1 John 1:1).

The presence of the Holy Spirit in a human life is not characteristically evidenced in some exotic way, such as speaking in tongues, but in inner qualities of character and outward ministry. The fruit of the Spirit includes love, joy, peace, patience, kindness, goodness, faith, gentleness, and self-control (Gal 5:22). Where the Spirit is, there is freedom (2 Cor 3:17), love (Rom 5:5), peace, and joy (14:17), hope, joy, and peace (15:13). The work of the Spirit is known in the fellowship of the church (2 Cor 13:14). It is by the Spirit that we know the deep things of God (1 Cor 2:10-13). In scripture, those who "spoke from God" are ones "moved by the Holy Spirit" (2 Pet 1:20ff.). Being "filled with the Spirit" is evidenced not in self-serving ways but in ministry to others. When filled with the Holy Spirit, Zechariah preached (Luke 1:67). Filled with the Holy Spirit, Barnabas sold a field and gave the money to care for the poor (Acts 4:36ff.; 11:24). Stephen, "full of faith and of the Holy Spirit" (Acts 6:5), gave his life for his witness to Christ. Empowered by the Holy Spirit, Jesus' followers are to be his witnesses to the end of the earth (Acts 1:8). With the Spirit upon Jesus, he proclaimed his vocation in terms of ministry to human need at every level (Luke 4:18ff.), inclusive of persons as far away as a Sidonian widow (4:26) and a Syrian leper (4:27).

See also BAPTISM; BAPTISM OF FIRE; CREATION; FELLOWSHIP; FLESH AND SPIRIT; GOD; HOLINESS IN THE NT; HOLINESS IN THE OT; INCARNATION; JESUS; REVELATION, CONCEPT OF; SANCTIFICATION; TONGUES; TRINITY.

Bibliography. C. K. Barrett, *The Holy Spirit and the Gospel Tradition;* W. Eichrodt, *Theology of the Old Testament*; R. Otto, *The Idea of the Holy*; H. W. Robinson, *The Christian Experience of the Holy Spirit*; N. H. Snaith, *The Doctrine of the Holy Spirit*; F. Stagg, *The Holy Spirit Today.*

—FRANK STAGG

Justification   [MDB 483-84]

•Justification. The biblical teaching of justification by faith was the main doctrine of Christianity for the Protestant Reformers and has retained its place of prominence in Protestant denominations since the sixteenth century. The Reformers rediscovered in the Bible, especially in the letters of PAUL to the Galatians and the Romans, the reality that one is justified by God apart from any works of merit. Key passages which state this fact are Rom 3:21-31, Gal 3:11, and Eph 2:8-9. The writings of Paul contain the clearest biblical teaching regarding justification by faith.

Though Paul's teaching clearly has direct meaning for the individual sinner who wants to know how to become acceptable to God, the context in which Paul developed his teaching regarding justification by faith was the conflict in the first-century church between Judaizing Christians (see OPPONENTS OF PAUL) who insisted that Gentile converts should be circumcised and obey Jewish food laws and those who did not so believe. As Stendahl says, "Paul's doctrine of justification by faith has its theological context in his reflection on the relation between Jews and Gentiles, and not within the problem of how *man* is to be saved, or how man's deeds are to be accounted" (26). Dahl likewise claims that "the framework which Paul uses to locate the doctrine [of justification by faith] is social and historical rather than psychological and individualistic" (110).

In brief, Jews and Judaizing Christians argued that Gentiles may become part of God's chosen people by becoming part of the Jewish people. Since CIRCUMCISION was a sign of God's covenant with his people, Gentile Christians should therefore be circumcised. Paul argued in Romans and Galatians that Christ makes salvation available for everyone who has faith, whether Jew or Gentile. Gentile Christians therefore do not need to become Jews. The teaching of justification by faith enabled Paul to affirm the universality of the gospel. Unfortunately in the history of the church, the social context in which Paul developed his teaching was forgotten once the church became a Gentile church. The doctrine of justification by faith has become limited to personal religious experience and salvation. A careful study of Paul's letters in their historical setting reveals an often neglected social dimension in the doctrine of justification by faith.

This doctrine is based on the assumption that all people are sinners and need to be saved (Rom 3:9-18). It is also based on the belief that God is righteous/just, faithful, and truthful (Rom 3:1-8); God keeps his commitments. And God's commitment to Abraham was the following: "Scripture, foreseeing that God would justify the Gentiles by faith, preached the gospel beforehand to Abraham, saying, 'In you shall all the nations be blessed' " (Gal 3:8). So Paul's teaching of justification by faith is not primarily anthropological, that is, answering how the guilty sinner can be saved. It is primarily theological, defending God's moral integrity. God has not required of Gentiles something different than he required of the Jews or of Abraham. Abraham was saved through faith, not through works of the Law (Rom 4). Similarly all people—Jews and Gentiles—are justified through faith. The coming of Christ showed God's righteousness, his moral integrity, in that through the death of Christ God made salvation available for all through faith, just as he had promised to Abraham (Gal 3:6-9, 14-18).

Justification is entirely an act of God (Rom 8:33) and is based on the death of Jesus Christ, "who was put to death for our trespasses and raised for our justification" (Rom 4:25). Paul writes that "God shows his love for us in that while we were yet sinners Christ died for us. Since, therefore, we are now justified by his blood, much more shall we be saved by him from the wrath of God" (Rom 5:8-9).

The imagery of justification is a legal one, but as the parallelism between Rom 5:9 and 5:10 demonstrates, justification and RECONCILIATION are different metaphors describing the same reality. To reconcile means to put an end to enmity; to justify means to put an end to legal contention. Much discussion of the doctrine of justification throughout the history of the church has focused on whether justification confers on the believer a new status or a new character. Does justification bear the stamp of a legal conception (a status) rather than of an ethical conception (a real change in character)? Or, in other words, does justification mean that believers have only a new standing before God and are considered righteous, or are they also made righteous?

Since English has no verb "to rightwise" or "to rightify," we use the Latin "justify." But "to justify" in English does not mean "to make right." Biblical words for justification, however, are used for making right in the sense of rectifying a relationship. So justification is the action by which God rectifies the relation between himself and people.

See also RIGHTEOUSNESS IN THE NT; RIGHTEOUSNESS IN THE OT.

Bibliography. G. Bornkamm, *Paul;* N. A. Dahl, *Studies in Paul;* F. Stagg, *New Testament Theology;* K. Stendahl, *Paul among Jews and Gentiles.*

—ROGER L. OMANSON

Law in the New Testament [MDB 501-502]

•Law in the New Testament. "Law" is used in the NT in a variety of ways. The term can refer to any part or all of the OT (1 Cor 14:21), all or part of the Pentateuch (Matt 11:13), specific commands (1 Cor 9:8-9), the will of God (Rom 8:7), and Jewish tradition (Acts 22:3; cf. 1 Cor 9:20). Some would translate "law" (νόμος) as "principle" in texts like Rom 3:27, but this is debated. Because of the various nuances of the term, care should be taken in interpretation to determine how "law" is being used in each specific context.

Law occupies a different role in the NT than in the OT and in Judaism. In both the OT and Judaism the Law stands at the center of the relation between God and the people. In the NT JESUS Christ occupies this position. Christ's coming clearly marks the end of an era. However, the OT Law is still a major focus of the NT writings, and one ought not conclude that the Law is no longer in force. The same writers who declare that change has taken place with the coming of Christ also affirm the continuing validity of the Law (Luke 16:16-17).

Understandably then, many of the 195 references to law in the NT appear in contexts of debate. The conflicts between Jesus and the religious leaders of Judaism often centered on interpretation of the Law. Many of the debates within the early church were over the relevance of the OT Law for Christians. Especially well known are Paul's confrontations with "Judaizers" (see OPPONENTS OF PAUL) who wanted to make Gentile Christians observe the Jewish Law. In fact, more than half of the occurrences of "law" in the NT are in Romans and Galatians.

The OT did not teach salvation by works and was not inherently legalistic. The Law in the OT was an expression of the COVENANT relation with God. In fact, the meaning of TORAH (ET = "law") is primarily "instruction" or "direction."

Likewise Judaism was not inherently legalistic and did not necessarily teach salvation by works. Salvation was not so much earned as it was a result of being born Jewish or converting to Judaism. In the NT era Jews focused more on those aspects of law that separated them from other races. Consequently emphasis was placed on circumcision, Sabbath keeping, food laws, and rituals of purity. The desire for purity led Jews to place a "fence" around the Law to lessen the danger of transgression. This "fence" was an explanation and application of the Law to every part of life. While there were many godly Jews, this type of devotion led often to legalism because the intent of the Law was frequently lost.

Jesus and the Law. All four Gospels present Jesus as expressing a very positive attitude toward OT Law (even though Mark never explicitly uses the word "law"). Jesus asserted that he came to fulfill the Law, not destroy it (Matt 5:17). He stressed the permanence of the Law (Matt 5:18) and expected that people should obey it (John 7:19). When people asked him how to find eternal life, he instructed them to obey the commandments (Matt 19:17; Luke 10:26-28). The Gospel writers themselves seem to hold this same high view of the Law. They understood that the Law pointed to Jesus (John 1:45).

At the same time, Jesus is presented as one who broke the Law as far as the Jews were concerned. He repeatedly violated their understanding of the Sabbath. He ate with tax collectors and sinners, which for Jews was defiling. He set aside their understanding of the Law on issues such as divorce, food laws, and ritual cleansings.

Jesus was not, however, a new lawgiver. He came as the authoritative interpreter of the Law. Like the prophets before him, Jesus took the Law much more seriously than most of the Jewish people. He told the people their righteousness had to exceed that of the Pharisees (Matt 5:20). Then in the antitheses ("You have heard it said, but I say to you" sayings) of Matt 5:21-48 Jesus explained the true intent of God's Law. Where murder and adultery had been viewed as violations of the Law, Jesus argued that attitudes of anger and lust were violations as well. Where people had used the OT to legitimate divorce, Jesus prohibited it. Where people had used oaths as ways of avoiding the truth, Jesus required truth all the time. Where people used the OT to legitimate retaliation, Jesus asked people to turn the other cheek and show mercy.

All these teachings about law are based on two assumptions: that God's people should take their character from God; and that the Law is encompassed in the love commands. Since God displays mercy and goodness even on the unrighteous, his people should also. They are to love even their enemies (Matt 5:44-45). They are to be perfect as their heavenly father is perfect (Matt 5:48). This is not a call to perfectionism; it is a call to follow God.

Jesus' focus on the Law is not some form of legalism. Like Judaism before him and Paul and James after him, Jesus summarized the Law with the love commands. The essence of the Law is "You shall love the Lord your God with all your heart, and with all your soul, and with all your mind," and "You shall love your neighbor as yourself" (Matt 22:37, 39). All else is commentary. That is why the "golden rule" is seen as a summary of the Law and the Prophets (Matt 7:12) and why Jesus could tell the Pharisees that they had neglected the weightier matters of the Law: justice, mercy, and faith (Matt 23:23).

The question still must be asked whether Jesus did not violate the OT Law itself in addition to violating the Jewish understanding of the Law. Some would see Jesus' teaching on divorce as a contradiction of Deut 24:1-3, but this text does not legitimate divorce. It recognizes that divorce occurred and attempted to prevent a woman from remarrying her first husband after the death of, or divorce from, a second husband. The only place where Jesus appears to contradict the OT is in his statement "Not what goes into the mouth defiles a man, but what comes out of the mouth, this defiles a man" (Matt 15:11). While Matthew refers this saying to eating with unwashed hands, the Marcan parallel adds the comment, "In saying this, Jesus declared all foods clean" (Mark 7:19). At least in Mark, Jesus implies that the violation of OT food laws is not defiling; rather, what defiles is sinful actions and speech.

This change is indicative of Jesus' approach to the Law. He was not tolerant of the Law's concern for external purity and separation. He focused on the Law's concern for inner righteousness and for proper relations between people and with God. His was an ethic of principle rather than an ethic of rules, and the dominating principle for him was the love command.

Paul and the Law. PAUL's comments on the Law have caused debate up to the present time. Hardly anything derogatory was said about the Law by other NT writers, but Paul made surprisingly negative statements about the Law. In his theology, the Law brings a curse (Gal 3:13), is not a means to being declared righteous before God (Rom 3:20), works wrath (Rom 4:15), actually leads to the increase of sin (Rom 5:20), is associated with sin to create transgression and death (Rom 7:8-11), is the power of sin (1 Cor 15:56), becomes a tyrant from which people need to be freed (Rom 7:1, 6), and has a ministry of condemnation (2 Cor 3:9).

At the same time Paul made the most positive statements about the Law. The Law is holy and the commandment is holy, righteous, and good (Rom 7:12). The Law is spiritual (Rom 7:14) and gives knowledge of sin (Rom 3:20). The righteous requirement of the Law is to be fulfilled (Rom 8:4) and doing the Law as opposed to merely hearing it is a factor in being declared righteous (Rom 2:13). Contrary to what is often asserted, Paul did not argue that Christ brought the Law to an end. In Rom 3:31 Paul asserted that his understanding of faith did not nullify the Law; rather it established the Law. Rom 10:4 is the verse cited most often to show Paul viewed the Law as obsolete, but this verse should probably be translated "For Christ is the *goal* (τέλος) of the law for righteousness to everyone who believes" (cf. the use of "goal," τέλος, in 1 Tim 1:5).

Paul quoted the Law as validation for his arguments (Gal 3:13). He expected people to obey its ethical injunctions and saw the Law as encapsulated in the command to love one's neighbor as one's self (Rom 13:8-10). Paul did not explain how he made distinctions in the Law, but he clearly did. He saw the love command as universally binding, but he rejected the Law's focus on circumcision, food laws, and sabbath keeping. Apparently those items that separated Jews from Gentiles were the items he saw as no longer binding. The Law was no longer determinative; Jesus Christ was. In fact, Paul saw Christian acts of love as fulfilling the "law of Christ" (Gal 6:2).

One key to understanding Paul's statements on the Law is in seeing the context in which Law is placed. When viewed in connection with sin and the flesh (by which Paul means humanity apart from God), the Law is negative. It brings people to subjection and death. But this is contrary to God's intention. The Law has, in fact, become a tool that sin has commandeered to cause rebellion and transgression (Rom 7:7-13). When, however, the Law is viewed (as God intended) in connection with faith and God's Spirit, then the Law is positive and is to be lived (Rom 8:4).

While most of Paul's references to law refer in some way to the OT, he also speaks of the "law written on the heart." By this he means the moral conscience that is available to all humans. Paul's statements are a recognition that some people who had not encountered the revelation in the OT still had come to similar moral beliefs and practices.

Other NT Writers. The Book of Hebrews is the only NT writing to comment explicitly on the cessation of the sacrifices detailed in the OT Law. (However, note Matt 12:6-7 and 1 Cor 5:7-8.) The writer of Hebrews had a positive view of the OT Law, but saw it as the shadow of the good things coming in Christ (10:1; cf. Col 2:17). He understood the old priesthood of Aaron as replaced by a new one, that of Christ. Christ offered the one perfect sacrifice, and therefore, no other sacrifice is necessary (10:1-18). The change in priesthoods effected a change in the Law (7:12) so that the first covenant of God with Israel was replaced with the new covenant prophesied in Jer 31:31-34 (8:8-13). The laws in this covenant are placed in the minds and written on the hearts of God's people. The prophecy of Jer 31 has been fulfilled by the work of Christ.

The author of James agreed with Paul that Christians should be doers of the word and not hearers only (1:22; cf. Rom 2:13). The Law is to be performed. Pure and untainted religion is embodied in the care of widows and orphans and in keeping oneself undefiled from the world (1:27). The focus on doing, however, does not lead to legalism or a view of the Law as drudgery. The author was enamored with the Law. Surprisingly, he described the Law as the perfect law of liberty, meaning the law that gives freedom. Into this law one should inquire and in it one should remain (1:25). Doing leads to happiness. The Law is "the royal law" and is summarized by the command to love one's neighbor as oneself (2:8). Christians are to live with the recognition that they will be judged on the basis of this law of liberty (2:12).

Conclusion. The NT evidence indicates that the Law has a much more positive role in the lives of Christians than Reformation theology has often allowed. The understandings of law as external form, as legalism, or as a way to earn salvation were never legitimate. The Law is always susceptible to being used by sin to foster rebellion and pride. The OT Law was only a shadow of the good things coming in Christ. But the intention of the Law always has been found in the commands to love God and neighbor. The high call of the Law to orient one's being and actions around the love of God and neighbor is a call that still needs to be heard.

See also COVENANT; JESUS; LAW IN THE OT; PAUL; TORAH.

Bibliography. R. Badenas, *Christ the End of the Law: Romans 10:4 in Pauline Perspective*; R. Banks, *Jesus and the Law in the Synoptic Tradition*; C. L. Blomberg, "The Law in Luke-Acts," JSNT 22 (1984): 53-80; C. E. B. Cranfield, "St. Paul and the Law," SJT 17 (1964): 43-68; W. D. Davies, *Torah in the Messianic Age and/or the Age to Come*; D. P. Fuller, *Gospel and Law: Contrast or Continuum?*; R. A. Guelich, *The Sermon on the Mount*; H. Hübner, *Law in Paul's Thought*; J. Jervell, "Law in Luke-Acts," HTR 64 (1971): 21-36; R. S. McConnell, *Law and Prophecy in Matthew's Gospel*; D. J. Moo, "Paul and the Law in the Last Ten Years," WTJ 49 (1987); S. Pancaro, *The Law in the Fourth Gospel*; H. Räisänen, *Paul and the Law*; E. P. Sanders, *Paul, the Law, and the Jewish People*; G. S. Sloyan, *Is Christ the End of the Law?*; S. G. Wilson, *Luke and the Law.*

—KLYNE R. SNODGRASS

Letters/Inscriptions [MDB 509-10]

•**Letters/Inscriptions.** Recent years have witnessed the recovery of an abundance of inscriptional material from Syria-Palestine. Probably the most exciting was the recovery of the EBLA (Tell Mardikh) archives. Not only was this find significant because of its size (more than 4,000 tablets that were complete or nearly so, and a total of more than 17,000 fragments) and age (the majority of texts date to ca. 2400–2250 B.C.E.), but also because it provides significant historical data for the Old Canaanite period especially concerning a previously unknown kingdom in North Syria. Although not nearly so spectacular, many significant finds have also been made of inscriptions in the alphabetic scripts of Palestine.

Palestinian Inscriptions. While it is true that the quantity of finds of alphabetic scripts has not been as great as for the cuneiform archives, nevertheless many additional inscriptions in HEBREW, ARAMAIC, MOABITE, AMMONITE, EDOMITE, and PHOENICIAN have been recovered in Palestine. To date, the largest single corpus of Palestinian inscriptions is from ARAD where 112 Hebrew, eighty-five Aramaic, two Greek, and five Arabic inscriptions were unearthed. In addition thirteen inscribed weights and nine *lmlk* impressions were found. The longest single inscription from Palestine is the fragmentary DEIR 'ALLA text.

The list of major inscriptions now known from Palestine must include at least the following from the period of the Hebrew monarchy, about 1000–586 B.C.E.: Gezer calendar, MESHA STELA, Amman Citadel inscription, KUNTILLET 'AJRUD ostraca, SAMARIA ostraca, SILOAM Tunnel inscription, Shebna tomb inscriptions, Deir 'Alla inscription, Tell Qasile inscriptions, Meṣad Ḥashavyahu inscriptions, HESHBON ostraca, Gibeon jar handles, Arad ostraca, Lachish ostraca, Tell Siran bottle, Khirbet el-Qom inscriptions, Khirbet Beit Lei inscriptions, and a number of inscriptions from various excavations in Jerusalem (the most exciting probably being the Ketef Hinnom silver amulets bearing a variant form of the Aaronic benediction [Num 6:24-26] and dating to about 700 B.C.E.). From the earlier periods, one must include the Proto-Sinaitic inscriptions, Proto-Canaanite inscriptions from Lachish and Beth-Shemesh, the Izbet Ṣartah ostracon, and a number of inscribed javelin heads. Later finds include the Samaria papyri, Naḥal Ḥever, Wadi Murabbaat, and Qumran (DEAD SEA SCROLLS) material.

The value of these inscriptions for historical reconstructions and biblical interpretation is inestimable. A few examples will indicate their value.

The Mesha Stela provides much new information about King Mesha of Moab, previously known only from a few references in the OT. Furthermore, the stela also mentions OMRI, king of Israel, and provides a correspondence between the reigns of these two kings. Israel's God, Yahweh is mentioned on the stela, along with CHEMOSH, Moab's god. The language of the Mesha stela is very close to the Hebrew of the OT, so it provides very helpful parallels in studying the Hebrew language during the period of the monarchy.

The Meṣad Ḥashavyahu ostracon provides insights into the situation at the time of Josiah. The inscription illuminates the biblical command concerning garments taken in pledge (Exod 22:26-27). In the inscription a peasant complains that his garment has been taken without cause (apparently by an overseer) and he requests its return. A second matter of interest from the inscription is the availability of writing for a peasant. Either the peasant was literate or scribes were readily available even to a poor peasant. In either case, it is apparent a relatively small matter was put in writing and brought to higher officials for redress.

Letter Form. Among the many inscriptional finds from Palestine have been a number of letters. A study of these letters shows they have significant features in common.

(1) *Sender.* Some letters begin with the name of the person sending the letter. This feature is not very common, however, in Hebrew letters. Arad 16 begins in this manner: "Your brother Hananyahu sends (greeting) concerning the well-being of Elyashib and the well-being of your household."

(2) *Recipient.* Most Hebrew letters begin with the name of the recipient. Since letters would typically be sent by messenger, one must assume the recipient would know the sender from the messenger, or would recognize the writing or seal affixed to the letter. A typical recipient formula is simply "To _____ " (the name of the person intended). Often the relative rank of the recipient to the sender is indicated, for example, "To my lord Yaush" (Lachish Letter 2), in which the sender is definitely addressing a superior.

(3) *Greeting*. Most Hebrew letters included a greeting. Arad 16 mentioned above shows a common form of greeting. At times the greeting may be quite elaborate. Often Yahweh is invoked to bring well-being (*shalom*) and blessing on the recipient and the entire household.

(4) *Transition*. Many letters use a specific word to indicate the transition from greeting to the formal body of the text. Typically the Hebrew word *v'at*, "and now," marks the transition. This transition can readily be seen in Arad 18: "To my lord Elyashib, may Yahweh ask concerning your well-being. And now, give. . . . "

(5) *Body*. The body of the letter contains the purpose of the letter, perhaps a message, a report, a command, or a response to a previous communication.

(6) *Closing greeting*. None of the Hebrew letters from the period of the monarchy have this feature. But it does appear in Aramaic letters and later letters from the Bar Kochba period. *Shalom*, "well-being," is a typical closing word.

(7) *Signature*. Again, none of the Hebrew letters from the period of the monarchy have this feature. But it does appear in several later letters. Obviously the signature is unnecessary in letters that have the sender's name as the first element.

This letter form remains relatively unchanged into the NT period. Even the epistles of the NT show many of the same elements as the much earlier Hebrew letters. Note, for example, the elements in the Letter to the Galatians:

Sender: "Paul an apostle," 1:1
Recipient: "to the churches of Galatia," 1:2
Greeting: "Grace to you and peace," 1:3
Transition: (missing)
Body: "I am astonished," 1:6–6:10
Closing greeting: "See with what large letters I am writing with my own hand. . . . The grace of the Lord Jesus Christ be with you," 6:11-18.

The study of Hebrew letter forms can aid in interpreting NT materials by offering additional comparative texts.

Hebrew letters also indicate frequently the relationship between the sender and the recipient. One example has been noted above, as a sender addressed the recipient as a superior, "my lord." The sender who is of lesser status would use such terms as "your servant" and "your son." It is unclear whether all references to a son describe kinship, or may refer to the relative status of the two individuals. When the two individuals are of equal status, the term "my brother" was used. The use of this kinship term to indicate relative status without necessitating kinship suggests a similar use of the term "son." Furthermore, the use of kinship terms to indicate status may open anew discussion of kinship terms in the Bible.

See also MESHA STELE; SEMITIC LANGUAGES; SILOAM INSCRIPTION; WRITING SYSTEMS.

Bibliograhy. J. A. Fitzmyer, "Some Notes on Aramaic Epistolography," JBL 93 (1974): 201–25; D. Pardee, *Handbook of Ancient Hebrew Letters*.

—JOEL F. DRINKARD, JR.

Luke [MDB 529]

•**Luke.** Luke was the fellow traveler of Paul and the traditional author of the third Gospel and the Acts of the Apostles. His name (Gk. *Loukas*) is probably an abbreviation of the Latin *Lucius*. Luke is mentioned by name only three times in the NT, all in letters attributed to Paul: Col 4:14; Phlm 24; 2 Tim 4:11. The most important of these is the passage in Colossians, where Luke is called "the beloved physician" and is apparently distinguished from Paul's other coworkers "who are from the circumcision" (Col 4:11). That the writer of Luke-Acts was educated and could have been a physician is borne out by the vocabulary of Luke and Acts, as well as by the character of the contents of both writings. In the LETTER TO PHILEMON, sent to the same place as Colossians, Luke joins Paul's other "fellow workers" in sending greetings to Philemon. Finally, in 2 Tim 4:11 Paul writes, "Only Luke is with me," and asks Timothy to join him with Mark.

If Colossians and Philemon were written by Paul when he was a prisoner in Rome, then Luke must have accompanied Paul on his voyage as a prisoner to Rome, as described in Acts 27 and 28. These two chapters comprise one of the three WE-SECTIONS in Acts (beginning in Acts 16:10; 20:5 and 27:1) in which the author identifies himself as a participant in the narrative. If Luke was the author of Acts, then he must have joined Paul at Troas in 50 C.E. and traveled with him to Philippi (Acts 16:10-18). Here he appears to have been left behind, only to be picked up again some seven years later on Paul's trip to Jerusalem with the offering for the Judean Christians (Acts 20:5–21:18). It is conceivable that Luke was the "true yokefellow" whom Paul asks in Phil 4:3 to help resolve the differences between Euodia and Syntyche. Later still, possibly during Paul's second imprisonment in Rome, Luke is alone with Paul (2 Tim 4:11)—which may imply that Luke served as the amanuensis of Paul if the latter wrote 2 Timothy. This agrees with an early Christian tradition (the so-called Anti-Marcionite Prologue to Luke) that Luke the physician remained a faithful coworker of Paul until the apostle's martyrdom. What happened to Luke after this cannot be determined with certainty, but according to the same tradition Luke continued to serve the Lord without wife or child until he died in Boeotia in Greece at the age of eighty-four.

Some scholars identify Luke with one or both of the bearers of the name Lucius in Acts 13:1 and Rom 16:21. In Acts, however, there is no evidence to connect this Lucius with Luke the physician (Lucius was a common name in the Roman world). The Lucius mentioned in Romans as one of Paul's "kinsmen" is distinguished from Timothy, who is called "my fellow worker." It is difficult to see how the Gentile Luke could be regarded as a relative of Paul by kinship or race.

See also APOSTLES, ACTS OF THE; LUKE, GOSPEL OF; WE-SECTIONS.

Bibliography. C. K. Barrett, *Luke the Historian in Recent Study*; S. G. Wilson, *Luke and the Pastoral Epistles*; W. K. Hobart, *The Medical Language of St. Luke*.

—DAVID A. BLACK

Opponents of Paul [MDB 633-34]

•**Opponents of Paul.** From his letters, it is obvious PAUL had many opponents and enemies. Much internal evidence points to a group termed "the Judaizers," who composed the right wing of the Jerusalem church, as the major opponents of Paul. They viewed him as a "Johnny come lately" to the Christian movement—one who possessed little knowledge of the historical Jesus. They attacked him especially at the point of not being one of the twelve disciples.

The major issue, however, separating Paul and the Judaizers was the one concerning the CIRCUMCISION of Gentile converts. Judaizers emphasized three major points: (1) salvation belonged to the children of Abraham; (2) Gentiles could become adopted children of Abraham by accepting the initiatory rite of circumcision; and (3) converts should keep the Jewish Law with particular emphasis on the food laws, feasts, and fasts.

The great Tübingen critic F. C. Baur did much to emphasize the Judaizers as Paul's major opponents. As early as 1831 Baur raised questions concerning Paul's relationship to the Jerusalem disciples in reference particularly to the "Christ party" at Corinth (cf. 1 Cor 1:12). Baur believed even the most casual reader of the NT would notice the tension that existed between Paul and the Jerusalem church. Baur underlined that tension to the point of almost warlike proportions. Baur saw the conflict as between Paul, the champion of the Gentile movement, and JAMES along with PETER, the leaders of the Jerusalem church. These Jerusalem apostles and other members of their party followed Paul around on his various journeys. They attempted to correct his false teaching. In Baur's view, the majority of the NT books tried to cover over this conflict—especially the Book of Acts. Baur, in addition, viewed GALATIANS as Paul's major reply to his Judaizing opponents.

Other evidence points to GNOSTICISM as the background of Paul's opponents. Walter Schmithals has been the chief advocate of identifying Paul's opponents as Gnostic Jewish Christians. He based his theory on evidence that there were more than two parties in early Christianity: the Pauline and the Jerusalem apostles. He argued for a syncretistic group of Jews who had modified their Judaism with Gnosticism. He associated the Gnostic concept of primal man with the Messiah or Christ. Schmithals felt that the various Gnostic Christian sects evolved out of Gnostic Jewish sects. In fact he concluded that Judaism had been the most important mediator of Gnosticism to the West.

Schmithals pointed to Gal 4:9-10 as good support for his Gnostic theory. There Paul warned the Galatians not to return to the weak and beggarly elemental spirits. The reference to the worship of "elemental spirits" should be considered an evident overtone of Gnosticism. Gnosticism fostered a worship of those spirits through cultic practices (days, months, seasons) which would propitiate them.

W. Luetgert and J. H. Ropes took the position that Paul was opposed by two groups rather than one. Paul was caught between the legalists on one hand and the libertines on the other. The legalists called him too conservative. The Ropes-

Luetgert school made much of Gal 5:11. There Paul declared, "But if I, brethren, still preach circumcision; why am I still persecuted?" In their view, this would certainly not be a charge leveled at Paul by Jews from Jerusalem. The accusation that Paul was "preaching circumcision" would be made by a more liberal group such as the libertines. Paul viewed the libertine theology as much a threat as the Judaizers. The libertines felt the Jewish Law was not binding on them, and this attitude led to moral license. They accused Paul of giving in to the Judaizers and the authority of the Jerusalem church.

The two-front theory also recognized the role and influence of the Judaizers. Unlike Baur, Luetgert-Ropes rejected the identification of the Jerusalem Twelve with the Judaizers as Jewish Christians loosely connected with the church or even legalistic Gentiles.

Johannes Munck concluded that Paul's opponents, especially in Galatia, might have been Gentile converts rather than Jerusalem Jews. Paul converted the Gentiles without insisting on circumcision. Later these converts encountered the demands of the Law as revealed in the Jewish scriptures. Some felt that they were not true Christians because they had not received the seal of the covenant, circumcision. Thus they voluntarily accepted this rite and started preaching it to their fellow brothers. At the same time, they called into question the apostolic authority of Paul. These Gentile Judaizers felt that the Jerusalem apostles were still preaching circumcision and the Law. Thus there was a call to return to the orthodox teaching of Jerusalem and a mandate to brand the Pauline gospel as heresy.

Who were Paul's opponents? Many answers have been given over the years by NT scholars. Were they the Jerusalem Twelve, Gentile Christians, Jewish Gnostics, Jewish Christians at Jerusalem or some combination of these groups? Perhaps, the answer depends on whether one were in Galatia or Corinth. The Jerusalem Judaizers seem to be the best choice for Galatia. It is hard to oppose F.C. Baur at that point. Although he exaggerated his case, he saw the basic theological cleavage between Paul and the Jerusalem church. At Corinth, the opponents seem to have more of a Gnostic background. The so-called Christ party was a group that separated the body from the soul. These enthusiasts believed that what you did in the body could not affect the soul. This attitude led to the excesses at Corinth. The best approach to the problem, then would be to see many Pauline opponents coming from a multitude of backgrounds. Only study of the context of the writing can allow one to point to one group over against another.

See also CIRCUMCISION; GNOSTICISM; JAMES; PAUL; PETER.

Bibliography. F. C. Baur, *Paulus*; W. Luetgert, *Gesetz und Geist*; J. Munck, *Paul and the Salvation of Mankind*; J. H. Ropes, *The Singular Problem of the Epistle to the Galatians*; W. Schmithals, *Gnosticism in Corinth*.

—JAMES L. BLEVINS

Paul [MDB 657-62]

•**Paul.** Paul was a first-century non-Palestinian Pharisaic Jew who changed from being a persecutor of the earliest Christian church to become one of the most effective and influential missionaries in all of Christian history. He called himself an "apostle of Jesus Christ" to "the Gentiles," and, while it was primarily to non-Jews that he preached, his message had a profound impact even on the originally Jewish portion of early Christianity.

Paul's Life. (1) *Sources for the study.* The NT and other early Christian literature seem to provide a wealth of sources for reconstructing the life of Paul. More than one-half of the Book of Acts is an account of Paul's career from the time he was a persecutor of the church through his imprisonment in Rome toward the end of his life. Thirteen letters in the NT bear Paul's name as their author. Outside the canon of the NT many volumes of early Christian literature present themselves as other "letters" by Paul or offer further accounts of his "acts."

(a) *Problems.* When one turns to the early Christian literature in order to ascertain the life of Paul, one immediately encounters three serious problems. First, extensive as the sources are, they provide *insufficient data* for writing a "life" of Paul. For example, little, if anything, is known about Paul's birth, childhood, and early manhood; indeed, we do not even know with absolute certainty when, where, and how Paul died. Much remains shrouded in mystery, for the sources are simply inadequate for producing a Pauline biography.

Second, one must establish the *authenticity* of the sources. For example, no contemporary scholar judges that Paul wrote any of the number of extrabiblical letters that are attributed to him, correspondences like the *Epistles of Paul and Seneca*, Paul's *Letter to the Laodiceans*, and *3 Corinthians*. Clearly these were produced by others in the name of Paul. Moreover, because of matters of history, vocabulary, style, and theology, many scholars (frequently the majority) judge that as many as six of the thirteen letters in the NT attributed to Paul were written by his colleagues and students, not the apostle. These are 2 Thessalonians, Ephesians, Colossians, 1 and 2 Timothy, and Titus. Only seven letters are judged undisputedly to be authentic. Thus, many scholars conclude that all of the NT letters attributed to Paul are not of equal value for reconstructing the life of the apostle.

Third, it is sometimes *impossible through harmonization to reconcile statements* made in even the most reliable sources. For example, Acts 9 recounts that when Paul was struck down on the road to DAMASCUS, he was "immediately" active there (in Damascus) preaching in the synagogues that Jesus was the Son of God. After "many days," Acts says, he went to Jerusalem in an effort to join the disciples; but they were afraid of him, because they doubted his sincerity, and so they avoided him. Then, one learns from Acts that BARNABAS took Paul to the apostles who accepted him. The result was that Paul preached, going in and out among the Jerusalem Christians and even down to CAESAREA, so that "the church throughout all Judea and Galilee and Samaria had peace and was built up" (Acts 9:31).

In contrast, Gal 1:11-24 (esp. vv 15-24) is a statement by Paul declaring his independence as an apostle. He avers here that the gospel he preached did not come from any human, instead it came through a revelation by God of the risen Jesus Christ. Paul claims he was ordained by God, that he did not confer with "flesh and blood," i.e., any human agent. He insists that when he was called by God he did not go up to Jerusalem to the apostles for their approval but went to Arabia and later returned to Damascus. He says that after three years he visited Cephas (Simon Peter) in Jerusalem for fifteen days; but he declares that he saw "none of the other apostles except James the Lord's brother" (Gal 1:19). Indeed, Paul claims that he departed after this visit "still not known by sight to the churches of Judea" (Gal 1:22).

Frequently accounts of early Christianity provide a harmonization of these passages. But this is bad method! One cannot simply take a secondary source (here, Acts) and derive from it a framework into which a primary source (here, Galatians) must be made to fit. The result of such harmonization is abusive of primary material and produces a distorted picture of early Christianity.

(b) *Methods.* There is a way to work through the rough spots in the reconstruction of Paul's life, but in order to do so, one must be guided by sound method. Briefly stated the critical method that guides most contemporary Pauline studies is this:

(i) The primary sources always have priority. Moreover, the soundest basis for understanding Paul is laid by using the seven undisputed letters of Paul: Romans, 1 Corinthians, 2 Corinthians, Galatians, Philippians, 1 Thessalonians, and Philemon. The other letters may be consulted in an ancillary capacity—though they add little if anything to one's knowledge of Paul's life.

(ii) The secondary source, Acts, may be used cautiously as a supplement to the primary materials when it is not in conflict with the letters. Indeed, agreement of the primary and secondary materials gives one certainty, for the author of Acts shows no knowledge of Paul's letters or even that Paul wrote letters.

(iii) Other early Christian documents are almost useless for the purpose of reconstructing Paul's life. These works are highly legendary in character. They illustrate matters that are best regarded as debatable or unknown. For example, extrabiblical early Christian literature offers competing stories about Paul's death. This diversity probably indicates that the exact manner of Paul's death was not widely known among subsequent Christians and that because of their curiosity these later Christians formulated a variety of accounts by interpreting freely, using pious imagination, the evidence that was available to them.

(c) *Results.* By taking the autobiographical material in Paul's letters, comparing that information with Acts, and then considering the extrabiblical sources, one distinguishes two kinds of material. First, one isolates reliable information that allows one to compose Paul's story in outline. This account is nothing like a biography, the sources do not provide such extensive information; but one gets an impression of the man and develops a sketch of his career as an apostle. In the form of a sentence outline, the sketch appears as follows.

(i) The man's name was *Paul*, a Greek name.

(ii) He had a Jewish name, *Saul*. (Having two names was not uncommon for Jews who lived outside Palestine in the first century.)

(iii) Paul was born in TARSUS, a city in southeastern Asia Minor.

(iv) He came from a family of PHARISEES of the tribe of Benjamin and was named for the tribe's most illustrious member, King Saul.

(v) Paul's letters show familiarity with both *rabbinic* methods for interpretation of scripture and *popular Hellenistic philosophy* to a degree that makes it likely that he had formal education in both areas.

(vi) He was probably, as an adult, a resident of Damascus.

(vii) He was an active persecutor of the early Christian movement (probably because he perceived it to be a threat to Torah obedience).

(viii) Paul became a Christian, an apostle, through a dramatic revelation of Jesus Christ.

(ix) His first years as a Christian, spent in Arabia are a mystery.

(x) Three years after his call Paul went to Jerusalem to visit; he saw Peter and James.

(xi) Later (after fourteen years), he returned to Jerusalem for a meeting often referred to as the "Jerusalem Conference" or the "Apostolic Council."

(xii) Paul was a vigorous evangelist, traveling and preaching in Achaia, Arabia, Asia, Cilicia, Galatia, Judea, Illyricum, Macedonia, Syria, and making plans for Italy and Spain.

(xiii) On the mission field he: worked with a group of trusted colleagues (Aquila, Prisca, Silvanus, Sosthenes, TIMOTHY, TITUS, and others); supported himself with his craft, tentmaking; was often in danger and abused; and suffered from a "thorn in the flesh."

(xiv) Along with evangelization, Paul worked among his non-Palestinian congregations on a major project, a collection for the "poor" in Jerusalem, which he hoped would reconcile the non-Law-observant Christian givers and the Law-observant Christian recipients.

(xv) While actively engaged in evangelization of a region, Paul wrote to churches he had founded earlier in other areas to address problems experienced by those congregations.

(xvi) Paul's clear self-perception was that he was an "apostle of Jesus Christ to the Gentiles," i.e., one sent to proclaim the good news of Jesus Christ among non-Jews.

(xvii) One probably loses sight of Paul in the primary sources as he is imprisoned in Caesarea writing to Philemon and to the church at PHILIPPI (cf. the chronological sketch below). Nevertheless, with all but certainty one may conclude that while in prison (under Felix and then Festus), he appealed to be tried before

Caesar (Nero) and was sent to Rome for a hearing. Subsequently, he died there as a martyr.

Even in this material there is some uncertainty. For example, because of the ambiguity of his statements, when Paul says "then after three years" (Gal 1:18), and "then after fourteen years" (Gal 2:1), one cannot be sure exactly what he means. He could be indicating two points in time, both dated from his call—to paraphrase, "then three years after my call" and "then fourteen years after my call." But, he could mean "then three years after my call" and "then fourteen years later"—in other words, *seventeen* years.

A second kind of information isolated in this study is that information in the secondary sources about which the interpreters of Paul must express reservations. For example, Acts 2:3 informs the reader that Paul was brought up in Jerusalem at the feet of GAMALIEL—in other words, Paul was a student in Jerusalem of one of the most famous rabbis in Jewish history. But, Paul himself never mentions these credentials. This is striking, for there are places in his letters where he lists his "Jewish" credentials at length. The mention of Gamaliel in these listings would have amplified Paul's point concerning his former zeal for and status in Judaism, but he does not mention the connection. It is possible that Paul studied with Gamaliel in Jerusalem, but since he does not mention this himself, it is safest to omit this item when reconstructing his life. Moreover, from Paul's own letters Paul himself says he "went up to Jerusalem to visit" and that he "returned to Damascus" (Gal 1:18, 17). From this manner of reference, serious students of Paul's life and work understand that he was, as an adult, a resident of Damascus, not Jerusalem. Even more problematic is the claim in Acts that Paul received an endorsement from the apostles in Jerusalem. Not only does Paul not say this, he flatly denies it in Galatians.

In conclusion, by delineating and practicing a sound method for the use of sources in the reconstruction of Paul's life, one achieves valuable results. On the one hand, one exposes information that allows a more sophisticated reading of the NT documents in relation to one another. On the other, one develops a sketch of the life of Paul. This sketch may, through the conservatism of the method, be a minimal one; but it is absolutely reliable, admitting no debatable material. The sketch will be useful for the remainder of this study.

(2) *The pattern of Paul's life and work.* Toward the end of his ministry Paul says, "I have been able to bring to completion [the preaching of] the gospel of Christ from Jerusalem around as far as Illyricum" (Rom 15:19). In modern terms he claims to have preached the "good news" from Israel through Lebanon, Syria, Turkey, Greece, as far as portions of Bulgaria, Albania, and Yugoslavia. How could Paul have done this in twenty to twenty-five years of his ministry?

The usual image of Paul is of an energetic, tenacious, individual preacher, but one should recognize that Paul's missionary activity was teamwork. His letters reveal that he coordinated the activity of a systematically organized band of missionaries and that his method was fairly consistent. Paul would move with a group of seasoned missionary colleagues to the capital city of a Roman province.

Upon arrival he and his associates would approach the local SYNAGOGUE, and if possible set up a base therein for the proclamation of the gospel. If no synagogue existed, the team would seek out the so-called "God-fearers" (see Acts 10:2, 22; 13:16, 26), i.e., Gentiles who were attracted to the theology and morality of Judaism but who had not become full converts. If there were no God-fearers, Paul and his companions would take the message to the local marketplace. In the process of moving into a city Paul would gather any Christians who already lived there and incorporate them into the missionary enterprise, thereby expanding his staff. While Paul seems to have remained in the capital city and its immediate area, his fellow workers appear to have dispersed themselves throughout the other cities, towns, and villages of the region in order to establish satellite congregations. Paul would remain in one location until the job he set out to do was done (he was in CORINTH a year and a half and in EPHESUS two years and three months) or, more often, until he became embroiled in a controversy that forced him to leave the region. Paul then moved on to repeat this process in a new location. But, he did not loose contact with the churches he founded. Indeed, he paid checkup visits to the churches when he deemed it necessary. Moreover, he used the writing of letters as a part of his missionary strategy, employing the written communication (like a modern "bishop's letter") to influence and build up the congregations he addressed.

Some scholars attribute this method of organizing missionary work to the church at Antioch of which Paul was a member, and which itself was extremely active in early Christian missionary work. This may be the case; or, if Paul was a Jewish missionary before he was Christian, perhaps he adapted the technique from Jewish missionary activity. It may even be that Paul devised the strategy himself. Knowing the source of Paul's missionary style would be enlightening, but not knowing this does not detract from understanding Paul's work and appreciating its effectiveness.

(3) *Chronological outline.* In attempting to map a Pauline chronology—i.e., to locate times and places in the life of Paul—one immediately finds a lack of real detail for the task. Moreover, even with regard to some of the available details there are uncertainties. For example, how long was Paul in Arabia (Gal 1:17)? Or when he writes in Philippians and Philemon that he is in prison, in what city is the prison located? And when he says he is confident of his impending release, is he merely being optimistic? or does he have some reason to believe he will be freed? or is he playing a bluff to motivate those to whom he writes?

Because of the lack of specific information and in light of the difficulties associated with using what material is available, many scholars argue that no more than a relative dating of Paul's letters is possible. And even here there are problems, for the preserved copies of Paul's letters are not dated. Moreover, the claims of some scholars to recognize developments in Paul's thinking from one letter to another are not persuasive, being locked in as they are to the presuppositions that Paul's thought evolved and that he could not change his mind.

• Outline of Paul's Life •

35 (or 32)	Paul is called by God's revelation of Jesus Christ (problem of "three" and "fourteen")
35–38	Missionary activity in Arabia (Gal 1:17) and Damascus (2 Cor 11:32)
38	Paul visits with Peter (and James) in Jerusalem (Gal 1:18)
38–48	Missionary activity in Cilicia and Syria (Gal 1:21)
48	So-called Apostolic Council in Jerusalem (Gal 2:1-10; Acts 15)
48 or 49	Incident with Peter and others in Antioch (Gal 2:11-14)
49	Missionary activity in Galatia (Acts 16:6)
50	Missionary activity in Philippi, Thessalonica, and Beroea (Acts 16:11–17:14)
late 50	Travel to Corinth via Athens (Acts 17:15; 18:1); writing of 1 Thessalonians
late 50 to May 52	Missionary activity in Corinth (Acts 18:11)
summer 52	Travel to Caesarea; then Antioch; then passing through Asia Minor he paid a second visit to Galatia on the way to Ephesus (Gal 4:13; Acts 18:18-23)
late 52 to spring 55	Missionary activity in Ephesus (Acts 19:1, 8-10, 22); writing of Galatians, 2 Cor 6:14–7:1; 1 Corinthians, and the letters preserved in 2 Cor 8 and 2:14–6:13, 7:2-4
(54)	Visit to Corinth (presupposed in 2 Cor 13:1)
late 54–55	Writing of letter preserved in 2 Cor 10–13
summer 55	Travel through Macedonia to Corinth; writing of letter preserved in 2 Cor 1:1–2:13; 7:5-16, and of the final "Collection Letter", 2 Cor 9
late 55 to early 56	Stay in Corinth; writing of Romans
56	Travel to Jerusalem with the collection; arrest and imprisonment
56–58	Imprisonment in Caesarea; writing of Philippians and Philemon
58	Felix replaced by Festus; Paul appeals to Caesar and is sent to Rome
58–60	Imprisonment in Rome (Acts 28:30)
60+	Martyrdom

From these cautionary remarks one might gather that the prospect of working out a Pauline chronology is bleak. But, these warnings should not completely deter an attempt at correlating dates and places for Paul's career. Indeed, one firm date for Paul's activity is ascertainable (though recent work by Jewett, Luedemann, and Murphy-O'Connor draws conclusions that differ from this scholarly consensus). From Acts 18:12-18 one learns that Paul was in Corinth when GALLIO was proconsul. An inscription found at Delphi (an ancient Greek town) permits dating of Gallio's term as proconsul to the period from May of 51 C.E. to May of 52 C.E. By correlating Acts and the Delphic inscription, one learns when Paul could possibly have appeared before Gallio. At the earliest it was the summer of 51 and at the latest the spring of 52. Scholars mount arguments for both extremities, but they have not settled the issue which is perhaps unresolvable. Since there is nothing in Acts 18:12 to indicate that Gallio had taken office only recently (Acts 18:11 is a simple atemporal summary and does not indicate past time), for convenience we will make use of the later date—although recognizing that one may adjust the ensuing reconstruction by moving back the dates almost one year.

The information concerning Paul's imprisonment in Caesarea under Felix and then Festus is another "definite" moment in Paul's life. Some scholars correlate the information in Acts 24–26 with other material from Roman history concerning the family of Felix, but this is quite complicated and the case is fraught with difficulties, even improbabilities, and is merely speculative. Thus it is best to use the information in Paul's Letters and Acts to work forward and backward from the dating of Gallio's proconsulship. Also to be considered are the conditions for travel in the ancient Greek world. For example, those who traveled on foot, as Paul no doubt did, could cover about twenty miles per day; few sea voyages took place during March, April, May, September, and October, and from November through February the Mediterranean was effectively closed for travel. Taking all these factors into the calculation, one achieves the chronological outline above.

(The conclusion that Paul did not write the six disputed letters lies behind this particular reconstruction. The decisions concerning the authorship of these letters are not related to chronology, however; and those who conclude that Paul did write the disputed letters can easily factor their conclusions into this account of Paul's life by locating 2 Thessalonians shortly after 1 Thessalonians, late in 50 or early in 51 C.E. from Corinth. Furthermore, most scholars who accept Colossians, Ephesians, and the Pastoral Epistles as authentic Pauline letters usually and most aptly regard them as coming from the time of Paul's Roman imprisonment. If one concludes that any or all of these is/are genuine Pauline correspondences, one may set the letter[s] in the period 58–60+ C.E.).

Paul's Letter Writing. Since Paul's Letters are what remain directly from his labors as an apostle, one should examine them in terms of their organization and style to see if they offer further insight into the character of their author. To perceive the genius of Paul's Letters it is helpful to know something about letters and letter writing in antiquity (see also EPISTLE/LETTER and LETTERS/INSCRIPTIONS).

(1) *Ancient letters.* Education, commerce, and travel in the Hellenistic era created a context for letter writing. There was even a semiprofessional class of letter writers called scribes or amanuenses. Letters moved surprising distances in Paul's day. The first "traveling" letters were official communication regarding governmental and military matters, but with improved conditions all sorts of letters were produced. These included public decrees by rulers, official letters between authorities, business letters, friendly communications, and brief notes of all sorts.

In Paul's day, as today, letters were written in standard forms. Normally, there were five sections to the letter: (1) a Salutation in three parts which name the sender, the addressee, and offer a greeting; (2) a Thanksgiving; (3) the Body of the letter; (4) Final Instructions (Parenesis); and (5) the Closing in two parts which offers final greetings and the parting word. The letters are frequently dated and addressed.

(2) *Paul's modifications to standard letter form.* It is helpful to compare Paul's briefest letter, Philemon, as an example of Paul's letter-writing style, with the standard form of the Hellenistic letter. When this is done, one readily recognized how Paul's letters are similar and dissimilar to other letters of his day.

Salutation
>> *Sender(s)*:
>>> "Paul, a prisoner for Christ Jesus and Timothy our brother"
>> *Recipient(s)*:
>>> "to Philemon our beloved fellow worker and Apphia our sister and Archippus our fellow soldier and the church in your house"
>> *Greeting*:
>>> "Grace to you and peace from God our Father and the Lord Jesus Christ."

Thanksgiving
>> "I thank my God always when I remember you (singular, indicating Philemon) in my prayers."

Body of the Letter
>> Paul discusses the return of Onesimus, a runaway slave.

Final Instructions (Parenesis)
>> Throughout the letter Paul has exhorted Philemon: "receive him" (v 17); "charge that to my account" (v 18); "refresh my heart in Christ" (v 20). His final instructions are in v 22, "prepare a guest room for me."

Closing
>> *Greetings*:
>>> "Epaphrus, my fellow prisoner in Christ Jesus, greets you (singular) [and] Mark, Aristarchus, Demas, and Luke, my fellow workers."
>> *Parting word*:
>>> "The grace of the Lord Jesus Christ be with your spirit."

Yet, as similar as the letters of Paul are to other Hellenistic letters, one should notice how Paul subtly altered the style of the standard letter for his own purposes. These alterations reflect the peculiarly Christian character of Paul's Letters and reveal how thoroughly his relationship with Jesus Christ affected him. Indeed, God's revelation of the risen Christ gave Paul a new emphasis and left its stamp on everything he did, even the writing of letters. It is instructive to view the anatomy of some of Paul's changes of the form of a standard letter. For example, *in the opening* of his letters Paul identifies himself in relation to God and Christ. Moreover, he identifies those to whom he writes in terms of their own roles as Christians. Furthermore, he alters the language of the normal greeting and expands it into a lofty but practical wish for the recipients. The usual salutation in Hellenistic letters is the word *greetings*. But, Paul does not send his readers "greetings"; he salutes them by saying, "grace and peace." The words *greetings* and *grace* resemble one another in Gk.: "greetings" = *chairein* and "grace" = *charis*. Thus, Paul's salutation begins with a wordplay that reveals the effects of God's activity, and he develops his altered greeting by coupling a common Jewish greeting, "peace" (*shalom*), with "grace."

Finally, one should recognize that Paul was not a casual letter writer. His are not simple friendly communications. He wrote to address specific situations that existed in particular churches. With his letters he sought to extend his influence (often in an authoritative fashion) in order to assure desired results. He always strives to build up the congregation addressed. Thus, for Paul the letter was an instrument of his apostleship.

Paul's Religious Background and Thought. (1) *Judaism.* Paul the Christian had once been Paul the Jew. It is clear from both his own letters and the story of his ministry in Acts that Paul was not merely a Jew but a Pharisee. He boasts from time to time in his letters of his Jewish past in rebuttal to other missionaries who caused problems in the churches that he had founded (see Phil 3 and 2 Cor 11). In so doing Paul reveals that prior to being a Christian he was a zealous Pharisee. Acts 22:3 preserves a tradition that associates Paul with Rabbi Gamaliel I, one of the most influential figures in first-century Judaism. While Paul does not mention this striking association when rehearsing his Jewish credentials, the association of Paul with formal rabbinic education seems likely, for in his writings Paul manifests signs of "rabbinics": he does midrashic exegesis of the Hebrew Bible; he demonstrates a clear perception of the Law as the heart of Judaism; and the contrast he draws between Christ and the Law shows his disavowal of human, systemic righteousness which he had once practiced with confidence and contentment. These features of Paul's writings locate him within the stream of first-century Pharisaic Judaism; they do not, however, amount to evidence for the assertion that Paul was a rabbi.

(2) *Hellenism.* As it is clear that Paul's past was in Pharisaic Judaism, it is also certain that Paul was a Hellenized Jew. According to Acts he was born outside Palestine in the Greco-Roman trade city of Tarsus. Indeed Paul's own writings show signs of Hellenistic education. The basic mastery of the skills of reading, thinking, argumentation, and expression in writing are the hallmarks of Hellenistic education.

Moreover, the letters are filled with telltale signs of Paul's Hellenistic heritage. From his quotation of Jewish scripture one sees that Paul read the Bible in its Greek version, the LXX. Paul is thoroughly familiar with the conventions of popular Hellenistic philosophy and methods of literary interpretation. Moreover, he calls himself Paul (Gk. *Paulos*), not Saul (Heb. *Sāul*); and his metaphors are drawn from the Greco-Roman world of sports and military.

(3) *Debate.* These observations illustrate a basic problem for those seeking to understand Paul, namely, what background best accounts for Paul's own understanding of what he did and said? Formerly, scholars drew hard lines between three areas that putatively influenced Paul. Since he was certainly a Pharisee, rabbinic or Palestinian Judaism was thought to provide the key to interpreting Paul. His use of apparently technical language in reference to tradition he had received and delivered (1 Cor 15:3) to the churches he founded was taken to indicate his self-understanding and his attitude toward the tradition itself. Moreover, Paul's practice of midrashic exegesis (cf. Paul on Exodus in 1 Cor 10 or on Abraham in Gal 3) was thought to reveal his approach to the OT while his concern with the contrast between Christ and the Law was determined by his past participation in Pharisaism.

Yet other scholars have argued that Hellenism was the most appropriate background for viewing and interpreting Paul. That Paul did allegorical exegesis was said to show still another attitude and approach toward the Hebrew Bible (see Paul on Sarah and Hagar in Gal 4). Furthermore, it was held that by casting Paul in the context of Hellenism one found the prerequisite cause for understanding such basic Pauline notions as the sacraments and Christology. Since Paul was thoroughly Hellenistic in heritage, this meant he would interpret baptism and the Lord's Supper in relation to the practices of Hellenistic MYSTERY RELIGIONS, and he would have understood Christ in terms of a general, Hellenistic myth of a descending and ascending redeemer figure.

(4) *Apocalyptic thought.* A third approach to Paul designated apocalyptic Judaism as the determinative background for understanding his writings. Paul's language bespeaks an apocalyptic perspective in focusing on wrath, judgment, and the day of the Lord. He displays a yearning for the messianic age that characterized all apocalyptic writing. He shows an awareness of living on the boundary of two worlds, one dying and one being born. Further he has a sense of special urgency derived from the apocalyptic conviction that his generation is the last. The clearest sign of Paul's thoroughly apocalyptic perspective is the presence in his writings of the dualistic doctrine of two ages. This doctrine maintains that the age to come breaks into the current age supernaturally through God's intervention and without human agency.

Scholars now recognize that these backgrounds are not exclusive of one another and that each makes a contribution to a balanced reading of Paul, for Paul was influenced by and drew upon all of them. Nevertheless, the question remains whether one of these is dominant.

It is becoming increasingly clearer through the work of several contemporary scholars (e.g., Beker, Käsemann, and Martyn) that the apocalyptic element provided Paul with the basic framework of his thought and determined his comprehension of the world around him. What is this apocalyptic perspective? When scholars are called upon for clarification one finds that remarkably different understandings of "apocalyptic" exist. In Gk. *apokalypsis* means "revelation." Paul uses this word to refer to his original encounter with the risen Jesus Christ (Gal 1:13). That dramatic revelation was the occasion of Paul's call. Moreover, it was the time and means of Paul's being taught or given the basis of the gospel which he preached (Gal 1:11-17). This disruptive intervention of God into Paul's life bespeaks the pattern of thought typical of first-century apocalyptic Judaism.

Apocalyptic is a special expression of Jewish eschatology that was characterized by the dualistic doctrine of two ages. On the one hand there is "the present evil age"; on the other, there is "the age to come." The "present evil age" is the world of mundane realities in which human beings live; the "age to come" is the supernatural realm of the power of God. There is no continuity between these ages. Indeed, apocalyptic Jewish thought held that at some future moment "the age to come" would break into the human realm by a supernatural act of God. In this moment of God's intervention the "present evil age" would pass away and "the age to come" would be established as a new reality, ordained and directed by God. Apocalyptic Judaism held that by this act of God evil would be annihilated and those who were righteous would be redeemed. Thus "the age to come" was the hope of those who believed in God but found themselves oppressed by the forces of evil in the present world. In Jewish apocalyptic literature the authors usually claim to live in the last days of "the present evil age." Their message to readers is the joint promise and warning that the intervention of God is about to happen.

Throughout his letters Paul's language and patterns of thought reveal elements of this apocalyptic eschatology. For example, Paul frequently uses apocalyptic language: "destined . . . for wrath," "the wrath to come," "the wrath of God," "the day of wrath," "the day of the Lord Jesus Christ," "the day of salvation," "redeemed," "redemption," "this age," "the rulers of this age," "the present evil age," and "the ends of the ages." Moreover, Paul reveals in his letters the conviction that he and his readers are part of the last generation of humanity (1 Thess 4:13-18, esp. v 17; 1 Cor 15:51-57).

Paul does not use the phrase "the age to come," and so some scholars deny the thoroughgoing apocalyptic character of his thought. But he speaks in distinctively Christian phrases of the same idea when he says "a new creation" and "the Kingdom of God." This difference in phrases indicates a slight, but fundamental, alteration on the part of Paul. He transforms the pattern of Jewish apocalyptic thought described above into a particularly Christian pattern of apocalyptic thinking which permeates all of his writings. In other words, Paul the apostle articulates an apocalyptic perspective that has been modified in light of the Christ-event.

Jewish apocalyptic eschatology thought in terms of two ages. These were distinct; one age ended and the other began by an intervening act of God. Paul has a similar, but distinct, view of time that stamps his entire thought process. He maintains the temporal dualism characteristic of Jewish apocalyptic, but he modifies the scheme in light of the Christ-event so that there are two distinct ages that are separated and joined by an interim.

For Paul the first temporal epoch is "the present evil age" (Gal 1:4; 1 Cor 2:6-8). This age is ruled by the god of this world (2 Cor 4:4), namely Satan, and by the elemental spirits of the universe (Gal 4:3; 1 Cor 2:8). Under the influence of its rulers this age is at odds with God (1 Cor 15:24-28; Rom 8:37-39). Nevertheless, this age is passing away (1 Cor 7:31). The second epoch is the "new creation" (Gal 6:14; 2 Cor 5:17). This new age comes as God in Christ defeats the forces in opposition to him (Gal 6:14; 1 Cor 7:31; Rom 5:21), and it is established as the *regnum dei,* apparently an age of glory (1 Thess 2:10-12; 1 Cor 15:20-28; 2 Cor 4:17; Rom 5:2, 21).

The present exists as the juncture of the ages or as a mingling of the ages (1 Cor 10:11; 2 Cor 5:16). Here 1 Cor 10:11 is important. In this verse Paul describes himself and other humans as those "upon whom the ends of the ages have met." Modern translations often obscure Paul's idea in this phrase, translating it as does the RSV, "upon whom the *end* of the ages has come." This rendering implies that Paul stands at the end of time and looks back at the ages (something like dispensations?) that have gone before—indeed, he does not. Paul perceives that he and other humans live at the juncture of the ages. This juncture came about as a result of the cross of Christ (1 Cor 1:17-18) and it will conclude, marking the absolute end of the present evil age, at the coming of Christ from heaven (1 Thess 2:19; 3:13; 4:13-18; 1 Cor 15:23-28).

Paul was called and he thought, worked, and preached in this interim. Much of Paul's message derives from his understanding of this juncture, for, as noted, it came about as a result of the cross of Christ (1 Cor 1:17-18). In essence Paul said:

(a) Sin has been defeated (Gal 1:4; 1 Cor 15:3; Rom 4:25).

(b) Death has been condemned (1 Cor 15:54-57; Rom 8:31-39).

(c) The Law has been exposed for what it is (Gal 3:24-25; Rom 7:7-12).

(d) Christ has discharged humanity from the curse of the Law (Gal 3:13-14); Rom 7:4-6).

(e) Although the battle goes on toward God's final victory, creation has been reclaimed by God (1 Cor 15:20-28; Rom 8:18-25).

(f) God's sovereignty has been established (Rom 8:31-39).

(g) Creation presently awaits the grand assize (1 Thess 5:2-11; 1 Cor 6:2-3; 15:20-28; 16:21; Rom 8:18-25), and while the Kingdom of God has *not yet* been fully established in glory, this is *already* the messianic age in which, for now, everything is to be viewed from the vantage point of the cross (2 Cor 5:16).

See also ACTS OF THE APOSTLES; ANTIOCH; BARNABAS; CAESAREA; CORINTH; DAMASCUS; EPHESUS; EPISTLE/LETTER; ESCHATOLOGY IN THE NT; FAITH; GALLIO; GAMALIEL; GENTILE, GENTILES IN THE NT; JERUSALEM COUNCIL; JUSTIFICATION; LORD'S SUPPER; MESSIAH/CHRIST; MYSTERY RELIGIONS; ONESIMUS; PHARISEES; PHILIPPI; PRISCILLA/AQUILA; RABBINIC LITERATURE; SILAS; SYNAGOGUE; TARSUS; TIMOTHY; TITUS.

Bibliography. J. C. Beker, *Paul the Apostle: The Triumph of God in Life and Thought*; G. Bornkamm, *Paul*; W. Bousset, *Kyrios Christos*; R. Bultmann, *Theology of the New Testament*; W. D. Davies, *Paul and Rabbinic Judaism*; W. G. Doty, *Letters in Primitive Christianity*; E. E. Ellis, *Paul and His Recent Interpreters*; E. Käsemann, *Perspective on Paul*; L. E. Keck, *Paul and His Letters*; J. Knox, *Chapters in a Life of Paul*; G. Luedemann, *Paul, Apostle to the Gentiles*; J. L. Martyn, "Epistemology at the Turn of the Ages: 2 Corinthians 5:16," *Christian History and Interpretation,* ed. W. R. Farmer et al.; W. A. Meeks, *The First Urban Christians* and *The Writings of St. Paul*; J. Murphy-O'Connor, "On the Road and on the Sea with St. Paul," BR 1 (Summer 1985): 38-47; C. Roetzel, *The Letters of Paul*; E. P. Sanders, *Paul and Palestinian Judaism*; A. Schweitzer, *Paul and His Interpreters*; M. L. Soards, *The Apostle Paul: An Introduction to His Writing and Teaching*; P. Vielhauer, "Apocalypses and Related Subjects," *New Testament Apocrypha,* ed. E. Hennecke and W. Schneemelcher.

—MARION L. SOARDS

Peter　　　　　　　[MDB 671-72]

•**Peter.** The surname *Peter*—which means "stone" or "rock"—appears 155 times in the NT in reference to a disciple of Jesus. According to Mark 3:16, Luke 6:14, and John 1:42 Jesus himself gave this name to his disciple. The Aramaic equivalent is *Cephas* which is found only once in the Gospels (John 1:42) and eight times in Galatians and 1 Corinthians (Paul uses the name *Peter* only in Gal 2:7-8). Peter's Aramaic given name was *Simeon* (Acts 15:14; 2 Pet 1:1[?]); its Gk. equivalent is

Simon (fifty times). These figures include the combinations *Simon Peter* (twenty times) and *Simon (who is) called or named Peter* (seven times).

The Aramaic name of Peter's father was Jonah (Matt 16:17), and its Gk. equivalent was John (John 1:42; 21:15-17). John 1:44 says Peter's home was in BETHSAIDA, whereas Matt 8:14, Mark 1:29, and Luke 4:38 indicate that he had a home in CAPERNAUM. The two villages were only a few miles apart near the Sea of Galilee. He and his brother ANDREW were fishermen by trade (Mark 1:16). He was married and evidently took his wife with him at church expense during some of his missionary travels (Matt 8:14; Mark 1:30; Luke 4:38; 1 Cor 9:5). His brother ANDREW was a follower of JOHN THE BAPTIST before he began to follow Jesus (John 1:35-42), and it is probable that Peter was also. Acts 4:13 does not indicate that he was illiterate, only that he did not have rabbinical training. His native language was Aramaic, but as a native of "Galilee of the Gentiles" he could certainly speak Greek.

The Gospels, Acts, and Pauline Letters picture Peter as the leader of the apostles. His name heads each of the lists of the apostles (Matt 10:2; Mark 3:16; Luke 6:14; Acts 1:13). He was one of the so-called inner circle of the apostles (e.g., Mark 5:37; 9:2; 13:3; 14:33). He was their spokesman and representative (e.g., Mark 9:5; 10:28; 11:21; 14:29).

There is, however, some difference in emphasis among the sources. Mark's description is often uncomplimentary, the most notable instances being 8:33 where Jesus calls Peter "Satan" and perhaps 14:71 where the meaning may be that Peter invoked a curse on Jesus rather than himself. Luke omits both of these. Matthew includes the curse but omits the characterization of Peter as Satan. Indeed, Matthew exalts Peter more than any other NT writer, especially in connection with Peter's confession of Jesus at CAESAREA PHILIPPI not only as the Messiah but as "the Son of the living God" (16:16). The promise of Jesus to build his church on Peter and/or on Peter's confession and similar confessions (Matt 16:18) is unparalleled.

In addition to omitting most of Mark's derogatory statements, Luke honors Peter by his unique accounts of the miraculous catch of fish (5:1-11), Jesus' prayer for Peter (22:31-32), and a resurrection appearance to Peter (24:34). Moreover, in the first half of Acts Peter is the leading character without a trace of criticism. Peter is the most frequently mentioned disciple in John's Gospel, but in terms of significance he takes second place to the BELOVED DISCIPLE. The latter is the disciple who most closely follows Jesus and is the model for others. In the Pauline Letters Peter is acknowledged as a leader of the Jerusalem church (Gal 2:7, 9), a source of information about Jesus (if that is the meaning of Gal 1:18), the apostle to the Jews (Gal 2:7-8), and the subject of a resurrection appearance (1 Cor 15:5), but he is also rebuked for wavering about accepting Gentile Christians as equals (Gal 2:11-14).

For about a decade Peter was the leader of the Jerusalem church. Then he became an itinerant evangelist in Palestine (Acts 9:32; 11:18). At this point JAMES the brother of Jesus assumed the leadership. Acts 12:17 would seem to imply that James was already the leader when Peter was forced to flee for his life in 44 C.E. Certainly

James was the leader when the Jerusalem Council met (Acts 15). About that time Peter was at Antioch (Gal 2:11). First Cor 1:12, 3:22, and 9:5 may indicate that Peter came to Corinth. First Pet 1:1 may indicate that he ministered in Asia Minor and 5:13 that he came to Rome (Babylon is almost certainly a code name for Rome). Of his other movements the NT mentions nothing.

Two NT books claim to have been written by Peter. The authorship of 2 Peter was disputed in the early church, and that of both is disputed by contemporary scholars.

Early Christian tradition confirms the implication of 1 Pet 5:13 that the apostle went to Rome; it also claims that he founded the church there, served as its first bishop, and died a martyr's death during the persecution of Nero in 64 or 65 C.E. (cf. John 21:18-19; 2 Pet 1:14-15). Some of the sources give Paul an equal role in founding the church, which is certainly false (there was already a church in Rome when Paul wrote to it, and at that time he had never visited the city). The claim of Peter founding the church and serving as its first bishop may be questionable, but there is nothing improbable about the claim that he died as a martyr in Rome.

A part of the early Christian tradition is the APOCRYPHAL LITERATURE that was falsely ascribed to Peter. This includes the *Preaching of Peter* (KERYGMA PETROU), APOCALYPSE OF PETER, the GOSPEL OF PETER and the ACTS OF PETER.

See also ANDREW; ANTIOCH; APOCRYPHAL LITERATURE; CAPERNAUM; GALATIANS, LETTER TO THE; KERYGMA PETROU; PETER AND THE TWELVE APOSTLES, ACTS OF; PETER, ACTS OF; PETER, ACT OF (BG); PETER, APOCALYPSE OF (ANT); PETER, APOCALYPSE OF (NH); PETER, GOSPEL OF; PETER, LETTER OF, TO PHILIP; PETER, LETTERS OF; THE TWELVE.

Bibliography. R. E. Brown, et al., *Peter in the New Testament*; F. F. Bruce, *Peter, Stephen, James, and John*; D. W. O'Connor, *Peter in Rome*; O. Cullman, *Peter: Disciple-Apostle-Martyr*.

—JAMES A. BROOKS

Righteousness in the New Testament   [MDB 765-66]

•**Righteousness in the New Testament.** The concepts of righteousness and JUSTIFI-CATION have been important throughout the history of NT interpretation. Much of their importance springs from their place in Paul's discussion of salvation. Luther's emphasis on salvation by grace elevated Paul's discussion of righteousness through faith to one of the cornerstones of Protestant theology. In Paul, Luther found an ally whose polemic against the idea of righteousness through works supported his own polemic against a Roman Catholic emphasis on works-based salvation.

Ordinary Meaning of Righteousness. A dictionary of the day would probably have shown two basic meanings for the word in the first century. One of those would certainly have referred to righteousness within the judicial system. To be considered righteous or innocent meant that one conformed to the prevailing legal and moral system of one's society. Righteousness could be used to mean both the standard to which one conformed and one's status with regard to society. One aspect of that status was the judgment of one's peers. To be righteous was as much a social as a legal perception. A second meaning of righteousness, though, went beyond the sense of a legal obligation to a moral or philosophical obligation. To be righteous meant that one possessed certain qualities that contributed to the moral fiber of society. As such, righteousness became a virtue to be cultivated, the mark of a productive member of society.

The Concept of Righteousness in the OT and Judaism. The Hebrew concept of righteousness found in the OT emphasized the idea of relationship; righteousness characterized Yahweh's behavior in a covenant context. God was righteous because God upheld the covenant and was faithful to Israel (2 Chr 12:6). Such faithfulness meant that God would watch over Israel to see that it was protected from those who would take away its rights. Israel also called upon God to judge according to God's upright character. Often Israel called on God to vindicate it in the presence of enemies, although Israel claimed that God had been wronged (Ps 68). God's covenant responsibility included not only the protection of Israel as a nation, but the protection of those whose individual rights under the covenant had been denied (Ps 146:7-9). Here again, the emphasis was upon God's upright restoration of the person's rights; any punishment of the wrongdoer was a natural consequence of that restoration. The attitude that characterized a righteous person in relationship with God was an attitude of faith. When one trusted wholly in God for one's vindication, one was considered to be righteous.

The Babylonian Exile brought a new emphasis on one's individual rights and responsibilities before God. An individual's righteousness was measured by one's covenant relationship with God. Increasingly, one's covenant responsibility became defined in terms of keeping the commandments of the Law. Within the context of political and economic oppression, the idea that God would vindicate the downtrodden gave a special righteousness to those who helped the poor. Righteousness could be gained by doing acts worthy of merit, and God would weigh one's merits against one's demerits. Paul seems to have reacted against such a righteousness based on works, although some scholars have questioned the idea that Rabbinic Judaism demanded works for salvation. Whether or not Judaism demanded works for salvation, the context for the NT use of righteousness focused on one's relationship with God within the covenant. This included one's responsibility to obey the Law in order to maintain one's place within the covenant community.

Important NT Terms. Most of the words in the NT which convey the concept of righteousness come from the same root, and the translations "righteousness," "righteous," and "to make righteous" (for the Gk. words δικαιοσύνη, δίκαιος, and δικαιόω convey this relationship. Depending on the context, however, these words can also carry such meanings as innocence/innocent, right, upright, to justify, and justification, among other related meanings. In addition to these positive terms, the NT writers used negative terms such as "unrighteous" (ἄδικος) which shed light on the meaning of the concept of righteousness in the NT (Luke 16:11).

Aspects of the Meaning of Righteousness in the NT. Three different aspects of the word "righteousness" are important for a balanced understanding of the NT usage.

(1) *Relational.* The NT maintains the idea that righteousness was an integral part of one's covenant relationship with God. To be righteous demanded that one stand in the proper covenant relationship with God. That covenant relationship, however, could only be reestablished by God; this God did in Christ. The demands of this new covenant were twofold. To enter into the covenant, one must admit one's failure to uphold the previous covenant (repentance) and acknowledge that one's relationship with God is a matter of God's grace rather than human works (faith). One's fellowship with God demanded a subsequent fellowship with other members of the covenant community, and each person was responsible for maintaining that fellowship.

These relational aspects of righteousness are often emphasized in the NT. Many people are referred to as righteous as a result of their proper attitude toward God. Cornelius, for instance was characterized as "righteous" or "upright" to Peter (Acts 10:22), because he worshipped God, even before Peter had a chance to share the gospel with Cornelius. Others were termed righteous or unrighteous depending on their attitude toward God. Those who approach God within the context of a proper covenantal relationship are called righteous; those who ignore that relationship are characterized as unrighteous.

In the same way, those who keep their promise within the covenant community are righteous; those who break their promise are unrighteous. The ideas of righteousness and faithfulness between members of the community are linked because of God's faithfulness within the covenant. As God is faithful, so should the members of his community act with faithfulness toward each other. Often, the concept of righteousness is used to discuss actions which will destroy fellowship or relationship within the covenant. Actions such as anger, lust, and hate are unrighteous more because they destroy covenant relationships than because they violate a moral or legal code (Matt 5).

(2) *Forensic.* Another aspect of the NT use of righteousness was drawn from the use of the word in a secular legal context. One's legal righteousness was a result of one's innocence, often construed as conformity to societal or legal norms. The forensic, or legal, aspect of righteousness involved a verdict of "not guilty." For much of the history of NT interpretation, the forensic view of righteousness was dominant. Many scholars reconciled God's righteousness with forgiveness of sinful humanity by assuming that justification meant that God imputed righteousness to human beings; even though they remained guilty sinners, they were "considered" righteous or innocent. God met their guilty plea with a verdict of "not guilty" because of Jesus' atonement. More recent discussions, though, have emphasized the relational aspect of righteousness, which seems to agree with even a forensic understanding of righteousness. The fact that God proclaims one to be "righteous" presupposes a restored relationship with God and the covenant community.

(3) *Ethical.* A third aspect of righteousness in the NT is its ethical dimension. Not only have scholars chosen to emphasize the relational concept of righteousness over the forensic, a general dissatisfaction has arisen with the idea that God's justification involves a judgment of innocence without an accompanying change in the character of the one justified. In fact, many have concluded that God does more than impute righteousness to an undeserving sinner; the gift of God's righteousness actually involves a change in the status of the sinner (Rom 4:5). This change involves a new relationship, as the sinner is reconciled to God. Moreover, God has the power to change the status of the sinner, not only declaring one righteous, but making one righteous. This new status makes ethical demands on the Christian. Righteousness is not just a new status in the presence of God; it is a new way of living. The one who has accepted the gift of righteousness through grace by faith must now live in such a way as to be worthy of that grace. These ethical demands function within the context of the covenant. Righteousness is not the result of good works, but good works are the result of righteousness.

The Righteousness of God. One of the important phrases for the understanding of Paul's writings is the phrase "righteousness of God" (δικαιοσύνη θεοῦ). Most of the discussion surrounding the concept of righteousness in the NT has concerned different interpretations of what Paul meant by the righteousness of God. Grammatically, one may choose to interpret the phrase as either the righteousness that comes from God or that righteousness which God possesses. Even after one chooses a translation, one must still attempt to understand this phrase within the context of Pauline theology.

Martin Luther interpreted the phrase to mean that power by which God makes people righteous through Christ. Luther also combined the ethical and relational aspects of righteousness, noting that one's new righteous status (a gift of God through faith in Christ) allows one to live a righteous life in Christ. Later theological developments in church history led to an increasing emphasis on the righteousness of God as a divine quality, to the detriment of the idea that God's righteousness provided the power for the act of salvation and justification.

The most recent scholarly discussion of the phrase "righteousness of God" may be traced to an address by Ernst Käsemann, in which he proposed the idea that righteousness was both the gift of God in justifying humanity and the power of God which accomplishes that justification and sanctification. Käsemann's position has evoked both significant support and opposition. The resulting discussion has affirmed the tension between God's righteousness as an attribute of his being and God's righteousness as a part of his saving work in the world.

Conclusion. Righteousness in the NT must be seen within the context of the covenant relationship. At its foundation, righteousness involves reconciliation between God and humanity, a reconciliation initiated by God through Christ. Not only is one declared to be righteous within that covenant relationship, one accepts a new status of righteousness. One also accepts a new way of life which may be termed as righteous, since one lives in Christ and is in the process of being sanctified in Christ. Righteousness is both gift and demand.

See also JUSTICE/JUDGMENT; JUSTIFICATION; RIGHTEOUSNESS IN THE OT; SALVATION IN THE NT; SALVATION IN THE OT.

Bibliography. P. J. Achtemeier, "Righteousness in the New Testament," IDB; M. T. Baruch, "Perspectives on 'God's Righteousness' in Recent German Discussion," *Paul and Palestinian Judaism,* E. P. Sanders, ed.; R. Bultmann, *Theology of the New Testament*; H. Conzelmann, *An Outline of the Theology of the New Testament*; N. A. Dahl, "The Doctrine of Justification: Its Social Function and Implications," *Studies in Paul*; R. A. Kelly, "Righteousness," ISBE; W. G. Kümmel, *The Theology of the New Testament*; G. Schrenk, δίκη, κτλ., TDNT; F. Stagg, *New Testament Theology*.

—STEVEN M. SHEELEY

Slavery in the New Testament   [MDB 831]

•**Slavery in the New Testament.** In the legally and socially complex world of the NT, "slavery" designates the various systems of compulsory labor and dependency in which at any one time as many as one-third of the urban population was owned by a large number of the others. Another one-third were enslaved earlier in their lives; under Roman, Greek, and Jewish laws, slaves were freed quite frequently. Slaves of Roman citizens were usually set free (manumitted) by age thirty and routinely granted Roman citizenship.

In contrast to "New World" slavery, these slaves were not distinguished from free persons either by race, religion, kinds of work, clothing, ownership of property (including other slaves), or formal schooling, being often better educated than their owners. For these reasons a modern reader needs a solid understanding of this pivotal social institution (far more than can be given here) in order to comprehend what is said about human relationships in the NT or the metaphors of "bondage" and "freedom."

In contrast to the first century B.C.E. when the chief means of enslavement were capture in war and kidnapping by pirates (1 Tim 1:10), slaves mentioned in the NT were most likely born to slave mothers (Gal. 4:21-31). Sometimes parents of free-born children were forced to sell them into slavery to pay oppressive debts. In the early Roman Empire large numbers of people sold themselves into slavery, usually to escape the insecurity of life as a free day-laborer, to obtain special jobs, or to climb socially. For example, Erastus, a Christian, the "city treasurer" of Corinth (Rom 16:23), probably sold himself to the city to gain that responsible position. Paul had such self-sale in mind when exhorting the Corinthians: "You were bought with a price; do not become slaves of men" (1 Cor 7:23). Yet in the next generation some Christians did sell themselves into slavery to obtain funds to manumit some from oppressive owners and to feed others (*1 Clem* 55:2).

All ancient moral teachers took owning persons as slaves for granted, including the Stoic philosopher Epictetus who was educated while in slavery. No plan to abolish slavery motivated any of the major slave rebellions in the Mediterranean area, all of which occurred during 140–170 B.C.E. Slaves performed a wide variety of functions, some quite sensitive, ranging from streetsweepers to executives, fieldworkers to administrators of large estates, handworkers to foremen, including teachers, physicians, and household managers. When set free, most slaves continued their previous work. "Slave-only" jobs were reserved for convicted criminals who as slaves of the empire were expected to die as mine laborers or galley oarsmen.

The NT gives direct evidence that some early Christians were slaves or owners of slaves, e.g., Philemon and his slave Onesimus, the famous text in 1 Cor 7:21, and the exhortations to mutual respect between slaves and their owners in Col 3:22–4:1/Eph 6:5-9 (cf. 1 Tim 6:1-2; 1 Pet 2:18-21). A slave's treatment was dependent entirely on the character of his or her owner. Neither Jesus, nor THE TWELVE, nor the 120 at Pentecost appear to have been slaveowners. When Paul described himself (Rom 1:1) and Timothy (Phil 1:1) as "slaves of Christ Jesus" he stressed not only their full spiritual dependence on Christ but also their place of honor in the OT tradition of Abraham, Moses, and David.

See also ONESIMUS; PHILEMON, LETTER TO; SLAVERY IN THE OT.

Bibliography. S. S. Bartchy, *First-Century Slavery and the Interpretation of 1 Cor 7:21*; K. R. Bradley, *Slaves and Masters in the Roman Empire: A Study in Social Control*; M. I. Finley, *Ancient Economy*; N. R. Petersen, *Rediscovering Paul: Philemon and the Sociology of Paul's Narrative World*; A. Watson, *Roman Slave Law*; T. Wiedemann, *Greek and Roman Slavery*.

—S. SCOTT BARTCHY

Theophilus [MDB 908]

•**Theophilus.** [thee-of'uh-luhs] Theophilus was the person to whom the GOSPEL OF LUKE and the ACTS OF THE APOSTLES were addressed or dedicated (Luke 1:3; Acts 1:1). The name means "friend of God." The third evangelist follows the Hellenistic practice of dedicating books to patrons, benefactors, or persons interested in the project who often aided in the distribution of the work. The address "most excellent" (Luke 1:3) is used in Acts 23:26, 24:2, and 26:25 for Roman officials but was not limited to such people in the Mediterranean world of the time. There is, then, no necessity of viewing Theophilus as a Roman official, although he could have been such.

The phrase "concerning which you have been informed" (Luke 1:4) may be read two different ways. It may be taken to mean Theophilus was a non-Christian who had received reports about Christianity and needed confirmation or clarification or, more likely, that he was a Christian who had already been instructed and who needed certainty about such. In the absence of any concrete data about this person numerous theories have been offered: e.g., it is not the name of an individual but that of any friend of God, the average Christian reader, the typical catechumen (so Origen); it is a baptismal name for an individual, not a real name but rather a pseudonym to conceal the person's true identity to avoid persecution; it is the real name of an individual such as was commonly used among both Greeks and Jews.

None of these theories has enough evidence to support its weight. All that can be known is what is available from Luke 1:1-4. Later legend that depicts Theophilus as the bishop of Antioch or Caesarea is unsubstantiated.

See also APOSTLES, ACTS OF THE; LUKE, GOSPEL OF.

—CHARLES H. TALBERT

We-Sections [MDB 954-55]

•**We-Sections.** "We-sections" refers to four passages in Acts in which an unexpected shift from third-person to first-person pronouns occurs: 16:10-17, a sea voyage from Troas to Philippi; 20:5-15, a sea voyage from Philippi to Miletus; 21:1-18, a sea voyage from Miletus to Jerusalem; and 27:1–28:16, a sea voyage from Caesarea to Rome.

Several explanations for this shift have been advanced. The traditional view, supported by IRENAEUS, as well as by some modern scholars, interprets the first-person pronouns as a reference to the author himself. When an account occurs in first person, the author of Acts is indicating he was an eyewitness of the events recorded. Proponents of this view claim this is the most natural way to understand "we/us" and is how the original readers of Acts would have understood the reference. According to this view, then, the author of Acts was an occasional companion of Paul. The breaks in the narratives in which first-person pronouns do not occur indicate the author was not with Paul on those occasions. On the basis of Phlm 24, Col 4:14, and 2 Tim 4:11, many readers have surmised that LUKE was this traveling companion of Paul and thus the author of Acts.

Among the problems associated with identifying the author of Acts (and of the we-sections) as a companion of Paul are discrepancies between events described in Acts and in the letters of Paul, discrepancies between the theology of Paul as presented in Acts and as found in his own writings, and the unexplained abruptness of the appearance and disappearance of the we-sections. These problems have led many scholars to abandon the traditional explanation and posit new hypotheses. One alternative hypothesis states that the author of Acts is dependent in the we-sections on a written source, possibly an itinerary of Paul's journeys or a diary kept by one or more of his traveling companions. A major problem with this view is that no stylistic differences exist between the we-sections and the surrounding texts. The we-sections were authored or at least heavily edited by the same individual who wrote the rest of Acts. If the author of Acts so heavily edited the we-sections as to recast them into his own style, why did he not change the first-person pronouns to third person to conform to the surrounding texts? No satisfactory explanation has been given.

A more attractive suggestion is that the use of first-person pronouns is an intentional literary device of the author of Acts. One such proposal states that by adopting the first-person style the author attempted to impart credibility to the accounts by intimating he was an eyewitness of the events described. Another way of understanding the first-person narratives as a literary technique has been suggested by a comparison of the we-sections with ancient accounts of sea journeys. A specific genre of literature, sea voyages, in which the account is told in first person, seems to have existed in the ancient world. The writer of Acts, aware of this genre, shaped the accounts of Paul's sea voyages to conform to this literary genre. Readers of the first century C.E. would have expected a first-person narration of the voyage, regardless of whether the author was an actual participant or not.

Although no completely convincing solution to the problem of the we-passages has yet been demonstrated, the variety of scholarly opinions indicates that the presence of first-person pronouns in the Book of Acts does not necessarily provide information about authorship of Luke-Acts.

See also APOSTLES, ACTS OF THE; LUKE.

Bibliography. J. Dupont, *The Sources of the Acts*; E. Haenchen, " 'We' in Acts and the Itinerary," JTC 1 (1965): 65-100; V. K. Robbins, "By Land and By Sea: The We-Passages and Ancient Sea Voyages," *Perspectives on Luke-Acts,* ed. C. H. Talbert.

—MITCHELL G. REDDISH

Witness   [MDB 965-66

•**Witness.** Someone who is knowledgeable about the facts under question and who speaks about them at a legal proceeding is a witness. The use of witnesses in various legal cases was legislated in Deuteronomy at various points. Common to all of these cases was the stipulation that a conviction could not be obtained on the basis of a single witness (Deut 19:15). The use of such witnesses is described in Prov 19:28; Isa 8:2; and 1 Kgs 21:9-13. Serving as a witness of this sort was seen in Israel as a religious and civic duty; willfully giving false testimony was strongly condemned (Exod 20:16; 1 Kgs 21:5-29; Deut 19:16-19).

A witness also served as an attestation that a transaction was legal and had been completed. The elders of a village often served in this capacity (Deut 25:9; Ruth 4:4, 9-11) but other responsible citizens also performed this function (Jer 32:9-15).

A type of witness closely related to the latter was the memorial or monument which served as a physical reminder of an agreement made or an event of moment. The cairn erected by Jacob and Laban in Gen 31:44-54, the Reubenite altar in Joshua 22:21-34, and the proposed altar of Isaiah (19:19-20) were witnesses of this type.

In the NT, the term "witness" (Gk. *martüs*) came to refer specifically to one who had seen Jesus during his lifetime or had seen the risen Lord (Luke 1:2; 24:8; Acts 1:22). Witness to the truth of the gospel was expected of all believers, a witness supported by the Spirit (Rom 8:16). Martyrs in later Christian history were witnesses, testifying to the truth of Christian faith by their readiness to die holding fast to that faith.

See also TESTIMONY.

—RAY SUTHERLAND

Women in the New Testament   [MDB 966-68]

•Women in the New Testament. Recent studies have contributed greatly to renewed awareness regarding the status of women in the NT. In addition to standard historical-critical methods, the approaches of sociological analysis, literary criticism, and feminist critical hermeneutics are proving to be constructive in gaining a more sharply delineated picture.

Women in the First-Century Mediterranean World. Christianity was born into a complex social milieu which felt primarily the influence of Greek, Roman, and Jewish religiocultural mores. These societies were patriarchal in orientation, relegating women to subordinate roles in religion, government, education, and domestic concerns. Although there were notable exceptions such as women's participation in the syncretistic mystery cults (which were more inclusive than traditional Greek religion or sectarian Judaism) and the writings of Plutarch (which challenged the double standard), the *paterfamilias* structure was normative. Considerable unrest over these strictures characterized the world in which the NT was written. The education of women, for instance, inevitably provoked conflict over their public and private roles. It is understandable that the NT reflects both a tension and an accommodation with these perspectives as it sought to articulate the gospel story of Jesus the Christ and chronicle Christianity's subsequent missionary activity in the Mediterranean world. In this matrix the church made decisions about the role of women within the Christian community that still influence contemporary thinking and practice.

The OT provided a rich paradigmatic repository and substructure for much of the NT. The legal stipulations, in particular, underscored Israel's patriarchy. Barred from full participation in the religious sphere, the woman's existence was defined by her relationship to father, husband, or children (preferably sons). Occasionally women functioned in nontraditional roles, e.g., DEBORAH the judge (Jdgs 4–5) and HULDAH the prophet (2 Kgs 22:14ff.), but visions of gender equality were missing from most of the texts. Some among the prophets saw beyond this repressive society and proclaimed a new day for God's people in which religious and personal disabilities would no longer characterize the existence of women (cf. Joel 2:28-29; Hosea 4:14; Jer 31:22).

Postexilic Judaism struggled to preserve its identity amid an increasingly Hellenized culture through elaborate regulations and precise cultic prescriptions. Women were more restricted during this epoch than they had been in the OT. Rabbinic literature was particularly misogynistic in outlook; women were not only portrayed as the origin of evil but the locus of its continuing embodiment (*m.Abot* 2, 7; *b.Ketub* 65a). Diaspora Judaism was generally more tractable concerning the position of women, but in no wise could be considered egalitarian.

Women and the Ministry of Jesus. The extent to which women figured in the ministry of Jesus is remarkable given the religiocultural background. His prophetic message, inclusive concern, and unrelenting challenge to religious perversions display a radical discontinuity with OT and postbiblical Jewish precedents. Jesus' willingness to teach women (John 4:27; Luke 10:29) directly countered the rabbinic dictum against permitting a woman to study Torah.

Clearly women were among the disciples called by Jesus. His proclamation of the KINGDOM OF GOD (inbreaking in his ministry) offered a new vision for humanity where the walls of partition were no longer determinant. In the new "family" Jesus was forming (Mark 3:31ff.), sisters and brothers would participate in a "discipleship of equals," as Elisabeth Schüssler Fiorenza describes it (140ff.). The technical words used for disciple ("following," Mark 8:34; "serving," Mark 15:40-41; Luke 10:38-42) are freely applied to the women who responded to Jesus' message. Although excluded from THE TWELVE for symbolic and pragmatic reasons, i.e., to demonstrate the continuity of his message with the life of the covenantal nation Israel, and the itinerant nature of his ministry, respectively, the participation of women in Jesus' ministry is expressly noted by the four evangelists. From the beginning of the Galilean proclamation to the resurrection vindicating Jesus' claim, women accompanied and assisted this one who welcomed their contributions.

At times, the Gospel writers portray women as more exemplary disciples than men, a radical departure from first-century expectations. This recounting must surely reflect the indisputable challenge of Jesus to the patriarchal ethos—the evangelists would not likely create or embellish these stories. Mark 12:41-43 portrays Jesus' commendation of the poor widow to the disciples as an example of generosity and utter self-giving. Likewise the action of MARY of Bethany, anointing Jesus "for burial" (Mark 14:3ff.; Matt 26:6ff.; John 11:2), is presented as evidence of her sensitive discipleship, comprehending the approaching passion of her Lord while others were seemingly oblivious.

The clearest expression of Jesus' affirmation of women occurs in his commissioning of them as witnesses to his resurrection. All four Gospels record the presence of women at the tomb and Jesus' instruction to them to "go and tell the brethren" (Matt 28:1-10; Mark 16:1-8; Luke 24:1-12; John 20:1-18). In a culture where the word of a woman was not considered a trustworthy witness, how amazing that Jesus would entrust the climax of the good news, God's power to overcome the power of sin and death, to these marginalized messengers! In this context the Gospel of John takes pains to render Mary of Magdala as a true disciple (20:11-18). As one of Jesus' own, she recognizes him when she hears his voice (cf. John 10:4-5). She and the BELOVED DISCIPLE are the ones who believe without hesitancy, unlike Simon Peter and Thomas. Many NT scholars regard Mary as the first witness to the resurrection, the one to whom Jesus first appeared.

The Gospels not only reflect events during the life of Jesus but also the actual practice of the Christian communities in which the evangelists wrote. Clearly a theological momentum which allowed more equal status to women in home, church, ministry, and society finds its genesis in the ministry of Jesus. That it continued is the witness of the Gospel writers.

Women in the Early Church. The NT presents diverse views on the role of women in the early church, reflecting the varied times and circumstances of its composition. The Christian communities, in the main, followed the example of their Lord by according to women fuller participation in both private and public spheres.

The Acts of the Apostles and the Pauline letters give evidence of a greater freedom for women in relation to domestic concerns. No longer is the existence of the single woman (either VIRGIN or WIDOW) a despised and precarious one, rather her singleness affords her unique opportunities for ministry. The four virgin daughters of Philip, the widow Tabitha, and Paul's instructions to the unmarried (Acts 21:9; 9:36ff.; 1 Cor 7:32ff.) offer approbation to the single status as a viable (at times even preferable) means to discipleship for women. Whereas the life of the single woman in the OT had few prospects, these writings of the primitive church greatly elevate her status. The story of one woman, LYDIA of Thyatira (Acts 16:14ff.), is narrated without reference to her family relationships. The emphasis is upon her resourcefulness is helping give birth to the church in Philippi.

The married woman also has new egalitarian possibilities. She is seen as a full partner in marriage sexually (1 Cor 7:3ff.), economically (Acts 18:2-4), and in parental responsibility (Eph 6:1ff.). Often the household rules of Eph 5:22–6:9; Col 3:18-41; 1 Pet 3:1-7 are interpreted in a prescriptive way; actually they evidence the theological momentum engendered by Christ. These are conservative injunctions socially, and the usual order of society is not broken down, but the Christian understanding is clearly moving away from the old order to new relationships of mutual responsibility of love and respect. The movement is toward a model of marriage in which neither partner dominates the other; neither seeks personal growth at the expense of the other. Each partner is to act toward the other as he or she would toward the Lord. Neither is independent of the other; both find their fullest joy in serving one another in ways that show the self-emptying love of Jesus (cf. Phil 2:5-11).

Further, the married woman no longer participates in the religious community in a vicarious manner as the OT prescribed. The worshipping community of the early church forsook the exclusivistic structures of Temple and synagogue worship, where women were sequestered away from the men, even farther than the Gentiles. Acts and the Letters record the struggle religiously and culturally to incorporate women in the work of the church (1 Cor 11:2-16; 14:34-35; 1 Tim. 2:12ff.). Marriage did not preclude an itinerant ministry for women; couples such as Priscilla and Aquila and Adronicus and Junia (KJV, NRSV; Junias, RSV, Rom 16:7) travelled in the service of the gospel. Progress came more easily, however, for those more influenced by Greco-Roman customs than for the Jewish-Christian communities. The chief struggle for the latter seemed to be the question of the Law and Gentile Christians; the Hellenistic Christians addressed the role of women more fully.

As in the ministry of Jesus, women were quite active in the missionary activity of the early church. They were teachers such as Priscilla (Acts 18:26), deacons like Phoebe (Rom 16:1), church workers as Euodia and Syntyche (Phil 4:2), apostles like Junia (Rom 16:7), and prophets (1 Cor 11:2-16; Rev 2:20), to mention some of the more prominent ones.

That all Christians (including women) received the Holy Spirit (Rom 12:6ff.; 1 Cor 12:4-11; Eph 4:11-12) and served in a variety of ways in the early church is evident. However, a difficult question for NT scholarship and contemporary ecclesiastical polity is the degree to which women were a part of the official ministries of the church. The full development of a hierarchy of church offices is postbiblical, thus historical reconstruction in the first century is speculative.

Quite often contemporary interpreters will extrapolate the following argument: Jesus selected only men to comprise THE TWELVE; the Twelve constitutes the foundational leadership for the early church; therefore, the church's leadership today should be only male, as Jesus intended. This argument is flawed, however, for it accords a role to the Twelve that is beyond the evidence of the Bible. The early church was founded upon the apostolic witness, which was not restricted to men. It is the apostolic witness, further, that serves in a paradigmatic way for all subsequent ministries. The function of the Twelve is more limited, "eschatological and symbolic, not ministerial," according to Tetlow (121).

While in the OT priestly ministry (from which women were excluded) was focal, it falls into the background in the NT. The only NT reference to this genre of ministry is in Hebrews where it refers to Christ's priesthood (Heb 4:14–5:10). In Christ the priesthood has reached its culmination, needing no further representation. This cultic institution, with its rigorous exclusionary parameters, has become obsolete because of the priestly sacrifice of Christ (Heb 9:11-14).

The PASTORAL EPISTLES (and a few other isolated passages) note the presence of deacons (1 Tim 8:8-13), elders (1 Tim 5:17-20; cf. Jas 5:14-15), and bishops (1 Tim 3:1-6; Titus 1:5-9). The titles and functions of the offices are quite fluid; it is not until the patristic period of the church's history that each was given a distinct identity. One who looks to the NT for a blueprint for enduring church polity will be disappointed. Only general guidelines about Christian character and responsibilities are to be found. These guidelines do not preclude the participation of women. Further, the chief criterion determining church leadership appears to have been the particular community's situation and need. The presence of spiritual gifts and the willingness to employ them in the service of the church dictated the development of church leaders much more than gender did.

Life and ministry in the Christian community were Christological in origin and character. Being conformed to the crucified and risen Christ defined the existence of the Christian. The NT emphasis is upon the ministry of Jesus which included both women and men. Empowered by the Spirit of the exalted Lord, Christians were to offer themselves in both the ministry of the word and the ministry of service. According to the evidence of the NT, the exclusion of women from ecclesiastical ministry is neither in accord with the teaching or practice of Jesus nor with that of the first-century church.

See also DEBORAH; FEMINIST HERMENEUTICS; HULDAH; LYDIA; MARY; PRISCILLA AND AQUILA; SOCIOLOGY OF THE NT; THE TWELVE; WOMEN IN THE OT.

Bibliography. G. B. Caird, "Paul and Women's Liberty," BJRL 54 (1971): 269-81; A. Y. Collins, ed., Feminist Perspectives on Biblical Scholarship; J. Danielou, The Ministry *of Women in the Early Church*; E. S. Fiorenza, *In Memory of Her* and "Women in the Pre-pauline and Pauline Churches," USQR 33 (1978): 153-66; E. Freed, "The Women in Matthew's Genealogy," JSNT 29 (1987): 3-19; R. Gryson, *The Ministry of Women in the Early Church*; E. M. Howe, *Women and Church Leadership*; J. Kopas, "Jesus and Women: Luke's Gospel," *Today* 53 (July 1986): 192-202; E. Moltmann-Wendel, *The Women Around Jesus*; C. F. Parvey, "The Theology and Leadership of Women in the New Testament," *Religion and Sexism*, ed. R. R. Ruether; S. M. Schneiders, "Women in the Fourth Gospel and The Role of Women in the Contemporary Church," BTB 12 (1982): 35-45; E. Schweizer, "Traditional and Ethical Patterns in the Pauline and Post-Pauline Letters and Their Development," *Text and Interpretation*, ed. E. Best and R. L. McL. Wilson; A. Spencer, *Beyond the Curse*; E. Stagg and F. Stagg, *Women in the World of Jesus*; L. Swidler, *Biblical Affirmation of Women*; E. M. Tetlow, *Women and Ministry in the New Testament*; R. C. Wahlberg, *Jesus and the Freed Woman*.

—MOLLY MARSHALL

Acts

Mikeal C. Parsons   [MCB 1083-1122]

Introduction

The Acts of the Apostles is the only book that presents the story of the early church in the apostolic age. As such it is a foundational document for understanding the life and work of the earliest Christian communities much as the four Gospels are the foundational documents for understanding the life and work of JESUS of Nazareth. The placement of Acts in the NT CANON between the fourfold gospel and the collection of Pauline epistles is reflective of its function in the canon: Acts is a bridge between the time of the founder of the community and the time of his first followers.

Authorship

Early Christian tradition argues that Luke the physician, the traveling companion of PAUL (see Col 4:14; 2 Tim 4:11; Phlm 24), was the author of Acts (see Irenaeus, *AdvHaer* 3.14). Although this traditional view still has its ardent supporters (see Fitzmyer 1981, 35–51), many scholars today are skeptical about identifying the author of Acts with any certainty. Since Cadbury, appeals to the "medical language" of Acts to support the traditional view of Lukan authorship is neither fashionable nor persuasive. Even the view that Luke and Acts were written by a gentile author has met strong resistance by those who view the conflict in Acts as an inter-Jewish problem. The identity of the author will probably remain a point of contention, but accepting an anonymous author in no way detracts from the message of the book. The name "Luke" is used throughout this commentary as a matter of convenience to refer to the implied author of Acts without any assumptions about the identity of the real author.

Relationship between Luke and Acts

Acts is the sequel to the Gospel of Luke. As such, one document is best read in light of the other, much like the fourth Gospel is best understood in the light of the Johannine Epis tles. That Luke and Acts were written by the same person seems indisputable; to argue that these two writings comprise a single, continuous narrative (represented by the hyphenated title "Luke-Acts"), however, is to make too much of the evid ence. There is no manuscript evidence that these two writings ever existed as one document in a "precanonical" form. In fact, the longer Western text of Acts supports the notion that the writings enjoyed basically independent reception in the early church and were probably composed as discrete, although interrelated, narratives. In other words, the separation of Luke from Acts in the NT canon is not simply the result of a "botched" job by the "canonical" editors, but rather an accurate reflection of the independent character of each writing. Maintaining the individual character of each Lukan writing allows the reader to see both the similarities and the differences between the Gospel of Luke and the Acts of the Apostles.

Date and Place

Most scholars assume Acts was written after the third Gospel and near the end of the first century C.E., although the date assigned ranges from as early as pre-70 C.E. to as late as 150 C.E. The concerns reflected in Acts are similar to those of the Pastoral Epistles and tend to support a late first-century date. ACHAIA, CAESAREA, ANTIOCH, and more recently EPHESUS have been suggested as the locale of the Lukan community. Still others argue there was no one "Lukan community" but that Luke was addressing Christians in various locales. As with authorship, however, the questions of date and place remain unsettled; furthermore, a detailed understanding of those issues is essentially irrelevant for purposes of interpretation.

Genre and Literary Forms

The form of a writing helps interpret its content. Unfortunately, the genre of Acts is a much disputed issue. The book contains features often found in ancient biography, history, and novel, and scholars variously assign Acts to one of those forms. Although the overall genre of Acts is difficult to establish, understanding the constituent literary forms may be helpful in the reading process. The speeches, travel narrative (including the WE-SECTIONS), miracle stories (including "punitive" miracles), stories of edification, and summary statements all share literary conventions typical of other ancient literature, al though Luke has given his material a distinctive Christian "spin." Whatever sources were at Luke's disposal, the Book of Acts reflects an author in control of his materials. Above all, Acts is a story and employs literary conventions typical of ancient narrative.

For Further Study

In the *Mercer Dictionary of the Bible*: APOSTLE/APOSTLESHIP; APOSTLES, ACTS OF THE; BARNABAS; CHRISTOLOGY; FELLOWSHIP; HOLY SPIRIT; JAMES; JERUSALEM COUNCIL; LUKE; LUKE, GOSPEL OF; MIRACLE STORY; PAUL; PETER; PHILIP; RESURRECTION IN THE NT; ROMAN EMPIRE; SEVEN, THE; STEPHEN; TWELVE, THE; WE-SECTIONS; WOMEN IN THE NT.

In other sources: J. Chance, "Luke," *MCB*; J. Fitzmyer, *The Gospel according to Luke I–IX*, AncB; R. Funk, *The Poetics of Biblical Narrative*; S. Garrett, *The Demise of the Devil: Magic and the Demonic in Luke's Writings*; D. Gill, "The

Structure of Acts 9," *Bib* 55:546–48; E. Haenchen, *The Acts of the Apostles*; G. Krodel, *Acts*, AugCNT; J. Polhill, *Acts*, NAC.

Commentary

An Outline

The Sense of a Beginning, 1:1–5:42

The Beginning of the Church, 1:1-26

The opening chapter of Acts refers to the previous story of the founder of the earliest Christian community, Jesus of Nazareth, and sets the stage for the emergence and spread of that community. Acts 1:1-14 orients the reader to the story, and the remainder of chap. 1 (vv. 15-26) tells of the defection of Judas and the selection of his successor.

1:1-14. Introduction. Acts contains a brief, retrospective summary that describes the contents of the third Gospel (vv. 1-2). A prospective outline of the contents of Acts is given in v. 8 (this pattern is one of several used in narrative writings in antiquity: see, e.g., Polybius, *Hist* 2.1.4-8; 3.1.5–3.3.3; Philo, *Life of Moses* 2). Significantly, the outline is given by Jesus and is couched in the narrative as a promise.

The ascension account in Acts (vv. 6-11) follows the form of Greco-Roman assumption stories, while its terminology is heavily dependent on the assumption story of ELIJAH (2 Kgs 2:1-12). Just as ancient assumption stories accentuate the elevated status of their subjects, the ascension of Jesus underlines his exaltation. It is the fitting conclusion to the ministry of Jesus (so Luke 24:50-53); and here, it makes the life of the church both possible and intelligible. The ending of the story of Jesus then serves as the appropriate beginning of the story of the church.

Although after chap. 1 Jesus is absent as a character from the narrative of Acts (but see Acts 7:56), his influence throughout the rest of the narrative is profound.

The name of Jesus occurs no less than sixty-nine times in Acts. He is at the center of the church's controversy with the Jews. He guides the church in its missionary efforts; he empowers the disciples to perform miracles. The ascended and exalted Christ, although absent as a character, is present throughout the narrative.

The ascension is significant for Luke's story and theology, but these opening verses actually focus on the response of the disciples to Jesus. This second section (vv. 6-11) contains two parts, and each one concludes with a reproof of the disciples (vv. 7, 11a) followed by a promise to them (vv. 8a, 11b; see Talbert 1984, 6–7). Despite the reproaches, the fact that both dialogues end with promises to the disciples invites a favorable judgment of the disciples by the audience.

In the summary of vv. 12-14, Luke lists the disciples who have gathered together in the *room upstairs*. The names of the disciples in Acts 1 are the same as those in Luke 6:13-16, although the order is slightly different. The list of followers is extended in Acts to include women and the family of Jesus. To mention women in ancient genealogies is unusual. Mary, the mother of Jesus, stands as a bridge figure between the women who followed Jesus (see Luke 8:2; 23:49, 55; 24:10) and the family of Jesus, who, except for James, receive no further mention in the text. The omission of Judas's name from the list, of course, prepares the reader for the report of his death and the choice of his replacement.

1:15-26. The death of Judas and the election of Matthias. Before Luke narrates the fulfillment at Pentecost of Jesus' promise that the disciples will be empowered by the Holy Spirit, Luke addresses what was for him a problem of the first magnitude. The circle of THE TWELVE has been broken and must be restored.

Peter stands in the midst of the believers to address this problem (v. 15). The situational irony of this first apostolic speech in the post-Easter community should not be lost. The irony is created by the similarities in the pre-Easter actions of JUDAS and PETER. Judas betrayed Jesus (Luke 22:47), thus fulfilling Jesus' prophecy (Luke 22:21-22). Peter denied knowing Jesus three times (Luke 22:54-62), thus fulfilling Jesus' prophecy (Luke 22:34). The actions of both Judas and Peter were associated with the work of Satan (Luke 22:3; 22:31). And so in Acts v. 15, we have the ironical predicament of the one who denied Jesus standing up to retell the story of the one who had betrayed him.

Before leaving v. 15, we should note the narrator's use of a narrative aside to address the reader directly about the size of the assembly gathered with Peter: *together the crowd numbered about one hundred twenty persons*. The number is significant since 120 is not only a multiple of the Twelve but also because 120 males were required to constitute a local Jewish SANHEDRIN or council (Sanh 1.6). Luke may be arguing that the early church is also a "properly constituted" community according to Pharisaic standards. Regardless, it is clear that in this newly formed community, women also count (see v. 14; also Luke 8:1-3; 23:49).

Peter's speech (vv. 16-22) turns upon the OT quotation cited in v. 20. The first half of the quotation taken from Ps 69:26 deals with the demise of Judas; the second half, a citation of Ps 109:8, addresses the election of Judas's successor. The double use of the verb for divine necessity (δεῖ) in vv. 16 and 21 is the narrative clue for dividing the speech into these two parts.

Peter depicts the defection of Judas and his subsequent judgment in the language of economics (Johnson 1977, 179–81). Judas does not repent and return the betrayal money (contra Matt 27:3-5), but rather purchases a farm (v. 18). This purchase not only stands in contrast to the believers who sold their farms and laid the proceeds at the apostles' feet (see 4:32-35); it also is juxtaposed to Peter who, along with James and John, "left everything" to follow Jesus (see Luke 5:11). Judas's purchase of property is a symbol of his apostasy from the circle of the Twelve.

Ironically, Judas dies on this same property. There is no hint of suicide here (as in Matt 27). The death is apparently the result of divine judgment, and the field is called the *Hakeldama, that is, Field of Blood* (v. 19). And just as the purchasing of a field symbolized Judas's defection, so also the fact that his property is doomed to perpetual desertion (v. 20) is a sign of his judgment.

Joseph and Matthias are put forward as apostolic candidates, and the assembly prays for divine guidance in the selection process. Matthias is chosen as the replacement. Note the play on words throughout this scene: Judas has forfeited his "share" (κλῆρος) in the apostolic ministry and gone to his own "place" (τόπος). In contrast, the "lot" (κλῆρος) now falls to Matthias, and he takes his "place" (τόπος) alongside the eleven in the apostolic ministry. The scriptures are fulfilled, the circle of Twelve is reconstituted, and the stage is set for Pentecost.

Pentecost, 2:1-47

The Holy Spirit descended on Jesus at the outset of his public ministry (Luke 3:22; 4:1; 4:14). Now the Holy Spirit comes upon the disciples at the inauguration of their public ministry. The disciples are worthy successors of Jesus.

2:1-13. The miracle of Pentecost. All narratives have gaps in the telling of a story, and what a narrator decides *not* to say is sometimes as important as what is said. The story of Pentecost is such a story. The story itself fills a gap created when Jesus instructs the disciples to stay in the city for an indeterminate length of time until they *receive power when the Holy Spirit has come upon* them (1:8). In v. 1 the length of time is fifty days. That time has not been idle time for the disciples: they spend forty days being instructed by the risen Lord about the kingdom of God (1:3) and an unspecified time electing Judas's replacement.

But gaps still remain within the story itself. In this Pentecost narrative, the reader encounters rather large lacunae over the nature of the miracle of glossolalia and the overall background against which the passage should be read. How one chooses to fill those gaps will determine in large measure the interpretation assigned to this particular passage.

What is the nature of the miracle recorded in Acts 2? The coming of the Spirit is joined by two manifestations: a loud noise and *tongues, as of fire*. But the function of these audial and visual signs in this narrative is unclear. When the apostles speak "in other tongues" (v. 4 RSV; NRSV *languages*) are they speaking in ecstatic, unintelligible speech (see 1 Cor 12–14), or are they speaking in the languages of the many foreign peoples gathered together there? There is evidence for both interpretations. Those gathered there heard in their own languages (vv. 6-7); but others mistook the disciples as drunk (v. 13), suggesting that, at least for some, the apostles' speech was unintelligible. The weight of the evidence seems to favor a miracle of hearing, but the "correct" interpretation is perhaps finally undecidable. Such rich ambiguity may underscore the multilayered understanding that Luke himself had of this event.

In the Pentecost narrative, the reader, standing at a crossroads, is faced with choosing among these various options. The road signs are few, and the exegetical path one chooses will determine the direction of interpretation when one encounters the next crossroad. Reading the passage against these various backgrounds at times sheds new light; at other times, such choices perpetuate certain misreadings.

Whichever of these paths the interpreter chooses to follow, one often-neglected emphasis of this passage remains constant. Alongside the theme of the Holy Spirit empowering the disciples (Acts 1:4) is the countertheme that Pentecost also hints at the benefits of waiting, of being patient (Luke 24:52; Acts 1:8, 12; 2:1). So Pentecost celebrates both an empowered church as well as a patient God who endures the church's abuse of that power. Filling the interpretive gap left by the Pentecost narrative with an emphasis on the patience of waiting disciples and a faithful God also picks up on a major point of the text from Joel, which serves as the basis for Peter's sermon.

2:14-40. Peter's Pentecostal sermon. Peter's interpretation of the Pentecost experience is almost three times longer than the narrative detailing the event itself. The speech divides into two main parts (vv. 17-21; 22-36), with an introduction (vv. 14-16) and conclusion (vv. 37-40).

Peter stands again (see 1:15-22) to strengthen the brothers and sisters (vv. 14-15). The narrator's introduction (v. 14a) anchors the speech firmly within the narrative framework of 2:1-13. The linguistic connections are strong. Peter raises his *voice* (φωνή, v. 14) in harmony with the *sound* (φωνή, v. 6) that had drawn the multitudes to the company of believers in the first place. Furthermore, the word Luke uses to describe the address of Peter to the crowd is the same word used to describe the inspired speech the Spirit gave to the believers who were speaking in "other tongues" (see 2:4). Not only are the "tongues" at Pentecost divinely inspired, but Peter's interpretation of that event is likewise authoritatively inspired.

The introduction to the speech itself is a response to the exasperated question some of them were posing to one another, *What does this mean?* (v. 12). If Peter rejects the mockery of some that the believers are drunk (v. 15; see v. 13), he also affirms the understanding of others that the believers are rehearsing the *God's deeds of power* (v. 11). This citation of Joel 2:28-32 (LXX 3:1-5) functions as the bridge both to what precedes and follows it.

Note first the inclusive nature of this citation. This community Joel speaks about and that Peter says is realized in the earliest Christian community is remarkably inclusive. It is gender inclusive: *your sons and your daughters* (v. 17); *my slaves, both men and women* (v. 18). It is age inclusive: *your young men* and *your old men* (v. 17). And if we are to take seriously the opening of this citation (*all flesh*, v. 17), then this community is also destined to be ethnically inclusive.

The Joel citation has been modified by the addition of several significant terms and phrases. That this new community itself is an eschatological sign is underscored by the change from "after these days" in the LXX text of Joel (cf. Joel 2:29) to *in the last days* found here in Acts. That this sermon is inspired speech is further underscored by the addition in v. 17 of *God de clares*. Peter had assumed the role of the narrator in this speech, but quickly yields the floor to Joel who in turn defers to God. The effect of these narrative lay ers—Luke said that Peter said that Joel said that God said—is to reinforce the utterly reliable and authoritative character of the speech here. This point is made again by the next Lukan addition to the quotation at the end of v. 18: *and they shall prophesy.* This promise is fulfilled not only in the Pentecost event; Peter is fulfilling it himself in this very speech.

The last element added to the Joel citations, *signs* (v. 19), is perhaps the most significant addition. The phrase "wonders and signs" or SIGNS AND WONDERS becomes something of a refrain throughout the first half of Acts. It first recurs in the context of this very speech when Peter refers three verses later to *Jesus of Nazareth, a man attested to you by God with deeds of power, wonders, and signs . . .* (v. 22). Jesus is the primary referent to the prophecy that God would work wonders and signs as eschatological portents of the coming Day of the Lord.

But Jesus is not the only referent. Later in this chapter we find wonders and signs being done through the apostles (cf. 4:30; 5:12). Stephen, one of THE SEVEN Hellenists selected to assist the Twelve (see 6:1-6), is himself described as one who *did great wonders and signs among the people* (6:8). Stephen next describes Moses as *having performed wonders and signs in Egypt, at the Red Sea, and in the wilderness for forty years* (7:36). Philip also works *signs* (8:6—note the absence of "wonders"). Finally, the Lord grants *signs and wonders to be done* by the hands of Paul and Barnabas (14:3; see 15:12).

Signs and wonders, then, accompany the ministries of the leaders of God's community in unbroken succession, from Moses to Jesus, to the Twelve, to Stephen and Philip the Hellenists, and to Paul and Barnabas, the leaders of the gentile mission. Luke demonstrates that the early church has been more faithful to the tradition of Moses than other groups making the same claims. Membership in this radically inclusive community is restricted in only one way: *Then everyone who calls on the name of the Lord shall be saved* (v. 21). The identity of this "Lord" is explored in the second part of this sermon (vv. 22-36), and the call to "be saved" is the focus of the invitation at the end (vv. 37-41).

Acts 2:22-36 is marked with several appeals for attention that serve as indicators of rhetorical shifts. This part of the speech forms the following chiastic structure (Krodel 1986, 83):

A   the kerygma, 22-24
   B   proof from scripture, 25-28
      C   interpretation of scripture, 34a
         D   exaltation of Jesus and the
            mediation of the Holy Spirit, 32-33
      C'   interpretation of scripture, 29-31
   B'   proof from scripture, 34b-35
A'   the kerygma, 36

The heart of the Pentecost sermon is to be found in vv. 32-33. Peter identifies the unnamed Christ as Jesus (v. 32), which distinguishes early Christian messianic exegesis from that of Jewish contemporaries. The identification is further strengthened by the use of resurrection language. David foresaw and spoke of the *resurrection of the Messiah* (v. 31) who is *this Jesus God raised up* (v. 32a).

These verses also serve to link the speech with the Pentecost narrative and its interpretive framework provided by the Joel citation. The reference to the *promise* Jesus *received from the Father* (v. 33) recalls the Pentecost event; v. 33 identifies that promise as the *Holy Spirit*. That Jesus *poured out this that you both see and hear* (v. 33) echoes the Joel prophecy ("I will pour out my Spirit," Joel 2:28) and explicitly interprets Pentecost as a miracle of both sight and sound.

The conclusion of Peter's sermon (vv. 37-39) is interrupted by the audience who are cut to the heart and ask Peter and the rest of the apostles, *Brothers, what should we do?* (cf. Luke 3:10). Peter then offers a soteriological conclusion to his sermon: *Repent, and be baptized every one of you in the name of Jesus Christ so that your sins may be forgiven* (v. 38a). He also promises that they too will receive the "gift which is the Holy Spirit" (v. 38b, author trans.). This promise (see v. 33) is not only for Peter's audience, but for their children and *for all who are far away* (v. 39). The final phrase of Peter's speech, *everyone whom the Lord our God calls to him*, takes the last phrase of the Joel citation (v. 21=Joel 2:32) and turns it on its head. The invitation to salvation is reciprocal: "Everyone who calls on the name of Lord" will be those "whom the Lord our God calls to him."

2:41-47. Narrative summary. Luke concludes this section with the first of a series of long summary statements. Some summaries, such as Acts 1:12-14, are brief (see 6:7; 8:14; 9:31-32; 11:19-20); others, such as vv. 41-47, are longer and more detailed (cf. 4:32-35; 5:12-16). These summaries are quite common in the early chapters of Acts and serve a double purpose. They divide the narrative into segments but serve also as connective tissue or "narrative glue," shaping the episodes into a continuous account.

The summary begins and ends with reference to the numerical growth of the community (vv. 41b, 47b). In between, the narrator depicts the shared life of the community, which for Luke is the life of the Spirit. The believers who accepted the word and were baptized, now devote themselves to the teaching of the apostles, to the shared life, to the breaking of bread, and to prayer. These four elements characterize the life of the Spirit and are illustrated by the examples given in vv. 43-47.

The Healing of a Lame Man, 3:1–4:31

This section is clearly set off from the rest of Acts by narrative summaries on either side (2:41-47; 4:32-35). The passage itself displays a certain internal coherence and is divided into four segments or scenes that are marked by shifts in space, time, and/or participants (Funk 1988, 83). While these changes in time, setting, and characters provide clear rhetorical markers for dividing the text into four scenes, these segments are also united by several thematic links. The theme of healing is found in every scene, either with specific reference to the lame man at the Beautiful Gate (3:7, 16; 4:9-10, 22) or to healing in general (4:30). Likewise, references to "the name of Jesus" are found throughout this stretch of narrative on the lips of Peter (3:6, 16; 4:10, 12), the religious leaders (4:7, 17, 18), and the community of believers (4:30).

3:1-10. Scene 1. At the Beautiful Gate. The opening verses (vv. 1-2) particularize the general description of the community of believers found in the preceding narrative summary. Two of these apostles, PETER and JOHN, are going to worship in the Temple on a specific day at a specific time, three o'clock in the afternoon, the hour of prayer. With the setting, time, and characters in place, the stage is set for a specific *sign* of healing (2:43; see 4:22).

This beggar sits at the Beautiful Gate of the Temple doing the only thing he knows to do: he begs for alms. But to his surprise, he receives the mercies of God. *I have no silver or gold*, Peter responds, *but what I have I give to you; in the name of Jesus Christ of Nazareth, stand up and walk* (v. 6). The name of Jesus Christ is introduced into this story for the first time and will remain the focus of attention throughout this stretch of narrative. The lame man's feet and ankles are made strong, and Peter and John, like Jesus before them (Luke 5:17-26) and Paul after them (Acts 14:8-18), command the lame to walk, confirming and extending the programmatic ministry of Jesus (Luke 7:22).

The once-lame man leaps and praises God (echoing Isa 35:6; see also Luke 7:22). A third group of participants now enter the scene, *all the people*, who recognize the man as the one who sat for alms (vv. 9-10). For the second time, the Beautiful Gate of the Temple is mentioned. With this second reference to the gate, one wonders if the narrator may be less interested in its specific locale and more interested in working a wordplay between the repetition of *hour* (ὥρα, *hour of prayer*, v. 1) and the Beautiful (ὡραῖα) Gate. Within the semantic domain of this word is the meaning "opportune moment" or "timely" (see Rom 10:15 quoting Isa 52:7). Could the narrator be hinting that this ninth hour (three o'clock in the afternoon), the hour of prayer, is the "timely" moment of opportunity for this lame man who sits begging, ironically, at the Gate of Opportunity?

3:11–4:4. Scene 2. In Solomon's Portico. The change in locale from the Beautiful Gate to Solomon's Portico indicates a scene change (v. 11). The pattern of Pentecost is repeated here: a miraculous event (vv. 1-10; cf. 2:1-4) draws a crowd (v. 11; cf. 2:5-12) and Peter delivers a speech (vv. 12-26; cf. 2:14-40).

The outer frame of the first half of Peter's speech (vv. 12-16) deals with the healing of the lame man (vv. 12, 16) which is interpreted by the inner frame, a traditional christological kerygma (vv. 13-15). This kerygmatic statement is arranged in a chiastic pattern:

A *The God of Abraham, the God of Isaac,*
  and the God of Jacob . . .
    has glorified his servant Jesus, 13a
  B *whom you handed over and rejected*
    in the presence of Pilate, 13b
  B' *But you rejected the Holy and Righteous One*
    . . . and you killed the Author of life, 14-15a
A' *whom God raised from the dead,* 15b

The loaded christological titles, *servant, Holy and Righteous One,* and *Author of life,* along with this traditional kerygma, provide the foundation for the correct interpretation of the healing of the lame man. Some observers of this sign might conclude that Peter and John through their *own power or piety . . . made him walk* (v. 12), but Peter denies this interpretation and argues rather that "the faith that is through Jesus has given him this perfect health in the presence of all of you" (v. 16).

And now, friends is the rhetorical clue that marks the beginning of the second half of Peter's sermon (vv. 17-26). Here Peter extends an invitation to repentance undergirded by various citations of and allusions to scripture. He begins by acknowledging that his audience, although culpable for the death of Jesus, *acted in ignorance, as did also your rulers* (v. 17). Still, this ignorance produces a guilt that stands in need of repentance (v. 19).

The call to *repent, therefore* is accompanied by the promise of a number of benefits (vv. 19-22). These benefits carry with them the responsibility to listen to the prophet like Moses (v. 22). The addition in v. 22 of the words *tells you* in this quotation from Deut 18:15-20, is a rhetorical device the Lukan Peter employs to sharpen the challenge to his audience. The speech ends on a salvation-historical note: God, having raised up his servant (see v. 12), *sent him first to you* (v. 26), hinting at least at the gentile mission that will soon follow in Acts led by Peter himself (see Acts 10).

In the concluding verses to this scene (4:1-4), new participants are introduced—priests and the captain of the Temple and the SADDUCEES—who take Peter and John into custody for "teaching the people and proclaiming that in Jesus there is the resurrection of the dead" (v. 2). It is late, so their interrogation will have to wait until tomorrow. The major temporal break between the first two scenes and the last two does not occur, however, before the narrator reports in a brief aside that *many of those who heard the word believed; and they numbered about five thousand* (v. 4). Even in the face of danger, the community of believers continues to add to its numbers.

4:5-22. Scene 3. Before the Sanhedrin. The next two scenes take place on the following day, and a formidable group of religious leaders gather for the interrogation of Peter and John (v. 6). The apostles are set in their midst, and the inquiry by the leaders links with Peter's previous speech: *By what power* (see 3:12) *or by what name* (see 3:16) *did you do this?* (v. 7). Before recording Peter's response, the narrator reports that Peter was *filled with the Holy Spirit* (v. 8), thus fulfilling Jesus' words of encouragement that when his followers are oppressed "the Holy Spirit will teach you at that very hour what you ought to say" (Luke 12:12). Peter, then, recapitulates his previous speech, echoing the traditional christological kerygma: the one "whom you crucified, whom God raised from the dead" (v. 10; see 3:13, 15); reiterating the rejection of Jesus by his audience: *This Jesus is the stone that was rejected by you, the builders* (v. 11; see 3:13-14); and underscoring the fact that the healing was through *the name of Jesus Christ of Nazareth* (v. 10; see 3:16).

Peter introduces a new element into his summary; he identifies the healing as a *good deed*, or "benefaction" (v. 9). Later in Acts, Peter will characterize the healing ministry of the earthly Jesus with the same word (10:38). This is the technical word associated with the benefactor/client system so prominent in the social structures of the ancient Greco-Roman world. Benefactors gave support, financial and otherwise, to individuals, groups, and sometimes whole cities. In return the recipients of such benefaction pledged and gave their loyalty to these benefactors (Danker 1982). The disciples here have taken over the role of benefactor, and, like Jesus, that which they have to give— wholeness of life—is far more precious than the typical benefits of *silver and gold*.

Unable to rebuke Peter and John because the lame man stood beside the apostles as empirical proof of the truth of Peter's words, the religious leaders order them out of the council (SANHEDRIN) and discussed what they should do. This scene heightens in tension when the council reaches the conclusion to issue a restraining order to the apostles (v. 17).

The apostles are called back in and warned *not to speak or teach at all in the name of Jesus* (v. 18). They respond with the boldness the SANHEDRIN has already observed: *we cannot keep from speaking about what we have seen and heard* (v. 20). The narrator depicts Peter and John speaking these words in unison (v. 19), highlighting the unity of the apostolic witness. The Sanhedrin further threatens them and then releases them, unable to follow through on their threats because of the people (v. 21).

This scene ends with a reference to the healing event of 3:1-10 (v. 22). The reader learns that the lame man was more than forty years old, although the narrator does not disclose the significance of that reference. Is he old enough to be a reliable witness to the event? Does his age underscore the miraculous nature of the healing of this one who had been *lame from birth* (3:2)? The reader must fill this gap.

More significant, perhaps, is the reference to this event as a *sign of healing* (v. 22) linking this miracle closely to the *wonders and signs* done through the apostles (2:43). The Sanhedrin had just acknowledged that this healing was *a notable sign* (v. 16). Earlier Peter had made the connection between this man who had been *healed* (σώζω, v. 9) *by the name of Jesus Christ* and his soteriological conclusion that *there is no other name under heaven given among mortals by which we must be saved* ("saved" = σωθῆναι, v. 12). The use of this word, which bears the double meaning of "heal" and "save," suggests that this healing story is more permeated with soteriological content.

The healed lame man has become the paradigm of salvation through Jesus' name in Acts. Just as the blind man who regains his sight in John 9 is a model disciple in the fourth Gospel where believing is symbolized as a kind of seeing, so the lame man who walks in Acts 3 is the symbol of salvation in a story where journey narratives occupy much narrative space, and where the Christian movement is referred to simply as "the Way" (see 9:2; 19:9, 23; 22:4; 24:14, 22).

4:23-31. Scene 4. Reunited with friends. The finale to this episode is set in some unnamed place in Jerusalem where the apostles return to *their friends* (Gk. "their own") and recount to them what the reader already knows about the threats of the chief priests and elders. This recapitulation prompts the community to pray with one voice to God in a show of solidarity with their beleaguered colleagues.

The prayer (vv. 24b-30) begins with an invocation of the Sovereign Creator. Psalm 2 is then interpreted in light of the passion of Jesus. The kings (HEROD and Pontius PILATE) and rulers (by inference the Sanhedrin, see 4:5) gathered with the gentiles and the peoples of Israel against the Lord and his Anointed. Of course, even these acts are according to God's hand and plan that God *predestined to take place* (v. 28; see 2:23).

But this psalm is also interpreted in light of the present circumstances of the believers. The believers pray that the Lord will *look at their threats* and grant to his servants *to speak your word with all boldness* (v. 29). The final verse of the prayer is a precis of many of the issues already addressed in this episode: *While you stretch out your hand to heal, and signs and wonders are performed through the name of your holy servant Jesus* (v. 30), with emphasis placed on the role of Jesus as the power source for the wonder-performing servant.

The entire episode is brought to a close in v. 31. The place in which they were gathered was shaken, and they were filled with the Holy Spirit (recalling Pentecost, 2:1-4). The first part of their petition, to speak *the word of God with boldness*, is fulfilled. In fact, this theme of speaking the word of God with "boldness" or "openness" (παρρασίας) is another dominant theme not only in this episode (see vv. 13, 29, and here in v. 31), but throughout the Book of Acts (see 2:29; 9:28; 13:46; 14:3;

18:26; 26:26; 28:31). Such boldness will surely be needed, as in the next episode the believers face conflict both within and without the community.

Tensions Within and Without, 4:32–5:42

Attention is turned again by way of a narrative summary (4:32-35) to the shape of this company of believers. Two case studies follow, providing positive and negative examples of how believers dealt with their possessions and commitments within the community. The final episode, 5:12-42, depicts the life of the community from an outsider's perspective. Here many of the themes found in 3:1–4:31 are repeated: the apostles are found healing the sick (5:12-16; cf. 3:1-10), which prompts the religious authorities to arrest them again and to bring them before the Sanhedrin for their second interrogation (5:17-42; cf. 3:11–4:22, see Tannehill 1990, 59–79). As the community is marked by unity and tension within, so it is characterized by similar challenges from without.

4:32–5:11. Tensions within. In 4:32-35, Luke reiterates the point of emphasis of the summary in 2:41-47. But this summary also provides an interesting variation to the themes found in chap. 2. Now, the believers took the proceeds from their sales and *laid it at the apostles' feet* (v. 35). To assume the posture of being at another's feet is a gesture of submission in the OT (Josh 10:24; 1 Sam 25:24, 41; 2 Sam 22:39; Pss 8:7; 110:1). Luke also employs this language of being at another's feet as a symbol of submission (Luke 7:38, 44, 45, 46; 8:35, 41; 10:39; 17:16; 20:43; Acts 2:35; 10:35; 22:3). So here in v. 35, laying the proceeds at the apostles' feet is more than just a way of taking care of an administrative detail. As Luke Johnson has noted: "When the believers lay their possessions at the Apostles' feet, therefore, they were symbolically laying themselves there, in a gesture of submission to the authority of the Twelve" (Johnson 1977, 202). In just such an act of submission, Barnabas lay his gift at the apostles' feet (vv. 36-37—see further comment on Barnabas at 11:19-30; 12:25).

Not everyone submitted themselves to the authority of the apostles, as the story of ANANIAS and Sapphira indicates (5:1-11). This story is linked linguistically to the previous two scenes by the words *at the apostles' feet* (v. 2) and depicts a negative example of community life. Ananias and Sapphira sell a piece of property, but they mock the community's Spirit of unity, and they usurp the authority of the apostles when they lay only a part of the proceeds at their feet.

Peter assumes the role of prophet when he confronts Ananias with the conspiracy (v. 3). Like Judas, Ananias has fallen prey to Satan (v. 3; cf. Luke 22:3), and like Judas, Ananias will not live to enjoy the material gains of his deceit (v. 5; see 1:17-18). Although Ananias has not lied verbally, the act of conspiracy itself was a *lie to the Holy Spirit* (v. 3).

Peter's remaining questions suggest that Ananias and Sapphira were not required to dispose of their property in this way, but could have retained authority over it (v. 4). But by taking this duplicitous action, they usurped the authority of the apostles. The offense was not simply against the community, Peter argues; it was against God. The problem was not simply a human one; it had serious spiritual dimensions, and as Ananias soon found out, serious repercussions. Upon hearing Peter's words, *he fell down and died* (v. 5).

After the disposal of Ananias and an interval—the narrator tells us—of *about three hours* (v. 7), Peter confronts Sapphira in what resembles a legal trial. The story drips rich with irony because the reader has knowledge Sapphira does not possess: the conspiracy is broken. Unknowingly Sapphira compounds the conspiracy with a verbal lie. Yes, she tells Peter, they sold the land *for such and such a price* (v. 8).

Peter's role as prophet becomes even more active when he predicts that this one who with her husband conspired against the community and God would now suffer the same fate as he (v. 8). And the final note of irony: Sapphira falls dead at Peter's feet. She who had feigned to lay her possessions at the apostles' feet now literally does fall at Peter's feet. The submission to apostolic authority she failed to give in life, she now gives permanently in death.

This grizzly story fulfills the threat of Peter's earlier sermon: *everyone who does not listen to that prophet will be utterly rooted out of the people* (3:23). No wonder that a *great fear seized the whole church and all who heard of these things* (v. 11).

5:12-42. Tensions without. This third and final summary (vv. 12-16), which describes the Jerusalem church, in several ways recalls a previous episode (3:1–4:31). First, there is the setting of Solomon's Portico that was the site of Peter's speech and the apostles' arrest (3:11–4:4). Second, the other half of the believers' prayer that *signs and wonders* be performed (4:30) is now fulfilled when the narrator reports: *Now many signs and wonders were done among the people through the apostles* (v. 12). Finally, the healing of one man in chap. 3 has now been generalized so that people carried their sick into the streets (vv. 14-15) where the apostles continue their benefaction (see 4:9), and *they were all cured* (v. 16). And, of course, the narrator does not miss an opportunity to record that *more than ever believers were added to the Lord, great numbers of both men and women* (v. 14). This summary is, however, distinct from the previous two in at least one important way. In contrast to the previous summaries (2:41-47; 4:32-35), "which looked inward at the internal life of the community, Luke's new summary looks outward at the public effect of the apostles on the Jewish people" (Krodel 1986, 124).

The public character of this summary scene is presumed in the closing episode of the chapter, vv. 17-42. The reader now learns of another response to the apostles than that of the people who *held them in high esteem* (v. 13). The high priest and the party of the Sadducees were *filled with jealousy* (v. 17). This response also explains further the timidity of the people who dared not join the believers (v. 13).

There is also remarkable redundancy between vv. 17-42 and Acts 4:1-22 (Tannehill 1990, 59–79). Both include the arrest of the apostles, their appearance before the Sanhedrin, short speeches that highlight the apostolic witness to Jesus and their commitment to obey God rather than the Sanhedrin, deliberation by the Sanhedrin out of the presence of the apostles, and the decision to release the apostles with the warning not to preach in Jesus' name. But variations in detail between these two accounts serve to heighten the tension of the narrative between the believers and the religious establishment. How will the church respond to these challenges from without?

In this closing episode, the conflict broadens: all of the apostles are placed in prison, not just Peter and John (cf. 4:3). This scene also adds the new dimension of divine intervention with an ironic twist. The narrator winks at the reader when he reports that the apostles are released from prison by an "angel," whose very existence the Sadducees deny (see 23:8). On the next morning, the officers find the prison guards standing watch over an empty cell (v. 23). The liberated apostles are found teaching in the Temple as they were instructed to do (v. 20), and they are quietly returned to the Sanhedrin (vv. 25-26).

The stage is set for the second interrogation (vv. 27-32). The old charge of teaching *in this name* (v. 27; cf. 4:7) is coupled with a new reaction by the Sadducees to the accusation that the apostles' teaching is intended to *bring this man's blood on us* (v. 28). The stakes have been raised considerably since the last confrontation. Peter responds with a confession similar to the one he made at the first interrogation (see 4:19): *We must obey God rather than any human authority* (v. 29). What had been a conditional sentence becomes a divine imperative, and the duet of Peter and John now becomes an apostolic chorus led by Peter.

They then employ the christological kerygma typical of the previous speeches (2:23-24, 36; 3:13-15; 4:10): *The God of our ancestors raised up Jesus, whom you had killed by hanging him on a tree* (v. 30). But rather than calling down this man's blood upon the Sadducees as the high priest had feared, the apostles argue that the exalted Jesus is the Leader and Savior who gives repentance and forgiveness of sins (v. 31). The speech concludes with the apostles reaffirming in unison their role as witnesses along with *the Holy Spirit whom God has given to those who obey him* (v. 32).

The apostles' insistence on the culpability of the religious leaders in Jesus' death, the need for Israel's repentance, and the reference to the gift of the *Spirit* (in which the Sadducees also did not believe—see 23:8) now not only annoys the Sadducees (see 4:2), but enrages them to the point of contemplating murder (v. 33). GAMALIEL, a PHARISEE member of the Council who was *respected by all the people*, swiftly stands and orders the apostles taken outside. In this tense moment, he offers a brief speech marked by restraint and caution. Citing the historical examples of Theudas and Judas the Galilean who were leaders of revolutionary movements that *came to nothing*, Gamaliel advises the council that *if this plan or this undertaking is of human origin, it will fail; but if it is of God, you will not be able to overthrow them* (vv. 38-39).

Of course, Luke's reader already knows from the divine intervention, the miraculous healings, and other signs and wonders, that *this plan* and *this deed* are, indeed, *of God*. The only conclusion to be drawn from the narrator's point of view is that the Sanhedrin has already been found opposing God (v. 39). An angel had intervened earlier on behalf of the apostles in freeing them from prison; now the agent of intervention is a human one, a Pharisee, who compels by the wisdom of his argument.

So the Sanhedrin took Gamaliel's advice and released the apostles (v. 40). Again, the religious leaders charge them not to speak in the name of Jesus (see 4:18), but the conflict is heightened as the threats turn into beatings. Once again, the apostles boldly defy the Sanhedrin's instructions, and every day in their expressions of corporate worship, publicly in the Temple and privately at home (see 2:46), the apostles *did not cease to teach and proclaim Jesus as the Messiah* (v. 42). This plan and this deed must surely be of God.

Problems and Personalities, 6:1–12:25

The first five chapters of Acts focus on the action in and around Jerusalem, and the second half of Acts (chaps. 13–28) narrates the spread of the gospel by focusing on the places where the apostle Paul and his companions travel. These middle chapters, however, explore personalities more than places. The adventures of STEPHEN, PHILIP, PAUL, PETER, and BARNABAS fill these pages. Of course, the success of the gospel in overcoming problems in the community is still the underlying theme that holds these stories together (see the INCLUSIO formed by the references to the spreading of the word of God in 6:7 and 12:24), but this middle division provides perhaps the best justification for the title assigned to this work in the second century, the "Acts of the Apostles."

Stephen: His Witness and Death, 6:1–8:3

6:1-7. Structures and the spirit. This first scene serves two purposes: to provide another example of how conflict in the early Christian community is resolved (and schism thus avoided) and to introduce Stephen and Philip into the narrative.

To fulfill the first purpose, Luke employs a narrative pattern remarkably similar to the OT form for choosing auxiliary leadership (Exod 18 and Num 27): (1) statement of the problem—a grumbling among the Hellenists that Greek-speaking Jewish-Christian widows were being excluded from table fellowship (vv. 1-2; cf. Exod 18:14-18; Num 27:12-14); (2) the proposed solution—the apostles thus propose that they continue to devote themselves to *serving the word* (v. 4b) and that the newly appointed auxiliary leadership be responsible to *wait on tables* (vv. 2c-3; cf. Exod 18:19-23; Num 27:15-17); (3) requisite qualifications for new leadership—they are to be *of good standing, full of the Spirit and of wisdom* (v. 3), and, judging from their Greek names, they came from the part of the church that had complained about mistreatment of some of its constituency (v. 3b; cf. Exod 18:21; Num 27:18-21); (4) *setting apart the new leader ship*—the Seven are set apart by prayer and the laying on of hands (vv. 5-6; cf. Exod 18:25; Num 27:22-23; on this pattern, see Talbert 1984, 29).

This unit ends with a second reference to the way *the number of the disciples increased greatly in Jerusalem* (v. 7; cf. v. 1). The point is further emphasized by the notice that "the word of God grew" (author trans.: on this phrase, see the comments below, at 12:24). The narrator goes on to add that *a great many of the priests became obedient to the faith* (v. 7). The upshot for Luke, of course, is that despite the conflicts that threaten the unity of the fledgling community, the church is able to solve its problems and continues to grow.

6:8–7:1. The controversy. The tensions between the followers of Jesus and the leaders of the Jewish community, recounted in Acts 4 and 5, now continue with the story of Stephen, one of THE SEVEN. Stephen, whom the narrator again reminds the reader is *full of grace and power* (v. 8) and *wisdom and the Spirit* (v. 10) performs signs and wonders like the apostles before him (4:30). Stephen is soon engaged in a dispute by some diaspora Jews (originally from various places, but probably belonging now to one synagogue; cf. v. 9) who stir up the people and bring him before the Council (v. 12).

The scene before the Sanhedrin parallels (and intensifies) the encounters of the apostles with the Council with one significant variation. In the previous conflict scenes, the "people" sided with the apostles (cf. 4:21, 5:26; see Tannehill, 84); here the people are stirred up against Stephen, thus removing the buffer that had previously protected the apostles. Instead, the scene now more closely parallels the arrest and trial scene of Jesus. Like Jesus, Stephen is led into the Sanhedrin (v. 12; Luke 22:66); and the people are stirred first against Jesus, now against Stephen (see Luke 23:13-25).

The tension has escalated here in Acts to unprecedented proportions. Only during the ministry of Jesus had such tensions been previously experienced, a fact that only intensifies the suspense for the readers.

The charge of blasphemy against Stephen (see Luke 5:21) is specified by false witnesses: Stephen had proclaimed that Jesus would destroy the Temple and change the customs of Moses. Stephen will ultimately address both these charges (see comments on the speech below). The charges do not die with Stephen; they will resurface later against Paul (21:28). In response to the high priest's question regarding the validity of the charges, Stephen speaks.

7:2-53. The speech. The speech of Stephen is the longest in Acts and is very important for understanding the nature of the conflict in the Jewish community about the role and purposes of Jesus. The speech is not a comprehensive retelling of Jewish history; in fact, it is very selective. Nor is the story a dispassionate, neutral account; it is revisionist history from a Christian perspective. As is the case in so many discourses, both oral and written, the purpose of Stephen's recounting Israel's history comes into focus only at its conclusion. At the end of the speech, Stephen accuses his listeners of *opposing the Holy Spirit, just as your ancestors used to do* (v. 51). Specifically, just as the ancestors had persecuted the prophets, so now their descendants had betrayed and murdered the Righteous One whose coming the prophets had foretold (v. 52). Both ancestors and contemporaries had rejected the law they had received. In short, Stephen argues that the death of Jesus fit into the overall pattern of rejection that was characteristic of Israel's history. All that goes before this part of the speech leads, in one way or another, to this climax.

The speech itself is organized into five parts: (a) the story of Abraham, vv. 2-8; (b) the story of Joseph and the patriarchs, vv. 9-16; (c) the story of Moses in three parts of forty years each, vv. 17-29, 30-34, 35-43; (d) the story of the tent and the Temple, vv. 44-50; and finally (e) the invective against Stephen's listeners, vv. 51-53. In the speech, Stephen at times will quote the LXX, summarize its content, or at least in one significant instance, expand the story with more explicit details. All of the parts fit together to make up Stephen's Christian interpretation of Jewish history.

MOSES receives more attention in the speech than any other OT character. His life is divided into three periods of forty years each (see above). Although Jesus is not explicitly mentioned until v. 52 (and even there not by name), the retelling of Moses' story has striking similarities to the story of Jesus. These parallels are most clearly seen in the first and last units (vv. 17-29 and 35-43). In Stephen's reconstruction, the infancy and childhood of Moses is parallel with that of Jesus. Moses was beautiful before God (v. 20; cf. Exod 2:2); Jesus was in favor with God (Luke 2:52). Moses was instructed in wisdom (v. 22) as was Jesus (Luke 2:52). As an adult Moses, like Jesus, was "powerful in words and deeds" (v. 22; cf. Luke 24:19; Acts 2:22).

In the last unit (vv. 35-43), the parallels continue. Both Jesus and Moses (and Stephen—see v. 8) performed signs and wonders (v. 36; see 2:22). Both Moses and Jesus are prophets. The typology is made explicit in Moses' words to the Israelites, *God will raise up a prophet for you from your own people as he raised me up* (v. 37).

This theme of Jesus as the *prophet like [Moses]* (see 3:22) is the most important parallel and lies at the heart of the Stephen speech. The ignorance of the people regarding Moses' call (v. 25) and their subsequent rejection of him (v. 35) foreshadow the rejection of Jesus by the people (v. 52).

The rejection of God's representatives is no less than a rejection of God himself. That is the point made at the end of the episode about Moses. Not knowing what had happened to Moses (v. 40), the people turn to idolatry, making a calf and sacrificing to it (v. 41). God then turns away from them and gives them up to their idolatry (vv. 42-43). The people have not only rejected Moses; they have rejected God.

The Moses' episode also contains Stephen's first response to his accusers that Stephen had claimed that Jesus would change the *customs that Moses handed on to us* (6:14). The rhetoric of Stephen's argument indicates that the Jewish leadership, not the followers of Jesus, are responsible for abandoning Moses and the law (v. 39; cf. v. 53). From Stephen's (i.e., Luke's) perspective, the Christian community is the "true Israel," i.e., the group within Judaism that is authentically preserving the customs of Moses as they reflect the purpose and destiny of what it means to be the people of God.

The second charge against Stephen, that he claimed that Jesus would destroy *this place* (6:14, i.e., the Temple), is addressed in the next unit (vv. 44-50). Here Stephen's complaint is not against the existence of the Temple per se, but rather against the view that God's presence is limited to a particular place. To worship God in "this place" was not to be understood as limiting God's self-disclosure to the Temple. Although Stephen does not make explicit the conse quences for violating the purposes of the Temple as he did the claim that God would judge the people's misunderstanding of Moses and his *customs* (6:14; cf. vv. 42-43), Luke's readers no doubt understood this invective against the background of the destruction of the Temple. Luke, then, in Stephen's speech, is not only drawing on the content of OT history, he is employing the familiar pattern of the Deuteronomistic history of disobedience, punishment, call to repentance, and restoration to make sense of the Temple's destruction. The people had defied the purpose of Temple worship and suffered then the destruction of that institution.

The climax of the speech, as we noted above, occurs here at the end. Both ancestors and contemporaries were guilty of *forever opposing the Holy Spirit* (v. 51). They had rejected the prophets from Moses to Jesus, they had an inadequate understanding of where and how they were to worship, and they had rejected the laws and customs of Moses. They had not kept the things that had been *ordained by angels* (v. 53), and now they were about to reject the one whose *face was like the face of an angel* (6:15).

7:54–8:3. The martyrdom. The speech results in the stoning of Stephen (reminiscent of the stoning of NABOTH in 1 Kgs 21:8-13). Earlier in the Pentecost sermon, Peter had leveled similar accusations against his listeners that *cut to the heart* (2:37) and led to their repentance. Here those whose hearts and ears are *uncircumcised* (7:51) harden their hearts and cover *their ears* (v. 57) and drag Stephen out of the city to stone him, with one Saul aiding and abetting them.

Actually this violent action only occurs after Stephen has recounted his vision of *the Son of Man standing at the right hand of God!* (v. 56). The term SON OF MAN, occurs only here outside the Gospels, and the curious detail that the Son of Man is standing rather than sitting (see Luke 22:69) may be taken in a juridical sense where Jesus stands as in advocacy for Stephen before God.

The last words of Stephen continue the parallels with Jesus begun in 6:8-15: *Lord Jesus, receive my spirit*, spoken by Stephen in 7:59 is reminiscent of Jesus' word from the cross: "Father, into your hands I commend my spirit" (Luke 23:46); and Stephen's final words, *Lord, do not hold this sin against them* (v. 60), echo Jesus' prayer: "Father, forgive them, for they do not know what they are doing"

(Luke 23:43). Stephen, like Jesus in the third Gospel, dies the death of an innocent martyr and thus takes his place as yet another example of a prophet who, because he spoke of *the coming of the Righteous One* (7:52), is the victim of *stiff-necked people* who continue to persecute the representatives of God (7:51).

Luke concludes this section (8:1-3) with the notice that this persecution was not limited to Stephen, but was against the whole Jerusalem church (v. 1). Chief among those persecuting the church is one Saul who by dragging the believers to prison (v. 3; cf. Luke 21:12) is inadvertently contributing to the growth of the Word, as the next unit indicates.

Philip: A Man on Mission, 8:4-40

Philip is the other member of the Seven who, with Stephen, plays a major role in the story. With Philip's ministry, the gospel enters the area of the Samaritans. In chap. 8, he is the focus of two very important episodes and is in dialogue with two of the most interesting characters in Acts: SIMON MAGUS and the ETHIOPIAN EUNUCH.

8:4-25. Philip and Simon: miracles vs. magic. From the second century, Simon has been characterized as the first Gnostic and archrival to Christianity (Justin, *Apol* 1.26.1-3; 1.56.2; *Trypho* 120; Irenaeus, *AdvHaer*, 1.23). The text of Acts, however, is silent on the final destiny of Simon, and unfortunately these later reflections have preoccupied most interpreters of Acts 8. Comments here will be limited to what can be gleaned from the narrative of Acts itself (see Garrett 1989, 61–78, for a detailed exposition).

One of Luke's purposes in recording Philip's encounter with Simon was to respond to charges that the signs and wonders performed by early Christian missionaries were indistinguishable from the magical practices of antiquity. Luke concedes (contra later apologists) that outwardly there are similarities between Christian miracle workers and magicians, but then argues that the similarities are only superficial: at a deeper level there are profound differences between "Christian miracles" and "pagan magic." Luke makes this point forcefully in the Simon Magus episode.

On first reading there are striking parallels between the acts of Philip and Simon. Only closer reading of the text demonstrates the fundamental difference between the two: Simon's deeds point to himself in an act of self-aggrandizement; Philip's signs point to the kingdom of God and corroborate his proclamation of the Christian gospel. In fact, the opening passage about Philip ties his words and deeds very closely together: *The crowds with one accord listened eagerly to what was said by Philip, hearing and seeing the signs that he did* (v. 6). What was the content of this message? Luke fills it out later in the narrative claiming that Philip *was proclaiming the good news about the kingdom of God and the name of Jesus Christ* (v. 12).

So to preach the gospel for Philip was to proclaim (1) that Jesus was the "Christ," the one God had anointed for *doing good and healing all who were oppressed by the devil* (as Peter would put it in 10:38); (2) that the KINGDOM OF

GOD, inaugurated in the ministry of Jesus, would be completed when all of Christ's enemies—surely including Satan himself—had been brought into submission at Christ's feet (cf. 2:34); and (3) that this proclamation "in the name of Jesus" would issue forth in the forgiveness or liberation from sin and Satan's authority to the power of God. In other words, "Philip's message about the Christ, the Kingdom of God, and the name of Jesus was implied also to be a message about release from Satan's authority" (Garrett 1989, 65). Hence, Philip's signs and wonders—the healings and exorcisms—were outward signs reinforcing his message: Satan is being overcome, and the kingdom of God is being established.

In contrast to Philip, the deeds of Simon Magus were performed only to bring glory to himself. In a flashback (v. 9), the readers learn that Simon had been amazing the Samaritans with his magic and that they have designated him as the *power of God* (vv. 9-11). This claim stands in direct contrast to Luke's depiction of Jesus. From Luke's perspective, *the power of God* (v. 10) was in Jesus, or upon Jesus, or with Jesus, but the power of God was always distinct *from* Jesus. That Simon does not reject this title (as Paul and Barnabas do in Acts 14:11-15) but rather encourages it through his magic, places him in the tradition of the "false prophets" who throughout Jewish history, and now in Christian history, reject the way of God (now most clearly revealed in the ministry of Jesus and his followers) in favor of idolatry (cf. Luke 6:22-23; Acts 7:51-52). As such, Simon is depicted as an agent of Satan who is an opponent to God and the "true prophets" of Christianity. Nonetheless, this section ends with Simon believing, being baptized, and being constantly amazed (cf. v. 11) at *the signs and great miracles* of Philip (v. 13).

The sincerity of Simon's conversion has long been questioned because of this closing climactic scene. The opening notice (vv. 14-17) that the Jerusalem apostles prayed for the new believers and that they received the HOLY SPIRIT *after* their BAPTISM stands in contrast with the sequence in Acts 2:38 and argues against basing any *rigid* doctrine of the relationship between baptism and the gift of the Spirit on Acts.

More important, however, is Luke's report that Simon tried to buy the Holy Spirit from the apostles (v. 18). This detail confirms the earlier impression that Simon is portrayed as a false prophet, an agent of Satan. Magicians practiced their art for money, and as Hermas noted, the false prophet "accepts rewards for his prophecy, and if he does not receive them he does not prophesy" (*Man* 11:12). Although it is true that here Simon is offering money and not receiving it, clearly if he is willing to pay money for the use of the Spirit, he will later accept payment when he employs its power. In contrast, Peter makes it clear that the apostles would never take money for what they do (see 3:6). "Thereby Luke demonstrates that the Christians do not share one of the most widely recognized traits of practitioners of magic" (Garrett 1989, 70).

The fate of Simon is ambiguous. The language of Peter's curse is reminiscent of OT curses of idolatry (see esp. Deut 29:17-19). Either Simon is to repent of his wickedness, i.e., his idolatry, or he (and his money!) is to be condemned to eternal destruction at the judgment (vv. 20-22). Although he has supposedly entered the Christian community, Simon is still in *the chains of wickedness* (v. 23), i.e., still under the authority of Satan, and has not fully experienced Philip's message of liberation from sin. Simon beseeches Peter and John to pray for him that he might be spared this judgment. Luke perhaps does not know the fate of Simon and thus leaves the conclusion uncertain. More important to Luke is the fact that in this encounter Satan and his agent have been overcome, and the path is cleared for the preaching of the gospel in Samaria. So Peter and John (one of the two who had earlier offered to call fire down to consume the Samaritans! Luke 9:54) do indeed proclaim *the good news to many villages of the Samaritans* (v. 25).

8:26-40. Philip and the Ethiopian eunuch: What hinders me? The next pericope involving Philip is foundational to Luke's theology and certainly is the most exotic in its details. Philip is characterized as a prophet and preacher, and his entrance and exit in the story is reminiscent of ELIJAH and EZEKIEL (1 Kgs 18:12; 2 Kgs 2:16; Ezek 11:24). The story also echoes another foundational story in Luke and Acts: the two on the road to EMMAUS (see also the parallels with Luke 4:16-30 and Acts 13:13-43). Just as Jesus opens the scriptures to CLEOPAS and his companion, so Philip explains Isa 53:7-8 to the eunuch. Both Jesus and Philip make quick exits from the story (Luke 24:31; Acts 8:39). Finally the two stories relate to the two or-dinances of the church—the Emmaus story to the LORD'S SUPPER and the Ethiopian eunuch episode to Baptism. Also noteworthy are the parallels between this episode and the other three conversion stories recorded in this immediate context: the conversion of the Samaritans (8:4-13), the conversion of Paul (9:1-31), and the conversion of CORNELIUS (Acts 10:1–11:18). Most striking is the way Luke intensifies the element of divine intervention and providence in the last three epi-sodes as the Spirit directs Philip, Paul (and Ananias), and Peter (and Cornelius; for other parallels with the Cornelius episode, see Tannehill 1990, 110–11).

Another way of understanding the meaning of the passage is by probing its form. Most scholars agree that a chiastic structure shapes the unit, although they dis-agree about its details. At the heart of any structure, however, lies the citation from the OT and the eu nuch's questions. The quotation of Isa 53:7-8 is the only time in Luke or Acts when the narrator quotes the OT directly, apart from the lips of an in-dividual character. Philip uses this OT text to tell *the good news about Jesus* (v. 35).

This kind of messianic exegesis was not as unusual as is sometimes thought. In first-century Judaism, interpreters were using a method of messianic exegesis to interpret the Hebrew scriptures, often providing messianic interpretations of scrip-tures that originally were not messianic prophecies. The messianic exegesis of Christians was not unique because they saw the Messiah foretold in the scriptures (their Jewish contemporaries saw that as well); the uniqueness lay in the fact that they believed this Messiah had already come in the person of Jesus Christ. Convinced of the truth of Philip's message, the eunuch lets forth with the refrain of an unhindered gospel that runs throughout Acts: *Look, here is water! What is to prevent me from being baptized?* (v. 36; cf. 10:47; 28:31). How is it, though, that the story of the Ethiopian eunuch bears witness to this "unhindered" gospel?

The answer may be found in the very description of this new convert: the Ethiopian eunuch. Implicit in each of those words are two very important characteristics. First, he is an Ethiopian, which informs the readers of the geographic and ethnographic significance of this conversion. Ethiopia was viewed by people of antiquity as lying at the southernmost end or limit of the earth (see e.g., Homer, *Iliad* 23.205–97; Herodotus, *Hist* 3.114–15; Strabo, *Geog* 1.2.27–28; 2.2.2). Thus the conversion of an Ethiopian represents "the symbolic (and partial) fulfillment of Acts 1:8c of mission to 'the end of the earth' " (Martin 1989, 120). Second, it is also well documented in ancient literature that skin color was an Ethiopian's most distinctive feature. Homer (*Odyssey* 19.244–48), Herodotus (*Hist* 2.29–32; 3.17–24; 4.183, 197), and Seneca (*Naturales Questiones* IV A. 218), among others, all refer to the dark skin of the Ethiopians. What is the ethnographic significance of the Ethiopian's conversion? Clarice Martin (1989, 114) argues that "the story of a black African . . . from what would be perceived as a distant nation to the south of the empire is consistent with the Lukan emphasis on 'universalism,' a recurrent motif in both Luke and Acts, and one that is well known."

The Ethiopian is also a eunuch, from which the readers infer two additional items. He is, first of all, an outsider, since Deut 23:2 forbids a castrated person from entrance into the assembly of the Lord and probably precluded even proselyte status. In the Acts passage, he has just returned from Jerusalem where he had gone to worship and was, no doubt, relegated to the outermost chambers of the Temple. For Luke, then, the Ethiopian eunuch is a God-fearing gentile and, as such, is the first gentile convert to Christianity. Commentators who resist this conclusion normally do so to preserve Cornelius as the first gentile convert and Peter as the founder of the gentile mission. The significance of Cornelius notwithstanding, the conversion of the Ethiopian eunuch is Luke's report of how, through Philip, the gospel reached the "end of the earth" and the gentile mission was initiated. Again, the reader is put in the superior position of knowing more about the story of the early church's progress than any of its characters.

Philip in these two stories is depicted as a man on mission. He is pressing the boundaries, with the apostles scrambling to keep up. He preaches the gospel, and Samaritans and a representative from the "ends of the earth" are converted. Evidently, it will take the Jerusalem church some time before it comes to the same position and then only through the insistence of the apostle to the gentiles, Paul. Later, Paul finds Philip in Caesarea (21:8) where the narrator left him. But now Philip is not alone; he has four unmarried daughters *who had the gift of prophecy* (21:9), and no doubt Philip's encouragement to exercise it. Not only is Philip's adventuresome spirit reaffirmed for the reader, but his openness to the fresh winds of God's Spirit has been passed on to another generation.

Paul: His Conversion and Call, 9:1-31

It would be difficult to overestimate the significance of the conversion of Paul for the narrative of Acts or, indeed, the course of early Christian history. Acts 9 is the first of three accounts in Acts of Paul's conversion (see chaps. 22 and 26). The accounts are slightly different in detail and tone (see the comments on chap. 22 for a discussion of the variations), but the repetition of the event indicates its importance for Luke. The passage in Acts 9 is not only about the conversion of Paul; it is also the narration of his call and commission to become the "apostle to the gentiles." As such, it shares similar formal features with other commissioning stories, both within Luke and Acts (e.g., Luke 1:5-25, 26-38; 2:8-20; 24:36-53; Acts 5:17-21; 10:1-8, 9-23; 16:9-10; 18:9-11; etc.) and throughout the biblical narratives (see e.g., Gen 17:1-4; Exod 3:1–4:16; Judg 6:11-24; 1 Kgs 19:1-19a; Matt 28:1-8; Mark 16:1-8; John 20:19-23; see Hubbard for other references and a list of the formal features associated with the commissioning story). Acts 9 then is about the conversion of Paul from a persecutor of Christ to one persecuted for Christ and Paul's call to be apostle to the gentiles.

9:1-25. Paul in Damascus. The unit is organized into two parts. The first part describes the events in and around DAMASCUS; the second details Paul's preaching ministry in JERUSALEM. The following chiastic arrangement for this first unit has been suggested (see Talbert 1984, 40):

A   Paul plots against the Christians in Damascus, 1-2
    B   Paul sees the vision, is blinded, and fasts, 3-9
        C   Ananias sees a vision,
                is commissioned to go to Paul, 10-14
            D   Paul's mission is foretold by Christ, 15-16
        C'   Ananias goes to Paul, reports his vision, 17
    B'   Paul's sight is restored,
        he is baptized and eats, 18-19a
A'   Paul preaches Christ in Damascus,
    the Jews plot to kill him, 19b-25

Paul reappears in the opening verses of chap. 9. He was last mentioned in 8:3 where he was *ravaging the church*. Here in chap. 9 he is still *breathing threats and murder against the disciples of the Lord* (v. 1) and seeks permission to extend his persecution beyond Jerusalem to Damascus. The description of Paul here recalls Stephen's invective against those who *are forever opposing the Holy Spirit* (7:51-52).

Paul is not the only character to receive a vision in this episode; the Lord also visits Ananias, a disciple in Damascus (vv. 10-14). This "double vision" provides for Paul a (reluctant) deliverer from his blindness. Ananias's vision also supplies the content of Paul's call (vv. 15-16). In the CHIASM above, these verses lie at the heart of the passage and should be taken as its primary focus. Two points are made: (1) Paul is to be an *instrument whom I* [Christ] *have chosen to bring my name before*

Gentiles and kings and before the people of Israel (v. 15) and (2) that Paul *must suffer for the sake of my name* (v. 16). Paul's call to the gentile mission cannot be separated from his call to suffer. His entire ministry throughout Acts is characterized by a mission in which he experiences rejection and persecution (cf. 13:46-47; 20:19-21; 22:15-18). As such, he stands in the long line of persecuted prophets that extend from Moses to Jesus and more recently to Stephen. But Paul does not have to wait until his "first" missionary journey to experience this suffering. His first preaching tour in Damascus ends with a narrow escape from his persecutors in a basket.

9:26-31. Paul in Jerusalem. This emphasis on the suffering character of Paul's ministry continues in this next episode of Paul in Jerusalem. The events in Damascus and Jerusalem are almost exact parallels (Gill 1974, 547–48).

Damascus	Jerusalem
Ananias hesitates to believe that Paul has been converted, 13-14.	The disciples fear Paul, "not believing that he is a disciple," 26.
The Lord reassures him, 15-16.	Barnabas reassures them, 27.
Ananias goes to Paul, cures, and baptizes him, 17-192.	
Paul is *with* the disciples in Damascus, 19b.	"Paul was *with* them going in and out at Jerusalem," 28a.
Paul preaches immediately in the synagogues, 20-22.	Paul speaks freely in the name of the Lord, 28b-29a.
The Jews plot to kill Paul, 23-24.	The Hellenists try to kill him, 29b.
Paul escapes, 25.	Paul escapes, 30.

Gill has commented on the significance of this parallelism: "The Jerusalem episode acts out for a second time the theme of preaching and persecution which Luke has placed as a heading over the whole chapter" (Gill 1974, 548). The zealous persecutor of Christ and his church has become the zealous missionary persecuted in Christ's name and for his church.

Peter: His Words and Deeds, 9:32–11:18

The next three scenes, the healing of AENEAS, the raising of Tabitha, and the conversion of Cornelius, may all be grouped under the larger heading "the acts of Peter." Theologically, all three stories serve to underscore the inclusive nature of the gospel, as well as to reveal further the complex character of PETER. Pairing stories of men and women is typical of Luke. Further, to join two shorter stories with a longer third one to make basically the same point is not uncommon to Luke. In fact, these stories are similar to Luke 15 where we have the two briefer stories of the lost sheep and the lost coin standing alongside the much longer story of the lost sons—with all three describing the joy in the kingdom when that which was lost is found. As with these three parables, readers can also detect the movement in these three stories in Acts to open the gospel to all persons.

9:32-43. Peter's raising of Aeneas and Tabitha. While evidently on a preaching tour, Peter encounters a paralyzed *saint* in Lydda who had been bedridden. Now for the second time (see Acts 3:1-10), Peter heals a lame man. The story is bare and unadorned with details; the narrator gets right to the point. Peter informs Aeneas that "Jesus Christ heals you; get up and make your bed!"

The reader is led to empathize more deeply with Tabitha and her mourners in the next scene. Tabitha (which the narrator tells us means DORCAS or "Ga zelle") is described as one who is *devoted to good works and acts of charity* (v. 36—cf. the description later of Cornelius in 10:1 of the next episode). The products of her benevolence are made explicit when the widows who are mourning her death show to Peter *the tunics and other clothing Dorcas had made while she was with them* (v. 39). Quite possibly, they are wearing the garments (the verb is in the middle voice); for the widows to lose Dorcas was to lose their benefactor.

Once again, the problem of helpless Greek-speaking Jewish-Christian widows resurfaces in the narrative (cf. 6:1). Peter orders everyone outside (like Jesus, see Luke 8:51) and commands, *Tabitha, get up* (again reminiscent of Jesus' words in Mark 5:41). She, too, is raised, and he presents her alive to the saints and widows (v. 41).

These two stories share much in common: they echo the ELIJAH-ELISHA cycles of 1–2 Kings, as well as events in the career of Jesus (Acts 9:32-35 = Luke 5:18-26; Acts 9:36-43 = Luke 8:40-56). Further, unlike most healing stories in Luke and Acts, the healed persons here are named (contra Luke 5:17-26; 11:14-23; 18:35-43; Acts 3:1-10; 14:8-18). Both Aeneas and Tabitha are healed through divine power (vv. 34, 40). In their respective locales, both healings result in many conversions to the faith (vv. 35 and 42).

Finally, the raising of a lame man and the resuscitation of a dead woman are more similar than might appear at first glance. In the ancient Mediterranean world, the body was divided into three symbolic zones: (1) the heart-eyes, which is the zone of emotions and thoughts; (2) the mouth-ears, which is the zone of self-expressive speech; and (3) the hands-feet, which is the zone of purposeful action (Pilch 1991, 204). Aeneas's healing obviously falls into the zone of purposeful action. But resuscitations are also related to this zone; the dead can perform no purposeful act (Pilch 1991, 205). Thus, both healings share in the same symbolic zone; Aeneas and Tabitha are healed so they can resume their places as contributing members of the Christian community and walk in *the Way* (9:2).

10:1–11:18. The conversion of Cornelius and Peter. Many scholars focus in this story on the significance of the conversion of CORNELIUS and his household for the spread of the gospel to the gentiles in Acts. This episode does represent a critical turning point in the narrative of Acts. Equally as important, though, is the conversion of Peter to a new point of view, namely, that salvation knows no human boundaries and that *God shows no partiality* (v. 34). The chapter divisions here (as in many other places in scripture) are misleading. The episode actually divides into seven scenes (see Haenchen 1971, 357–59), interrelated by much repetition (the vision of Cornelius is reported four times; Peter's vision is twice related; and all of chap. 11 is basically a summary of chap. 10).

Scene 1. 10:1-8. Cornelius's vision in Caesarea. Cornelius, a centurion (see Luke 7:1-10), is favorably described by Luke as a *devout* man who practiced traditional Jewish piety in almsgiving and prayer, although he was himself a gentile "God-fearer." In this opening scene, Cornelius has a vision in which he is told his prayers and alms have been heard and accepted (v. 4) and that he should send to Joppa for a certain Simon Peter. Without further question, Cornelius complies by dispatching two personal servants and a soldier to fetch Peter. Throughout the narrative the activities are directed from above (cf. chap. 9), but that does not mean there is no human response to this divine activity. Rather, the pattern here is that the divine revelations or epiphanies of both Cornelius and Peter are incomplete (Tannehill 1990, 129) and are only understood after further reflection and interaction with other human characters. Revelation here is depicted in contextual and interrelational terms, which means that both Cornelius and Peter have to move with the light they have before they can receive further illumination.

Scene 2. 10:9-16. Peter's vision in Joppa. Peter, like Cornelius, experiences a vision while at prayer (v. 10). This vision, too, is incomplete. Three times Peter is shown a sheet with all kinds of animals on it and is commanded to eat. Three times he refuses, claiming, *By no means, Lord, for I have never eaten anything that is profane or unclean* (v. 14). Is he thrice resisting temptation (cf. Luke 3) or thrice denying his Lord (cf. Luke 23)? The final response of the heavenly voice makes Peter's resistance clear: *What God has made clean, you must not call profane* (v. 15). What remains unclear is the subject of this vision. Is Peter to disregard Jewish dietary laws or is something else at stake?

Scene 3. 10:17-23a. Cornelius's men in Joppa. While Peter is wondering about the vision, Cornelius's emissaries arrive in JOPPA. The puzzled Peter is still obedient enough to respond to the Spirit's call to go with these men *without hesitation* (v. 20) or "without discrimination" (author trans.). Peter takes the first step in understanding his vision by extending hospitality to these gentile visitors and giving them a night's lodging.

Scene 4. 10:23b-33. Peter in Caesarea. The vision comes more into focus with Peter's visit to CAESAREA. After correcting Cornelius's mistaken assumption that Peter is a god (vv. 25-26), Peter takes the next step in correctly interpreting his vision when he sees the crowd of gentiles gathered in Cornelius's house and says, *You yourselves know that it is unlawful for a Jew to associate with or to visit a gentile* [Peter now has done both], *but God has shown me that I should not call anyone profane or unclean* (v. 28; cf. the restrictions of *Jub* 22:16; *JosAsen* 7:1).

Sociologists use the term "map" to designate "the concrete and systematic patterns of organizing, locating, and classifying persons, places, times, actions, etc. according to some abstract notion of 'purity' or order" (Neyrey 1991, 278). Peter understands that the vision of the sheet is not just about what can or cannot be eaten, that is, a cultural "map of the body"; but more importantly it addresses the question of who is and is not clean, i.e., the question of a radically new cultural "map of persons." Just as Stephen proposed a new map of holy places (which did not limit "holy space" to the Temple), so Peter is being directed to draw a new cultural map of people which was radically inclusive and gave gentiles a place on the map. The issue of the vision is not whether gentiles can be included in salvation: Peter has heard Jesus say as much (Luke 24:47) and has himself preached it (Acts 2:39; 3:25-26). The obstacle for the Jewish Christian to launch the gentile mission is gentile uncleanness that obstructs Jewish-gentile social relationships. The vision of the sheet now removes that obstacle.

Scene 5. 10:34-43. Peter's speech. After Cornelius recounts his vision (vv. 30-33, now for the third time), Peter responds to Cornelius's invitation to address the assembly. His speech falls into three parts: the introduction (vv. 34-36), the kerygma (vv. 37-41), and the conclusion (vv. 42-43). Peter's conversion to this new perspective of gentile cleanness is completed in the opening line of this speech: *I truly understand that God shows no partiality* (v. 34).

The next two verses are grammatically troublesome, and their meaning is obscured by both RSV and NRSV. Perhaps the best way to understand these verses is reflected in the following translation:

> Truly I perceive that God shows no partiality, but in every nation anyone who fears him and practices righteousness is acceptable to him. This [namely, the statement just made] is the word which he sent to the children of Israel, preaching good news of peace through Jesus Christ—He is Lord of all (vv. 34b-36, cited by Krodel 1986, 196).

This translation makes "He is Lord of all" the centerpiece of the thought unit rather than a disruptive or intrusive phrase (in parentheses in RSV). Both God (who "shows no partiality") and Jesus (who is "Lord of all") support Peter's perspective on the radically inclusive nature of the Gospel. The kerygma that follows (vv. 37-41) characterizes Jesus' ministry as one of benefaction, a particularly appropriate image for a gentile audience familiar with patronage and especially the audience in Cornelius's house who no doubt had personally enjoyed the benefits of Cornelius's benefaction.

Peter ends his speech (vv. 43-44) by returning to the theme of universality: *everyone who believes in him receives forgiveness of sins through his name.*

Scene 6. 10:44-48. The gentile Pentecost. Before Peter could finish speaking (v. 44), a second Pentecost occurs: the Holy Spirit falls on these gentiles. As in the first Pentecost, the gift of the Spirit is con firmed for the "circumcised believers" when *they heard them* [the gentiles] *speaking in tongues and extolling God* (v. 46). Peter strikes a major theme of Acts again when he asks, "Is anyone able to hinder the water for baptizing these who have received the Holy Spirit just like us?" (author trans.). The answer for Luke is, of course not. Just as earlier nothing could hinder the Ethiopian eunuch from being baptized (8:36) and later not even prison could hinder Paul from preaching the gospel (28:31), so now the barrier of gentile uncleanness could no longer hinder the inclusion of gentiles into the kingdom although it would indeed be the subject of one more debate (see chap. 15).

Scene 7. 11:1-18. Reporting to the Jerusalem church. The conversion of Cornelius and his household, as noted earlier, is important not because Cornelius is the first gentile converted in Acts (that honor belongs to the Ethiopian eunuch), but because his is the first gentile conversion publicly acknowledged by the Jerusalem church. Most of chap. 11 is a recapitulation (with some interesting variations) of the events reported in chap. 10. Most important are the opening verses that set the context: Peter is asked to defend his actions, not of ordering these gentiles to be baptized, but of eating with the "uncircumcised," i.e., of rewriting the "cultural map" of persons (see above). After recounting the incident (again the repetition points out the significance of this event for Luke), Peter asks, *Who was I that I could hinder God?* (v. 17; on "hinder" see the comments on scene 6 above). The question is not intended to be rhetorical, and the silence is finally broken when these Jewish Christians from Jerusalem praise God saying, *Then God has given even to the Gentiles the repentance that leads to life* (v. 18).

The issue of gentile inclusion in the church is by no means resolved, as Acts 15 demonstrates, but at least Peter's conversion is as complete as that of Cornelius and his household. For Peter, at least, as far as Jews and gentiles were concerned, God *has made no distinction between them and us* (15:9).

Barnabas, Peter, and Herod: Contrasting Examples, 11:19–12:25

In Luke's version of the last supper, a dispute arose among the disciples as to who was to be regarded as the greatest. In Luke 22:25-26, Jesus says, "The kings of the Gentiles lord it over them; and those in authority over them are called benefactors. But not so with you; rather the greatest among you must become like the youngest, and the leader like one who serves." In a sense, this episode (Acts 11:19–12:25) provides an exegesis by example of the saying in Luke 22. The contrasts between displays of divine and earthly power are striking.

11:19-30; 12:25. Barnabas and the church at Antioch. Luke presents the fledgling church at ANTIOCH as a case study of the mission of the early church. The church at Antioch receives considerable attention from Luke. It is established just after the conversion of Cornelius. Antioch was primarily a "Hellenistic city" (although there was a significant Jewish population of between 25,000 and 50,000). Antioch's population of 500,000 to 800,000 ranked it third largest in the Roman Empire (Polhill 1992, 268–69). The church was founded by Hellenists who *were scattered because of the persecution that took place over Stephen* (v. 19). Although some Hellenists spoke only to Jews, Christians from Cyprus and Cyrene evangelized the gentiles in Antioch. These Hellenistic Jewish-Christians who themselves had grown up in the gentile environment of the dispersion were sensitive to the cultural back ground of the Antiochenes and spoke not of Jesus as the Jewish Messiah, but rather proclaimed *the Lord Jesus* (v. 20), a title more familiar to those gentiles.

After the church was established and then encouraged and confirmed by BARNABAS and PAUL (vv. 22-26), the church at Antioch had the opportunity to minister to the believers in the church at Jerusalem, a clear sign that those first missionaries encouraged mission not only *to* but *with* the Antiochenes.

The Antiochenes' sensitivity to the plight of Judea is remarkable for several reasons. First, the famine was not confined to Judea, but rather evidently Antioch itself was gripped by famine during this time (ca. 46–47 C.E.). Second, the city of Antioch had experienced numerous disasters itself over the past one hundred years that must have left their mark on the collective memory of the inhabitants. In the midst of their own suffering, the Antiochene Christians reached out to those in need, not out of plenty but out of want.

Barnabas embodies this spirit of generosity so characteristic of the Antiochene Christians. When the disciples decide to send relief *to the believers living in Judea,* they send it by the hands of Barnabas and Saul (vv. 29-30). Like Saul (Acts 7:58), Barnabas makes a cameo appearance before assuming the center stage of the gentile mission (4:36-37; see Acts 11, 15). He provides a concrete example of those believers who demonstrated their commitment to the apostles' authority by laying the proceeds from the sale of his property at the apostles' feet (4:35).

The narrator supplies several interesting details about Barnabas; he is a LEVITE (who in the OT had no portion in the land!—see Deut 12:12; 14:29) and a native of Cyprus. But the most important detail is that the apostles have given him a surname, Barnabas. That the apostles have given this name is another indication that Barnabas has submitted himself to the authority of the apostles.

> By having one of the two great leaders of the gentile mission express submission to the Twelve by receiving from them a new name and laying his goods at their feet, Luke is subtly but effectively creating an image in the reader's mind: the image of the Gentile mission under the authority of the Twelve (Johnson 1977, 202).

Also noteworthy is the translation the narrator provides for Barnabas's name, *Son of encouragement* (4:36). The significance lies less in the etymology of the Aramaic than it does in the role Barnabas will play later in this story. Barnabas is a sign both of submission to the apostles and of encouragement to fellow believers. While the Jews plot to kill Saul and the believers are afraid of him and doubt that he is a disciple (9:23-27), Barnabas takes the risk of befriending Saul, bringing him before the apostles, and confirming Saul's Damascus-road experience before them (9:27). When the church in Jerusalem hears about Greeks who had *turned to the Lord* in Antioch (vv. 19-21), they send Barnabas to Antioch, and he "encouraged [see 4:36] them all to remain faithful to the Lord with steadfast purpose" (v. 23, author trans.).

But Barnabas's submission to apostolic authority is not blind loyalty. When he turns his attention to the gentile mission, he is sent out, not by the apostles, but by the Holy Spirit (13:4; see also 13:43, 46, 50). The active role of Barnabas in the

Apostolic Conference (chap. 15) is direct testimony to the way in which he (and Paul) held respect for the apostles' authority in tension with submission to the guidance of the Holy Spirit. This Barnabas who is (not blindly) loyal to the apostles and a continuing source of encouragement to the community (see also 15:36-40) stands in sharp contrast not only to the story of Ananias and Sapphira, but to the following story about Herod.

12:1-24. Herod: unmasking the powers. With the note of true Christian benefaction ringing in their ears, the readers are introduced to the manufactured benefaction of a tyrant, HEROD. In between is sandwiched the story of Peter's deliverance from prison. This chapter is one of the most delightful in Acts, but it is not only entertaining; it is also profitable, for it demonstrates Luke's understanding of the nature and locale of true power.

In the opening scene (vv. 1-5), Herod (whom the first- and twentieth-century reader might mistakenly identify as the wicked king of the Gospels) had JAMES, John's brother, *killed with the sword* (v. 2). Seeing this curried the favor of the Jews, Herod determines to serve them Peter as well. Perhaps aware of Peter's reputation as an escape artist (see 5:19-26), he places Peter under close watch around the clock (v. 4).

In an aside, the narrator notes that the arrest of Peter occurred during the PASSOVER (v. 3). This detail is important for several reasons. First, it accounts for the reason Peter did not immediately suffer the same fate as John; Herod wished to avoid a tumult of the people (see v. 4). This setting also parallels this deliverance scene with the passion of Jesus, which also occurred during the festival of Unleavened Bread (Luke 22:1, 7). (By now, the reader has noted the frequency with which the experience of the church parallels the experiences of Jesus.) Finally, the setting creates the biting irony of Peter in chains during the very festival that celebrated the deliverance of Israel from bondage in Egypt (see Pervo 1990, 41). This should not be surprising to the readers since Luke in his first volume had already described the passion of Jesus as an "exodus" (Luke 9:31).

The Passover setting, then, is very important in understanding the next scene, the deliverance of Peter from prison (vv. 6-11). The Exodus imagery continues, particularly in Luke's choice of language: *the night before* (v. 6; Exod 12:12); *Get up quickly* (v. 7; Exod 12:11); *put on your . . . sandals* (v. 8, Exod 12:11); *the Lord has rescued* (v. 11; Exod 18:4, 8-10). As in the Cornelius episode, everything is directed "from above" by an angel of the Lord who gives specific instructions to Peter even on how to dress himself. Peter's passivity is emphasized by the fact that he thought what was happening was another vision (cf. chap. 10), not realizing the reality of the situation. He does at least respond again to the call, *Follow me* (v. 8). Clearly, this is the story of Peter's divine deliverance from bondage (like the Israelites), not his escape.

Realizing finally the reality of his deliverance, Peter goes to the house of Mary, mother of John Mark, where the believers have gathered to pray (v. 12). This scene is filled with drama, punctuated with irony and comic relief. Peter encounters a second gate, only this time it does not open miraculously (cf. v. 10). Vulnerable to anyone who might see him, Peter knocks and a maidservant named *Rhoda* or "Rose" comes to answer. In Luke and Acts, this is Peter's second encounter with a maidservant (cf. Luke 22:56-57), neither of which is very successful. Rhoda is so overjoyed at recognizing Peter's voice that she runs inside to tell the others, leaving Peter standing at the gate (v. 14). The believers who presumably had gathered to pray for Peter (see vv. 5, 12) refuse to believe that their prayers have been answered. Rather, they inform Rhoda that she is out of her mind and suggest that what she has seen is not Peter but his ghost. This is evidently another sign that they did not trust that God would deliver Peter since, in popular Jewish tradition, it was believed that a person's "guardian angel" often appeared immediately following the person's death. As Polhill remarked, "They found it easier to believe that Peter had died and gone to heaven than that their prayers had been answered" (1992, 282). Like the two on the road to Emmaus, these believers refused to believe female testimony (cf. Luke 24:22-23).

But Peter continues to knock, and finally they open the gate and find him there, much to their amazement (v. 16). After recounting his rescue, Peter asks them to tell these things to James (presumably the brother of Jesus) and the believers. This is the key verse in this scene since it marks the beginning of the changing of the guard in the Jerusalem church from Peter to James, a transition that will be completed in chap. 15. Peter then departs, and Herod's frustrated search for Peter ends in the death of the guards from whom he escaped (vv. 18-19). With this note, attention turns again to Herod.

Already Herod has killed the other James, imprisoned Peter with the intentions of putting him to death, and executed the four squads of guards (a total of sixteen men) who had watched over him. Now he cuts off food supplies from the people of Tyre and Sidon (in Phoenicia) because he is angry with them for some unspecified reason (v. 20). After negotiations between the king and the Phoenician citizens brokered by the king's personal servant Blastus result in reconciliation, a celebration is held for the king to receive the people's praise for his benefaction (which, of course, is only necessary because of Herod's own vindictiveness). His speech garners the people's favor, and he is hailed as a god (v. 22). When Herod accepts this praise without protest and without giving "glory to God," he receives his own tap from an angel (v. 23; see v. 7) and meets the fate he intended for Peter. Like other tyrants (according to Josephus, *Ant* 19.343-52), Herod dies a grisly, worm-infested death.

The story of Peter is the second of three rescues from prison, and the demise of Herod is the third punitive miracle where the opponent of God is struck down (see JUDAS and ANANIAS and SAPPHIRA). These stories "unfold in inverse symmetry" (Pervo 1990, 43). The result is that the earthly powers, here represented by Herod, are unmasked for the impostors they are, and the power of God is demonstrated through the Antioch church, Barnabas, and Peter. Like the seed sown on good earth (see Luke 8:4-15), the *word of God* (meant here by Luke as figurative language to refer to the church) *grew* in the face of opposition and continued to produce a remarkable yield, just as it did at the beginning of this section (v. 24; see 6:7).

Paul's Mission to the Gentile World, 13:1–19:41

This next major division of Acts narrows its vision from the activities of the Twelve and the Seven to focus on the gentile mission of PAUL and his apostolic company. To speak of these chapters as Paul's "three missionary journeys" is inaccurate since Luke himself never refers to Paul's campaigns in such fashion. In fact, only Paul's first "foray" into the gentile world (13:1–14:28) has the character of an intentional journey, in this case a round trip beginning in and returning to Antioch. The second section revolves around the controversy surrounding Paul's missionary efforts and its resolution (15:1-35). The next three sections focus on Paul in MACEDONIA (15:36–17:15), the Achaian cities of ATHENS and CORINTH (17:16–18:17), and EPHESUS (18:18–19:41). The shift then is from persons (chaps. 5–12) to places (chaps. 13–19), but the spread of the gospel remains the central theme.

Paul's Initial Missionary Campaign, 13:1–14:28

13:1-12. Commissioned and tested. This scene begins with the commissioning of Paul and Barnabas by the church at Syrian Antioch (vv. 1-3). Two things are noteworthy about this opening. First is the diversity of the Antiochene church evidenced by this short list: SIMEON or Niger, a black person, perhaps from North Africa; Lucius, who is originally from CYRENE and perhaps among those broad-minded enough to evangelize among the gentiles (see 11:20); and Manaen, who is of aristocratic Jewish stock, having been brought up in the court of Herod Antipas (see Luke 3:1; Acts 4:27). Barnabas and Saul are also counted as prophets in this list. The second important feature is the role of Holy Spirit in the commissioning. Luke wants it clear that just as the Holy Spirit was involved in the beginning of Jesus' public ministry, the Antiochene church sets Saul and Barnabas apart only under the direction of the Holy Spirit (v. 3).

The parallel between Paul and Jesus continues in the next scene (vv. 4-12). Saul and Barnabas are sent out by the Holy Spirit (v. 4) after their commissioning, as was Jesus (see Luke 4:1). For the second time in Acts, a Christian missionary confronts a magician (see Acts 8). Here the opponent is Bar-Jesus, known also as ELY-MAS, a *Jewish false prophet* (v. 6). Elymas, who is in the service of a leading Roman official—Sergius Paulus—fears that Sergius might be persuaded to turn to the Christian faith by Paul and Barnabas so he opposes them (vv. 7-9). Elymas is closely related to Satan in Paul's curse where he is called *a son of the devil* and an *enemy of all righteousness*. He is also described as being *full of all deceit and villainy* (v. 10).

The confrontation here is between Paul, a true prophet full of the Holy Spirit, and Bar-Jesus, who seeks to make *crooked the straight paths of the Lord* (v. 10)—thus undoing the work of another true prophet, JOHN THE BAPTIST. It is nothing less than a confrontation between the Holy Spirit and the devil and echoes the conflict between Jesus and Satan at the beginning of Jesus' public ministry (Luke 4). Paul's curse of blindness on Elymas is especially fitting: as an idolater who serves as an agent of Satan, Elymas is cursed to the darkness from which he has come (see Deut 28:28-29; 1 QS 2:11-19).

Note also the irony here: Paul, who has himself just made the transition from darkness to light (see chap. 9), now pronounces a curse of "mist and darkness" that causes Elymas to search for *someone to lead him by the hand* (v. 11). The point of this scene for the ministry of Paul is crucial: Like Jesus, Paul has demonstrated his authority over the forces of Satan and thus has proven himself worthy of the mission set before him. The conversion and commission of Paul that began in chap. 9 is now complete, and perhaps this explains why from this point on, Saul is consistently referred to as Paul (see v. 9). With the fulfillment of his change in status from one who opposed God to one who now serves him comes a change in name (see Garrett 1989, 85). That the church also gains a prominent convert in Sergius Paulus is a nice by-product of this encounter, but by no means the central focus.

13:13-52. Paul's speech at Pisidian Antioch. This next scene has three parts: (1) the setting (vv. 13-16), (2) the speech (vv. 17-41), and (3) the aftermath (vv. 42-52). After a whistle stop in Perga, Paul and his company come to Antioch of Pisidia. As would prove to be his pattern in Acts, Paul enters the synagogue on the Sabbath (v. 14). After the reading of scripture (see Luke 4), Paul is given the opportunity to speak and delivers the first of the major addresses in Acts (cf. Acts 17:22-31; 20:18-35).

Paul's inaugural speech (vv. 17-41) is remarkably similar to Jesus' inaugural address in Luke 4 and Peter's first major speech recorded in Acts 2 (see Tannehill 1990, 160). All three speeches use scripture to interpret the mission (Luke 4:18-19; Acts 2:17-21; 13:47) and include gentiles in God's salvation (Luke 4:25-28; Acts 2:39; 13:45-48). The speech itself narrates God's promises to Israel (vv. 16b-25), the fulfillment of those promises in Christ (vv. 26-37), and an invitation and warning (vv. 38-41). Each of these units is introduced with a form of direct address (*You Israelites . . .* [v. 16b]; *my brothers . . .* [v. 26]; *my brothers* [v. 38]). These direct addresses make it clear that Paul is addressing Jews (*you Israelites*) and those who are deeply interested in Judaism (*others who fear God*).

The first part of the speech (vv. 16b-25) is similar to Stephen's speech in that it recounts Israel's history; its focus however differs by concentrating not on Israel's rebelliousness, but rather on God's faithfulness. After this brief summary of Israel's history from the ancestors to David, the central claim of the section is made in v. 23: *Of this man's* [David's] *posterity God has brought to Israel a Savior, Jesus, as he promised.* Paul then cites the words of John the Baptist as corroborating evidence to support his claim that God's faithfulness has climaxed in Jesus.

That Jesus is the fulfillment of God's promises to Israel is worked out in more detail in the second part of Paul's speech (vv. 26-37). Having appealed to the content of Jewish history (vv. 17-22) and the witness of John the Baptist, Paul now employs two favorite scriptures (Pss 2, 16) and the rules of Jewish messianic interpretation (see comments on Acts 8). But Christian messianic exegesis once again takes a startling turn (see 3:20); this Messiah, whom God promised and to whom the scriptures point, has already come in the person of Jesus (vv. 32-33).

The conclusion of the sermon is twofold. First, Paul extends an invitation for the hearers to receive the forgiveness of sins that can come only through Jesus, not through the Law of Moses (vv. 38-39). He also issues a prophetic warning (quoting Hab 1:5, cf. 1QpHab 2:1-10) that to reject Paul's message is to reject God's salvation and to be condemned to play the part of *scoffers* whose fate it is to *perish* (v. 41).

Immediately following the sermon, the people urge Paul and Barnabas to return the next Sabbath, and in the meantime the people follow these Christian missionaries who continue to exhort them (vv. 42-43). The rest of this unit falls into two parallel scenes (vv. 44-48; 49-52) summarizing Paul's ministry in Antioch (see Talbert 1984, 59; Krodel 1986, 246–47).

A   The gathering of the whole city
          to hear the word of the Lord, 44
     B   The rejection of unbelieving Jews, 45
          C   Response of Paul and Barnabas:
                    turning to the Gentiles, 46-47
               D   The Gentiles rejoice, 48
A'   The word of the Lord
          spread throughout the region, 49
     B'   Unbelieving Jews stir up persecution
               against Paul and Barnabas, 50
          C'   Response of Paul and Barnabas:
                    shaking off the dust from their feet, 51
               D'   The Disciples are filled with joy, 52

This pattern of (1) the proclamation of the gospel that leads to (2) division among those listening, (3) rejection by the unbelievers, (4) withdrawal by the Christian missionaries, and, finally, (5) Luke's report of the progress despite the opposition continues to the end of Acts. It will be repeated in the very next scene of Paul and Barnabas in Iconium.

14:1-28. Paul in Iconium, Lystra, and elsewhere. The description of the scene in ICONIUM (vv. 1-7) prevents the readers from reducing Paul's ministry to the simple formula of rejection by the Jews and success among the gentiles (Tannehill 1990, 176). Rather, Luke reports that a *great number of both Jews and Greeks became believers* (v. 1). Likewise, both Jews and gentiles persecute the apostles (v.

5) who withdraw to the surrounding country and continue to preach the good news
(vv. 6-7). Paul's words in 13:46-47 are not to be understood in any rigid sense; division is not always along ethnic lines, certainly not in Iconium. The division is not
between Jews and gentiles, but between those who hear the word and accept and
those who reject the message and persecute the messengers.

In LYSTRA, Paul heals a man lame from birth (vv. 8-10; cf. Acts 3:1-10). As a
result, the crowds cried out that *the gods have come down to us in human form* (v.
11), specifically Zeus (Barnabas) and Hermes (Paul). This story echoes an ancient
legend no doubt familiar to the ancient reader that Zeus and Hermes had once
visited the region of Phrygia and Lycaonia but had not been recognized nor warmly
received until they came upon an elderly couple Baucis and Philemon (see Ovid,
Metamorph. 8.626). Perhaps the hasty conclusion reached here by the Lycaonians
was an attempt to avoid making the same mistake twice.

In sharp contrast to Simon Magus (Acts 8) and Herod (Acts 12), Paul and
Barnabas are quick to deny their newly acquired divinity. In a quickly composed
speech that anticipates the AREOPAGUS address (Acts 17), Paul is still barely able
to restrain the people from honoring them with sacrifice. This turmoil gives way
quickly to more serious trouble when Jews from Antioch and Iconium who have
been pursuing Paul and Barnabas persuade this fickle crowd to join them in stoning
Paul, dragging him outside the city, and leaving him for dead (v. 19). Suffering for
Christ's name, foretold to Ananias in an epiphany (9:16), now becomes a painful
reality. Surrounded by the support of other disciples, Paul gets up and continues his
ministry in DERBE. This symbolic death and resurrection bear witness again to the
"unhindered" nature of the gospel.

Luke quickly narrates the story of how Paul and Barnabas retrace their steps,
and this episode ends in Syrian Antioch where it began, forming a literary inclusio
(vv. 21-28). On this first missionary endeavor, Paul had fulfilled his calling first
revealed to Ananias that Paul would *bring* [Jesus'] *name before Gentiles and kings
and before the people of Israel* and that *he must suffer for the sake of* [Jesus'] *name*
(9:15-16). So in Antioch, they reported to the church how God *had opened a door
of faith for the Gentiles* (v. 27). Very shortly, however, some in the church would
seek to close that door or at least severely limit its access.

The Conference in Jerusalem, 15:1-35

Acts 15 stands at the center of the Book of Acts both literarily and theologically. Finally the issue of gentile inclusion into the family of God is addressed and resolved. The episode is structured in four scenes: a description of the nature of the
conflict (1-5); the debate in Jerusalem focusing on the three speeches by Peter, Paul,
and Barnabas, and James (6-21); the solution (22-29); and the report to Antioch (30-
35).

15:1-5. The conflict. The success of Paul and Barnabas reported in Acts 13 and
14 prompts some unnamed individuals to come down from Judea to Antioch to
assert the official position of the Jerusalem church: *Unless you are circumcised*

according to the custom of Moses, you cannot be saved (v. 1). *No small dissension and debate* (v. 2) between them and Paul and Barnabas resulted, and delegates were sent to Jerusalem to resolve the matter.

Verse 2 introduces the major players: the circumcision party (whom Luke refers to as *believers who belonged to the sect of the Pharisees* [v. 5]) which has no individual spokesperson but rather speaks as a group; the apostles, represented by Peter; and the elders, represented by James. The only group missing are the Hellenists, and Luke may intend for the reader to understand that Paul and Barnabas have been appointed by the Antioch church to represent their concerns (v. 2; cf. 13:1). The issue is stated sharply by the sect of the PHARISEES: GENTILES cannot become Christians without first becoming JEWS, that is, they must be circumcised and observe the Law of Moses.

15:6-21. The debate. The other representatives are then allowed to present their position. Peter speaks first. By recounting briefly the Cornelius story (without mentioning his name), Peter appeals to his own experience to justify including without restrictions the gentiles within the family of God. Two points are of special interest in Peter's speech. First, Peter's argument is not a mere autobiographical argument from personal experience; it is a theological argument (Tannehill 1990, 184). The speech throughout de scribes what God was doing in those events. God is the subject of most of the verbs and participles in this speech: God made a choice; God knows the human heart; God testified to them (gentiles); God gave them the Holy Spirit; God cleansed their hearts; God has made no distinction between them and us (vv. 7-9). The upshot is that God, not Peter (or Paul), is responsible for the inclusion of the gentiles. In light of this appeal to divine mandate, Peter's question, *Why are you putting God to the test by placing on the neck of the disciples a yoke that neither our ancestors nor we have been able to bear?* (v. 10), reduces the assembly from *much debate* (v. 7) to *silence* (v. 12).

The other point of emphasis in Peter's speech is on justification by grace through faith. The speech ends with these words: *we believe that we will be saved through the grace of the Lord Jesus, just as they will* (v. 11; cf. v. 9). The emphasis is, of course, a very common theme in Paul's letters (cf. e.g., Gal 3:15), but it is also found in the message of the Lukan Paul. At the end of his synagogue speech in Antioch, Paul asserts "everyone who believes is justified" (13:38-39, author trans.). Peter then represents the most liberal position on this issue: gentiles need only to believe in order to be saved. Salvation is an act of God's grace, not the result of human effort.

After Paul and Barnabas support Peter by relating the *signs and wonders that God had done through them among the Gentiles* (v. 12), James, representative of the Jerusalem elders, addresses the assembly. As Peter had offered a theological argument for gentile inclusion on the basis of his personal experience, James offers a theological argument based on another source of authority—scripture. James begins his speech with a reference to Peter's speech: *Simeon has related how God first looked favorably on the Gentiles to take from among them a people for his name* (v. 14). The Greek word for "people" is used in Luke almost exclusively for the Jews, but here it unmistakably identifies believing gentiles with God's chosen "people."

James argues further that the inclusion of gentiles into the people of God was foretold by the prophet Amos. James's interpretation of Amos 9:11-12 rests on the LXX version of that passage, which claims that the house of David will be restored *so that all other peoples may seek the Lord—even all the Gentiles over whom my name has been called* (v. 17; cf. Amos 9:12 where the sense is very different). Since no mention is made in Amos of the gentiles being circumcised or obeying the Mosaic law, James concludes that scripture confirms Peter's experience that the gentiles should not have to become Jews in order to become Christians: *we should not trouble those Gentiles who are turning to God* (v. 19).

James does, however, go one step further toward compromise with the sect of the Pharisees by suggesting that the council write to the gentiles, instructing them to observe certain dietary laws (v. 20). The council is persuaded by James's words and decides to communicate its decision to the gentile believers in Antioch, Cilicia, and Syria (15:23). But what exactly have they decided? Is this last addition by James a soteriological requirement or social compromise? In other words, has James removed circumcision only to substitute dietary laws as a requirement for gentile salvation, or is he addressing a social problem of how gentiles and Jews are to live together peaceably in the church? A closer examination of the decree itself and the context of Acts in general may help resolve this question.

15:22-29. The solution. The four requirements demanding abstention from food offered to idols, from sexual immorality, from meat of strangled animals, and from blood (possibly based on Lev 17:8–18:18) are repeated in the letter composed for gentile consumption. The immediate context of the letter suggests these requirements should not be viewed as necessary for salvation, since the letter has been sent to correct those *certain persons who have gone out from us, though with no instructions from us,* and who *have said things to disturb you and have unsettled your minds* (v. 24). Further, these four requirements are "all basically ritual requirements aimed at making fellowship possible between Jewish and Gentile Christians" (Polhill 1992, 331). This view is supported by other clues in the text. In 16:1-3, Timothy (whose mother is Jewish and father Greek) is circumcised by Paul, not to insure his salvation, but to remove any obstacle that would hinder fellowship with the Jews with whom he came into contact. These regulations are recalled again in 21:21, where Paul is accused of leading Jews living among gentiles to *forsake Moses.* The situation has changed: "The problem is no longer the demands being made on Gentiles to become Jews but the pressure being felt by Jews to conform to a Gentile way of life" (Tannehill 1990, 191). The problem is still basically a social one of fellowship between Jewish and gentile Christians.

15:30-35. The report distributed. The appointed delegation—Paul, Barnabas, Judas BARSABBAS, and SILAS—depart, and the letter is delivered to the church at Antioch. It achieves the desired results: the congregation read it and *they rejoiced at the exhortation* (v. 31). The gentile mission has won a significant dispute; and, equally important for Luke, the church has resolved another major dispute in an orderly and peaceable fashion. Once again, church unity has been restored, and Paul and Barnabas can return to the task of teaching and proclaiming the word of the Lord (v. 35).

Paul in Macedonia, 15:36–17:15

15:36–16:10. Paul and the Apostolic company. Following the conference, Paul proposes to Barnabas that they retrace the steps of their first missionary campaign to see how the fledgling churches are faring (v. 36). This plan does not materialize because of a dispute about whether John Mark should accompany them. Again the conflict produces a positive result. The division actually leads to a multiplication of missionary efforts: Barnabas and Mark sail to Cyprus; and Paul and Silas travel through Syria and Cilicia, *strengthening the churches* (v. 41).

Paul's choice of traveling companions, Silas (15:40) and Timothy (16:1-3), deserves further comment. Timothy's mother was a Jewish Christian (on his circumcision, see comments on 15:22-29 above), and he himself *was well spoken of by the believers in Lystra and Iconium* (16:2). As a companion of Paul, he insured that the concerns and interests of these newly founded churches would be well represented. Silas, along with Judas, was one of the *leaders* of the Jerusalem church (15:22) who had been chosen to bear the apostolic decree to the gentile churches. In Antioch, Silas had shown his mettle by saying much *to encourage and strengthen the believers* (15:32). In fact, Luke identifies him as a *prophet.* Rather than exclude the Jerusalem church from further participation in the mission because they were on the losing side of the debate, Paul chooses to include Silas in his apostolic company. Silas, therefore, embodies the Jerusalem church's commitment to support the Jewish-gentile mission of Paul (see Tannehill 1990, 196).

So when Luke reports that *they went from town to town,* delivering the accord reached by apostles and elders in Jerusalem (16:4), it is significant that the *they* includes both a member of one of these diaspora churches and a member of the Jerusalem congregation. As a result of such strategy the churches grew daily both qualitatively (*in the faith*) and quantitatively (*in numbers* [16:5]).

Despite these positive references, Luke does not avoid reporting the limitations and failures of Paul's mission. With Paul and his company traveling as it were by trial and error, Luke twice reports that Paul was forbidden by the Spirit, first from speaking the word in Asia (16:6) and next from entering into Bithynia. The floundering mission is finally given focus in Troas when Paul experiences a vision (cf. chap. 10) in which a Macedonian man pleads with Paul to travel to Macedonia to *help us* (16:9). Guided now by the conviction that the campaign had divine endorsement, Paul sets sail for Macedonia (16:10).

Actually, the text says *we immediately tried to cross over to Macedonia* (16:10). Here Luke introduces the first of several so-called WE-SECTIONS, where the narrator seems to become a participant in the story. The use of first-person narration is important because: "Geographically, it is prominent in the Aegean coastal region, but not limited thereto. Thematically, it emphasizes major moments and events. Literarily, the 'we' brings readers into the story. Its intimacy makes this story *our story*" (Pervo 1990, 56). The use of the first person, then, signals that important events are about to follow.

16:11-40. Conversions and imprisonments. The reader is certainly not disappointed, for what follows is another household conversion story (vv. 11-15; cf. Acts 10–11), an exorcism (vv. 16-24), and the third rescue from prison (vv. 25-40). Paul and his companions pass quickly through Samothrace and Neapolis to Philippi, *a leading city of the district of Macedonia and a Roman colony* (vv. 11-12), where they encounter some women at prayer, the most notable of whom is LYDIA (vv. 13-14). The story of Lydia actually frames this unit (vv. 13-15, 40).

The reader learns several things about Lydia: she is a *worshiper of God* (like Cornelius, a devout gentile who had not yet fully converted to Judaism [cf. 10:2]) and a dealer in purple cloth from Thyatira, which indicates that she is a rich businesswoman (v. 14). After she and her household are converted, she adopts the role of a gracious Christian hostess and patroness (see Rom 12:13; Heb 13:2; 3 John 5-8) in opening her home to and sharing her possessions with Paul and his company.

During their time with Lydia, Paul and his companions encounter a slave girl with *a spirit of divination* whose fortune-telling was very lucrative for her owners (v. 16). She rightly identifies the missionaries as *slaves of the Most High God, who proclaim to you a way of salvation* (v. 17). After *many days* of this, Paul commanded the spirit to leave the girl, reminiscent of Jesus's exorcisms (v. 18; cf. Luke 4:34; 8:28).

With the departure of the spirit went also the fortune of the slave-girl's owners. Once again, the material effect of the missionaries efforts leads to adverse results. The owners drag Paul and Silas into the marketplace before the authorities and hide their rage at economic loss behind political charges that will stick: *These men are disturbing our city; they are Jews and are advocating customs that are not lawful for us as Romans to adopt or observe* (vv. 20-21). The crowds join in, and the local authorities acquiesce. Stripped and flogged, Paul and Silas are thrown into prison where they are put in the innermost cell, what we would call the dungeon (vv. 22-24).

The next scene resembles a rescue-from-prison scene, but there is a significant difference. Prayers, hymn singing, and an earthquake lead not to the rescue of Paul and Silas from prison, but rather the deliverance of the Philippian jailer and his household to salvation. When the jailer awakens to discover the prison doors opened, he draws his sword to take his own life before the local authorities can (cf. 11:18-19). But Paul interrupts; the earthquake had opened the prison doors and unfastened the prisoners' fetters, but Paul and Silas were still there (vv. 27-29). Trembling, the jailer asks, *Sirs, what must I do to be saved?* (v. 30). Paul and Silas respond with the kerygma in a nutshell, *Believe on the Lord Jesus, and you will be saved, you and your household* (v. 31). In the middle of the night these words come true. Both parties receive cleansing waters—one for wounds, the other for baptism—and a symbolic Lord's Supper follows as the jailer sets food before them (vv. 32-34). Like Lydia, the jailer demonstrates the authenticity of his faith by acting as the proper host.

The scene has come to a proper denouement with the conversion of the jailer, but Luke has one more important detail to report. Only now in the story does the reader learn that Paul and Silas have been illegally beaten and imprisoned—they are Roman citizens (v. 37). This disclosure of citizenship comes too late in the story to offer protection, but it does set the stage for later encounters with political authorities when Paul's Roman citizenship becomes important again (22:25). This scene ends where it began, in Lydia's house (v. 15) with Paul and Silas strengthening the brothers and sisters there.

17:1-15. Conflict in Thessalonica. Paul and Silas's journeys next take them to THESSALONICA where there is a Jewish synagogue (v. 1). Luke reminds us that it was Paul's custom to speak in the synagogue; he has not yet abandoned the Jewish mission. His message is strikingly similar to the message of the risen Christ in Luke 24 (Tannehill 1990, 206): Paul "opens" the scriptures (*explaining and proving,* v. 3a; see Luke 24:32); he speaks of the necessity of the Messiah's suffering (v. 3b; Luke 24:26, 46). The result is that a few of the Jews were converted as well as *a great many of the devout Greeks and not a few of the leading women* (v. 4).

The notice given to these women converts is interesting. Although Luke has consistently given attention to the role of women in the Christian community (e.g., 1:14; 5:14; 8:12), they receive even greater attention in chaps. 16–18 (see 16:13-14, 16; 17:4, 12, 34; 18:2, 18, 26). The notice of leading women in the Macedonian churches is "very much in keeping with inscriptional evidence that in Macedonia women had considerable social and civic influence" (Polhill, 361). Even more important for the role of women in these churches, no doubt, was the gospel of freedom and radical inclusion that Paul preached.

A familiar pattern emerges in Acts 17:5-8. The Jews become jealous and join with some *ruffians* to form a lynch mob against Paul and Silas. When their searching fails to turn up Paul, they settle for Jason and some other believers instead (v. 6). Knowing that religious differences will matter little to the city authorities, they hurl political charges again (see 16:21), claiming the Christians *have been turning the world upside down* and that they *are all acting contrary to the decrees of the emperor saying that there is another king named Jesus* (vv. 6-7; see 1 Thes 1:1-20; 5:3). The officials are disturbed, but choose only to fine Jason and the others before releasing them (v. 8).

Meanwhile, Paul and Silas are carried off to Beroea where they repeat the pattern of going to the synagogue (v. 10). Luke reports that these Beroean *Jews were more receptive than those in Thessalonica* (v. 11). Whereas in Thessalonica only *some* Jews be lieved, Luke reports that in Beroea *many of them believed,* along with *not a few Greek women and men of high standing* (v. 12). Although the Beroean Jews are receptive, the Thessalonian Jews are equally persistent; they come to Beroea and again stir up the crowds (v. 14; cf. 14:19-20). And again, believers intervene, accompanying Paul ultimately all the way to Athens (v. 15). These believers receive instructions from Paul that Silas and TIMOTHY (who had been left behind, v. 14) are to join him as soon as possible, and they depart (v. 15).

Paul in Achaia, 17:16–18:17

This next episode takes place in the region of ACHAIA. In Athens, Paul gives his only missionary speech addressed to a gentile audience. As such it stands as a model for preaching to the gentiles. Paul next spends an extended period of time in Corinth. Both of these cities were well known in the ancient world. ATHENS, although it had faded from its period of prominence (4th–5th century B.C.E.), was still highly regarded as the cultural and intellectual center of the ROMAN EMPIRE, and CORINTH had emerged as the largest, most cosmopolitan city in Greece. Thus, in Achaia Paul continues his pattern of evangelizing in significant urban centers.

17:16-34. Paul in Athens. The scene in Athens is divided into three parts: the setting leading up to the sermon is described in some detail (vv. 16-21); the sermon itself is the centerpiece of the episode in Athens (vv. 22-31); and the scene ends with a report of the responses to Paul's message (vv. 32-34).

While waiting for Silas and Timothy to join him, Paul has the opportunity to see Athens. Rather than being impressed by its magnificent art and architecture, Luke reports that Paul was "infuriated" (author trans.) to see the city full of idols (v. 16), a point Paul will address in his sermon. Again Paul follows the normal pattern of arguing with the Jews in the synagogue, but Luke goes on to say that he also engages in debate with people, especially Epicurean and Stoic philosophers, in the marketplace or agora (v. 17).

The EPICUREANS and STOICS represented two of the leading philosophical schools of the day. The Epicureans were committed to an ethical system that tolerated the existence of gods, but gave them no vital role. The Stoics were pantheists who held a more dynamic view of the gods, believing that the divine "spark" was present in all of creation. Paul will allude several times in his speech to certain views of these philosophers.

Evidently, Paul had not been terribly successful in communicating his views, for his audience assumed that he, too, was a pantheist presenting his view about Jesus (which in Greek is grammatically masculine) and his consort "Anastasia" ("Resurrection," which in Greek is grammatically feminine). Before he was through, however, Paul would dispel any notions that he was a polytheistic thinker.

Enamored with intellectual fads (see Demosthenes, *Oration* 4:10), the Athenians took Paul to the AREOPAGUS to present his new ideas (vv. 19-21). There is some debate whether Luke means that Paul was taken to a hill located beneath the acropolis and above the agora called the Areopagus (see, e.g., the KJV "Mars Hill") or whether he had in mind the court known by that name (an analogy is "Wall Street," which may refer either to the place or the stock exchange named after the street).

Internal evidence, such as the conversion of Dionysus, a member of the court of Areopagus (v. 34), suggests that Paul addressed the court of the Areopagus (which by this time was probably meeting in the *Stoa Basileios* or Royal Portico) in the northwest corner of the agora (Polhill 1992, 368). This view is further supported by the possible parallel that the ancient reader might have drawn between Paul's experience and the trial of Socrates. The accusation that Socrates had "introduced" other new gods (Plato, *Apologia* 24B) may be echoed in the description of Paul "introducing" a *new teaching* (v. 19) that had earlier been identified as *foreign divinities* (v. 18). Paul, of course, escapes here the fate of Socrates, and one does not have to posit a formal trial before the Areopagus to acknowledge the parallels with Socrates' trial.

The Areopagus sermon is the fullest and most dramatic speech of Paul's missionary career (vv. 22-31). Anticipated by the shorter address in Lystra (14:15-17) and consistent with the kerygma Paul presents to the gentiles in his letters (cf. Rom 1; 1 Thes 1), this address provides a window into how Paul dealt with the gentiles in other places. The speech itself is composed of five couplets following a chiastic pattern (see Polhill 1992, 37).

A   Introduction: evidence of the ignorance
         of pagan worship, 23-24
    B   The object of true worship
             is the one Creator God, 25-26
        C   Proper relationship between humanity
                 and God, 26-27
    B'   The objects of false worship are the idols
             of gold, silver, or stone, 28-29
A'   Conclusion: the time of ignorance
         is now over, 30-31

The sermon begins with a typical convention of ancient rhetoric, the *captatio benevolentia*, in which the speaker attempts to curry the favor of his audience with a compliment. Here Paul says, *Athenians, I see how extremely religious you are in every way* (v. 22). His evidence is taken from his tour of the city, during which he has seen an altar with the inscription *"To an unknown god"* (see Pausanias 1.1.4; Philostratus, *Life of Apollonius of Tyana* 6.3.5). But within the compliment is an implicit criticism, *What . . . you worship as unknown* [or perhaps in ignorance], *this I proclaim to you* (v. 23). The Athenians had been worshiping an object not a personal God, a "what" not a "whom."

Paul then claims that this unknown God is none other than the Creator God (vv. 25-26). There is no other god worthy of worship; indeed, Paul would argue, there is no other God. Although Paul does not quote scripture, his monotheism is biblically grounded (e.g., Paul's description that God *does not live in shrines made by human hands* (v. 24)—cf. 1 Kgs 8:27; also Acts 7:48-50), as is his language used to speak of God creating all nations *from one ancestor* (presumably Adam) as well as the human response to search for God (vv. 26-27).

What Paul does quote, however, is not the OT, but rather the Stoic philosopher Aratus: *For "in him we live and move and have our being"; as even some of your own poets have said, "For we too are his offspring"* (v. 28). Here then is the basis for Paul's attack on idolatry that follows: since humans are God's offspring and in the true image of God, then no image *formed by the art and imagination of mortals* could possibly be anything other than a distortion of the image of the one, true God (v. 29).

Paul concludes his sermon by announcing that the time of ignorance is over. God will no longer *overlook* this ignorance (cf. 14:16; Rom 3:25); now is the time for repentance (v. 30). Just as God had made all the nations *to inhabit the whole earth* from *one ancestor* (v. 26), so God will judge the world through *a man* whom God appointed (cf. Rom 5). That this man is Jesus is confirmed when Paul says that God raised him from the dead (v. 31).

The sermon gets mixed reviews (vv. 32-34). The resurrection is viewed as "folly" by some of the Greeks in Paul's audience (v. 32; cf. 1 Cor 1:23), but to view the Areopagus speech as a failure would be a mistake. Some pledge to hear Paul speak again (v. 32); others, Dionysius and Damarius among them, became believers. Neither Paul nor the gospel failed in Athens; only those who heard the good news and did not respond in faith have failed.

18:1-17. Paul in Corinth. In the opening section (vv. 1-4), Paul leaves Athens and travels to Corinth. There he meets PRISCILLA AND AQUILA who had recently come to Corinth from Italy where they and other Jews had been expelled by the emperor Claudius (cf. Suetonius, *Life of Claudius* 25.4). Like Paul, they were tentmakers (v. 3). Paul stayed and worked with them (see Acts 20:34; cf. 1 Cor 4:12; 1 Thes 2; 2 Cor 11:7), while continuing to follow his customary pattern of trying to persuade Jews and gentiles that Jesus was Messiah (v. 4).

The rest of this passage preserves three "type scenes," defined as "when a basic situation, with similar characters and plot elements, recurs several times in a given literature" (Tannehill 1990, 202, 221–29). The first type scene is a kind of "synagogue rejection" that occurs three times in Acts and in which Paul turns to the gentiles in the face of Jewish rejection. The first such scene takes place in Pisidian Antioch (13:44-47); the third occurs in Paul's speech to the Jews in Rome (28:23-28; cf. also 19:8-9; 22:17-21). In each instance, Paul makes a speech in which he announces that from that point on he is turning to the gentiles (13:46; 19:6; 28:28). Why does Paul continue to preach to the Jews in the face of such resistance? His prophetic act of shaking the dust off his feet (cf. 13:51; Luke 9:5) combines with his prophetic words *Your blood be on your own heads* (v. 6; cf. Ezek 33:4) and his symbolic shift from the synagogue to the house of a believer, Titius Justus, to demonstrate that Paul is fulfilling his responsibility as witness to the Jews. The Jews are responsible for their reaction. In fact, individual Jews continue to convert (witness Crispus the synagogue ruler and his household in this very scene, v. 8). Paul is obligated only to present the gospel; he cannot coerce converts.

The second type scene is that of a "divine commissioning" (see Tannehill 1990, 223). This scene was familiar to the readers from their reading of the OT (Exod 3:2-12; Josh 1:1-9; Jer 1:5-10; Isa 41:10-14) and Acts (5:17-21; 9:10-18; 16:6-10; 27:23-24). The scene consists of a confrontation (v. 9a, *The Lord said to Paul in a vision*), the commission to undertake a task (v. 9b, *speak and do not be silent*), reassurance (esp. prominent here in vv. 9-10, *Do not be afraid . . . for I am with you, and no one will lay a hand on you to harm you*), and a conclusion where the commissionee usually fulfills the assigned task (v. 11, *He* [Paul] *stayed there a year and six months, teaching the word of God among them*). Paul can continue his mission in the confidence that the Lord is present with him. The reality of this presence is felt in the next scene.

The third type scene has been identified as a scene of public accusation before an official, here Gallio (vv. 12-17). Twice already the reader has encountered this pattern (16:19-24; 17:5-7; cf. also 18:23-41) that has three elements (Tannehill 1990, 202): (1) Christians are compelled to appear before an official person or body (v. 12); (2) they are accused of wrongdoing, political or religious (v. 13); (3) the outcome is reported (vv. 14-17). This scene differs from the others in the outcome because, rather than being beaten and imprisoned (16:19-24) or fined (17:5-7), Paul is acquitted and SOSTHENES, the official of the synagogue, is beaten instead. Perhaps the difference in outcome is due to the fact that in the first two "public accusation" scenes, the charges are political; here they are religious—*This man is persuading people to worship God in ways that are contrary to the law* (v. 13)—giving Gallio an excuse to pay *no attention to any of these things* (v. 17). In any case, this scene proves the truthfulness of the previous unit: at least in Corinth no one will lay a hand on Paul.

Paul in Ephesus, 18:18–19:41

The final episode (18:18–19:41) of this division (chaps. 13–19) focuses on the city of Ephesus. The unit is organized into the following scenes: (1) Paul visits EPHESUS, JERUSALEM, and ANTIOCH (18:18-23); (2) the baptism of John (18:24–19:7); (3) Paul and the sons of Sceva (19:8-20); (4) Paul's resolve (19:21-22); and (5) the riot in Ephesus (19:23-41).

18:18-23. Paul visits Ephesus, Jerusalem, and Antioch. The first scene is transitional and could as easily be included at the end of the preceding section. Paul returns to Antioch where he began these missionary endeavors (15:35-41), but he also makes a quick stop in Ephesus where he leaves Priscilla and Aquila and enters into a quick debate with the Jews in the synagogue there (v. 19). Along the way, Paul shaves his hair to fulfill a vow (a Nazirite vow?—see Num 6:1-21), signifying that he continues to be a practicing Jew despite charges otherwise (see Acts 21:21). Paul also stops in Jerusalem to greet the church (v. 22); the tie between the gentile mission and the Jerusalem church remains unbroken. This passage then looks back to Antioch where Paul began his missionary career and forward to Ephesus where he will spend his last three years as a free man.

18:24–19:7. The baptism of John. The connection between the next two scenes, 18:24-28 and 19:1-7, may not be immediately obvious. In the first, Luke does a rare thing by shifting the spotlight away from Paul to APOLLOS. Apollos is described in glowing terms. He is *an eloquent man, well-versed in the scriptures. . . . instructed in the Way of the Lord* (vv. 24-25). He "spoke being fervent in the Spirit" (author trans.), and *taught accurately the things concerning Jesus* (v. 25). The only thing lacking is that Apollos *knew only the baptism of John* (v. 25).

Here then is the point of contact with the next unit (19:1-7) where Paul encounters some disciples in Ephesus who likewise have only experienced the baptism of John (v. 3). In both cases, "those knowing or having experienced John's baptism have their knowledge (18:26) or experience (19:4-6) completed by the associates of Paul (18:26) or by Paul himself (19:6)" (Talbert 1984, 81).

Nonetheless, there are significant differences in these two stories. Apollos is depicted much more favorably than the "disciples" encountered by Paul. The disciples were not only limited to the baptism of John; they had not heard that there was a Holy Spirit! (19:2). Apollos, on the other hand, spoke, "being fervent in the Spirit" (18:25). Further, these Ephesian disciples had to be instructed about the meaning of John's baptism for the coming of Jesus, while Apollos, limited as he was to John's baptism, is still able to teach *accurately the things concerning Jesus* (18:25). Further, with a little fine-tuning instruction from Priscilla and Aquila (note a woman instructing an evangelist here in a post-Pauline document, cf. 1 Tim 2:12), Apollos is able to secure a letter of recommendation from the Ephesians to continue his ministry in Corinth (18:27-28; 19:1).

These contrasts explain why the Ephesian disciples needed to receive baptism in the name of Jesus and the gift of the Holy Spirit (confirmed again by glossolalia, cf. 2:21-24; 10:44-48) while Apollos did not, even though both knew only the baptism of John.

19:8-20. Paul and the sons of Sceva. In this scene, the pattern of synagogue rejection continues. After three months, Paul's sermons in the Ephesian synagogue are met with such resistance by the Jews that he leaves and takes up residence elsewhere, in this case, the lecture hall of Tyrannus, where he preaches both to Jews and Greeks (18:8-10). As in the portrayal of Philip, Paul's healing ministry (vv. 11-12; cf. 8:6-7; also 5:15) confirms his message. By healing illnesses and casting out unclean spirits, Paul confirms the Christian kerygma that the authority of Satan has been overturned (on this passage, see Garrett 1989, 89–99).

Now for the third time (see Acts 8, 13), a Christian missionary confronts a practitioner of magic. In Ephesus, *some itinerant Jewish exorcists tried to use the name of the Lord Jesus over those who had evil spirits* (v. 13). The language used to describe the activities of these *seven sons of a Jewish high priest named Sceva* (v. 14) echoes magical practices of antiquity, especially "exorcist" and "adjure." That these exorcists are using the formula *the Jesus whom Paul preaches* probably implies that they, like Simon Magus, have mistaken Christian miracles for feats of magic. Thus they try to use Jesus' name in a way typical of magical technique, but Luke makes it clear that Jesus' name is not some magical name vulnerable to manipulation. Rather there is a close tie between Jesus' authority and the authority of the one calling upon his name. In Acts 16:16-17, e.g., the spirit in the slave girl recognizes Paul and his companions as *slaves of the Most High God*. But here the evil spirit replies to the sons of Sceva, *Jesus I know, and Paul I know; but who are you?* (v. 15). The demon does not know them, i.e., does not acknowledge their authority, and therefore refuses to obey them. Instead, the demon becomes master over them, sending them out of the house *naked and wounded* (v. 16). "The seven sons failed to mobilize Jesus' power because they lacked the authority to invoke his holy name, and so the demon remains in control" (Garrett 1989, 94).

The defeat of the sons of Sceva makes the accomplishments of Paul's exorcisms even more impressive, a fact not lost on the Ephesians (vv. 17-19). This incident demonstrates that the name of Jesus cannot be manipulated and therefore is worthy of praise (v. 17). Further, these Jews and Greeks had already heard the word of the Lord (v. 10) and seen the defeat of Satan confirmed in the healing ministry of Paul (vv. 11-12); now they reckon with the fact that magic itself is obsolete. "The magic books are useless now—emblems of a defeated regime—and so must be burned" (Garrett 1989, 95). The value of the books burned (*fifty thousand silver coins*) has been reckoned as having a current market value of about $1 billion.

The burning of the magical books is not to be viewed as an act of believers who had secretly practiced magic until now, but rather as part of the act of repentance on the part of those who, as a result of this incident, forsake their belief in and practice of magic and become believers. Thus, Luke uses lan guage—"extol" and "awestruck"—that is intimately associated with conversion (cf. 9:31; 10:46). Furthermore, as noted earlier (see on 12:24), the phrase that concludes this section, *the word of the Lord grew mightily,* is one way Luke refers to the addition of believers to the church (see also 6:7, 12:24). Ironically, the victory of the demon over Sceva's sons is actually a defeat for the devil, because both sides serve Satan. Satan's kingdom is divided and thus doomed (Luke 11:18), and the Word of the Lord continues to grow.

19:21-22. Paul's resolve. In the next unit composed of only two verses (vv. 21-22), Luke anticipates the rest of Paul's ministry as it is recorded in Acts. Paul resolves in the Spirit (v. 21) to go through Macedonia and Achaia (see 20:1-12), to visit Jerusalem once again (see 21:15-38), and finally to go to Rome (see 28:14-16).

The language is quite strong; Paul says that he *must* see Rome, a word characteristically used in Acts to describe divine purpose. As such it is reminiscent of Jesus'
resolve to go to Jerusalem (Luke 9:51). Although suffering is not mentioned explicitly, there is good reason to see here that the parallels between Jesus' journey to
Jerusalem and Paul's journey to Rome include the dimension of suffering. For Paul,
this insight becomes clearer the farther he journeys (20:22-24), but here we have the
first step taken by Paul in understanding his divine destiny to travel to Rome.

19:23-41. The riot in Ephesus. Although Paul is largely absent from this scene,
he remains at the center of controversy. The unit opens with one DEMETRIUS, a sil-
versmith who made shrines of ARTEMIS, the Asian mother goddess of nature,
addressing his fellow artisans. Demetrius has accurately perceived that Paul's in-
vectives against idols would be bad for business (v. 26). To this economic
argument, Demetrius adds a religious one: *the temple of the great goddess Artemis
will be scorned, and she will be deprived of her majesty that brought all Asia and
the world to worship her* (v. 27).

Even here, economics is not far beneath the surface; the temple of Artemis was
a central pillar in the financial structures of Asia (Dio Chrysostom, *Oration* 31.54)
as well as one of the seven wonders of the world bound to beef up the tourist
industry in Ephesus.

Demetrius is successful in stirring up the crowd who drag GAIUS and Aristarchus, two of Paul's companions, into the theater. In the midst of mass confusion and
shouts of *Great is Artemis of the Ephe sians!* Paul is urged by some officials of
Asia, who were friendly to him, to stay clear of the theater (v. 31). Finally,
Alexander, a Jew, stepped forward to *make a defense before the people* (v. 33). Did
Alexander intend to disassociate the Jews from the Christians or to defend Jewish
rejection of idols? We will never know, but the crowd at least identifies this Jew
with the Christian rejection of idols and drown him out in a verbal filibuster,
resuming their chant: *Great is Artemis of the Ephesians!* (v. 34).

A speech by Demetrius began the riot; finally a speech by the town clerk ends
it (Tannehill 1990, 243). With appropriate rhetorical flourish (cf. Acts 17:23), the
town clerk begins by identifying with the point of view of the crowds, speaking of
the *great Artemis* whose statue *fell from heaven* and whose temple is entrusted to
the keeping of the city of the Ephesians (v. 35). In Gamaliel-like fashion, he points
out the innocence of Gaius and Aristarchus and that the danger to the Ephesians was
not Paul, but rather *the danger of being charged with rioting* (v. 40).

This scene shares similarities with previous public accusations (in chaps. 16, 17,
and 18). Here, as in the first scene in Philippi, the accusers are gentiles (Jews are
accusers in Thessalonica and Corinth, see Tannehill 1990, 202–203), making it a
mistake to view opposition to the Christian movement as only and characteristically
Jewish. The scene also bears remarkable similarity to the riot in the Jerusalem
Temple (21:27-36). Especially similar is the reason for the riot in both instances:
"Members of an established religion are protesting the effect that Paul's mission is

having on their religion and its temple" (Tannehill 1990, 242). The riot subsides, order is restored, and Paul is prepared to make his final journey to Jerusalem and Rome (Acts 20–28).

Paul's Farewell Journey, 20:1–28:31

This last division of Acts (20–28) narrates Paul's farewell journey. For much of this part of the story Paul is under arrest, and the narrative is punctuated with Paul's defense speeches.

Paul's Last Journey to Jerusalem, 20:1–21:16

This first section describes the beginning of Paul's journey to Jerusalem (20:1-16), recounts his farewell address to the Ephesians (20:17-38), and records the resolve of Paul to continue to Jerusalem despite several warnings otherwise. Throughout the section, Paul exchanges good-byes with those whom he thinks he will never see again.

20:1-16. The beginning of the farewell journey. After the riot in Ephesus has been quieted, Paul gathers the disciples, encourages and bids them good-bye, and heads for Macedonia (vv. 1-6). Paul is accompanied by seven named companions who represent various areas of the gentile mission. Perhaps the number "seven" not only indicates a certain completion or fullness of the apostolic company, but represents the gentile mission itself (cf. the "seven" appointed to represent the concerns of the "Hellenists" in Acts 6). Yet another of Paul's companions reappears here when the narrator employs the first-person narration, the second such "we-passage" in Acts (cf. 16:17). This farewell ministry is characterized by the continued opposition of the Jews to Paul's witness (v. 3) and Paul *had given the believers much encouragement* (v. 2).

This encouragement is given further detail in the next scene (vv. 7-12). Paul's companions, separated at Philippi, are reunited in Troas, where they stay for a week (v. 6). Paul meets with the believers there on Sunday to share in the Lord's Supper, to *break bread* as Luke preferred to call it (v. 7; see Acts 2:42, 46). Since this was his last message to these believers, Paul continues to preach until midnight (v. 7). A young man named EUTYCHUS ("Lucky") has the misfortune of falling asleep and then falling out of a window of the upstairs room where they had met (v. 9). Pronounced dead by the time Paul gets to him, Paul takes the boy in his arms (cf. 2 Kgs 4:34) and announces that *his life is in him* (v. 10). Like Jesus (Luke 7:11-17) and Peter (Acts 9:36-42) before him, Paul now restores to life one who was presumably dead.

This story has a symbolic dimension: in the context of Paul's passion Luke places a story that foreshadows the resurrection power of the gospel to overcome death. Along these lines, the seemingly irrelevant detail about the *many lamps* in the meeting place (v. 8) may be read both literally, as an explanation of why, in the face of heat and lack of oxygen, Eutychus went to the window, and symbolically, as a contrast between the meeting room where the Word of God was proclaimed and the Lord's Supper as a place of light (13:47; 26:18, 23) and the place of death and darkness where Eutychus falls when he falls asleep. Eutychus's story is an exegesis by example of Paul's later admonition to the Ephesians to "stay awake" (author trans.) in his absence (v. 31). They may not be so fortunate as Eutychus ("Lucky"), who had Paul to reverse the misfortunes of his lack of moral diligence.

The story ends with Luke's report that the Troas believers were "not a little encouraged" (v. 12, author trans.), picking up on the word used to describe Paul's ministry throughout Macedonia and Greece (v. 2). The encouragement here derives from the integrity between Paul's *word* through preaching and sacrament (v. 11) and his *deed* in raising Eutychus.

The episode ends with a brief summary of Paul's travels from TROAS to MILETUS (vv. 13-15). The readers learn that a temporal goal has been added to Paul's spatial goal: he hopes to be in Jerusalem by the day of Pentecost (v. 16). He also chooses not to stop in Ephesus (because he dreaded the grief of leaving that Christian community again?) but rather sends for the leaders of the community to join him in Miletus (v. 16).

20:17-38. Paul's farewell address to the Ephesians. Sandwiched between the report of the arrival (v. 17) and departure (20:26-38) of the Ephesian elders is the speech given by Paul to them (vv. 18-35). Before examining the structure and content of the speech itself, it may help the reader to place the speech in several contexts. First in the context of Acts, this speech is the third by the Lukan Paul. The first in Antioch of Pisidia (Acts 13:16-41) is addressed to Jews; the second is the Areopagus speech delivered to the Greeks in Athens (17:22-31). The audience partly determines the shape and content of those first two speeches, and this is no less true for this last speech addressed to the Christian leaders from Ephesus who had gathered in Miletus to hear Paul. This speech serves as a window on the problems not only associated with the Ephesian church during Paul's day, but also with the problems faced by Luke's community in a post-Pauline time period. Luke's story about the time of Paul now gives way to Paul's story about Luke's time. As such, this speech has much in common with the Pastoral Epistles (1, 2 Timothy; Titus) that, like Acts, evidently address ecclesiastical problems in a post-Pauline situation. These problems will be given more attention in the exploration of the speech itself.

In form, the speech shares many similarities with the ancient genre of the farewell address. Farewell speeches were common in late Judaism (Gen 49; Josh 23–24; 1 Sam 12; Tob 14; *AsMos*; *T.12 Patr.*) and early Christianity (Mark 13; John 13–17; Luke 22:14-38; 2 Tim 3:1–4:8; 2 Pet) and shared certain constituent elements: (1) the assembling of the speaker's family and/or friends; (2) notice that the speaker is about to leave or die; and (3) a speech that exhorts the listener to emulate desired behavior and predicts events that will follow the speaker's departure/death (Polhill 1992, 423). The Miletus address reflects all these features.

The speech itself defies neat organization, although Talbert (1984, 85) has offered the following helpful proposal (here slightly modified). The speech divides into three parts (18b-27; 28-31a, 31b-35), each with its own chiastic or concentric structure.

1. Defense and Prediction, 18b-27
   A   Paul's review and defense of his past ministry
        with the Ephesians, 18b-21
        B   Paul's prediction of his future suffering—
             marked by "and now," 22-24
        B'   Paul's prediction of his death—
             marked by "and now," 25
   A'   Paul's defense of his past ministry, 26-27
2. Exhortations and a Prediction, 28-31a
   A   Exhortation to elders to watch
        over the church, 28
        B   Prediction that heresies will arise, 29-30
   A'   Exhortation to elders to "stay awake," 31a
3. Exhortation and a Blessing, 31b-35
   A   Paul's past exhortation, 31b
        B   Paul's present blessing, 32
   A'   Paul's past example, 33-35

At the heart of this speech lie the predictions that heresies will arise (vv. 29-30). These predictions function at two levels; a narrative level in which the predictions are fulfilled within the course of Acts, and a historical level in which these predictions have already come to pass in Luke's community. Thus, within the narrative itself there is good reason to view those external opponents (*savage wolves will come in among you,* v. 29) as Jews, such as the ones who in the very next episode (21:27-28) are found in opposition to the church (note that in 21:27 these Jews are identified as being from Asia, strengthening this argument), and the internal opponents as Jewish Christians or gentiles influenced by Judaism (21:20-21). There is also ample historical evidence for heresy in Ephesus at the end of the first century (see Eusebius, *EccHist* 3.32.7-8). The crisis faced here is how, in the face of internal and external pressures, to insure that the Christian traditions are preserved in the passing from one generation to the next.

21:1-16. Warnings to avoid Jerusalem. With tears and farewells, Paul and his company set sail again. After passing through Cos, Rhodes, and Patara, they land at Tyre to unload the ship's cargo (vv. 1-3) and stay there seven days. *Through the Spirit* the believers at Tyre gave Paul his first warning *not to go on to Jerusalem* (v. 4), probably because they, like Paul, knew that suffering and persecution were awaiting him there (cf. 20:23). Still, in spite of this weighty testimony to the contrary, Paul persists in continuing his journey to Jerusalem (vv. 5-6).

After a brief stop in Ptolemais, Paul and his company arrive in Caesarea and encounter several characters already familiar to the readers. They stay in the home of Philip the evangelist (see Acts 8) who has *four unmarried daughters who had the gift of prophecy* (v. 9). While it is unclear whether Paul will make it to Jerusalem by Pentecost, it is clear that already in Caesarea he is seeing evidence of the fulfillment of Pentecost prophecies, in this case, that both *sons and . . . daughters shall prophesy* (Acts 2:17).

Paul also meets with the prophet AGABUS who had prophesied a famine in Judea (11:27-30). Through Agabus, the Holy Spirit again describes the persecution awaiting Paul in Jerusalem (cf. 20:23). Like an OT prophet, Agabus combines a prophetic sign, binding his own hands and feet with Paul's belt, with a prophetic warning: *This is the way the Jews in Jerusalem will bind the man who owns this belt and will hand him over to the Gentiles* (v. 11). This time, the believers, not the Holy Spirit, interpret this sign as a warning to Paul not to continue the journey to Jerusalem.

In the face of this third prediction of his passion (20:23; 21:4, 11), Paul remains resolute: *I am ready not only to be bound but even to die in Jerusalem for the name of the Lord Jesus* (v. 13). Unlike Peter who made a similar promise (Luke 22:33) but failed to fulfill it (at least in the narrative of Luke), Paul remains true to his oath. Seeing they could not persuade him otherwise, the believers pray that *the Lord's will be done* (v. 14). In language that echoes Luke 22:42, Paul is depicted here as facing his own Gethsemane, where he, like Jesus, finally prays, "Lord not my will, but yours be done."

This scene ends with some of the disciples from Caesarea escorting Paul and his company to the house of Mnason of Cyprus with whom they lodged in Jerusalem (v. 16).

21:17-40. Paul's arrival and arrest in Jerusalem. Paul and his companions are warmly received by the Jerusalem believers (v. 17), and on the next day, Paul meets with James and the Jerusalem elders (v. 18). In a scene reminiscent of the Jerusalem conference (Acts 15), Paul recounts what *God had done among the Gentiles through his ministry* (v. 19). The Jerusalem elders, in turn, invite Paul to see *how many thousands of believers there are among the Jews* (v. 20). But herein lies the problem: the Jewish believers have been told that Paul was teaching Jews living among gentiles to forsake Moses and abandon Jewish customs (v. 21).

This is the third church conflict involving Jewish-gentile relations (see Tannehill 1990, 268). First the question of baptizing gentiles was resolved in Acts 11. Then the controversy over requiring gentiles to be circumcised was addressed in Acts 15. The problem before the church now has to do with pressure, real or perceived, on Jewish Christians to forsake their Jewish customs, values, and practices. Paul is at the center of this problem because as leader of the gentile mission, he is creating a social situation that is not particularly supportive of Jewish Christians who wish also to honor their Jewish heritage. As the gentile mission continues to be successful and the Jewish population in the church becomes more and more of a minority, this problem intensifies.

The solution proposed by James and the elders is for Paul to demonstrate tangibly his support for Jewish Christians to live as Jews (v. 23). Paul is to join four Jewish believers who are under a vow in going through a seven-day rite of purification in the Temple (vv. 23-24). This will provide the evidence needed to dispel the rumors about Paul. Further, they argue, this solution in no way compromises the agreement reached at the Jerusalem conference regarding the gentiles (v. 25). Paul, despite all the Spirit's previous warnings of persecution and suffering, agrees and engages in the very public act of Temple purification (v. 26).

While Luke reports nothing of the response by Jewish believers to Paul's acts, he has much to say about the reaction of the Jewish community. Jews from Asia, who had seen Paul in the Temple and had also previously seen the gentile TROPHIMUS from Ephesus with Paul, jump to the conclusion that Paul has defiled the Temple by taking Trophimus into it (vv. 27, 29). Thus they stir up the crowd milling around the Temple charging that Paul is *the man who is teaching everyone everywhere against our people, our law, and this place* (v. 28)—charges similar to the ones leveled against Stephen (cf. 7:13). These Asian Jews incite a riot that would rival the one Paul had just endured in Ephesus. Paul was dragged from the Temple, and the Temple doors ominously were shut, never to be open to Paul again (v. 30).

Only the intervention of a Roman tribune prevents Paul from meeting his death (vv. 31-32). Paul is arrested and bound (cf. Agabus's prophecy in v. 11), and efforts by the tribune to learn Paul's identity are thwarted by the uproar of the crowd (v. 34). Instead, the pursuing mob becomes so violent that Paul has to be carried away by Roman soldiers in the midst of shouts of *Away with him!* (v. 36), the very cry of the crowds who called for Jesus' death (Luke 23:18).

While Jesus went to his death with no defense speech, Paul requests to address the crowd (vv. 37, 39). The tribune is surprised to learn that Paul speaks Greek, for he had mistakenly supposed that Paul was an Egyptian insurrectionist (v. 38). Paul identifies himself to the Roman tribune as a Jew from a leading city and then stands to clarify his identity to the Jewish mob (v. 40).

22:1-29. Paul addresses the crowd and the Roman tribune. Paul gestures for the crowd to be silent, but when they hear him speaking in their own language they become even more quiet (v. 2). Paul's speech addresses three issues: his Jewish piety and former life (vv. 1-5), his conversion (vv. 6-12), and his divine commission to go to the gentiles (13-21).

In the first unit (vv. 1-5), Paul again follows the conventions of ancient rhetoric and tries to identify with his audience: he is a pious Jew. He makes this point by (1) speaking in Hebrew (probably here meaning Aramaic), (2) addressing the audience as *brothers and fathers* (v. 1), (3) claiming immediately to be a Jew (v. 3), (4) recounting his impeccable Pharisaic education at the feet of Gamaliel (v. 3; cf. 5:34-38), (5) claiming to share a zeal for God with his audience (v. 3), and (6) appealing to the high priest and the whole council of elders as witnesses to his persecution of the church (vv. 4-5).

This affinity with his audience continues as Paul recounts his conversion experience in the form of a commissioning story, a form familiar to an audience steeped in the similar stories found in scripture (vv. 6-11). This is the second time Paul's conversion is narrated in Acts (see Acts 9:1-18), and there are both significant similarities and differences between the two accounts (and the third to be related later in chap. 26). Many of the differences may be explained by the fact that the audience with whom Paul is trying to relate to is Jewish (see Polhill 1992, 459–61 for a discussion of other differences). The dialogue between Paul and Jesus in the two accounts is nearly verbatim (compare vv. 7-8 with 9:4-5). The addition of *of Nazareth* to Jesus' name (v. 8) is appropriate for such a Jewish audience. Likewise, the description of Ananias as a pious Jew (v. 12) rather than a devout Christian (as in 9:10) again helps Paul establish his Jewishness with this Temple mob.

Also important in explaining the differences is the fact that Paul, not an omniscient narrator (as in chap. 9), is recounting the story, and thus Paul relates events as they unfolded to him. Hence the commission to go to the gentiles comes to Paul (vv. 17-21) and not to Ananias (9:15-16).

Again, Paul, like a good Jew, is praying in the Temple when Jesus commands him, *Go, for I will send you far away to the Gentiles* (v. 21). The brief mention of Stephen's stoning (where Paul was present, giving his approval, v. 20) prepares the readers for the response of the crowd.

Once Paul mentions the gentile mission, the mob is stirred against him again, throwing off their garments, tossing dust in the air, and shouting, *Away with such a fellow from the earth! For he should not be allowed to live* (vv. 22-23). In that sense, Paul's *defense* (as he calls it in v. 1) is a failure; his efforts to prove his "Jewishness" to the crowd finally give way to his conviction that he is called to be apostle to the gentiles.

Once again the tribune intervenes and decides to get to the bottom of this conflict by literally beating the answers out of Paul (v. 24). But just before he is to receive lashes, Paul reveals to the centurion what the reader already knows (see 16:37), namely, that Paul is a Roman citizen (v. 25), and flogging a Roman citizen was simply not an acceptable practice (see, e.g., Cicero, *Verrine Orations* 2.5.66). Paul has not purchased his Roman citizenship as did the tribune (who probably mentions the fact out of suspicion that Paul is lying); even better, he is a citizen by birth. Realizing he has bound and nearly flogged a Roman citizen, the tribune looks for an alternative plan for finding out the nature of the differences between Paul and the Jews.

22:30–23:11. Paul before the Sanhedrin. The tribune convenes a meeting of the SANHEDRIN and places Paul before them to speak (22:30). Paul begins with the assertion, *Brothers, up to this day I have lived my life with a clear conscience before God* (23:1). He is saying, in effect, that he has been obedient to his calling to the gentile mission (cf. 26:19). The high priest simply cannot accept that Paul's mission is indicative of his obedience to God and so orders Paul struck on the mouth (v. 2). Paul immediately responds with a sharp retort, *God will strike you, you white-washed wall! Are you sitting there to judge me according to the law, and yet in violation of the law you order me to be struck?* (v. 3). When observers point out to Paul that he has insulted the high priest (v. 4), Paul's tone changes rapidly, *I did not realize, brothers, that he was high priest; for it is written, "You shall not speak evil of a leader of your people"* (v. 5). The reader who notes a little irony here is probably not mistaken: Paul did not recognize the high priest (for whose organization he previously worked) because he was not acting like one might expect the leader of the people to act.

Paul then notices that both Sadducees and Pharisees are present on the council, and he attempts to redirect the focus of the debate from whether or not Paul is an observant Jew to a weighty theological issue, the question of the resurrection of the dead. Paul is really attempting to do more, however, than simply start a controversy among members of the Sanhedrin. Rather, his concern about *hope and resurrection* raised here continues to be an important theme throughout the defense even when it no longer creates controversy (see 24:15, 21; 28:20; see Tannehill 1990, 286–87). Nonetheless, Paul's words about resurrection here do spark a debate between the Sadducees who deny the doctrine of resurrection (as well as the existence of angels and spirits) and the Pharisees who affirm it. Note that Paul is speaking about a final eschatological resurrection of the dead (plural), not specifically of the resurrection of Christ. The Lukan Paul is seeking to emphasize the similarities between Christianity and segments of Judaism and thus lay the groundwork for more explicit claims later about the resurrection of Jesus (26:23). The Pharisees proclaim Paul's innocence (v. 9), much as Pilate, Herod, the penitent thief, and the centurion pronounced Jesus innocent (cf. Luke 23).

Once again, the tribune, fearing for Paul's safety, has him delivered back to the barracks. This scene ends with Paul as the recipient of yet another nocturnal christophany: *That night the Lord stood near him and said, "Keep up your courage! For just as you have testified for me in Jerusalem, so you must bear witness also in Rome"* (v. 11). The reason for the divine necessity for Paul to go to Rome is made clear: he is to *bear witness* there as he has in Jerusalem.

23:12-35. An ambush avoided. The resolve of the Jerusalem Jews against Paul is demonstrated by the next scene in which forty Jews take a solemn oath neither to eat nor drink until they had killed Paul (v. 12). They approached the Temple establishment (Saducean chief priests and elders) with a plan to take Paul by ambush (the absence of the more sympathetic Pharisees from this conspiracy is noteworthy).

The plan is thwarted by Paul's nephew, his sister's son. The young man reports the conspiracy first to Paul and then to the tribune with detailed accuracy (vv. 16-21). The tribune again acts decisively in Paul's behalf. After ordering Paul's nephew to tell no one of their conversation, the tribune orders an impressive guard (200 soldiers, seventy horsemen, and 200 spearmen) to transport Paul to Caesarea where the procurator FELIX resides (vv. 23-24). In addition, the tribune drafts a letter to be delivered to Felix.

This letter is interesting for both its form and content. In form, the letter follows the threefold salutation typical of ancient letter writing: the sender, the recipient, and the word of greeting. For the first time, the readers learn the tribune's name, CLAUDIUS LYSIAS (v. 26). Lysias is a complex character. He has acted decisively in Paul's behalf, thrice intervening in life-threatening situations (21:31-36; 23:10; 23:23-25). He has also been persistent in his investigations to learn the facts about Paul, and he has been willing to accept new information about Paul (to believe that he was an Egyptian insurrectionist, to accept that he was a Roman citizen, and now to believe the reports of Jewish conspiracy to kill Paul). But his letter reveals that Lysias also is willing to rearrange and suppress the facts to put himself in a better light. In the letter to Felix, Lysias suggests that he intervened in Paul's behalf after learning that he was a Roman citizen (v. 27). If this account were true, Paul presumably would not have been bound. But the reader knows that Lysias had at first thought Paul was a revolutionary and learned of Paul's citizenship only *after* he had placed him in chains and nearly had him flogged. Lysias's self-assurance in decision making is marred with interests of self-protection. Other political figures encountered later will demonstrate a similar complexity in character.

Both Paul and the letter are safely delivered to Felix (vv. 31-33). After learning that Paul is from Cilicia and within his jurisdiction, Felix promises to give Paul a hearing when his accusers arrive. Meanwhile Paul is kept under house arrest in Herod's headquarters (v. 35).

Paul before Felix, Festus, and Agrippa, 24:1–26:32

This section is filled with legal scenes and defense speeches. Here Paul confronts the political establishment—the Roman officials Felix and FESTUS and the Jewish king AGRIPPA. But a close reading of these passages reveals that Paul is not the only one "on trial": he is joined by the Christian gospel. Paul not only defends himself; he bears witness to the Christian faith whether before the Jews, the Roman PROCURATOR, or even Caesar himself.

The political establishment presents a less than consistent picture. On the one hand, the Romans protect Paul and testify to his innocence. On the other, they are willing to distort the facts in order to portray themselves in the most favorable light—this is true of Lysias, Felix, and Festus. Both Felix and Festus withhold justice from Paul, despite his innocence, in their desire to "do a favor for the Jews" (see 24:27). Each episode is examined in more detail below.

24:1-27. Paul before Felix. When Ananias and some of the elders arrive in Caesarea some five days after Paul, they bring with them their own attorney, TER-TULLUS, who uses his persuasive skills in oration to present the case against Paul to Felix (v. 1). There are several interesting points about Tertullus's speech. The *captatio benevolentia*, in which Felix is praised, is nearly as long as the formal complaint lodged against Paul (vv. 2-4). Further, this section of praise is excessive. Tertullus uses all the right phrases to curry Felix's favor. Felix has brought much *peace* to the Jews (v. 2). He has enacted reforms that grew out of his *foresight* or "providence" (v. 2). And, Tertullus continues, all Jews everywhere and in every way are grateful to Felix for his benevolence (v. 3). The reader who knows the facts of Felix's reign, flawed as it was with countless rebellions by disgruntled Jews, however, will see through this poorly veiled attempt to influence Felix through flattery (see Tacitus, *Ann* 12:54; Josephus, *Ant* 20.181-182).

When Tertullus finally gets to the charges against Paul, the reader notes that the accusation has taken a decidedly political direction from the complaints lodged earlier in 21:21. Here Tertullus combines the charge that Paul is profaning the Temple (v. 6) with the more serious charge, from Felix's point of view, that Paul is a *pestilent fellow* who is *an agitator among all the Jews throughout all the world, and a ringleader of the sect of the Nazarenes* (v. 5). This charge of sedition would not be taken lightly by Felix, in light of the previous Jewish riots in Felix's territory of Judea (see Josephus, *BJ* 6.124-28). Tertullus concludes his speech by inviting Felix to examine Paul for himself, but Tertullus does not supply any supporting evidence or witnesses for his accusations (a point Paul will capitalize on in his rebuttal). The best Tertullus can do is produce other Jews who simply maintain the truth of his charges (v. 9).

Rather than conduct his own investigation at this point, Felix nods to Paul (v. 10) to present his defense, which he does (v. 10-21). Like Tertullus, Paul begins with a *captatio benevolentiae*, but Paul limits his "praise" to the simple acknowledgement that Felix's experience as *judge over this nation* ought to qualify him to judge the veracity of the charges brought against Paul (v. 10). Paul counters Tertullus's sweeping and ambiguous charges with a detailed narration of the events of twelve days ago. Paul had no past history of inciting people to riot (v. 12); Paul had come to Jerusalem to worship, not stir up a rebellion (v. 11). His accusers have no way of making their case stand up under scrutiny (v. 13).

After this string of denials, Paul is willing to make a confession: he is a member of *the Way,* what the Jews call a *sect,* and as such, Paul confesses, he worships *the God of our ancestors, believing everything laid down according to the law or written in the prophets* (v. 14). Such a confession could hardly be found objectionable to Paul's opponents.

Paul then goes on to point out that he shares a hope in the resurrection of the dead with his accusers (Sadducees notwithstanding). Then in vv. 17-19, he re sponds to Tertullus's charge that he had tried to desecrate the Temple (v. 6). To the contrary, Paul was conducting himself as a pious Jew, bringing alms, making sacrifice, and completing the rite of purification—all without any disturbance (v. 18). The uproar, Paul claims, was caused by Jews from Asia who are not even at the trial to bring their charges firsthand (v. 19).

Paul concludes his speech by making explicit the true nature of the charge against him. His crime, he says, *was this one sentence that I called out while standing before them, "It is about the resurrection of the dead that I am on trial before you today"* (v. 21). Paul is not guilty of political sedition or even violation of Jewish law. What is at stake here is the *resurrection of the dead*—the "fundamental issue that unites Pharisaic Judaism with Christianity and divides non-Christian Judaism" (Krodel 1986, 441).

Felix's decision to postpone judgment until Lysias arrives appears at first reading to be a cautious and reasonable choice by a competent judge: he is, after all, *rather well informed about the Way* (v. 22). Felix even gives Paul some freedom under a loosely designed house arrest and arranges to hear him again (v. 23). But this initial favorable impression of Felix changes quickly.

Felix and his Jewish wife Drusilla (on the infelicities of this marriage, see Josephus, *Ant* 20.139-44) hear Paul *speak concerning faith in Jesus Christ* (v. 24). However offensive such talk may have been to the Jewess Drusilla is left to the imagination of the reader. What does disturb Felix is Paul's discussion of *justice, self-control, and the coming judgment* (v. 25). Felix's own inadequacy in the area of self-control is revealed in his hope to receive bribe money from Paul, a desire that motivates frequent conversations between Felix and Paul. His lack of justice is demonstrated when he leaves Paul in prison for two years in order *to grant the Jews a favor* (v. 27). "Thus Roman justice is undermined by an unjust administrator" (Tannehill 1990, 302).

25:1-12. Paul before Festus. The change in administration from Felix to Festus raises new hope that justice may be done for Paul. This hope is sustained when Festus refuses to grant a favor to the Jews against Paul, a favor they no doubt had come to expect from the Roman procurator through their dealings with Felix. Underlying the request to transfer Paul to Jerusalem was the old plot to ambush him along the way (v. 3). Festus replies that Paul would stay in Caesarea and if they had any accusations against Paul, those with authority should travel there along with Festus and present them personally before him (vv. 5-6).

In little more than a week, both Festus and the Jews have arrived to hear Paul (v. 6). Unsubstantiated charges are once again hurled against Paul (v. 7). And within these eight or ten days, Festus has evidently learned the political necessity of doing favors for the Jews (v. 9; see Tannehill 1990, 306-307) and asks Paul if he wishes to go to Jerusalem for trial. Paul's response is no little shock: rather than a simple yes or no, Paul once again maintains his innocence and appeals to Caesar for his trial (v. 11). That Paul is aware that he can receive no fair trial at the hands of Festus is hinted at in his words, "No one can *grant* me as *a favor* to them [the Jews]," echoing the narrator's statement that Festus wished "to grant the Jews a favor" (author trans.).

Historically, Paul's appeal to the emperor, the *provocatio*, is shrouded in mystery. Whether Paul thought he could have a fairer hearing before the emperor (then Nero) than before Festus is probably less important than his desire to fulfill his destiny to bear witness to the gospel before the emperor in Rome (19:21; 23:11;

27:24). Festus and his council, sensing an opportunity to rid themselves of a difficult case, formally ratify Paul's request with the terse judgment, *You have appealed to the emperor; to the emperor you will go* (v. 12).

25:13–26:32. Paul before Agrippa. After a few days, King Agrippa and his sister, Bernice, arrive to greet the newly appointed Festus (v. 13). Festus uses this opportunity to involve Agrippa in the proceedings against Paul, and more importantly, to offer a public defense of his own actions. In these two speeches by Festus (25:14-22 and 24-27), Luke subtly discloses Festus's hypocrisy without explicitly labeling it as such (see Tannehill 1990, 310–15). Like Lysias and Felix before him, Festus tries to put his public image in the best light possible. His concern for justice that permeates his speech is notably absent from the narrator's account (25:1-12). His summary of the events surrounding Paul are decidedly biased toward his own self-interests. Festus correctly reports that he refused to turn Paul over to the Jews without a proper trial (25:16), but he glosses over his real purpose in proposing a Jerusalem trial for Paul (to gain the favor of the Jews, 25:9) by claiming that he *was at a loss how to investigate these questions* (25:20). Agrippa responds by requesting an audience with Paul, which Festus promptly arranges (25:22).

In his second address, however, Festus continues his distortion. First he exaggerates the pressure he is under from the Jews. He claims that the *whole Jewish community . . . both in Jerusalem and here* [Caesarea], petitioned him (25:24), while the narrator indicates only *the high priests and the leaders of the Jews* brought charges against Paul (25:2). Despite this (albeit exaggerated) pressure, Festus claims that Paul *had done nothing deserving death* (25:25). But when Paul had appealed to Caesar, there was nothing Festus could do but grant the request. If one takes Festus's remarks at face value, then Paul's request is incomprehensible. If, however, his speeches are understood as a cover-up, then Paul's appeal to Caesar to escape the incompetence if not corruption of this judge is even more understandable.

The decision to send Paul to Rome relieves one problem but creates another. Festus is no longer responsible for rendering a judgment in Paul's case, but he must specify the charges against Paul in a letter to the emperor. Perhaps his motivation to include Agrippa in the process is grounded in the desire to have someone to share the responsibility should the emperor determine the charges against Paul are of no substance, but rather are due to the incompetence of the local administration. Whatever the reason, Paul's address before Agrippa is "his most important speech before his most distinguished audience. The King Agrippa scene is as close as we shall get to seeing a speech before the king at Rome" (Pervo 1990, 87).

Indeed, Paul's speech in this scene allows him to fulfill the words of Jesus directed at his followers: "You will be brought before kings and governors for my name's sake" (Luke 21:13). The speech falls into five parts: (1) the *captatio benevolentiae* in which Paul (again following convention) curries the favor of Agrippa (26:2-3), (2) a summary of his Jewish background and credentials (26:4-8), (3) his work as persecutor of Christians (26:9-11), (4) a recounting of his conversion that here has more of the character of a prophetic call or commissioning (26:12-18), and (5) a brief summary of his missionary activity (26:19-23). The speech climaxes with Paul's assertion that the *Messiah must suffer* and be *the first to rise from the dead* (26:23). Paul's defense speech has a thorough christological grounding.

Festus interrupts Paul's speech at this point and accuses him of being *out of your mind* (26:24). For the first time in this scene, Paul addresses Festus, but only to make the point that Agrippa is fully aware of the things about which Paul speaks. None of the things associated with the Christian community has been *done in a corner* (26:26); rather Paul has made his case publicly in the marketplace and in the synagogues.

Agrippa replies to Paul's question about whether he believes the prophets with a sharp retort: *Are you so quickly persuading me to become a Christian?* (26:28). Paul concludes his defense with an object lesson: *Whether quickly or not, I pray to God that not only you but all who are listening to me today might become such as I am* [i.e., a follower of Jesus]—*except for these chains* (26:29).

But Agrippa has heard enough and rises to leave with Festus and Bernice. He does not depart without making this observation, *This man is doing nothing to deserve death or imprisonment* (26:31), and for the fifth time Paul's innocence is declared (see 23:9, 29; 25:18-19, 25). By now, the response that Paul could have been set free if he had not appealed to the emperor (26:32) sounds more than a little lame. The readers have no reason to think that Festus and Agrippa would have released Paul, regardless of his innocence or his appeal. The voyage to Rome begins.

The Sea Voyage to Rome, 27:1–28:31

In the last unit of Acts, the long-awaited journey to Rome is narrated. Luke returns to his use of first-person narration in these chapters, and much of the material shares common features with other sea voyage stories: shipwreck, narrow escapes, suspense, conflict, and high drama. This unit falls into two parallel panels, with the first and last being the most detailed.

> A   Paul journeys to Malta, 27:1-44
>   B   Paul in Malta, 28:1-10
> A' Paul journeys to Rome, 28:11-16
>   B' Paul in Rome, 28:17-31

Of course, Paul's voyage to Malta is determined by where he and his companions are washed ashore while his voyage to Rome has been an intentional destination for much of the second half of Acts. These units are examined in more detail below.

27:1-44. To Malta. The journey begins in Caesarea when Paul is entrusted to the custodial care of a centurion named Julius, who shows kindness to Paul (vv. 1-3). Verses 1-12 are both a prologue and a summary: in eight verses Luke describes Paul and the others on board setting sail for Italy and stopping at four different ports along the way, culminating with Paul's warning not to continue past *Fair Havens*.

The storm (vv. 13-38) and shipwreck (vv. 39-44) are narrated in detailed and technical nautical language.

In a way typical of sea-voyage stories, Luke describes a variety of settings through which Paul and his fellow prisoners, the sailors, and Julius and his fellow soldiers pass: Sidon, Myra (in Lycia), Cnidus (or nearby), Fair Havens (on Crete), and Malta. In the process, they pass near several other cities, regions, or islands: Cilicia and Pamphylia, Lasea, Phoenix, Cauda, and Syrtis. But the one setting that remains constant throughout this voyage is the sea (both the Mediterranean and the Adriatic), and this setting is the most important for understanding the significance of this passage.

In both ancient Jewish and Greek literature, the sea was viewed sometimes as an evil or hostile place of chaos and confusion, sometimes as a vehicle through which divine forces punish wickedness. Homer tells how Odysseus's crew was killed in a shipwreck as punishment for destroying Helios's cattle (*Odyssey* 12.127-41, 259-446). In Chariton's *Chaereas and Callirhoe*, evil persons are drowned at sea and the just are spared (3.3.10, 18, 3.4.9-10; cited by Talbert 1984, 101). In the OT, God uses the sea to reverse creation and judge evil humanity (Gen 6–8); God uses a sea to destroy the Egyptians and rescue the Israelites (Exod 14); God employs a storm to persuade a recalcitrant prophet to speak (Jonah 1). The same view is held in postbiblical Judaism. In the Babylonian Talmud (*B.Mes.*, 58b-59), Rabbi Gamaliel is spared from the raging sea only after declaring his innocence before God (see Talbert 1984, 102).

Thus, both Greek and Jewish readers would understand the potential disasters involved here. If Paul perishes at sea, he is no doubt guilty of the charges leveled against him; if he is spared, then he is honored with divine vindication. The closing note to this section, where Paul and his traveling entourage are brought safely to land, reveals God's evaluation of Paul and his mission (v. 44).

Luke also uses this sea voyage with all its colorful details and rich imagery to depict the symbolic death and resurrection of Paul, much as he narrates the imprisonment and release of Peter in Acts 12. Both prison and shipwreck are common metaphors for death in antiquity. Night, the disappearance of heavenly luminaries (v. 20; cf. Luke 23:44-45), and the loss of hope (v. 20; cf. Luke 24:21) all echo the passion of Jesus and allude to Paul's symbolic death. On the other hand, references to daylight, the third day (21:19), a shared meal (vv. 33-35; cf. Luke 24:30-31), and Paul's deliverance from the tomb of the sea (v. 44) all point to a kind of symbolic resurrection.

Luke also deepens the characterization of Paul as a Christian benefactor through a description of his words and deeds. Two are especially noteworthy. After taking harbor in *Fair Havens* (v. 8), Paul predicts the dangers that lie before him and his fellow travelers: *Sirs, I can see that the voyage will be with danger and much heavy loss, not only of the cargo and the ship, but also of our lives* (v. 10). Like a prophet of old, Paul's words are ignored by his audience (vv. 11-12), and finally under divine direction he modifies his original prophecy to assure his companions that *God has granted safety to all those who are sailing with you* (v. 24). Still, Paul's heroic role as leader and visionary is strengthened by these words of prophetic insight, not to mention that Paul alone is granted direct discourse throughout this passage.

Equally important is the scene described in vv. 33-35 where Paul urges his companions to take food. The eucharistic symbolism of this passage is quite apparent: *After he had said this, he took bread; and giving thanks to God in the presence of all, he broke it and began to eat* (v. 35; cf. Luke 22:19). While perhaps not strictly bespeaking an observance of the Lord's Supper since most of the company are not believers, this meal anticipates deliverance in some sense similar to the promise of deliverance present in the Lord's Supper. This position is supported by the repeated references to "salvation" or "deliverance" throughout this section (vv. 20, 31, 34, 43, 44; 28:1, 4), no doubt "a reminder to a Christian reader that the same God who delivered the storm-tossed voyagers from physical harm is the God who in Christ brings ultimate salvation and true eternal life" (Polhill 1992, 527).

28:1-10. In Malta. Paul and all his companions are delivered safely from the shipwreck and find themselves on the island of Malta. Here the theme of Paul's vindication continues. Just as nature was understood to be a vehicle of divine vindication or retribution, so also was the animal kingdom (see *t.Sanh.* 8:3; *y.Ber.* 5:1; cited by Talbert 1984, 102). Paul survived the shipwreck, but will he survive the bite of the viper who fastened itself to Paul's hand while he gathers firewood (vv. 2-4)? The natives think not, assuming the snakebite is punishment for some heinous crime such as murder and that Paul is being punished by the Greek goddess of "Justice" (v. 5). But once gain, Paul is vindicated by God, and, unharmed, he shakes the serpent into the fire. By now there is no need to correct for the reader the native's misperception that Paul is a god (v. 6; cf. 10:25-26; 14:11-15).

The final act of Paul on Malta also confirms his role as a righteous representative of a beneficent God. When the leading man of the island, Publius, falls ill, Paul cures him *by praying and putting his hands on him* (v. 8). In return, Paul the Christian benefactor is the recipient of great honor and provisions at the hands of the Maltese. Christians, Luke seems to say, have no corner on hospitality and benefaction.

28:11-16. To Rome. After three months of winter, Paul and company set sail again. Three days in Syracuse, one day at Rhegium, and they join a community of believers in Puteoli where they lodge for a week. Paul next travels to Rome and takes the decisive step in fulfilling the earlier theophanic prophecy (*Do not be afraid, Paul; you must stand before the emperor*, 27:24). Having literally survived hell and high water (symbolized by the Satanic serpent and the storm at sea), Paul and crew finally come to Rome (see Pervo 1990, 92). The scene ends with a reminder that Paul, despite his immediate past heroism, is still a prisoner: *When we came into Rome, Paul was allowed to live by himself, with the soldier who was guarding him* (v. 16).

28:17-31. In Rome. The end of a book is no less important than its beginning. Luke chooses to end this narrative neither with a confrontation between Paul and the emperor, nor with a narration of Paul's martyrdom, but rather by focusing on Paul's dialogue with the Roman Jews. The closing scene is organized into three parts: Paul's first (vv. 17-22) and second (vv. 23-28) encounters with the Jews, and the final summary statement about Paul's ministry in Rome (vv. 30-31).

In the first encounter with the Roman Jews, Paul recounts the events of Acts 22–26. In so doing, Luke preserves what is most important for his readers to retain from that long stretch of narrative and speeches. Most important is Paul's claim that he *had done nothing against our people or the customs of our ancestors* (v. 17). Further, his appeal to Caesar did not mean that Paul intended to bring a charge against the Jewish nation (v. 19). To the contrary, Paul insists that *it is for the sake of the hope of Israel that I am bound with this chain* (v. 20). Throughout this speech, Paul maintains that he has remained a loyal Jew and that his mission to the gentiles is not based on an anti-Jewish foundation. The Jews respond by saying that they would like to hear more of Paul's thinking, especially regarding the Christian *sect* that is spoken against everywhere (v. 22).

In the second encounter with the Roman Jews, a familiar pattern emerges: Paul is first heard favorably by the Jews, is then resisted, and finally turns to the gentiles (see 13:42-48; 18:5-7; 19:8-10). Once again, his proclamation of Jesus divides his audience: *Some were convinced by what he had said, while others refused to believe* (v. 24). In his parting statement to them Paul quotes Isa 6:9-10, a harsh indictment of the dullness of ears, eyes, and heart of the Jewish people. Individual Jews may continue to believe, but Israel as a nation, at least at the time of Luke's writing, has rejected the new thing God has done in and through Christ Jesus. Now for the third and final time, Paul turns to the gentiles and thus opens up the *salvation of God* to all who would come (v. 28; cf. 13:46; 18:6).

The Book of Acts ends with the notice that Paul spent the next two years living under house arrest at his own expense (v. 30). Mention of *two years* in Acts often refers to periods of special blessing (see 18:11; 19:10; see Talbert 1984, 104; although cf. 24:27). The last claim of the book is that Paul preached the kingdom of God (cf. 1:6) *without hindrance* (v. 31), or "unhindered." The focus subtly shifts from Paul the messenger to the message he is proclaiming, the Christian gospel.

Frank Stagg has persuasively demonstrated that this final word—unhindered—sums up the message of Acts: the Gospel has overcome all human-made prejudice and every geographical, social, ethnic, gender, and theological barrier (Stagg 1955). In this regard, Pervo's words are apropos: "Luke's own last word is a perfect summary of his writings, a one-word closure, i.e., at the same time, an opening, a bright and invigorating bid to the future, an assurance that 'the ends of the earth' is not the arrival at a boundary, but realization of the limitless promises of the dominion of God" (Pervo 1990, 96).

The gospel is unhindered because of the sovereignty of God who ultimately insures its triumph in the face of adversity. But from Luke's perspective, this "unhindered" gospel remains an "unfinished" gospel. The gospel is unfinished because of the grace of God who ultimately insures that its completion can occur when all have had the opportunity to hear about the "kingdom of God" and the "Lord Jesus Christ." Unfettered yet unfinished, the gospel can only be completed when the readers finally take up the challenge to fulfill the prophecy uttered at the beginning of the first of Luke's two volumes proclaimed by John the Baptist (who also quotes the words of the prophet Isaiah): "all flesh shall see the salvation of God" (Luke 3:6).

Works Cited

Danker, Frederick. 1982. *Benefactor: Epigraphic Study of a Graeco-Roman and N.T. Semantic Field.*

Fitzmyer, Joseph A. 1981. *The Gospel according to Luke I–IX.* AncB.

Funk, Robert. 1988. *The Poetics of Biblical Narrative.*

Garrett, Susan R. 1989. *The Demise of the Devil: Magic and the Demonic in Luke's Writings.*

Gill, David. 1974. "The Structure of Acts 9," *Bib* 55:546–48.

Haenchen, Ernst. 1971. *The Acts of the Apostles.*

Krodel, Gerhard. 1986. *Acts.* AugCNT.

Johnson, Luke T. 1977. *The Literary Function of Possessions in Luke-Acts.* SBLDS 39.

Martin, Clarice J. 1989. "A Chamberlain's Journey and the Challenge of Interpretation for Liberation," *Semeia* 47: 105–35.

Neyrey, Jerome H. 1991. "The Symbolic Universe of Luke-Acts: 'They Turned the World Upside Down'," in *The Social World of Luke-Acts: Models for Interpretation,* ed. Neyrey, 271–304.

Pervo, Richard I. 1990. *Luke's Story of Paul.*

Pilch, John J. 1991. "Sickness and Healing in Luke-Acts," in *The Social World of Luke-Acts,* 181-209.

Polhill, John B. 1992. *Acts.* NAC.

Stagg, Frank. 1955. *The Book of Acts.* 1990. "Apostles, Acts of the," MDB.

Talbert, Charles H. 1984. *Acts.* Knox Preaching Guides. 1990. "Luke, Gospel of," MDB.

Tannehill, Robert C. 1990. *The Narrative Unity of Luke-Acts.* Vol. 2. *The Acts of the Apostles.*

Romans

Dan O. Via [MCB 1223-1162]

Introduction

Across the centuries the Christian church has found Paul's letter to the Romans to be one of its richest theological resources.

Genuineness, Unity, and Place in the Canon

Genuineness and unity. Scholars have generally concluded that PAUL was in fact the author of the whole original letter as established on the basis of the best manuscripts. Although the argument is inevitably somewhat circular, Romans is held to be in broad agreement with the other letters considered to be genuine writings of Paul in style, vocabulary, and thought. We shall see below that in light of the textual (i.e., manuscript) evidence there has been debate about whether the original letter was composed of chaps. 1–14, 1–15, or 1–16.

One should note that there have been some exceptions to the general consensus that Paul is the author of the whole original letter and that the letter is a coherent unity. Three examples will be mentioned. Rudolf Bultmann argued that Romans contains several later glosses (2:1; 2:16; 6:17b; 7:25b; 8:1; 10:17; 13:5) (Bultmann 1967). Walter Schmithals maintained that our Romans is composed of two earlier letters of Paul plus some fragments. According to Schmithals, letter A contained Rom 1:1–4:25; 5:12–11:36; 15:8-13, and letter B consisted of 12:1-21; 13:8-10; 14:1–15:4a, 7, 5-6; 15:14-32; 16:21-23; 15:33 (Schmithals 1975, 180, 189). Gloss and partition theories are not supported by ms. evidence.

Perhaps the most radical challenge to the genuineness and unity of Romans came from J. C. O'Neill, who argued that not only had short marginal comments of others been taken into the text but also editors had supplemented the text with substantial interpolations. Among the extensive sections that O'Neill denied to Paul are 1:18-32; 2:1-16; 2:17-29; 5:12-21; 7:14-25; 9:1-29; 10:16–11:36; 12:1–15:13 (O'Neill 1975, 14, 41–42, 49, 53, 96, 131–32, 155, 177, 192). O'Neill strained hard to explain why the manuscript evidence does not support his position (O'Neill 1975, 14–15) and generally based his argument on three questionable presuppositions: (1) that Paul always argued in a single-mindedly logical line and that, therefore, any inconsistencies have to be attributed to someone else; (2) that an author (Paul) is more likely to be consistent than a commentator; and (3) that Paul always used terms in the same sense.

Canonical Location. The individual title "To the Romans" suggests that Paul's letters became widely known as parts of a collection with a comprehensive title something like "The Letters of Paul." The most plausible explanation for this collection is that Paul's associates began a continuing "Pauline school" that sought to preserve and extend his influence. The first clear evidence for the existence of the Pauline collection, however, is provided by the second-century semi-gnostic MARCION, whose arrangement places Romans after Galatians and 1 and 2 Corinthians (Knox 1982, 356–57; Gamble 1985, 41).

While Marcion gives us the first definite evidence, it seems probable that the collection originated earlier, in the late first or early second century. Had Marcion's collection been the first one, there would likely have been "orthodox" suspicion of Paul. But there is no indication of second-century hostility to Paul except from heterodox Jewish Christianity. Moreover, the reference of IGNATIUS (early second century) to "Paul in every letter" suggests that he knew a Pauline collection. The order of letters in this early collection was based on the length of the letters, but there seem to have been two editions of the collection based on the fact that length was assessed in different ways. In both cases the order ran from longest to shortest. The first approach regarded all letters to a given community as one unit and produced the order 1–2 Corinthians, Romans, Ephesians, 1–2 Thessalonians, Galatians, Philippians, Colossians (Philemon?). The second approach considered each individual letter as a separate unit and produced the order Romans, 1 Corinthians, 2 Corinthians, Ephesians, Galatians, Philippians, Colossians, 1 Thessalonians, 2 Thessalonians, (Philemon?) (Gamble 1985, 40–45; Knox 1982, 356–57).

Place of Writing and Date

Place. As Paul draws to the conclusion of the letter, he tells his readers that he has evangelized the Mediterranean world from JERUSALEM to ILLYRICUM (roughly the former modern Yugoslavia and Albania) and therefore has no more place to work in the East (15:19, 23). He hopes to extend the preaching of the gospel to Spain and to visit Rome on his way there (15:23-24, 28), but first he must go to Jerusalem to carry the money that he has collected in MACEDONIA and ACHAIA for the poor among the Jerusalem Christians (15:25-26).

Where is he as he writes? CORINTH is the most likely place. In the CORINTHIAN CORRESPONDENCE Paul is also concerned about the offering to be sent from the gentile churches of Achaia and GALATIA to Jerusalem, and he contemplates that he may make the trip to Jerusalem himself (1 Cor 16:1-4; 2 Cor 8:1-14; 9:1-5). In addition, PHOEBE, whom he recommends and who may be the bearer of the letter, is a deacon in the church of CENCHREAE, the port of Corinth (16:1-2). Beyond that GAIUS, his host (16:23), may well be the Gaius of 1 Cor 1:14, one of Paul's Corinthian converts. And ERASTUS (16:23) also could be loosely associated with Corinth (Acts 19:21-22; 2 Tim 4:20).

Date. Paul was apparently in Corinth three times, and Romans would have been written during the third of these sojourns. That means the writing occurred late in his life. The three-missionary-journey scheme in Acts would call for dating the letter late in the third journey (Acts 20:1-3). While the Acts format may contain individual items that are historically accurate, the scheme as a whole, and especially its stress on Paul's dependence on Jerusalem, is historically suspect. Nevertheless, Paul's letters confirm that he was a travelling missionary and suggest that he wrote Romans late in his career.

The one certainly datable event during Paul's missionary activities is the proconsulship of the Roman GALLIO in Corinth, whose tenure in office lasted from the spring of 51 to the spring of 52. During his first stay in Corinth Paul was haled before Gallio, according to Acts 18:12-17, by hostile Jews. It is plausible to suppose that the third visit to Corinth, the occasion for writing Romans, was sometime around 55 or 56.

Manuscript Evidence and Destination

Paul did not found the church in Rome and had not visited it prior to the writing of the letter. Why did he write this letter to Rome? Did he in fact write it *to Rome*? It seems altogether probable that the original letter was addressed by Paul directly to the Roman church, but that contention has not gone unchallenged.

One reason for challenging an original Roman destination is that the words "in Rome" are omitted in 1:7, 15 in a few manuscripts of a Western textual type. If this omission were the original reading, then it might be argued that Paul wrote the letter as a circular one, not intended for any one particular church. But the evidence is strongly in favor of including "in Rome" in the text. The great preponderance of manuscript evidence supports it. Romans 1:13 shows that the letter is written to a particular church that he has wanted to visit but has thus far been prevented from visiting. It can also be demonstrated that Romans as a whole can be rather specifically connected with a particular situation in the church at Rome.

The major textual problem in Romans is that the final doxology (16:25-27) appears in several different places in the manuscript tradition. The doxology itself is probably post-Pauline (see commentary), but it must have been composed quite early, and its placement bears on the question of the various versions of Romans that circulated in the early church. The complex manuscript tradition supports the following six configurations.

(1) 1:1–16:23 + doxology
(2) 1:1–14:23 + doxology + 15:1–16:23 + doxology
(3) 1:1–14:23 + doxology + 15:1–16:24
(4) 1:1–16:24
(5) 1:1–15:33 + doxology + 16:1-23
(6) 1:1–14:23 + 16:24 + doxology (Metzger 1975, 534)

The evidence suggests that at an early date three versions of Romans were in circulation: Rom 1–14, Rom 1–15, and Rom 1–16. Each will be briefly assessed.

Romans 1–14 is probably not the original. The manuscript evidence is weaker than it is for the other alternatives, and the thought of 15:1-13 shows no break with that of chap. 14. A tradition going back to ORIGEN says that Marcion cut off chaps. 15–16, and we can understand why he might have. He would have wanted to remove the personal material in 15:14-33 and chap. 16. And his antipathy for the OT would have prompted him to excise 15:1-13 as he did chaps. 4 and 9–11 (Manson 1991, 9–11).

A somewhat stronger case can be made for Rom 1–15 as the original. Only one manuscript supports it (the PAPYRUS P^{46} which shows the concluding doxology after 15:33), but it is the oldest Greek manuscript of Paul (ca. 200) and represents the early Alexandrian text, generally considered the best. Moreover, Rom 16 with its many greetings to named individuals and its biting criticism of false teachings in 16:17-20a seems very different in content from chap. 15. The preceding factors have generated some arguments that Rom 16 was a separate letter of Paul and that it was sent to EPHESUS, not Rome. (1) Paul knows more people than he would have known in Rome, but he would have had many friends in Ephesus where he had a long ministry. (2) Some of the people greeted in Rom 16 are explicitly connected with ASIA, the province surrounding Ephesus: Prisca and Aquila (Acts 18:24-26; Rom 16:3), Epaenetus (Rom 16:5). (3) Paul knows some of these people too well for them to belong to a church he has never visited. For example, he knows who have house churches meeting in their homes (16:5, 15) and knows the identity of household groups (16:10, 11). (4) Rom 16:17-20 is inappropriately sharp for the Roman situation but could have been directed to a church like Ephesus where Paul had long worked. (5) Rom 15:33 has the solemn tone of a conclusion (Kümmel 1965, 222–26; Knox 1982, 364–68; Manson 1991, 12–13).

Similar arguments can be used to support the view that Paul wrote all of Rom 1–16 to Ephesus and 1–15 to Rome (Manson 1991, 11–13).

On the other side arguments have been brought forward against a connection between Rom 16 (or 1–16) and Ephesus and against the independence of chap. 16. (1) While there are other examples of letters composed primarily of greetings, there seems to be no other case in the Pauline corpus of combining letters to more than one church. (2) Inscriptions support the currency of the names Urbanus, Phlegon, Persis, and Asyncritus in Rome in the first century but not in Ephesus. (3) Paul seems not to have singled out individuals for greetings in churches that he did found. (4) Rom 15:33 is not a characteristic Pauline conclusion. Typically the peace wish (Rom 15:33) preceded (Gal 6:16; 1 Thes 5:23) the concluding benediction, which always makes reference to grace, an element lacking in Rom 15:33 (Lampe 1991, 216–17; Gamble 1977, 53–54, 84, 90; Ziesler 1989, 21). It should be pointed out, however, that this is not a strong argument because it could be held that an original fifteen-chapter version of Romans contained a grace benediction following 15:33.

John Knox maintained that the arguments for Ephesus and Rome cancelled each other out and that neither should be regarded as the destination of Rom 16. Rather that chapter was written after Paul's time by someone in the Roman church in order to claim Paul's authority in the fight against false teaching (Knox 1954, 364–68). Knox's position has a good bit to commend it. However, the strongest manuscript evidence places the final doxology at the end of chap. 16. Moreover, in recent years additional arguments have been articulated in favor of connecting Rom 16 with the situation of the Roman church and of regarding that chapter as an integral part of Paul's original letter to the Romans. That is now the consensus position (Donfried 1991a, lxx).

These arguments in support of it may here be considered: (1) Paul might well have known many people in the Roman church because Jewish Christians expelled from Rome by the edict of CLAUDIUS (see next section), whom Paul met in Ephesus (and elsewhere), could have returned to Rome after Claudius' death. (2) Movement was easy in the ROMAN EMPIRE. (3) Paul need not actually have known all whom he greeted. (4) Rom 16:1-2 does resemble a letter of recommendation, but there are other examples of notes of recommendation within the conclusions of longer letters. (5) Other letters of Paul display the same concluding structure: (a) travel plans (1 Cor 16:5-9; Rom 15:22-29); (b) recommendation of a third party (1 Cor 16:10-11, 15-18; Rom 16:1-2); (c) final greeting (1 Cor 16:19-21; Rom 16:3-16) (Gamble 1977, 47–51, 85, 87, 89; Donfried 1991b, 48–49). (6) As for 16:17-20 the sterner tone may suggest that Paul realizes there are other issues in Rome than the ones he had addressed or he may have outside infiltrators in mind. Changes of tone within Paul's letters are not unusual (1 Cor 16:22; Phil 3:2, 18-19; 1 Thes 2:15-16), and in any case his addressing the readers here as "brothers" shows that his posture is not strongly polemical (Ziesler 1989, 23; Lampe 1991, 219; Wedderburn 1991, 15; Gamble 1977, 52).

Paul's purpose for the multiple greetings is to support the individuals who are named but even more to undergird his own credibility by associating himself with these people whom the Roman church knows and trusts. This would be important to do in a church that he did not establish (Lampe 1991, 219; Gamble 1977, 48, 92).

We have seen that it is quite plausible to suppose that Paul knew a number of people in the Roman church and that he knew at least some of them well and was in close touch with them. That would be because mobility was high in the Roman Empire and mail communication was quick and easy—seven or eight days between Corinth and Rome. Paul then could have had a good deal of specific knowledge about the situation of the church at Rome.

Occasion and Purpose

A good case then can be made for connecting Romans closely to a specific situation in the Roman church. But Paul's own situation and the one that he addresses in Rome both have many aspects, and the purposes that motivate his writing of the letter are more than one.

In assessing the occasion and purpose we have to take account not only of the situation in Rome but also of Paul's own situation and experiences. How do his successes, hardships, and conflicts in Galatia, Corinth, Ephesus, and elsewhere and his sense of having completed the evangelization of the East affect his posture? What impact do his intentions to visit not just Rome but also Jerusalem and Spain have on the content of the letter? And we must consider the character of the letter itself. While it is not at all a full, constructive statement of Paul's theology, it is relatively systematic and tightly argued. Whether or not it was Paul's intention to write such a letter, that nevertheless defines its nature. And while a convincing case can be made that the letter addresses a particular situation in Rome, it is by no means immediately obvious in what precise ways that situation is reflected in the letter.

Sometimes those who argue for a close relationship to a precise historical setting speak as if the only two alternatives are that the letter either is totally conditioned historically or is a timeless theological compendium unrelated to a specific setting. But that is not an adequate grasp of our interpretive task. The letter *is* historically conditioned. Thus the two real alternatives become is its meaning exhausted by its historical connectedness or does the meaning both reflect and transcend the setting? The more probable alternative is that the historical situation affects the meaning but does not account for everything in it.

Because the historical and theological context is complicated and the precise relationship of the letter to the Roman situation is not obvious, many have found the governing key to the meaning and purpose of Romans in some other factor: (1) it is a general theological treatise; (2) it reflects *Paul's* situation; (3) it has the imminent trip to Jerusalem primarily in view; (4) it is controlled by the hope of a mission to Spain. No one of these alone is an adequate explanation for the letter, but each must be considered for what it contributes to our understanding of it.

(1) According to Anders Nygren, Paul in Romans is dealing with a great theological issue on which hangs human life itself. It would be a misunderstanding of Romans and a constriction of its meaning to try to interpret it in the light of the accidental circumstances of the Roman setting, of which Paul had very little knowledge anyway (Nygren 1949, 4–8). Günther Bornkamm in a famous article held that while Paul had only a general knowledge of the Roman church, the letter grew out of the specifics of *Paul's* situation and is not a timeless theological treatise. However, Bornkamm ended up asserting that Romans lifts Paul's theology above the moment of definite situations and conflicts and into the sphere of the

eternally and universally valid (Bornkamm 1991, 20, 21, 28). This unexpected turn in Bornkamm's argument shows how hard it is to confine the meaning of Romans within any specific historical situation.

(2) That Romans is to be explained not in light of the Roman situation but in light of Paul's own was also argued by T. W. Manson. Paul sums up the position that he had reached as a result of his controversies in Galatia and Corinth over the relationship of law to gospel (Manson 1991, 14–15). Robert Karris sees Romans as dealing with theological and ethical issues in the light of solutions to problems Paul had reached in his earlier missionary work, and Karris questions why we should assume that all of Paul's letters must have been addressed to specific church situations (Karris 1991a, 82–123; 1991b, 127).

(3) Peter Lampe maintained that the purpose of the whole letter was to gain the confidence of the Romans so that they would support Paul's mission to Spain (Lampe 1991, 218). Paul does want their support (15:24, 28)—spiritual, material, or both. This reference, however, is too brief and casual and Paul's concern to clarify his understanding of the gospel for its own sake is too strong for the Spanish mission to be a major part of Paul's purpose (Klein 1991, 33).

(4) The collection that he was about to carry to Jerusalem was important to Paul because it grew out of his agreement with the Jerusalem leaders (Gal 2:10) and symbolized the oneness of Jewish and gentile believers. Jacob Jervell argues that the prominence of Jewish issues in Romans—the status of the law (7:7), whether Israel has an advantage (3:1), the ultimate fate of Israel (11:1, 11-12) and others—shows that the content of Rom 1:18–11:36 is the defense Paul expects to make in *Jerusalem*. He presents it to the Romans because he wants them on his side when he goes to Jerusalem (Jervell 1991, 56, 62–64).

It is certainly the case that Paul wants the Roman church to pray for his Jerusalem mission, to pray that the unbelieving Jews will not harm him and that Jewish Christians in Jerusalem will be willing to accept his offering (15:30-31). Paul is intently looking over his shoulder at Jerusalem as he writes to Rome, and that undoubtedly affects the content of the letter, but the prominence of Jewish issues is also explained by his own origin in Judaism and by the gentile-Jewish conflict in the Roman church. And that brings us to Rome.

The intended visit. Although Paul's past longing to visit Rome has been thwarted (in chap. 1 he does not say why), he now intends to come for the purpose of exercising his apostleship by preaching the gospel and gaining a harvest of obedient faith (1:5-7, 13, 15). The Romans fall within his obligation to preach to all categories of people (1:13-15). He modestly—or prudently—suggests also that he expects to receive a spiritual blessing from them (1:11-12).

How does this eagerness to preach in Rome square with Paul's statement in 15:20 that it has been his intention to preach where Christ has not already been named? This principle of action he now offers as the explanation for why he has not been able to come to Rome (15:22). He was preaching where the gospel had not been heard. But since Christ has been named in Rome and the church has been established independently of Paul, how can he now come to preach in Rome since he does not want to build on another's foundation (15:20)?

Most scholars have taken his statement in 15:20 to be a fixed policy. And if that is the case, there seems to be a conflict between that policy and his present hope to preach in Rome. Can the conflict be resolved?

According to Günter Klein, Paul's non-interference policy does not renounce all missionary activity in already Christianized areas. He will not build on another's foundation, but if there is a church that in Paul's view lacks an apostolic foundation, he is free to preach there. What is at stake is whether the church in Rome has actually been founded on Christ (see 1 Cor 3:10-11). Paul will preach in Rome because the Roman church lacks the fundamental kerygma (proclamation) and grounding in Christ (Klein 1991, 38–43).

This is an attractive theory that could explain much in Romans. But if Paul's posture in principle were that he could preach wherever a church was not founded on the apostolic preaching of Christ, and if Rome were such a church, he could have gone to Rome at any time. He need not have waited until he had evangelized the East (15:19-22).

Peter Stuhlmacher deals with the issue by connecting Paul's eagerness to preach in Rome (1:15) with his *past* desire in 1:13: he *had* intended to come and preach, but having been prevented, that is no longer his hope, and he will be satisfied with the mutual sharing of faith described in 1:11-12. That is not in conflict with the noninterference policy (Stuhlmacher 1991, 236–37).

But Paul's concrete elaboration of his strong sense of obligation to preach to all and the use of the present tense in 1:14 make it difficult to relegate his eagerness to preach in Rome in 1:15 to the past.

Karl Donfried has suggested the most convincing approach (Donfried 1991c, 45). Paul is not stating an unexceptionable policy in 15:20 but simply explaining why he has not been able to come to Rome. It has been his first responsibility to preach to those who have not heard the gospel. But now that he has completely evangelized the East—according to his understanding of his calling—and has no further place to work there, he is free to come to Rome where the gospel has already been heard. The purpose of Paul's visit will be to preach in Rome.

The visit and the letter. For the Hellenistic world generally and for Paul in particular a letter is understood as a substitute or surrogate for the presence of the sender and also the recipient. Paul states at one point that what he says by letter when absent, he does when present (2 Cor 10:11). In a somewhat formal and in-direct way a letter represents what happens in face-to-face human meetings: greeting-dialogue-farewell (Funk 1967; Petersen 1985, 53–55). The purpose of the letter then is the same as the purpose of the visit: to preach the gospel—in light of the Roman situation, his own situation, the intended missions to Jerusalem and

Spain, and in light of the capacity of the gospel to generate a certain logic or structure of thought irrespective of a particular situation.

The specific setting in the Roman church. This now needs further attention. The following scenario has been gaining increasing acceptance as the situation in the Roman church that Paul was addressing.

The Roman writer Suetonius (ca. 75–160) reports that the emperor CLAUDIUS expelled the Jews from Rome (in 49) because of rioting instigated by Chrestus. Chrestus is probably a corruption of Christus, and Suetonius may have thought that Christ was there in Rome at the time. These disturbances in the Jewish community probably refer to the conflict between law-abiding Jews and Jews who had come to believe in Jesus as the Messiah and had freed themselves from the Law of Moses. Among the Jews forced to leave the city would have been a number of Jewish Christians. There is no evidence that Claudius's edict of expulsion was ever re-scinded, but it was probably allowed to lapse after his death in 54, and that would have made it possible for Jews who had left Rome to return. We can imagine that many Jewish Christians availed themselves of the opportunity. Jewish Christians were then returning to a Christian community that had for several years been entirely—or almost so—in the hands of gentile Christians. Differences would have been present, and tensions would have developed. Paul's purpose is to interpret the gospel so as to present the theological basis upon which these groups with different experiences and theological positions can live with mutual acceptance and love as one body in Christ (12:3-8; 14:1; 15:7-10). How are the gentile majority and Jewish minority to relate to each other (e.g., Donfried 1991c, 48–49; Wiefel 1991, 92–96; Ziesler 1989, 11–12; Dunn 1988, xlviii–xlix, liii; Wedderburn 1991, 55–56)?

The composition of the Roman Christian community needs to be further ex-amined. The Jewish quarrels that Claudius addressed show that Christianity was in Rome by the 40s. We do not know who the first missionaries were, but the fourth-century writer "Ambrosiaster" suggests that they were Jewish Christians faithful to the Law of Moses, and that may well be correct. It could be that the absence of a central governing council for Roman Jews made it easier than it might have been for Christian missionaries to win converts from individual synagogues (Wiefel 1991, 108). By the time of Paul's letter, we may suppose that there were at least five groups in the Roman Christian community, representing at least three different theo-logical positions: (1) Jewish Christians who were faithful to the Law of Moses; (2) Jewish Christians who were law-free; (3) gentile Christians who were law-abiding because of deep attachment to the synagogue prior to their conversion to Christiani-ty; (4) gentile Christians who were law-free; (5) gentile Christians who stretched Paul's belief that salvation is by grace and not by works of the law to mean that the Christian stands under no moral obligation. Paul appears to assume that the Roman church was composed primarily of gentiles (1:5-6, 13-15; 9:3-4; 10:1-3; 11:13, 17-18, 24, 28, 30-31; 15:15-16, 18). But that it also contained Jewish members is seen in 15:7-12; 16:3, 7, 11. It would seem probable that the various house churches were marked and divided by these differing theological and ethnic characteristics.

We may also observe other social differences. Chapter 16 suggests that women had important places of leadership. If the Roman Christian community reflected the general population, it would have contained about two-thirds slaves and freedpersons and one-third free. Probably a majority of the members would have been from the lower socio-economic strata and a small minority from the upper classes (Lampe 1991, 222–30).

The letter is pervaded by Paul's concern about Jewish-gentile relationships (1:16; 2:12-16, 25-29; 8:33; 9:1–11:32; 15:8-12). His defense of the law and affirmation of God's faithfulness to Israel (3:1-8; 3:31; 7:7a, 10a, 12, 14a, 16; 11:1-2, 11, 23, 28-29) bespeak his own conviction about the continuity of the Christian community with Israel (4:11-12; 11:17-18). And he hereby supports the commitments of law-abiding Jewish Christians and gentile Christians who had firm attachments to JUDAISM as well as opposes the antinomian position (that faith has no moral requirements) of some. At the same time his proclamation of the gospel and his critique of the law (3:19-30; 4:1-5; 6:14; 7:1-6, 7b-9; 9:30–10:4) expound his own conviction about salvation by GRACE, not works of the LAW, and support the position of law-free gentile and Jewish Christians as well as confront his law-affirming Jewish Christian opponents.

The discussion up to this point may be summarized in the following way. Paul purposes to offer the Romans a universally valid gospel that is the power of God for the salvation of all humankind and in fact of the whole cosmos. This gospel, which has been worked out through his own experiences, is addressed to Rome for the sake of the gospel's own truth and for the well-being of the Romans. That is, Paul hopes to win converts to the Christian faith (1:5-6, 14-15) and to strengthen the faith of believers (15:14-15). And because of the all-encompassing capacity of the gospel, it can be the key for resolving the gentile-Jewish tension in the Roman church. At the same time Paul also wants to win the Romans' assent to his understanding of the gospel in the interest of gaining their support for his trip to Jerusalem and his Spanish mission.

Three additional topics that bear on the question of the letter's relationship to its historical situation call for brief discussion.

Historical setting and theological structure. Neither all of the elements in Romans nor the way they are related or structured can be accounted for—at least not exhaustively—by the historical situation. For example, it cannot be demonstrated, as is sometimes suggested (Campbell 1991, 252–53, 258–60), that the purpose of the gospel is the transformation of Jewish-gentile relationships.

It is clear from the syntactical indications of purpose in 3:25-26 that the *purpose* of the gospel is the demonstration of God's righteousness and the justification of believers. The new equality of Jews and gentiles (3:28-30) is the result of carrying out this purpose. It will also be argued in the commentary that justification and faith (3:21–4:25) have a structural relationship to life and freedom (5:1–8:36) that grows out of the inner logic of Paul's gospel and not out of the Roman situation.

Historical setting and letter type. The evidence of a certain sub-type of the letter genre in the first century augments the probability that Romans does both respond to a specific historical situation and also transcend that situation. A letter belonging to the sub-genre known as the letter-essay is addressed to a real situation and has the framework of a regular letter (greeting and closing), but what is framed inside is more nearly a treatise than a personal message. This type of letter has an instructional purpose that reaches beyond the immediate addressees (Stirewalt 1991, 147–48; Donfried 1991d, 121–25; Dunn, lix).

Paul apparently felt free to mix genres, and evidence of this is seen in the fact that what is framed inside the greeting and closing of Romans displays certain characteristics of the *logos protreptikos* or "speech of exhortation." This type had the purpose of winning the hearers to a particular way of life or thought and had the following parts: (1) a critique of other ways of life or thought (Rom 1:18–3:20); (2) a positive presentation of the true way (Rom 3:21–15:13); (3) a personal appeal (15:14-33) (Aune 1991, 278–82, 295–96).

Historical setting and diatribe style. Karl Donfried has acknowledged that the claim that Romans was addressed to a specific situation would be undermined if it could be shown that the diatribe exercised a pervasive influence on the letter. However, Donfried has argued that the diatribe was not a definite genre but rather a series of rhetorical devices, that it did not seriously influence Romans, and that it does not in fact bring into question the historical specificity of the letter to the Romans (Donfried 1991d, 112–19; 1991b, lxx). We need to consider Stanley Stowers's work on the relationship of Romans to the diatribe.

The most distinctive feature of the diatribe is its dialogical nature. If the objections of the one who questions the speaker/writer in the dialogue grow out of a misunderstanding of the *subject matter*, then these objections do not need to be explained by the *situation* of the letter. The objector is a literary, not a historical, figure (Stowers 1981, 2). Is that the case for Romans?

With regard to the social setting an older scholarship held that the diatribe was a type of popular moral or philosophical propaganda directed to the masses by wandering preachers with the intention of converting the former. Stowers' own view is that the setting from which the diatribe emerged is the philosophical school (Stowers 1981, 18, 35, 44–48, 75–76).

The diatribe was not a fixed form or technical genre but was a distinct style though subject to variation. It was first of all the record of a school lecture or discussion and not a literary tractate (Stowers 1981, 29, 44, 47–48, 75).

The dialogue proceeded by address from the teacher, objections from the students, and response to the objections. When there were no real questions or objections, the teacher manufactured them. The mode of discussion was not polemical, for the teacher was not trying to damage the student/opponent or his credibility. He did want, however, to expose and indict his error and lead him to truth. The goal was not simply to impart knowledge but to transform the student. The concern of Paul's questioning objections throughout Romans is what is to become of the law if JUSTIFICATION is by faith and not works (Stowers 1981, 20, 40, 56, 76–77, 105–106, 117, 166).

What gives the diatribe its rhetorical effect is the interplay between two audiences: the real one and the one that provides the fictitious objectors (Stowers 1981, 106, 140). We might imagine that the real audience identifies sympathetically with the indictment of the fictitious one because it thinks it is not being indicted. Then when it discovers that it is, there is no escape.

In summary fashion we may note that the following diatribal features appear in Romans: (1) address to the imaginary questioner or interlocutor as distinguished from the real addressees (2:1-5, 17-24; 9:19-21; 11:17-24; 14:4, 10); (2) objections to or false conclusions drawn from the writer's position (3:1-9; 7:7, 13-14); (3) dialogical exchange between writer and questioner (3:27–4:2) (Stowers 1981, 79, 119, 128–29, 134, 155, 164).

In Stowers's view, these similarities show that Paul was dependent on the diatribe in Romans though he adaptively made it his own. The diatribe element in Romans is not an accident, not Paul's preaching style unconsciously coming through, but is rather central to his message and his self-presentation as a *teacher* (Stowers 1981, 176–79).

Stowers concludes that the objections and false conclusions that Paul cites in Romans do not reflect specific positions of the addressees of the letter. The dialogical interaction grows out of Paul's theological argument and represents what is typical for Paul. But the typical is addressed to a specific historical situation of whose pedagogical needs Paul has some knowledge (Stowers 1981, 180).

The issue of rhetoric having now been introduced, a somewhat more comprehensive look at the relationship of Romans to Greco-Roman rhetoric is in order.

Romans and Rhetoric

The term "rhetoric" refers both to the use of and critical reflection about persuasive language. It has been strongly recognized in recent years that rhetoric as spoken or written discourse is a matter of argumentation and persuasion and not of stylistic ornamentation. Style, of course, is a part of rhetoric, but for the best speakers and critics style should serve argument and not be gratuitous ornamentation. The speaker/writer hopes to modify a situation of exigence or urgency by using discourse to change human attitudes or action (Mack 1990, 14–15; Kennedy 1984, 25, 34–35; Wuellner 1991, 128; 1987, 449). When "rhetoric" is used to refer to reflection about discourse, it deals with the rules that a society agrees are acceptable for debate and argumentation (Mack 1990, 16, 19).

Rhetoric emerged in the Greek city-states during the sixth and fifth centuries B.C.E. By the first century B.C.E., it pervaded the Greco-Roman world, permeating both the system of education and public discourse (Mack 1990, 25, 28). Rhetoric would have been a part of the cultural air breathed by Paul and the Evangelists (Kennedy 1984, 9–10).

While Donfried considers the indispensability of rhetorical criticism on Romans an open question (Donfried 1991b, lxxi), Wuellner clearly believes it is the necessary wave of the future. Studies of the literary form of the letter can illuminate the letter frame but not the structure and nature of the body. Rhetorical criticism will allow us to grasp the structure of the argument found in the letter body as addressed to a particular situation. Rhetorical criticism will enable us also to comprehend the letter as a social act inseparable from other social relationships as well as to appreciate the role of rhetoric in appealing to our emotions and imaginations and not just to our rationality (Wuellner 1991, 129–32; 1987, 453, 461; Jewett 1991, 266).

Ancient rhetoricians identified three species, genres, or types of rhetoric on the basis of the kind of judgment the speaker is seeking. Each may take a positive or negative form. (1) In forensic or judicial rhetoric the speaker is trying to persuade the audience to make a judgment about past events. It may take the form of prosecution or defense. (2) In deliberative rhetoric the attempt is to move the audience to take some action in the future. It may take the form of exhortation or dissuasion. (3) In epideictic or demonstrative rhetoric the writer wants the audience to accept or reaffirm some value or point of view in the present. It may take the form of praise (encomium) or blame (invective) (Kennedy 1984, 19–20). This present-time perspective is a frequent but not necessary characteristic of epideictic (Beale 1978, 223).

It seems reasonably obvious that Romans belongs primarily to the epideictic genre. Paul wants to persuade the Romans to accept and/or reaffirm his understanding of the gospel and salvation right now in the present. Some would say that Romans is thoroughly epideictic (Wuellner 1987, 460) on the ground that the moral teaching in Romans (12:1–15:13) has to do with belief and attitude and not with action (Kennedy 1984, 154). It is true that Paul praises such attitudes or dispositions as humility (12:3), love (12:9), and self-consistency (14:5, 22-23). But his exhortations about paying taxes (13:1-7) and eating and drinking (14:15, 20-21) pertain to specific actions and refer to possible future behavior and so take certain parts of the letter over into the sphere of deliberative rhetoric.

It has recently been argued that the main defining feature of epideictic rhetoric is "rhetorical performative." Epideictic participates in or performs the action to which it refers, and brings the audience to participate in the community act that is the speech (Beale 1978, 225–26, 236). This accords well with Paul's claim in Romans that the gospel which he presents in the letter is the power of God.

For Further Study

In the *Mercer Dictionary of the Bible*: GRACE; JUSTIFICATION; PAUL; RIGH-
TEOUSNESS IN THE NT; ROMAN EMPIRE; ROMANS, LETTER TO THE; ROME; SALVATION
IN THE NT; SIN.

In other sources: C. K. Barrett, *A Commentary on the Epistle to the Romans*;
C. E. B. Cranfield, *A Critical and Exegetical Commentary on the Epistle to the
Romans*, ICC; K. P. Donfried, ed., *The Romans Debate*; J. D. G. Dunn, *Romans 1–8*
and *Romans 9–16*; H. Y. Gamble, *The Textual History of the Letter to the Romans*;
E. Käsemann, *Commentary on Romans*; S. K. Stowers, *The Diatribe and Paul's
Letter to the Romans*; A. J. M. Wedderburn, *The Reasons for Romans*.

Commentary

An Outline

I. Letter Opening, 1:1-15
   A. Paul's Greetings to the Saints
      in Rome, 1:1-7
   B. Paul's Thanksgiving
      for the Roman Community, 1:8-15
II. Theme: The Gospel of Righteousness
    as Power, 1:16-17
III. The Revelation of God's Righteousness,
     1:18–4:25
   A. Righteousness as Wrath, 1:18–3:20
   B. Righteousness as Justification
      by Faith, 3:21–4:25
IV. Life as Liberation
    from Victimizing Powers, 5:1–8:39
   A. Transition from Justification
      to Peace and Life, 5:1-11
   B. Freedom from Adam, 5:12-21
   C. Freedom from Sin, 6:1-23
   D. Freedom from the Law, 7:1-25
   E. Freedom from Death and Flesh,
      8:1-39
V. God's Word and the Destiny of Israel,
   9:1–11:36
   A. God's Rejection of Israel, 9:1-29
   B. Israel's Rejection of Righteousness
      through Faith, 9:30–10:21
   C. The Final Salvation of all Israel,
      11:1-36

VI. God's Mercy (Righteousness) and the
    Behavior of Believers, 12:1–15:13
   A. Ethical Renewal as the Appropri-
      tion of Mercy, 12:1-2
   B. Love in One Body in Christ,
      12:3-21
   C. The State and Taxes, 13:1-7
   D. Love as the Fulfillment
      of the Law, 13:8-10
   E. The Pressure of the Imminent End,
      13:11-14
   F. Eating and Drinking among the
      Weak and the Strong, 14:1–15:13
VII. Concluding Personal Statement,
     15:14-32
   A. Paul's Feelings about the Roman
      Church and his Self-evaluation,
      15:14-21
   B. Travel Plans, 15:22-29
   C. Emotional Appeal
      for Their Prayers, 15:30-32
VIII. Closing, 15:33–16:27
   A. Peace Wish, 15:33
   B. Commendation of Phoebe, 16:1-2
   C. Greetings, 16:3-23
   (Interrupted by Exhortation, 16:17-20a)
   D. Grace Benediction,
      16:20b or 16:24 or both
   E. Doxology, 16:25-27

In the Greco-Roman period there was no sharp distinction between a private, personal letter and a public, literary one (epistle). The most ordinary personal letters were shaped by stylized letter-writing conventions. Paul's letters were personal in that they were written to real household churches, but they were meant to be read publicly in the whole assembly and perhaps circulated in other cities (Stowers 1989, 18–19).

The structure and content of Romans conforms broadly to the shape of the Greco-Roman letter form: greeting, prayer or thanksgiving, body, and closing. The outline above includes both greeting and thanksgiving in the opening. Items II–VII form a connected argument and should all be regarded as parts of the body. Especially should the ethical part not be excluded from the body since it has both a logical and syntactical ("therefore") relationship to the preceding theological parts—which themselves contain ethical implications. The personal statements in 15:14-32 close the body of the letter while 15:33–16:27 is the closing for the letter as a whole.

For the conventional term "greetings" (*chairein*) in the Greco-Roman letter Paul has substituted his theological term "grace" (*charis*, 1:7). Paul also preserves a characteristic of the semitic letter when he adds a peace wish to the greeting: grace to you and peace (1:7). Instead of the conventional "farewell" at the end Paul uses a benediction such as *The grace of our Lord Jesus Christ be with you* (16:20b) (Stowers 1989, 21–22).

The Greco-Roman letter genre was constituted by adding an initial greeting and final closing, as a frame, to the form of a proper speech as defined by the rhetoricians (Kennedy 1984, 141). The structured argument of Romans, then, can be illuminated by displaying its relationship to the speech form. This form had the following parts although speeches would not necessarily have all the parts.

(1) The *proem* or *exordium* (introduction) seeks to obtain the attention and good will of the audience.

(2) The *narration* provides the facts or background information.

(3) The *proposition* or *thesis* states the major contention to be proved and is followed immediately by a justifying reason. The thesis is the transition from exordium and/or narration to the proof.

(4) The *proof* or *confirmation* contains the arguments to support the thesis. Arguments could be creatively invented or could be "non-technical" proofs drawn from the traditional stock of laws, contracts, scripture, witnesses, and the like. The distinction between invented and non-technical proofs seems not to have been a firm one. The kinds of material available were classified as historical examples, analogies, and fables.

(5) The *refutation* neutralizes opposing views.

(6) The *epilogue* or *peroration* summarizes the argument and seeks to arouse the emotions of the audience to take action or make a commitment (Kennedy 1984, 23–24; Jewett 1991, 272–74; Mack 1990, 32–40; Wuellner 1991, 133–46).

Because the theological argument of Romans is complex and because the letter's theological intention is the chief item of debate within contemporary Romans scholarship (Donfried 1991a, lxxii), it seems well to begin the commentary proper by presenting a tentative "rhetorical-theological" overview of the letter as a whole.

The greeting (1:1-7) has already taken on a rhetorical function since it contains brief narration about both Paul himself and the SON OF GOD who is the content of the gospel. The rhetorical exordium corresponds to the letter thanksgiving in which Paul seeks the good will of the Romans by thanking God for their faith which is proclaimed worldwide and by expressing his strong desire to see them. This also continues the narration about Paul.

Paul's thesis (1:16-17), which is the letter theme, is that the gospel is the power of God unto salvation for all who believe. This claim is grounded on the justifying reason that in the gospel the righteousness of God is revealed. The commentary will show that the thesis truly is a transition closely connected syntactically to both exordium-narration and proof.

The rhetorical proof (1:18–15:13) corresponds to the letter body except for the body's concluding personal statement (15:14-32). Several fundamental proofs are offered for the power of God's righteousness.

(1) It is demonstrated in God's wrath that delivers rebellious human beings to the ruinous consequences of their own actions (1:18–3:20).

(2) It is seen in God's providing justification equally for Jews and gentiles (3:21–4:25). This section displays Paul's use of Abraham as a historical example.

(3) God's power is manifested in God's liberating deliverance from the victimizing power of Adam (5:12-21), sin (6:1-23), the law (7:1-25), and flesh and death (8:1-39). Justification opens up freedom as a new quality of life, a relationship to be examined in the commentary.

(4) God's righteousness will finally be able to save all Israel despite the rebellion of the latter (9:1–11:36). In this section we find Paul using analogies with the potter and his clay (9:19-24) and with the olive tree (11:17-24) in order to clarify the human situation (Jewett 1991, 272–74).

(5) The ethical section is also a proof because it is God's power that enables ethical renewal (12:1–15:13).

Paul has taken the refutation of opposing views up into his proof by his employment of the diatribe style. At certain points he mentions objections to or false conclusions drawn from his positions and then refutes these mistakes (3:1-9; 3:31; 4:1-2a; 6:1-3, 15-16; 7:7, 13-14; 9:14-15, 19-20; 11:1-3, 11; 11:19-20) (Stowers 1981, 119–22).

The rhetorical peroration corresponds to the personal conclusion of the letter body (15:14-32). Here Paul compliments the Romans for their spiritual achievements yet affirms his right to instruct them. This moves into a favorable evaluation of his own ministry, which in turn melds into a brief narration (recall the exordium) of the scope of his past mission. Then he "narrates" the future as his hope to visit the

Romans on his way to Spain and his present need to go to Jerusalem first. Finally he makes an emotional appeal for their prayers.

The letter closing (15:33–16:27) continues the rhetorical function of the peroration—to cement personal connections.

Letter Opening, 1:1-15

Paul's Greetings to the Saints in Rome, 1:1-7

Paul's greeting expands the simplest conventional greeting form (Theon to Tyrannus, greetings): *Paul to God's beloved in Rome, grace and peace from God our Father and the Lord Jesus Christ*. The Romans are designated as saints, set apart for God.

Paul introduces two expansions into the greeting. (1) He identifies himself as set apart for the GOSPEL, as the OT prophets had been set apart or elected to preach (Isa 49:1; Jer 1:5), and identifies himself as an apostle. A NT apostle is one sent with an authoritative commission to represent the sender. For Paul the commission is from the risen Lord to preach to the gentiles (1:5; Gal 1:15-16). According to Acts 1:21-22 to be an APOSTLE one must have been a follower of the earthly Jesus and a witness to his RESURRECTION. Paul did not meet the first of these criteria, but he was fully convinced that his having seen the risen Lord and having been commissioned by him was quite enough to make him an apostle equal in authority to the others (Rom 1:1, 5; 1 Cor 9:1; 15:8-11; Gal 1:15-16).

(2) In addition Paul defines the gospel in terms of a Christological confession that he probably received from the tradition existing before or alongside him. This confession portrays Jesus' mission as moving in two stages (not two natures): (a) according to the flesh—in his historical phase—he was the descendant of David; (b) then he was appointed or installed (*not* declared to be who he already was) SON OF GOD in power in the spiritual realm by the resurrection of the dead. Notice it is not by *his* resurrection from the dead but because he anticipates the future general resurrection of the dead. The CHRISTOLOGY of this early confession is broadly adoptionistic. Jesus was not eternally Son of God but became Son at a certain point. However, there is no assertive denial of his pre-existence.

Paul provides a frame for this confession. He introduces it as a confession about the Son, thereby anticipating its second part, and he concludes by naming the Son, Jesus Christ our Lord, the one to whom the believer owes total obedience. For Paul the term Son of God connotes Jesus' close bond with God and his role as redeemer, but it is probable that no Pauline passage clearly connects pre-existence with the title Son. In Rom 1:3, 9 the content of the gospel is the Son while in 1:16-17, it is the righteousness of God. This shows that for Paul the inner meaning of christology is the standing of human beings before God.

Paul's Thanksgiving for the Roman Community, 1:8-15

Paul first of all thanks God for the faith of the Roman Christians and assures them of his prayerful concern for them. Apparently in his enthusiasm he forgets to follow up "first" with a "second." (On Paul's desire to visit Rome see Introduction: Occasion and Purpose, The Intended Visit.)

Paul wants to preach in Rome because his obligation to preach is unlimited. He must preach to those who have been cultivated by the use of the GREEK LANGUAGE and those who are barbarian. He is a debtor to both wise and foolish. Hence he is eager to proclaim the gospel in Rome. In the thematic statement that follows—his thesis—he begins to explain further the reason why.

Theme: The Gospel of Righteousness as Power, 1:16-17

Paul wants to preach in Rome because he is not ashamed of the gospel. "I am not ashamed" might have a psychological tone. He is not tempted to think he will be shamed for having trusted something unreliable. Or the term might be confessional and be roughly equivalent to "I confess" or "I acknowledge" (see Mark 8:38). Paul is not ashamed of the gospel because it is the power of God for salvation. The gospel proclaimed is not words *about* God's power but *is* God's power in action (see 1 Cor 1:18, 21, 24). Salvation— ultimate well-being—is characteristically future for Paul (5:9-10) but can also be past (8:24) and present (1 Cor 1:18; 2 Cor 2:15).

The righteousness of God means God's action in being faithful to God's COVENANT intention, and faith is the human appropriative response to this. Righteous or righteousness when attributed to human beings refers to being in a right relationship. But see the commentary on 3:21-31 for a fuller discussion of these important terms. Paul finds the essence of the gospel to have been expressed in Hab 2:4—the one righteous by faith shall live. Paul is able to do this by changing the meaning of the prophetic passage. The Greek text of the Habakkuk passage should probably be translated "the one righteous by my (God's) faithfulness shall live." And the Hebrew text of the prophet should probably be translated "the righteous one shall live by his (own) faithfulness." But for Paul the meaning is that the one righteous by faith (in Paul's sense of faith) shall live.

The strong interconnections linking the end of the thanksgiving, the thesis as transition, and the beginning of the letter body are noteworthy. Verses 16-18 are closely tied to v. 15 by a fourfold use of the word *for* (i.e., "because"; vv. 16a, [16b], 17a, 18a), and this formation overarches the formal distinctions involved. Verse 15 belongs to the thanksgiving, vv. 6-17, to the theme or thesis, and v. 18, to the beginning of the body. The causal sequence binds these three together.

Verse 16a states why Paul is eager to preach in Rome (v. 15): because he is not ashamed of the gospel. Verse 16b states why he is not ashamed of the gospel: because it is the power of God. *Gospel* has to be understood as the subject of *is* in v. 16b. Verse 17a explains why the gospel is the power of God: because the righteousness of God is revealed in it. Verse 17a is dependent on v. 16b because the *it* of v. 17a has to have *gospel* as its antecedent. The gender agreement of *it* is with *gospel*, not with *salvation* or *power*.

In the light of both terminology and concept, v. 18a would seem to be parallel to v. 17a: wrath is conceptually related to righteousness (both refer to God's actions), and righteousness in v. 17a and wrath in v. 18a both have the same predicate: *for . . . the righteousness of God is revealed* is parallel to *for the wrath of God is revealed*. Therefore both would be dependent on v. 16b and would thus express causes for the gospel's being the power of God: because righteousness is revealed in it and because wrath is revealed.

Although the terminology and parallelism seem to support that conclusion, some of the conceptual content points in another direction. Righteousness and wrath have a different *temporal* qualification here. The righteousness of God has been manifested in the *present* eschatological moment—now (3:21). But 1:18-32 shows that the wrath of God has been happening *since creation* (1:20). Therefore, although it goes against the parallel structure (meanings and interpretations are rarely, if ever, certain), 1:18 is best referred back to v. 15 as another cause for Paul's wanting to come to Rome: because the WRATH OF GOD is being revealed. He hopes that his coming with the gospel—God's power—will save some from that wrath. Thus Paul has both positively and negatively stated reasons for coming—to bring the gospel and to save from wrath. And since the letter is a substitute for his presence, these are also his reasons for writing.

The Revelation of God's Righteousness, 1:18–4:25

Righteousness as Wrath, 1:18–3:20

1:18-32. Against the gentiles or all humankind. The wrath of God is being revealed against the ungodliness and wickedness of *all* human beings. This is not unjust of God. All are without excuse (v. 20) regardless of their religion or culture because God has made God's eternal power and deity known and perceptible in the created order since the beginning. But human beings in the interest of having finite gods (idols) that they can manipulate (vv. 23, 25) have refused to thank and honor God and have suppressed the truth of God which they have (vv. 18, 21, 25). The result is that the senseless human mind has become darkened and futile (vv. 21b, 22b). Thus, the human situation is that universal knowledge of God is a possibility only in principle—a possibility "before the fall" so to speak and still a latent possibility. The actual situation in historical existence is that people do not have knowledge of God (vv. 21b, 22b; 1 Cor 2:10-14). But the possibility in principle is enough to hold people responsible (v. 20), for the lack of knowledge results from their *choice* not to have it.

The wrath of God here is God's reaction to humankind's rejection of the truth and knowledge that God has plainly revealed in creation. It is not just a cosmic principle of retribution working automatically in the moral universe (Dodd 1954, 21–24) but God's personal action, God's giving people up (vv. 24, 26, 28) to the consequences of their rebellion.

This giving up has three manifestations.

1. God gave them up to the dishonoring of their bodies in homosexual relationships (2:24-27). HOMOSEXUALITY then is not in Paul's view so much SIN itself as a consequence of sin, and yet it is evil for Paul in that it is destructive of the human self.

Present knowledge makes it difficult to agree with Paul that sinful rebellion is the sole or even a primary cause of homosexuality. But Paul's apparent underlying principle may be right. Rebellious rejection of God deforms the inner depth of human life where the roots of all sexuality lie.

Some Greek moralists defended pederasty (sexual relations between adult men and young boys) as superior to heterosexuality. Among the arguments were: (1) it contributes to the wisdom of youth; (2) it is more masculine; and (3) it is more "according to nature" (Scroggs 1983, 44–49). Other moralists condemned pederasty with such arguments as: (1) it is effeminate; (2) it lacks mutuality and permanence; (3) it is exploitative; (4) it is the expression of insatiable lust; (5) it is contrary to nature (Scroggs 1983, 49–65; Furnish 1979, 62–66).

Paul essentially agreed with the opponents of pederasty. He held homosexuality to be generated by insatiable lust—consumed with passion (v. 27). And he believed that it was chosen—they exchanged (v. 26). And perhaps most emphatically he held it to be contrary to nature, against God's created intention as an order immanent in the world and humankind (Cranfield 1980, 125–26; Käsemann 1980, 48).

People will debate whether homosexuals are more lustful than heterosexuals. That homosexuality is simply chosen and not biologically or socially determined is too facile an assumption. What about "contrary to nature"?

For Paul and the ancient world generally there is no such thing as a homosexual nature or orientation. There is one nature—what we would call a heterosexual one. Thus what Paul is condemning as unnatural is homosexual acts by people whom he takes to have a heterosexual nature. His underlying principle, then, is that people when they act sexually should do so in accordance with their nature. If Paul then could be confronted with the reality of a homosexual nature, he would not be consistent with himself if he claimed that homosexual acts by people with a homosexual nature are contrary to nature.

2. God gave them up to a base mind—a mind that cannot tolerate crisis and that collapses under testing (v. 28). The wrath of God is that God ratifies the darkened thinking that people visit on themselves (vv. 21b, 22b) and turns it into a destiny that they cannot escape on their own.

3. God gave them up to improper conduct (v. 28). The vices that Paul then lists as illustrative of this conduct are behaviors that destroy the coherence of the social order and turn it into a tissue of conflict and reciprocal hostility (vv. 29–32).

2:1-16. Against the Jews—or all humankind. In v. 1 Paul addresses every person who judges another, and he tells such a person that he or she is without excuse because in judging another, one condemns oneself. This is because the judge is guilty of the same offenses. Who is the "man" whom Paul addresses here in the second person as the guilty judge?

In v. 1 Paul has shifted from the third person description of 1:18-32 to second person address—you, O man, the judge. The *you* is not the real letter audience—usually designated as "brother/brothers" (cf. 1:13; 16:17) by Paul—but the imaginary questioner of the diatribe. Such a shift of addressee along with a strong indictment, as here, is typical of the diatribe style. Paul indicts the false conclusion that some are in a position to judge others. This address to "you" personalizes and concretizes the "them" of 1:18-32. Yet despite the slight distance created by the insertion of the imaginary questioner the real audience is still in view (Stowers 1981, 81–86, 91, 96, 106, 110–12). Who is it?

The initial *therefore* in v. 1 suggests a close relationship between 1:18-32 and vv. 1-16. In the former he is describing primarily the situation of the gentiles, but the allusion to *Israelite* IDOLATRY in 1:25 (see Ps 106:20; Jer 2:11) shows that he has Jews also in mind. Thus the *you* in v. 1 includes everybody.

However, as the gentile is primarily in view in 1:18-32, the Jew is primarily in view in vv. 1-11, and for these reasons: (1) He is explicitly referring to the Jew in 2:17-29, and 2:1-11 is similar to 2:17-29 in that both criticize inconsistent behavior. (2) The standard of judgment in 2:1-16 is Jewish in nature—works or deeds in obedience to the law (vv. 6, 12-13). (See Pss 18:20-24; 62:12; Prov 24:12; Job 4:9-10; Sir 16:12-14.) (3) Rom 2:4 seems to criticize the Jewish attitude described in Wis 3:9-10; 4:15; 11:9-10, 23; 12:8-11, 19-22; 15:1-6; 16:9-10. These passages suggest that Israel will be judged but with mercy, and Israel will accept the opportunity to repent. The gentiles, on the other hand, are judged without mercy and do not accept the opportunity to repent. Paul's position is that Israel has not repented but is as guilty as the gentiles.

While the wrath of God that Paul describes in 1:18-32 is the historical anticipation of the final judgment, vv. 5-10 speak about that future day of wrath and retribution itself. God will repay people according to their works (*erga*). Those who do good will receive ETERNAL LIFE, but those who do evil will get anguish and fury. This is the situation for both Jew and Greek (vv. 9-11).

The term "works" (v. 6, author trans.) has a very specific meaning for Paul and can hardly be thought to mean something like acts of *faith* or looking beyond human achievement (Barrett 1957, 45–48). Works of the law are human achievements, and here Paul seems to allow that some will be justified by doing the law (v. 13). This appears to contradict his statements elsewhere that no one can be justified by works of the law (3:20, 28; 4:2-5; 9:30–10:3).

On the other hand, here in vv. 6-13, Paul may be speaking hypothetically, speaking from the Jewish point of view for the sake of argument. If the law is the medium of the divine-human relationship, as Judaism says, then only obedient works count for salvation. Since the Jews have not been obedient, they are out on their own terms. But Paul's own real position is that the law is not and cannot be the medium of the divine-human relationship (3:21). For Paul it is in fact possible to be perfectly obedient to the law (Phil 3:6), but fallen human beings will turn that righteousness of the law into a claim of self-salvation rather than accepting righteousness as a gift from God (Phil 3:4b, 6, 9; Rom 9:30–10:3). The righteousness of the law is not the righteousness of God.

To underline the equality of Jew and gentile Paul states that while the gentile does not have the law as the Jew does, gentiles—or some gentiles— nevertheless do by nature what the law requires and thus show that the work of the law is written on their hearts (vv. 14-15). No one, regardless of religion or culture, is without moral sensibility.

Paul is not necessarily expressing the Greek belief that the reason of every person is stamped by the divine cosmic reason. He may rather be stating that the transcendent will of God encounters gentile as well as Jew in concrete situations (Käsemann 1980, 63–64) and is affirmed from within.

Whether the gentile is obedient to this inner law is judged by CONSCIENCE. For Paul and the ancient popular philosophy from which he learned the concept of conscience, the latter is the self in its *judging* mode. Conscience does not *determine* what is right or wrong but is the self judging itself on the basis of a standard of right that is independent of conscience. Here the standard is the law written on the heart, and it is distinct from conscience, whose judging function is expressed in the conflicting thoughts which accuse or excuse.

The statement about the law on the heart in vv. 14-15 should probably be taken as a parenthesis. If it is, then v. 16 flows from v. 13 in a smooth and natural way. The doers of the law will be justified (v. 13) on the day when God carries out the judgment (v. 16). The operation of conscience then (vv. 14-15) is something that goes on in history prior to the judgment day and perhaps anticipates it. But if 2:14-15 is not taken as a parenthesis, it interrupts the flow and makes the operation of conscience coincident with and a kind of ratification of God's final judgment. That is probably not what Paul wanted to say. For Paul conscience has a relative authority and should be heeded (1 Cor 8:7-12). But it is not infallible and is subject to correction by God's judgment (1 Cor 4:4-5).

2:17-29. Religion, obedience, and circumcision. Here Paul explicitly addresses the Jew: the Jew who has persuaded himself that because he knows the law he has a secure relationship with God on which he can depend and a right to instruct others about how to live in the light. But this Jew who knows the law and the will of God and preaches against theft and adultery does the very things he condemns. Paul indicts this discrepancy between religious claims and moral performance. Again only obedience counts if the Jew is faithful to his own position.

It occurs to Paul that some Jew will say: we have circumcision that counts for us with God. Paul rejoins that circumcision is a benefit only if you obey the law, but disobedience renders it void. You have been disobedient, so circumcision is of no value. Moreover, real circumcision is a matter of the heart. The uncircumcised person who keeps the law is better than the circumcised person who breaks it. True Judaism is an inward and spiritual matter.

3:1-8. Then has the Jew any advantage? We more-or-less expect Paul to say "no." He has argued that the Jew—despite knowing God and the law, despite being mercifully given the opportunity to repent, despite offering moral instruction to others and having the gift of circumcision—is as disobedient and as subject to wrath as the gentile. So what advantage has the Jew? Paul surprises us with "much in every way." The Jews were entrusted with the oracles of God. Paul does not say that the law (*nomos*) is an advantage but that the oracles (*logia*) are. The Jewish scripture is more than law. The Jews know from scripture that if some of them were unfaithful God is still faithful. Paul uses three terms in this context to express the reliability of God—faithfulness (*pistis*, v. 3), righteousness (*dikaiosynē*, v. 5) and truth (*alētheia*, v. 7). This knowledge is the Jews' advantage.

All of this seems to mean that our unrighteousness brings out the righteousness of God. That will prompt some diatribal objector to ask then whether God is not unjust to condemn us. Paul replies "absolutely not" (v. 6, author trans.), for how could God judge the world if he were unjust. Paul's answer could mean that since God is surely judge of the world, he must be just. Or it might mean that God could not be a just judge if he did not take into account the intention of people—to do evil—and not just the result—the confirmation of God's righteousness.

The fact that human unrighteousness leads to the faithfulness of God might also prompt some people to the closely related assertion—which Paul says some people slanderously attribute to him—let us do evil in order that the good might come. Paul does not really deal with this problem here; he dismisses it contemptuously. But he raises the issue again in 6:1 and then gives a substantive theological-ethical response.

3:9-20. Are we Jews then any better off? The meaning of the verb translated "are we better off?" is very problematical, and only the briefest account of the possibilities can be given (see the longer commentaries). The verb could have three possible meanings: (1) Are we making a defense? (2) Are we excelled, at a disadvantage? (3) Are we better off, at an advantage? The first two possibilities seem ruled out by what precedes. The third makes most sense in context even though the middle voice of the verb with this sense is not attested elsewhere. But there are cases of other verbs in the middle voice with an active sense.

Paul's answer to the question is also ambiguous. It could mean either "not absolutely" or "absolutely not." The latter seems more probable in context. Thus question and answer should read: Are we Jews any better off? Absolutely not!

Romans 3:1 and 3:9 then stand in a paradoxical relationship to each other. The Jews have an advantage but are no better off. Their knowledge of God's faithfulness from scripture does not mean that they are any less sinful than the gentiles. The Jews are no better off because all people, Jews and gentiles, are equally under the power of sin. When Paul uses "sin" in the singular, as here, it means, not an act, but a power that controls human beings, especially since he speaks of people as being *under* it. And yet Paul can also speak of sins in the plural to mean acts (4:7; 7:5; 11:27). Sin as power produces sin/sins as dispositions and acts.

Not even one person is righteous. Paul quotes scripture to illustrate and confirm this universal sinfulness. The sin/sins that he details embrace both dispositions and actions. They are both religious and moral. Humankind is without understanding (v. 11). Religiously speaking people do not fear or seek God (vv. 11, 18). Morally speaking they show no kindness but rather deceive, curse, poison, and shed the blood of their neighbors (vv. 12-15).

Interestingly, none of these OT passages comes from the books of the law. They are primarily from Psalms but also from Ecclesiastes and Isaiah, and yet Paul comprehensively includes them under the category of law (v. 19). The accusations against all Jews and Greeks in vv. 10-18 are the accusations of the law (v. 19), for the purpose of the law is precisely accusation—to stop every mouth (undermine every self-defense) and hold the whole world accountable to God. Proper works of the law are implicitly defined as fear of God and concern for the neighbor—the opposite of the offenses here condemned. But none can be justified by such works because the law's purpose is to hold people guilty, knowingly guilty. The law brings knowledge of sin (v. 20); it does not bring obedience.

But the law can make people aware of their sin only because they have in fact sinned, violated the law, and the law also has a role in the latter connection. The knowledge of sin that the law gives is the knowledge that comes from *doing* it. That is, the claim that the law gives knowledge of sin for Paul means that the law makes people sin (Rom 7:5, 7-8; see commentary on Rom 7).

Since the theme of the works of the law has been introduced by Paul and since Paul's interpretation of Israel's law is one of the most hotly contested issues in Romans scholarship (Donfried 1991a, lxii, lxxi), it seems well to look at the debate at this point.

Excursus: The Law in Paul

In recent years, certain claims have been made that minimize Paul's differences with his ancestral religion and his critique of the law and thus challenge the so-called "Lutheran" interpretation of Paul. Some of these arguments for the "non-Lutheran" Paul will be presented here.

1. Palestinian Judaism in Paul's time had no legalistic merit doctrine of salvation. Election into the covenant people—getting in—and ultimately salvation are by God's grace. E. P. Sanders states that obedience is *either* a response to electing grace *or* a meritorious means of salvation. The correct interpretation of the

Jewish sources is that obedience to the law is a response to grace and a means of staying in the covenant, not a way of earning salvation. Thus Paul is not attacking the righteousness of the law on the grounds that it leads to self-righteousness and pride (Sanders 1977, 81–83, 420, 422, 426; Dunn 1988, lxv; Ziesler 1989, 42–43).

2. The works of the law that Paul does oppose are not meritorious acts that earn salvation but such sociological boundary markers as circumcision, sabbath observance, and food laws that mark Israel off from other peoples and give her a sense of privilege or special status. Such an attitude fails to see that what God demands is the obedience of the heart (Dunn 1988, lxv–lxxi, 124, 137, 191–92, 382, 627).

3. Paul did not reject the law as the way to salvation because of any inherent flaw in the law itself, but because of two other factors that grow out of Paul's Christian theological standpoint. (a) Salvation is for all and therefore cannot be by the law because only the Jews have the law. Salvation by the law would exclude the gentiles. (b) Salvation cannot be by the law because dogmatically, as a matter of definition, it comes through Christ, through faith in Christ (Sanders 1977, 489–90, 496–97; 1983, 20, 27, 31–35, 47, 155).

The following counterarguments can be made.

1. Let it be gladly affirmed that grace is an important theme in first-century JUDAISM. That, however, does not mean that Judaism was not legalistic. The two modes of obedience—obedience as response to grace and obedience as a meritorious condition for salvation—are by no means an "either/or" but rather a highly ambiguous "both/and." It is not possible to separate the two experientially, and theo-*logically* grace as enabling power and salvation by works—theological legalism—go hand in glove. By theological legalism is meant the religious belief that human behavior, obedience, performance of God's requirements, counts with God as a condition for salvation.

In Leviticus Israel's salvation depends on the grace of atonement provided by God (17:11). On the other hand, Israel must maintain herself in life in the land by obedience to the law (18:5; 20:22; 23:11; 26:3-39). Similarly in Deuteronomy God chooses Israel out of God's love and not because of Israel's merit, and God graciously intervenes in history on Israel's behalf (1:30-32; 7:7-8; 8:17; 9:4; 10:15). Israel's OBEDIENCE then is the appropriate response to GRACE (5:6-21; 6:20-25; 7:6; 8:4; 14:1-2; 26:5-11; 27:9-10). On the other hand, Israel maintains herself in the land and purges her guilt by right actions (4:1, 5; 6:18; 7:12; 8:1; 11:26-28; 16:20; 21:9). This legalistic strand can be seen in many places (Job 34:11; Pss 18:20-24; 62:12; Prov 24:12; Jer 17:10; Hos 12:2; Tob 4:9-10; Sir 16:12-14): performance issues in salvation.

Stating this point is not a chauvinistic effort to make Christianity look better than Judaism. The NT also has its legalistic strand. For example, despite Paul's strong polemic against JUSTIFICATION by works, his appeal to judgment on the basis of deeds (Rom 14:11; 2 Cor 5:10) is legalistic. Even more strongly in Matthew, while grace is a reality (13:16, 17, 20, 23, 37-38) that enables the response (7:16-20;

12:33-37; 13:23), human beings must achieve salvation by their own efforts (5:20; 6:14-15; 7:24-25; 16:27; 18:35). Given the legalistic strand in the daughter religion (Christianity) it would be strange indeed if it were not in the parent (Judaism). The paradoxical theo-logic running through all this material is that God's grace as forgiveness and power enables people to do what *they* must do to be saved.

2. Returning to Paul, acts performed to express Jewish separateness, like circumcision, cannot be neatly distinguished from meritorious acts to gain salvation since God could be expected to approve such boundary markers. Moreover, Paul does not say that people seek the righteousness of the law—perform works of the law—in order to mark themselves off as distinct but in order to have something of their own to trust (Rom 9:30–10:3; Phil 3:4, 9): a righteousness of their own based on the law. This boasting or trust in self (3:27) is not before other people but before God (10:2). And while works of the law include cultic boundary markers (Gal 2:11-16), they also include strictly religious attitudes and moral acts as the commentary on 3:19-20 showed. Works of the law for Paul are cultic, religious, and moral acts performed in order to gain a standing with God based on one's own achievements.

3. Paul did not reject the law as the way to salvation *because* salvation by law would have excluded the gentiles. It would not have excluded them, because all are under the law already. There is an obvious sense in which the Jews have the Law of Moses, and the gentiles do not. But there is a running subtext in Paul that reveals that in the actual struggles of existence the gentiles are as much under the law in principle as the Jews. For example, what the law requires is written on the hearts of gentiles (2:14-15). It is the purpose of the law to hold everyone accountable, all the world; therefore all are under the law (3:19-20). The "all" of 3:19-20 are the same as the "all" of 3:9: Jew and gentile. Since the whole church—Jew and gentile—is said to have died to the law (7:4), all must have been under the law. In 5:12-14 the command to Adam is equivalent to law, and ADAM symbolizes the whole human race.

4. Nor did Paul reject the law as the means of salvation because by definition salvation is through faith in Christ. He rather rejected it because there is a substantive opposition between the righteousness of the law and the righteousness of faith. The righteousness of faith is not relatively better but is a qualitatively different antithesis. The righteousness of faith is willing to receive from God while the righteousness of the law asserts itself against God and is an instance of living according to the flesh (see commentary on 9:30–10:3).

5. The pursuit of salvation or justification by works of the law is not just a failure to see that God requires the obedience of the heart but is a deformation of the heart, a rupture of the wholeness of the self, in which three different levels of self-awareness are both in conflict with each other and out of touch with each other. These levels are: (1) I am righteous and wise (Rom 3:27-28; 1 Cor 1:29; 3:18-21). (2) Why then do I compulsively pursue righteousness and wisdom (Rom 10:2-3; 1 Cor 1:20-22; Gal 1:13-14; Phil 3:4-6, 8-9)? (3) My righteousness and wisdom are

really foolishness and wickedness—trash (Rom 3:10, 20, 23; Phil 3:6, 8-9; 1 Cor 3:19) (see Via 1990, 29–33).

6. Paul makes positive statements about the law: it is connected with faith (9:30-32) and promises and promotes life (7:10, 14a, 16b, 22-23). But he also makes negative statements: the law causes sin (7:5, 7-10). This is only an apparent contradiction because Paul is not stating opposing things about the law under the same category but is distinguishing yet relating two different categories—intention and result. Paul's basically consistent position, which accounts for most of his statements on the law, is that the law intends faith and life, but human beings as flesh try to use the law to save themselves with the result that they subvert the law's original intention and produce sin. Romans 5:13-14 and 5:20 are in conflict with the generally consistent position (see commentary).

7. God's original intention for the law is subverted not only because human beings as flesh try to make themselves secure through a righteousness of their own (Rom 8:3, 7; Phil 3:4, 9-10) but also because the law as a personified power deceives people (Rom 7:10-11). Paul associates the law with sin and death (1 Cor 15:56) and death with the demonic cosmic powers (1 Cor 15:24-26; Rom 8:38). Thus by implication the law is a demonic power that seduces people into the false belief that it is the source of salvation (7:10; 9:30–10:3) (Via 1990, 38–44, and commentary on 8:31-39).

Righteousness as Justification by Faith, 3:21–4:25

3:21-26. Righteousness, faith, and grace. But *now*— now when the *future*, final, eschatological revelation has become a *present* reality—God has manifested his righteousness apart from the law. Righteousness, faith, and grace will be distinguished for analysis, but for Paul they are inseparable parts of the divine-human transaction. Although manifested apart from the law, Paul shows (for example, in 1:17: 4:1-25; 10:5-13) how this righteousness is continuous with the law and prophets that bear witness to it. Righteousness must come apart from the law since the law has left all people sinful without distinction. Sin as falling short of the glory of God may refer to humankind's loss of the image of God (1 Cor 11:7). (On sin, see commentary on 1:18-32; 5:12-21; 7:1-25.)

Paul's understanding of righteousness is derived from OT and Jewish usage. In the OT we may discern three senses: (1) God's righteousness is God's character or nature—readiness to be faithful to the covenant relationship. (2) God actively manifests this character by intervention in human affairs to establish life. This manifestation of righteousness is salvation (Isa 46:12-13; 51:5-6; 61:11; 62:1-2; Ps 98:2-3). (3) Since God's righteousness or salvation can be received by people, it is also referred to as *theirs* (Isa 62:1-2; 54:17).

Paul essentially repeats these three usages. (1) Righteous is something God is (Rom 3:26)—God's character. (2) This character is revealed in action: God's righteousness is manifested (1:17; 3:21). (3) People who receive God's righteousness exist in the righteousness of faith—the state of human beings who have a right relationship with God (Rom 4:3, 5; 9:30). The righteousness of the law is the attempt of human beings to establish a relationship with God based on their own works (Rom 10:3; Phil 3:9; Williams 1980, 259–65; Wedderburn 1991, 116–23).

God's manifestation of his covenant righteousness occurs as the justification of the believer (3:22, 24, 26). In Greek the righteousness family of words and the justification family have the same root (*dikai-*). Justification is God's establishment of the new right relationship. It is not making the sinner *ethically* righteous in either action or intention. Nor is it treating the sinner *as if* he or she were ethically righteous—a legal fiction. Justification is rather a *relational* term, and its social setting is the law court. To justify is to acquit. Paul's usage begins in the law court but surpasses that frame of reference, for the OT forbids that a guilty person be acquitted (Isa 5:22-23; Prov 17:15) and asserts that God will not acquit the wicked (Exod 23:7). But that is exactly what Paul says God has now done: God justifies, acquits, pronounces not guilty the one who is sinful, ungodly, guilty (vv. 23-24; 4:5). This is not a legal fiction but a relationship that is real. The guilty person has with the judge the relationship of a not guilty person that cannot be broken (8:33-36). The unacceptable one is accepted.

Faith is the human acceptance or reception of God's justifying action (vv. 22-25). It is the opposite of works: that is, it is receiving from God rather than depending on one's own righteousness (9:30-32). Faith involves two closely connected moves: (1) It is willingness to believe that the proclaimed death and resurrection of the Son of God constitute God's saving action. (2) It is a surrender to this divine action and a reversal of self-understanding based on it, a renunciation of boasting or self-trust. The two acts of faith merge into one because Paul came to know Jesus as Lord and Son of God in coming to understand himself as having nothing on which to depend for salvation (Phil 3:6-11; Gal 2:19-20) (Bultmann 1951, 300–301).

Faith as response to God's justifying act is a *human* decision. It is acceptance of the preached word *as* word of God (1 Thes 2:13); therefore faith involves a committed interpretation of the human word that is the vehicle of God's righteous action. That faith is a human decision for which people are responsible is seen in the fact that Paul puts his readers under the *imperative* to have and live by faith (1 Cor 7:29-31; 2 Cor 5:20; Rom 11:20-22). Yet faith is not a posture human beings produce in themselves but one that God generates in them through the power of the preached word (Rom 1:16; 10:8, 17). Faith is given—"graced" (Phil 1:29). Both sides are seen in Phil 2:12-13: *you* work out your *own* salvation *because God* is working in you.

Faith in Jesus (Christ) (vv. 22, 26) is more literally translated "faith of Jesus Christ," and it has been argued that it means the "faithfulness of Jesus Christ" that is the medium of the divine activity rather than the faith of the believer in the divine activity (Hays 1981, 168, 196; Williams 1980, 271–76; Cousar 1990, 39). Actually the expression and its contexts (see also Gal 2:16) are ambiguous and it could mean one as well as the other, or both. It is not possible to determine that one of these meanings is the only right one.

Grace for Paul is both God's act in which God gives faith as response to the saving event and the act that is the saving event itself. These are two sides of the same event. Grace underlines the *gift*—undeserved—character of the event. Grace as event and gift extends what Paul has expressed in his understanding of the righteousness of God as the justification—acquittal—of the sinner: justification by grace. The eventful gift is the redemption accomplished in the sacrificial death of Christ Jesus.

The term "redemption" (*apolytrōsis*) was used for the liberation of slaves or prisoners of war and could be an allusion to the deliverance of Israel from Egyptian slavery. Therefore, it images Jesus' death as a liberation from sin.

The background of "sacrifice of atonement" by his blood has several facets. The term "sacrifice of atonement" (*hilastērion*) is generally used in the LXX (and in Heb 9:5) to refer to the mercy seat, which was the cover of the ark of the covenant in the holy of holies in the Temple (Exod 25:21). This is where God's presence is manifested (Exod 25:22; Lev 16:2) and where the blood of the sin offering is sprinkled to atone for sin (Lev 16:11-16). Closely associated with the sin offering is the ritual in which the scapegoat bears away Israel's sins into the wilderness (Lev 16:20-22). Romans 3:25 probably makes some reference to this material although "mercy seat" is too restricted a meaning, especially since *hilastērion* could mean "expiation" more broadly (4 Macc 17:22).

In Isa 53:6, 10, 12 the death of God's servant is a sin offering and a bearing of Israel's sins. It is difficult to believe that the NT text makes no allusion to this, even though Jewish sources did not interpret the Isaiah text as teaching expiatory vicarious suffering (Williams 1975, 111, 120).

In 4 Macc 17:22 (see also 1:11; 6:28-29) the deaths of the Jewish martyrs are interpreted as a *hilastērion* that preserves and purifies Israel. This Hellenistic-Jewish text was probably influenced by the classical Greek notion of a hero or heroine dying for the city, fatherland, family, or piety. Either directly or through such a Jewish source as 4 Maccabees this idea reached early Christianity (Williams 1975, 111, 120, 145–63, 230, 233). It should be pointed out that Rom 3:25-26a or 3:24-26 is probably a pre-Pauline confession.

The term *hilastērion* can mean either *propitiation* (a human act to appease or placate God—primarily in nonbiblical sources) or *expiation* (a divine act to deal with sin—primarily in the LXX). In Paul there is a hint of the idea of propitiation. The death of Jesus does after all avert the wrath of God (Rom 5:8-9). But the overall context in Paul shows that expiation is much the stronger sense: it is what God does to cover and forgive human sin. This interpretation is supported by several points.

(1) In speaking of Christ's death for human beings Paul does not say that it was *in place of* us (*anti*) (to appease God's wrath) but rather *for our sakes* or *in behalf of* us (*hyper*) (to affect us: Rom 5:8; 1 Cor 15:3; 2 Cor 5:14; Gal 3:13).

(2) Christ does not die in our place. Rather *our* old self also must die, and Christ's death is for us in that it draws us into itself and enables us to die to the old person we were (Rom 6:4-6; 7:4, 6; 2 Cor 5:14-15).

(3) It is humankind that needs to be reconciled, not God. We are the enemy, not God (Rom 5:10; 2 Cor 5:18-19).

(4) The cross confronts us as word (1 Cor 1:18) and as sacrament (Rom 6:4-6; 1 Cor 10:16; 11:26). The cross as word becomes effective by creating faith in us (Rom 10:8-9, 17). The cross as word, then, is toward us and affects us. It is not directed toward God.

In vv. 25b-26 the purpose of God's expiating act is to demonstrate God's own righteousness. God needs to make this active move because in the past God has passed over (not forgiven) former sins in God's restraint or inactivity (see Isa 63:15; 64:10-12). That is, God has not dealt with the sinful situation of the past (Williams 1975, 21–34). Perhaps the main reason for seeing the past as negative or neutral (unforgiven) is that it is contrasted with the present which is positive: righteousness is *now* demonstrated. The manifested righteousness has a dually stated purpose: in order for God (1) to be righteous, and (2) to justify the one who has faith in Christ (or the one redeemed by Christ's faithfulness). Since the latter purpose is positive, the fact that the former is mentioned at all probably (or possibly) means that it is a negative contrast. That is, the demonstration of God's righteousness entails judgment or justice as well as acquittal. This judgment is not in addition to justification by grace but is included within it. When one accepts the *undeserved* gift of a new standing with God, no longer under condemnation (8:33-34), then one must acknowledge—judge—oneself as *undeserving*.

In recent years René Girard has developed a complex theory to explain the origin and structure of both societies and religions. In his view societies project their internal, reciprocal violence and hostilities onto a sacrificial victim or scapegoat in order to remove from the society the violence that would otherwise destroy it. By deciding unanimously to kill the scapegoat, the society's violence and the guilt for it are transferred to the sacrificial victim. Thus social conflicts are eliminated or curtailed and the community can exist in accord. The victim is regarded as both guilty and sacred. The community conceals from itself the fact that it is really the violent and guilty party. The great difference that the biblical tradition inserts into this picture is that guilt is shifted away from the victim and back onto society where it belongs (Girard 1986, 27, 38, 101–103, 109–10, 117; 1989, 3–4, 7–8, 53, 94–96, 104).

Whatever one may think of the generalizability of Girard's theory, the structure of Romans, with its own modifications and transformations, reflects Girard's depiction of the development of religion and society. In the letter the whole human community is portrayed as totally divided (1:18-32) and involved in ruinous, reciprocal violence (3:10-18). In this situation God acted redemptively through the sacrificial death of Christ (vv. 21-26). Paul understands the social violence as sin (3:9), and the way to freedom from the violence of sin is to die sacramentally with the sacrificial victim (6:4-6). This communal participation in baptism creates a unified community—one body in Christ (12:5). But the redemption, both individual and communal, is never complete; and the individual is exhorted to keep redemption in process by the continual appropriation of the death to sin (6:11-12); and the church is exhorted to continue cementing communal bonds (12:3, 6, 9).

3:27–4:2. Boasting, faith, and the validity of the law. This section is a diatribal exchange in which Paul deals with the impact of justification by grace on the continuing validity of the law (Stowers 1981, 164–65). The dialogue is generated by the interlocutor's question about what has happened to boasting if justification is through faith.

To boast is to put one's confidence in or to affirm one's confidence in. It is virtually synonymous with to trust in (*peithō*) (Phil 3:3). The object of this confidence can be God (Jer 9:24) or Christ (1 Cor 1:31; 2 Cor 10:17; Gal 6:14; Phil 3:3), on the one hand, or one's own achievements—wisdom, power, righteousness (Jer 9:23; 1 Cor 1:29; Phil 3:3, 9), on the other hand (Bultmann 1951, 242–43; Käsemann 1980, 69–70). Paul's questioner wants to know what has become of our basis for having confidence in our own righteousness based on the law. What becomes of boasting?

Paul answers that it has been excluded on the law or principle of faith. The word translated "law" here is Paul's normal word for law (*nomos*). But it could mean principle, norm, or order. On the other hand, Paul could be understood as saying *law* of faith. That is, boasting is excluded on the basis of the Law of Moses understood, not as demanding works, but as intending faith (see commentary on 9:31-32). There is *one* God, of Jew and gentile; therefore, there is *one* condition for justification, for both Jew and gentile. It is faith.

Paul's questioner then asks: do we overthrow the law, since justification by faith rules out works performed in obedience to the law as a way to justification. Paul answers: absolutely not, we rather establish the law.

The interlocutor then wonders how justification by *faith* can uphold the law since ABRAHAM belongs to the law but was justified by *works* and thus has something of his own to boast about. JUDAISM understood Abraham as the prime example of the devout Jew who was received as righteous because of his faithful obedience to the law (Jub 23:10; 1 Macc 2:52; Kidd 4:14) (Dunn 1988, 196). Paul replies that whatever boastful claims Abraham might have been able to make, they would have no standing with God.

In the remainder of chap. 4 Paul proceeds to develop the point that justification does not overthrow the law because justification by faith is already in the law in the case of Abraham. Clearly Paul understands the law as including much more than demands, and he is going to interpret Abraham very differently than his fellow Jews did.

It is true that Paul affirms the continuity between Israel and Christianity in Rom 4 (Dunn 1988, 197). Paul does this, however, by Christianizing Abraham. He does not say: proper Christian faith is like the faith of Abraham, the father of Israel. He rather says: Abraham, the father of Israel, already had Christian faith. That is, Paul finally defines Abraham's faith as *resurrection* faith. Since Paul's strategy is to use Abraham to prove that the Christian gospel of justification by faith does not overthrow but rather establishes the law, he logically has to argue that Abraham already had the faith of justification by faith.

4:3-15. Abraham's faith is reckoned as righteousness. For Paul it was not Abraham's works but his *believing* God that was reckoned to him as righteousness. Paul interprets the faith and righteousness attributed to Abraham in Gen 15:6 as being qualitatively the same as the righteousness of faith that Christians have.

In vv. 4-5 Paul makes a clear distinction between the self-understanding that accompanies works and the one that accompanies faith. The person who does works for salvation regards these works as meritorious; that is, the reward from God is a debt or obligation (*opheilēma*) which God owes to the worker. But the one who simply accepts in faith the new relationship that God establishes, knows herself or himself as *ungodly*, not deserving.

Verses 7-8 connects the *reckoning* of righteousness with not *reckoning* sin in Ps 32:1-2 (Ps 31 in LXX). Thereby Paul identifies justification with the forgiveness celebrated in the Psalm. But this LXX quotation is the only place where Paul uses this common verb for "forgive" (*aphiēmi*).

Paul goes on to underscore the non-meritorious quality of Abraham's righteousness by pointing out that his faith was reckoned as righteousness *before* he was circumcised. Then he was circumcised as a seal of the righteousness. Therefore, Abraham can be the father of the gentiles, who have faith but are not circumcised, and of the Jews, who are circumcised but also follow the example of Abraham's pre-circumcision faith.

4:16-25. Abraham's faith as faith in the resurrection. The specific promise of God that Abraham believed and as a result had his faith reckoned as righteousness was the promise that he would have many heirs. The promise was given at a time when he was old and Sarah was barren and they had no legitimate heir.

The fact that Paul describes the God in whom Abraham believed as the one who gives life to the dead and calls into existence the things that do not exist shows that Paul is interpreting Abraham's experience of God in the light of the Christian experience of the God who raised Jesus from the dead (v. 24). The Abraham story may also have contributed to his understanding of Jesus' death and resurrection. The dialectical interaction between the two is seen in the fact that the discussion of Abraham moves immediately into the kerygmatic (preaching) statement about Jesus' death and resurrection for our justification.

Paul's appropriation of the Abraham story is a clear case of his Christian under-standing governing his reinterpretation of the pre-Christian past.

We could say that Paul posits a "resurrection situation" in Abraham's history and a corresponding faith arising from it. The resurrection situation is what the Christians' and Abraham's situations have in common—the promise of life in the midst of death.

The broader import of Rom 4 is that for Paul the death-resurrection-faith situation is a possibility—in principle and in actuality—at any point along the line of the history of God's saving acts. Not only Abraham but also other Israelites had the kind of faith Abraham had (4:11-12). Yet Paul can speak of the time before Christ as the time before faith came (Gal 3:23-25). These two points of view can be reconciled by pointing out, with Käsemann, that salvation history is not uninterrupted but contains discontinuities (Käsemann 1971, 88). The "before faith came" does not mean there had been no instances of Christian faith before Christ but that these instances had come intermittently, separated by gaps. There were times of faith before Christ but also times before faith came.

Romans 4 constitutes a certain modification—or deconstruction—of Paul's customary position. Generally faith in Christ (Rom 3:22; Gal 2:16) or in his death and resurrection (Rom 10:9; Gal 2:20; 3:1-2, Phil 3:9) is the condition for salvation. Being in a right relationship with God comes through faith in Christ (Rom 10:10). Faith in Christ is *in itself* the way to, or the consequence of (Phil 1:29), salvation. But in Rom 4, faith in Christ is not itself the way to justification. Rather faith in Christ has become a paradigm or model for other analogous situations that are not specifically faith in Christ but are qualitatively similar to it. If that were not Paul's real point, he would not be able to show that the faith of justification was present in Abraham and thus does not overthrow the law.

The medium for this shift in Paul's position is the hermeneutical move of interpreting X *as* Y; that is, interpreting Abraham's faith in God's promise (X) *as* the Christian's faith in the death and resurrection of Jesus (Y). The substance of the shift is that faith in Christ has ceased to be the focus and has been replaced in the center by the category of having righteousness reckoned to one. This is what happened for both Abraham and the Christian believers—the reckoning of righteousness. What the two have in common is that faith is reckoned as righteous-ness (vv. 22-24a).

The focus or fundamental category is having faith reckoned as righteousness, and the faith in which righteousness—a right relationship with God—becomes a reality has a certain character. Having this faith is the content of salvation, and this content is what Paul wants to define here. But the faith in which righteousness becomes a reality does not have to be faith in Christ. It has to be *like* faith in Christ. It has to be holding in hope to God's promise of life in the face of the impossible. Faith in Christ is the paradigm for faith as righteousness but not the only actual access to the right relationship.

Life as Liberation from Victimizing Powers, 5:1–8:39

Romans 5:1 is an important transitional verse. *Since we are justified* sums up 3:21–4:25, and *peace* encompasses the new *life of freedom* that 5:1–8:39 will unfold. Paul makes the discussion in Rom 5–8 engage issues connected with the Jewish-gentile conflict in the Roman church—for example, the ethical dimension of the gospel (6:1-4, 12-13; 8:13) and the role of the law (chap. 7). That historical connection, however, is not the generating source of Rom 5–8, for both the juxtaposition of 5–8 to 1:18–4:25 and the content of 5–8 flow theo-*logically* from the content of 1:18–4:25. For Paul the new relationship with God—JUSTIFICATION—issues in a new quality of life—FREEDOM; and yet that freedom is experienced ambiguously. Therefore, it is necessary to explicate the powers that assail the life of freedom: ADAM, SIN, the LAW, flesh, and death. But Paul's real interest is in affirming deliverance from the destructive powers. In his paradoxical and dialectical way Paul both declares that the liberation has occurred (6:6-8; 7:6; 8:1-2) and expresses the hope that it will occur (5:5; 8:20-25). In the ending of each of the major subdivisions of this section he affirms that life has come to believers in and through Christ (5:21; 6:23; 7:25a; 8:39).

Justification and liberation are not identical with each other, but they do merge into each other in the process of SALVATION. Justification gives the sinner the new *relationship* of a sinless person, no longer under condemnation. The new relationship confers upon the believer's life a new center—Christ (2 Cor 5:15)—rather than oneself. Thus the believer no longer lives toward achieving his or her salvation through good works. Since it was this misguided effort that brought one under the power of sin and the law (7:13-25), the justification that provides the new relationship is also a deliverance into a new kind of life. Proceeding from the other direction, it is the liberation from the power of sin and death—the overwhelming ruinous drive to manipulate all reality—that makes it possible to accept the new relationship. Faith is a gift.

Justification and liberation are immanent in each other, but they are not identical. By analogy the relationship of justification is the shape of the new life, and freedom from the powers is the content that is shaped. Moreover, justification sees the guilty sinner as freely and responsibly rejecting God and pronounces him *not guilty*. The *justified* sinner is still *sinner*. Deliverance sees the sinner as the victim of superhuman powers and frees her from these powers. The liberated sinner has a new character, is on the way toward not being sinner. Justification and liberation continue to interact with each other in salvation understood as an ongoing process (2 Cor 3:18; 4:16).

Transition from Justification to Peace and Life, 5:1-11

Romans 1:18–4:25 is unified on the basis of its depiction of the negative (wrath) and positive (justification) sides of God's righteousness. Romans 5:12–8:39 coheres on the basis of its portrayal of the interconnected destructive powers—Adam, sin, law, FLESH, DEATH—and the proclamation of God's liberation from these through Jesus Christ. Romans 5:1-11 points transitionally in both directions.

Our transitional passage looks backward to justification and grace (vv. 1-2, 9), Jesus' death for sinners (vv. 6-9), salvation (vv. 9-10), and wrath (v. 9). It points forward to the hope of sharing eschatological glory (v. 2; 8:18, 21), suffering (v. 3; 8:18), ethical concerns (v. 4; 8:4-5, 13-15), and the death of Christ (vv. 6-9; 6:3; 7:4, 25a; 8:3).

According to some manuscripts Paul says "since we are justified by faith, therefore *we have* (indicative mood) peace." According to other manuscripts (slightly better) he says "since we are justified by faith, therefore *let us have* (subjunctive mood) peace." In terms of the larger context of Rom 5–8, either is compatible with Paul's thought. He can refer to God's salvation in human beings as an accomplished reality (6:3-4) or he can put believers under the imperative to make it a reality (6:11-13). Justification and peace are related as cause and effect—justification, therefore PEACE. They are not identical.

Peace does not mean the subjectivity of peace of mind. Its background is the Hebraic concept of *shalōm*—total well-being. Within the context of Romans, it refers to the reconstitution of the deformed self (1:21-23, 24-28; 3:23) and the restructuring of a society torn by reciprocal hostility and violence (1:29-32; 3:10-18).

Having strongly criticized boasting (trusting) in our own works, Paul proposes boasting in the hope of sharing God's glory as the fitting Christian posture. More than that, believers boast in their afflictions. Suffering is not a contradiction to standing in grace but the condition in which grace is effective (Dunn 1988, 264). We boast in our suffering because suffering leads through endurance and character—the quality of being proved by testing—to HOPE. And hope does not disappoint us because—it would seem—of our strength of character. But Paul surprises us. Hope does not disappoint us because the LOVE of God has been poured in our hearts by the Holy Spirit. It is God's love for us, not our love for God, which the HOLY SPIRIT has established in our hearts, the inner core of our being.

The Spirit for Paul is the power of God that makes God's reality and action present in human experience. In this context the action of God that the Spirit makes present is the love God demonstrated by sending God's Son to die for humankind. Our radical undeservingness of this love Paul underscores by means of a vivid contrast. While a person will hardly die for another who is righteousness (correct according to law or moral principle), a person perhaps would dare to die for someone who is good (more than correct). But Christ died for us ungodly sinners who are neither righteous nor good.

As in 3:24-25, the consequence of Jesus' saving death is expressed as justification (v. 9)—a new relationship. This is paralleled in v. 10 by defining the new situation as RECONCILIATION. This category takes its meaning from the reality of personal, group, and national hostilities, and it draws out the significance of peace with God in v. 1. In reconciliation hostility is overcome, and here it is human beings, not

God, who are the enemy that needs to be reconciled. Justification and reconciliation overlap in meaning. Reconciliation is neither identical with nor the consequence of justification. Each describes the new situation that results from Christ's death, with reconciliation underlining the personal element in the relationship between God the judge and the justified sinner (Cranfield 1980, 265–67; Dunn 1988, 259).

Now that justification and reconciliation are a present reality through the love of God, total salvation in the future is assured. Paul typically, but not always, uses the term salvation for the future completion of redemption.

Freedom from Adam, 5:12-21

With this section the theme of sin takes on a new intensity and a somewhat different focus. Prior to this, sin is seen as universal but primarily as a matter of individual responsibility. Now with the role of Adam the supra-individual cause of sin comes clearly into the picture. Romans 6:1-23 then treats sin as a concrete everyday problem and struggle in the life of the believer. Chapter 7 deals with the relationship of sin to the law and chap. 8, with its connections to flesh and death. Yet throughout the discussion all these destructive powers are interconnected.

Adam is not the originating *source* of sin, but he is the agent through which sin as a demonic personalized power entered the world and infected all humankind and brought death in its wake. And yet death spread to *all* because *all sinned*. Paul maintains the paradox that sin and death are both freely chosen and fated, but the fated side is emphasized in vv. 12-21.

Structurally v. 12 is the first member of a comparison between ADAM and Christ, the second member of which occurs only at v. 18b: *as* through the one man Adam sin came (v. 12), *so* through the other one's act of righteousness justification came (v. 18b). Verses 13-17 is a parenthesis clarifying the difference between Adam and Christ, and v. 18a essentially repeats v. 12 as a preparation for the second member in v. 18b (Cranfield 1980, 272–73).

For Paul the presence of the law makes sin a transgression, makes it guilt-laden, causes it to count or incur wrath (vv. 13-14; 4:15). Adam's sin was such a guilty transgression because God's command to him not to eat from the tree (Gen 2:16-17) was the functional equivalent of law. But Paul holds here that between Adam and Moses' giving of the law, since there was no law, although people sinned and died, this sin was different from Adam's and was not counted. That declaration contradicts Paul's more general position in two ways. (1) There are many indications in Paul elsewhere that the whole human race has always been under the law in principle (see excursus on the law in the commentary on 3:9-20). Thus there could be no time when sin was not counted. (2) For Paul death is the wages or *result* of *sin* (Rom 6:23; 8:5-6); therefore, since Paul grants that death did in fact rule from Adam to Moses (when there was allegedly no law) and holds in 6:23 that death is the wages of sin, he cannot say consistently in v. 13 that sin is not counted. The reality of death shows that sin did count.

If Adam was not the originating *source* of sin, he is nevertheless the *cause* of the plight of all other human beings. His sin causes the sin (v. 19), death (vv. 15, 17), and condemnation (vv. 16, 18) of all others.

Adam and Christ are alike in that in each case what the one does affects the many—all others—and each of them represents the whole (or potentially the whole) of humankind. On the other hand, while Adam began a history, the history of sin, Christ reversed that history. Thus Adam represents humankind as sinful and Christ, humankind as righteous. And the righteousness of Christ does not just balance the sin of Adam and its consequences. It much more overbalances them, producing justification and life (vv. 15b, 16b, 17b, 18b, 19b).

In v. 16b the word signifying the opposite of condemnation should be translated justification, as it is. But in Greek it is not Paul's usual word for justification (*dikaiōsis*) but rather the cognate term *dikaiōma*, which ordinarily means requirement or righteous deed. *Dikaiōma* has a more normal meaning in v. 18 where it is used of Christ's righteous deed as a synonym for his obedience (v. 19).

Paul probably believed Adam to have been the first historical man, a difficult belief in the modern world. Nevertheless, Adam is also profoundly employed by Paul as a symbol for what the human situation always is in historical existence. In Rom 7 Paul can use the Adam story to express his own implication in sin and also to say what is true typically for other individuals. At the same time Adam symbolizes the whole of humankind, the structural human situation, the totality that overwhelms the individual. As Paul Ricoeur puts it, Adam is the always already there of evil in every situation into which the individual enters (Ricoeur 1969, 241, 243, 251, 257–58).

It has been held that Paul bases the participation of all humans in Adam on the physical-psychic solidarity of the human race and that he thinks of the participation of all in Christ in an analogous way. There is only the slightest hint of the role of faith. All share in Christ's work as a matter of the unity of the race (Best 1955, 35–37).

But Paul does *not* treat the effects of Adam's and Christ's actions in an analogous way. When he speaks of our involvement with Adam, he uses the past (aorist) tense and indicative mood—signs of factuality (vv. 15a, 17a, 19a, 21a). But when he speaks of the effect of Christ's obedient righteousness, although he once states that grace has already abounded (v. 15b), he characteristically here speaks of our involvement in Christ by using the future tense or subjunctive mood (vv. 17b, 19b, 21b)—signs of possibility. And he implies that this possibility—not a natural fact—will become a reality when it is *received* by faith (v. 17b).

Paul concludes the Adam section by stating that the law slipped or stole in *in order that* (probably a purpose rather than a result clause) the trespass might increase or become greater. This contradicts Paul's more typical position that sin is the *result rather than* the *purpose* of the law (see excursus on the law in commentary on 3:9-20). But the good news is that when sin increased, grace superabounded; and the purpose of this grace is that it might reign through righteousness to produce eternal life. Grace, righteousness and eternal life are compactly distinguished and related. Grace (the gift and act of God) establishes righteousness (a right relationship with God) that issues in eternal life.

Freedom from Sin, 6:1-23

In Rom 6:1 Paul has his diatribal questioner draw a false conclusion, phrased as a question: What then shall we say? If grace superabounds where sin increases, should we not remain in sin in order that grace might abound? Paul answers "absolutely not" (author trans.). He then spends this chapter giving his reasons why the believer should not continue in sin. Thus he takes up in a substantive way the question that he summarily dismissed in 3:8. Sin in Rom 6 is both a personalized power (vv. 6-7, 12, 16, 20) and deeds of rebellion (vv. 12, 19, 21).

What are the reasons for not remaining in sin? It has been argued that since Paul rejects the law as a standard for performing good works that merit salvation and since he does not appeal to the inherent authority of the law, he has no logical basis for claiming that the believer must not continue in sin (Knox 1954, 471). Paul, however, does have powerful arguments of a different kind to justify his contention that the believer should live an ethical life. It is not Paul's position that the believer in consequence of his or her renewal will necessarily live an ethical life but rather that the morally responsible life is now a possibility that ought to be enacted—and for good reasons.

6:1-14. Sin and baptism. Paul tells the Romans that Christians should not sin because in BAPTISM they have shared in Jesus' death and potentially in his resurrection. Jesus' death was a victory over sin (v. 10); therefore, our baptismal participation in his death frees us from sin (vv. 6-7). We should enact in our daily ethical lives what we have become in baptism—freed from sin. The believer should not continue in sin because to do so shatters wholeness or integrity, ruptures the correspondence between what we are in baptism and what we are in our daily lives. Sin violates the newness (v. 4) and life (v. 13) that have been created in us in consequence of the death of our old self (v. 6).

Baptism has a real effect. It is not just a pointer to a faith experience that happens independently of baptism. It is a symbol in which the meaning or effect is actualized in and through the symbol. Since in baptism we are united with Christ's death (v. 5), the benefits of that death are extended to us, and we are freed from sin (v. 7). Baptism does something.

This freedom from sin, however, is not a fixed, inalienable condition or possession. It is a reality but a reality that is a possibility that must be appropriated by the believer. You must become what you are. The believer is placed under the imperative to understand herself as dead to sin and alive to God (v. 11) and to yield her members to God and not to sin (v. 13).

The movement of this section is from indicative affirmations about the reality of freedom from sin (vv. 1-10) through imperative calls to appropriate this reality-possibility (vv. 11-13) and back to the affirmation in v. 14 that sin will not lord it over you because you are not under law but under grace. Since the law is the power of sin (1 Cor 15:56), if it is done away with (v. 14b), sin is reduced in power (v. 14a).

It is important that for Paul while the believer has already shared in Christ's *death* through baptism (vv. 4a, 5a, 6a, 7) sharing Christ's *resurrection* is *"reserved"* (Käsemann 1980, 166–67) for the future (v. 5b). Through sharing Christ's death a new quality of life is possible in this life (vv. 4, 6), but we are not yet raised with Christ (Phil 3:10). This means that salvation is never possessed but is a continuing process in which grace and faith interact (2 Cor 3:18; 4:16).

It has often been held that the MYSTERY RELIGIONS of the ancient world (the worship of Attis, Osiris, Dionysus, etc.) focused on a dying-rising deity with whom the worshiper could attain unity and deification through ritual acts. By means of the cultic celebration the worshiper passed from death to life with the deity. This influenced Paul's view of baptism.

It has been questioned, on the other hand, whether any sources truly substantiate the idea that the mysteries were in existence in Paul's time, and real differences have been pointed out between Paul's understanding of baptism and the mystery rites.

For example, the mystery rites were believed to be effective in themselves, automatically, while for Paul baptism is effective only when appropriated by faith. Or in the mysteries the worshiper is absorbed into the deity while in Paul the believer retains his or her identity but has a new relationship with God (Best 1955, 47–48; Wagner 1967, 117–18, 195, 198, 202, 212, 217).

Whatever the chronological relationship between Paul and the mysteries and however many very real differences there were between them, they had one important thing in common. Redemptive power extends from the deity to the worshipers by means of symbolic acts. This is also true in Judaism where, for example, the liberating power of the EXODUS is re-experienced through the celebration of PASSOVER.

6:15-23. Sin and death. Paul begins his discussion of the second reason for not remaining in sin by repeating the initial words from 6:1: *What then? Should we sin because we are not under the law but under grace?* And again: "Absolutely not." The central point is that one should not sin because sin produces death.

Paul interweaves four kinds of material in this section: theological reflection, indicative affirmations about their being set free from sin, the imperative to be righteous, and observations about the Romans' past way of life.

Paul's theological reflections deal with the paradoxical interaction of freedom and slavery. A person is the slave of whatever lord or power he or she obeys. But the choice to acknowledge and obey *no* lord is not a human possibility. As finite creatures human beings must obey some higher power. The only choice is whether one will obey sin or obey God (or righteousness) (vv. 16, 18, 22). To be free from sin is to be the slave of God or righteousness. But to be free from sin is at the same time to be free for God and obedience, which one was not when one was a slave of sin (v. 20). Real freedom for Paul is slavery to the power that can give life (v. 22). Romans 6 emphasizes that freedom from sin is *slavery to God* which is *freedom for God* and obedience. But 1 Cor 3:21-23 adds that one who belongs to Christ and God is grounded in a reality beyond the world. On the basis of this ground the believer is also free *for the world*, free to engage in the totality of the world's reality without being enslaved by it.

Paul declares to the Romans that they have in fact been liberated from sin (vv. 18, 22). But as is typical of him, he also places them under the imperative to make that freedom/slavery—which is both a reality and a possibility—into an actuality. Present your bodily members as slaves to righteousness which leads to sanctification (v. 19c).

Käsemann has argued that for Paul the righteousness that God establishes in believers includes obedience. The ethical imperative does not stand alongside the indicative statements about the reality of justification or righteousness but coincides with them or is integrated into them (Käsemann 1980, 174–75). SANCTIFICATION is the believer's being for God in his or her everyday existence in the secular world (183), and for Käsemann justification includes sanctification; they coincide (174, 183). Or he can say that gift (justification) and task (sanctification) coincide (175). Obedience must verify the gift (174). Christ is no longer the Lord of the one who does not obediently serve him (175). If one fails at the task, he or she loses the gift.

Käsemann's interpretation ignores the fact that for Paul it is the *ungodly* or *sinful* person who is justified (3:23-24; 4:5). The person who is justified is still sinful. The justified believer who performs acts deserving of condemnation is still justified by God and is still the object of the crucified and risen Christ's intercession (8:33-34). Nothing can separate us from the love of Christ (8:35-39).

At the same time it is certainly the case with Paul that the proper and intended result of justification is sanctification. Righteousness is toward or into sanctification (v. 19; but also, see commentary on 14:10-12).

The one who is justified by grace without regard to his or her religious or moral achievements is nevertheless not to continue in sin because to do so: (1) causes the self to be divided against itself and (2) produces death. The juxtaposition of these two reasons implies that one dimension of death is self-division. The other—and more fundamental—dimension of death is that it is hostility to and estrangement from God (8:6-8). To go on in sin is to be both against God (vv. 16, 18, 22; 8:7) and against oneself (6:2, 4, 6; 7:5, 9; 8:10). The fundamental sinful reality is being against God (1:21a, 23, 25), and being against oneself is its consequence (1:21b, 24b, 27). Death is the slave wages paid by sin when one serves sin.

The free gift of God is life—a new relationship of reconciliation with God, the reconstitution of a shattered society and the reuniting of the divided self.

Freedom from the Law, 7:1-25

7:1-6. A death frees from the law. Paul introduces this topic by stating a broad principle (v. 1) which he illustrates (vv. 2-3) and then extends into its theological application (vv. 4-6). The connections of the parts are far from obvious or smooth, but the whole thing may hold together better than it appears to. And the main point is clear: the believer has been freed from the law.

The principle taken literally is a truism. A person is freed from obligation to the law by his or her own death. In the illustration a wife is freed from the legal requirement to be faithful to her husband by her husband's death. Thus one person is freed from the law by the death of another (vv. 2-3).

The theological application (7:4-6) makes metaphorical use of both preceding motifs, one's own death and the death of another. Under the conditions of fallen existence—the flesh—sinful passions aroused by the law worked in our members to produce death. But believers have been discharged from the law by dying to it. They are dead as far as the law's enticement to earn salvation by works is concerned. The old self has died through the body of Christ—probably a reference to Christ's death. The believer participates in the redemptive effects of Christ's death by dying with him (6:4; 2 Cor 5:14-15).

7:7-25. The law, sin, and internal conflict. First Corinthians 15:56 states concisely that the law is the power of sin, and Rom 7 probes that relationship in an elaborate way. Both sin and the law are personified by Paul as cosmic powers, suprahuman persons. Sin has dominion, reigns, enslaves (Rom 6:6-7, 12-14, 16, 20). It lies dead, revives, deceives, and kills (vv. 8-9, 11). Similarly, the law comes in (5:20; 7:9), arouses sin (vv. 5, 7), takes us captive (v. 6), and promises life but deceives by serving up death (v. 10).

Sin uses the law (vv. 8, 13). But the law as the instrument of sin is so closely tied to sin as a power, sin as the initiator of sinning, that the law itself can appear as the initiator. Sin employs the law, but the law is the power (7:5; 1 Cor 15:56) that brings latent sin to active life (v. 9). Therefore, the law itself can be spoken of as the provoker that causes sin (v. 7) and that, installed in the flesh, works against God's redemptive intention (vv. 22-23).

The law provokes or arouses sin (vv. 7-14), and existence under the law is rent by internal conflict (vv. 15-25). Paul makes use of the Adam myth to interpret his own experience as typical of humankind. There are three questions (which interpenetrate each other) to be pursued in interpreting this passage.

1. What phase of Paul's life is he talking about when he speaks of himself as engaged in all kinds of covetousness and torn asunder by conflict between intention and result?

He can hardly be referring to his Jewish life because as a Jew he saw himself as blameless regarding the righteousness of the law (Phil 3:6). It can also be argued that his description ill fits his Christian life. While there are other places where he attributes conflict to the Christian life (8:10), in such places the redemptive forces are victorious (8:11, 16). But in Rom 7 the law and sin seem to have the upper hand. Moreover, the structure of Romans suggests that he is not talking about Christian experience in this chapter. Just as 1:18–3:20 provides a negative foil for 3:21–5:11, and 5:12-21 provides a negative foil for 6:1-23, and 9:1–10:21 does for chap. 11, so 7:1-25 provides a negative foil for 8:1-39 (Käsemann 1980, 205, 210).

The most likely possibility is that since Paul as a Jew felt blameless (Phil 3:6), Rom 7:7-25 is describing his past Jewish life from the standpoint of his Christian faith. Looking back on his pre-Christian past he sees that he was in fact sinful and self-divided, but prior to his conversion he was unconscious of his true condition. Here he is describing the human situation as fallen—fleshly—and under the power of sin (v. 14), a part of cosmic fallenness (1:18–3:20; 8:22-23) (Bultmann 1951, 246–49; Käsemann 1980, 192, 199).

The chief problem with the immediately preceding interpretation is that the past tenses with which Paul has been describing his experience in vv. 7-13 are replaced by the present tense when he begins to speak about his inner conflict (vv. 14-24). Must we not then say that the present tense verbs present his pre-Christian and unconscious self-dividedness as if it were present and conscious. Does not the present tense in fact extend the inner conflict into the present of Paul and his Christian readers? Believers are only in the process of being renewed (2 Cor 3:18; 4:16). As long as they bear the image of the old Adam (1 Cor 15:39) and do not have Christ fully formed in them (Gal 4:19), which means as long as time lasts (Phil 3:10-11), they struggle with sin and self-division.

2. What exactly is the nature of the sinful covetousness or desire that Paul describes or in exactly what sense does the law provoke sin?

The most obvious answer is that the law provokes acts of covetousness. That wrong acts are in view is supported by the fact that the passions of sin aroused by the law are plural (7:5). Also the reference to members of the body and fruit for death (7:5) alludes to the similar language in 6:19, 21 where sin is rebellion upon rebellion.

The law is not sin, yet Paul would not have sinned but for the law. The very prohibition against coveting generated every coveting in him (vv. 7-8). The dynamic is that the law as a demand for obedience is a reminder of human limitations and thereby provokes in people a will not to submit (8:7).

At the same time vv. 9-10 seems to be a transition to sin in a different sense incited by the law (Theissen 1987, 209–10). *Sin* (v. 9) is closely related to the fact that the law promises life but causes death (v. 10). The law promises life, and under the conditions of fallen existence (in the flesh) people assume that life is attained by doing the law (10:5). They attempt a righteousness of the law that is a righteousness of their own (10:3; Phil 3:9), a human righteousness that puts God in their *debt* (Rom 4:4). This also is a refusal to submit to God (10:3). The law incites sin in the sense of offering a means to establish one's own righteousness, which is a rejection of God's righteousness.

Perhaps the connecting link between these two dimensions of sin is the function that Paul assigns to the law in 3:19—to shatter every self-defense and hold people accountable. The law provokes sin in the sense of overt acts of disobedience. Then people, knowing from the law that they are accountable and without a word to say, attempt to establish their own righteousness by obedience to the law and to put God in their debt.

3. What is the nature of the inner conflict Paul describes in vv. 15-24? Its nature is governed by the two dimensions of sin that Paul has brought to light. It is not an either/or but a both/and.

Paul in anguish declares that he does not do what he intends but rather does what he hates. He can will the good, but he cannot do it (vv. 15, 18-19). He rather does evil.

This self-division is in some part moral. The law was for Paul as a Jew, and still is in some sense, an ethical standard (13:8-10; 1 Cor 7:19). Paul wills to do the moral good that the law requires but finds that he lacks the resources and does the opposite.

With this sense of failure—at some level of consciousness—he then tries to use the law to establish righteousness and life for himself. Here the conflict is existential. He agrees that the law is good and spiritual (vv. 14, 16). He appropriates its promise to give life (v. 10a) but discovers that it gives death instead (v. 10b). The good he wills is life—salvation—but the evil he achieves is death, because he pursues his own righteousness rather than accepting God's.

We have seen that broadly speaking Paul evaluates the intention of the law positively but sees its results in the context of fallen human existence as negative. This paradoxical view of the law is seen in Rom 7. The law is not sin but is holy, just, good, spiritual, and promises life (vv. 7, 10, 12, 14, 16). Yet the law is the cause of sin (vv. 8-9) and deception and finally issues in death (v. 10). This ambiguity is seen compactly in vv. 22-23. He delights in the law in his inner person or mind—the law in its redemptive intention. But at war with this law there is another law, the law of sin in his members, the law misunderstood as demanding works. This law takes him captive.

Paul calls out in his wretchedness—the wretchedness of his pre-Christian but also Christian existence—and asks who will deliver him from this body of death, the death of self-division. And now in his explicit Christian voice he offers his thanks to God through Jesus Christ for deliverance (v. 25a). But in the last sentence of this discussion he returns with great realism to the self-dividedness that even existence in faith never escapes during this historical life: I serve in my mind the law of God, but in the flesh—the condition of fallenness—I serve the law of sin (v. 25b).

Freedom from Death and Flesh, 8:1-39

8:1-11. Law, flesh, death, Christ, and Spirit. The affirmation that there is therefore now no condemnation for those in Christ is based on the rescue from the law accomplished by Christ (7:25a) despite the continuing struggle of the life of faith (7:25b). The ground of this absence of condemnation is further specified as our liberation from the law of sin and death by the law of the Spirit. The law of the Spirit and the law of sin and death could mean two principles of reality or two ways of understanding the Law of Moses—in terms of its intention (to give life and the Spirit) and in terms of its result (to cause death).

The law is a *power* that overpowers human beings and entices them against their wills into sin. But the ambiguity of the law expresses itself in yet another way. The law is also *weak*. Its weakness is its inability to do what God intended it to do—give life and faith. This weakness was caused by the flesh—human being in its fallenness—which is also a power. But God has done what the law could not do by sending his own Son.

The sending is probably not thought of as a sending from a preexistent heavenly state. There is no reference to a preexistent mode of being or activity, as in Phil 2:6; Col 1:15, 17; 1 Cor 8:6; Heb 1:2. The sending is more like an earthly appointment, as in the commissioning of the prophets (Isa 49:1, 5-6; Jer 1:5, 7) or the sending of the son to the vineyard in the parable of The Wicked Tenants (Mark 12:6; Fuller 1978, 41-44). That Jesus was sent in the *likeness of sinful flesh* does not mean that Paul questions Jesus' real humanity. Jesus was a man of flesh (1:3) and suffered the human condition under the power of wrath or curse (Gal 3:13) and the law (Gal 4:4). But Paul's insertion of the word *likeness* suggests that in the case of Christ the sin that is endemic to the flesh was overcome (2 Cor 5:21).

The purpose of sending the Son is that the law's requirement (*dikaiōma*) might be fulfilled in us who walk according to the Spirit. This requirement is probably the faith that the law intends. But the reference to walking also includes the ethical life that both the law and faith have in view.

For Paul flesh is not a *part* of human being but the *whole* self from a certain point of view. Paul has deepened and developed the OT notion of flesh as weakness (Ps 56:41; Isa 31:3; Davies 1948, 18–20) and given it a range of meanings. The flesh is the visible or physical (1 Cor 15:39; 2 Cor 12:7) and as such is weak and perishable in comparison with God (Gal 4:13; 1 Cor 15:50; 2 Cor 4:11). Yet it is the sphere of human existence created by God in which believers and all others live, and it is not judged to be evil (Gal 2:20; Phil 1:24). But the concept takes on a darker connotation when it is denied that believers still live in the flesh (Rom 7:5; 8:9). Then flesh becomes fully evil, virtually identical with sin. The mind of the flesh is hostile to God, refuses to submit, and those in the flesh cannot please God (vv. 6-8). The mind of the flesh prefers its own righteousness to God's (10:1-3). Observe that when the flesh is physical it is not evil, and when it is identical with sin it is not physical. The flesh as evil is a stance of the whole self. It is the self as trusting in itself or in some other aspect of finite reality. Paul's term for mind here (*phronēma*) does not just mean thought but the orientation or direction of one's whole existence (Käsemann 1980, 219).

This direction of one's existence *is* death. Death is not a punishment added to this hostility to God, but death is already present in it.

The power that liberates from flesh and death Paul refers to interchangeably as the Spirit, Spirit of God, Spirit of Christ, and Christ in you (vv. 9-10). The tension and ambiguity of existence in faith are still in view: although *your* body is dead because of sin, the Spirit of *God* is life because of the new relationship that is righteousness. Clearly here the Spirit of the one raising Jesus from the dead is the power of God operative in human existence to give life to dying bodies.

The body for Paul, like flesh, is not a *part* of a human being but is the *whole* self or person from a certain point of view. The body is the person in his or her physicality as a part of the material world (1 Cor 12:12-26; 13:3; 2 Cor 10:10; Gal 6:17). This shades off, however, into the body as the whole person, something one *is*, not something one has (Rom 6:12; 12:1). More specifically the body is the self in its *relatedness* in principle to other dimensions of reality (Bultmann 1951, 192–96, 201–203; Käsemann 1969, 135; 1971, 17–23).

In the relationship of self to self the body is perhaps most characteristically the self as the object of the self's will (Rom 6:12-14; 12:1; 1 Cor 9:27; 13:3; Phil 1:20). But the body as having deeds of its own is also subject (Rom 8:13). In fact the parallelism between body and spirit in 1 Cor 6:15, 17 shows that the body has a spiritual dimension. It is the place where death and resurrection with Christ is both understood and actualized (2 Cor 4:7-12).

A part of the meaning of body is its identity with flesh (1 Cor 6:16; 2 Cor 4:10-11). As such it is the self as the object of the world's physical violence (Gal 6:17; 2 Cor 11:23-29) and the self as sexually related (1 Cor 6:16). But the body is also the self as intended for the Lord (1 Cor 6:13, 15). The body can be given over to the power of death (Rom 7:24; 8:10-11), but the body is also the vehicle of eternal life (1 Cor 15:44), the spiritual body, the self fully assimilated to the realm of the Spirit. Here its fleshly physicality is explicitly denied (1 Cor 15:44-50). The *identity* of the self in relation to God and self is maintained in the resurrection, but *not* its *physicality* (Via 1990, 68–70).

8:12-17. Life in the Spirit as an obligation or task. In the previous section the Spirit's overcoming of the believer's death and self-division is spoken of as an assured reality. But in this passage the transformation of death into life is a task and obligation of the believer. It is in some way not certain that the believer will carry out this task.

Paul says: *If you live according to the flesh*—and you *will* (a condition determined as true)—*you will die.* But immediately thereafter he also states: *If by* (or in) *the Spirit you put to death the deeds of the body*—and you *will* (again a condition determined as true)—*you will live.* Each of these conditions is stated as equally possible. Paul perhaps leans toward the latter since he moves on to affirmative statements about the leading and witness of the Spirit. Body here is the equivalent of flesh in its evil sense (see Gal 5:16-17, 19).

Thematically for Paul (eternal) life is the gift of GRACE (Rom 1:16-17; 5:21; 6:23), but in 8:13 life is conditioned on the believer's putting an end to sinful acts. The believer must do what God has done in him or her.

The role of the Spirit here is to make being a child of God a *present* reality. The Spirit bears witness to our spirit that we are in fact God's children. The human spirit here is not a fragment or apportionment of the divine Spirit, but the strictly human spirit. The Spirit in bearing witness with our spirit is not talking to itself; rather, divine and human spirits are distinguished.

The human spirit is not a *part* of the self but the *whole* self from a particular standpoint. The spirit is the self as knowing subject. As spirit the self knows itself (1 Cor 2:11) and knows the public world and other people (1 Cor 16:18; 2 Cor 2:13; 7:13). Perhaps most importantly, as Rom 8:16 shows, the human spirit is the self in its openness to the testimony of God's Spirit (Via 1990, 70–73).

If we are children of God, we are fellow heirs with Christ, provided we suffer with him in order that we might be glorified with him. This note of suffering becomes the theme of the next section.

8:18-27. Suffering the wait for redemption. Present suffering cannot be compared to the overcompensating GLORY to be revealed—glory being Paul's term for the full manifestation of eschatological redemption. Glory is the substance of resurrection existence that believers will finally share with Christ (8:17; 2 Cor 3:18; 4:17; Phil 3:20-21).

Just as human beings struggle and groan against the power of sin, law, flesh, and death, so the nonhuman creation waits and longs for release from the decay and futility that God has allowed the cosmic powers to impose on the world. The human and non-human creation form a solidarity—they struggle and groan together—so that neither will be fully redeemed apart from the other (cf. Gen 3:17-19; 4 Ezra 7:11-14). In 8:14-16 being a child of God is a *present* reality. But in vv. 22-23 while the Spirit gives a *foretaste* of this reality, full adoption as a child of God is identified with the resurrection of the body and is projected into a future for which we wait. Yet we wait with the hope in which salvation resides. Although we do not yet see our full redemption, hope is confident about the future which is in God's hands.

8:28-30. God's predetermining purpose. According to some manuscripts (reliable and diversified) Paul states that *all things* work toward the good—a happy outcome—for those who love God. According to other manuscripts (reliable but less numerous and less diversified) he says that *God* works with all things toward the good for those who love God. Whichever reading one takes, Paul has God's sovereign intention in view. Things do not work on their own. The *all things* probably refers especially to the suffering struggle in which believers are engaged.

The good is worked for those *who are called according to [God's] purpose*. These people God foreknew and predestined. God's redemptive intention is always there ahead of us. The eternal purpose of God becomes concrete historical reality in calling and justification, which have already happened. But here Paul goes further and also affirms our glorification—our final resurrection existence—as a part of the salvation that has already happened. This is in tension with his general tendency to reserve glorification for the future.

8:31-39. The certain security of the believer. What then shall we say? What is the outcome of our being already glorified (8:30)—despite being not yet glorified (8:17; Phil 3:21)? The outcome is that nothing can undo our redemption. Even if we do something deserving of condemnation, God's giving his Son for us guarantees our justification against which no charge can stand. Christ who died and was raised is interceding for us at God's right hand. This mythological image gives concrete expression to the never ending validity of Christ's death for us. Nothing can separate us from the love of Christ (v. 35) or, interchangeably, from the love of God in Christ (v. 39).

Our own deeds that are worthy of condemnation cannot separate us (vv. 31-37). Neither can the afflictions and reversals of the historical process separate us (v. 35). Nor can anything that life or death, present or future, might hand out separate us (v. 38). Not even cosmic fate can pull us away from the love of God. That is what Paul means by the principalities and powers (vv. 38-39). Paul presupposed the worldview of his time, which held that there are personal, hostile, supernatural powers that victimize and control human beings. Christ has overcome them (Via 1990, 40–44).

God's Word and the Destiny of Israel, 9:1–11:36

This section is not a parenthesis or excursus in which Paul merely indulges his Jewish patriotism by claiming for Israel a permanent place in the purpose of God. Paul rather addresses here an issue that grows essentially out of the preceding discussion. Can the word of God be trusted? For Paul the gospel of the righteousness of God as justification by faith is the fulfillment of God's promise to save Israel (Rom 4:13, 16, 20). *Israel* is the people of the COVENANT, the LAW, the sonship, the promises (9:4-5). But when the promises were fulfilled in the manifestation of God's justifying RIGHTEOUSNESS the result has been that most Jews are not justified believers while most believers are gentiles. Is justification by faith apart from the law then a nullification of God's promise to save Israel? Is God's promise unreliable? Has the word of God failed (9:6)?

Paul develops a threefold argument to show that the word of God has *not* failed. This demonstration is of great theological importance to Paul, for if God's promising word to Israel is not reliable, then God's word is not reliable for anyone.

God's Rejection of Israel, 9:1-29

9:1-5. Paul's deep sorrow about his people. Paul is in anguish because most of his kinspeople according to the flesh—the Israelites—stand outside the realm of salvation. He would give up his own salvation for them if that were possible. It is ironical that Israel is mostly lost, for these are the very people who have had the tokens of salvation—sonship, the covenants, the law, the patriarchs, the promises.

And from Israel the Christ is physically descended. To the word "Christ" (NRSV *Messiah*) Paul adds *who is over all, God blessed forever. Amen.*

How God is related to Christ here is a difficult interpretive problem (for various possible readings see Cranfield 1981, 464–70; Metzger 1975, 520–23) because the lack of punctuation in the original manuscripts leaves the relationship ambiguous. The two main alternatives are as follows: (1) Understand God as in apposition to Christ and read "Christ, who is God over all." (2) Put a period rather than a comma after Christ thus separating God from Christ in an independent doxology and read " . . . Christ. God who is over all be blessed." Probably syntax and Pauline style favor the first. But the Pauline theological pattern seems to favor the second. Nowhere else does Paul directly identify Christ with God, and in 1 Cor 15:24, 27 he clearly subordinates the Son to God the Father.

9:6-29. The sovereign electing will of God. God's word promised salvation to Israel (Rom 4:16-18) (see commentary on Rom 11 for Paul's ambiguity regarding the constitution of the saved Israel). But most of Israel is not saved. Does that mean that God's word has failed? *No.* Here Paul gives his first argument to support the reliability of God's promise. It has never been the case that all of Abraham's descendants are saved. God's dealings with Israel have been consistent, for God has always distinguished among the descendants of ABRAHAM between the physical descendants and the children of the promise who alone are the children of God. Everything depends on God's electing will; nothing depends on human position or performance. Paul makes much use of the OT throughout this section.

For example, when twin sons were born to the patriarch ISAAC and his wife REBECCA, before they were born or had done anything good or bad, God chose JACOB and rejected ESAU. Only God's decisive action counts, not human works. This action of God can be spoken of as his promise (vv. 6-8), his calling (vv. 11-12), or his purpose of ELECTION (v. 11). All of these are expressions of his will (v. 18). God's will prompts God to show MERCY toward some (vv. 15-16) and to harden the hearts of others (vv. 17-18).

If then everything comes from God in deciding salvation or rejection and nothing from human beings—Paul's diatribal questioner will ask—how can God find fault since no one can resist his will (v. 19)? Paul's answer is that people have no more right to question God than the clay has to question the potter who molds it. But Paul does go on to say that in all of this God's purpose has been to create vessels of mercy destined for glory from among both gentiles and Jews.

The salvation of the gentiles Paul grounds on the promise in Hos 1:10; 2:1, 23 that God will make his people from those who are *not* his people. Paul, however, has changed the meaning of the OT text, for in HOSEA, the "not my people" refers to unfaithful, sinful Israel and not to the gentiles. Paul grounds the salvation of the relatively few believing Jews on the prediction that he attributes to Isaiah (but which actually amalgamates Isa 10:22-23 and Hos 1:10) that only a REMNANT of the huge number of Israelites will be saved.

God's word has not failed because from the beginning (with Abraham) until now the identity of Israel does not depend on birth (not all of Abraham's descendants are children of God) nor on performance of works, but solely on who God says it is by the exercise of his sovereign electing will. The failure of most of Israel to be saved is determined by God's doing, and God has been consistent.

Israel's Rejection of Righteousness through Faith, 9:30–10:21

It is then highly paradoxical when Paul states as his second argument against the failure of God's word that Israel has missed out on salvation because *Israel* has rejected God's way of dealing with humankind. Everything depends on God; everything depends on Israel.

9:30–10:4. Israel's pursuit of righteousness by works. Paul notes an irony. The gentiles, who did not pursue righteousness, attained righteousness by faith. Israel, on the other hand, did pursue the law that affords righteousness. This pursuit of the law was not a mistake in itself, for the law can lead to righteousness.

The law as limit (Rom 7:7) and as accuser (3:19) makes people aware of their finitude and guilt and thus should point them in faith to God as the source of salvation. But under the conditions of fallen existence the law enticed Israel to attempt her own salvation. That is, Israel wrongly thought that the law called for works rather than faith. Thus Israel failed to attain the *law*. This shows that the real intention of the law was faith.

Paul acknowledges Israel's zeal for God but denies that her zeal is enlightened. In ignorance of the righteousness that comes from God Israel sought to establish her own righteousness by means of the law. What is wrong with the righteousness of the law for Paul is that it asserts itself to establish a right relationship with God rather than receiving the relationship from God. It does not submit (*hypotassō* in the passive) *to God's righteousness* (10:3). This is parallel to Paul's statement in 8:7-8 that *the mind that is set on the flesh is hostile to God [and] does not submit* (*hypotassō* in the passive) *to God's law*, that is, to the intention of the law to evoke faith. The parallelism between the two passages shows that pursuing the righteousness of the law is an expression of the mind of the flesh in its hostility to God.

Paul then says "for Christ is the end (*telos*) of the law, leading to righteousness for every believer" (author trans.). The *for* (*gar*) does not express the reason for what Paul has just said. That is, Christ's being the end of the law is not the reason for Israel's not submitting. Rather it is the reason for something that Paul implies but does not state: Israel *should have* submitted to God's righteousness, *for* Christ is the end of the law (Williams 1980, 283–84).

Christ is the end of the law (10:4) in two senses, corresponding to Paul's dialectical—yes and no—understanding of the law. Christ is the *fulfillment* of the law's intention—to evoke faith and give life. But Christ is the *termination* of the law from the standpoint of its result—its being understood as a demand for works that produces death.

There is a difference between the attitude that Paul criticizes here—trusting in one's *obedient* works of the law as able to establish one's own righteousness with God—and the attitude he criticizes in 2:17-24—trusting that one is secure with God because one knows God's will in the law and approves what is excellent while at the same time *disobeying* the law. It should be remembered that Paul regards *all* people as under the law in principle; therefore, these sinful postures toward the law are not peculiarly Jewish but rather characteristically human.

10:5-13. Word, faith, and resurrection. Here Paul draws a line through the OT distinguishing between what is invalid and valid in the Jewish scriptures. To MOSES in Lev 18:5 he attributes the view that the righteousness of the law promises life to those who live by achieving obedience (v. 5; see Käsemann 1980, 285). *But* (adversative *de* indicating a contrast, v. 6) the righteousness of faith—replacing Moses as the speaker in Deut 30:11-14—calls, not for the achievement of obedience, but for believing and confessing the word. Paul interprets this word in Deuteronomy as the saving proclamation of Jesus' lordship and resurrection.

The very surprising thing about Paul's interpretation of Deut 30:11-14 is that the "word" in the Deuteronomy passage means the "law" (30:11, 14)—just as Leviticus speaks about the law—and not the righteousness of faith. Paul has read a fully Christian understanding of word back into the Deuteronomy passage, but his interpretation is not wholly arbitrary. "Word" in Deuteronomy does mean "law," but it also means the effective preaching about the God of Israel who gives life by bringing people through death (Deut 32:1-3, 6-13, 19-35, 36-43; esp. 32:39). This theme would have had a close affinity with Paul's preaching of the death and resurrection of Jesus. Thus while Paul clearly over-Christianized Deut 30:11-14, we can understand why he saw a connection between his preaching and the message of Deuteronomy. As in Rom 4 so also here he finds moments of the gospel in the OT.

Judaism prior to and in Paul's time used Deut 30:11-14 to speak about the inaccessibility of WISDOM. Wisdom is accessible only to God, but God has brought her near in the law (Bar 3:29–4:1). Paul may have Baruch as well as Deuteronomy in mind. In Rom vv. 6-8 Paul uses spatial imagery—up, down, near—of both the resurrected Christ and the preached word. Thus Christ and the word are in effect made identical. The word of the righteousness of faith says: Do not seek the risen Christ in a cosmically distant place but seek him in the near word which enters your heart and brings you to faith.

Paul personifies the righteousness of faith and has it speak of the nearness of the resurrected Christ in vv. 6-9. Righteousness first speaks of the nearness of Christ in negative terms (not far) and then in positive terms. But the fact that the category of nearness holds together the negative and positive ways of speaking suggests that they both have the same subject. Speaking negatively righteousness says: Do *not* seek the risen Christ up there in heaven to bring him down or down there in the abyss among the dead to bring him up (vv. 6-7). Then when righteousness speaks of the nearness of Christ positively or directly, it replaces the risen Christ with the preached word (v. 8). Righteousness does not say that Christ is near but that the word is near, on your lips and in your heart.

It is evident from the negative expression of Paul's theme (Christ is not far) that his point is the nearness of *Christ*. Therefore, it makes no sense to speak of the nearness of the *word* if the word does not represent Christ. Thus when Paul replaces Christ with the word, puts the word in Christ's place, he is interpreting the risen Christ *as* the power of the proclaimed word about Christ to bring people to faith (vv. 8, 17). Faith calls upon the Lord who is present in the heart by means of the word. Everyone who calls upon this Lord will be saved.

10:14-21. Preaching, faith, and understanding. Paul unfolds a series of stages that are necessary to lead to salvation: the sending of preachers, preaching, hearing, believing, and calling upon. Paul then affirms, by appealing to the predictions of scripture rather than to historical evidence, that preachers have been sent, have preached, and have been heard. But not all of Israel has obeyed or believed what was heard (v. 16). Paul then at v. 19 introduces a new category into his series—understanding. Did Israel not understand? He answers the question by again appealing to the OT. The gentiles who were not seeking God have found God. Evidently Paul means to say that the gentiles at least have understood. But Israel has been disobedient and contrary.

Paul's point is less than clear, and his answer to the question whether Israel understood and his view about how understanding is related to believing (faith) can be interpreted in two ways.

(1) Paul distinguishes faith from understanding and means to say that since the gentiles understood the gospel surely Israel understood it although they did not (all) believe it.

(2) For Paul faith and understanding overlap extensively. Understanding is the intellectual element of faith itself and like faith shapes human existence (Rom 12:1-2; 2 Cor 3:12-18). Thus Israel no more understood than she believed, and that is made all the more ironical by the fact that the gentiles did understand and believe. This seems to be the more probable interpretation.

Paul has argued that only a few Jews are believers: (1) because God alone has decreed who among the descendants of Abraham shall be the spiritual Israel and (2) because Israel in the interest of self-assertion has neither believed nor understood. The relationship between these two opposing explanations can be understood in at least two ways.

1. The relationship is radically paradoxical. From one side God's act of will determines everything, and from the other side it is totally a human decision. If this is not seen as a hopeless contradiction, both sides are taken as necessary to account for the mystery of human destiny while acknowledging that there is no way to explain how they meet and interact.

2. There is finally an insoluble paradox, but to some extent the divine and the human can be seen as fusing and their point of contact, as definable. This pre-

supposes that the divine and human are to some degree commensurate and comparable.

In 1 Cor 1:18 and 2 Cor 2:14-16 the divine, initiating activity occurs in the preaching of the gospel and thereby creates a situation in which a decision is inescapable for those who hear. Some respond with a "yes" and gain life while others respond with a "no" and inherit death. These are human decisions. The opposite destinies of the gentiles and Israel depend on how *they* decide (vv. 19-21; cf. 9:30-32). Yet the divine action in preaching made the decisions inescapable and necessary, determined that the decisions would in fact be made. Therefore, the yes leading to life and the no leading to death are at the same time in some sense divine actions or divine determinations.

The Final Salvation of All Israel, 11:1-36

Paul's third argument in favor of the reliability of God's promise to Israel is that in the end God will save all Israel.

11:1-6. The present salvation of a remnant. Paul himself—a saved Israelite—is proof that God has not abandoned God's historical people. Beyond that there is now, as in the past (Elijah's time), a REMNANT chosen by grace, not rewarded for works.

11:7-10. Election and hardening. Israel (as a whole) did not attain the right relationship with God (9:31-32) that it sought, but the elect attained it. The rest were hardened. Note that Israel contains both the elect and the hardened. Paul reiterates the point made in 9:14-18 that both the election of the saved and the hardening of the lost are God's doing. Using scripture Paul underlines the assertion that the failure of the hardened to see and to understand God's intention was visited upon them by God. The wrong choice establishes an inescapable destiny.

11:11-16. The stumbling of Israel and the salvation of the gentiles. Israel has stumbled but not so as to fall, that is, not so as to be finally lost. Israel's stumbling, her temporary rejection of and by God, has provided the opportunity for the salvation of the gentiles. The purpose of the gentiles' salvation is to make Israel jealous, and that will lead to the salvation of *some* Jews by means of Paul's apostolic ministry. Evidently Paul's point is that Israel's seeing the gentiles' attaining the salvation promised to Israel will make her want to claim her own lost heritage. If Israel's rejection has had beneficial results for the gentiles and the world, how much more consequential will be her inclusion. It will bring about—or be brought about by—the resurrection from the dead.

In v. 16 Paul states a principle that will turn out to have far-reaching implications (see commentary on 11:25-32). In the OT (Num 15:17-21; Lev 23:14) a holy offering to God from the first fruits released the rest of the harvest for general or *non-holy* uses. Paul reversed this and stated that the holiness of the first fruits makes the whole *holy*. But the principle is the same in both cases, and it is reiterated with the root and branches image. What is true for the part is also true for the whole to which the part belongs. What is actual in the part—first fruits and root—is latent or potential in the whole—the full lump or harvest and the branches. The part represented by the first fruits and root is probably Abraham and/or the believing Israelite remnant through the centuries. The whole imaged in the full harvest and the branches is all Israel. Before drawing out the implications of this (in 11:25-32) Paul continues—in 11:17-24—his specific address to the gentile Christians in Rome, which he began at v. 13.

11:17-24. The relationship of saved gentiles to the historical Israel. Here Paul takes the root and branches image of 11:16 and develops it into an allegory of the history of salvation in which the people of God throughout history are portrayed as a cultivated olive tree (vv. 17, 24) or its root (v. 18), unbelieving Israelites are represented as branches cut off from this tree, and believing gentiles are imaged as *a wild olive shoot* grafted into the tree.

Several indications of diatribe style are seen here. (1) The gentile Christians are identified with the personified *wild olive shoot*. (2) This olive shoot is the diatribal interlocutor who raises an objection (v. 19). (3) Paul issues admonitions and warnings (Stowers 1981, 99–100).

Olive cultivation of the time included both grafting wild shoots into cultivated trees and cultivated shoots into wild trees (Cranfield 1981, 565–66; Dunn 1988, 661). Paul's meaning depends less on particular agricultural practices than on his metaphorical use of them. He does seem to want to suggest that there is something unnatural—unexpected—about finding gentiles among the Israelite people of God (v. 24).

In this passage the believing community, which extends from Abraham down into the church of Paul's time, does not exist because individual believers decide to get together and form it. Rather the historical community is always there prior to the individual, and individuals are saved by being placed in the community by God. The root (the historical believing community) supports the grafted in shoots, not vice versa.

The gentile Christians are not to think themselves superior to the Jews (branches) who have been cut off. The latter were cut off because of their unbelief, and the gentile Christians are in only because of their faith. They are dependent on both the prior existence of the tree and God's gift of faith. But *they* have a responsibility to continue in faith. If they let thinking highly of themselves replace awe and faith, God will cut them off also.

However strongly Paul affirmed in 8:31-39 that nothing can separate believers from the love of God, here he allows that believers may in fact renounce faith and be cut off. From the standpoint of God's intention salvation is certain. From the standpoint of possible human lack of resolution, salvation is not so certain. And yet since faith is *God's* work in believers as well as the latter's own decision, can faith finally be renounced?

Paul makes a transition to the next section by reminding the gentile Christians that if they have been unnaturally grafted into the saved community, how much more will God graft the cut off natural branches (Jews) back into the tree.

11:25-32. The mystery of Israel's final salvation. Having pronounced severe judgment on the Jews (chap. 2) and declared that most of them now stand outside of salvation (9:30–10:3; 10:18-21; 11:7-10), Paul here affirms that once the hardening of Israel allows the full number of gentiles to come in, then all Israel will be saved. By *the full number of the Gentiles* he probably means all the elect among the gentiles or gentiles as a whole. By *all Israel* Paul probably means Israel as a whole but not necessarily every single Jew. That would be consonant with the contemporary Jewish understanding of "all Israel" (Mishnah, *Sanh* 10). Paul anticipated this development in 4:16 where he says that grace is to avail for *all* the seed of Abraham— those who belong to the law and those who share the faith of Abraham.

Evidently Paul believes that the salvation of Israel will be accomplished by the eschatological return of Christ (vv. 26-27), whose preaching will bring Israel to faith. Faith is the only way that either gentiles (1:16-17; 3:21-26; 9:30-31) or Jews (1:16-17; 3:19-20; 4:12; 10:6-10, 13; 11:5-6) have ever come to salvation. So will it be at the end.

It is not possible that all Israel would not be finally saved because in choosing the patriarchs God has irrevocably called all Israel. The call, the covenant, the promises (9:4-5) cannot be nullified (vv. 28-29).

Paul concludes his argument and his vision of the future with the affirmation that God has consigned all to disobedience in order that he might have mercy on all. Mercy can be fully appropriated only when sin has been fully experienced and acknowledged (3:19-20; 7:7, 13, 15, 24-25). This belongs to the purpose of God. When Paul reaches this stage of his argument, it is no longer just that all Israel will be saved. It is now that *all human beings* will finally be the recipients of God's mercy (v. 32).

This vision of the future moves Paul to praise God for God's riches, wisdom, and inscrutable ways whose depths are unknowable to humankind and to give God glory.

In the course of Rom 9–11 Paul's thought about ELECTION undergoes a decided change. He moves *from* a quantitative division of human beings in which some are chosen and others are rejected (9:6-18) *to* a qualitative division in which rejection (disobedience) and election (mercy) are two stages through which *all* pass (11:32). It is impossible to say how conscious Paul might have been of the shift.

This change is mediated by the principle articulated in 11:16 that what is actual in the part is latent in the whole. Some Jews and some gentiles have actual faith; therefore, all Jews and all gentiles have latent faith and ultimately will have actual faith (v. 32). Romans 11:16 in the context of Paul's thought leads by an inevitable logic to v. 32—the salvation of all human beings as the recipients of God's mercy.

The change in point of view leaves some tensions in Paul's theological argument. In 2:4, 17-18, 22-24 he criticizes Jews who presume upon the kindness of God and assume that their relationship with God is secure whether or not they are obedient. He implicitly condemns the assumption that being a member of the covenant people (9:4-5) places one among the elect (11:5-7). And yet he himself takes the position that belonging to the covenant people constitutes an irrevocable call (11:28-29) to salvation.

The affirmation of the salvation of all stands in tension with Paul's frequently expressed clear belief that God will execute a final judgment that will leave some outside of God's kingdom in final death (6:23; 14:10-12; 1 Cor 6:9-10; 2 Cor 5:10; Gal 5:19-21; 6:7; Phil 3:18-19; 1 Thes 5:3).

Perhaps both sides of these tensions are necessary to disclose the mystery of human destiny as Paul sought to grapple with it and to express the uncertain certainty of existence in faith. Paul's logic leads to the affirmation of universalism, the salvation of all people. But it would be presumption and an offense against God's sovereignty to tell God that God *will* save all human beings individually. The final judgment motif protects against that presumption. Yet the sweep of Paul's argument makes it impossible to assert that any particular individual will not be saved. One is assured of the final salvation of all (11:32) but must not assume one's own security (2:4, 17-18, 22-24). One is assured of the final victory of God's intention to save all (11:32) and redeem the cosmos (8:18-25), but in the course of the historical process one is not sure whether one belongs to the true believing remnant (11:5-7). The believer hopes (8:24-25; Phil 3:10-14)—with confidence (Rom 5:3-5).

God's Mercy (Righteousness) and the Behavior of Believers, 12:1–15:13

The *therefore* of 12:1 demonstrates a close relationship between Paul's theological interpretation of salvation in chaps. 1–11 and the ethical exhortation which he is going to give in 12:1–15:13—salvation, and for that reason, moral action.

Ethical Renewal as the Appropriation of Mercy, 12:1-2

Paul uses the expression *the mercies of God* (v. 1) to summarize the meaning of the gospel as he has developed it in Rom 1–11. The word for *mercy* here (*oiktirmos*) is different from the root for mercy which he used prominently in chaps. 9–11 (*eleeō* and *eleos*), but the two are synonymous (9:15).

Mercy represents the event of grace which changes human existence and *enables* the ethical posture which is called for. This *enablement* generates and implicitly contains a *motive* or justifying reason for the action or disposition required. The motive is wholeness or integrity: to be and act in accord with the new self or life which one has become through the mercies of God.

The required ethical stance is a *result of* the new life and is not identical with the latter (1 Cor 5:7; Gal 5:25), but it is the expected and appropriate result. The relationship of new life to ethical behavior is paradoxical. The new life given through God's mercy in justification and liberation is a reality and not just a possibility. Yet the very existence of the imperative—*become* what you are by presenting your bodies as living sacrifices—shows that the new life is not quite real but is a possibility to be realized in the process of moral action (Via 1990, 50–51).

Body for Paul means the *whole self* in its *relatedness* to the multiple dimensions of reality. By use of the cultic terms *sacrifice* and *service* (*latreia*) Paul extends worship to include the behavior of the body-self in all of its life relationships in a way pleasing to God.

The ethical imperative is extended in the call to *not be conformed to this world but [to] be transformed by the renewing* of the mind. One's whole existence is changed by the reshaping of the mind. This entails a move from the old age of sin and law to the new eschatological time. Mind here means the power of critical judgment, the ability to test and differentiate (Käsemann 1980, 330), and also suggests moral perceptiveness (Cranfield 1981, 609).

The transformation of the self by the renewal of the mind is something that the believer is to do. It is his or her own responsibility: transform yourself. This possibility, however, has been enabled by God's enacted mercy.

The renewal of the mind reverses the situation of a person in sin and under the wrath of God as portrayed in 1:18-32. Paul's use of cognate terms makes this clear. Humankind tested reality and chose (*dokimazō*) not to have God in its knowledge (1:28a). In consequence God gave it up to a mind that cannot cope with the tests of reality (an *adokimos* mind) (1:28b). But now in the eschatological time of salvation the realizable purpose of the mind's renewal is that it might discover or discern (*dokimazō* again) the will of God. For Paul the ethical norm is the will of God. That will, however, has not been exhaustively given in ethical rules but must be newly discovered in the changing situations of life.

Love in One Body in Christ, 12:3-21

The quality of *sober judgment*, which is to characterize the believer, Paul borrows from the Greek philosophical tradition where it connotes moderation, restraint, or a sense of proportion. For Paul, however, the content of this moderation will be drawn from the renewal of the mind through the gospel and the believer's sense of his or her place in the Christian community, imaged in this passage as one body in Christ.

The application of moderation that Paul makes here is the avoidance of excessive self-estimation. The key to this is the unity and diversity of the community. The church is *one* entity, not because of good feelings the members have for each other, but because they are all grounded together in a single reality that transcends them all—the crucified-risen Christ in his self-identification with his people. Common participation in Christ enables risky involvement with one another.

But as in the human body, so in the one body in Christ the members have different functions. Each member has a gift (*charisma*) given by grace, and each gift includes a role or calling and a function: a servant serves, a teacher teaches, et cetera. That these gifts are *different* from each other is a consequence of *God's grace*. Therefore, no one gift in its difference can be regarded as more or less important than another.

An additional check on over self-estimation is the suggestion that God has given each person a measure of faith that accords with that person's capacities. One's self-evaluation is to be in line with the measure of faith one has been given (v. 3b). The gift of grace then that comes with faith confers both a calling and a limit (Käsemann 1980, 334). Each gift is to be exercised by carrying out the function that is proper to it, and one should not attempt more functions than one has been given. The teacher, for example, exercises his or her calling by teaching and should not think of himself or herself too highly by claiming the functions of other callings.

That love should *be genuine* takes on here (v. 9) a thematic significance. Heretofore in Romans Paul has used the term *agapē* of God's love (5:5, 8; 8:39) in its surprising concern for the radically underserving. Now Paul uses *agapē* for the love that believers should extend both to fellow members of the body (vv. 9-10) and to enemies on the outside (vv. 14, 20). The love that believers have received they are to share.

For Paul love as an ethical disposition and mode of action means to seek the good or advantage of the other person rather than one's own. Paul expresses this in a number of places and with different vocabulary (15:1-2; 1 Cor 10:24, 33-34; 13:5; Phil 2:4; 1 Thes 5:15). This central ethical norm is an open or formal one. What constitutes the good of the other is left undefined and is to be determined in differing social contexts (Via 1990, 60–63). In this particular passage seeking the advantage of the other takes such expressions as showing honor (v. 10), meeting physical needs (v. 13), emotional identification (v. 15), living in harmony (v. 16), and renouncing vengeance (vv. 19-20). Love does not passively accept evil but overcomes it (v. 21).

The State and Taxes, 13:1-7

Paul calls on *every person [to] be subject to the governing authorities*. Paul's terms (*exousia*—13:1; *archōn*—13:3) are subject to varying interpretations. Some think that he has in mind primarily or exclusively human officials (Cranfield 1981, 656–59) while others hold that the terms refer both to the civil rulers and the cosmic or angelic powers that act through them (esp. Cullmann 1957, 63, 66, 98). Probably both dimensions are in view with the emphasis being on the human.

The political rulers have authority at all because it has been delegated to them by God, the ultimate source of authority, for the purpose of preventing wrongdoing and promoting the common good (vv. 1b, 4). Since God has appointed the rulers, to resist them is to resist God.

A part of the believer's responsibility is to pay taxes, both direct (taxes—*phoros*) and indirect (revenue—*telos*). The admonition to pay taxes and to show respect and honor to all to whom they are due may mean that Paul is addressing an actual situation in the Rome of the fifties—unrest about the collection of indirect taxes (Wedderburn 1991, 62).

Paul offers here—explicitly or implicitly—four reasons for being subject to the authorities. (1) It should be done out of respect for the authority of God (vv. 1-2). (2) One should obey in order to escape punishment from the rulers, which is also an instrument of the wrath of God (vv. 2b-5). (3) One should obey for the sake of conscience. This assumes that those addressed know that they have an obligation to obey and would have a painful conscience if they did not (v. 5b). (4) Paul implies that one obeys and pays taxes in order to promote the good of the socio-political order (v. 4).

Paul affirms that God's governance of the world requires the political order in *principle*, but since he can also be critical of *particular* government officials in *particular* circumstances (1 Cor 2:8; 6:4), he is not saying that the believer is obligated to support any and every particular political system.

Since Paul's admonition to obey *the governing authorities* and pay taxes (vv. 1-7) is surrounded (12:9; 13:8-10) and framed by his affirmation of the love principle, these two motifs interpret each other. Paying taxes is seen as an expression of love—the seeking the advantage of the other that flows from receiving the undeserved love of God. And in the exhortation to pay taxes love is seen to have expressions that are public, political, and unsentimental.

Love as the Fulfillment of the Law, 13:8-10

If the believer pays all of his or her debts—respect, honor, taxes—the only remaining—and continuing— obligation is the obligation *to love one another*. That obligation can never be exhausted. Love to the neighbor is the fulfillment and summing up of all the individual commandments in the law. This probably does not mean that all the commandments of the law are still to be obeyed as such but now with a loving attitude. It rather means that love to the neighbor has superseded the many individual commands of the law because it actualizes what the law has always intended—not to do any harm to the neighbor. And yet the OT commandments of God retain a certain relative validity for Paul (7:7-12; 1 Cor 7:19) 7:7-12) in that they suggest how love can be made concrete. The individual laws are traces of God's will (Via 1990, 63–65). And Paul uses an OT command—"love your neighbor as yourself" (Lev 19:18)—to disclose the full intention of the whole law.

The Pressure of the Imminent End, 13:11-14

Paul reminds his readers to wake up because salvation is nearer than when we first believed. Salvation here means the return of Christ, the final judgment, and the eschatological completion of redemption, the resurrection of the body. Having moved from dealing with a specific ethical issue (political involvement) and a broad ethical norm (love for the neighbor) Paul now interprets the situation of believers in the temporal process both theologically and ethically by using the imagery of *night* and *day*. The night is far advanced and day has drawn near. Believers live in this in-between time that is no longer darkest night but is not yet quite day. Yet the day—the last day—is near enough to put pressure on the believer to live as if it were day. Cast off the works of darkness—drunkenness, debauchery, quarreling—and walk (live) as in the day. The principle is that the believer is to live in a way that is appropriate to his or her situation in the temporal process of salvation. The problem is that while the present situation of salvation is ambiguously neither night nor day, the moral demand is to live unambiguously as in the day.

That the believer is not yet fully in the day is underscored by the imperative to *put on . . . Christ* (v. 14). If one is told to put on Christ, then one has not yet put him on. But Paul can also tell baptized believers that they have already put on Christ (Gal 3:27) and are already "children of the day" (1 Thes 5:5). Living in the day and putting on Christ as the power of new life is both an actualized reality (1 Thes 5:4-5; Gal 3:27) and an unactualized reality (Rom 13:11-14)—the possibility of actualization through moral living.

Eating and Drinking among the Weak and the Strong, 14:1–15:13

This passage seeks to promote mutual acceptance (14:3-4, 13; 15:7), peace and harmony (14:19; 15:5), and mutual upbuilding (14:19) between two groups in the church at Rome that hold different opinions and apparently live in some tension with each other.

Paul designates them as the *weak in faith* (14:1) and the *strong* (15:1) and includes himself among the strong (15:1). The weak are vegetarians (14:2) who observe certain holy days (14:5) and apparently reject the drinking of wine (14:21). The strong eat anything (14:2, 21), consider all days alike (14:5), and drink wine (14:21). The meat avoidance seems not to be a matter of rejecting meat from animals sacrificed to idols, as at Corinth (1 Cor 8:1, 4, 7, 10), but rather to be a vegetarian rejection of all meat.

Regarding the history-of-religious sources of these differences the strong would be Christians of either gentile or Jewish background who had accepted a law-free position similar to Paul's that permitted their behavior on these issues. The weak are more difficult to categorize. Jews observed holy days, the SABBATH and other festival times, but Jews did not characteristically reject wine drinking. And while certain animals were forbidden as food (Lev 11), and Judaism permitted animals had to be slaughtered in the proper cultic manner (Lev 17:14; Deut 12:16, 23), Judaism did not reject the eating of meat in principle (Lev 11:1-3; Deut 12:15). On the other hand, some gentile religions did teach vegetarianism (e.g., Orphics and Pythagoreans).

Yet there is some evidence (Dan 1:12, 16; *Testament of Isaac* 4:5, 6, 41) that certain Jewish groups living under the pressure of a gentile environment did adopt vegetarianism and teetotalism (Wedderburn 1991, 33–34). Moreover, since 15:7-13 makes the point that the purpose of Christ's mission was to save both Jews and gentiles, it seems probable that the two groups designated as the weak and the strong were primarily, though not exclusively, respectively Jewish Christians and gentile Christians. Paul offers three perspectives for their living together in peace.

14:1-12. The theological perspective. That the weak person is weak specifically *in faith* suggests that he or she feels that faith alone is not sufficient for salvation but must be supplemented by the behaviors at issue here (Dunn 1988, 798). Interestingly Paul does not go on to condemn this position though he distinguishes himself from it (15:1—*we . . . are strong*).

The strong are not to treat the weak with contempt; the weak are not to condemn the strong. The important thing is that each should be convinced in his or her *own* mind that he or she is doing the right thing (v. 5).

The basis for this mutual acceptance is that both groups do what they do to honor the Lord. Moreover, all persons must finally *stand before the judgment seat of God* and give an account of themselves to God (vv. 10-12). Being accountable to the judgment of God lifts one above the position of being judged by a fellow human being. It is a Pauline paradox that God confronts us as both gracious redeemer (3:21–4:25) and demanding judge (1 Cor 6:9-11; 2 Cor 5:10; Gal 5:16-24).

14:13-23. The ethical perspective. Paul clearly believes that certain *ethical* acts and dispositions are inherently wrong (1:28-32; 1 Cor 6:9-10; Gal 5:19-21). But he rejects the Jewish distinction between cultic cleanness and uncleanness that rests on the belief that certain *physical* objects (like foods, Lev 11) or processes (like menstruation, Lev 15:19; marital sex, Lev 15:18; or childbearing, Lev 12:1-5) are inherently unclean (Via 1985, 88–96). Thus when he that *nothing is unclean in itself* (v. 14, emphasis added) Paul means nothing like food or drink. But such things are unclean to those who think they are unclean (v. 14b).

Paul is concerned that the strong should not cause harm to the weak who think that meat and wine should be avoided. Since meat and wine are not unclean in themselves (vv. 14, 20), he will not deal with the issue in terms of such unexceptionable rules as: do not eat meat, do not drink wine, observe the sabbath.

Paul rather applies the love principle (v. 15)—seek the good of the other—to this situation. It *is* wrong to eat meat or drink wine *if* it causes the ruin of a brother or sister for whom Christ died. It is all right to eat or drink if your faith's self-understanding allows it (vv. 22-23). But the person of weak faith believes it is wrong. If by your example you entice your weak brother or sister to eat meat or drink wine, you cause his ruin, cause her to fall or stumble (vv. 15, 20, 21). That is, you cause the weak one the inner pain of doubt and self-judgment because he or she will be going against what his or her own faith permits (vv. 22-23). The weak sin if they eat meat, not because it is wrong in itself, but because it violates what their faith allows; it violates the unity of their being. The strong do wrong if they cause this to happen to the weak.

Paul calls for mutual acceptance, but he really asks more of the strong than of the weak because they are capable of more. The strong have the freedom to eat meat and drink wine or not without suffering internal disruption. The weak do not have that much freedom. If they want to avoid inner conflict, they are free only not to eat or drink. So the strong are called on to give up their freedom to eat or drink in those situations where it causes harm to the neighbor.

15:1-13. The Christological perspective. Here the strong are specifically asked to bear the weaknesses of those who are not strong and not to please themselves. This appeal is based on the model of Christ who *did not please himself.*

The weak and strong are admonished to accept each other as Christ accepted both of them. Christ became a servant in order to confirm God's faithfulness to his promises to Israel's forefathers and to bring the gentiles to glorify God.

Concluding Personal Statement, 15:14-32

Paul's Feelings about the Roman Church and His Self-Evaluation, 15:14-21

Paul is satisfied with the spiritual stature of the church at Rome but also claims justification for having written to them boldly on the ground that God's grace has made him *a minister . . . to the Gentiles* (v. 16). Paul describes his preaching of the gospel as priestly activity, and the offering he makes to God through the gospel is the gentiles. The term he uses of himself as *a minister* (v. 16, Gk. *leitourgos*) means priest in Neh 10:39; Isa 61:6; Sir 7:30; Heb 8:2. The verb *hierougeō* (serve as a priest) underscores this.

Paul believes that his work for God is something to boast about (v. 17). The word he uses for boasting (*kauchēsis*) is the same word that he uses for the boasting that is excluded by justification by grace in 3:27. But here in v. 17 he is proud, not of his attainments, but of what Christ has achieved through him.

For further discussion of this section see Introduction: Occasion and Purpose, The Intended Visit.

Travel Plans, 15:22-29

On this passage see the discussion of Paul's plans to visit Jerusalem and Spain in Introduction: Occasion and Purpose.

Emotional Appeal for Their Prayers, 15:30-32

This last part of the concluding personal statement (body closing) fulfills the rhetorical function of making an emotional appeal to the Roman church for their prayerful concern about Paul.

Closing, 15:33–16:27

For the issues raised by chap. 16, see above, Introduction: Manuscript Evidence and Destination. And for the structure of the Closing, refer to the outline at the beginning of the commentary. Only a few brief comments will be made here.

It could be that Paul intended to end the letter with the grace benediction in 16:20b and that Paul's scribe *Tertius* (16:22), added the greetings from Paul's associates, requiring a repetition of the grace benediction in 16:24. Manuscripts differ on the placement of this benediction (Gamble 1977, 91–94).

Among those for whom Paul requests greetings are *Andronicus and Junia*(s) (16:7) whom Paul designates as fellow Jews and as persons who are well known among the apostles. The Greek name Iounian, as far as spelling is concerned, could be the accusative case of the male name Iounias (Junias) or the accusative of the common Roman female name Junia. But apart from this verse there is no evidence for a male name Junias (Cranfield 1981, 788). The name should be read as the female Junia, and it should be recognized that there were women apostles.

The final doxology (16:25-27) is probably a post-Pauline addition. Such terminology as *the eternal God* (*tou aiōniou theou*), *the only wise God* (*monō sophō theō*), and *the mystery . . . made known* (*mystēriou . . . gnōristhentos*) is not characteristic of Paul. Especially strange is the idea of the gospel as a mystery kept secret through the ages but now made known through the prophetic writings (Kümmel 1965, 223). Paul's own position in Romans is that the righteousness of faith, recently made manifest through the redemption in Christ Jesus (3:21-26), was already proclaimed in the law (10:6-8), and actualized by Abraham (4:3-8).

Works Cited

Aune, David E. 1991. "Romans as a *Logos* Protreptikos," in Donfried 1991a.

Barrett, C. K. 1957. *A Commentary on the Epistle to the Romans*, BNTC.

Beale, Walter H. 1978. "Rhetorical Performative: A New Theory of Epideictic," *Philosophy and Rhetoric* 11/4 (Fall 1978): 221–46.

Best, Ernest. 1955. *One Body in Christ*.

Bornkamm, Günther. 1991. "The Letter to the Romans as Paul's Last Will and Testament," in Donfried 1991a.

Bultmann, Rudolf. 1951. *Theology of the N.T.*, vol. 1. 1967. "Glossen im Römerbrief," *Exegetica*.

Campbell, William S. 1991. "Romans III as a Key to the Structure and Thought of Romans," in Donfried 1991a.

Cousar, Charles B. 1990. *A Theology of the Cross, Overtures to Biblical Theology*.

Cranfield, C. E. B. 1980. *A Critical and Exegetical Commentary on the Epistle to the Romans*, 2 vols., ICC.

Cullmann, Oscar. 1957. *The State in the N.T.*

Davies, W. D. 1948. *Paul and Rabbinic Judaism*.

Dodd, C. H. 1954. *The Epistle of Paul to the Romans*.

Donfried, Karl P. 1991a. *The Romans Debate*, rev. ed. 1991b. "Introduction 1991: The Romans Debate since 1977," in Donfried 1991a. 1991c. "A Short Note on Romans 16," in Donfried 1991a. 1991d. "False Presuppositions in the Study of Romans," in Donfried 1991a.

Dunn, James D. G. 1988. *Romans 1–8*. 1988. *Romans 9–16*.

Fuller, Reginald H. 1978. "The Conception/Birth of Jesus as a Christological Moment," *JSNT* 1 (1978): 37–52.

Funk, Robert W. 1967. "The Apostolic Parousia: Form and Significance," *Christian History and Interpretation.*

Furnish, Victor Paul. 1979. *The Moral Teaching of Paul.*

Gamble, Harry. 1977. *The Textual History of the Letter to the Romans.* 1985. *The N.T. Canon,* GBS/NT.

Girard, René. 1986. *The Scapegoat.* 1989. *Violence and the Sacred.*

Hays, Richard B. 1981. *The Faith of Jesus Christ,* SBLDS 56.

Jervell, Jacob. 1991. "The Letter to Jerusalem," in Donfried 1991a.

Jewett, Robert. 1991. "Following the Argument of Romans," in Donfried 1991a.

Karris, Robert J. 1991a. "Romans 14:1–15:13 and the Occasion of Romans," in Donfried 1991a. 1991b. "The Occasion of Romans: A Response to Professor Donfried," in Donfried 1991a.

Käsemann, Ernst. 1969. *New Testament Questions of Today.* 1971. *Perspectives on Paul.* 1980. *Commentary on Romans.*

Kennedy, George A. 1984. *N.T. Interpretation through Rhetorical Criticism.*

Klein, Günter. 1991. "Paul's Purpose in Writing the Epistle to the Romans," in Donfried 1991a.

Knox, John. 1954. "The Epistle to the Romans," *IB.*

Kümmel, Werner Georg et al. 1965. *Introduction to the N.T.,* 14th rev. ed.

Lampe, Peter. 1991. "The Roman Christians of Romans 16," in Donfried 1991a.

Mack, Burton L. 1990. *Rhetoric and the N.T.* GBS/NT.

Manson, T. W. 1991. "St. Paul's Letter to the Romans—and Others," in Donfried 1991a.

Metzger, Bruce E. 1975. *A Textual Commentary on the Greek N.T.*

Nygren, Anders. 1949. *Commentary on Romans.*

O'Neill, J. C. 1975. *Paul's Letters to the Romans.*

Petersen, Norman R. 1985. *Rediscovering Paul.*

Ricoeur, Paul. 1969. *The Symbolism of Evil.*

Sanders, E. P. 1977. *Paul and Palestinian Judaism.* 1983. *Paul, the Law, and the Jewish People.*

Schmithals, Walter. 1975. *Der Römerbrief als historisches Problem.*

Scroggs, Robin. 1983. *The N.T. and Homosexuality.*

Stirewalt, Martin Luther, Jr. 1991. "The Form and Function of the Greek Letter-Essay," in Donfried 1991a.

Stowers, Stanley Kent. 1981. *The Diatribe and Paul's Letter to the Romans.* 1989. *Letter Writing in Greco-Roman Antiquity.*

Stuhlmacher, Peter. 1991. "The Purpose of Romans," in Donfried 1991a.

Theissen, Gerd. 1987. *Psychological Aspects of Pauline Theology.*

Via, Dan O. 1985. *The Ethics of Mark's Gospel.* 1990. *Self-Deception and Wholeness in Paul and Matthew.*

Wagner, Günther. 1967. *Pauline Baptism and Pagan Mysteries.*

Wedderburn, A. J. M. 1991. *The Reasons for Romans.*

Wiefel, Wolfgang. 1991. "The Jewish Community in Ancient Rome and the Origins of Roman Christianity," in Donfried 1991a.

Williams, Sam K. 1975. *Jesus' Death as Saving Event*, HDR 2. 1980. "The Righteousness of God in Romans," *JBL* 99/2 (June 1980): 241–90.

Wuellner, Wilhelm. 1987. "Where Is Rhetorical Criticism Taking Us?" *CBQ* 49/3 (July 1987): 448–63. 1991. "Paul's Rhetoric of Argumentation in Romans," in Donfried 1991a.

Ziesler, John. 1989. *Paul's Letters to the Romans.*

First Corinthians

Marion L. Soards   [MCB 1163-1189]

Introduction

First Corinthians is considered one of Paul's four *great* letters (along with Romans, 2 Corinthians, and Galatians) in part because of the actual length of this letter in comparison to the other writings attributed to Paul in the NT; but even more, 1 Corinthians is regarded as a great epistle because of the range of the topics and the depth of the reflections that it contains. The "great letters" are regarded by all students of Paul's writings as the central documents for the interpretation of the apostle's theology, and 1 Corinthians is particularly significant for its treatment of important aspects of basic Christian faith and practice.

Authorship

Since the writing of *1 Clement* in the late first century the letter we refer to today as 1 Corinthians has been attributed to the apostle Paul (see *1 Clem* 47.1-7). No one has ever seriously questioned whether Paul wrote this letter. Even the most radical critics, F. C. Baur and his so-called Tübingen School, accepted 1 Corinthians as authentic. From time to time isolated scholars have raised questions about the unity of the letter, sometimes suggesting either that the epistle as we know it was composed from parts of several letters by Paul that were assembled by a later editor or that it contains a significant number of major and minor glosses that were written into the letter by later scribes. Such broad theories have not attracted a following, though scholars regularly question the authenticity of a few verses of the letter. (We shall consider these verses as we work through the sections of the letter in the commentary that follows.)

Paul and the Corinthians

First-century CORINTH existed because the city had been reconstructed by order of Julius Caesar in 44 B.C.E., long after the Romans destroyed old Corinth in 146 B.C.E. In antiquity Corinth lay in a particularly crucial location on the isthmus that connected the mainland of Greece with the Peloponnesian peninsula that separated the Corinthian Gulf of the Adriatic Sea on the west from the Saronic Gulf of the Aegean Sea on the east. The new city was reestablished as a strategic military and economic outpost for Rome. The population of new Corinth was originally composed of Italian freedmen, given their freedom as a reward for military service. Other merchants and traders looking for new and rich opportunities joined the former soldiers, so that the new city had a complex, cosmopolitan population despite an initially shallow culture. The goods of the East and the West moved through Corinth's harbors and across the short roadways connecting them. The city was an exciting place—genuinely pluralistic with a penchant for SYNCRETISM; fortunes and fame were made and lost in Corinth.

From PAUL's letters to Corinth and from a judicious reading of Acts, especially Acts 18, we can reconstruct a portrait of Paul's experiences in Corinth and of his dealings with the members of the Corinthian church. Apparently, shortly after Paul arrived in Corinth he sought out the Jewish quarter of the city where he met Prisca and Aquila (see PRISCILLA AND AQUILA), a Jewish couple recently arrived in Corinth as part of the emperor Claudius's expulsion of certain Jews from Rome. Historians conclude that Prisca and Aquila were Jewish Christians, indeed that the Jews expelled from Rome were the Christian Jews who created a disturbance in the capital of the ROMAN EMPIRE by preaching the gospel of Christ among the Jews. This couple shared both their faith and their trade of tentmaking with Paul, and we learn as no surprise that Paul lived and worked with this couple in Corinth.

In the time that followed, Paul, Prisca, Aquila, TIMOTHY, SILAS, and perhaps others who remain unnamed, preached to Jews in the SYNAGOGUE that Jesus was the Christ. The success of this mission is clear from the memory that Crispus, the leader of the synagogue, and his household became Christians. Severe opposition arose, however, so that the mission moved out of the synagogue into the house next door that belonged to a God-fearer named Titius Justus (Acts 18:7). According to Acts many Jews and God-fearers came to believe through the preaching of Paul and his colleagues. This work in Corinth lasted for eighteen months before the unbelieving Jews launched a united attack against Paul and his colleagues. They brought him before the Roman tribunal of the proconsul Lucius Junius Annaeus GALLIO, whose term of office extended either from 1 May 51 to 1 May 52 or 1 May 52 to 1 May 53 C.E. Gallio refused to hear the case, which produced a sharp outcry and demonstration by Paul's Jewish adversaries.

According to Acts, Paul stayed in Corinth "many days longer" (18:18 RSV), although eventually he departed from Corinth with Prisca and Aquila. After a time of travels, Paul and his companions settled in EPHESUS for over two years. From Ephesus Paul wrote a series of letters to the Corinthians, and he even had conversations with representatives of the Corinthian congregation who visited him in Ephesus. From 1 Cor 5:9 we see clearly that prior to the writing of 1 Corinthians Paul had already written at least one other letter to the Corinthians. Scholars debate whether that earlier letter is completely lost or whether it may, in part, be preserved in 2 Corinthians. Whatever the case, we should understand that our canonical work, 1 Corinthians, is at least the "second" letter to the Corinthians. At the time that Paul wrote our 1 Corinthians, he had been in Ephesus for an extended period, for he mentions his plans to leave Ephesus in 1 Cor 16:5-9.

The Situation and the Problems

As Paul lived and worked in Ephesus, he learned of the situation in Corinth both from visitors and from a letter that the members of the Corinthian congregation sent to him. First, near the beginning of the letter, in 1:11, the apostle mentions *Chloe's people* with whom he has been in conversation. This designation indicates members of the household of Chloe and could be a reference to family members, slaves, or both. Later, near the end of the letter, in 16:17, Paul names *Stephanus and Fortunas and Achaicus* who had visited him, and so, made up for the absence of the other members of the congregation. We cannot determine whether the early reference to *Chloe's people* are to be identified with the three men (apparently the letter delegation) named toward the end of the letter, but we do see that Paul had firsthand observations concerning the circumstances in Corinth. In the course of the letter Paul refers explicitly to matters of which he learned from his visitors—see 5:1-2 (and perhaps the material in 5:3-6:20). Second, at 7:1 Paul refers directly to the letter with the phrase *Now concerning the matters about which you wrote*. Subsequently he uses the phrase *now concerning*, still apparently referring to the letter from the Corinthians, in 7:25, 8:1, 12:1, and 16:1. The items considered in relation to the letter from Corinth include sex and marriage, food offered to pagan idols prior to being sold in the market for consumption, the GIFTS OF THE SPIRIT, and the method for the collection that Paul was assembling for the poor in Jerusalem.

Behind all the issues Paul addresses in 1 Corinthians lies a preoccupation of the Corinthians with wisdom. The wisdom with which they were concerned was not mature or reasonable judgment, but special information that gave those "in the know" special status in relation to others who did not share those data. The Corinthians wanted involvement with supposedly deeper meanings and lofty unseen things. Some of them apparently thought of their life in Christ as if it were participation in MYSTERY RELIGIONS. Paul pejoratively calls such wisdom "human wisdom" (1:20; NRSV *wisdom of the world*), and he contrasts it with God's powerful wisdom, shown in the cross of Christ, in order to castigate the Corinthians for their inappropriate attitudes and behaviors.

Paul's remarks reveal that he understands the preoccupation with wisdom to result from the basic will of the Corinthians to boast. By claiming to have wisdom the Corinthians elevate themselves above others who do not share their information. Indeed, the will to boast of one's status through possession of wisdom was so great one group of Corinthians even compared their wisdom over against another's, to establish their spiritual superiority (or the other's inferiority). Throughout this letter Paul criticizes the particular actions of the Corinthians, but above all he denounces the will to boast. The will to be superior and to brag about it was the fundamental problem that generated the other symptomatic problems in Corinth.

Date

Since we know from the mention of Gallio in Acts 18 that Paul was active in Corinth sometime between 1 May 51 and 1 May 53 C.E., by taking 1 May 52 as a starting point and by tracing Paul's travels up to the time he arrived in Ephesus (Acts 18–19), we can safely understand that Paul arrived in Ephesus in late 52. He labored in Ephesus until the spring of 55. Moreover, from 1 Cor 16:5-9 we learn that Paul wrote 1 Corinthians toward the end of his Ephesian sojourn, so that this letter was most likely written early in 55 (or, less likely, very late in 54).

Primary Themes

First Corinthians presents a kaleidoscope of themes, touching on various aspects of basic Christian faith and practice. Among the prominent topics treated are the forming of factions in the church, the value of human wisdom versus divine wisdom or power, the nature of spirituality, blatant forms of misconduct, sex and marriage, social status, the eschatological character of Christian existence, food offered to pagan gods prior to sale in the marketplace, the nature of Christian freedom, orderly worship, the gifts of the Spirit, the church as the BODY OF CHRIST, the superior way of love, TONGUES and PROPHECY, resurrection, the collection for the SAINTS in Jerusalem, and Paul's future plans. In the course of reflecting on these topics, Paul comments on a number of items of concern for people today—to name but a few: the essence of the GOSPEL, the shape and substance of Christian ministry, Christian involvement in lawsuits, appropriate and inappropriate sexual relations, DIVORCE, SLAVERY, the role of women in the life of the church, charismatic practices, the reality of Jesus' resurrection, and Christian giving.

For Further Study

In the *Mercer Dictionary of the Bible*: CORINTH; CORINTHIAN CORRESPON-DENCE; EPISTLE/LETTER; ESCHATOLOGY IN THE NT; GIFTS OF THE SPIRIT; LOVE IN THE NT; MEAT SACRIFICED TO IDOLS; PAUL; RESURRECTION IN THE NT; SUFFERING IN THE NT; WISDOM IN THE NT.

In other sources: C. K. Barrett, *The First Epistle to the Corinthians*, HNTC; J. M. Bassler, "1 Corinthians," *WmBC*; R. B. Brown, "1 Corinthians," BBC; H. Conzelmann, *1 Corinthians*, Herm; G. D. Fee, *The First Epistle to the Corinthians*, NICNT; R. A. Harrisville, *1 Corinthians*, AugCNT; E. Fiorenza, "1 Corinthians," *HBC*; J. Murphy-O'Connor, "First Letter to the Corinthians," NJBC, *1 Corinthians*, and *St. Paul's Corinth*; W. F. Orr and J. A. Walther, *1 Corinthians*, AncB; C. H. Talbert, *Reading Corinthians*; M. E. Thrall, *First and Second Letters of Paul to the Corinthians*.

Commentary

An Outline

I. Salutation, 1:1-3
  A. Senders, 1:1
  B. Recipients, 1:2
  C. Greetings, 1:3
II. Thanksgiving, 1:4-9
  A. The Corinthians' Endowments, 1:4-7a
  B. The Lord's Faithfulness, 1:7b-9
III. Body of the Letter, 1:10–15:58
  A. The Gospel and Wisdom, 1:10–4:21

  B. Specific Problems and Questions,
     5:1–11:1
  C. Orderly Worship
     and Spiritual Gifts, 11:2–14:40
  D. The Truth of the Resurrection, 15:1-58
IV. Parenesis, 16:1-18
  A. Future Plans, 16:1-12
  B. Principles for Life, 16:13-14
  C. Saluting Special Persons, 16:15-18
V. Closing, 16:19-24

Salutation, 1:1-3

The letter opens with a fairly standard greeting, presenting the normal three elements an ancient reader would have expected at the beginning of a letter: sender(s), recipients, and a greeting. Although standard, these verses are pregnant with theological significance through Paul's adaptation or modification of the basic letter form.

Senders, 1:1

In naming the senders, Paul refers to himself as *an apostle*. For modern readers this word has become a technical title, so that we miss Paul's point that he is a "sent one," which is the literal sense of the word "apostle" (ἀπόστολος) in Greek. Not only is Paul one who is sent, he was sent in behalf of Christ Jesus. Moreover, his being sent came about through God's will, not by Paul's own choice. Thus, Paul says he was *called*, meaning that God intervened in his life and established the priority of God's own will. Furthermore, Paul does not write alone, for he works in conjunction with others whom God also directs into action. Here, Paul names *Sosthenes* as his coauthor. Remarkably, Sosthenes is the name of the leader of the Jews who brought charges against Paul before Gallio in Corinth (Acts 18:17). If the Sosthenes named here is the same person about whom we read in Acts, he surely experienced a radical change of heart and a reorientation of his life.

Recipients, 1:2

Paul refers to the Corinthians in a nuanced fashion. They are a *church* (ἐκκλησία). The Greek word can mean "church," or "congregation," or "assembly." In Greco-Roman literature it indicated a political assembly, but as Paul would have known the word from its use in the Greek translation of the Hebrew Bible, ἐκκλησία was used for the Hebrew word קהל that named the children of Israel both in their EXODUS wanderings and in their worshipful assemblies at the Temple. Paul says the church is *the church of God*—that is, God has priority in the formation of the congregation, so that only secondarily does the apostle refer to the geographical location of the church *in Corinth*. Moreover, he declares the Corinthians are *sanctified in Christ Jesus*, indicating that the Corinthians were made holy by Christ—not by their own efforts. The Corinthians are (literally) "called saints," as Paul was (literally) "called apostle." Paul and the Corinthians share the experience of God's calling them and actually naming the purpose of their lives. Furthermore, Paul refers to the Corinthians as being saints *together with all those who in every place call on the name of our Lord Jesus Christ, both their Lord and ours*. With these phrases Paul recognizes the common bond of the Corinthians with all other Christians. They are not an isolated holy group simply set apart from the world; rather, the Corinthians (and Paul and Sosthenes) live in a dependent relationship to Christ that establishes a mutuality that transcends the normal boundaries of human relations.

Greetings, 1:3

The greeting pronounces *grace* and *peace* upon the Corinthians *from God our Father and the Lord Jesus Christ*. Thus, we see the true source of GRACE and PEACE. Grace is a divine gift that produces the divine result of peace in the lives of those who experience it.

Thanksgiving, 1:4-9

Scholars have long recognized that as a formal element of Paul's letters the thanksgiving (or, thanksgiving-prayer) serves several purposes. First, the thanksgiving terminates the opening portion of the letter. Second, it signals the basic theme or themes of the letter that will follow. Third, the thanksgiving can sometimes even outline the major topics to be treated in the epistle. Here, for example, Paul acknowledges God's grace as active among the Corinthians to the end that they are *in every way . . . enriched in* [Christ Jesus], *in speech and knowledge of every kind*. Among the Corinthians the real gifts of "speech" and "knowledge" are at the heart of their problematic thoughts and actions. At once Paul names the genuine strengths and weaknesses of the Corinthian church. The members experience the endowments of grace, but, as the remainder of the letter reveals, their concern with and use of these gifts is completely out of hand.

The Corinthians' Endowments, 1:4-7a

Paul acknowledges and qualifies the spiritual gifts with which the Corinthians have been blessed. The goal of God's gifts of speech and knowledge relates to the testimony about Christ that comes to confirmation among the Corinthians. As God endows the Corinthians with spiritual gifts, God demonstrates the reality of God's gracious work in Christ. The Corinthians experience grace unto the glory of Christ, not for their own aggrandizement. God's authority is recognized in the words *the grace of God . . . has been given you*; God gave grace, the Corinthians merely (though really) received it.

The Lord's Faithfulness, 1:7b-9

The true status of the Corinthians becomes clear in these verses; they are *waiting* for the revelation of the Lord Jesus Christ. *Already* they experience grace, but *not yet* is the Lord fully present. The Corinthians live in relation to a promise. The full experience of God's grace lies beyond the present in the future, and the sole basis of hope in that future is that *God is faithful.* The grace that the Corinthians experience in the present is not the guarantee of their hope for the future; rather, God who grants grace now is himself the hope of the future. Grace is no guarantee; it is a sign of God's goodness, a manifestation of God's faithfulness, which itself underwrites the future. God called the Corinthians into communion with Jesus Christ and, in turn, with one another. The fellowship they experience is not of their own doing; it is God's work. The church is not theirs; it is God's—by will and by work. The Corinthians are called into the community of faith created by God's grace at work in the Lord Jesus Christ. Seeing this much should inform the Corinthians who they are as a church; and so, they should see how they are to live.

Body of the Letter, 1:10–15:58

The Gospel and Wisdom, 1:10–4:21

This first major portion of the body of the letter is a coherent reflection treating basic matters of Christian belief and the particular situation in Corinth. Paul argues against an understanding of the gospel as a kind of esoteric or mysterious wisdom teaching, especially a teaching that would elevate those who have the information above the masses to whom the teaching would not be available.

1:10-17. Factions in the congregation. At the outset Paul takes up the issue of factions (*divisions*, v. 10; *quarrels*, v. 11) in the Corinthian church. He expresses his astonishment at the situation and implies his disapproval of the matter, but he does not yet offer a full resolution to the problem. Paul's choice of vocabulary (*appeal*, v. 10) indicates his earnestness in admonishing the Corinthians, and his reference to *the name of our Lord Jesus Christ* expresses the means and authority of his appeal. Paul's goal for the Corinthians is that they will be united in thought and disposition.

As Paul talks about the factions in Corinth, he identifies the groups in relation to prominent persons: PAUL, APOLLOS, Cephas (PETER), and CHRIST. It is not clear whether he means to name three or four groups, for it is not certain whether there is a "Christ party" or whether Paul means that all, regardless of their relationship with Paul, Apollos, or Cephas, are related to Christ. At root the problem is that the Corinthians have turned relationships into status-giving identities or positions. Paul works to inform the Corinthians that they have direction in life, they do not merely have positions to defend or declare. The three rhetorical questions in v. 13 are answered "yes," "no," and "no." The first question about the division of the church names the problem, and the following two questions make it clear that the situation is absurd.

At first reading, the statements in vv. 14-16 seem to display a shockingly cavalier regard for BAPTISM. There is certainly sarcasm in the remarks as Paul attempts to jolt the Corinthians out of their boastful comparisons concerning their status in the church. Yet, as one sees by continuing to read Paul's words in v. 17, he is able to relativize the importance of baptism (which the Corinthians value as giving them special identities and status) because he understands his call as a call to preach. Baptism is a part of the larger picture of Christian faith and practice, but for Paul proclamation of the gospel is the cutting edge. Given the particular problem in Corinth with its baptismal parties and boasting, Paul is genuinely thankful that baptism per se was not his primary ministry. Further clarification comes in his words contrasting "wisdom" and the CROSS. The good news of God's saving work in the cross of Christ is not a slick message that is sold through elegant packaging. Sheer manipulative eloquence is not a medium that can bear the weight of the message of the cross. Above all, the shocking claim that God saves humanity in the cross of Jesus Christ demonstrates that God works in defiance of this world's norms.

1:18-25. God's peculiar, powerful way. God works in a most peculiar way—not only in defiance of the standards of this world, but also in such a powerful way that it incapacitates, reverses, even turns upside down the values (objectively established) of this world. Paul declares this way of God's working as a fact. In v. 18 Paul sets up a rhetorical contrast scheme that drives home the heart of the gospel as he understands it. In relation to the theme of "the word of the cross," that is, the proclamation of the saving death of Jesus Christ, Paul refers to humanity in two groups. On the one hand, there are those who regard the word of the cross as *foolishness*; Paul says they are perishing. On the other hand, there are those who are *being saved*. The passive voice of the verb indicates that God is doing the saving here. Moreover, in the scheme of this contrast with *perishing* versus *being saved*, one finds *foolishness* contrasted with *the power of God*. The natural opposite of *foolishness* in this context would be *wisdom*. Remarkably Paul says that it is what God does, not what humans know, that saves. God acted in the cross of Christ and it produces a division among humanity that itself implies God's power.

To make this argument Paul quotes Isa 29:14, although he changes the verb in the quotation from "conceal" to *thwart* (v. 19). With this slight alteration Paul makes the citation fit more exactly the context to which he writes. As the apostle offers a scriptural precedent for the way God works through the cross of Christ, he does more than prooftext his point. His use of scripture shows that he understands scripture to be absolutely authoritative, absolutely essential for comprehending God's ways, but of an ultimately penultimate significance. God's work in Christ directs the use of the Bible; the Bible does not control God.

The argument here locates where the wisdom of the merely human wise one, scribe, and debater originate—in *this age*. God's "age," however, exposes the shallowness and inaccuracy of merely human wisdom. Even the loftiest theology that is disengaged from the primary revelation of God in Jesus Christ is *foolishness*. Humans do not reason their way to God; God saves humanity (and the world!) by the cross of Christ, which is, by this world's standards, *foolishness*. Christ preached as crucified brings a crisis of separation. Denial of the saving significance of the cross reveals that one is in bondage to "this world," whereas "those who believe" are shown to be called by God, to be grasped by the power of God—a demonstration that Christ is God's "wisdom." Verse 25 summarizes the whole section saying that God's wisdom or power expressed in the cross of Christ renders worldly wisdom into foolishness as a demonstration of the reality of the power of God.

1:26-31. Before and after God's call. In these theologically loaded verses, Paul calls the Corinthians to consider themselves both *before* (or, at) the time of their call and *after* (or, in) their calling. Before their calling Paul suggests that in a variety of ways the Corinthians were for the most part nobodies; after being called by God, however, the Corinthians are instruments of God's power with Christ Jesus as the source of their lives. To make this argument Paul engages in a careful, deliberate play on the LXX version of Jer 9:22-24. The reference to scripture is clear in v. 31, but already in vv. 28-29 the language echoes Jeremiah, especially in the reference to "the wise" and "wisdom" and to "the powerful" and "the strong." Paul's contrast scheme is designed to humble the Corinthians in order to heighten their appreciation for the saving work of God in Jesus Christ. Paul tells the Corinthians that in light of what God has done in Jesus Christ the only legitimate boasting that Christians do is about what God has done—not about what humans know, do, are, or achieve.

2:1-5. Paul's apostolic ministry and message. This section is an exposition of Paul's *apostolic* message and ministry. It comes in two moves: First, vv. 1-2 demonstrate the continuity between the form and content or the style and substance of the apostle's proclamation. Second, vv. 3-5 demonstrate the continuity of the message and the demeanor of the preacher or messenger. Paul's language is intensely personal. The statements make clear that his approach and practice of ministry were deliberate. The statements are, nevertheless, ambiguous. Paul is not saying, "I preached only the cross instead of the cross plus something more." Rather, he insists that he laid aside all other devices for persuasion and proclaimed the cross without frills.

Paul's portrait of himself refers to *weakness* and explains this idea by using the traditional Jewish image of *fear and trembling*—a reference to the reverent recognition of the reality of God! Paul says that his message was such that his speech allowed the Spirit and God's power to show themselves as they worked through his message. The Corinthians came to believe, not by showy human effort, but by the very working of God's power. Although humans are God's agents, God alone is the one who saves humanity.

2:6-16. Meditation on the operation of revelation. These verses are an excursus on the wisdom of God and the spiritual discernment of Christians, or a meditation on the operation of REVELATION. Interpreters ask whether Paul contradicts himself here. Does he have a two-leveled message with one word for some and a "deeper" teaching for others? No. One should recall that Paul designated his message "the word of the cross" (1:18 RSV). Clearly he interprets the saving significance of the cross throughout his letters by regularly applying the meaning of the cross to the lives of his readers. The cross is not only something that happened to Jesus. Paul declares that by the mysterious grace of God the cross affects, or effects (!), the lives of Christians. Paul does not have a special teaching for some. He can, however, explicate more to some than to others because of the differing degrees of their own spiritual maturation. This situation seems to be the basis for Paul's distinction between the "mature" and the "spiritual" on the one hand and the "unspiritual" or "natural" on the other.

Paul declares that God's wisdom is not available simply to inquiring minds. Paul refers to the scriptural precedent for this teaching, although it is impossible to identify precisely the passage he cites. His "quotation" in v. 9 seems to be a pastiche from perhaps Ps 3:20; Isa 52:15; 64:3-4; 65:16-17; Jer 3:16; Sir 1:10; and *AscIsa* 11.34. The depths of God's will and work come to humanity only as God chooses to reveal them through the Spirit. Paul explains the necessity of divine revelation through an argument on the principle of "like by like"—saying that a person is the only one who knows the inner secrets of himself or herself. It is likewise with God. Paul states that an unspiritual human is unable to receive the things of the Spirit of God because these things are only discernible by the Spirit. Moreover, in vv. 12 and 16 Paul boldly declares that Christians have the *Spirit that is from God* and *the mind of Christ*, so that they have God's wisdom imparted to them through the Spirit.

3:1-17. Working toward unity and edification. Paul ties together what he has said to this point in vv. 1-4 in order to show why he did not impart God's wisdom to the Corinthians. The chief implication of his remarks is that the Corinthians are immature, as is seen in their factionalization. Notice, however, that Paul at least regards the Corinthians as *infants* (v. 1) so that he does not completely deny they are persons of faith. Paul's words would prove insulting, nevertheless, for he repeatedly says the Corinthians are *of the flesh*. Although the Corinthians value wisdom and declare their status as mature believers or "spiritual ones," Paul refutes their claims.

Then, Paul takes up a series of metaphors in order to instruct the Corinthians. The entire set of remarks is aimed at correcting the Corinthians' misunderstandings and at directing them toward unity and mutual edification. In vv. 5-9 Paul offers a lesson by taking himself and APOLLOS as examples. Paul and Apollos are cast as field servants who serve the higher authority of their Lord. Their assignments are different, though they are both merely functionaries. The reality of divine farming is that God does the growing while the field hands simply execute God's will. As servants Paul and Apollos are equal and they get paid according to their labor. The NRSV provides a helpful translation of v. 9. Other translations may read "we are

God's fellow workers" (RSV), an idea that makes little sense in the context of the previous lines; but the NRSV more accurately renders the ambiguous Greek as *we are God's servants, working together*. God's servants labor together; they do not form competitive groups, for they are united in their efforts under the sole authority of God. Paul recognizes God's authority over the apostles and over the church in Corinth, which he calls *God's field*.

At the end of v. 9 Paul shifts metaphors. Not only are the Corinthians *God's field*, they are also *God's building*. With that image established, Paul assumes the point of view of a sophisticated master builder and tells of the foundation he laid, the foundation of Jesus Christ. That foundation cannot be changed, although now others may erect an edifice on the foundation. Yet, Paul declares that even in the activity of building on the foundation of Jesus Christ, not all buildings are equal. Verse 12 catalogues a variety of building materials. Then, the following discussion promises a testing of the materials, an eschatological testing in the future, promised *Day* (of the Lord). Those who built on the foundation of Jesus Christ may anticipate reward or loss in accordance with the quality and durability of the material they used. Paul means to admonish the Corinthians to a careful selection of materials, that is, to a way of life as a church that is fitting for the foundation of Jesus Christ. Christian works may not bring salvation—God accomplished that in the cross of Christ—but what Christians do with their lives makes a difference in God's eyes. As Paul applies the metaphor of *God's building* to the Corinthian situation, he informs them of their identity as God's Temple as they experience the indwelling of the Holy Spirit among them. Finally, Paul plainly warns that a just reward will be given to any who *destroy* God's Temple. Behavior that destroys the church will ultimately be destroyed by God.

3:18-23. Evaluating by God's standards. In these verses Paul returns to the original issues he identified and began to discuss at 1:18-25, namely, the contrast between God's mysterious saving activity in the cross of Christ and the elitist attitude of the Corinthians that resulted from their preoccupation with "wisdom." Paul identifies the behavior of the Corinthians for what he perceives it to be, sheer self-deception. By focusing on their own knowledge as a key to their spiritual standing, they have shunned the amazing power of God. Paul calls for the Corinthians to take a proper attitude toward wisdom: in comparison with the saving power of God it is of little value. In order to establish his point Paul cites Job 5:13 and Ps 94:11 (93:11 LXX). Here Paul is essentially underscoring his argument with prooftexts. The citation from JOB is very loosely related to the original text; literally the LXX refers to God as "the one who takes the wise ones in [their] prudence," whereas Paul names God as "the one who catches the wise ones in their craftiness" (v. 19b NASV). Paul comes closer to the psalm text in v. 20, simply altering the word "humans" in the psalm to read *wise*.

Having scored his basic point and documented it from the LXX Paul continues by informing the Corinthians that they do not claim enough. By dividing themselves into cliques or factions they fail to embrace the larger reality that God has called into being through the saving and unifying cross of Christ. The Corinthians belong to Christ, and because Christ belongs to God all that belongs to God belongs to Christ; so that all this is available to the Corinthians as they are faithful followers of Christ. In and through Christ God unifies a redeemed creation, and the Corinthians are called to a new life in that grand unity.

4:1-5. God as the only real judge. Nothing about Christian life leads to boasting. Paul illustrates why. He also identifies Christ as the only real or true judge. The lines begin by informing the Corinthians how they are to regard Paul, Apollos, Cephas, and all other early Christian workers. They are merely *servants* and *stewards*, called to serve Christ as agents of the proclamation of the mysteries of God's GRACE. Only one key quality must characterize stewards, trustworthiness or, more literally, faithfulness. God requires that Paul and the others be faithful executors of the charge with which they have been entrusted. What the Corinthians think of God's stewards is actually of little or no importance. In fact, Paul says the opinions God's stewards have of themselves is irrelevant. Why? Because of one simple fact: The Lord is the one who does the judging. In a sense Paul is freed by the Lord's being his sole judge, for he needs neither to worry about what others think nor even to be obsessed with evaluating his own performance. Paul is free to strive to be faithful, not worrying about his success, for in the end Christ will judge him (and all others) and then God will mete out whatever praise is appropriate.

The promise of judgment comes in striking eschatological form. The language is that of apocalyptic eschatology. Paul expects the coming of Christ in the end. That coming will create a separation of "light" and "darkness," apocalyptic language for good and evil. Christ's final judgment will be universal, disclosing and exposing all things, even *the purposes of the heart*. Then, in the end the focus turns to God who enacts the results of the judgment that Christ effected.

4:6-13. Exposing inappropriate boasting. Paul has illustrated matters with reference to himself and Apollos, but what he has said was intended to apply to the Corinthians, as is clear from v. 6. This verse, while stating that Paul wanted the Corinthians to draw a lesson from his discussion of himself and Apollos, is difficult to comprehend precisely. The grammar seems to suggest that Paul wants the Corinthians to learn for two purposes: (1) so that they will understand and apply the saying, *"Nothing beyond what is written"* (v. 6); and (2) so that they will not form factions because of arrogant prejudices. While these purposes are plain, exactly what lesson Paul would have the Corinthians gain from his metaphors about farming and building is not immediately apparent; and the meaning of the quoted saying itself is not clear. By *what is written* Paul most likely is referring to the scripture he quoted in the sections prior to the metaphorical arguments in 4:1-5. If that is the case, we can return to Paul's basic point in 3:18-23, namely, by forming factions the Corinthians defy the unity that God in Christ is creating and to which the Corinthians themselves are called.

Paul's argument in the ensuing verses comes in two strokes. Verse 7 lays the basis for an attack on the Corinthians' practice of judging, comparing, and boasting. Verses 8-13 form the attack. At the outset in v. 8 Paul is quite sarcastic, mocking the Corinthians for their pride, or false pride as Paul would see it. In the face of Corinthian arrogance Paul counters with the example of the apostles themselves. Paul insists that God uses the real oppression of the apostles to a positive end. He then contrasts the state of the apostles with the claimed status of the Corinthians to show that something is wrong in their lives. His rhetoric is patterned: we . . . you; we . . . you; you . . . we. Paul's wording draws the attention of the Corinthians away from themselves and creates focused emphasis on the sufferings of the apostles. Thus, he lays out the nature of a genuine apostolic style of ministry characterized by "weakness."

This line of argument raises a question: What is the purpose of the suffering that the apostles endure? The last two clauses of v. 13 speak to this question, but they are notoriously difficult. The NRSV translates the verse, *We have become like the rubbish of the world, the dregs of all things, to this very day*. Thus, the translators take Paul's statement to indicate that the apostles have become "rubbish" and "dregs" in their sufferings, that is, Paul offers two negative descriptions in apposition. Orr and Walther (1976), however, suggests translating v. 13, in part, "until now the dirt scoured from the world, that which cleanses all"; so that Paul's phrases are read as a negative image that is superseded by a contrasting positive one. Remarkably, the Greek word (περικαθάρμα) translated as "rubbish" or "dirt scoured" occurs in Prov 21:18 (LXX) and means "expiation" or "ransom," and the Greek word (περίψημα) translated as "dregs" or "that which cleanses" occurs in Tob 5:19 and means "ransom" or "scapegoat." Rather than ending with two negative images in apposition ("rubbish," "dregs") or in a negative image that is superseded by a contrasting positive one ("dirt scoured," "that which cleanses"), Paul may ultimately define the positive meaning of the genuine suffering he and the others apostles endure. Thus, perhaps one should translate v. 13: "Being slandered, we call out, having become like an expiation for the world, a ransom for all until now." If this reading is correct, then, Paul is not saying that Christian suffering is a bad fate that can be endured; rather, Christian suffering plays a vital role in reconciliation.

4:14-21. A paternal appeal and threat. Paul's tone changes as he explains his motives for writing and issues an appeal to the Corinthians. The apostle employs the image of a "father" in relation to the congregation. Paul cites the special relationship he has with the Corinthians, and he recognizes this intimate association to be the natural result of his having founded the church through the preaching of the gospel of Jesus Christ. Paul works with the image of a father in terms the Corinthians would easily comprehend. As the father of the Corinthian church Paul is an example whom the Corinthians are to imitate. They are urged to take on Paul's *ways in Christ Jesus*. In order to direct the Corinthians Paul sends his "beloved and faithful child" Timothy, who in the pattern of relations named here would be a sibling to the Corinthians. Paul's call to imitation may seem egotistical, but we see later in 11:1 that Paul is urging the Corinthians to Christlike living (*Be imitators of me, as I am of Christ* [11:1]). The call here is an appeal for the Corinthians to take up or return to the standards of life that informed all of the congregations Paul founded.

Again, the Corinthians are called away from idiosyncratic, arrogant behavior as Paul reminds them they are part of the larger church that God in Christ is calling into being. Then, with the directions given, Paul continues in vv. 18-21 to write as a father to rowdy children as he issues a clear, pointed parental threat.

Specific Problems and Questions, 5:1–11:1

This lengthy and important part of the letter takes up a remarkable complex of materials that may be viewed as three major clusters of material: First, 5:1–6:20 treats a set of concrete misunderstandings. Paul has taught and written the Corinthians, but they have not accurately interpreted his remarks. Second, 7:1-40 deals with the topics of marriage, divorce, and social status. Again, the behavior of the Corinthians indicates that they have not taken the teachings of Paul to heart for the living of everyday life. Third, in an extended and spiraling segment of this section of the letter, 8:1–11:1, Paul discusses Christian rights and responsibilities in order to correct and direct the activities of the Corinthians.

5:1-13. Shocking sexual immorality. Verses 1-5 identify an incident of sexual immorality in the Corinthian congregation, wherein literally "someone has his father's wife." Paul declares his shock and announces that he has already passed judgment; he instructs the church about what to do and tells them why.

The problem is unclear in many ways. The situation is most likely that a man is living with his former stepmother. From Paul's discussion the man's father is quite likely dead. In turn, the language related to Paul's judgment, his instructions to the Corinthians, and his explanation are difficult and produce a number of challenges for interpretation.

First, Paul's directions concerning the action the Corinthians are to take are worded ambiguously. Yet, since Paul wrote to the "holy ones in Christ Jesus" (author trans.) at 1:2 and since he believes in the presence and the active power of the Risen Lord, one should probably take 5:4-5 to read, "When you are assembled in the name of the Lord, and I am with you in spirit along with the power of our Lord Jesus, give this one to Satan . . . " (author trans.).

Second, what is Paul's purpose in telling the Corinthians, literally, "Give this one to Satan unto destruction of the flesh, in order that the spirit may be saved in the day of the Lord?" What does "unto destruction of the flesh" mean? Whose "spirit" is it that "may be saved"? There are no easy solutions, but one should avoid interpretations that attribute to Paul ideas such as that Christians receive an indelible character in BAPTISM or that salvation comes by death.

In vv. 6-8 Paul turns on the community and their problem of boasting. The arrogance mentioned in v. 2 is a theme. Here Paul criticizes the Corinthians' boasting by using the image of leaven in relation to his directions for expulsion of the flagrantly immoral member. Paul's point is that a little undesirable boasting goes a long way. He advances his argument by employing the Jewish ritual of PASSOVER housecleaning to insure the full removal of all "leaven," that is, immorality and boasting.

Paul continues by declaring the motivation for Christian purity and discipline, namely, Christ, the paschal lamb. This traditional image registers the reality of the saving significance of Jesus' death and reminds the Corinthians that what God has done in Christ calls forth an altered manner of living for those who hear and believe the message of Christ.

A new, related line of thought comes in vv. 9-13. Paul refers to a former letter he says the Corinthians badly misunderstood. Paul means for the Corinthians to dissociate themselves from immoral persons in the church, not from those outside. Paul says that God attends to those outside the church. The directions not to eat with the immoral probably assume the context of the LORD'S SUPPER, which will occupy Paul in detail in chap. 11. Here, v. 13 is crucial. This verse is a quotation of Deut 17:7, although Paul uses the second person plural form of "drive out" rather than the second singular of the LXX. Thus, Paul tailors the biblical word to the Corinthians' situation, so that v. 13 helps one to comprehend Paul's difficult directions in 5:4-5. By expelling the immoral member from the church, the Corinthians assure that he comes under God's judgment. His condition is not, therefore, hopeless, but hopeful. The church, as those called by God in Christ, cannot tolerate such immorality; but if the church does allow such behavior, the sinner has no cause for change and no hope of reconciliation to God. God, on the other hand, can judge and call the sinner to the righteousness of faith.

6:1-11. Going to judgment before non-Christians. Having raised the issue of the relations of Christians both to other Christians and to those outside the church, Paul's mind seems to move to the matter of how Christians relate to one another outside the life of the church. Paul's discussion focuses on the issue of Christians suing each other in pagan courts of law. One cannot determine how Paul knows about this problem, nevertheless, he discusses the matter in some detail. Interpreters regularly refer to these verses as an excursus, although the discussion is not simply a digression from the main lines of thought.

Paul views Christians taking one another into pagan courts over lawsuits as an example of the degree of the Corinthians' lack of understanding, or better, lack of love, as will become clear later in the letter (chap. 13). The image of the "saints" judging the world adapts a motif of Jewish apocalyptic eschatology found in DANIEL, ENOCH, and the WISDOM OF SOLOMON. Does this statement contradict what was said about the church's capacity to judge in 5:9-13? No, for the judgment in view here is an anticipation of future judgment. Paul's argument is from greater to lesser, from future to present. If Christians will judge the world in a great apocalyptic future judgment, then, Paul argues, they should certainly be capable of exercising judgment over their own affairs here and now. Paul admonishes the Corinthians to take the full extent of life in Christ's community seriously.

In vv. 7-8 Paul advances his argument by declaring bluntly that the will to assert one's own rights at the expense of others—and at the expense of the general image of the community—is defeat. Verses 9-11 offer a catalogue listing in an illustrative, not exhaustive, manner certain characteristics and conditions that will not gain entry into the kingdom of God. The section becomes a brief meditation on "unrighteousness" (ἄδικος). The NRSV translation of *wrongdoers* (for ἄδικοι) rightly catches Paul's focus on actions, but this accurate translation runs the danger of minimizing Paul's point throughout this discussion that improper behavior results from a faulty theological attitude. Verse 11 is the most important statement in the section. From a frank recognition of the character of "some" of the Corinthians before their conversion, Paul elaborates why they now are—and, in turn, ought to be—different. They are *washed, sanctified,* and *justified* (v. 11); that is, Paul locates the Corinthians theologically, identifies them in relation to Christ, and recognizes the priority of God in their salvation and, now, in the conduct of their lives. In hearing this line, the Corinthians would likely think of their baptism, the gift of the Holy Spirit, and their new, right relationship with God. All of this transformation that the Corinthians have experienced comes, as the passive verbs show, through the work of God in Christ.

6:12-20. The character of Christian freedom. These nine verses form a complex segment of the letter. One finds here quotations from the Corinthians and a citation of the LXX. The verses are largely cast in the diatribe style of popular Hellenistic philosophy. One also encounters traditional elements of early Christian "doctrine." All of this material is woven together in service to Paul's deliberate line of argumentation.

Paul builds and argues a case in vv. 12-17 in response to the thinking and declarations of the Corinthians. As the NRSV and other translations recognize by placing the statement *All things are lawful for me* in quotations, Paul employs a pattern of rhetoric wherein he quotes the position of those with whom he is in imaginary dialogue in order to respond to their thinking. The conversation goes back and forth:

> [Corinthians] *All things are lawful for me,*
> [Paul] *but not all things are beneficial.*
> [Corinthians] *All things are lawful for me,*
> [Paul] *but I will not be dominated by anything.*
> [Corinthians] *Food is meant for the stomach and the stomach for food,*
> [Paul] *and God will destroy both one and the other.*

The Corinthians' slogan literally says, "All things [are] to me permissible." They may have learned this statement from Paul himself, for he never denies its validity; rather, he qualifies the idea with his argument. For the Corinthians, what they know or think they know has given them an abstract principle that can and has produced less than desirable results. Paul concretizes this idea. Freedom, according to Paul, is characterized by pursuing what it best; freedom does not lead to a new form of slavery. The Corinthians mistakenly claim an inner freedom that places them above the mundane realities of the world, and they are eager to demonstrate their liberation.

If Paul's remarks about the Corinthians' attitude toward food and sexual activity is accurate, the will to display freedom had gotten completely out of hand (although one should not forget that Paul creates deliberate distortions in his arguments in order to score his points). The Corinthians seem to assume that freedom means they are at liberty to gratify their every appetite. Paul expresses mild shock that from the notion that all foods are fit for consumption by those who are aware of their freedom, some in Corinth engage in casual sex with prostitutes in celebration of their freedom.

Paul's critique calls the Corinthians into a responsible relationship to "the Lord." Freedom, Paul tells the Corinthians, is "for the Lord," not merely for personal pleasure. To make his point with all possible force, Paul alludes to Gen 2:24 in v. 16b. On the one hand, he uses scripture to denounce involvement with prostitutes; on the other hand, the citation sets up a crucial statement of the nature of the spiritual union of Christians with the Lord.

In vv. 18-20 Paul's rhetoric takes the form of a clear frontal attack. He directs the Corinthians to *Shun fornication!* Then, he informs the Corinthians that their *body is a temple of the Holy Spirit within [them]*. Paul bluntly tells the Corinthians, *You are not your own*. Why? Because they *were bought with a price*. The language is a metaphorical reference to redemption as "ransom," and it alludes in an undeveloped way to the death of Jesus.

That the Corinthians belong to God is the ultimate qualification of their freedom. One should see that throughout this section Paul jabs his readers with the rhetorical refrain, *Do you not know . . . ?* The implication is that the Corinthians do not know what they ought to know. Paul writes to factor into the Corinthians' thinking new information that should correct their ignorance.

7:1-7. General remarks on marriage. Paul's statements in these verses are more often misunderstood than grasped and appreciated for what they say. At the outset, one should recognize that in v. 1 Paul is taking up the letter sent to him from Corinth with its variety of inquiries. Paul refers to the letter and, then, as the quotation marks in the NRSV around the words *"It is well for a man not to touch a woman"* recognize, he quotes a line from the letter. It is the position of some of the Corinthians that "It is well for a man not to touch a woman." Obviously the point was debated, for now the Corinthians have written to get Paul's own thinking on this point. Paul's position comes in v. 2. In Greek Paul uses an imperative in this statement, so that literally he declares, "Because of instances of sexual immorality, let each man have his own wife and let each woman have her own husband" (author trans.). This position is often called a concession, but the imperative force of the declaration calls that description into question.

From this opening exchange with the Corinthians Paul continues in v. 3 working with the assumption that people are already married. If so, then Paul instructs the husbands to give the wives their due and, likewise, the wives to give their husbands their due. At issue are so-called conjugal rights, which Paul assumes do exist. Verse 4 offers the social or anthropological assumptions behind Paul's directions. Remarkably, at this point Paul assumes a genuine mutuality in marital relations. The *authority* over each spouse's body is attributed to the other marital partner. There is little to no historical or cultural precedent for what Paul says here.

In v. 5 Paul initially encourages sexual union in the context of marriage, but he does allow for abstinence for special times of devotion *to prayer*. Some of the Corinthians seem to assume that ascetic restraint is a clear indication of spirituality, but Paul does not follow their line. Refraining from sexual union in a marriage is not the path of spirituality, although Paul allows for limited abstinence in special circumstances. When in the following verse Paul says, *This I say by way of concession, not of command*, he is merely qualifying his previous statement in v. 5 that allowed for sexual continence for prayer. In other words, Paul himself does not think that married persons need necessarily to refrain from sexual activity *by agreement for a set time* in order to devote themselves to prayer.

The heart of Paul's thinking about marriage and sex in marriage comes through in v. 7. Chastity, the capacity not to marry, freedom from a desire for sex in the context of a marriage, is a spiritual gift from God. For Paul, not marrying is preferable only if the capacity to remain single is given by God, but the gift of chastity is not universal and it is not necessary. Paul's own prejudices come out clearly in his remarks here, for he understands the gift of remaining unmarried to be an opportunity for freedom from marital responsibilities. Paul develops this dimension of this thinking later in 7:32-35.

7:8-9. Directions to the unmarried. Having discussed marriage, the advisability of sexual union in marriage, and the spiritual gift of remaining single, Paul turns directly to the unmarried members of the Corinthian congregation. He declares that he himself considers it better to remain unmarried than to marry, and his manner of expression shows that Paul is offering his own thinking on this subject. Later in this chapter he explains that he is of this opinion because of the eschatological character of the time in which he believes he and the Corinthians live. Nevertheless, Paul informs the unmarried members of the church that they should marry in certain circumstances. Paul reasons here from the assumption that the capacity to remain unmarried is a spiritual gift. The translation of this line in the NRSV and other translations, *But if they are not practicing self-control, they should marry*, is easily misunderstood. Paul is not saying, "If you cannot control yourself, get married." In Paul's well-known list of the fruit of the Spirit at Gal 5:23 one finds the noun "self-control" (ἐγκράτεια), so that although Paul uses the verbal form of "self-control" here (ἐγκρατεύεσθαι meaning "to practice self-control"), he is referring to a Spirit-empowered directing of one's self. If an unmarried person in Corinth does not have the Spirit-given ability to be chaste, then Paul says that person should marry.

7:10-11. Directions to the married. In turn, Paul writes again to the married. As he begins his remarks, Paul makes plain that he is not simply giving his own opinion; instead, he is delivering a word from the Lord to the Corinthians. The tradition to which Paul refers may lie behind the materials in passages such as Mark 10:2-9 and Luke 16:18 or Matt 5:32. This dominical word is a firm denial of the validity of DIVORCE. The NRSV correctly places v. 11 in parentheses. The statement is not an exception clause, however; rather, it provides directions in the event that persons practice divorce despite the word from the Lord. Remarkably Paul does not turn the Lord's word into a new law. Moreover, facing the possibility of a divorce that is obviously contrary to the advice from the Lord, Paul does not denounce the divorced person. He has other advice. Paul's comments at this juncture once more assume that in marriage both wives and husbands have responsibilities and can take initiatives.

7:12-16. Regarding "mixed" marriages. Having directed remarks to unmarried Christians and to Christians married to each other, Paul writes *to the rest*, that is, to those Christians who are married to *unbelieving* partners. Paul works from the assumption that divorce is contrary to the teaching of the Lord (7:10-11); yet, he recognizes that the involvement of an *unbelieving partner* in a marriage creates a different set of circumstances. Paul's advice to the Christian partners is that they remain in their marriages if their non-Christian spouses agree. Paul's reasoning supports or maintains Christian freedom, although the ideas of reconciliation and peace are the foundations of his thought. Peace, not the conflict of a divorce, is the characteristic of Christian life.

Verse 14 is enigmatic. Paul probably assumes that non-Christian spouses are involved in pagan religions and makes these statements to recognize that no pagan deity plays a part in the Christians' dealings with pagan spouses. Thus, his reference to the children of "mixed" marriages aims at illustrating the ultimate power of the Lord. Christians are not defiled by pagan spouses, rather the Christian's presence in the family and the Spirit's presence in the life of the believer actually sanctifies the relationship. In turn, v. 16 summarizes the reason Paul advises Christians to remain married to pagans. Critical editions of the Greek text suggest the two sentences are questions, not assertions as the NRSV translates. The basic sense of the sentences is clear whether the words are taken to declare or to inquire, and what Paul says may seem peculiar at a glance. One sees clearly from Paul's total writings that he does not think humans ever save themselves or one another, God does the saving through Christ; so these lines are best understood to say that God may work through a Christian spouse to save an unbelieving partner.

7:17-24. God's gifts and the Corinthians' calling. The reference *to the rest* in v. 12 probably indicates that having addressed the question of how men and women are to relate in terms of sex, Paul thinks he is done with that topic. Nevertheless, he sums up the matter and elaborates a bit in this next segment of the letter. Paul tells the Corinthians they are to live according to the gift the Lord gave them in the state in which they were called. Paul applies this idea to CIRCUMCISION and to SLAVERY. The concluding lines of this section reiterate the basic idea that the Corinthians are to remain before God in the state in which God called them. How is a modern reader to take this notion? Some observations may aid comprehension. One should notice that Paul offers an off-balance contrast in v. 22:

(A) a Christian slave is the Lord's free person *in the Lord*;

(B) a free person is the Lord's slave.

The idea of being *in the Lord* transcends simple social conventions. Moreover, Paul's thought here is completely relativized in relation to his thoroughgoing apocalyptic eschatology as is clear from 7:31b, *For the present form of this world is passing away*. For Paul, God saves regardless of worldly social status, and remaining in the social state in which one was called demonstrates that it is not something that humans do that effects salvation; indeed, worldly social change is not equivalent to salvation.

Finally, the calling of Christians by God creates real freedom. All who are called are freed, in spite of social circumstances, to obey God (v. 19). The saving work of God actually eliminates the boundaries of sacred and profane, for God's saving work knows no confines.

7:25-40. Issues and eschatology. These verses are a contorted series of statements about "virginity," the eschatological nature of the time, and the death of a spouse. An amazing variety of issues are treated in rapid succession. Verses 25-28 are difficult, in part, because of the uncertain (for us) identity of the VIRGINS. Verse 25 clearly states that Paul is offering his opinion, not a word from the Lord, but he suggests his opinion is informed and valuable. Paul's thinking is determined by his eschatological conviction that the worldly future is to be but a brief span of time. Therefore, Paul advises the virgins to stay as they are, as everyone else should; but Paul says if the virgins marry they do not sin.

Paul's eschatology becomes more explicit in vv. 29-31. All of human existence is relativized in light of the conviction that God's work is bringing this world to its end. The passage should be taken in relation to Paul's earlier teaching about freedom and the aim of Christian life to glorify God. Paul's point: The time left is short, so live it fully for God. In turn, vv. 32-35 are well intended (v. 35) but odd advice. Paul's attitude is decidedly ascetic. There are certainly other possibilities that simply do not occur to Paul. The apostle seems capable of understanding marriage only as a responsibility that will create anxiety. Paul writes out of his own Spirit-endowed gift of singleness with little understanding of the broad range of possible relationships in marriage. The idea that the love and mutual support of a marriage might actually foster more effective Christian living does not appear to cross Paul's eschatologically riveted thinking.

The enigma of the virgins comes around again in vv. 36-38, although the NRSV resolves the matter (rightly) by rendering the Greek *fiancée* rather than "virgin." The language of these lines reflects the male-dominant character of the first-century culture in which Paul wrote. Although the focus and the language are somewhat different from the earlier discussion in 7:8-9 and 7:25, Paul's thinking is consistent: if passions are strong, then marry; whoever marries does well, but whoever is able to remain single does better.

8:1-13. Eating meat sacrificed to idols. Paul takes up a theme here that, despite the seeming lack of coherence, continues through 11:1: Christian rights and responsibilities, especially regarding "knowledge" and "freedom" in relation to idol sacrifices. As the opening words show, Paul is again responding to an issue brought to his attention by the Corinthians. He probably quotes the Corinthians' own position as the NRSV recognizes with the quotation marks around *"all of us possess knowledge."* Paul's critique of this declaration follows as he contrasts "knowledge" and "love." Paul remarks that knowledge is of no value in itself. The appropriate criterion is not knowledge but love for God. To focus on knowledge demonstrates an inadequate understanding. What really matters is to be known by God; and the evidence of God's knowing a believer is the believer's love for God. God's will and work must be the first priority of a believer, not a self-inflated estimation of the value of what one knows.

In v. 6 Paul offers a confessional statement that seems creedal in character. This "creed" assumes a Christian perspective and focuses on creation, call, Christ, and redemption. From the discussion one sees that the Corinthians had turned the confession into a speculative thesis that led to an artificially sophisticated lifestyle that easily denied the reality of *idols*. Paul, by contrast, takes pagan gods and lords more seriously than do the Corinthians. Later, at 10:20, Paul relates such gods and lords to demons, so that he considers them to be dangerous entities.

Verse 7 explicitly refutes the Corinthians' claim concerning knowledge. Every believer does not share the conviction that idols are not real. Paul's concern is to correct the arrogant behavior of those denying idols toward "weak" believers who assume the idols are real. Those who deny the idols insist their knowledge frees them to eat meat that had been previously sacrificed to idols (as most meat for sale had been), despite the objections of other believers who believed in idols and were scandalized by the eating of idol meat. Paul teaches that freedom is not abstract, but concrete. Real freedom is being freed from the necessity to assert only, or primarily, one's own rights. Knowledge alone is dangerous. What ultimately matters is that believers will the well-being of others rather than simply insist on their own rights and privileges.

9:1-27. Illustrative observations on the "rights" of an apostle. This chapter may appear to be an intrusion into the discussion of idols and eating idol meat, but Paul simply takes himself and the matter of his rights as an apostle as an illustration of a proper demeanor for Christians. Paul declares his freedom in a rhetorical question.

Then, he explains the real meaning of freedom in his own life. Paul reminds the Corinthians that he could make claims as others do (vv. 4-5) or as soldiers, planters, and shepherds (v. 7). Moreover, he recognizes that God ordained that the apostles be able to derive their living from the work they do as ministers. To underscore this point Paul offers a midrashic exposition on Deut 25:4 in vv. 9-11. Yet, he continues by stating that he does not use the right of support by the churches, lest his taking pay for his ministry be misunderstood as bilking the congregation (v. 12). Paul elaborates the matter of his right to support by referring to the practice of supplying the needs of those in Temple service from the proceeds given to the Temple. Then, in v. 14 he cites a word from the Lord (cf. Luke 10:7) to the effect that *those who proclaim the gospel should get their living by the gospel.* Yet, Paul explains that he does not take his rightful support. Amazingly, Paul's reward is that he takes no reward! Paul preaches because he was commissioned to do so, but by not taking his due he gives up his own rights as an offering to God.

In vv. 19-23 Paul describes the style of his ministry and its motivations. He reiterates his freedom and declares that while he is free from all, nevertheless, he enslaves himself to all. Paul reports that he varies his personal behavior depending upon his audience. In relation to Jews who are *under the law* (v. 20) Paul takes on their patterns of living, although he himself is not under the law. In relation to those *outside the law* (v. 21) he lives as they do, but he is not free from God's law because he lives under "Christ's law." Paul says he varies his behavior in order to "win" both Jews and those outside the law. Paul strives to become all things to all people in all ways so that he may serve as God's agent in saving "some." Paul's remarks in v. 23 show that the power of the gospel presides over Paul; it is the senior partner in a partnership. Thus, the gospel is not relativized to worldly social conditions that are no more than contemporary social structures and sensibilities; rather, the apostle himself becomes relativized in order to preserve the integrity of the gospel.

Paul brings his discussion of apostolic rights to a conclusion in vv. 24-27. He takes up a set of athletic images as metaphors, explaining and advocating discipline. Paul's metaphors are inexact and should not be allegorized. First, Paul writes of *runners.* Basically he seeks to admonish the Corinthians to an active and disciplined life. Appropriate Christian living takes definite direction. With that point in mind Paul shifts to the image of boxing. He says he does not "fan the air" in the style of an untrained fighter; he works like an expert pugilist whose punches count because they hit their mark. Paul is focused through discipline.

Paul's final comments on boxing are almost shocking. He reveals that his opponent is himself. Surely this is a lesson for the Corinthians whose attitude leads to the kind of easy, self-indulgent living that merely presumes upon God's grace and does not relate in obedience to God's saving acts. Paul explains that he "blackens the eye of [his] body" (v. 27, author trans.) lest he be disqualified himself—a strong word of warning to the readers.

10:1-13. Relating the Exodus experience to Christian life. Having raised the frightening, serious matter of disqualification, Paul moves immediately to deliver a midrash on the EXODUS that is laced with scriptural allusions. Paul applies the Exodus story to the Corinthian situation as a further word of warning. Then, he specifies the heart of his concern by again taking up the matter of eating meat that had been offered to idols. Paul returns to the Corinthians' slogan about freedom and offers further rebuttal, clarification, and directions.

Verses 1-5 form the midrash. One finds here allusions to the book of Exodus, selected Psalms, the Wisdom of Solomon, and Numbers. Paul's style of biblical interpretation may strike modern readers as strange, but this manner of interpreting the biblical materials is neither unique nor was it unusual in Paul's day. Indeed, both PHILO and the RABBIs developed the idea of a peripatetic or divine rock. Paul may simply be "christianizing" a standard theme of Jewish wisdom teaching, or he may appropriate images and ideas from developed wisdom traditions in his own creative reflection. The idea of Christ's preexistence is inherent in Paul's comments, although preexistence per se is not the focus of the discussion.

The application of the Exodus imagery is made through typological analogy (see τυπικῶς in v. 11). The typological analysis and application lay the foundation for the stark warning that comes in v. 5, where *nevertheless* says a great deal. Indeed, in spite of the ancestors having been *baptized into Moses* (v. 2) and having participated in an archetypal LORD'S SUPPER, God was not pleased with most of them and they were overthrown in the wilderness. Thus, according to Paul, baptism and participation in the Lord's Supper are not unequivocal assurances against negative divine judgment. The sacraments are not magical charms that guarantee an absolute claim on salvation.

Verses 6-13 make further application of the midrash by adding and applying other Exodus materials to the exhortation. Primarily the story is brought to bear on the Corinthians in relation to the issue of idolatry, especially in relation to the theme of idol-meat. Verse 6 introduces the application in a general manner. Verse 7 applies the scriptural lesson directly to the issue of idolatry and in doing so quotes a portion of Exod 32:6 verbatim. Finally, vv. 8-10 form a trilogy of negative directions against immorality, testing the Lord, and grumbling. These verses also report the terrible results of such wrongful behavior—the death of *twenty-three thousand . . . in a . . . day* (v. 8, although in Num 25:9 one reads that "twenty-four thousand" died). Verse 11 explains the application, and one should notice two items. First, Paul's exegesis clearly reveals that he understands the scriptures to be typological as a result of the Christ-event. Second, Paul locates himself and the Corinthians at the juncture of the ages, as the NRSV recognizes with the correct translation, *they were written down to instruct us, on whom the ends of the ages have come.* This line is generally mistranslated and misunderstood as a reference to either a general summary of all previous times or epochs (*ends of the ages* [v. 11]) or a general summary of all previous nonepochal time ("end of the age"). But, these understandings fail to take seriously Paul's apocalyptic eschatological temporal dualism. From this perspective Paul understands that he and the Corinthians live at the point where "the present evil age" (Gal 1:4) and the "new creation" (2 Cor 5:17) are both *already* and *not yet* present. They live between the cross and the coming of Christ at a time when the ages are mingled. In this interim the old is already dying and the new is already being born, though the old has not yet passed away and the new has not yet fully arrived.

Verse 12 issues a sobering warning, probably because of Paul's convictions about the danger of the volatile times, that recognizes the continuing threat of opposition to God. More directly, v. 13 declares that the real crisis (temptation) besetting the community is indeed manageable and conquerable. Paul proclaims the theological basis of such management: God is faithful. God provides the antidote to the temptation. While there is no avoidance of the problem, mixed with the problem in this mingling of times is God's saving provision. Paul's confidence is in God's sustaining grace. Although one can imagine different ways in which Paul would name this divine provision—the Spirit, Christ, the power of God—the apostle does not name God's grace; rather, he declares God's faithfulness. Above all, Paul establishes here the necessity of the relationship of the Corinthians to God who saves.

10:14-22. Directions against idolatry. Paul elaborates and makes even more direct application of his warning to the Corinthians. He understands himself to be building on his preceding remarks and inferring conclusions in relation to them as is evident in his first word in this section, *Therefore*—or better, "On account of" (Διόπερ). Paul tells the Corinthians to *flee from the worship of idols*. Then, he states in eucharistic metaphors the unified nature of Christian life (vv. 15-16). By analogy to Israel Paul identifies the demonic forces associated with pagan religion and, in turn, with sacrificial food (vv. 17-20). One should note that Paul's reference is to the food, not to the act of eating. Then, Paul doubly reiterates the exclusive nature of Christian life in terms of the elements of the Lord's Supper, mentioning the cup before the bread. Finally, he instructs the Corinthians through two rhetorical questions. Paul informs them that their *eating*, an insistent practice of personal freedom, may and does provoke God. Thus, the apostle contrasts human and divine strength in such a way that he issues an indirect threat.

10:23–11:1. Further clarification of the nature of Christian freedom. Verses 23-24 repeat the Corinthians' slogan from 6:12, but this time there is no *for me* with the words *All things are lawful*. As in chap. 6 Paul states and qualifies this slogan twice. First, he repeats and qualifies exactly as in 6:12, *but not all things are beneficial*. Then, he repeats the slogan and qualifies it in relation to edification or "building up." This reasoning recalls 3:10-15, so one sees that, above all, Paul desires the unity of the church. Paul builds on these qualified statements by declaring a maxim, *Do not seek your own advantage, but that of the other*. In other words, he teaches them to live so that each may say, "Not my good but your good be done."

Verses 25-30 make practical application of this principle. In fact, one sees Paul pluck a principle out of the thin air of abstraction and put it down with the power of particularity in the actual affairs of the Corinthians. In so doing, the principle of Christian freedom is maintained; but, the matter of one's conscience is not raised as governing one's actions! Rather, the conscience of others is brought in relation with one's freedom so that freedom is interpreted as an established opportunity for putting others before one's self.

In 10:31–11:1 Paul sums up and concludes by again declaring the goal of Christian life to be the *glory of God* in all that believers do. Paul continues to make matters concrete by reference to his own attitude, aim, and style of ministry. He calls for the Corinthians to imitate him as he imitates Christ. Thus, he issues a call to Christlikeness.

Orderly Worship and Spiritual Gifts, 11:2–14:40

This third major section of the body of the letter contains reflections on a variety of topics that are particularly interesting for contemporary Christian practices. Here, Paul discusses the role of women in worship, the celebration of the Lord's Supper, charismatic gifts and practices, and the essential traits of Christian life and relationships.

11:2-16. Keeping church customs. The section opens with a commendation that may or may not be in response to a claim the Corinthians have made about their own preservation of tradition as Paul delivered it. Verse 3, however, follows by taking exception to a practice Paul views as outside the boundaries of normal church *custom* (cf. v. 16). Paul begins his argument by articulating a scheme of priority of authority. There are three distinct and related statements, but the scale here is not a simple stepladder or hierarchy:

Christid	>	the head	>	of every man
Christ	>	the head	>	of every man
the husband	>	the head	>	of his wife
God	>	the head	>	of Christ

One should notice, above all, that the scheme begins with the authority of Christ and ends with the authority of God. While the notion of the husband having authority over his wife offends progressive sensibilities, Paul's point here is to recognize the authority of Christ over humanity and the ultimate authority of God. The scheme is a Stoic-like system of "natural order" that values order over chaos. Verses 4-6 unpack one line of argumentation concerning this scale in relation to the worship activities of praying or prophesying, specifically focusing on the practice of women wearing head coverings.

There are immediate problems for interpretation: Which instances of *head* are literal and which are metaphorical? Are all uses of *head* literal, all metaphorical, or is there some mix? Clearly the first occurrence of *head* in both v. 4 and v. 5 are literal because of the issue of covering and not covering. But, what of the second use of *head* in each verse? Are they metaphors for Christ and husband respectively, or are they literal? (The third mention of *head* in v. 5 in the NRSV is a supplying of the word by the translators. In Greek the perfect passive participle ἐξυρημένη "having been shaved" is simply preceded by the definite article τῇ, probably meaning "the woman," not "her head"; so that the line reads "it is one and the same thing as her having been shaved.") From what follows in v. 7, the explication of a man's not covering his head in terms of his existing as the image and the glory of God and the woman' covering her head in terms of her being the glory of man, one sees that the dishonored "heads" of vv. 4-5 are metaphorical.

The strange sense of the argument begins to make sense when one sees that Paul understands *nature* (v. 14) to *give indication* of the God-ordained pattern of life. Nevertheless, there are several problems raised by these verses that are not easily resolved: (1) How can a woman, veiled or otherwise, pray or prophesy if she is to be silent in the church as 14:33-35 indicates? (2) Has not Paul confused nature and humanly determined fashion? Are male and female hairstyles given by nature or set in style? (3) How is one to understand the amount of energy Paul invests in this section, vv. 2-16? Does the show of creative effort indicate the severity of the problem? Or, is Paul simply biased? (4) What kind of attitude do these lines reflect—Greek, Jewish, or Christian? It is easier to raise difficult questions than to find gratifying answers. One needs to follow the remaining course of the argument.

Verses 7-12 continue the argument from the perspective of a set of biblical texts. Verse 7 restates the idea with which Paul is working, bringing in the language of Gen 1:26-27; yet, the idea clearly controls the exegesis. Then, vv. 8-9 extend the argument by taking recourse to the creation story of Gen 2:18-22.

Verse 10 is an enigma. The opening words, *For this reason*, can relate either to previous or to ensuing comments. The words probably refer to what went *before* (vv. 8-9 or vv. 2-9), since still another *because of* ends the line. Thus, because of the relationship of men and women, women ought to have *a symbol of authority* on their heads, and this wearing of a symbol is related to *the angels*.

What does Paul mean by *because of the angels*? The statement is obscure. Perhaps he is thinking of the fallen angels of Genesis 6 who took human women for wives; or, perhaps he means the angels who were thought to be protectors of the order of creation and who are present, according to early Christian thought, in the assembly of Christians at worship.

Verses 11-12 form a statement in peculiar juxtaposition to what Paul has said to this point. One should note the all-important phrase *in the Lord*. This location allows the balanced statement in v. 12 to be made. Paul understands the situation concerning men and women as he did the issues of circumcision and slavery in chap. 7. *In the Lord* one recognizes the eschatological abrogation of sexual distinctions, but as Christians await the Day of the Lord they are not to act as if the Day has already come. One remains in the state in which one was called as the only valid demonstration of freedom.

Verses 13-16 put the issue before the Corinthians for a last time and from another angle. Paul calls for the Corinthians to judge the matter of a woman's being

unveiled at prayer. The basis of the evaluation is the teaching of nature; Paul understands that nature indicates God's will and how one is to style one's self as a copy
of nature. Paul surely did not reflect on this weak example or argument, for what
he attributes to nature is merely human fashion, reflecting culture, not necessarily
God—unless Paul thinks somehow that culture derives from nature and, in turn, that
fashion ultimately goes back to God. Strikingly, in denouncing his opposition Paul
cannot cite revelation or the Lord; rather, he is reduced to custom for his standards
and authorization. The issues here may elude resolution, although one should not
fail to see that v. 16 recognizes the potential denial of Paul's argument.

In sum, at its root the alteration of custom often (although not always) stems
from individualism, that is, the claiming of personal rights in the name of the
Lord—a problem already identified by Paul. Christians, Paul tells the Corinthians,
are "not to confuse a direct desecularization that is carried on by ourselves with the
eschatological desecularization brought about by Christ, but to maintain the
imperceptibility of this unworldliness—by dint of Christians wearing their hair normally and clothing themselves in normal ways" (Conzelmann 1975, 191).

11:17-22. Problems in the assembly. Paul identifies and criticizes a problem or
problems arising when the Corinthians *come together*. Paul says their gathering is
not for the better but for the worse. The results of the congregational assembly are
negative. Paul recognizes divisions among the members of the church. Oddly, he
rationalizes this problem by explaining that factions are necessary in order that those
who are approved may be recognized. It is debatable whether he is being sarcastic
or whether he discerns God creating confusion in Corinth.

Verse 20 broaches the matter of the LORD'S SUPPER, declaring that at their
assemblies the Corinthians do not eat a meal that can be so named. Then, vv. 21-22
identify individualistic self-gratification—in the extreme—as the social reality that
Paul opposes. But, he puts a theological twist on his denunciation by showing that
self-interest undermines community. Thoughtlessness toward others causes humiliation and, as becomes clear in what follows, is antithetical to love. From Paul's
rhetorical questions in v. 22 one must ask whether the Corinthians are interpreting
divisiveness as a pluralism that deserves praise. If so, Paul's remarks indicate that
unity is essential and without it diversity is meaningless.

11:23-26. Recalling the origins of the Lord's Supper. These four verses
recapitulate the early Christian tradition concerning the institution of the Lord's Supper. Paul reiterates this tradition as the foundation of his ensuing teaching in vv. 27-
34. In light of the Corinthian situation he explicates matters related to the tradition
but does not explain or theologize the tradition directly.

These verses are enormously important for the church in belief and practice,
and must be studied along with parallels in Mark 14:22-24, Matt 26:26-28, and
Luke 22:17, 19-20 for full appreciation of the tradition. A full-scale comparative
analysis is not attempted here.

Verse 23 claims the Lord as the ultimate source of this tradition since the words go back to the Lord whom Paul understands to be raised and who is alive in the Spirit. Paul's language concerning *receiving* and *handing on* is technical vocabulary in both Greek schools and Jewish synagogue thought. This manner of speaking establishes both the authority and reliability of the teaching. Remarkably, nothing in the tradition necessitates the PASSOVER setting found in the Gospels, but mention of the betrayal shows the fixed nature of this tradition and points to its association with the larger PASSION NARRATIVE.

Verse 24 narrates the first act. Thanksgiving and breaking of bread are Jewish table customs that were performed by the head of a household or a host. The words *this is my body* refers to the bread alone. Brokenness is not in view here. The emphasis is on the phrase *that is for you*, words that recognize the vicarious nature of Jesus' death. Some interpreters contend this clause is inherently sacrificial in focus, but that is not necessary. The words translated *do this in remembrance of me* are ambiguous in Greek, though they clearly interpret the ritual. In Greek the phrase literally says "do this unto my memory." Does this mean (1) that as Christians do and remember what Jesus said that they perceive the power and presence of Christ, or (2) that as Christians do these things, God's memory of Christ or Christ's own memory of his disciples is jogged toward realization of the parousia. Both interpretations are suggested by scholars, although the first option finds the most support.

Verse 25 narrates the second similar act. The focus is the cup, not its contents. This observation helps one see that the interpretation attaches to the administration of the Supper, not the elements themselves. Moreover, the acts stand separately as well as together as sacramental communications. One should notice that the COVENANT is related to the cup. The blood defines or establishes this covenant. The type of covenant is not determined by the statements, though the relationship of the covenant to blood recalls, in the context of 1 Corinthians (see 5:7), the motif of the paschal lamb. The motive of remembrance anticipates repetition of the acts.

Verse 26 extends the repetition theme and brings together the bread and cup in the declaration, *you proclaim the Lord's death until he comes.* These words hold open God's future in relation to the Lord's death as they refer to the Lord's coming. This note places the whole observation of the Lord's Supper in the larger conceptual framework of apocalyptic eschatology and takes the Supper as prescribed foundational behavior for life between the cross and the coming.

11:27-34. Proper and improper attitudes at the Supper. These verses are concerned with one's attitude toward the Supper. They give advice for eliminating an improper disposition at the celebration. The final lines, vv. 33-34, are practical and elucidate the more abstract materials in vv. 27-32.

Verses 33-34 begin *So then*, and aim at correction or circumvention of the previously named problem(s). Note the advice:

(1) *When you come together to eat, wait for one another*—from 11:21 one
    knows that the Corinthians individually or in small groups are going ahead
    with their meals.
(2) Parenthetically, Paul separates satiation of hunger from the community meal
    or celebration—cf. 11:22.
(3) Paul's advice aims at preventing condemnation ensuing from the inappropri-
    ate gathering in which the Corinthians are already engaging—cf. 11:17-19.

Thus, 11:33-34 and 11:17-22 form a bracket or INCLUSIO around Paul's reflections and directions on the Lord's Supper in the material between 11:23-32. This
fact grants a perspective from which to view vv. 27-32. First, a pair of negative
observations: (1) Paul is not directly or indirectly concerned with the nature of the
sacramental elements; (2) the matter at hand is not one's personal piety or lack
thereof. A second, positive observation is that Paul's concern is for an appropriate
attitude that fosters appropriate behavior.

Verses 27-32 take up the issue of appropriate attitudes and behavior. Eating and
drinking in an unworthy way is eating and drinking with an attitude of self-centeredness, individualism, or arrogance. Even hyperpious individualism would fall
under the rubric *unworthy*. Unworthy participation—coming to the Supper without
regard for the result of Christ's reconciling work that draws the Christian
community into a new selfless relatedness—makes one *answerable for the body and
the blood of the Lord*. To deny the reconciling, unifying effects of Christ's death
casts one into the role of those who crucified Jesus. Thus, one must examine one's
self to insure the appropriate Christ-like attitude and, then, in a spirit of self-giving
and interrelatedness one eats and drinks. Otherwise, Paul says, one participates in
the Supper unto judgment, that is, one casts one's self outside the pale of redemptive reconciliation into the context of God's eschatological wrath.

Verse 29 mentions *discerning* the body. This statement should not be reduced
to an abstract level. Rather, to discern the body (notice the absence of blood) means
to comprehend and appropriate into one's own life the transforming significance of
Christ himself. *Body* metaphorically identifies the Christ-event with its power to
transform lives and create the new Christian community of reconciliation. Furthermore, v. 30 is Paul's explanation of illness and death in the Corinthian community.
He speaks from the perspective of his belief in Christ's real presence in the *remembrance* of the Supper. Surely his explanation is descriptive and dramatic, not a
declaration. Finally, v. 31 mentions judgment—not eschatological, but present judgment in this world as in v. 30. This explains the importance of the Corinthians'
heeding Paul' directions.

12:1-3. The nature of Christian enthusiasm. This section addresses a new topic,
namely, *spiritual gifts* or the gifts of the "spiritual ones." The language at the outset
of the discussion is ambiguous in Greek, but the basic sense of Paul's remarks
comes through however one decides to translate the Greek word πνευματι-
κοί—translated *spiritual gifts* in the NRSV. A note in the NRSV indicates the

possible translation "spiritual persons." One should notice that throughout the remainder of the section Paul continues the discussion by referring to spiritual gifts (χαρίσματα, an unambiguous designation); so the initial reference (to πνευμα- τικοί) is most likely to "spiritual persons."

Verse 1 shows that the Corinthians brought this topic to Paul's attention. Paul's stated wish may imply that the Corinthians do lack adequate information. Then, vv. 2-3 identify the problem as the practice of ecstasy. Ecstasy may be contrasted with enthusiasm to explicate Paul's point here. Ecstasy is the effort to "stand outside" oneself, to grasp or be grasp by a vital power that provides one with an extraordinary experience. Enthusiasm is the result of one's being indwelt by the power of God, so that one's quality of experience is transformed. At a glance it is hard or impossible to distinguish the frenzy of ecstasy from the empowering of enthusiasm, but according to Paul genuine enthusiasm affirms the lordship of Jesus whereas the practice of ecstasy generates behavior contrary or hostile to the affirmation of Jesus' lordship. The recognition of the lordship of Jesus is the criterion that forms the parameters of legitimate enthusiasm.

One should notice that Paul assumes the reality of extraordinary spiritual experiences. He battles a particular theological explanation given to the experiences, not the experiences per se. The situation seems to be that the Corinthians are taking spiritual gifts as the grounds for comparison that leads to ranking of gifts and boasting. The more flamboyant gifts according to the Corinthians, are to be cherished and more highly esteemed. Some people apparently become so elevated in their spirituality that they have no use for, indeed they even express disdain for, the all-too-human Jesus who suffered the disgrace of dying on the cross. Paul will have none of this kind of spiritual expression.

12:4-11. Unity and diversity of gifts. This section argues concerning the spiritual gifts that there is a unified purpose in a variety of expressions because of the common divine origin of one's gift. The gifts Paul discusses here are not natural, birthright propensities.

In vv. 4-6 there are three parallel statements based on an underlying triad of Spirit/Lord/God. In relation to each of these three "persons" Paul recognizes variety. There are varieties of gifts of grace and there is one Spirit; there are varieties of services and there is one Lord; there are varieties of activities and there is one God. Diversity in the human sphere exists, relates to, and is unified by unity in the sphere of the divine. By drawing these phrases together Paul creates the theological matrix for valid interpretation of the phenomenon of *spiritual gifts*. Ultimately all gifts extend from God and are given for the good of the church. These gifts are not rendered according to the disposition of those who receive them. They are given and established under the Lordship of Jesus the Lord.

Verses 8-10 catalogue gifts without offering an exhaustive inventory. The list seems, in light of the rest of the letter, particularly relevant to the situation in Corinth. In this list, *discernment of spirits*, that is, the capacity to judge rightly for which Paul calls throughout the letter, is itself recognized to be a charismatic reality (v. 10).

12:12-31a. The body of Christ. In three striking movements these verses introduce (vv. 12-13), develop (vv. 14-26), and apply (vv. 27-31) Paul's best-known ecclesiastical metaphor: *body of Christ*. Scholars debate the exact background from which Paul may have drawn inspiration for developing this memorable image for the church. His contemporaries, certain Stoic philosophers, spoke of the cosmos in its unity as a body, and Jewish wisdom thinking often reflected upon the idea of corporate personality among a whole people. While Paul's image is not unique, his thinking does not exactly match any background, and his use of the image of "body" is extraordinary. One should notice that this metaphor applies both to the local church and to the church universal (see Romans 12). Furthermore, philosophically, being a "body" is the very basis of human relation; and, in context, as Paul speaks of "body" he refers to the absolute antithesis of that over which the Corinthian pneumatics were in orbit, namely, "spirit."

The metaphor BODY OF CHRIST serves to explicate a powerful thesis, *So it is with Christ!* Christ means variety but essential unity. From the outset of this discussion it is clear that this metaphor is possible because of the unifying work of the Spirit. The emphasis on unity cuts sharply across all social boundaries. Then, as Paul develops the metaphor, he ponders the significance of "body" from alternating points of view. First, vv. 14-19 approaches the metaphor from the perspective of *differentiation* of body members. Paul elaborates this perspective and articulates the necessity of differences. He states that such differences are by divine design and volition and, then, concludes by summarizing the necessity of differences. Second, vv. 20-26 return to the perspective of *unity*. Again, Paul elaborates his thought and declares that unity reflects divine design. Paul declares that unity is necessary, relating his thought to the motif of mutual care in the church. Paul concludes this phase of the meditation by summarizing the value of relatedness in the church.

Verses 27-31a apply and explain the metaphor in specific relation to the Corinthians' situation. Paul delineates the godly order of spiritual gifts, probably placing speaking in TONGUES last in order to devaluate the desirability of this flamboyant gift. Paul pursues the theme of the necessity of differentiation or variety of gifts in rhetorical questions (vv. 29-30). Then, in v. 31a he states his desire for the Corinthians. Even though the gifts are granted by God, Paul advises, the Corinthians to aspire toward the "greater" gifts!

12:31b–14:1a. The superlative way of love. These verses are often referred to as an excursus on love, and there are good reasons for this description. From Paul's admonition to aspire for the greater gifts—literally, he says, "Earnestly seek the higher gifts of grace" (v. 31a)—Paul declares that he shows the Corinthians *a still more excellent way* (v. 31b). The transition from v. 31a to 31b is awkward, and the material that follows in 13:1–14:1a is remarkable. First, it intrudes. 1 Cor 12:31a flows well into 14:1b; and the theme of *love* in chap. 13 relates only indirectly to the particular situation being addressed to this point in the epistle. Second, the material on love seems to be a self-contained, quite polished unit. Third, there are comparable Greek and Hellenistic-Jewish parallels to this meditation on love found in such diverse materials as Tyrtaeus, Plato, Maximus of Tyre, and especially 3 Ezra 4:34-40. Fourth, the chapter seems unconcerned with Christ. This array of observations produces a variety of suggestions; but, in any case the material seems to be an originally independent piece (or, originally independent pieces) of developed tradition that Paul inserted into this context and applied to the Corinthian situation. Paul is likely to have worked minor adaptations on this material in order to fit it into this letter, and it is not impossible that the piece, although originally independent, was composed by Paul himself.

Verses 1-3 establish the necessity of love, for love alone confers worth to all other spiritual gifts. The mention of *tongues* has immediate relevance to the Corinthian situation, and the *gong* and *cymbal* are naturally associated with pagan religious ecstasy; so that Paul's words form a poetic critique of the Corinthians' behavior as one knows it from the previous chapters. Yet, in the next lines *prophetic powers* names a gift highly regarded by Paul. Thus, even manifesting a gift Paul values is useless without love, so one sees here no simple condemnation of those who have values different from the apostle and his cohorts. In turn, the reference to FAITH in v. 2 seems odd. In this line *faith* seems to be something akin to "miraculous power," a traditional definition, rather than Paul's own understanding of faith as "fruit of the Spirit" (Gal 5:22; 1 Cor 12:9).

A minor textual problem makes it uncertain whether Paul says that without love it is no gain to hand over one's body "in order to boast" (13:3) or "in order to be burned" (see NRSV mg.). Whichever reading is original, the sense of Paul's statement is that either the pride or the selflessness of sacrifice is worthless without the authenticating motivation of love. Paul's twin verdicts here are that without love *I am nothing* and *I gain nothing*. Whatever characterizes human lives and whatever achievements humans attain are ultimately judged by the presence or absence of love.

A change of style occurs in vv. 4-7. The content and style are those of Jewish parenesis, and the form is didactic (instruction) not hymnic (praise). The phrase "Love *is*" supplies the verb in English which is absent in Greek, but the translation accurately captures the descriptive intention of the lines. In brief, vv. 4-6 create a listing that is epitomized in v. 7. Love is presented as the essential Christian characteristic: Love is selflessness and is not self-centeredness. Love is patient and kind. It is not jealous, boastful, arrogant, rude, irritable, and resentful. The lines critique the Corinthian situation elegantly but abstractly. Then, with a shift from the nature of love to the activities of love, one finds that love does not insist on its own way or rejoice at wrong; rather, love rejoices in the right, bears all things, believes all things, hopes all things, and endures all things. In short, love defines and directs Christian life.

Once again the style shifts in 13:8–14:1a. Now instead of pithy wisdom sayings one encounters elaborated arguments. The preceding verses of this meditation on love took the position that charismatic gifts are worthless without love, but now love and the charismatic gifts are set over against each other with the end of establishing the enduring, eternal, eschatological nature of love. Verse 8 opens with a contrast between love and prophecy, tongues, and knowledge—declaring the enduring quality of love and indicating that prophecy, tongues, and knowledge will come to an end or will cease. One recalls 1 Cor 7:31 where Paul said *the present form of this world is passing away*; so that one infers that prophecy, tongues, and knowledge belong to this world, not to God's new creation. Thus, v. 9 can identify the basis for the cessation of knowledge and prophecy—they are imperfect.

Verse 10 declares the eschatological end of imperfection and promises survival of that which is perfect, so that one recalls 1 Cor 3:10-15. This point is dramatized through the metaphor of putting away childish things. Immaturity gives way to maturity. Moreover, the ensuing metaphor of seeing in a mirror *dimly* articulates a contrast between current existence and the promised eschatological vision of seeing *face to face*. In these metaphors Paul states the idea of knowledge seen in earlier chapters. Current knowledge is labeled *partial*, whereas eschatological knowledge is promised to be *full*. Here, Paul writes that all full eschatological knowledge, as well as current partial knowledge, is based on our being fully known by God, so that one learns again of God's genuine priority in salvation. As stated in chap. 1, what matters is not what humans comprehend but what God has done and will do.

Finally, 13:13–14:1a heightens and concludes the previous lines of thought. There is a slight contrast between these statements and what went before, for now one hears of the three highest gifts—faith, hope, and love. Faith was mentioned in 13:2, but it is not clear that the same sense of "faith" is intended here. Nevertheless, faith becomes the foundation for Christian life. In turn, hope emanates from faith (13:7); but as the lines continue one sees that the point here is to establish the superiority of love, as stated in 12:31b. Interpreters debate whether 13:13 means that (1) faith, hope, and love are and remain valid eternally or (2) faith, hope, and love are now valid, but only love will endure eternally. In either case, one should see the superior and eternal character of love. The supreme characteristic and motivation—now and forever—for Christian life is nothing other than love.

14:1b-40. Practicing the gifts and maintaining orderly worship. This chapter returns to the direct consideration of spiritual gifts that was left off after 12:31a. Paul's general concern is with orderly worship, but there are bends and turns to the argumentation that are hard to follow and highly debated.

At the outset (vv. 1b-5) Paul compares and contrasts only two of the gifts, *tongues* and *prophecy*. His discussion makes clear that so-called TONGUES are unintelligible assertions (glossolalia), not foreign languages. He declares his own strong preference for PROPHECY over tongues. In his consideration of these two gifts Paul informs the readers that those who speak in tongues do not address people but

God, and no human understands them because they utter the mysteries of the Spirit; whereas those who prophesy speak to humans for the edification, encouragement, and consolation of their hearers. Paul tells the Corinthians that tongues edify the one speaking and prophecy edifies the whole church. Paul states that he wants all to speak in tongues, but even more he desires that all prophesy. Paul's concern is not so much with the content of tongue-speech and prophecy as with the mode and orientation of these utterances. Paul declares the superior merit of an utterance that is oriented away from one's self to speech, even spiritual speech, that merely serves one's self.

In vv. 6-12 Paul shifts into a diatribe style of disputation, issuing a series of rhetorical questions in various forms that are followed by illustrative analogies and a concluding exhortation. Verse 6 begins with a false first person statement, declaring an irreality to make the point that giving one's self to the practice of glossolalia necessarily precludes one from engaging in sensible, understandable communication. Paul refers to the flute, harp, and trumpet and the muted playing of such instruments to illustrate the unintelligibility and inferiority of speaking in tongues (vv. 7-8). Tongues are no more useful than indistinct music, for one is as good as *speaking into the air* (v. 9).

Paul continues to illustrate his point with a similar analogy indicating the pointlessness of speaking in a foreign language to those who do not understand the language (vv. 10-11). Finally, v. 12 redirects the energies of the Corinthians. Paul calls for them to excel in edification as genuine manifestation of the Spirit. He reiterates his earlier point (see 12:31a) that the Corinthians are to seek the preeminent gifts, not merely the flashy ones. While the point is clear, Paul's phraseology is not, for his sentence could mean either "Seek spiritual gifts that edify the church in order to excel" or "Seek to excel in the spiritual gifts that edify the church." Given the thrust of the general argument against self-directed spiritual practices, the second option is preferable over the first.

Paul continues (vv. 13-19) by explaining his position. He offers an argument against a sheer enthusiasm that would be indistinguishable from ecstasy. In genuine enthusiasm one's mind stays engaged. A Christian caught up in the Spirit does not unplug the mind and feel a lot. Rather, the concern for others, both Christians and non-Christians—named here as "outsiders," or more literally, "the uninitiated"—orients the enthusiast and grounds enthusiasm in sensible reality. Paul reports his own practice of tongues and his clear preference for prophecy. He speaks in tongues and is thankful to God for it, but in church he prefers that which makes clear sense to others. One suspects that Paul must, therefore, have practiced glossolalia privately, though he does not impose such a restriction on the Corinthians' speaking in tongues. Nevertheless, the degree of Paul's preference of prophecy over tongues is clear from the numbers he articulates: five words with the mind are better than ten thousand words in a tongue—odds of two thousand to one. The reason for this preference is that in church prophecy benefits others whereas tongues edify only the self.

A further section of the reflection follows in vv. 20-25 with language and concerns reminiscent of 2:6 and 3:1. Paul calls the Corinthians away from childishness—perhaps meaning a fascination with things that dazzle—to maturity. He literally calls for them to "become perfect" or "complete ones," and in an aside he expresses his desire that they be naive in terms of evil. In v. 21 the apostle cites Isa 28:11-12 as a text on the topic of tongues. The citation is a very loose paraphrase that alters vocabulary, word order, subjects, and verbs alike, as is necessary since the original passage in Isaiah referred to foreign languages, not to glossolalia. Nevertheless, Paul finds in Isaiah a scriptural precedent for his position, and the citation leads into his next statements.

Verses 22-25 are striking. The individual sentences are clear, but the sequence of thought is nevertheless hard to follow. Verse 22 states a principle, claiming to do exegesis of the cited biblical passage ("then" or "thus"; Gk. = ὥστε). From the citation Paul concludes that tongues are a *sign* to unbelievers, not to believers; yet, prophecy speaks to believers, not to unbelievers. The way forward in this application should be clear, but it is not. From this lead, given that the whole church assembles and all speak in tongues and the uninitiated or unbelievers enter, one would expect that the uninitiated would be struck by the *sign* (and moved to believe?); but, instead Paul says that the uninitiated will say that the tongue-speaking believers are raving mad. Furthermore, given that all believers prophesy and the uninitiated enter, one expects that the uninitiated would not perceive; but, instead Paul says the uninitiated will be convicted by all, held accountable by all, and they will worship God and say that God is truly among the believers. Some sense for this strange sequence of statements comes clear if, for Paul, *sign* in v. 22a means "that which is obscure," not that which indicates something. Yet, v. 22b remains cryptic. In any case, Paul is marshaling still another argument for the preference of prophecy to tongues.

In vv. 26-33a Paul delineates regulations for orderly assembly and worship. He names certain elements of worship: HYMNs, lessons, revelations, tongues, and interpretations. All of these must produce edification. Thus, Paul restricts the practice of tongues to two or three tongue-speakers per assembly. Moreover, he allows tongues only if someone is present who can interpret the tongues, for otherwise glossolalia is unintelligible, useless, and so, not permissible. Similarly, two or three prophets may speak in a single assembly, and curiously some prophecy is recognized to be more urgent than other prophecy. Here, v. 32 is difficult. Paul means either "each prophet controls the spiritual gift he or she possesses" or "one who prophesies is subject to evaluation by other prophets who are present." Given (a) that 12:10 recognizes *discerning the spirits* as an identifiable gift of the Spirit and (b) the emphasis on mind and Spirit in 14:13-19 and (c) the expectation that tongue-speakers can limit their expression to instances when interpreters are present, the first option seems most likely. Most importantly, however, Paul articulates the central theological position that underlies what he has said and will say, namely, *for God is a God not of disorder but of peace.*

No verses cause more difficulty in the late twentieth century than vv. 33b-36. The problems are complex for exegetical and sociological reasons. Thus, some preliminary observations are in order.

First, the phrase *the churches of the saints* in v. 33b is peculiar, for in the context of the undisputed Pauline letters there is no such designation. Rather, churches are referred to as the church(es) of God or Christ and as the church(es) of a region or city. Thus, divine proprietorship and geographical setting are the normal ways of identifying Pauline congregations.

Second, the command to silence in vv. 34-35 seems to contradict the expectation in chap. 11 of women praying and prophesying, albeit they should be veiled.

Third, the verb *to speak* in vv. 34-35 is *not*, as some commentators suggest, equivalent with "to chatter" as an activity distinct from other sensible speech or prayer or prophecy. Through the rest of chap. 14 *to speak* refers to inspired speech (cf. vv. 2, 3, 4, 5, 6, 9, 11, 13, 18, 19, 21, 23, 27, 28, 29, 39).

Fourth, the issue in chap. 11 is somewhat different in focus. There the focus was on "men and women," but here, as v. 35 makes clear, the issue concerns "husbands and wives."

Fifth, at 11:6 one finds that it is "shameful" (αἰσχρόν; NRSV *disgraceful*) for a woman to be shorn, whereas in 14:35 it is *shameful* (αἰσχρόν) for a wife to speak in church.

Sixth, some few and inferior manuscripts transpose vv. 34-35 to a position after 14:40. While the manuscript evidence is not strong, it shows both (a) scribal grappling with the illogical intrusion of these verses in the discussion of worship from the perspective of tongues and prophecy (two specific forms of verbal expression) and (b) the scribal recognition of a naturally smoother transition from 14:33a to 14:36.

Seventh, a very similar position is articulated in 1 Tim 2:11-12.

What can be made of the evidence? Because of the unusual character of the language and the textual problems associated with these verses, a strong case can be mounted that this section of the letter is an interpolation, perhaps of an early scribe's marginal gloss. Or, the shift of focus from men and women to husbands and wives may provide a key, indicating that Paul is advocating the preservation of traditional Jewish patterns of family relations. This understanding is problematic since Paul is writing to Corinth, which is not a Semitic social context. Or, the speaking of the wives to which these verses refer may be simply a specific instance of enthusiasm that amounts to no more than the importing of pagan ecstasy into the context of Christian worship, so that Paul's advice applies only to a single situation and is not meant to be followed elsewhere. Still other solutions, none entirely gratifying, are offered by various interpreters. The lack of specific information about the situation(s) Paul faced in Corinth may make it impossible for later readers of the letter to understand these lines—even if they do come from Paul. Of late, however, the increasing tendency among both conservative and radical scholars is to regard the verses as an interpolation into Paul's original text.

In any case, the fact that the argument in v. 33b and v. 36 is based purely on custom, not on revelation or a word of the Lord, gives the statements a restricted force. Moreover, it is astounding that these verses (coupled with 1 Timothy 2) became the church's norm when one finds in 11:11-12, Gal 3:28, and in the frequent mention of prominent Christian women ministers in Paul's letters both declarations and assumptions about women taking active roles of leadership in the life of the church.

Finally, in vv. 37-40 Paul boldly confronts the Corinthians. He states a criterion that puts the burden of proof on anyone wishing to disagree. Agreement, by contrast, would verify one as a prophet or a spiritual one. It is not clear how Paul relates his teaching to a *command of the Lord*, although the point of discussion is concerned with the issue of prophecy, not with the immediately preceding matter of wives speaking in church (see v. 39). The passive form *is not to be recognized* in v. 38 suggests God's involvement in the life of the church. Ultimately tongues are permissible but prophecy is preferable and all is to be decent and orderly. Such are God's ways, and such is God's will.

The Truth of the Resurrection, 15:1-58

The letter moves toward its conclusion with the long, crucial discussion of the resurrection in chap. 15. In general this section is a long defense of the truth of the resurrection and its intrinsic importance for all of Christian belief and life.

15:1-11. Back to the basics. Paul takes the Corinthians back to the basics, to the very foundation of their faith. In vv. 1-2 he identifies what follows in vv. 3-11 as *the good news that I proclaimed to you*, and he qualifies this gospel with the phrases *which you in turn received, in which also you stand*/have stood, and *through which also you are being saved*. Then, he recognizes the troubling possibility that the Corinthians may have believed *in vain*. It is a moot point whether Paul refers to a reality or an irreality when he says the Corinthians may have believed *in vain*.

Verses 3-8 communicate the foundational content of the teaching of Paul in Corinth. Interpreters generally recognize that in these verses there are one or two early Christian confessional formulae to which Paul adds his own commentary. When the apostle says he delivered this tradition to the Corinthians *as of first importance* (ἐν πρώτοις), he may mean either that he delivered this teaching logically "above all" or temporally "in the first instance." The lines, in either case, state Paul's starting point.

Paul recalls the substance of his primary teaching in a complex that finds its structure in a series of "that" (ὅτι) clauses: *that Christ died . . . that he was buried . . . that he was raised . . . that he appeared*. These phrases form the backbone of the confessional material in vv. 3-5, and there is additional information both embedded in this basic framework and attached to it in vv. 6-8. Thus, some interpreters suggest perhaps two "competitive" confessions are amalgamated and adapted—although no polemical note occurs in the lines and the phrase *that he appeared* is merely extended through the ensuing series of *he appeared . . . then he appeared* statements in vv. 6-8.

Of interest and importance is the material that is embedded in vv. 3-5. First, in v. 3 one learns of Christ's vicarious, sacrificial, atoning death (*for our sins*) that occurred as part of God's will and work (*in accordance with the scriptures*). In v. 4 one learns of the timing of Jesus' resurrection (*on the third day*), which also occurred as part of God's will and work (*in accordance with the scriptures*); and in v. 5 one learns of the initial appearance to *Cephas*, a partial explanation of the prominence of PETER in the life of the early church. One also learns of the subsequent appearance to *the twelve*, an odd note since for a time after the demise of Judas Iscariot there were only eleven disciples in the inner group. Nevertheless, one sees the early presence and importance of *the twelve*. Thus, one finds here evidence of the early interpretation of Jesus' death and resurrection and an indication of the early church's recognition of authorizing appearances that actually identified and formed the structures of the church.

The additional information in vv. 6-8 reports the appearance to *five hundred [believers] at one time* and declares that most of them were *still alive* at the time Paul wrote. These lines both document the reality of the appearances by taking them out of the realm of private hallucination and register the point that even those who saw the risen Lord die. Moreover, the mention of JAMES (the brother of the Lord) recognizes and perhaps explains his prominence in the early church; indeed, the remark may explain his being a believer since he was not a disciple of Jesus. Commentators remark, "James' new status as a believer offers an indirect proof that there was nothing he could remember from his acquaintance with Jesus in the family that would make such belief impossible" (Orr and Walther 1976, 322). But, the facts of James' coming to leadership in the early church cut two ways: That *James* did not believe before and without this appearance is a direct proof that there was nothing he knew from the family or from his acquaintance with Jesus that compelled him to believe in Jesus!

The mention in v. 7 of the appearance to *all the apostles* seems to name a central criterion, perhaps *the* criterion, for apostleship from Paul's perspective. Then, v. 8 tells of the final appearance of the risen Lord, this one to Paul. This appearance occurred after the appearances to the others, but at the time of Paul's writing to Corinth, this last appearance had taken place about twenty years earlier. Paul's language is that of violent metaphor. He literally says he was born as of an abortion. Thus, he aims at communicating the abnormal manner in which he became an apostle.

In turn, vv. 9-11 explicate Paul's point so that there is no need to speculate about the sense of his metaphorical language. Paul tells of his behavior that should have disqualified him as an apostle. Then, he grounds the reality of his calling in the reality of God's transforming grace. The degree of the power of God's grace is clear in that Paul was not merely redirected, so that his own zeal took new directions; rather, God's grace grasped his life and made it into something new and different. Throughout this section, Christ's death, burial, resurrection, and appearances are taken in their full soteriological force; they are not reported as isolated propositions.

15:12-19. Controversy in Corinth. These verses move from the foundational issues to a controversy in the Corinthian church, and the verses declare in a tough-minded logic the invalidity of the Corinthians' position. The problem is that some of the Corinthians said *there is no resurrection of the dead*. Perhaps they meant (1) there is no resurrection at all, or (2) they advocated "immortality" rather than "resurrection," or (3) they denied a future resurrection and claimed a fully realized this-worldly resurrection (as in 2 Thess 2:1-2 and 2 Tim 2:17-18). Option two is not likely given the full discussion by Paul. Option one makes the plainest sense of the words; but given the Corinthians' penchant for enthusiasm, sacramentalism, and the futuristic christocentric argument that follows in this chapter, option three may be preferable.

This whole section resists viewing Christ's resurrection in isolation as a mythic theme or as an eternal timeless truth. Paul's argument exposes the errors of the Corinthians' denial of a future resurrection of the dead. Paul argues a tight logical loop: *Christ is raised* > the gospel is preached > the Corinthians have faith > the dead in Christ are raised > *Christ is raised*. To falsify one element of this loop is to invalidate the whole, and to invalidate the loop exposes the testimony of the apostles as false testimony about God. If, moreover, the testimony about God's gracious saving work is false, then, the dead are lost and Christians have no hope, but are to be pitied as deluded.

15:20-28. Christ, the resurrection, and the end. These verses form a remarkably rich section of Paul's reflections and teachings about resurrection (see RESUR-RECTION IN THE NT). One encounters quotations of and allusions to several passages from the LXX, and Paul employs other traditional materials in formulating his argument. Despite the seemingly straightforward nature of the lines, they are subtle. In vv. 20-22 Christ is presented as the one through whom there is a resurrection of the dead, but one should notice that *all will be made alive in Christ* (emphasis added). Resurrection is reality in Christ, but the resurrection of others—dead or living—is cast as a future phenomenon. Moreover, commentators debate who the *all* of v. 22 are—the "all" who die in Adam certainly refers to all humanity; but does *all* [who] *will be made alive in Christ* indicate all humans or merely all believers? The matter cannot be settled simply from the words in these verses or even from examining these lines in the context of the entirety of 1 Corinthians. Paul's remarks in 1 Thess 4:13-18, 5:1-11, Phil 2:5-11, and Rom 9–11 are critical parallels for interpretation.

Verses 23-28 delineate the events of the end, though Paul is probably not concerned here with a strict chronological ordering. Rather, all Paul's teaching follows from Christ's having been raised by God. In rapid succession these lines tell of the PAROUSIA (Christ's so-called second coming), the destruction of the forces set in opposition to Christ, Christ's delivery of the kingdom to God, Christ's reign that is now underway, and death as the last enemy of Christ. The implication of Paul's scenario is that Christians necessarily face death as an inevitable foe until Christ's achieves the end. Though Christ reigns and defeats his foes, including death, one should not miss the thoroughly theological cast of Paul's teaching. As v. 27 makes clear, God and God's power are active in Christ's accomplishing that good of which Paul tells and even predicts. Finally, v. 28 clarifies the ultimate purposes of God's power at work in Christ: *so that God may be all in all!*

15:29-34. Arguments against misunderstanding. Paul offers another set of arguments against the Corinthians' denial of resurrection. He makes statements and asks questions in a loose sequence, with all that he says aimed to refute and reverse the Corinthians' position. In form and thrust the argument is similar to vv. 12-19.

Through rhetorical questions Paul attempts to bring the thinking of the Corinthians into proper line. First, in v. 29 he uses two questions about a practice of the Corinthians to expose the inconsistency between their activities and the denial of the resurrection. Exactly what Paul means by referring to people *who receive baptism on behalf of the dead* is not clear. Dozens of theories have been proposed, and none is fully satisfactory. Whatever Paul means we should (1) note that he does not criticize or deny the practice but uses it to score his point: The dead will rise; and (2) resist any interpretation that bases its understanding on either the idea of necrobaptism or a doctrine of baptismal regeneration, for elsewhere Paul demonstrates no such thinking (compare 1 Cor 1 and Rom 6).

Verses 30-31 pose another question: Why would Paul jeopardize himself for a hopeless lie? He would not, but he does risk his very life for the sake of calling the Corinthians and others to believe the gospel truth of Jesus Christ's death and resurrection. Thus, the resurrection is no lie. In turn, v. 32 uses another question to illustrate the serious degree of Paul's perils in ministry. One cannot know whether Paul's reference to fighting with beasts is literally true or hyperbolically metaphorical, although the difficult phrase *with merely human hopes* (κατὰ ἄνθρωπον) may signal the metaphorical nature of the remark. Nevertheless, even if he speaks in picture language Paul means to identify the seriousness of the threat he faced. Paul cites Isa 22:13b to establish the necessity of the truth that the dead are raised. The apostle's remarks have been labeled "opportunistic," but when read in their specific context the statements are in no way unscrupulous.

Paul quotes a well-known Greek proverb from the poet Menander in v. 33 to make the point that association with those in Corinth who deny the resurrection presents a danger to those forming such affiliations. This proverb leads into a blunt upbraiding in v. 34. The call to sobriety is plain enough, and such language was standard rhetoric for urgent eschatological exhortations in early Christianity; literally Paul says, "Sober up righteously and by all means don't sin!" He avers that some have an active lack of knowledge about God (ἀγνωσία, usually translated "no knowledge"). There is a difference between ignorance that actively disregards the truth and naivete that is simply as yet uninformed.

15:35-49. Pondering the reality of resurrection. Paul offers another complicated segment of his argument that quotes the LXX; alludes to stories from Genesis; and develops analogies related to seed, fleshes, body and glory, and Adam. The lines open in the style of a diatribe with a dialogical argument. Verse 35 states the question from Paul's supposed opponent, and v. 36 issues the first, scoffing reply that leads into an analogy on seed. Paul's point becomes clear in v. 38: God is sovereign and supreme in relation to all creation.

This argument in v. 38b sets up the analogies following in vv. 39-41, which themselves lead to the summary application of all the analogies in vv. 42-44. Paul's point is that the resurrection or "spiritual" body is a kind of its own, unique as are other bodies; but the spiritual body is like all other bodies in that it is given by God (v. 38a).

The series of arguments concludes with a discussion using Adam typology (vv. 45-49). Paul uses this new style of reasoning and this fresh illustration to underscore three items: (1) The spiritual body will be distinctive; (2) God gives the spiritual body; and (3) the resurrected *will* have/be/get this body in the future as they are transformed by God from being like Adam to being like the risen Christ.

15:50-58. Concluding comments. Verse 50 introduces a new idea or line into the reflection. Naturally, from Paul's statement that *flesh and blood cannot inherit the kingdom of God*, one would ask, "Then how?" Paul assumes that unstated question and uses the following lines to answer the query.

The anticipated transformation of *flesh and blood* into the God-given spiritual body is *a mystery*. This mystery is not known by reason but, if at all, by God's revelation of this truth. Thus, Paul scores the point that the transformation of earthly existence into spiritual reality is purely God's work. Paul writes in traditional terms and language of divine transformation, using mysterious images designed to inspire awe and confidence. He continues by extending his reasoning in a didactic fashion. Verse 53 gives a prophecy that *will* be fulfilled. Paul offers a prooftext for his point from Isa 25:8, and to amplify his position Paul adds the words *in victory* to Isaiah's *death has been swallowed up*. The victory is God's, through Christ, and this divine victory has implications for Christian hope and life (v. 54). Paul continues in v. 55 with a quotation from Hos 13:14, and again he adapts it to suit the context. Both quotations from the LXX relate to the statement made earlier in 15:26.

Verse 56 is Paul's own exegesis of the quotations from the prophets, as is clear from the mention of "law" at the end of the line. Paul continues with a doxological declaration of the meaning of all that he has written (v. 57). Then, v. 58 builds a final admonition (*Therefore*) on the tradition. This statement is not a mere work ethic, but an assurance of the Lord's preserving of vital Christian efforts (cf. 3:10-15). Thus, Paul argues for the reality of resurrection, basing his argument on God's work in Christ and calling for the Corinthians to embrace his teaching as the basis for their future hope and current living.

Parenesis, 16:1-18

Chapter 16 concludes the letter, offering a parting report about the apostle's personal appointment book and expressing his ultimate regard for the church in Corinth.

Future plans, 16:1-12

16:1-4. The collection. Paul may or may not be responding to an inquiry at this point, but the words *Now concerning* identify a topic that was likely brought to Paul's attention by the letter or the delegates from Corinth. Paul moves to discuss the collection he was assembling for the poor saints in Jerusalem. One sees that giving in the church had not yet been systematized. There was no standard timetable and there was no formula for how much one should give. Tithing apparently was not yet an idea in the church. Paul does, however, say that he did not wish to do fund-raising when he arrived in Corinth. Moreover, he wanted the giving to be done naturally and willingly, so that generosity was more charismatic than duty-bound. Similarly, Paul's plans for delivering the collection were open to development or to the guidance of the Spirit.

16:5-9. Paul's travel plans. Paul's travel plans seem cryptic to twentieth-century readers, but they are related to the seasonal conditions of travel in the first-century Mediterranean world. Paul intended to spend the winter, the season when travel was impossible, in Corinth; then, when spring came and travel was possible he could go either East or West as the Spirit directed. Paul refers to his stay in Ephesus, indicating success and opposition; yet, he sees that the end of that stay is at hand. In speaking of his work in Ephesus, Paul says, *a wide door for effective work has opened to me.* The form of the statement shows that Paul understood both opportunities and successes in ministry to be the results of God's own involvement in his life and work.

16:10-12. Mentioning fellow workers. Paul refers to Timothy and Apollos as he moves toward the end of his letter. Timothy was apparently working on or was about to work on some commission, probably from Paul, and apparently the Corinthians requested Apollos to come to them. But, Paul says this development (literally) "was not the will." Whose will, Apollos's or God's? The sentence is ambiguous. In any case, Paul and Apollos could and did discuss the matter, plainly disagreed with each other, but continued to relate without friction.

Principles for Life, 16:13-14

These two verses are a bit of stock parenesis. The tone is traditional and eschatological. The Corinthians are admonished to *watch*. They are told to stand courageously "in their faith"—the foundation of their existence—and they are to do everything *in love*—the chief criterion for all Christian living (see chap. 13).

Saluting Special Persons, 16:15-18

Paul passes out praise for the prominent Christian workers in Corinth. The *household of Stephanas* (see STEPHANAS) especially shows spiritual gifts and should be rightfully acknowledged, not because of status, but because of the presence and the power of the Lord at work in their lives. Moreover, the Corinthians who visited Paul in Ephesus (*Stephanas and Fortunatus and Achaicus*) are praised for representing the Corinthians and bringing Paul encouragement on the mission field. Paul declares that these persons who have served faithfully are worthy of recognition.

Closing, 16:19-24

Paul passes greetings in vv. 19-24. He mentions t*he churches of Asia*, conceiving the distinct assemblies in a region (see ASIA) as a network of congregations. *Aquila and Prisca* (see PRISCILLA AND AQUILA) send greetings through Paul to the Corinthians. Paul offers a generally greeting, and, then, he mentions an enigmatic form of greeting, the *holy kiss*. Though many have guessed what this *holy kiss* was, no one really knows.

The last lines are Paul's autograph. A scribe had written for Paul to this point, but now Paul takes pen in hand and gives the letter a truly personal touch. As he writes he couples a curse (ἀνάθεμα) on those who oppose the Lord with an eschatological cry for the Lord to come (μαράνα θά), a cry that shows the proper attitude toward the Lord. Although the anathema is in good Greek and the eschatological call is Aramaic transliterated into Greek, the words form a sound pair that contrast spiritual discord and spiritual concord. The last line of the letter is remarkable, for Paul ends with an unusual passing of his love to all the Corinthians in Christ Jesus.

Works Cited

Conzelmann, Hans. 1975. *1 Corinthians*. Herm.
Orr, William F., and James Arthur Walther. 1976. *1 Corinthians*. AncB.

Second Corinthians

W. Hulitt Gloer [MCB 1191-1206]

Introduction

While no Pauline letter demands more from its readers, none rewards its readers more fully than 2 Corinthians. Forged in the crucible of controversy, it has been called the "paradise and the despair of the commentator" (Martin 1986, x). Writing with an unmistakable intensity and urgency, Paul sets before his readers an unusually vivid picture of himself in this most personal of all his letters. At the same time he sets before us a most powerful portrayal of the nature of the gospel and the lifestyle of all who would be its ministers. In 2 Corinthians we discover the essence of what Paul understood the gospel and the nature of ministry to be.

First-Century Corinth

First-century CORINTH was a teeming urban center of relatively recent vintage. Once the chief city of the Achaian League, it had been destroyed by the Romans in 146 B.C.E. Recognizing its strategic military and commercial significance, Julius Caesar refounded the city in 44 B.C.E. and populated it with Roman freedmen. Beginning in 27 B.C.E. it functioned as the capital of the Roman province of ACHAIA. Archeological and literary evidence suggests that the city grew rapidly during the first century and was home to tens of thousands by the time of Paul's arrival.

Located on a narrow isthmus connecting the Peloponnesus with the mainland of Greece and separating the Gulf of Corinth and the Saronic Gulf, Corinth was situated at the crossroads of trade and travel. It controlled all trade and travel between the Peloponnesus and the mainland, and with its two harbors, one leading to Asia (Cenchreae) and one leading to Italy (Lechaeum), it controlled the safest and most direct trade route between Italy and ASIA.

As a result of its location, the city played host to tradespeople from all over the world and grew rich from taxes levied on the movement of goods it supervised and controlled. Its coffers were further lined as a result of banking, the production of bronze, an active terra-cotta industry, and the production of pigments, lamps, and small bone implements. In addition to all this, every two years Corinth played host to the Isthmian games, which brought to it people from all over the Mediterranean world.

Corinth was a microcosm of first-century religious life. Pagan cults of every stripe were represented: Apollo, Athena, Poseidon, Hera, Heracles, Jupiter Capitolinus, Asklepius, Isis, and Serapis. The city was especially well known as a center for the worship of Aphrodite whose temple stood high above the city atop the Acrocorinth, and throughout the Roman world the mention of Corinth elicited images of sexual license and excess. Philosophers of all persuasions plied its streets, and the presence of a Jewish colony is well attested. Paul's proclamation of the gospel added yet another ingredient to this diverse religious mix.

The Corinthian Church

PAUL founded the Corinthian church during his initial eighteen-month visit to the city during his second missionary journey (Acts 18:1-18). The fact that this visit coincides in part with the term of the Roman governor GALLIO (who ruled July 51–June 52 C.E.) suggests that Paul probably first arrived in Corinth early in 50 C.E.. During his stay he preached Christ crucified (1 Cor 2:1-2), and his preaching was accompanied by "a demonstration of the Spirit and of power" (1 Cor 2:4; cf. 2 Cor 12:12). While he began his ministry in the SYNAGOGUE, opposition from the Jews eventually compelled Paul to move next door to the home of Titius Justus. An effort on the part of the Jews to bring charges against Paul for preaching an unlawful religion was rejected by Gallio, after which Paul stayed in Corinth for "many days" continuing his ministry.

While the church was born as a result of Paul's preaching in the local synagogue, it is likely that its membership was made up of both Jews and gentiles (1 Cor 1:22-24). Sociologically the membership seems to have been reflective of a cross section of the urban society from which it was drawn. Some of its members represent positions of high social standing: Crispus (Acts 18:8; 1 Cor 1:14) was a synagogue ruler who had a house; SOSTHENES (Acts 18:17; 1 Cor 1:1) was a synagogue ruler; Erastus (Rom 16:23) was the city treasurer; GAIUS (Rom 16:23; 1 Cor 1:14) had a house large enough to accommodate the whole church. Many, perhaps most of its members, however, did not enjoy such a position in their society and seem to have been drawn from the lower classes (1 Cor 1:26-29).

Paul's Continuing Ministry to the Corinthians

While the NT contains two Corinthian letters, a careful reading of the CORINTHI-AN CORRESPONDENCE suggests that Paul may have written as many as five letters to the church in Corinth. The following scenario, based on the Corinthian correspondence and the Acts narrative, details Paul's continuing ministry to the church after his initial visit and the place of the letters in that ministry.

Leaving Corinth after the founding of the church and an eighteen-month ministry there, Paul returned to JERUSALEM by way of EPHESUS and then proceeded to ANTIOCH. After a brief stay in Antioch he returned to Ephesus for an extended ministry of two and one-half years from autumn of 52 to spring of 55 (Acts 18:18ff.).

While in Ephesus he wrote his first letter to the Corinthians urging them not to associate with Christians who were immoral, greedy, idolaters, slanderers, drunkards, or swindlers. This letter, which we will call *Corinthians A*, is the "previous" letter mentioned in 1 Cor 5:9.

Subsequently, Paul learned from visitors from Corinth of factiousness in the church (1 Cor 1:11), and received a letter from the Corinthians asking for advice and counsel regarding a number of issues (1 Cor 7:1ff.). He responded to the oral report and the letter by writing *Corinthians B* (our 1 Corinthians, 54 C.E.). Paul sent TIMOTHY on a special mission to Corinth (1 Cor 4:17; 16:10), and Timothy returned with news of a crisis fomented by a ringleader who had launched a personal attack on Paul (2 Cor 2:5-11; 7:8-13). Paul made a *painful visit* to Corinth to deal with the crisis (2 Cor 2:1). He was humiliated and returned to Ephesus (spring 55) where he wrote a "tearful" or "severe" letter (*Corinthians C*) calling on the Corinthians to take action against the one who had offended him thereby demonstrating their influence in the matter and their affection for him (2 Cor 2:3-4; 7:8, 12). He sent this letter (which is either lost or partially preserved in 2 Cor 10–13) with TITUS (summer 55).

Anxious to learn of the Corinthian's response to his "severe letter," Paul left Ephesus hoping to meet the returning Titus in Troas. Though he found an "open door" for ministry there, when Titus did not appear, anxiety prompted Paul to leave for MACEDONIA in hopes of intercepting Titus there (2 Cor 2:12-13).

Upon meeting Titus in Macedonia and learning that the crisis was over and the rebellion quelled (2 Cor 7:6-16), Paul wrote *Corinthians D* (our 2 Corinthians) either in part (chaps. 1–9) or, less likely, in its entirety (in which case chaps. 10–13 are aimed at clearing up any remaining pockets of resistance) and sent it from Macedonia with Titus and two other brothers (2 Cor 8:16–9:5; fall 55).

Sometime later Paul learned of a renewed crisis in Corinth prompted by the arrival of "false apostles" who challenged his authority and introduced a rival teaching (2 Cor 10:10; 11:27; 12:6-7). He then wrote *Corinthians E* (2 Cor 10–13) to answer the accusations of the *false apostles* (2 Cor 11:13), dispel suspicions, and warn the Corinthians of a planned third visit when he would demonstrate his authority in no uncertain terms (2 Cor 12:14; 13:1-4, 10; 56 C.E.). This third visit is probably reflected in Acts 20:2-3.

Paul's Opponents in 2 Corinthians

Paul's polemic in 2 Corinthians is directed at a group he refers to as *super-apostles* (11:5; 12:11), *false apostles, deceitful workers* (11:13), ministers of Satan in disguise (11:14-15), *fools* (11:19), and *peddlers* of the word (2:17) who preach a *different gospel* about *another Jesus* that results in a *different spirit* (11:4). While he gives no systematic description of their teaching and practice, careful reading suggests they are outsiders (11:4) who have invaded Paul's mission field attempting to take credit for what he has done (10:13-18). Arriving with *letters of recommenda-*

tion (3:1), they claim to have a special relationship with Christ (10:7), a superior apostolate (11:5; 12:11), superior knowledge (11:6), and superior rhetorical abilities (11:6; 10:10). Flaunting their Hebrew pedigree (11:22), they refer to themselves as *ministers of righteousness* (11:15) and *of Christ* (11:23) who carry out their mission on the same basis as Paul (11:12). They place great significance in *visions and revelations* (12:1), and emphasize the importance of *signs and wonders* as the true signs of apostleship (12:11-13; 5:12).

These *super-apostles* criticize Paul, charging that he acts in a "worldly manner" (10:2), that Christ does not speak through him (12:3, 19), that he does not perform the SIGNS AND WONDERS that are the true signs of an apostle (12:12), that he lacks a commanding presence (10:9-10), is unimpressive as a speaker (10:10; 11:6), and has an inferior knowledge (11:6). Furthermore, they suggest that Paul is bold when absent but that this boldness disappears when they are face to face (10:1), that his unwillingness to receive support from the Corinthians indicates a lack of love for them (11:7-11), and that he has been duplicitous with regard to his travel plans (1:17ff.) and the Jerusalem collection (12:14-18).

Efforts to identify these opponents have focused in three basic directions. While some have identified them as Judaizers, the absence of the kind of polemic found in Galatians makes such an identification questionable. Others have identified them as Gnostics and while they exhibit some traits characteristic of later GNOSTICISM, these traits are also common to Hellenistic thought in general, including Hellenistic JUDAISM. It is probably best to see them as Jewish-Christian propagandists who have been influenced by the HELLENISTIC WORLD and have incorporated into their own understanding of apostleship certain Hellenistic ideas such as a stress on rhetorical skills and a fascination with signs and wonders, visions and revelations.

In essence, there are two fundamental differences between Paul and his opponents in Corinth. The first relates to the nature of the GOSPEL itself. From Paul's perspective, his opponents preach *a different gospel* presenting a different Jesus by which *a different spirit* is received (11:4). Thus, the very nature of the gospel is at stake in the controversy reflected here.

The second difference relates to the nature of apostleship and the criteria by which it is evaluated. Paul's opponents present a triumphalist perspective in which the apostle is authenticated by his or her impressive bearing, commanding presence, eloquent speech, the performance of signs and wonders, the reception of visions and revelations, and displays of apostolic power. In such a view there is no place for weakness and suffering.

Paul, on the other hand, presents a perspective in which it is precisely in our weakness and suffering that the power of God is made manifest for all to see, in which the true apostolic ministry is recognized by its fruits (3:2-3), and in which one shares in Christ's sufferings (4:8-12; 11:23-28). Those who preach the gospel of Christ crucified as Lord will exemplify in their ministry both the weakness in which Christ was crucified and the power exercised by Christ as risen Lord (4:7-12; 12:9-10; 13:3-4).

Thus, while in no way denying the importance of power and authority, Paul understands that these do not inhere in the apostle. They depend wholly on the activity of God who chooses to allow his power to rest upon the servant in his/her weakness and thereby to manifest that power (12:9-10). Such a perspective set Paul in direct opposition to the cultural conventions of his day, conventions that undergirded his opponents' view and must have made that view seem reasonable and very attractive to the Corinthians.

Authenticity and Integrity

The authenticity of 2 Corinthians has never been seriously questioned. The internal evidence supporting Pauline authorship is so strong that it is accepted without debate. The writer claims to be Paul and the letter is unmistakably Pauline in vocabulary, style, tone, and character.

The integrity of 2 Corinthians, however, has been the subject of much debate especially with regard to the relationship between chaps. 1–9 and 10–13. Because of the marked difference in tone that characterizes these two sections, there is widespread consensus that these two sections of our canonical 2 Corinthians represent two separate letters. Chapters 1–9 are confident, conciliatory, and full of praise for the Corinthians. They appear to be a response to a crisis resolved, a crisis precipitated by the actions of an individual. Chapters 10–13, on the other hand, are characterized by anxious pleading, defensiveness, and sharp attacks on rival apostles who are undermining Paul's ministry in Corinth. In short, chaps. 10–13 reflect a crisis brought about by a group of intruders referred to as *false apostles* that is far from being resolved, and the scathing rhetoric of these chapter is quite unexpected after the tactful, carefully reasoned remarks of chaps. 1–9.

Proponents of the unity of the letter (see, e.g., Hughes) point to the fact that there is no manuscript evidence that any part of our canonical 2 Corinthians ever circulated independently or as a part of another letter. They argue that the supposed differences between chaps. 1–9 and chaps. 10–13 are overdrawn and can be explained without resorting to a partition theory. After writing chaps. 1–9 Paul received distressing news of a deteriorating situation in Corinth and then penned chaps. 10–13 before sending chaps. 1–9, or chaps. 10–13 are addressed to a recalcitrant minority in Corinth, or the dramatic difference in tone can be attributed to the ups and downs of the apostles' mercurial temperament.

Proponents of a two-letter theory fall into two camps. On the one hand there are those who argue that chaps. 10–13 are to be identified with the "tearful" or severe letter mentioned in 2 Cor 2:3-4, 9, and 7:8, 12 which was written before chaps. 1–9 (see, e.g., Talbert). Those who hold this view suggest that certain things in chaps. 10–13 seem to precede chaps. 1–9: 12:11 precedes 3:1 and 5:12; 13:2 precedes 1:23; 13:10 precedes 2:3, 4, 9; 10:6 precedes 2:9 and 7:15. Furthermore, in 3:1 and 5:12 Paul speaks of commending himself *again* suggesting that he is thinking of his boasting in chaps. 10–13, and his announcement in 10:16 that he is looking forward to preaching *in lands beyond you* makes more sense if he is writing from Ephesus than from Macedonia from which he writes chaps. 1–9.

Others argue that the identification of chaps. 10–13 with the "tearful" or severe letter is too problematic. First, chaps. 10–13 make no reference to the one thing that we are certain must have been in the "tearful" letter, namely, the demand that a certain offender be punished (2:5-6; 7:12). Second, chaps. 10–13 promise an imminent visit and are written so as to make the impending visit more productive (10:2; 12:14; 13:1-2), but the "tearful" letter was sent so that Paul would not have to make a painful personal visit (1:23; 2:1). Third, when Paul describes what the "tearful" letter has achieved (7:5-12) there is no mention of the subject that dominates chaps. 10–13, the threat to the Corinthians' faith and to Paul's apostleship posed by the false apostles. Fourth, 12:18 assumes that Titus has made at least one visit to Corinth to assist in the collection, thus presupposing 8:6a or 8:16-19. Fifth, Paul is aware in chaps. 10–13 of suspicions that he is collecting money for the Jerusalem church under false pretenses (12:14-18) and that there are rumors of deceit and fraud (14:16-17), yet there is no suggestion of such suspicions in chaps. 8 and 9, but rather a confidence that the process he is engaged in will prevent any such suspicions from arising (8:20).

Factors such as these have led to an emerging consensus among recent commentators that chaps. 10–13 represent a separate letter written sometime after chaps. 1–9 when Paul had received news of another crisis in Corinth (Barrett, Bruce, Danker, Furnish, Kruse, Martin). The two letters probably became joined early in the manuscript tradition by an editor who removed the closing of one and the opening of the other in a kind of redactional activity employed by editors of other ancient letters. This is the view adopted in this commentary.

Noting a certain redundancy in Paul's discussion of the collection in chaps. 8 and 9, Paul's use of Greek particles in 9:1 (*peri men gar* similar to the *peri de* used to introduce new topics in 1 Corinthians), the fact that 9:2 is addressed to *Achaia* rather than Corinth, and the different reasons given for the sending of *the brothers* in 8:20 and 9:3-5, some have argued that these two chapters do not belong together and that chap. 9 represents a separate letter. However, given that Paul is not above redundancy, that there is no evidence that *peri men gar* would be recognized as a formal introduction, that 1:1 indicates the letter is also addressed to the churches of Achaia, and that the two reasons given for the sending of *the brothers* are not incompatible, it seems best to see chaps. 8 and 9 as a single, integrated treatment of the collection. Furthermore, when Paul mentions *the brothers* in 9:3, 5 he assumes his readers know about whom he speaks, yet they are only identified in 8:6, 16ff.

Noting a somewhat abrupt transition and a seeming lack of thematic continuity between chap. 7 and Paul's introduction of the collection in chap. 8, and pointing out that while in chap. 7 Titus has just returned from Corinth and in chap. 8 he is preparing to leave for Corinth, some have argued that chap. 8 does not go with chap. 7. Careful reading of the text, however, reveals that the two chapters are linked by the repetition of key terms (earnestness/zeal [*spoudē*], 8:7, 11 and 7:11, and boasting [*kauchēseōs*], 8:24 and 7:14), and an emphasis on Paul's love for the Corinthians and his request for their affection in return (6:11-13; 7:2; 8:7-8). The allusions to Titus are understandable if chaps. 1–9 were written after Titus's return from Corinth with good news and in preparation for his upcoming trip to Corinth in connection with the collection. This commentary assumes that chaps. 8 and 9 stand together with chaps. 1–7.

Some have argued that 2:14–7:4 constitutes an interpolation because the lengthy defense of Paul's apostleship that is contained in these verses seems to interrupt the flow of thought between 2:13 and 7:5. While in 2:12-13 Paul is discussing his travel plans with regard to Corinth, in 2:14 he launches into a lengthy discourse concerning apostleship that continues until 7:4. In 7:5 he returns to the subject of his travel plans. However, Paul's references to *Macedonia* in 2:13 and 7:5 would be unduly repetitive if they stood side by side. Furthermore, there is a strong verbal linkage between 7:4 and 7:5-7 as three of the words employed in 7:4 are repeated in some form in 7:5-7 (*paraklēsis, chara/charēnai, thlipsis/thlibomenoi*). There is thematic continuity as well as the idea of comfort in affliction found in both 1:1–2:13, and 7:5-16 runs like a thread through 2:14–7:4. We shall assume, therefore, that chaps. 1–7 are a unity consisting of an apology (2:14–7:4) framed by two sections of itinerary (1:18–2:13 and 7:5-16).

Finally, much attention has also been focused on 6:14–7:1. It has been argued that Paul's admonition against being mismated with immoral and idolatrous pagans can be seen as a self-contained unit that interrupts the flow of thought of the surrounding context. Furthermore, when these verses are removed, 6:13 joins easily with 7:2. Thus, these verses have been seen as an interpolation. Some have held that these verses represent a fragment of the lost letter to the Corinthians mentioned in 1 Cor 5:9 in which Paul had charged them not to associate with Christians who were living an immoral lifestyle.

Noting the presence of eight key words not found elsewhere in the NT and the presence of certain elements that resemble the language and thought of Qumran (the dualistic antitheses, the reference to Beliar, the idea of community as a temple, the conflation of OT citations, and the general emphasis on separation), others have argued that the passage is a non-Pauline fragment that has been incorporated into the text by a later editor.

While these verses contain features characteristic of Qumran, these features were not peculiar to Qumran. Furthermore, Paul is perfectly capable of digressing and these verses may represent an intentional digression (known in classical rhetoric as an apostrophe). In this case while pleading for a mutual openheartedness Paul reflects that the reason for the lack of openheartedness among the Corinthians lies in their unwillingness to break with idolatrous associations as he had charged them to do in 1 Cor 10:14ff. ("Therefore, my beloved, flee from idolatry . . . ").

Literary Form

Our canonical 2 Corinthians falls naturally into four sections after the pattern of a typical first-century letter. A *salutation* in which Paul includes a brief self-description (1:1-2) is followed by a *thanksgiving* that functions to introduce the main theme(s) and express Paul's perspective on the theme while inviting the readers to share in that perspective (1:3-11). The *body* of the letter follows and falls into three main sections. In 1:12–7:16 Paul defines the nature of his ministry. In 8:1–9:15 he challenges the Corinthians to complete their participation in the collection for the saints in Jerusalem. In 10:1–13:10 Paul defends his ministry in response to the criticisms of *super-apostles* who are seeking to undermine his authority. Finally, the *closing* of the letter consists of final exhortations and greetings followed by a benediction (13:11-13).

For Further Study

In the *Mercer Dictionary of the Bible*: ACHAIA; APOSTLE/APOSTLESHIP; CORINTH; CORINTHIAN CORRESPONDENCE; EPISTLE/LETTER; GNOSTICISM; HELLENISTIC WORLD; MACEDONIA; OPPONENTS OF PAUL; ROMAN EMPIRE; SATAN IN THE NT; SUFFERING IN THE NT.

In other sources: W. Baird, *1 Corinthians/2 Corinthians*; C. K. Barrett, *A Commentary on the Second Epistle to the Corinthians*; G. R. Beasley-Murray, "2 Corinthians," *BBC*; E. Best, *Second Corinthians*, Interp; H. D. Betz, *2 Corinthians 8 and 9*; F. F. Bruce, *I and II Corinthians*, NCB; F. Danker, *II Corinthians*; V. Furnish, *II Corinthians*, AncB; P. E. Hughes, *Paul's Second Epistle to the Corinthians*, NICNT; C. Kruse, *2 Corinthians*; R. Martin, *2 Corinthians*, WBC; J. Murphy-O'Conner, "The Theology of the Second Letter to the Corinthians," *RE* 86/3 (1989); C. H. Talbert, *Reading Corinthians*; F. Young and D. Ford, *Meaning and Truth in 2 Corinthians*.

Commentary

An Outline

Salutation, 1:1-2

As a typical first-century Greek letter, 2 Corinthians begins with the identification of the author and the recipient(s) followed by a short greeting. Writing to a congregation where his apostleship was being challenged, PAUL includes a brief self-description that functions as a clear statement of his apostolic authority. He is *an apostle of Jesus Christ*, that is, Christ's commissioned representative, not by human appointment but by *the will of God*. With these words Paul sets the stage for the defense of his apostleship that will occupy much of what follows. At issue in Corinth is the nature of authentic apostleship, and it is to address this issue that Paul writes. The mention of TIMOTHY indicates that Timothy endorses what is written.

The letter is addressed to the Corinthian church and *all the saints throughout Achaia*, the Roman province of which Corinth was the capital including, for example, the Christians at Cenchreae (cf. Rom 16:1). As *saints* ("holy ones") they are set apart for obedience to the will of God, and if Paul is an apostle by the will of God this means allegiance to him and the gospel he proclaimed to them. Therefore, what is at stake in Corinth is not so much the apostleship of Paul but the genuineness of the faith of the Corinthians.

In 1:2 Paul combines the conventional Greek greeting (*grace*) with the traditional Hebrew greeting (*peace*) and indicates that these gifts come from God through Jesus Christ.

Thanksgiving, 1:3-11

In these verses, which take the form of a typical Jewish benediction ("Blessed be . . . "), Paul introduces the central theme of the letter: *the consolation of God in the midst of affliction and suffering*. He gives thanks to God for the fact that both he and the Corinthians have experienced God's consolation in the midst of affliction. This God is the *father of mercies* (i.e., the most merciful Father, one whose outstanding characteristic is mercy; cf. Ps 86:5, 15; Mic 7:18) and *God of all consolation* (i.e., encouragement and cheer), a description of God that goes back to the OT (Ps 103:13, 17; Isa 51:12; 66:13). Paul has experienced the reality of God's consolation in the midst of affliction so that he will be able to console others in their affliction with the same consolation with which he has been consoled, that is, the consolation of God (v. 4). In short, Paul's ability to console others is a direct result of God's prior work in his life. Furthermore, God's consolation for us in our affliction is sufficient, that is, abundant, even as Christ's sufferings for us are sufficient, indeed abundant. Thus, we can count on God's consolation to be abundant even as we have counted on Christ's sufferings to be abundant (v. 5).

In vv. 6 and 7 Paul writes that his afflictions and consolations would doubly benefit the Corinthians. First, whether he is afflicted or consoled, the result is the same: their comfort. Second, the Corinthians can also experience this consolation if they *patiently endure* the kinds of afflictions Paul is experiencing. This "endurance" is not Stoic resignation nor the power of positive thinking. It is the obedient faith of those who trust in God's power to sustain and deliver his people in affliction. Paul knows that those who share in his experience of suffering will also share in his consolation precisely because where God is at work there is consolation in the midst of affliction.

In vv. 8-11 Paul explains why he is so sure about the reality of God's consolation by recalling for his readers a recent example of his affliction. The occasion and nature of this affliction in Asia is unknown (some have identified it with the experience mentioned in 1 Cor 15:32). Whatever it was, his suffering was so severe that he saw no way out but death; and, helpless in the face of this *deadly . . . peril*," Paul was forced to trust no longer in himself but in God who raises the dead.

Paul sees his deliverance from this death as a type of the resurrection. Just as Christ was called in his death to trust in God who raises the dead, so Paul was called in the face of death to trust this God whose deliverance of Paul became a demonstration of his power. In short, it is Paul's suffering that becomes the revelatory vehicle by which the power of God is made known so that it is precisely in his suffering that the legitimacy of his apostleship is demonstrated. In his affliction and consolation he becomes an embodiment of that truth first seen in Christ's death and resurrection, that God's power is made known and perfected in our weakness (cf. 12:9).

Paul concludes his thanksgiving by calling for the continuing prayers of the Corinthians so that many will join in thanking God for his suffering and deliverance, for it is precisely in this that the power of God is made known. To all who would deny his apostleship on the basis of his suffering, Paul announces that it is in his suffering that his apostleship is authenticated.

Defining the Nature of His Ministry, 1:12–7:16

Responding to Charges, 1:12-14

Paul moves to respond to charges of vacillation in his relationship with the Corinthians because he has postponed a promised visit. His CONSCIENCE is clear because his actions have been motivated by *the grace of God* and not by *earthly wisdom* (lit. "the wisdom of the flesh"). He has acted with *frankness* and *godly sincerity* and is not hesitant to write openly about his recent change of plans in the hope that the Corinthians will hear him out and understand him fully.

Reaffirming His Credibility, 1:15-22

The charge of vacillation (v. 17) stems from a change in Paul's travel plans. While he had originally planned to visit Corinth after passing through MACEDONIA (1 Cor 16:5), he later indicated that he would visit Corinth both before and after passing through Macedonia (vv. 15-16). But after the first of these projected visits he decided not to make *another painful visit* (2:1) and sent a stinging letter instead (2:3-4). Thus, the charge of vacillation, of making *plans according to ordinary human standards* (v. 17, lit. "according to the flesh"), of being ready to say "yes, yes" and "no, no" at the same time.

Paul's questions in v. 17 are constructed in Greek so as to require "no" for an answer. He responds by saying that just as God is faithful to his people, so he has been faithful to the Corinthians (v. 18). He is concerned, however, lest questions about his credibility lead to questions about the credibility of the gospel. He insists there is no equivocation in this gospel (v. 19). Indeed, all the promises of God find their *yes* in Jesus (v. 20) and it is through him that we are able to say *amen* to the glory of God. It is this God who has established Paul, his colleagues, and the Corinthians in Christ, anointing them with his Spirit which functions as both God's seal (the mark of his ownership) and *a first installment* guaranteeing their full participation in the blessings of the age to come (vv. 21-22).

Explaining His Actions, 1:23–2:4

Having argued that his change of plans was a result of his faithfulness to God and to the Corinthians, Paul explains that his change of plans was to spare the Corinthians *another painful visit* (1:23; 2:1). Instead, he wrote them *out of much distress and anguish of heart and with many tears* to let them know of his abundant love for them (2:4).

Restoring the Offender, 2:5-11

The circumstances surrounding Paul's painful visit to Corinth and prompting the severe letter are implied in vv. 5-11. During his *painful* visit to Corinth a member of the Corinthian church had acted in some way so as to injure Paul and, by derivation, the whole congregation (v. 5), and the congregation had neither supported Paul nor reprimanded the offender. Rather than make a return visit Paul had written the severe letter *to test* the obedience of the whole congregation (v. 9). This letter had prompted the majority to take sufficient disciplinary action against the offender (v. 6), and Paul, whose concern is reconciliation rather than retaliation, calls for forgiveness (v. 7) and love (v. 8) to be extended to the repentant offender lest their disciplinary action fail to be redemptive. Failure to respond in this way would be to fall prey to Satan's designs of destroying the love and forgiveness that are to characterize God's people as the sign of God's redemptive work (v. 11).

Going to Macedonia, 2:12-13

Anxious for news of the Corinthian's response to his severe letter (2:3-4), Paul left EPHESUS and went north to Troas, the embarkation point for Macedonia, hoping to intercept the returning Titus there. Though a *door was opened* for him as he preached the gospel there, his anxiety was so great that he left Troas and crossed the Aegean Sea hoping to find Titus in Macedonia.

Being Led in Triumph, 2:14-17

Interrupting the account of his movements, Paul launches the most detailed defense of his apostleship to be found in any of his letters, a defense that runs through 7:4. In v. 14 he employs a striking image of apostolic service that sets the tone for all that follows. In the Greek term *thriambeuein* (translated *leads us in triumphal procession*) Paul's readers would recognize an allusion to the Roman "triumph" in which a victorious general would parade through the streets of Rome leading a long procession of captives whose afflictions and sufferings became a demonstration of the power and glory of the conqueror.

While it is possible Paul sees himself as a partner with Christ in his triumph, it seems more likely that in this context Paul sees himself as a captive of Christ whose ministry, beset by afflictions and sufferings as it is, becomes a demonstration of Christ's power and glory. This image becomes a graphic expression of the significant role suffering plays in apostolic ministry, a significance rejected by Paul's critics in Corinth. Yet it is precisely through Paul's ministry of suffering that God *spreads in every place the fragrance that comes from knowing him* (v. 14), that is, through Paul's ministry the knowledge of God is spread abroad and the suffering apostle becomes *the aroma of Christ* (v. 15).

Paul knows that not all will respond positively to this understanding of the nature of ministry even as all do not respond positively to the word of the cross. In fact, Paul describes the reaction to this understanding of ministry in terms of the same twofold response described for the word of the cross in 1 Cor 1:18-25. For those who acknowledge that God reveals himself in Paul's suffering, this aroma is the fragrance of life. For those who reject it, the fragrance is the smell of death. To those being saved, suffering is an appropriate expression of apostleship. To those who are perishing, it is foolishness (vv. 15-16).

This reflection on the nature of apostolic ministry prompts Paul to ask, *Who is sufficient for these things?* (v. 16). Who, that is, is adequate for such a ministry? While his answer does not come until 3:5-6, in 2:17 he makes it clear that the "sufficient one" is not a *peddler of the word*, that is, someone who preaches and teaches for his or her own gain, even adulterating the message to make it more marketable. Those who are "sufficient" speak in Christ as persons of sincerity, as persons who speak for God (saying what God wants said), and as persons who speak as if standing in the presence of God (i.e., with God as judge, cf. 5:10).

Acknowledging His Commendation and Competence, 3:1-6

Paul raises two questions in v. 1 that are intended to distinguish him from those who have come to Corinth bearing letters of recommendation. The implied answer to both is "no." He need not commend himself and does not need letters of recommendation because the Corinthians themselves are his letter of recommendation, authored by Christ, *written . . . with the Spirit of the living God . . . on tablets of human hearts* (vv. 2-3; for the background of this image see Jer 31:33; cf. Ezek 11:19-20; 36:26-27). This letter is *to be known and read by all*.

In short, the Corinthians owe their very lives as Christians to the ministry of Paul and to deny his apostleship would be tantamount to denying their conversion. Their experience legitimates Paul's apostleship. Indeed, there is no better evidence of the validity of Paul's ministry than the existence of the Corinthian church.

The Corinthian church is itself the basis for Paul's confidence (v. 4), but he is quick to point out that his competence for this ministry is not in himself but from God *who has made us competent to be ministers of a new covenant*, a covenant not of letter but of spirit *for the letter kills, but the Spirit gives life* (v. 6). Thus, Paul sets up a contrast between the old covenant and the new, and implies that his ministry is an essential part of the dawning of the new age promised in Jer 31:33 and Ezek 11 and 36. This new spiritual covenant served by his ministry is the subject of 3:7-18.

Ministering under the New Covenant, 3:7–4:6

In a *midrash* on Exod 34:29-35 Paul develops further the contrast introduced in 3:6. In 3:7-11 he employs the rabbinic principle of arguing from the lesser to the greater (*qal wa-homer*) to demonstrate the surpassing glory of this new COVENANT and the ministry that accompanies it. While the old covenant is *chiseled in letters on stone tablets* (cf. 3:3 and Exod 31:18), the new is written *on tablets of human hearts* (3:3). While the old covenant results in *condemnation*, the new results in *justification* (3:9). While the ministry that accompanies the old covenant is *the ministry of death* (3:7), the ministry of the new covenant is *the ministry of the Spirit* (3:8) that *gives life* (3:6). While the old covenant has been *set aside* (3:11), the new covenant is *permanent* (3:11). While the old covenant came with *glory* (3:7, 9, 10, 11), the new covenant has come with *greater glory* (3:8, 9, 10, 11) so that *what once had glory has lost its glory* in the light of the new that has come.

As a minister of this new covenant, Paul acts *with great boldness* (3:12), unlike Moses who put *a veil* over his face to conceal the temporary character of the glory of the old covenant (3:13). In 3:14 and 15 this *veil* becomes a metaphor for the spiritual blindness that lies over the hardened minds of those who continue to live under the old covenant. When they turn to the Lord, however, this veil is removed and they are able to see *the glory of the Lord* as it is revealed in Jesus, and beholding him to be *transformed into the same image from one degree of glory to another* (3:18).

Paul reaffirms the fact that he is engaged in this ministry of the new covenant as a result of *God's mercy* (4:1; cf. 3:5). Therefore, he does not *lose heart* despite the suffering he may experience. The nature of this ministry is then described both negatively and positively. Those engaged in this ministry do not resort to methods that bring shame when exposed. They do not engage in deceptive methods for their own advantage and they do not adulterate the message to make it more palatable. Rather they commend themselves to the conscience of everyone in the sight of God by *the open statement of the truth* (4:1-2).

If Paul's message is veiled, it is veiled only to unbelievers who lack the enlightenment of the Spirit and have been blinded by *the god of this world*. In this blindness they see only Paul's suffering and are blind to the power of his message (4:3-4).

Paul's message does not center on himself. He preaches nothing but *Jesus Christ as Lord* and unlike those who would exploit the congregation, he postures himself as their "slave" (4:5). The basis for both his message and the manner of his ministry is to be found in his own experience of discovering *the light of the knowledge of the glory of God* [i.e., all that God is and wills] *in the face of Jesus Christ* (4:6).

Recognizing Treasure in Clay Jars, 4:7-15

In v. 7 Paul employs another powerful image for the apostolic ministry. *We have this treasure in clay jars.* In the ancient world treasure was often buried in clay jars. The jar was fragile and expendable and often had to be broken so that the treasure inside could be revealed. So the treasure of apostleship is carried within the life of a fragile human being *so that it may be made clear that this extraordinary power belongs to God and does not come from us* (v. 7). In the weakness and the brokenness of the vessel the power of God is made manifest, and, therefore, weakness and suffering are integral to authentic apostolic ministry.

In support of this view Paul presents a list of the tribulations accompanying his ministry in vv. 8-10. He is *afflicted, perplexed, persecuted,* and *struck down,* and in these sufferings he is carrying in his own body the death (lit. "dying") of Jesus. But he is *not crushed, driven to despair, forsaken,* or *destroyed* because the power of God sustains him, and, therefore, the life of Jesus is *made visible in [his] mortal flesh.* In short, Paul's apostolic sufferings are a manifestation of Jesus' death and resurrection, and his suffering to bring the gospel to the Corinthians assures them of life in Christ (vv. 11-12).

So Paul does not *lose heart* even though his ministry is beset by suffering. He has the same spirit of faith as the Psalmist who wrote, *"I believed, and so I spoke."* The quotation is taken from Ps 116, a hymn of thanksgiving for deliverance from death. What Paul believes that enables him to speak is the gospel that *the one who raised the Lord Jesus will raise us also with him, and will bring us with you into his presence* (v. 14).

Living in the Light of the Future, 4:16–5:10

In v. 16 Paul picks up on the theme of future glory as a reason that he does not *lose heart* amidst the suffering of his apostolic ministry. The contrast between present, momentary affliction, and future, eternal glory is a reason for apostolic confidence. While the *outer nature* (i.e., mortal existence) is passing away, the *inner nature* (i.e., identity as children of God) is being renewed day by day (4:16), and the affliction we encounter serves to prepare us for *an eternal weight of glory beyond all measure* (4:17). Thus, we are able to look beyond present, temporary, and seen affliction to the future, eternal, not-yet-seen glory that lies ahead (4:18).

In 5:1-5 Paul employs a series of metaphors to describe the resurrection life. In 5:1 he contrasts the transience of our *earthly tent* (a common idiom for life in the body) with the permanence of our *building from God,* a *heavenly dwelling* which is *eternal, not made with hands.* In 5:2-3 he employs the image of putting on a garment over a garment already being worn. Similarly in 5:4 he pictures the putting up of another tent around one already inhabited. In both cases, Paul's desire is to receive the new garment or tent without having to give up the old one so as not to be *naked* (5:3) or *unclothed* (5:4), that is, to avoid the threat of nonbeing (death).

So in this life we groan, longing for the mortal to be swallowed up by life, knowing that the Spirit of God that we have already received is the guarantee of the reality of this resurrection life (5:5).

In 5:6-8 Paul introduces yet another metaphor, that of being *at home* and *away from home.* To be *at home in the body* (i.e., mortal existence) is to be *away from the Lord.* It is to walk *by faith* and not *by sight.* While he prefers to be *away from the body and at home with the Lord,* his eschatological hope is the foundation of his confidence (5:6, 8). This eschatological hope is more than just a source of confidence. It is also a challenge to right living. Since we all must appear before the *judgment seat of Christ*, our aim, whatever our state, must ever be to please him (5:9-10).

Being Ministers of Reconciliation, 5:11–6:10

In 5:11-15 Paul discusses the motivation for his ministry. He carries out his apostolic ministry *knowing the fear of the Lord*, knowing, that is, that he will give an account for his service *before the judgment seat of Christ* (5:10). His motives and actions lie open before God and the Corinthians, who he hopes will listen to their consciences rather than to his critics (5:11). Paul's intention in writing is not self-commendation. His aim is to provide the Corinthians a basis for responding to his critics who boast in external appearances rather than the things of the heart (5:12).

In 5:13a Paul responds to charges that he is either mad (in which case he responds that his behavior is determined by his faithfulness to God) or that his ministry is not truly apostolic because it does not give sufficient evidence of ecstatic experiences (in which case he responds that such experiences are between him and God, and are not to be worn on one's sleeve as evidence of one's apostleship). Whatever his behavior, whether he is *beside* himself, or in his *right mind*, it is for God and his glory, and for the benefit of the Corinthians. Paul's primary motivation is *the love of Christ* (Christ's love for him), a love demonstrated in the fact that *one has died for all; therefore all have died*, died, that is, to a sinful, self-centered existence so that they might live a Christ-centered life (5:14-15).

The new life in Christ is characterized by two things. First, there is a new way of knowing (5:16) in which we no longer evaluate either Christ or others *from a human point of view* (lit. "according to the flesh," i.e., knowledge without reference to God and God's purposes). Second, there is a new way of being, *a new creation* (5:17). The old self-centered humanity *has passed away*; the new Christ-centered humanity has come (cf. Paul's treatment of the two humanities in Rom 5:12ff.). *All this is from God who reconciled us to himself through Jesus Christ* (5:18).

Reconciliation, a major soteriological motif in Paul (cf. Rom 5:10; Col 1:21ff.; Eph 2:11-22), is summarized in 5:18-21.

First, it is initiated and accomplished by God (5:18, 19).

Second, it is accomplished *through* (5:18), *in Christ* (5:19) who was made *to be sin* (5:21). While this phrase has been interpreted to mean (a) that God caused him to assume our sinful nature or (b) that God allowed him to be condemned as a sinner, it is probably best to understand it to mean that (c) God made him a sin offering. In any case, God has so acted that *in him* [Christ] *we might become the righteousness of God*, that is, sinners are given a righteous status before God through the righteous one who absorbed their sin and its judgment in himself.

Third, all who are reconciled become ministers of *reconciliation* (5:18), charged with announcing the *message of reconciliation* (5:19) as *ambassadors for Christ* (5:20).

This message contains the plea to *be reconciled to God*, a plea addressed in this case to the Corinthians whose alienation from Paul has become a denial of the reality of the gospel of reconciliation in their lives. This reconciliation is a relationship with God and others that must be continually reaffirmed and realized. Thus, quoting Isa 49:8, Paul exhorts the Corinthians not to accept the reconciling grace of God in vain by acting in a way that is contrary to their experience of God's grace for every day is the *today* of salvation.

Paul has attempted to live and minister so as not to hinder the message he proclaims. In 6:4b-5 he presents a catalog of afflictions that he has borne with *great endurance* (cf. 11:23-33 for a second and more detailed listing). In 6:6-7 he lists moral and spiritual characteristics necessary to conduct his ministry. These are the *weapons of righteousness for the right hand and for the left*. In 6:8-10 he gives seven pairs of antithetical ways of viewing his ministry that contrast the visible appearance and essential reality of that ministry. Those who evaluate on the basis of human standards will have one perception of Paul's ministry. Those who judge according to the standards of the new creation will have quite another perception.

Appealing to the Corinthians, 6:11-13

In all his dealings with the Corinthians Paul has spoken frankly with a heart wide open to them. If there is any lack of openness between Paul and the Corinthians, the fault lies with them (vv. 11-12). So as a father speaking to his children (cf. 1 Cor 4:14-15), Paul appeals to them to open wide their hearts to him (5:13).

Calling for a Holy Life, 6:14–7:1

These verses (seen by many as an interpolation: see "Integrity," above) are a digression suggesting that one reason for the Corinthians' alienation from Paul is that they are still accommodating too much to the pagan environment in which they live (a problem amply attested in 1 Corinthians). The passage begins with an exhortation not to be *mismatched with unbelievers*. The term *mismatched* means "unequally" or "unnaturally" yoked, such as harnessing an ox and an ass together (a practice prohibited in Deut 22:10). This is followed by five rhetorical questions presupposing a negative answer illustrating the incongruity of a believer being yoked to an unbeliever. Righteousness, light, Christ, believers, and God's temple have nothing in common with lawlessness, darkness, Beliar (an evil spirit in intertestamental literature, under, or identified with, Satan), unbelievers, and idols (6:14b-16a).

Verses 16b-18 characterize the church as God's *temple* and depict the nature of that community with a series of OT quotations (Lev 26:12; Isa 52:11; a combination of Ezek 20:34, Isa 43:6, and 2 Sam 7:14). The section closes with an exhortation in 7:1 to be a holy people in reverent fear of their God (cf. 5:10).

Continuing the Appeal, 7:2-4

In v. 2 Paul repeats his plea of 6:13. The basis for that appeal is found in vv. 2b-3. He has been totally honest in all of his dealings with the Corinthians, and his purpose for writing is not condemnation but an expression of his life-and-death commitment to them. Verse 4 is an expression of his confidence in the Corinthians.

Rejoicing in Reconciliation, 7:5-16

In v. 5 Paul resumes the account of his movements begun in 2:12-13. The affliction he had experienced in Troas (2:13) continued in Macedonia as he awaited Titus's return from Corinth with a report of their reception of his severe letter (2:3-4). On receiving Titus's report his regrets about sending the letter vanished (v. 8) and he was *overjoyed* (v. 4) because it had led the Corinthians to a *godly grief* that led them to repentance and salvation rather than a *worldly grief* which leads only to death.

As a result of his letter the Corinthians had (1) rallied to Paul's side and reaffirmed their solidarity with him (vv. 5-6); (2) acted to discipline the offender, realizing that the offender's actions not only injured Paul but ultimately the whole congregation (2:5-7; 7:11-12); and (3) lived up to Titus's expectations of them based on Paul's boasting about them as Titus witnessed their obedience to Paul's apostolic leadership (vv. 13-15).

Paul concludes this section with another affirmation of his *complete confidence* in the Corinthians (v. 16; cf. v. 4) that serves to set the stage for the request he is about to make in chaps. 8 and 9. Such expressions of confidence typically functioned to undergird the subsequent request by creating a sense of obligation through praise.

Challenging the Corinthians to Complete the Collection, 8:1–9:15

Chapters 8 and 9 focus on Paul's collection for the saints in Jerusalem (see 1 Cor 16:1-4 and Rom 15:25-27). Having expressed his *complete confidence* in the Corinthians (7:16), Paul calls upon them to fulfill their obligation to this collection.

Excel in Giving, 8:1-8

Paul challenges the Corinthians to follow the example of the Macedonian churches. Using the ancient rhetorical technique of comparison to evoke competition between two individuals or groups, Paul seeks to motivate the Corinthians by alluding to the generosity of the Macedonians. Though experiencing *a severe ordeal of affliction* and *poverty*, they have voluntarily given generously, even *beyond their means*, out of the overflow of their gift of themselves to the Lord and to Paul (vv. 1-5). So Paul encourages the Corinthians to demonstrate their commitment to the Lord and to him as he sends Titus to complete their gift to the collection (v. 6). Playing on their pride, he calls upon them to excel in this *generous undertaking* as they excel in everything else (v. 7). Here is an opportunity for them to demonstrate the *genuineness* of their love as the Macedonians have done (v. 8).

Follow Christ's Example, 8:9-15

In these verses Paul challenges the Corinthians to fulfill their obligation on the basis of the example of Christ who *though he was rich, yet for your sakes he became poor, so that by his poverty you might become rich* (v. 9) Paul advises them to match the eagerness they had previously shown with the necessary action to complete their gift (vv. 10-12). They are encouraged to give (1) according to their means and (2) in keeping with the principle of equality (vv. 13-15) whereby those who have share out of their abundance with those who have not so that there is a *fair balance*. Citing Exod 16:18 Paul finds scriptural support for this practice in the story of the gathering of the manna in the wilderness (v. 15).

Receive the Representatives, 8:16–9:5

Paul is sending a delegation to receive the contribution of the Corinthians. The delegation includes Titus (8:16-17), the brother *who is famous among all the churches for his proclaiming the good news* and who has been appointed by the churches to travel with them perhaps as a kind of independent auditor (8:18-19), and *our brother whom we have often tested and found eager in many matters* (8:22). These arrangements have been made so there can be no charges of deceit leveled against Paul or this project. The purpose for the delegation is clearly stated in 8:20-21:

> *We intend that no one should blame us about this generous gift that we are administering, for we intend to do what is right not only in the Lord's sight but also in the sight of others.*

Titus comes as Paul's representative, while the other two come as representatives of the churches (8:23). Paul encourages the Corinthians to show them proof of their love and the reason for Paul's boasting about them. In other words, complete the collection (8:24).

9:1-5 extend and support the commendations in 8:16-24 (for the view that chap. 9 represents a separate letter, see "Integrity," above), and together with 9:6-15 provide the conclusion for Paul's treatment of the collection in 8:1–9:15. The subject of Paul's *boasting* about the Corinthians is given in 9:1-2. He has boasted to the Macedonians about the eagerness of the Corinthians to participate in the *ministry to the saints*. They have been ready to participate *since last year*. This boasting has *stirred up most* of the Macedonians, and Paul hopes that his boasting about the Macedonians in 8:1-5 will stir up the Corinthians.

In 9:3-5 Paul gives a second reason for sending *the brothers* (Titus and the two unnamed brothers of 8:16-24; the first reason was given in 8:20-21). They will *arrange in advance* for the *bountiful* gift the Corinthians have promised so that neither the Corinthians nor Paul will be humiliated when he arrives with representatives of the Macedonian churches because the Corinthians, about whom Paul has been boasting, are not prepared with their gift.

Give Bountifully and Cheerfully, 9:6-15

Paul concludes his appeal on behalf of the collection by challenging the Corinthians to "sow bountifully" so that they may *reap bountifully* (v. 6; cf. Gal 6:7-8). To "sow bountifully" is to give *not reluctantly or under compulsion* but "cheerfully" (v. 7; cf. 9:5 and LXX of Prov 22:8a). To *reap bountifully* is to be *enriched in every way* (v. 11) by the God who is able *to provide you with every blessing in abundance*, not to be self-sufficient, but so that *having enough of everything, you may share abundantly in every good work* (v. 8).

In v. 9 Paul quotes from the description of the man who fears the Lord in Ps 112:9, whose *righteousness* [i.e., acts of piety, esp. almsgiving] *endures forever*.

The generosity of the Corinthians in sharing in the collection will supply the needs of the saints (v. 12) and will be a sign of their obedience to the gospel that will bring glory to God (v. 13). It will result in thanksgiving to God (v. 11b); in fact, it will overflow *with many thanksgivings to God* (v. 12b) because God is the ultimate source of both the spirit of generosity and the abundance from which the Corinthians are able to give.

All of our giving is done in light of and in response to God's *indescribable gift* (v. 15) for which Paul gives thanks as he closes this discussion. Romans 15:25-27 (probably written from Corinth after 2 Corinthians), suggests that the Corinthians heeded Paul's appeal with regard to the collection.

Defending His Ministry, 10:1–13:10

Because of the abrupt change of tone, there is a widespread consensus among NT scholars that chaps. 10–13 represent a separate letter. While some identify it as the "tearful" or "severe" letter referred to in 2:3-9 and 7:8-12 that was written before chaps. 1–9, a growing number of commentators—including the present one—argue that it was written some time after chaps. 1–9 in response to a fresh outbreak of trouble in Corinth precipitated by the arrival of *false apostles* (11:13) who were attempting to undermine Paul's ministry there (on the relationship between chaps. 1–9 and chaps. 10–13, see "Integrity," above). In any case, these chapters contain a passionate and vigorous defense of Paul's apostolic ministry.

Responding to Criticism, 10:1-11

Paul appeals to the Corinthians on the basis of *the meekness and gentleness of Christ* and in light of a series of criticisms leveled at him by his unnamed opponents in Corinth.

The first criticism, as reflected in vv. 1 and 10, is that while Paul is bold from a distance, he is weak and unimpressive in person. The charge probably reflects on his oratorical skills (cf. 1 Cor 2:3-4; 2 Cor 11:6), his physical appearance, and his behavior on the painful visit when in the face of opposition he left Corinth and, rather than returning in person, fired off the severe letter. Paul responds with the veiled threat in vv. 2 and 11, that he is prepared to back up his strong words with action if necessary when he arrives in Corinth.

The second charge is that he acts *according to human standards* (v. 2, lit. "according to the flesh"). This may mean either that he acts according to egocentric, worldly motives or that he acts without spiritual power. Paul responds that while he lives as a human being, he wields weapons with *divine power* (vv. 3-4a). Employing military images, he describes these weapons as capable of destroying *strongholds* (i.e., *arguments and every proud obstacle raised up against the knowledge of God*), taking captives (i.e., *every thought captive to obey Christ*) and punishing *every disobedience* (vv. 4b-6). While he wields these weapons in *the meekness and gentleness of Christ* (v. 1), this must never be confused with weakness. He will wield them in Corinth if necessary but hopes that the Corinthians will not force a showdown.

In response to the claims of his opponents, Paul reminds the Corinthians that he too belongs to Christ (v. 7) and that the Lord has given him the apostolic authority (v. 8) for the purpose of building up rather than tearing down.

Seeking the Lord's Commendation, 10:12-18

In v. 12 Paul focuses specifically on his opponents, ironically stating that he does not "dare" to compare himself with those who nonsensically measure themselves by one another and make themselves the measure of genuine apostleship. In reality no comparison is possible, for Paul sees them as *false apostles* who serve Satan rather than Christ (11:13-15). Unlike Paul, his opponents *boast beyond limits*, demonstrating the kind of excessive self-praise characteristic of the sham philosopher (v. 13). Furthermore, they boast *in the labors of others* (v. 15) and take credit for *work already done in someone else's sphere of action* (v. 16).

The clear implication is that Paul's opponents have invaded the sphere of action assigned to Paul and are seeking to take it over for themselves. In so doing they are not building up but destroying the Corinthian congregation (v. 8; 13:10). Paul, on the other hand, keeps within the field assigned to him (v. 13) preaching the gospel in places where it was not already known (cf. Rom 15:20-21). It was in keeping with that charge that Paul had come to Corinth as the first to preach the gospel there (v. 14). Corinth was, therefore, in his jurisdiction, and he now hoped to proclaim the good news in the lands beyond Corinth without boasting of work already done (v. 16).

Citing Jer 9:24 (LXX), Paul asserts that if any boasting is to be done it is to be boasting in the Lord, *For it is not those who commend themselves* [as do his opponents] *that are approved, but those whom the Lord commends* (v. 18). Once again Paul needs no letter of recommendation, for the very existence of the Corinthian church is evidence of the Lord's commendation, the only commendation that matters.

Playing the Fool for Love: the Fool's Speech, 11:1–12:13

This passage has been called Paul's "fool's speech" on the basis of Paul's introduction of it as *a little foolishness* (11:1) and his comment at the end, *I have been a fool* (12:11). The necessity of defending his apostolic status in the face of the boasting of his opponents forces Paul to engage in the kind of self-commendation he has just repudiated in 10:12-18. That such boasting is foolishness is clear; that it is necessary at this point is also clear, lest he lose the Corinthian congregation to even greater fools.

Careful reading of this "fool's speech" reveals that it is a devastating attack on Paul's boastful opponents. His emphasis throughout on the foolishness of such boasting (11:1, 17, 21; 12:1, 11) becomes an indictment of his opponents who practice such boasting. Furthermore, by boasting of humiliating experiences rather than of glorious accomplishments, he reveals the great gulf that separates his understanding of apostleship from theirs.

Having invited his readers to bear with him in *a little foolishness* (11:1), Paul explains that it is motivated by his concern for the Corinthians. Comparing himself to the father of a bride who has been betrothed, he sees his role as that of guarding his daughter's virginity between the time of the betrothal and the consummation of the marriage (11:2). He fears that the Corinthians are in danger of being led astray from *a sincere and pure devotion to Christ* by *super-apostles* who have come to Corinth preaching *another Jesus*, a *different Spirit* and a *different gospel* (11:3-5).

Paul emphasizes that he is in no way inferior to these *super-apostles*—an ironic designation of his opponents that makes light of their pretentious claims. Apparently Paul was being unfavorably compared with them on several accounts.

First, his style as a public speaker had been criticized because it lacked the rhetorical sophistication displayed by his opponents (11:6). This may also lead to the suggestion that he lacked the knowledge that according to his opponents an apostle should have. While not disputing his critics' evaluation of his eloquence, Paul will not allow their evaluation of his knowledge, a knowledge that has been made evident to the Corinthians in every way. In short, he is *not in the least inferior* to the *super-apostles*.

Second, in a culture where many considered it degrading for a philosopher to work, Paul's insistence on supporting himself while in Corinth with his refusal to accept support from the Corinthians had been seen as an indication of an inferior status and even as a lack of love for the Corinthians. Paul responds that his behavior was certainly not an indication of a lack of love; rather he has acted so as not to burden them (11:7-11). Finally, Paul will have nothing of his opponents' claim to an equal status with him (11:12). Disguising themselves as apostles of Christ, they are in reality *deceitful workers, false apostles, ministers* of Satan (11:13-15).

In 11:16 Paul repeats his plea of 11:1 asking indulgence for his foolish boasting. Nevertheless he will engage in the foolishness of boasting according to human standards as his opponents do (11:16-18). With powerful sarcasm he indicates that this is possible because in their "wisdom" the Corinthians *put up with fools* who would exploit them (11:19-20), something that he was *too weak* to do (11:21).

Paul begins his boasting by establishing that while his ethnic and religious credentials are no less Jewish than his opponents (11:22), his credentials as a minister of Christ are superior (11:23a). Ironically, the evidence he brings to support his claim is not a list of glorious triumphs but of the trials and hardships he has suffered as an apostle (11:23b-33). While some have understood this litany as an attempt at one-upmanship (the opponents bragged about what they had suffered for Christ, so Paul recounts what his service to Christ had cost him), the irony that pervades the context suggests that it is better seen as a kind of parody of the opponents' exalted claims. While they boast of things that demonstrate their strength, Paul boasts of things that show his weakness (11:29a-30) for in his weakness the transcendent power of God is made known (4:7-15; 12:9).

The incident at DAMASCUS (11:32-33) illustrates *danger in the city* (11:26). It stands as an example of Paul's weakness especially when viewed against the backdrop of the Roman *corona muralis* (wall crown) that was presented for valor to the first soldier to ascend the wall of an enemy city. The marked contrast between such a courageous ascent and Paul's inglorious descent of the city wall would not be missed by the Corinthians and could only have been seen as another evidence of his weakness and humiliation.

In response to the claims of his opponents, Paul finds it necessary to boast about *visions and revelations* (12:1). Using the third person (a reflection of his reticence about boasting of his own experiences), Paul tells of being *caught up to the third heaven* (considered in some Jewish cosmologies to be the highest heaven), which is here synonymous with Paradise. He says nothing of what he saw, and what he heard he cannot repeat because it was either inexpressible or impermissible to repeat (12:2-4).

While such experiences have a personal benefit for the one who experiences them, they have no real benefit for others. Therefore, Paul chooses to boast of his *weaknesses* (12:5-7) because he had learned that it is in weakness that God's power is made manifest. Paul had learned this from his experience of the *thorn . . . in the flesh* that had been given him to keep him from *being too elated*.

While the *thorn* has been the subject of much speculation, it is probably best understood as a physical illness or infirmity that left Paul open to public ridicule (cf. Gal 4:13-14). Paul's persistent plea for its removal was greeted by the promise of God's sufficient grace and the knowledge that God's *power is made perfect in weakness* (12:8). If this is the case, then it is not in our strength but in our weakness that God's power is revealed, and, therefore, it is in our weakness that we should boast (12:9). It is as we suffer *weaknesses, insults, hardships, persecutions, and calamities* that we become the showplace of God's power (12:10).

Thus, while Paul's vision had provided nothing that could be uttered for the benefit of others, the thorn in the flesh communicated the grace and power of God each day. In his weakness, therefore, Paul embodied the folly of the cross that reveals the power of God (1 Cor 1:18-31; 2 Cor 4:7-12).

Paul concludes his "fool's speech" by reasserting that he is in no way inferior to the *super-apostles* (12:11). He has performed the signs of a *true apostle* (12:12). His ministry was of both word and deed and had included *signs and wonders and mighty works* (cf. Rom 15:18-19). He has held back nothing from the Corinthians except that he has not asked them for support, and ironically he asks to be forgiven for not exploiting them as his opponents have (12:13).

Anticipating His Third Visit, 12:14-21

As Paul anticipates his third visit to Corinth, he makes it clear that he will continue his practice of not burdening the Corinthians. As a genuine apostle, he does not want what the Corinthians have but the Corinthians themselves. He cares for them as a parent for a child (v. 14) knowing that apostolic authenticity is demonstrated when one is willing *to spend and be spent* for the Corinthians (v. 15).

Verses 16-18 suggest that Paul has been charged with defrauding the Corinthians with regard to the collection for the saints in Jerusalem. Perhaps his critics were saying that while Paul asked for no money for himself, he was actually using the collection to line his own pockets. He responds by pointing to the exemplary behavior of his representatives (*Titus* and *the brother*). Just as they had not taken advantage of the Corinthians, neither had he.

Paul's concern is not for his own reputation but for the building up of the Corinthians (v. 19). As he approaches his third visit, he fears (1) that he may not find the Corinthians to be as he wished and that they might not so find him; (2) that there will be quarreling, jealousy, anger, selfishness, slander, gossip, conceit, and disorder; and (3) that the congregation will still be plagued by impurity, sexual immorality, and licentiousness (vv. 20-21).

Warning the Corinthians, 13:1-4

Citing Deut 19:15 Paul views his upcoming third visit as a third witness against his opponents and their followers. He had previously warned them on his second visit and then by means of the severe letter. When he arrives he will not be lenient but will vigorously assert his apostolic authority. He will give compelling evidence that Christ speaks through him in powerful action with regard to the unrepentant. Such powerful action is modeled after the pattern of Christ who was *crucified in weakness, but lives by the power of God* (v. 4).

> This does not mean that the crucifixion represents weakness and the resurrection power; the cross is the supreme expression of God's power (1 Cor 1:24) and the resurrection shows that what appears to be weakness (the crucifixion) is in truth the power of God (see Rom 1:4). Similarly the apparent weakness of Paul—his unimposing presence (10:10) and his suffering service (6:4-10; 11:25-29)—is in fact the sign that God's power is at work in his ministry (12:10). Since Paul shares the suffering of Christ

(Phil 3:10; Gal 2:10), he is "weak in him" (v. 4); since he shares the power of Christ's resurrection (Phil 3:10), he will exercise the power of Christ when dealing with the Corinthians (Baird 1988, 108).

Challenging the Corinthians, 13:5-10

Paul challenges the Corinthians who question whether Christ speaks through him to examine whether Christ lives in them (v. 5). While Paul hopes that they will recognize the authenticity of his apostleship and thus his authority (v. 6), his over-arching concern is that the Corinthians will do what is right, regardless (v. 7). He is happy to appear weak so long as the Corinthians are strong (v. :8) and prays that they will *become perfect* (v. 9; lit. "upright again").

In v. 10 Paul states the purpose for his writing. He has written so that when he comes he might not have to be severe in using the apostolic authority that had been given to him for the building up of the church.

Closing 13:11-13

Closing Exhortations and Greeting, 13:11-12

These verses contain the briefest of paraeneses (cf. Rom 12:9-13; 1 Cor 16:13-15; 1 Thes 5:12-22). Attention to Paul's fourfold admonition will allow the Corinthi-an church to become what God intends and will assure the Corinthians of God's presence.

Benediction, 13:13

This is the fullest Pauline benediction to be found in any letter. It is distin-guished from others by its clearly trinitarian form. The grace of the *Lord Jesus Christ* expresses and leads us to know the love of *God* whose *Spirit* produces com-munion with God and with one another.

Works Cited

Baird, William. 1988. *1 Corinthians/2 Corinthians*.
Martin, Ralph P. 1986. *2 Corinthians*. WBC.

Galatians

Charles H. Cosgrove   [MCB 1207-1215]

Introduction

Galatians is addressed to a group of gentile-Christian congregations founded by PAUL and located in central Asia Minor (modern Turkey). The date and place of composition are uncertain. Paul's so-called third missionary journey (ca. 52–56) is a possibility, in which case he may have composed the letter in EPHESUS, CORINTH, or in some part of MACEDONIA.

The Occasion of the Letter

Since Paul's founding visit, the Galatians have been influenced by certain persons who Paul claims are *confusing* them and wanting *to pervert* the gospel (1:7; cf. 5:10, 12). These persons may be Jewish-Christian teachers from JERUSALEM who disagree with Paul about the nature of the GOSPEL for the gentiles. They insist above all on CIRCUMCISION (5:2-6; 6:12-13), and will be referred to here as "the Circumcisers."

To judge from Paul's argument, the Circumcisers have urged the Galatians to accept the Law as a way of promoting the power and wondrous works of the Spirit (3:5). Paul's letter is an effort to refute this teaching and persuade the Galatians to return to the way of life in Christ that Paul first taught them.

Paul's Argument

Paul makes his appeal in three stages. The first stage is an "apostolic autobiography" (1:11–2:21) in which Paul claims that his apostolic authority and his gospel preaching come directly from God, the implication being that the Galatians had better listen to him. At the same time Paul depicts himself as the only apostle who has consistently defended the gentile cause in the gospel. The Galatians can trust him. Thus the primary aim of the apostolic autobiography is to encourage the Galatians to trust Paul, so they will accept his interpretation and logic in the central argumentation of the letter.

The second phase of Paul's appeal (3:1–4:31, with a certain anticipation in 2:15-21) consists largely of theological argument from scripture and Christian tradition. Paul argues that the Galatians enjoy eschatological life (manifest in the wondrous power of the Spirit, 3:5) solely because they believed Paul's gospel and not because of any relationship they may now have with the Law of Moses. In fact, if they practice works of the Law, they will put themselves under a curse and forfeit the blessing they now experience in Christ.

The third phase of Paul's appeal is an apostolic exhortation (5:1–6:10). Paul defines the relationship between the Law and FREEDOM in the Spirit. He admonishes the Galatians in a way that suggests their ethical life has been deteriorating—as if their adoption of the Law might itself be the cause of an increase among them of *works of the flesh*. In this way the exhortation functions as an implicit argument against Law-keeping.

Galatians and Anti-Judaism

In our time all Christian commentary proceeds in the shadow of the Holocaust, hence a word is in order about the impression Galatians gives today of sanctioning "anti-Judaism." For Paul, as for most Jews in his day, JUDAISM was defined by the Law, but in Galatians Paul says that all those "in the Law" are in slavery. That amounts to a harsh attack on Judaism, even if Paul was in some sense seeking to redefine Judaism on the basis of his conviction that the Messiah had come with a new revelation about the Law.

As part of the Christian Bible, Galatians has an anti-Jewish ring that is amplified by the political power of Christianity in the world. But when Paul wrote Galatians, the letter represented a critique that barely tinkled within the world of ancient Judaism; it certainly did not pose any social or political threat to Jews. As an ancient Jewish scholar Paul had every right to reinterpret Judaism by his own lights, and Jews and Christians of all ages have every right to quarrel with him about that reinterpretation. They also have an opportunity to learn from him.

For Further Study

In the *Mercer Dictionary of the Bible*: CIRCUMCISION; FREEDOM; GALATIA; GALATIANS, LETTER TO THE; JERUSALEM COUNCIL; LAW IN THE NT; NT USE OF THE OT; OPPONENTS OF PAUL; PAUL.

In other sources: H. D. Betz, *Galatians: A Commentary on Paul's Letter to the Churches of Galatia*, Herm; F. F. Bruce, *The Epistle to the Galatians: A Commentary on the Greek Text*, NIGTC; C. H. Cosgrove, *The Cross and the Spirit: A Study in the Argument and Theology of Galatians*; R. B. Hays, *The Faith of Jesus Christ: An Investigation of the Narrative Substructure of Galatians 3:1–4:11*, SBLDS; D. Lührmann, *Galatians: A Continental Commentary*; F. J. Matera, *Galatians*, SP; R. C. Tannehill, *Dying and Rising with Christ*, BZNW.

Commentary

An Outline

The Opening, 1:1-5

Instead of simply stating his name as "sender," Paul opens the letter by elaborating on his apostleship, declaring that he became *an apostle* directly through *Jesus Christ and God the Father*. What Paul means is that God has given him a direct commission to preach the gospel to the gentiles (1:16; cf. Rom 1:1-6, 13-14; 15:15-18), and in that commission God has also revealed the gospel to him (1:11-12). Being an apostle and knowing the gospel go together in Paul's self-understanding because he attributes both to the same source and revelatory moment.

The point of stating and defining his apostleship in the letter opening is to establish (probably by way of reminder) two things. First, the Galatians must heed what Paul says because he is God's messenger to them, the unspoken insinuation being that the Circumcisers have not gotten their message from God. Second, and by obvious implication, Paul's teaching is true because he got it straight from God.

Paul encapsulates that teaching in several brief expressions. He identifies God as *the Father, who raised* [Jesus] *from the dead* (v. 1), and he calls Jesus *the Lord*, who *gave himself for our sins to set us free from the present evil age*. The idea that the gospel means liberation from an EVIL cosmic condition (in which human beings are trapped) recurs elsewhere in the letter. That liberation, in Paul's understanding, comes to pass through Jesus' death, about which he will have more to say in 2:15-21, 3:10-14, and 6:14-15.

A Thanksgiving Parody, 1:6-10

In Paul's other letters rather elaborate "thanksgiving statements" follow his epistolary openings. But not in Galatians. Instead of celebrating their increasing growth and steadfastness in the gospel, Paul berates the Galatians for abandoning the gospel and turning to *another gospel*. He even goes so far as to pronounce a "curse" on anyone who might preach a gospel other than the one that he himself first taught the Galatians.

In the ancient Mediterranean world, it was widely assumed that the utterance of a curse, especially by a person who enjoyed special connections with the divine world (as Paul claims he does), could bring harm (including the possibility of death) to its object. Thus Paul is not simply expressing his own depth of concern; he is implementing his apostolic power (cf. 1 Cor 5:3-5) in a spiritual attack on his opponents (whom he later suggests—3:1—have themselves practiced witchcraft on the Galatians).

The Letter Body, 1:11–6:10

Apostolic Autobiography, 1:11–2:21

1:11-24. Paul's call and commission. In vv. 11-12 Paul claims that he did not receive his gospel *from* any human beings; it came directly *through a revelation of Jesus Christ*. This probably means a REVELATION by God of the risen Jesus. In 1 Cor 15:8 Paul reports that the resurrected Christ appeared to him, and in v. 16 he says that God "revealed his Son *in* me." We don't know exactly how Paul experienced this revelation (which may also be what he has in mind in 2 Cor 12:1-4), but clearly he understood it as a miraculous event in which God commissioned him to preach the gospel of Christ to gentiles without the requirement that they receive CIRCUMCISION and practice the Law of Moses. Admittedly, Paul does not say anything about the Law in vv. 11-24, but his insistence that he has always preached the same gospel (see esp. the stories that follow in 2:1-21) indicates that by *the gospel* he always means a gospel that does not require Law-keeping from gentiles.

According to some interpreters, the Circumcisers claimed that Paul received his apostolic commission from the Jerusalem apostles. In that case (so the argument goes) he would be obliged to conform his preaching to the Jerusalem version of the gospel, which the Circumcisers purport to represent. This conjecture seems very likely, considering the oath Paul takes in v. 20. But even if the Circumcisers did not claim that Paul stood under the authority of Jerusalem, Paul might well have made the argument he develops in the narrative of vv. 13-24. For that narrative backs up his claims to apostolic authority (vv. 1, 11-12) on the basis of which he instructs the Galatians about the gospel and the law, interprets scripture, and tells them how to live their lives in Christ.

Paul begins by describing his *earlier life in Judaism*, which provides a contrast to his life after receiving his call from God. It also implies that he knows more about the Law than the Circumcisers themselves do (see v. 14). Next Paul explains that after receiving his apostolic commission from God he had no contact with any of the apostles in Jerusalem. Instead he went directly to *Arabia* and then *returned to Damascus* (v. 17), which indicates that his call-revelation occurred in DAMASCUS. The point of vv. 13-17 is to refute any actual or potential claim that he received his knowledge of the gospel or any kind of commission from the Jerusalem church.

But three years later, Paul says, he did go up to JERUSALEM, evidently for the first time after receiving his call. His purpose was "to *see* Cephas" (v. 18, author trans.), Cephas probably being PETER. Paul uses a word in v. 18 (*historēsai*) that typically means to "inquire" or to "see someone about something." This shows that Paul is no longer at this point arguing that he didn't learn anything from any of the other apostles. When he says that he went up "to see Cephas" and that he didn't see any of the other apostles except JAMES (v. 19), he is making it clear that he had no meetings with the Jerusalem apostles that might be construed as occasion for any apostolic commissioning. Perhaps Paul finds it important to stress the unofficial nature of his meetings with Cephas and James because he has not yet arrived at the point in his life story where he began his apostolic ministry. His first mention of "preaching the gospel" appears only after the story of his first visit to Jerusalem, which was followed by trips to *Syria and Cilicia* (v. 21). Anyone who had been told (evidently correctly) that Paul began his apostolic ministry only after his first visit to the Jerusalem church might have inferred that the Jerusalem apostles commissioned him for this work. Paul makes it clear that he was party to no official meetings of the Jerusalem apostles, and he certifies this with an oath (v. 20).

2:1-10. God leads the Jerusalem apostles to confirm Paul's gospel. In vv. 1-11 Paul describes his first official meeting with the Jerusalem apostles. Whatever the Galatians may have been told about this meeting, Paul maintains that by the end of it, thanks to his own witness (v. 2), the chief Jerusalem apostles had come to full agreement with him about the nature of his apostleship and about the gospel for the gentiles (vv. 7-9).

Cephas, James, and JOHN may have invited him or even "summoned" him to Jerusalem. But Paul says that he went up in obedience *to a revelation* (v. 2), as if to ward off any impression that he was following directives from Jerusalem. At Jerusalem he presented his gospel, apparently in both public gatherings of the church and in private conferences with church leaders (v. 2). He did so, he says, in order to make sure that he had not been laboring for nothing (v. 2). But, as it turned out, *even Titus, who was with me, was not compelled to be circumcised, though he was a Greek* (v. 3). Verses 1-3 suggest that if the Jerusalem leaders had rejected Paul's understanding of the gospel for the gentiles and had insisted that TITUS be circumcised, then Paul would have accepted this as God's will. That seems surprising in the light of how Paul has argued thus far and how he continues to underscore his independence from Jerusalem in what follows. But it is nonetheless the impression Paul leaves, perhaps as if to say, "There came a time when God (to whom I am alone obedient) told me to go to Jerusalem and submit my gospel to the test of the Jerusalem authorities, and the result was, in God's providence, that the Jerusalem apostles approved my gospel." Nevertheless, the Jerusalem apostles were really only "seeing" and "recognizing" the activity of the divine "grace" already at work in Paul apart from any agency or authorization on their part (vv. 7-9).

But there were some *false believers* (v. 4) who *slipped in to spy on the freedom we have in Christ Jesus.* This FREEDOM must be the practice of living "free" from obedience to the Law. One guesses that the "false" believers saw Paul and BARNA-BAS breaking the Law (perhaps in their dietary practice) or discovered that Titus was not circumcised, and then denounced Paul and his party before the Jerusalem apostles (in order to *enslave us*, Paul says). But, as v. 5 describes it, Paul and his company stood heroically steadfast "in order that the truth of the gospel might be preserved for you" (RSV)—"you" being the Galatians, whom he has not yet even met! The rhetorical point of v. 5 is to imply that even before the Galatians became Christians, Paul was on their side. From first to last he remains the hero of the gentile cause.

By contrast the pillar apostles couldn't have been more affirming of Paul. Not, Paul says, that he cared anything about their status. He, like God, doesn't pay attention to such things (v. 6). But, we might add, Paul is in fact only too pleased to point out that the pillars affirmed his gospel. So he trades on their prestige at the same time that he denies owing them any obedience or special regard.

The pillars recognized that the same God who entrusted Cephas with the *gospel for the circumcised* (v. 7, meaning a gospel for the Jews) also entrusted Paul with the *gospel for the uncircumcised* (v. 7, meaning a gospel for the gentiles). The *gospel for the uncircumcised* is a Law-free gospel, and Paul probably assumed that since there is only "one" gospel, Jewish Christians are also not *required* by the gospel to keep the Law. The pillars at Jerusalem may have understood the agreement about the gospel (vv. 6-10) to mean that Jewish Christians must keep the Law while gentile Christians are not obliged to do so. That would explain how the controversy at ANTIOCH (2:11-21) could have arisen after the agreement made in Jerusalem. The understanding achieved at Jerusalem involved a fundamental misunderstanding between the two parties.

2:11-21. Paul champions the gentile cause at Antioch. In a story about the church at Antioch Paul again portrays himself as the hero who defends the gentile cause in the gospel. As he recounts it, Jewish and gentile Christians were accustomed to eating together in the Antioch church, evidently without observing any of the Jewish dietary laws. But when a certain group *from James* came, all the Jewish Christians (except for Paul but including Cephas, and even Barnabas) abandoned table fellowship with the gentiles. Paul accuses these Jewish Christians of *hypocrisy* (v. 13), meaning they acted in a way inconsistent with what they knew and affirmed to be the *truth of the gospel* (v. 14).

We should not assume that the party *from James* carried the same message to Antioch that the Circumcisers later brought to Galatia, except in the general sense that both groups promoted the Law and linked it positively with life in Christ. The Galatians were in a position to discern points of correspondence between the Antioch incident and their own situation. We can only guess about these similarities.

Paul accuses Cephas of "compelling" (v. 14) the gentiles to *live like Jews* (i.e., by practicing the Law). Cephas, Paul says, knows better than to pressure the gentiles into Law-keeping, for he himself lives *like a Gentile and not like a Jew*. And this way of living—which Cephas's present behavior so glaringly contradicts—is in accord with the truth of the gospel. That means that in Paul's understanding neither Jewish nor gentile Christians are obliged to keep the Law. Considered in the context of the Antioch incident, it also means that when Jewish and gentile believers are together, Jewish Christians ought to live as gentiles.

The theological rationale for Jewish-Christian freedom from the Law is found in a dense and obscure argument presented, ostensibly, as the speech Paul made at Antioch. Since it was a customary practice of the time to compose speeches in the course of a historical narrative, we need not assume that Paul reproduces in vv. 14b-21 exactly what he said at Antioch. That helps explain why it is difficult to see the immediate relevance for the Antioch controversy of everything he says in these verses.

According to Paul, Jewish Christians "know" that they owe their righteousness before God to the "faith of Jesus Christ" (v. 16; NRSV mg.). Paul does not say how they know this. The Galatians are to take his word for it, Paul himself being a Jewish Christian. The phrase, "the faith of Jesus Christ," is the most natural way to translate the Greek expression found here, which may refer to Christ's own faith or, more likely, to "Christian faith" as an eschatological way of salvation. The traditional translation, *faith in Christ* forces the Greek and should be avoided unless there is no other coherent way to interpret the phrase. In 1:23 Paul says that he preaches *the faith*. In 3:23, 25 he speaks of faith as a transcendent reality that comes into the world, like Christ himself. And in 3:22 he speaks of "what was promised from the faith of Jesus Christ" (author trans.). These texts suggest that "the faith" and "the faith of Jesus Christ" are names Paul uses for the way and means of salvation that God has brought in Christ.

In v. 20 Paul speaks of "the faith of the Son of God" (NRSV mg.), meaning the faith Jesus himself exercised, which may also be the sense of "the faith of Jesus Christ" in v. 16. In either case—whether the expression means Jesus' own faithfulness or stands in a larger sense for the way of salvation in Christ—the faith of Jesus Christ, according to Paul, effects what the works of the Law could not: it alone makes Jewish Christians righteous before God.

In his discussion of salvation, Paul uses a verb (*dikaioun*) that is used in the SEPTUAGINT in the passive voice to render Hebrew expressions that mean "be righteous" or "become righteous." It makes sense to follow this usage in translating the passive form of the verb (*dikaiousthai*) in Paul. Thus, we may render v. 16, "we know that a person does not become righteous by works of the Law but by the faith of Jesus Christ." The passive form occurs three times in v. 16. It is also found at v. 17, 3:11, 3:24, and 5:4.

Does righteousness (or JUSTIFICATION) by this faith imply that Jewish Christians are not obligated to keep the Law? In v. 17 Paul links seeking to be righteous in Christ with a way of living that leaves Christians open to the charge that they are sinners—sinners because they do not keep the Law. Presumably the party from James leveled this charge at the Jewish Christians at Antioch. Paul's answer to this charge is that if seeking to be righteous in Christ makes Jewish Christians sinners, then Christ himself is an agent of sin. That is, the rhetorical question in v. 17 is a *reductio ad absurdum*. As an argument it has force only if one already accepts Paul's premise that seeking to be righteous in Christ rules out seeking to be righteous by the Law. The party from James no doubt sees righteousness in Christ and righteousness in the Law as compatible. Paul doesn't. He "knows" that God commissioned him, a Jew, to evangelize and live among gentiles, without imposing the Law on them. This probably explains why he is so certain about the distinction between the righteousness provided in Christ—which both Jews and gentiles have—and the righteousness of the Law (which, according to Phil 3:6, he once had). According to v. 18, Paul would make himself a sinner before God only if he were to reinstate the requirements of the Law (*the very things that I once tore down*). The same holds for the Jewish Christians at Antioch, who have in fact reinstated those requirements, thus making themselves sinners before God by abandoning the righteousness they have in Christ—a righteousness constituted in part by their table fellowship with gentile Christians.

Verses 19-20 take another approach. In Christ, believers "die" to the Law, just as they die *with Christ* to the present world order (6:14; cf. Rom 7:4-6). They die *through the law* (v. 19) because Christ's death took place through the Law, namely, through the *curse of the law* (3:13). Thus, to be a Christian is to be *crucified with Christ*, which transfers one to the sphere of being in Christ. Only by dying with Christ does one come to experience eschatological life, signified in v. 19 by the Hellenistic Jewish expression *live to God* (cf. 4 Macc 7:19; 16:25). It follows from this interpretation of Christ's death that Christians are righteous because Christ lives through them and that they owe no obedience to the Law because they have died to it.

Paul closes off this argument with another *reductio ad absurdum*. If righteousness before God could be achieved through the Law, *then Christ died for nothing* (v. 21). Paul's point is that since Christ obviously did not die for nothing, righteousness must not be "from the Law." But this argument does not refute the view that righteousness before God depends on both the Law (as norm) and Christ (as source of atonement and moral power in the Spirit), which may be the theological opinion of the party from James (and the Circumcisers at Galatia).

Central Apostolic Argument, 3:1–4:31

3:1-5. Faith mediates the Spirit. With this paragraph Paul addresses the Galatians directly, suggests they have been *bewitched*, and gives some important clues about what he understands the "other gospel" (1:7) in Galatians to be. The passage moves from a question about the past to an inference about the present. The Galatians know that they received *the Spirit* (when Paul first preached to them) because they heard and believed, not because they began practicing the Law (v. 2). *Therefore*—the Greek text of v. 5 contains the illative particle *oun*—they should draw the same conclusion about the basis of their present experience of the Spirit: "Does the one who supplies you with the Spirit and works miracles among you do so because of the works of the Law or because you heard and believed [the gospel]?" (author trans.). The implied answer is that God's present provision of the Spirit and its mighty works has nothing to do with whether or not the Galatians keep the Law. Or, as vv. 3-4 suggest, if the Galatians continue on their present course with the Law they will end up with the flesh and, presumably, lose the Spirit (see FLESH AND SPIRIT).

This is the first argument aimed directly at the Galatians in their own situation, and it suggests that the Circumcisers told the Galatians that doing the Law mediates the power of the Spirit.

3:6-14. Faith brings the Spirit as the blessing of Abraham. In vv. 6-14 Paul develops a somewhat intricate argument to show that the blessing of the Spirit comes through the death of Christ alone, apart from the Law. First, he cites a scripture text that makes "faith" a basis for "righteousness" (Gen 15:6 quoted in v. 6) and concludes from this that *those who believe* (lit. "those from faith") are Abraham's children (v. 7). He then uses this bit of exegesis to interpret another, more famous, scriptural promise about all the gentiles (or "nations") being blessed through Abraham (Gen 12:3; cf. 18:18). By associating Gen 15:6 and Gen 12:3, Paul is able to draw the conclusion he needs to make his point: the blessing of Abraham on the gentiles belongs to those who share Abraham's faith, that is, to gentiles like the Galatians (v. 9).

But what is the blessing of Abraham? Since Paul seems to interpret this blessing in an all-encompassing sense in Rom 4:13 (as "inheriting the world"), we should perhaps not limit it in any way here. But the explicit content that Paul identifies as the substance of the promise to Abraham is *the Spirit* (v. 14). And we should note here the following implication of this identification: The blessing of Abraham is fulfilled among the Galatians in their present experience, namely, in God's ongoing gift of the Spirit to them, which includes *miracles* (v. 5).

Verses 10-14 develop the argument from Abraham in a way that relates that blessing to two of the letter's central themes: the Law and the cross of Christ. While it was a well-established Jewish tradition, based in the Bible, that faithfulness to the Law brings God's blessing, Paul radically disjoins the two. Those who *rely on* the Law fall *under a curse*, the Law's own curse upon the unrighteous (v. 10). This happens because "in the Law (i.e., in the sphere of the Law) no one is righteous before God" (v. 11a, author trans.; on the translation "no one is righteous," see the comments on 2:16). Paul does not attempt to prove this by arguing that no one can keep the Law perfectly. Instead he quotes the words of Hab 2:4 as proof that no one in the Law is righteous before God. *"The one who is righteous will live by faith,"* Paul declares (v. 11b), citing a version of Hab 2:4 that does not contain the possessive pronoun "his" (as the Hebrew scriptures do) or "my" (as the LXX does) before the word "faith." Nor does Paul mark it as a quotation from scripture by introducing it with a phrase such as "as it is written." He apparently expects the Galatians to recognize the words, probably because he himself made this text central to his foundation teaching (cf. Rom 1:17).

Scripture prophesies that the righteous person will *live by faith* (v. 11b). The Law, by contrast, *does not rest on faith* (v. 12a). As proof Paul now cites another scripture text, again without identifying it as such: "The one who does them [the works of the Law] will live by them" (v. 12b; author trans.). This is a paraphrase of Lev 18:5, a passage sometimes echoed in Jewish formulations of the Law's promise of life (cf. Neh 9:29; Ezek 20:13; Luke 10:28; CD 3:16; PssSol 14:3). The Circumcisers might have quoted this text to the Galatians as proof that doing the Law mediates eschatological life (the ongoing power of the Spirit). By contrasting Hab 2:4 and Lev 18:5, Paul demands that the Galatians choose between *faith* (meaning "Christian faith") and *works of the Law*, which comprise two ways of relating to God. The Circumcisers no doubt integrated these two ways by combining faith with works of the law. If so, Paul sharply distinguishes what they join. Nevertheless, nothing in the contrast itself, but only the preceding argumentation (in vv. 1-5 and vv. 6-9) and the weight of Paul's apostolic authority, are likely to persuade the Galatians to treat Hab 2:4 (and not Lev 18:5) as the definitive biblical word for the new age.

In v. 13 Paul declares that Christ *redeemed us from the curse of the law by becoming a curse for us.* According to the Law-text cited here (Deut 21:23), victims of crucifixion are an abomination (or "curse") in God's sight. Paul equates this curse with the curse of the Law already mentioned in v. 10. The death of Christ lifts this curse *for us*, a phrase that refers to those under the Law's curse and therefore may refer strictly to Jews.

With the transference of the curse to Christ the blessing of Abraham in Christ can flow to the gentiles (v. 14a) so that *we might receive the promise of the Spirit through faith* (v. 14b). Paul doesn't explain how the lifting of the curse from the unrighteous in the Law lets the blessing flow to the gentiles, with the reciprocal effect that "we" (which must mean we Jews who believe in Christ) receive the promise of the Spirit by faith. The Galatians are to take Paul's authoritative word for it. But they may also find his interpretation appealing, since it implies that Jewish Christians (such as the Circumcisers) enjoy the life of the Spirit solely by faith and only because God has first given this blessing to gentiles (such as the Galatians)!

3:15-18. Christ the sole heir of Abraham. Paul supplements his argument about how the blessing of Abraham (the Spirit) comes by comparing the Abrahamic covenant to a will. Even in human affairs it is illegal to add a codicil to a covenant (or a "will") once it has been ratified. God ratified the covenant with Abraham, in which God promised the inheritance to Abraham's offspring, long before God gave the Law. Therefore God could not, with justice, add the Law as a kind of later codicil, thus making the inheritance conditional upon keeping the Law. Since the very idea that God might attempt such an unfair thing is blasphemous, Paul qualifies his argument from the outset by explaining that he is going to speak "like a (mere) human being" (which is what v. 15 literally says).

The aim of vv. 15-18 is to reinforce Paul's contention that the Law has no say about the promise God made to Abraham, which Paul has already indicated is the *promise of the Spirit* (v. 14). God's promise to Abraham concerned an inheritance for a single *offspring* (v. 16), Paul says, quoting God's promissory words, *"And to your offspring,"* in Gen 13:15 (cf. Gen 12:7). In fact, the word *offspring* can be used in both the collective and the singular sense. In Gen 13:15 it is used as a collective (meaning "descendants"), but Paul interprets it as singular and takes it as referring to Christ. This exegetical move makes Christ the sole heir of the promise, thus excluding all those "in the Law" along with everyone else in the world! In 3:22-29 Paul explains how others come to be included with Christ as heirs of the promise.

3:19-22. The purpose of the Law. After disconnecting the Law from the promise and attributing to the Law the power only to curse and not to bless, Paul must explain why God gave the Law in the first place. He offers a brief and rather obscure answer to this question in vv. 19b-20. The Law was given "for transgressions" (v. 19b, author's trans.), which may mean to inhibit them. But, in view of Rom 5:20, it might mean "to create them" by making sin legally punishable as transgression. The remainder of vv. 19-20 poses an exegetical conundrum that continues to vex interpreters. Paul is perhaps arguing that the Law came only indirectly from God and therefore enjoys a lower status than the covenant with Abraham (which God made directly with Abraham).

In vv. 21-22 Paul seeks to dispel any impression that he views the Law as an opponent of the promise. The opponent is sin, which dominates all things (v. 22). The Law was never endowed with any power to *make alive*, hence it is not able to produce righteousness in a sin-enslaved world (cf. 1:4, *the present evil age*).

3:23-29. Becoming heirs with Christ. Having offered a brief defense of the Law in order to defend his own interpretation of its place in history, Paul now takes up an unfinished line of argument begun in 3:15-18. How can anyone become an heir of the promise to Abraham if Christ himself is the sole heir (3:15; cf. 3:19)?

Those under the Law are enslaved to sin. During this enslavement the Law serves as a kind of "guardian" (*paidagōgos*) until the arrival of Christian faith (3:23-25). In the Greco-Roman world the *paidagōgos* had charge of a boy during his minority, that is, until the boy came into his inheritance (see the comments on 4:1-11). Thus, being under the Law's guardianship, Paul says, coincides with the time of *waiting* for the inheritance. But now that *faith* has arrived (v. 25), this time of waiting under the guardianship of the Law is over.

The arrival of *faith* with Jesus Christ has transformed the Galatians into God's children (lit., "sons of God"). Through baptism they have "put on Christ" (RSV) and become "one" in Christ (vv. 27-28). That makes them part of the "one offspring" of Abraham, and in this process of unification with Christ they become heirs of the promise given to Christ alone (v.29).

4:1-11. The limited time of the Law. In 4:1-11 Paul explains what he meant by saying (in 3:23-25) that being under the Law is like being under a guardian. To be an heir during one's minority (childhood) is to be in a position no better than a slave, without access to the goods of one's inheritance. During this time the heir (typically a male) is under various overseers until a time set by his father. In the same way, Paul says, Jews and gentiles alike lived in a period of minority until the time of fulfillment set by God. But now that the *fullness of time* [has] *come* (v. 4), those redeemed by God through divine *adoption* receive the goods of the *inheritance*, namely, the Spirit itself (vv. 6-7).

In vv. 8-11 Paul equates serving the Law with bondage to the *elemental spirits* of the world. Many Jews in Paul's day attributed cosmic wisdom to the Law. Perhaps the Circumcisers taught the Galatians that by observing the Jewish calendar, informed by the Law's cosmic wisdom, Christians may live safely and prosperously in the present age (see v. 10). Paul calls this a path to cosmic bondage. Accepting the Law only brings the Galatians right back to the situation of futility in which Paul found them, when they were *enslaved to beings that by nature are not gods* (v. 8).

4:12-20. A "pathos" appeal. In 4:12-20 Paul makes an emotional appeal, what ancient rhetoricians called an argument from "pathos." He reminds the Galatians of the kindness and honor they bestowed upon him during his first visit (vv. 13-16), and wonders whether his letter, with its blunt truthfulness, will make him their enemy (v. 16). He attributes ulterior motives to the Circumcisers (v. 17) and describes himself, by contrast, as a mother who is perplexed by the fact that she is in labor pangs all over again with the same child (vv. 19-20)!

4:21-31. The law bears children for slavery. Before issuing apostolic exhortation to the community, Paul presents an allegorical interpretation of the story of Abraham's two wives and two sons. Paul identifies the slave wife HAGAR with the covenant of the Law from Mount SINAI. The Law, as a slavewoman, bears children for slavery. These enslaved children comprise the present Jerusalem, which stands for the Jewish people as a whole. The freewoman SARAH (who represents God's covenant with Abraham) stands, allegorically, for the heavenly Jerusalem, where the free children of the Spirit are born. This Jerusalem is *our mother* (v. 26), Paul says, including himself and the Galatians (v. 28) among her children.

The Mosaic covenant and the Abrahamic covenant are not only distinct, their children are at odds with each other: *But just as at that time the child who was born according to the flesh persecuted the child who was born according to the Spirit, so it is now also* (v. 29, quoting Gen 21:9), a citation that the Galatians are likely to construe as a call to expel the Circumcisers from their midst.

Apostolic Exhortation, 5:1–6:10

5:1-12. Stand fast in freedom. The logically inseparable themes of SLAVERY and FREEDOM have been running through the letter since the beginning (see 1:4; 2:4-5; 3:13, 22-25; 4:1-11, 21-31). According to Paul, Christ's death liberates people from slavery to sin. It redeems those under the Law from the Law's curse on the unrighteous. At the same time it also establishes freedom from the Law as a way of righteousness, an idea first broached in chap. 2 (2:4-5; 2:15-21). In v. 1 Paul calls the Galatians to stand fast in this (threefold) freedom to which Christ has set them free. He follows up this basic exhortation with a series of warnings (vv. 2-6). Accepting circumcision removes one from the sphere of Christ's blessing (v. 2). It also obligates a person to keep the entire Law (v. 3), which the Galatians may not realize if the Circumcisers have so far insisted only on circumcision and the Jewish calendar (cf. 4:10 and 6:12-13). In v. 4 Paul reiterates the point of v. 2, telling the Galatians that by becoming "righteous in the Law" (author trans.; on this translation, see the comments on 2:16) they lose Christ and fall from grace.

Next Paul describes his own view of Christian existence in ways that prepare for the ethical exhortation to follow. *For through the Spirit, by faith, we eagerly wait for the hope of righteousness* (v. 5). The words *hope of righteousness* probably mean the hope of salvation that belongs to righteousness and not the hope of becoming righteous. Thus far Paul has described the ethics of this righteousness only once. In 2:17 the expression *our effort to be justified in Christ* describes the way of life that Paul has adopted by giving up the practice of the Law in order to be in communion with gentile Christians. In v. 6 he defines the ethics of this righteousness as *faith working through love*. Paul would probably call the originally integrated community life at Antioch (2:12a) an expression of this love-working faith. In 5:13–6:10 he elaborates on his view that "love" is the basic form and guiding principle of righteousness in Christ.

Verses 7-12 resemble the "pathos appeal" of 4:12-20 in emotional tone and strategy. Paul celebrates the Galatians' beginnings in Christ, expresses confidence about their future, and blames the Circumcisers for the Galatians' defection from *the truth*. It may be that one of the Circumcisers is *confusing* the Galatians by telling them that in other churches Paul himself preaches circumcision (vv. 10-11).

5:13-26. Love as the way of freedom in the Spirit. Verses 13-26 show how the theme of *love* is related to basic themes of the earlier argumentation, namely, *freedom*, *the Law*, *the cross*, and *the Spirit*. Believers have died in Christ to the Law as a way of righteousness (2:17-20). The resultant freedom in Christ is to take ethical form as serving one another in love (v. 13). This is what it means to "walk by the Spirit" (v. 16 RSV; cf. v. 25). Opposed to this way of living is what Paul terms *the flesh* and its desires (v. 17), which he personifies as a kind of independent power. The passions of the flesh produce the *works of the flesh* described in vv. 19-21. These passions are in opposition to the Spirit, which produces the *fruit* described in vv. 22-23. The opposition of the flesh and the Spirit hinders Christians from doing what they *want* (v. 17). That means that the choice created for them by their freedom is to follow one of these two powers (cf. v. 13). If they *live by the Spirit* (i.e., yield to its desires, following the principle of love), they will not satisfy the passions of the flesh (v. 16).

Walking by the Spirit in love fulfills a basic intent of the Law (v. 14). In saying this Paul cites Lev 19:18, *You shall love your neighbor as yourself.* Early Christians identified Lev 19:18 as a summary of the Law, having learned to do so from Judaism (and especially from Jesus' own prophetic Jewish teaching). Paul is not saying that Christians must show love because the Law tells them to, but that the love commanded by the Spirit is in continuity with a basic interest of the Law itself. Dying with Christ (see the comments on 2:19-20) crucifies the flesh with its passions and cravings (v. 24). This enables believers to fulfill this way of love, which is embodied in the *fruit of the Spirit* (vv. 22-23). And, with a touch of wry humor, Paul comments that *there is no law* against such things as *love, joy, peace, patience, kindness,* and so forth.

6:1-10. Concluding exhortations. The ethical exhortation in vv. 1-10 presents additional and more specific admonitions. The community is to treat those who sin with gentleness and humility, renouncing spiritual rivalry (vv. 1-5). By bearing one another's burdens they will *fulfill the law of Christ* (v. 2). Paul does not define this law. Perhaps he expects the Galatians to recognize it as something he taught them about during his first visit. The law of Christ is probably the way of Christ exemplified in Christ's self-giving love (the way of Christ *who . . . gave himself for me,* 2:20; who "did not please himself," Rom 15:3; and who "became poor" for the sake of others, 2 Cor 8:9).

In vv. 7-10 Paul takes up the themes of the flesh and the Spirit once more (cf. 5:13-26), encouraging the Galatians to *sow to the Spirit* in order to inherit *eternal life* (cf. 5:21). Paul defines *sowing to the Spirit* in ethical terms as *doing what is right* (v. 9), which means *work for the good of all, and especially for those of the family of faith* (v. 10). The Greek expression behind *work for the good* is typically used in Hellenistic Jewish Greek to designate assistance to the poor, and this nuance (which echoes 2:10) should be heard in v. 10 as well.

A Personal Postscript, 6:11-18

The concluding postscript indicates that Paul followed the custom of having a trained writer (an *amanuensis*) take down the letter. But now at the end, as was also common, Paul inscribes something in his own (evidently clumsy) hand (v. 11). In this last word to the Galatians, Paul claims that the Circumcisers themselves don't even keep the Law (v. 13). Perhaps the Circumcisers think that only certain requirements of the Law (above all regarding CIRCUMCISION but apparently also the Jewish calendar; see 4:10) are obligatory for gentile Christians. In that case, Paul may be alleging, the Circumcisers prove themselves unfaithful to the very Law they are promoting. For circumcision (as Paul says in 5:3) obligates one to keep the entire Law, not just certain parts of it.

Paul also accuses the Circumcisers of seeking to avoid suffering for the cross (v. 12) and being interested only in their own glory ("boasting" in the Galatians' circumcised flesh, v. 13). He contrasts himself with them by declaring that he boasts only in *the cross of . . . Christ* (v. 14). The cross, Paul says, means death to the world (v. 14) and establishes a *new creation* in which *neither circumcision nor uncircumcision* counts for anything (v. 15; cf. 5:6). In Christ's death the present world itself also dies, at least as far as those in Christ are concerned. This implies that the community of those in Christ is the locus of the new creation.

Righteousness in this new creation constitutes itself in the erasure of distinctions between Jew and Gentile, male and female, slave and free (6:15; 3:28). These distinctions represent hierarchies by which the present age is ordered. But they come to an end in the death of the present world through Christ's crucifixion. Thus Paul closes his letter on a revolutionary note, declaring that the new social order, which embodies the apocalyptic hope of new creation, has already dawned in Christ. And the church is to be the place in the world where this new social order is sown.

Ephesians

Frank Stagg   [MCB 1217-1225]

Introduction

Ephesians is the most comprehensive writing in the NT on the church, both goal and instrument in God's *eternal purpose* to create in Christ Jesus *one new humanity*. It was *through the cross* that God broke down *the dividing wall* between Jew and gentile, replacing *hostility* with *peace*.

Opening with a doxology praising God for carrying through his redemptive purpose which antedates *the foundation of the world* and prayer for the illumination and empowering of the readers, the letter continues with an exposition of the origin, nature, and mission of the CHURCH, with a call to unity, freedom from old vices, and practice of virtues proper to God's people.

Authorship and Destination

PAUL as author is explicit in the first word of the text, supported by autobiographical references to bonds, afflictions, and *chains* (3:1, 13; 4:1; 6:20). Matters of style, word usage, and theology leave scholars divided as to whether authentically from Paul, a pseudonym, or an insoluble problem (see Tolbert 1990 and Kümmel 1975, 357-63). It does follow that the letter is from Paul or from some cogent, unknown writer with amazing insight into Paul's mind and experience.

No theory of destination is compelling. The superscription "To the Ephesians" was probably added when letters of Paul were first collected and published as a corpus. MARCION (ca. 140) listed this letter as "To the Laodiceans," probably influenced by Col 4:16. The words *in Ephesus* (1:1) are absent from the earliest known manuscripts (including p46, Vaticanus, and Sinaiticus) and were unknown to Tertullian and Origen, in which no place name appears. Nothing in the letter implies Ephesus. TYCHICUS, bearer of the letter (6:21), may have been authorized to insert a place name if the letter was to be read in various churches, but this is speculation.

Date

If not from Paul, there are no criteria for dating the letter. If from Paul, either his Caesarean or Roman imprisonment is likely. If, as held here, Ephesians is Paul's response to his eviction from the Temple and arrest in JERUSALEM, the likely date is around 60 C.E.

Relationship with Colossians

About one-third of Colossians appears also in Ephesians. Verbal parallels are found throughout the letter with the exception of 2:6-9, 4:5-13, and 5:29-33. Whether by common authorship or not, it is generally recognized that Ephesians is dependent upon Colossians and not vice versa. Both letters feature Christ and the church, differing in focus. In Colossians, Christ is the head of the church; in Ephesians, the church is the body of Christ. These two foci are not mutually exclusive or improbable for the same author, different situations calling for different emphases.

Occasion and Purpose

The theme that dominates Ephesians, God's purpose to reconcile Jews and gentiles to himself and to one another, in Christ Jesus and through the cross, also runs through Paul's undisputed writings, and it is emphatic in Romans and Acts. A flood of light falls upon Romans and Ephesians as well as Acts if it is perceived that Romans was written on the eve of Paul's visit to Jerusalem (cf. 15:25) and Ephesians after his eviction from the Temple and arrest leading to years of imprisonment in CAESAREA and ROME.

The *dividing wall* seen as *broken down* (2:14) seems to echo Paul's eviction from the Temple when charged that he has "actually brought Greeks into the temple and has defiled this holy place" (Acts 21:28). A wall separated the Court of the gentiles from that of the Jews, with plaques warning that anyone of another nation caught beyond that wall would be responsible for his death which would follow. That wall stood materially until the destruction of the Temple by Roman armies in 70 C.E.; but to Ephesians, that wall was in effect already broken down in that what it represented was rejected.

Before reading Ephesians, it is illuminating to read in Acts 20–28 Paul's last-recorded visit to Jerusalem and also Paul's own compulsion to make that visit as anticipated in 1 Cor 16:1-4, 2 Cor 8-9, and Rom 15:22-33 (see Stagg 1990, 259–78).

Wanting to go to Spain by way of Rome, Paul felt compelled to go first to Jerusalem with an offering called a *koinōnia* from MACEDONIA and ACHAIA for the poor among the *saints* in Jerusalem (Rom 15:26). Paul's strategy was to get gentile churches to give not only money but themselves to the Jews (2 Cor 8–9) and to get the Jewish saints in Jerusalem to accept not only the money but the gentile Christians who gave it (Rom 15:31). Thus, Paul's mission to Jerusalem intended both to provide relief for the poor and to unite Jew and gentile in Christ. Instead, the mission led to his eviction from the Temple and the closing of Temple doors not only to gentiles but also to a Jew such as Paul (Acts 21:30).

Paul was held prisoner for two years in Caesarea and under house arrest in Rome for at least two years (Acts 28:30). It is plausible that sometime during those years he looked back upon that traumatic experience in Jerusalem and wrote his classic on the Church. At the heart of Ephesians is the vision of "the broken wall" (Barth 1959). Along with the sign of the veil in the Temple "torn in two, from top to bottom" (Matt 27:51) stands that in Ephesians of "the broken wall." Much of the gospel is dramatized in these two signs.

For Further Study

In the *Mercer Dictionary of the Bible*: BAPTISM; CHURCH; COLOSSIANS, LETTER TO THE; EPHESIANS, LETTER TO THE; EPHESUS; MARCION; PAUL; RECONCILIATION; ROMAN EMPIRE; SLAVERY IN THE NT; SATAN IN THE NT.

In other sources: M. Barth, *The Broken Wall*; *Ephesians*; W. G. Kümmel, *Introduction to the N.T.*; N. H. Keathley, ed., *With Steadfast Purpose*; J. A. Robinson, *St. Paul's Epistle to the Ephesians*; A. Van Roon, *The Authenticity of Ephesians*.

Commentary

An Outline

I. Salutation, 1:1-2
II. Doxology and Prayer, 1:3-23
III. The Unity of All Humankind in Christ, 2:1–3:21

IV. Practical Exhortations, 4:1–6:20
V. Personal Words and Benediction, 6:21-24

Salutation, 1:1-2

The greeting is similar to that in Colossians, the most striking difference being the absence of a place name, except in later manuscripts. There is no compelling explanation for this absence. Origen took the phrase *tois ousin* ("those being") in an ontological sense, that is, "the saints who truly are!" The NRSV mg. reading is possible: "saints who are also faithful."

Doxology and Prayer, 1:3-23

1:3-14. Doxology. These twelve verses consist of *one sentence* in the Greek text. They fall into three strophes, each ending with *to the praise of his glory* (vv. 6, 12, 14). A trinitarian motif may be implied, for the first strophe praises *the God and Father of our Lord Jesus Christ*, the second praises *Christ*, and the third praises the *Holy Spirit*. This could argue for a post-Pauline development, but it is anticipated in 2 Cor 13:13. No formal doctrine of trinity appears, for the letter begins and closes with *God our (the) Father and the Lord Jesus Christ*, with no reference to the Holy Spirit.

The first strophe (vv. 3-6) traces our calling to a holy and blameless life and destiny as God's children to God's having elected us *before the foundation of the world*. ELECTION and destiny do not imply unilateral determination; they simply mean that God calls us before we are able to answer.

The second strophe (vv. 7-12) is laden with heavy theological terms about God's accomplishments *in Christ*. *Redemption* is liberation from the bondage of sin. This liberation is effected through Christ's *blood*, his life given for us. *Forgiveness* is not indulgence; it is not only acceptance of the sinner but overcoming of *trespasses*, all traceable to God's *grace*. In Christ is seen God's *plan for the fullness of time*, that is, *to gather up all things in him*.

The third strophe (vv. 13-14) praises the HOLY SPIRIT, the present possession of whom gives us the *pledge* (*arrabōn* = a down payment making a transaction binding) of our full redemption as God's people.

1:15-23. Prayer. This is one long sentence in Greek. It is a prayer that the readers be illuminated so as to know *the hope* implied in God's call, *the riches* of the *inheritance* God has offered, and the *power* which is inherently God's and which expresses itself in overcoming all resistance. It is the prayer that the readers experience within themselves the very power that *raised [Jesus] from the dead*.

The Unity of All Humankind in Christ, 2:1–3:21

Chapters 2–3 form the theological base for the CHURCH as the new humanity composed of Jew and gentile, God's new creation in Christ. With this is Paul's understanding of his own ministry to the gentiles and his prayer for his readers.

2:1-10. From death to life. Two foci appear: *You were dead. . . . But God . . . made us alive together with Christ* (vv. 1, 4-5). The emphasis is upon God's act of GRACE in giving new life to gentiles; but the *You* (v. 1) is expanded to *All of us* (v. 3), Jew and gentile alike, dead in sin until brought to life by God's grace.

In fact, several contrasts appear in this passage: Jew and gentile once dead, now made alive; Jew and gentile once divided, now together; not our work, but God's work; not by good works but for good works.

Trespasses (*paraptomasin*) refer to willful acts of disobedience. *Sins* (*hamartiais*) may refer to failure or "missing the mark," but even this term implies guilt. Sin is not only an act of disobedience, it results in spiritual death (Rom 6:23).

Paul shared the widely held view that powerful, evil spirits under an evil ruler (SATAN) are behind human sin, but this does not imply that we are mere victims and not *disobedient* sinners. He also saw that Jews as well as gentiles followed *the desires of flesh and senses*; but again, they were not merely victims. *Flesh* stands for disposition and life apart from God, with no special reference to the literal flesh (cf. Gal 5:19-21 for "the works of the flesh" as nonsensual as well as sensual). Also, Jews as well as gentiles are seen as *by nature children of wrath* (v. 3). This does not imply that they were mere victims of Adam's sin or of God's anger. "Wrath" to Paul was not God's anger so much as God's letting us follow our own choices even if they lead to our self-destruction (cf. Rom 1:18-32). Sinners "by nature" means that Jew and gentile alike are sinners in their natural state.

But God introduces the positive side of "from death to life." Salvation for gentile and Jew is new life and new life together, grounded in God's rich *mercy*, out of his *great love*, and by his *grace*. Sin and death are the works of Jew and gentile. Life, including life together with God and with one another, is God's act out of his love, mercy, and grace.

Verse 5 may intend that God makes each Jew and gentile alive *with Christ*. Probably it intends that "in the Christ" (so in p^{46}, Vaticanus, et al.), God makes Jew and gentile alive with one another. This parallels the picture in v. 6 (obscured in NRSV): "both raised together and seated together in the heavenlies in Christ Jesus" (author's trans.). This is the major theme of Ephesians. Overcoming hostility between Jew and gentile will *show the immeasurable riches of his grace in kindness toward us in Christ Jesus* (v. 7).

Salvation is *by grace* through the *faith* that is trust; and though not of our own doing, it is *for good works*. Jew and gentile as a new creation is in eternal design and achievement God's *poiema, what he has made us*!

2:11-22. One fresh humanity in Christ. Continuing his "before and after" theme, Paul contrasts the gentile status before Christ and now. They once were called *"the uncircumcision"* by those called *"the circumcision"* (v. 11). Paul himself had once built his faith and practice upon such an arbitrary and superficial distinction. He now exposes it in three Greek words: "in flesh, handmade." It is "in flesh," thus superficial; it is "handmade," thus artificial—a little skin removed with a knife.

The gentile's real privation was not genetic or cultic; it was the alienation from God and thus alienation from the people of God. The privation was not "uncircumcision" or being born gentile; it was being *without Christ*. It was in being *in the world* (a world like this) *without God*. Paul's word is *atheoi*, literally "atheists." Gentiles were not atheists in a philosophical sense; they were strangers to the true God, thus *strangers to the covenants of promise, having no hope*. They had their gods and their hopes; but they did not have "the hope of glory" (Col 1:27).

Verse 13 introduces the mighty newness *in Christ Jesus*. Those once *far off have now been brought near by the blood of Christ*. Again, the union of Jew and gentile in Christ is the overriding theme of Ephesians.

Verses 14-22 comprise the heart of Ephesians. This paragraph seems to look back on Paul's trauma of eviction from the Temple in Jerusalem, charged with having taken uncircumcised gentiles beyond the dividing wall separating the Court of the gentiles from that of the Jews (Acts 21:27-30). Although the wall stood materially until destroyed by Roman soldiers in 70 C.E., Paul saw that Christ Jesus had already in effect broken it down, rejecting the principles upon which it had been built.

Christ himself (*autos*) *is our peace*! This means peace with God, but the emphasis is upon peace between Jew and gentile, for *in his flesh he has made both groups into one*. Jesus not only rejected in words the holiness code that superficially ruled some "clean" and others "unclean" (cf. Mark 7:23); he rejected that code in his actions, touching a leper (Mark 1:41) and eating with "tax gatherers and sinners"

(Luke 15:1-2). He defined his true family in terms not of flesh but of obedience to the will of God (Mark 3:35).

Christ broke down the separating wall when he *abolished the law with its commandments and ordinances* (v. 15). He not only rejected such ordinances as kosher foods and purification rites but also the holiness code that rested upon externals (e.g., Lev 15:19-20; 21:18-24; Deut 23:1-6). He followed the tradition already found in such scriptures as Ps 24:3-6 and Mic 6:8. His holiness code had to do with moral and ethical principles and the attitudes and dispositions behind such principles and actions. When one holiness code replaced another, the dividing wall was broken down. (see HOLY SPIRIT).

Peace was made when Christ created in himself *one new humanity in place of the two* (v. 15). "Fresh" is a better rendering of *kainon* than "new." The church, the body of Christ, is not simply novel; it is a fresh kind of humanity where worldly criteria that separate are replaced by principles that unite. The old humanity was bent on excluding; the new humanity seeks to include.

The *one body* in which Jew and gentile are reconciled (v. 16) is the CHURCH. This is achieved *through the cross*, where the principle of self-serving is overcome by that of self-giving. The Jew-gentile hostility, like every hostility, was based on the self-serving principle. The CROSS is the ultimate in the self-denial which is salvation (Mark 8:34-35; John 12:24-26). The "enmity" (KJV; NRSV *hostility*) that is slain at the cross is life centered upon itself, the sin behind all sins.

The *peace* proclaimed to those *far off* and those *near* is peace between gentile and Jew; but it is first of all peace with God and peace with and within themselves (v. 17). This peace occurs when the love that serves and includes replaces the selfishness that exploits and excludes.

Jews and gentiles now have the same *access* to the Father, through Christ and *in one Spirit* (v. 18). Gone are the old courts, walls, barriers, and doors segregating Jews from gentiles, men from women, and priests from laypersons, as was built into the architecture of the Temple and imposed upon people. The "broken wall" and the "rent veil" mean now that all in Christ and by faith may enter the "Holy of Holies" into the very presence of *the Father*.

Using a political model, gentiles *are no longer strangers and aliens*, foreigners merely tolerated in another's land. They are *citizens with the saints and also members of the household of God* (v. 19). In Christ, Jews and gentiles alike are at home in God's house, unlike Temple discrimination.

The model having the church built upon *the foundation of the apostles and prophets* (v. 20) is seen by some as impossible to Paul, for whom the only possible foundation is Jesus Christ (1 Cor 3:11). The point is weighty and, to many, decisive against Pauline authorship of Ephesians. On the other hand, models are flexible; and different models are not necessarily competing. Ephesians holds to the centrality of Christ, whatever is intended here. *The foundation of the apostles and prophets* is ambiguous. This may intend either the apostles and prophets themselves as the foundation, or the foundation upon which they built. Christ is the unrivaled creator and lord of the church, the model here being *cornerstone*, not a mere ornamental stone but a keystone holding walls together.

Unlike the old Temple with dividing walls and veil, Jews and gentiles in Christ now form a new *holy temple*, built together into *a dwelling place for God* (vv. 21-22). God dwells in the fellowship of His people.

3:1-13. Paul's ministry to the gentiles. In 3:1 Paul began to pray, and then he paused to describe his role in ministry to the gentiles before resuming his prayer in 3:14 (each unit introduced with *Toutou charin*, "because of this"). In effect, vv. 2-13 form a digression, although highly relevant and instructive.

Identifying himself as *prisoner for Christ Jesus for the sake of you Gentiles*, Paul breaks off to give the background against which his prayer is best understood. NRSV obscures by seeing "this cause" (KJV; NRSV *reason*) as explaining Paul's imprisonment rather than why he presumes to pray for the gentiles.

To understand why Paul thus prays for the gentiles requires that they understand his special commission as minister to the gentiles. The explanation revolves around *the mystery* given him *by revelation* and his commission to proclaim the good news of God's eternal purpose to unite Jews and gentiles in Christ.

The commission given Paul translates *oikonomian*, a term for stewardship or management of a house. "Dispensation" (KJV) is misleading when confused with modern dispensational ideas. Paul simply means that the REVELATION given him carries with it a stewardship obligation to proclaim it (see 3:9). *Diakonos* (servant or minister) carries the same idea in v. 7. By the grace of God, Paul has received this revelation and the commission to proclaim it.

Paul calls this revelation a *mystery*, about which he has written briefly (v. 3), presumably in the early part of this letter (see also Col 1:26-27). This mystery is now an open secret, known first to God alone, and then revealed to his servant who is to proclaim it to Jews and gentiles. It is not apparent who were the *holy apostles and prophets* to whom this mystery was revealed. This understanding was offered the Twelve, but for the most part they resisted it (cf. Mark 9:38-41; Acts 1:6; 10:1–11:3; Gal 2:11-14). STEPHEN, PHILIP, and unnamed men from CYPRUS and CYRENE anticipated Paul in this VISION (Acts 6:8–8:1; 8:4-40; 11:20).

Verse 6 states the basic provision of the *mystery*, the union of Jew and gentile in Christ. NRSV interprets, but obscures some powerful wordplay: *gentiles have become fellow heirs, members of the same body, and sharers in the promise* (v. 6). The Greek text has it "heirs with and bodied with and partakers with." The second of these terms is possibly a new coinage, *syssōma* (synsomatic). These three terms strain to stress the oneness of Jew and gentile in Christ.

Verses 7-9 stress the marvel of Paul's part in showing forth the mystery. Of this mystery he became a *servant* (*diakonos*), and this by the *gift of God's grace* given him by the "energizing of his power" (author trans.). Seeing himself as *the very least of all the saints*, he marvels at the grace given him "to proclaim to the gentiles the untraceable (*anexichniaston*) wealth of Christ" (author trans.). He might strike its trail but could not trace it out, so vast it was.

In bringing to light this mystery, hidden in God for ages, *the wisdom of God in its rich variety* now could be made known to *the rulers and authorities in the heavenly places* (v. 10). This "multicolored (*polypoikilos*) wisdom of God" is seen at last *through the church*! Even the heavenly creatures do not understand God's wisdom until the emergence of the church, God's new creation out of hitherto hostile Jews and gentiles.

This great achievement was "according to the purpose of the ages" (NRSV *the eternal purpose*). God has had one plan through the ages, in Christ Jesus thus to unify Jew and gentile in giving them *access to God in boldness and confidence through faith* (vv. 11-12). Now that his readers see that Paul sees his mission to the Jews as God's gracious gift to him, they have no reason to *lose heart* over his sufferings.

3:14-19. Paul's prayer resumed. After several digressions in which Paul describes the mystery he is commissioned to proclaim, with its special relation to gentiles, Paul resumes the prayer begun in 3:1, repeating "For this cause" (*Toutou charin*).

A play on the words *Father* (*patera*) and *family* (*patria*) serves further to stress the theme of oneness. The intention may be "every fatherhood" rather than *family*, God seen as the archetype of all fatherhood. Either way, all peoples are seen as deriving from the same divine fatherhood, thus all "families" are united under "the Father of our Lord Jesus Christ." Although this sexually exclusive language is problematic today, the concern of Ephesians was elsewhere, to overcome ethnic bias.

The prayer is that they be strengthened in their *inner being* as Christ dwells within them. Salvation does not come as an abstraction; it comes only as Christ becomes a transforming presence within the inner self.

Paul next prays that not only may they be *rooted and grounded in love* (v. 17) but that they may be empowered *to comprehend, with all the saints* (v. 18) the love of Christ in its full magnitude: breadth, length, height, and depth. *The love of Christ* may be intended objectively, love *for* Christ, or subjectively, the love Christ has *for us*, presumably the latter. Such understanding is not for "loners," but for those who learn *with all the saints*.

To know the love of Christ is to know *that which surpasses knowledge* (v. 19). Again, here is a play on words, knowing which surpasses knowledge! To "know" the love of Christ is experiential knowledge, and it surpasses cognitive knowledge.

A reply to gnostic claims may appear in v. 19. Christ's love surpasses *knowledge* (*gnosis*) from which gnostics took their name and of which they were so proud. Again, in Christ gentiles and Jews *may be filled with all the fullness* (*plērōma*) *of God*. In Col 1:19, "all the fullness of God" was pleased to dwell in Christ, not in a gnostic hierarchy of eons or emanations. Also, where one is "in

Christ" and Christ dwells in that one, that one is *filled with all the fullness of God* (v. 19; cf. Col 2:10).

3:20-21. Doxology. Paul could not talk about God's grace and his marvelous "plan of the ages" without breaking into prayer and praise. He praises God for his power working within us, achieving *far more than all we can ask or imagine!*

Practical Exhortations, 4:1–6:20

Although theology continues, this section is primarily practical, with attention to the individual life, the life and work of the church, and guiding principles for the extended family: wives/husbands, children/parents, slaves/masters.

4:1-6. Basis for unity. In his capacity as *the prisoner in the Lord*, Paul calls for life worthy of *the calling* by which the readers were *called*. Salvation in Christ is our *calling* (*klesis*) or vocation. Initiative always is with God: creation, revelation, redemption. Calling and ELECTION refer to the same thing, divine initiative. God's calling opens the option, it does not dictate the response.

Those in Christ ought to be characterized by *humility and gentleness, with patience.* Humility was despised in the Greek world, proper to slaves alone. In the NT, servanthood and humility are seen as virtues, exemplified in Jesus and proper to his followers (John 13:4-5; Phil 2:3ff.).

Bearing with one another in love, is best rendered "holding back" or "forbearing," recognizing the fact that we tend to antagonize one another and strike back. It is *love* that gives us the disposition and strength to hold back.

Love demands more than simply holding back; it requires that we make every effort "to guard" (*terein*) *the unity of the Spirit in the bond of peace* (v. 3). Though unity is the divine provision, it is not unilaterally bestowed. It belongs to Christian vocation. *Peace* like *shalom* is well-being under the sovereignty of God.

Seven (the number for perfection) unities are named, in three groups: *one body, one Spirit, one hope; one Lord, one faith, one baptism; one God and Father of all* (vv. 4-6). The *one body* is the church, the body of Christ. Only context is clue to whether Spirit or the human spirit is intended. The *one hope* is "Christ in you" (Col 1:27). The one Lord is Christ. *One faith* is not one creed but one trust or faith commitment. *One baptism* is not only the one initiation rite but the commitment it signifies. *One God* is not only affirmation of the MONOTHEISM basic to OT and NT, but also the ultimate ground for the unifying of humanity.

4:7-16. Diversity in unity. The ascended Christ as prime minister of the church gives gifts of grace, varying with the individual, designed to equip all the saints for ministry. The receiving church is to be the serving church, both means and goal in the purpose of God.

The quotation, apparently from Ps 68:18, is freely adapted. The psalm celebrates the triumph of "the God of Sinai" as he came into "the holy place" and "ascended the high mount," that is, "the sanctuary," the "temple at Jerusalem." He did so "leading captives" and "receiving gifts," changed here to *gave gifts*. In Ephesians,

Christ both *ascended* and *descended*, the order unclear. The descent may be the incarnate experience leading to his death, the ascent being the resurrection and ascension. What is clear is that the descending and ascending one is the same. Christ is not dead but alive; not absent but present; not ghostly but embodied; not passive but active in the life and ministry of the church, his body.

Verses 11-16 form a classic statement as to the ministry of the church. Christ is *the Minister*. He gives to the church its various ministries, *some . . . apostles, some prophets, some evangelists, some pastors and teachers*. This catalogue is illustrative rather than complete, as comparison with other catalogues shows (Rom 12:6ff.; 1 Cor 12:28). There is no mention of bishops, presbyters, or deacons! These, too, although unmentioned here, belong to the equipping ministers of the Church. They are servants, not rulers.

The function of equipping ministers is *to equip the saints for the work of ministry* (v. 12). All in Christ are *saints*, ones set apart in Christ (with no implication of special sanctity). All are called to ministry. The whole Church is in intention the ministering body of Christ. Ministries vary with the gifts present in the members of the Body. The total ministry includes Christ, the equipping ministers, and all the saints.

The Church is intended to be both servant and minister and the goal of all ministry, itself "a perfect man, unto the measure of the stature of the fullness of Christ" (v. 13, author trans.). Unity and maturity are marks proper to the body of Christ, with each member functioning in terms of its role, and all members blended into one growing body. The saints are not to remain *children*, vulnerable to deceit; but they are to reach maturity and unity in variety. *Speaking the truth in love* could be rendered "holding the truth in love" or "being true in love."

4:17-24. Former vices to shun. Those *in the Lord* are no longer to live like *gentiles*, seen here as pagan (the readers were ethnically gentiles). The gentile plight was living *in the futility of their minds*. Alienated from God, their minds were not only uninformed but *darkened*, incapacitated and immoral. Those in Christ are called to a new quality of life, new and constantly *renewed*, a new creation in *the likeness of God in true righteousness and holiness*.

4:25–5:2. Sins of the spirit that destroy unity. A catalogue of wrong feelings, attitudes, and dispositions is matched in each case with positives. *Falsehood* is to be replaced with *the truth*. Since we are *members of one another*, in being true or false to others, we are that to ourselves. *Be angry but do not sin*? How? Anger is recognized as a reality; it is what we do with it that matters. To *let the sun go down on your anger* is to *make room for the devil*. It is to let anger eat away at us, even while we sleep. Stealing is to be replaced with honest work, providing not only for ourselves but *to have something to share with the needy*.

Evil talk is any talk that is like inedible fruit (*sapros*; cf. Matt 12:33, where "bad fruit" is not rotten but the wrong kind). In its place is to be talk *useful for building up* and for *giving grace*. There is no place for bitterness, wrath, anger, wrangling, slander, and malice. Instead, we should be kind, tenderhearted, and for-giving. All this follows, if as imitators of God, we *live in love, as Christ loved us.* This is the fragrant *sacrifice* to be offered to God.

5:3-20. Sins of sensuality that corrupt and degrade. Gross acts of sensuality like *fornication, impurity,* and *greed,* seen as pagan, are to be so far removed that they are not even mentioned among the *saints.* Even *obscene, silly, and vulgar talk,* making light of sensuality, is *out of place.*

The warning in v. 5 is severe (cf. 1 Cor 6:9-10). The Greek text may be im-perative, "This know ye, knowing" or indicative, "This ye know, knowing." The warning that *no fornicator or impure person, or one who is greedy* (worship of things seen as a form of idolatry) will inherit the kingdom of Christ is not softened. This is impossible to assimilate into the soteriology that equates salvation with what is perceived as confessional orthodoxy. For the most part, it is ignored as are such warnings as attributed to Jesus (cf. Matt 7:15-27; 25:31-46). Verse 5 is weighted on the side of orthopraxy rather than orthodoxy.

Light and *darkness* are the themes through vv. 6-14. The gentile readers were once *darkness,* but now they are *light* and *the children of light* (v. 8; cf. Matt 5:14-16). As in biblical usage generally, light and darkness are moral and ethical terms, not cognitive. A benighted person is evil, not necessarily ignorant; and an en-lightened person is good, not simply informed. To walk in darkness is to live in evil. To walk in light is to live in goodness.

Light and darkness are disclosed by their *fruit.* The fruit of light includes what is *good and right and true* (cf. Gal 5:22). Darkness, in fact, is *unfruitful* in that it bears no edible fruit.

It is the function of light to give light, exposing darkness and turning darkness into light (vv. 13-14). The darkness to be exposed are the *shameful* acts of darkness. The children of light are to be in action what they are in nature. The DEAD SEA SCROLLS belonged to a priestly group who saw themselves as "the sons of light," but they were hiding their light in their withdrawal at QUMRAN. Jesus countered as he addressed an ordinary group, saying: "You are the light of the world . . . let your light shine before others" (Matt 5:14-16).

Although light and darkness are moral and ethical terms, they are not indifferent to wisdom or foolishness. The children of light are to be *wise* and not *foolish* (vv. 15-17). For example, getting drunk with wine is not simply evil; it is foolish. Getting *filled with the Spirit* and "singing songs to God in praise and thanksgiving" (cf. Col 3:16) is both good and wise.

5:21–6:9. The extended family. This passage is a domestic code for the extended family: wife-husband, child-parent, slave-master. Parallels with commonali-ties and differences are found in Col 3:18–4:1; 1 Pet 2:13–3:7; Titus 2:1-10; and 1 Tim 2:1ff., 2:8ff.; 3:1ff., 3:8ff.; 5:17ff.; 6:1-2. The code in Ephesians seems to be built upon that in Colossians.

The extended family in the Greco-Roman world gave rise to codes designed to regulate relationships within domestic and civil structures of society, traceable in Aristotle (*Politics* 1.3) and Philo (*Hypothetica* 7.14). No direct dependence upon such codes is traceable here, but some influence is probable. The NT codes offer moral and ethical principles that should humanize and Christianize these relationships (Stagg and Stagg 1978, chap. 8).

Ephesians 5:21 is linked grammatically to what precedes, but in intention it governs what follows: *Be subject to one another out of reverence for Christ*. This applies to all who are in Christ; it is egalitarian; and it follows Jesus' basic law that, contrary to the pagan disposition to rule, his followers are to find their greatness in servanthood (Mark 9:33-37; 10:35-45). All codes must be subordinated to this principle.

All codes are historically conditioned, as here. Jewish and Roman law decreed that the husband was head of the family; and both laws gave slave owners legal authority over slaves. These were legal realities, whatever their injustices. The early church had no worldly power sufficient then to change such structures and laws. It did have the disposition to bring them under the claims of Christ.

Codes at best intend to articulate and apply values and principles in a given historical situation. They are never one and the same as such principles, and they are not failsafe. For example, kindness is a principle, universally and eternally valid. How kindness is expressed can never be defined in any code. Because all codes are historically conditioned and by nature not one and the same as that which they seek to apply, they are not to be uprooted from one situation and imposed upon another. Codes, like wineskins (Mark 2:22), are to be replaced as necessary if the "wine" of principle or value is to be preserved.

5:22-33. Wives-husbands. *Wives, be subject to your husbands* (NRSV) is a questionable translation, for there is no verb in the Greek text of v. 22. *Be subject* translates a participle in v. 21, and this carries over to v. 22, with imperatival force. In form it is middle voice and probably middle in force, "subject yourselves" instead of passive, "be subject." If middle voice, at least wives are recognized as responsible and competent to shape their side of the marital relationship, not subordinates to be commanded. If applied, v. 21 would call upon the husband to do likewise, with mutual choice of voluntary submission, each to the other.

In affirming husband as *head of the wife*, the code follows the legal structures then obtaining, not the ideal cited by Jesus from Gen 2:24: " 'For this reason a man shall leave his father and mother and be joined to his wife, and the two shall become one flesh.' So they are no longer two, but one flesh" (Mark 10:7-8). Significantly, the code itself gives way to the principle of Jesus in v. 31!

Christ as *head* and *Savior* of the church is the model here for wives as subject to their husbands. *In everything* heightens the demand over that in Col 3:18. Husbands normally were providers and protectors of the family, but surely a husband is not "savior" of his wife in the sense that Christ is Savior of the church. Many husbands are not themselves "saved," much less saving. The code is best understood within its own limits as historically conditioned. To absolutize the code as binding on wives today is to open the door to any abuse of which fallible husbands are capable and often disposed.

The appeal to "love" as the controlling principle in the husband's relationship with his wife follows what Jesus verified as "the first" commandment of all (Mark 12:29). A husband is to love his wife *as Christ loved the church and gave himself up for her.* Should a wife love a husband any less?

At this point, the focus turns to the church itself. What is intended by *cleansing her with the washing of water by the word* is difficult. Taken literally, this serves as a text for baptismal regeneration, as problematic as the contention that circumcision was a means to salvation, rejected outright in 2:11ff. *By the word* (NRSV) translates *en remati,* literally "in a word." This may imply a baptismal confession of the name of Christ (cf. 1 Cor 6:11), but this is speculation.

That a husband should love his wife "as his own body" may be understood two ways. He may love her the way he loves himself, or in loving her he does love himself, since the two have become one flesh.

Verse 31 recaptures the mutual and egalitarian ideal of v. 21. All are to be *subject to one another out of reverence for Christ,* and husband and wife are to become *one flesh.* It follows that husband should *love his wife* and wife should *respect her husband* (v. 33), but surely a wife should love her husband and a husband should respect his wife.

6:1-4. Children-parents. The code here differs somewhat from that in Colossians. In both letters, both parents are to be obeyed by their children; but "in everything" drops out in Ephesians! Instead, many manuscripts have *in the Lord*; but this phrase is absent in some strong Greek and Latin manuscripts and several early church fathers. Thus Ephesians does not impose obedience unconditionally, a significant factor today when many children are abused by their fathers and/or mothers.

Ideally, obedience to parents is *right*, for parental responsibility requires corresponding authority. Authority is forfeited when abused.

The text here builds upon the fifth commandment (Exod 20:12; Deut 5:16), *the first commandment with a promise.* Significantly, the egalitarian principle is in force here, for mothers and fathers are to be obeyed alike in the Decalogue and in Ephesians.

What precisely is intended by the promise *live long on the earth* is unclear. If individual longevity is the promise, it is unclear why many obedient children die young and many disobedient ones live long. In the Decalogue the promise may be long life "in the land" for a nation obedient to parents, not individuals.

Verse 4 goes beyond Colossians in adding a positive to the negative in discipline. Fathers are not only to refrain from provoking their children to anger, but also to *bring them up in the discipline and instruction of the Lord.*

Not including mothers here is in keeping with the distrust of mothers in much of the ancient world, deeming them unfit to teach even their own children. Such distrust of women does not accord with the manner of Jesus. Neither does it agree with the recognition that Timothy's "sincere faith" was in his maternal heritage, a faith that lived first in his maternal heritage, "a faith that lived first in your grandmother Lois and your mother Eunice" (2 Tim 1:5), not from his Greek father (Acts 16:1). Of course, there is no evidence today that mothers are less competent than fathers in teaching or parenting.

6:5-9. Slaves-masters. This part of the code parallels that in Colossians, with no significant variations. Slavery as such is not challenged, for whatever reason. What does concern the code is the quality service given by the slave, service which is a credit to a follower of Christ. As *slaves of Christ* they are to render service in deed and in spirit worthy of a servant of Christ. Ultimate reward is from the true Master, under whom the distinction between *slaves* and *free* persons is transcended (v. 8; cf. Gal 3:28).

Without condoning slavery, *masters* are warned that they are answerable to the ultimate "Master" for how they relate to those whom they hold as slaves.

6:10-20. The whole armor of God. This section sees the Christian as embattled, threatened by *cosmic powers* seen as *spiritual forces of evil in the heavenly places* (vv. 10-17), and also by human forces to whom the gospel is to be preached with boldness (vv. 18-20).

The present world retains the language about demonic forces, and there is yet sincere belief in the reality of such threats; but nothing today compares with fear in the ancient world of such powers believed to inhabit the stars, mountains, trees, and human beings. The word "disaster" preserves the belief that human sufferings are traceable to some star god. Modern space travel and even mining of mountains would be problematic to the ancient world, for fear of disturbing cosmic powers.

The *whole armor of God* implies nothing of worldly militarism. All the armor is defensive except the *shoes* that *will make you ready to proclaim the gospel of peace* (v. 15) and *the sword of the Spirit, which is the word of God* (v. 17; cf. Rev 1:16).

Defensive armor includes *the belt of truth*. The injunction anticipates our "fasten your seatbelts!" In a world like this, the Christian pilgrimage can be a rough ride. "Truth" is our defense, and it requires no defense. *The breastplate of righteousness* is a reminder that although we are not saved by our goodness, righteousness belongs properly to followers of Jesus. *Faith* is more than a shield, but it is that. *Salvation* is more than security, but it is that too.

Prayer rightly includes self, but there is a special duty to pray *for all the saints*. Paul includes himself in his prayer requests, but it is not a self-serving request. Imprisoned for preaching a gospel inclusive of Jew and gentile, he prays that he have the "boldness" to speak *the mystery of the gospel*, the very gospel for which he is *an ambassador in chains.* No threat is to silence him or cause him to modify his proclamation of "the mystery of the gospel" (cf. 3:1-6).

Personal Words and Benediction, 6:21-24

Tychicus is apparently the bearer of the letter (no postal system then for civilians). His further mission is to inform the readers more fully as to Paul's situation. This is for their encouragement in difficult times.

Peace, love, faith, and *grace* are primary in the benediction, as a reminder of what is received from *God the Father and the Lord Jesus Christ* and also of that by which *the whole community* is to be characterized. The final appeal is for *an undying love for our Lord Jesus Christ.*

Works Cited

Barth, Marcus. 1959. *The Broken Wall.* 1974. *Ephesians.*

Kümmel, W. G. 1975. *Introduction to the N.T.*

Robinson, J. A. 1904. *St. Paul's Epistle to the Ephesians.*

Roon, A. Van. 1974. *The Authenticity of Ephesians.*

Stagg, Frank. 1990. "Paul's Final Mission to Jerusalem," in *With Steadfast Purpose,* ed. N. Keathley.

Stagg, Evelyn, and Frank Stagg. 1978. *Woman in the World of Jesus.*

Tolbert, Malcolm O. 1990. "Ephesians, Letter to the," in MDB.

Philippians

Charles H. Talbert   [MCB 1227-1234]

Introduction

Philippians is one of thirteen letters attributed to PAUL in the NT. It belongs to the group of nine Pauline letters addressed to seven churches that is arranged in order of descending length. It is to devotional literature what Romans is to doctrinal and 1 Corinthians to ethical writing. The Marcionite prologue to Paul's letters (late second century) gives perhaps the oldest Christian view of the letter.

> The Philippians are Macedonians. They persevered in faith after [they] had accepted the word of truth and they did not receive false apostles. The Apostle praises them, writing to them from Rome from the prison, by Epaphroditus.

Genre

Philippians is both like and unlike ancient non-Christian letters (Soards 1990, 660). Like them, it begins with a salutation (A to B, greeting) followed by a prayer form (thanksgiving and petition), moves to a body, and ends with a conventional closing (e.g., greetings). Unlike them, its components are Christianized, for example, Salutation—*Grace and peace from God our Father and the Lord Jesus Christ* (1:2); Closing—*The grace of the Lord Jesus Christ be with your spirit* (4:23).

Author and Recipients

The letter's claim to be by Paul is universally accepted today. It is addressed to Christian converts in the Macedonian city of PHILIPPI. That church, founded during Paul's second missionary journey (Acts 16:9-40), stayed in close contact with the apostle (2 Cor 11:8-9; Phil 4:15-16; Acts 20:1-2, 3-6). It was basically gentile Christian in composition.

Integrity

There is diversity of opinion about whether or not Philippians is a unity. Some take 3:1b–4:3 as a fragment of a second letter. Others regard 4:10-20 as one note; 1:1–3:1 + 4:4-7 as another; and 3:2–4:3 + 4:8-9 as a third. If so, then these different letters were collected, edited, and published as one when the Pauline letter collection was made near 100 C.E. Still others believe that Philippians can best be explained as one letter. One's position on the matter of integrity affects one's decisions about other issues.

Date, Locale, and Occasion

If Philippians is not a unity, then its different components may come from different locales at different times and have different purposes. (1) If three independent letters are assumed, then 4:10-20 may be the earliest, written from an alleged imprisonment in EPHESUS, on the third journey, to thank the Philippians for their gift; 1:1–3:1 + 4:4-7 (perhaps 4:21-23) may be next, also from an Ephesian imprisonment, calling for unity and joy; while 3:2–4:3 + 4:8-9 may be the latest, written shortly after leaving Ephesus, perhaps from CORINTH, warning about false teachers (Koester 1976, 665–66). (2) If there were two original letters, then 1:1–3:1a + 4:4-23 may have been written from prison in Rome (Acts 28), Ephesus (an alleged imprisonment on the third journey), or CAESAREA (Acts 23:23–26:32) to thank the church for its gift and to exhort them to Christian unity; 3:1b–4:3 may have come from a time when Paul was not in prison, close to that of Galatians and warning about similar problems with false teaching (Michael 1928). (3) If the letter is a unity, it was written from prison in Rome, Ephesus, Caesarea, or elsewhere (2 Cor 11:23—Paul was imprisoned a number of times before the Caesarean imprisonment of Acts 23; *1 Clem* 5:5—Paul was imprisoned seven times) to serve multiple functions: giving thanks for a gift, encouragement to unity, warning about heresy, information about travel plans (Hawthorne 1983, xxix–xlviii).

Although no consensus exists, this commentary assumes the unity of Philippians, for which a good case has been made by Garland 1985, Kurz 1985, and Watson 1988. Again, although consensus does not exist and certainty is impossible, this reading of Philippians assumes a Roman origin, near the beginning of Paul's imprisonment there. The only serious obstacle against this ancient view, the great distance between Rome and Philippi that allegedly renders the travel undertaken and proposed difficult, is removed by the comment of Philostratus (*Life of Apollonius* 7.10), that the distance from Puteoli (near Rome) to Corinth (fairly close to Philippi) was crossed in five days. The similarities with Romans and Galatians are then explained by locating Philippians early in Paul's imprisonment in Rome. (For an outline of Paul's life and the place of his letters in it, see Soards 1990, 660.)

For Further Study

In the *Mercer Dictionary of the Bible*: PAUL; PHILIPPI; PHILIPPIANS, LETTER TO THE; PRISON EPISTLES.

In other sources. F. W. Beare, *A Commentary on the Epistle to the Philippians*, HNTC; W. G. Doty, *Letters in Primitive Christianity*; D. Garland, "The Composition and Literary Unity of Philippians: Some Neglected Factors," *NovT* 27 (1985): 141–73; G. F. Hawthorne, *Philippians*, WBC; H. Koester, "Philippians, Letter to the," *IDBSupp* 665–66; W. S. Kurz, "Kenotic Imitation of Paul and of Christ in Philippians," in *Discipleship in the New Testament*, ed. F. Segovia, 103–26; R. P. Martin, *Carmen Christi: Philippians 2:5-11 in Recent Interpretation*; J. H. Michael, *The Epistle of Paul to the Philippians*, MNTC; S. K. Stowers, *Letter Writing in Greco-Roman Antiquity*; C. H. Talbert, "The Problem of Preexistence in Philippians 2:6-11," *JBL* 86 (1967): 141–53; D. Watson, "A Rhetorical Analysis of Philippians and Its Implications for the Unity Question," *NovT* 30 (1988): 57–88.

Commentary

An Outline

I. Introduction, 1:1-11
  A. Salutation, 1:1-2
  B. Prayer, 1:3-11
II. Body of the Letter, 1:12–4:20
  A. Paul's Rejoicing, 1:12-26

  B. Paul's Exhortations, 1:27–2:16
  C. Paul's Plans: Travelogue, 2:17–3:1a
  D. Paul's Exhortations, 3:1b–4:9
  E. Paul's Rejoicing, 4:10-20
III. Conclusion, 4:21-23

Introduction, 1:1-11

Salutation, 1:1-2

The letter's beginning adopts and adapts the customary form of ancient letters: A to B, greeting. PAUL is the author but TIMOTHY (Acts 16:1-3; 19:22) is included to lay the foundation for his future visit (2:19-23) and to demonstrate Paul's humility (2:3-4; 3:17). The letter is sent *to all the saints in Christ Jesus* in Philippi; we would say to all the Christians there. *With the bishops and deacons* might better be translated "overseers and helpers" to convey the idea that they are not officials in the second-century sense but administrative functionaries manifesting the gifts of service (Rom 12:7—ministry [διακονίᾳ]; 1 Cor 12—helpers) and oversight (Rom 12:8—the leader; 1 Cor 12:28—administrators). These functionaries would be addressed because, in part, Philippians is a response to a gift sent to the prisoner Paul by the church and doubtless supervised by these overseers and helpers. The greeting of v. 2 invokes *God our Father* (Matt 6:9; Luke 11:2; Rom 8:15; Gal 4:6; 2 John 3) and the *Lord Jesus Christ* (Rom 15:6; 2 Cor 1:3; 11:31; Col 1:3), making it distinctively Christian.

Prayer, 1:3-11

As ancient letters often used a prayer form after the salutation. So does Paul. A THANKSGIVING (vv. 3-6) and a petition (vv. 9-11) are joined by an expression of personal affection (vv. 7-8). Thanksgiving and petition are organized in similar ways: reference to prayer followed by its two objects, ending with an eschatological note, the *day of Christ*. In this section one hears themes that will recur throughout the letter: Paul's joy, the Philippians' gift, the completion of salvation only at the last day, Paul's imprisonment, Christian growth.

1:3-6. Thanksgiving. Paul gives thanks for two things: (1) either for his every remembrance of them or for their every remembrance of him (the Greek allows either; so does the context), which is always in every prayer, for all of them, with joy (vv. 3-4); and (2) for their sharing in the gospel, that is, their gift to him in prison (v. 5; 4:10). The thanksgiving ends with a reference to their eschatological hope, the day of Christ, when God's saving activity in them, begun in the past, will find its completion (v. 6).

    1:7-8. Expression of personal affection. Paul's hope for the Philippians verbalized in v. 6 is grounded both in their sharing in God's grace (v. 7, here, ministry as in 1 Cor 3:10; Gal 2:9) and in Paul's deep affection for them (v. 8).

    1:9-11. Petition. Paul asks for two things for the Philippians: (1) that their love *may overflow* with knowledge and full insight (1 Cor 12:8, 10) so that they may *determine what is best* (vv. 9-10a), and (2) that, at the day of Christ, they *may be pure and blameless, having produced the harvest of righteousness.* The petition, like the thanksgiving, ends on the note of eschatological hope, the day of Christ.

Body of the Letter, 1:12–4:20

    The body of Philippians unfolds in a concentric pattern: A (1:12-26), B (1:27–2:16), C (2:17–3:1a), B' (3:1b–4:9), A' (4:10-20).

Paul's Rejoicing, 1:12-26

    This section, A in the pattern, is held together by an INCLUSIO: *spread/progress* (προκοπήν) in v. 12 and v. 25. It consists of two units, vv. 12-18 and vv. 19-26, the first focused on Paul's rejoicing in the present, the second on his rejoicing in the future.

    1:12-18. Paul's rejoicing in his present status. Being a prisoner and having heard that some preach out of bad motives does not keep Paul from rejoicing for two reasons: (1) because his imprisonment, rather than hurting the Christian cause, has advanced it among pagans (vv. 12-13; the *imperial guard* could refer to soldiers, members of the court, or officials of a government house, none of which were restricted to Rome) and Christians (v. 14); and (2) because even those seeking to afflict Paul advance the Christian cause (vv. 15-18; these opponents, whose message is acceptable but whose motives are questionable, are not those of 3:2-19, whose message is erroneous).

    1:19-26. Paul's rejoicing in the future. Whether he dies as a martyr or is released from prison will not keep Paul from rejoicing for two reasons: (1) because if he dies as a martyr, Christ will be honored and he will be with Christ (vv. 19-23; cf. 2 Cor 5:8); and (2) because if he is released, it will mean *fruitful labor* for him and glory for Christ (vv. 22-26; cf. 2 Cor 5:9).

Paul's Exhortations, 1:27–2:16

    This section, B in the pattern, consists of three paragraphs, 1:27-30, 2:1-13, and 2:14-16. The focus of the first is on the church's relation to the world while that of the second is on the community's inner life. The third offers general exhortations to round off the two prior paragraphs.

1:17-30. The church's relation to the world. Verse 27a is best translated: "Live, as citizens of heaven, worthily of the gospel of Christ." Just as the Philippians strove to live as citizens of Rome, worthily of their privilege in a Macedonian context, so the Philippian Christians, as citizens of heaven (3:20), are to live in line with their citizenship in this present evil age. Verses 27b-30 give two specific examples of what this means.

1:27b. Christian unity. To live in line with their heavenly citizenship in relation to the world means maintaining Christian unity. Military (*standing firm*) and athletic (*striving side by side*) metaphors describe the desired unity on behalf of *the faith of the gospel*. Paul calls for a new Macedonian phalanx and a new Olympic team of athletes to be formed, composed of Philippian Christians who manifest the same unity as successful military units and athletic teams do.

1:28a-30. Christian fearlessness. Living worthily of their heavenly citizenship means also fearlessness in the face of pagan hostility (v. 28a). Two bases for such fearlessness follow: (1) it is a sign to pagans of the ultimate outcome of history (v. 28b); and (2) not only faith in Christ but also suffering for Christ is a gift from God, as Paul's example shows (vv. 29-30; 1 Thes 2:2).

2:1-13. The community's inner life. This section is held together by an inclusio: the theme of vv. 1-2 echoed in v. 13. The section focuses on the inner life of the community. It is composed of three subsections, vv. 1-2, vv. 3-11, and vv. 12-13, each consisting of injunctions and their bases. All call for Christian unity.

2:1-2. Relate to one another as you are related to by God. Verse 1 offers four bases: "Since there is [1] *encouragement in Christ*, [2] *consolation from* God's *love*, [3] *sharing in the Spirit*, and [4] *compassion and sympathy* shown by God to us." The "if" clauses should be translated "if (and there is)" or "since." Verse 2 follows with four injunctions: (1) *be of the same mind*, (2) have *the same love*, (3) be *in full accord*, and (4) be *of one mind*. Relate to one another in a way that is consonant with the way God relates to you.

2:3-11. Relate to one another as Christ related to God. Verses 3-4 offer two injunctions: (1) *Do nothing from selfish ambition or conceit, but in humility regard others as better than yourselves*; and (2) *Let each of you look not to your own interests, but to the interests of others*. The problems Paul addresses were recognized by the philosopher Epictetus to be indigenous to the human condition. He said: "It is a general rule—be not deceived—that every living thing is to nothing so devoted as to its own interest" (*Discourse* 2.22.15).

The basis for these injunctions is in vv. 5-11. Verse 5 is missing a verb in the second half of the sentence. Translated literally, it reads: "Think this among yourselves, which also _____ in Christ Jesus." Different verbs may be supplied—either "was" or "think." This explains the difference in modern translations. If "think" is supplied, then the result is: "Let your bearing towards one another arise out of your life in Christ Jesus" (NEB). If "was" is supplied, then one finds: "The attitude you should have is the one that Christ Jesus had" (TEV). The RSV second edition reflects the former; the RSV third edition employs the latter. In terms of meaning, the former would mean, "Relate to one another as you relate to Christ" (i.e., with humility and submission); the latter, "Relate to one another as Christ related to God" (i.e., with humility). The former is an appeal to experience, the latter an appeal to tradition. The latter seems to fit the context better.

Verses 6-11 are almost universally regarded as an early Christian HYMN taken up and employed by Paul as the basis for his call to humility. The hymn divides into two parts, vv. 6-8 where Jesus is the subject of the action, and vv. 9-11 where God is the subject. In the first part, Jesus *humbles* himself, even to the point of death. In the second part, God exalts Jesus, giving him the name and position of Lord. Modern interpreters of the hymn disagree over whether vv. 6-8 refer to preexistence (v. 6), INCARNATION (v. 7), and death on the cross (v. 8), or only to Jesus' human existence as an antitype of Adam's experience in Gen 1–3: being in God's image (v. 6a; Gen 1:27); not trying to be like God (v. 6b; Gen 3:5); being obedient to God (vv. 7-8; Gen 2:16-17; 3:11). Either way, it is Jesus' humility that serves as the basis for the injunctions in vv. 3-4. Relate to one another as Jesus related to God, with humility.

2:12-13. Relate to one another, in obedience to Paul, as the God who indwells you enables you. In vv. 12-13 the two bases are split, v. 12a being the first, v. 13 the second. The injunction comes in v. 12b. It reads: *Work out your* [plural] *own salvation with fear and trembling.* This is not a call to personal salvation by works (Eph 2:8-9); the Philippians' salvation is assumed. Nor is it a call for individuals to grow spiritually (as in 3:12-15); it speaks rather about corporate wholeness. In Pauline thought, salvation involves not only individuals but also human community (Eph 4:1-16). Since groups as well as individuals sin, groups as well as individuals need to be delivered from sin. Moreover, groups as well as individuals need to grow spiritually. Here the community that has experienced God's saving power is asked to work out that initial deliverance from sin in all of the community's life. With a sense of seriousness, work out the implications of your corporate salvation in the many relationships of the community's life. The bases are two: (1) *For it is God who is at work in you* [plural], *enabling you* [plural] *both to will and to work for his good pleasure* (v. 13); and (2) *just as you have always obeyed me, not only in my presence, but much more now in my absence* (v. 12a).

2:14-16. General exhortations. Having exhorted the Philippians to right relations with the world (1:27-30) and proper relations within the community (2:1-13), Paul ends this section with the general exhortation *Do all things without murmuring and arguing*, that is, with cheerful obedience (v. 14; cf. 1 Cor 10:1-12; Exod 14:12; Num 16:41, 49). Two reasons for such behavior follow: (1) it benefits the world (vv. 15b; cf. Matt 5:14-16), and (2) it will benefit the Philippians (vv. 15a, 16a) and Paul (v. 16b).

Paul's Plans: Travelogue, 2:17–3:1a

Just as in 1 Cor 4:17-19 and 2 Cor 8:16-19, information about the travel plans of Paul and his coworkers appears in the middle rather than at the end of the letter (Rom 15:14-29). This paragraph functions as C, the centerpoint, in the concentric pattern of the letter's body. It consists of three parts: (1) about TIMOTHY (vv. 19-23), (2) about PAUL (v. 24), and (3) about EPAPHRODITUS (vv. 25-30). It is held together by an inclusio: "rejoicing" in 2:17-18, echoed in 3:1a.

2:19-23. Hope plus commendation. Paul hopes to send Timothy to see the Philippians soon to gather news about them. He will send Timothy because there is no one like him *who will be genuinely concerned* for their welfare. Others *are seeking their own interests* (2:4). Paul will send his best.

2:24. Paul's hopes for himself. In 1:24-25 Paul concluded that, since his remaining in the flesh was better for the Philippians, he expected to live and be released from prison. Here, in v. 24, he voices his *trust in the Lord that I will also come soon*. If he is to be released, it will be not because he wishes it but because God enables it.

2:25-30. Decision plus commendation. When the Philippians sent their latest gift to Paul (4:10), they not only sent it by Epaphroditus, but sent Epaphroditus himself to stay with Paul and assist him in his ministry while the apostle was in prison (vv. 25, 30). Epaphroditus became ill and nearly died (vv. 27, 30). Even though he survived, he became emotionally distraught, longing for home (v. 26). Paul, therefore, determined to send him back to Philippi. Lest the Philippians be unhappy with him on his return for not finishing his mission, Paul commends him for his labors and asks that he be welcomed and honored (v. 29).

Paul's Exhortations, 3:1b–4:9

This section is B' in the letter body's pattern, corresponding to Paul's exhortations in 1:27–2:16. The section begins with an introduction, 3:1b, and ends with a conclusion, 4:9. In between are two panels, each with three parts. Panel One appeals to apostolic example against error and consists of 3:2-11, 3:12-15, and 3:16–4:1. Panel Two utilizes apostolic teaching for the church's benefit and consists of 4:2-3, 4:4-7, and 4:8.

3:2–4:1. Panel one: apostolic example. In this segment of text Paul uses his own example to argue against three distortions of religious existence: legalism (vv. 2-11), perfectionism (vv. 12-15), and libertine behavior (3:16–4:1). Debate rages about whether these three issues reflect one, two, or three groups of opponents. Issues one and two could be explained by opponents who were either Jews or Jewish Christians. Issue three, if representative of the same group as one and two, requires a legalistic, perfectionistic, libertine opposition, perhaps Jewish-Christian GNOSTICISM. Unanimity reigns only on the conclusion that the opponents of chap. 3 are not the same as those of 1:15-18. In 1:15-18 Paul expressed reservations about his opponents' motives, not their message. In chap. 3 Paul defends against a wrong message.

3:2-11. Against legalism. A warning is issued, using terms of disparagement for the opponents: *dogs* (Rev 22:15; Matt 15:21-28), *evil workers* (Rom 2:17-24), *those who mutilate the flesh* (Rom 2:25-29). Christians are the true *circumcision* (Col 2:11). Paul then uses his own situation as a paradigm. He has every reason for confidence in the flesh—to trust human achievement to gain God's approval. A list of seven Jewish virtues is given (vv. 5-6), beginning with *circumcised on the eighth day* (Lev 12:3) and ending with *as to righteousness under the law, blameless.* Yet he regarded (perfect tense) them all as loss because of Christ (v. 7) and regards (present tense) everything as loss *because of the surpassing value of knowing Christ Jesus my Lord* (v. 8).

Paul's motivation for considering all things as rubbish is threefold : (1) *in order that I may gain Christ* (v. 8c; cf. Matt 13:44-45); (2) *in order that I may . . . be found in him* (Gal 3:27; Eph 4:24) with a righteousness not from law but from either the faith of Christ or faith in Christ (v. 9; Rom 3:21-22; 10:1-13; Gal 2:15-16); and (3) *I want to know Christ and the power of his resurrection and the sharing of his suffering by becoming like him in his death* (2:8; cf. Rom 6:5, 10), *if somehow I may attain the resurrection from the dead* (vv. 10-11; cf. Rom 6:8; 8:17). These three reasons are different aspects of the same reality—trusting Christ for one's relation with God instead of reliance on one's own achievements. Legalism, reliance on one's own productivity and achievements to gain a relation to God, is ruled out of order for the Philippians by Paul's example.

3:12-15. Against perfectionism. *Not that I have already obtained this or have already reached the goal* (v. 12). Paul claims to have experienced neither complete victory over sin nor the resurrection from the dead, as some perfectionists in the early church did (sinlessness—1 John 1:8; resurrection—2 Tim 2:18). Rather, like a long-distance runner, he presses on towards the goal (v. 14; cf. Eph 4:12-13; Heb 12:1-2). In Pauline thought, SALVATION involves three tenses: past ("We were saved"—Rom 8:24); present ("We are being saved"—1 Cor 15:2); and future ("We shall be saved"—Rom 5:9). It is inappropriate, then, to claim in the present what only belongs to the future. The paragraph concludes with the exhortation: *Let those of us then who are mature be of the same mind* (v. 15). Paul's example is again appealed to, this time against perfectionism.

3:16–4:1. Against libertine behavior. This unit is held together by an inclusio: 3:16, *Only let us hold fast to what we have attained*, and 4:1, *Stand firm in the Lord in this way.* Verse 17 begins with an explicit appeal to the Pauline example. *Brothers and sisters, join in imitating me, and observe those who live according to the example you have in us* (1 Cor 4:16; 11:1; 1 Thes 1:6; 2 Thes 3:7, 9). On the mission field, new converts need an embodied gospel. The apostle offers them himself and those who follow his example. Unlike those who make their belly their god (cf. Rom 16:18), with their minds set on earthly things (v. 19; 1 Cor 6:12-20),

Christians are citizens of heaven whose bodies will be transformed at the PAROUSIA to be like their Savior's glorious body (3:20-21; 1 Cor 6:14). This eschatological hope is the basis for Christians' standing firm in the Lord (4:1). Paul's point here is captured by the early Christian author of the *Epistle to Diognetus*:

> For the distinction between Christians and other men is neither in country nor language nor customs. For they do not dwell in cities in some place of their own, nor do they use any strange variety of dialect, nor practice an extraordinary kind of life. . . . Yet while living in Greek and barbarian cities . . . following the local customs . . . they show forth the wonderful and confessedly strange character of the constitution of their own citizenship. They dwell in their own fatherlands, but as if sojourners in them; they share all things as citizens, and suffer all things as strangers. Every foreign land is their fatherland, and every fatherland is a foreign country. . . . They pass their time upon the earth, but they have their citizenship in heaven (5:1-2, 4-5, 9; Lake 1970, 2:358–61).

Throughout the section, 3:2–4:1, Paul's example has been held up as a norm for the readers. "Keep your eye on the goal if you can see it. If not, keep your eye on one who knows the way to the goal and who is going there" (Robertson 1917, 118).

4:2-9. Panel two: apostolic instruction. In this segment of text Paul deals with three topics: (1) a specific need for Christian unity in the Philippian church (vv. 2-3); (2) the call for perpetual joy (vv. 4-7); and (3) an appeal to meditation on what is noblest and best (v. 8).

4:2-3. Christian unity. Two women in the Philippian church, Euodia and Syntyche, are urged to be of the same mind (1:27; 2:2; 3:15). An unnamed loyal companion, an individual, or perhaps the church as a whole, is urged to help the women agree (v. 3). They are worth the effort because they have *struggled beside me in the work of the gospel, together with Clement and the rest of my coworkers* (v. 3). Paul here makes no gender distinctions in ministry (cf. Rom 16:1-2, 7), just as he makes none in church membership (Gal 3:27-28).

4:4-7. Perpetual joy. The apostle asks for perpetual joy: *go on rejoicing in the Lord always* (v. 4). What follows are two injunctions and two promises.

Injunction: *Let your gentleness be known to everyone* (4:5a)

Promise: *The Lord is near* (4:5b).

Injunction: *Do not worry about anything, but in everything by prayer and supplication with thanksgiving let your requests be made known to God* (4:6).

Promise: *And the peace of God . . . will guard your hearts and your minds in Christ Jesus* (4:7).

"If anything is big enough to worry about, it is not too small to pray about" (Baille 1962, 47). Neither the hostility of others nor adverse circumstances need interrupt Christians' joy because of the resources provided by God: his nearness (either spatially, Ps 34:18, or temporally, 1 Thes 4:17; 1 Cor 15:52), his answers to prayer (cf. Ps 84:11; Jas 4:2; Matt 7:7), and his peace (cf. John 14:27).

4:8-9. Meditation on what is noblest and best. Just as the ancient Jew meditated on God, his acts and his precepts (Josh 1:8; Ps 1:2; 63:6; 77:12; 119:23, 48, 78, 97, 99, 148; 143:5), so the Christians are to think about things that are uplifting and ennobling. *Whatever is true, whatever is honorable, whatever is just, whatever is pure, whatever is pleasing, whatever is commendable, if there is any excellence* [and there is], *and if there is anything worthy of praise* [and there is], *think about these things.* The entire section of exhortations, 3:1b–4:9, ends with a generalizing command and a promise:

>Command: *Keep on doing the things that you have learned and received and heard and seen in me* (4:9a; cf. 3:17)
>
>Promise: *and the God of peace will be with you* (4:9b).

The apostle's concern is that his converts live according to what he taught and modelled. In this respect Paul mirrored the views of the philosophical schools of his time. The philosopher's word alone, unaccompanied by the act, was regarded as invalid and untrustworthy (Chrysostom, *Discourse* 70.6). Being a disciple meant imitating a teacher's acts and words so as to become like him (*Discourse* 55.4-5). "Plato, Aristotle, and the whole company of sages . . . derived more benefit from the character than from the words of Socrates" (Seneca, *Epistle* 6:5-6). Paul's appeal both to his words and to his deeds would have been what the Philippians expected from their apostle.

Paul's Rejoicing, 4:10-20

This section is A' in the body's pattern, corresponding to 1:12-26. It falls into two parallel panels (vv. 10-14 and 15-18) in which a rejoicing Paul (v. 10) thanks the Philippians for their gifts to meet his need, past (vv. 15-18) and present (vv. 10-14). The section concludes with a promise (v. 19) and a doxology (v. 20).

4:10-14. Panel one: present generosity. This panel is organized in terms of basically the same three components that will be found in panel two: (1) thank you, (2) but, (3) nevertheless.

4:10. Statement of the Philippians' act of generosity in the present. Now that an opportunity has presented itself for the Philippian church to give Paul material assistance again, they have done so. Paul rejoices in their concern for him.

4:11-13. Not that (οὐχ ο"τι) Paul speaks out of great want. He has learned *to be content* (αὐτάρκης) *with whatever I have* (v. 11). He knows how to deal both with plenty and with deprivation (v. 12). The Greek term translated *content* was widely used in Stoic circles to refer to a state of being independent of external circumstances. Epictetus, for example, praised Agrippinus, a distinguished Roman Stoic of the mid-first century C.E. because: "His character was such . . . that when any hardship befell him he would compose a eulogy upon it; on fever, if he had a fever; on disrepute, if he suffered from disrepute; on exile, if he went into exile" (*Fragment* 21). The Stoic discovered within himself the resources to allow contentment no matter what situation might arise. For Paul the resources came from his relation to Christ. Verse 13 might better be translated: "I have the strength for everything (poverty or plenty) in union with the one who infuses me with power" (cf. 2 Cor 12:9-10; Col 1:29). Paul's independence of circumstances came through his dependence on the Lord (cf. Heb 13:5-6).

4:14. Nevertheless the Philippians did well in sharing in Paul's distress. Even though he could have done without their gift, yet Paul affirms their care and concern shown for him by their contribution.

4:15-18. Panel two: past generosity. Three similar components to those in vv. 10-14 make up the second panel, vv. 15-18.

4:15-16. Statement of the Philippians' acts of generosity on two or more occasions in the past. Although Paul refused to allow the Corinthian church to give him money in order to avoid any charges of self-interest on his part (1 Cor 9:3-18; 2 Cor 12:13), he accepted aid from the Philippian church more than once prior to the present gift.

4:17. Not that (οὐχ ο"τι) Paul seeks the gift in and for itself. Paul does not want his acknowledgment of the Philippians' past generosity to be interpreted as his desire for more from them. It is what they gain by it that he seeks (cf. 2 Cor 8:1-5).

4:18. A pleasing sacrifice.. Commercial language used in v. 18a indicates that this part of the letter is Paul's receipt for the Philippians' gift (*paid in full*). Sacrificial language in v. 18b points to their gifts as their participation in the Christian liturgy of life (2:17; Rom 12:1-2).

4:19-20. A promise and a doxology. The conclusion to the two panels, 4:10-14 and 15-18, comes in the form of a promise and a doxology.

4:19. A promise. Verse 19 is a promise or a petition depending upon which textual variant is chosen for the main verb: *my God will fully satisfy every need* (future tense) or "may my God fully satisfy your every need" (aorist optative). The NRSV reflects the better textual alternative. Paul speaks as a prophetic figure, certain that God will act in a certain way because of who he is. *My God will fully satisfy every need of yours.* What follows is better rendered: "in a glorious manner in Christ Jesus." (Hawthorne 1983, 208). As in 2 Cor 9:6-11, Paul believes God gives prosperity to his children to enable their generosity.

4:20: A doxology. *To our God and Father be glory forever and ever. Amen.* For similar doxologies to end a letter, compare Rom 16:25-27; 2 Pet 3:18b; Jude 24–25. The letter ends (v. 20) as it began (1:2) with a reference to God the Father.

Conclusion, 4:21-23

The conclusion to a Pauline letter often contained one or more of the following: a peace wish, greetings, reference to the holy kiss, a grace or benediction. Two of these components are found here: greetings (vv. 21-22) and a grace (v. 23). *Caesar's household* refers to that body of officials and servants involved in imperial administration. They would be found in most of the great cities of the empire, for example, Rome and Ephesus. That the saints of Caesar's household greet you (v.

22) indicates how far the gospel had penetrated Roman society. Without Paul's imprisonment (1:12-13), would this have happened?

Works Cited

Baille, John. 1962. *Christian Devotion.*

Garland, D. 1985. "The Composition and Literary Unity of Philippians: some Neglected Factors," *NovT.*

Hawthorne, G. F. 1983. *Philippians.* WBC 43.

Koester, Helmut. 1962. "Philippians, Letter to the." IDBsup.

Kurz, W. S. 1985. "Imitation of Paul and of Christ in Philippians," in *Discipleship in the New Testament.*

Lake, Kirsopp. 1970. *The Apostolic Fathers.*

Michael, J. H. 1928. *The Epistle of Paul to the Philippians.* MNTC.

Robertson, A. T. 1917. *Paul's Joy in Christ: Studies in Philippians.*

Soards, M. 1990. "Paul." MDB.

Watson, D. 1988. "A Rhetorical Analysis of Philippians and Its Implications for the Unity Question," *NovT.*

Colossians

Frank Stagg [MCB 1235-1239]

Introduction

Colossians is a creative response to heresy. Instead of merely condemning it, PAUL exposed its fallacies and countered with a fresh statement of the Christian calling. Paul clarified his own theology and the moral and ethical practice it implied as he met what apparently was a strange new syncretism of pagan, Jewish, and Christian thought and practice.

Authorship

Whether Colossians is from Paul or his followers is debated. Arguments relate to style, word usage, and theology as compared with the undisputed letters of Paul. Variances are real, but theories accounting for them are not compelling. Extensive use of traditional materials (hymnic, paraenetic, domestic codes) plus Paul's dependence upon scribal help (cf. Rom 16:22) may account for the variants (Cannon 1983, chaps. 2–4). Seeming linkage with Philemon (probably the letter out of LAODICEA, 4:16) argues for Paul as author.

Time and Place

Paul's many imprisonments (2 Cor 11:23), leave uncertain the place from which he wrote Colossians. Options generally considered are ROME, CAESAREA, and EPHESUS. Evidence is not compelling for any one of these. Fortunately, this does not vitally affect interpretation. Date is tied to place; mid-fifties to early sixties, if written from Caesarea or Rome.

Occasion and Purpose

The threat at COLOSSAE was for Paul a *philosophy and empty deceit* (2:8), falsifying the nature of Christ, human nature, and the world, with dire implications for faith, worship, and practice. It subordinated Christ to a hierarchy of spiritual beings, teaching the worship of angels, ascetic disciplines, and bondage to a religious calendar. Paul contended for the all-sufficiency of Christ, the fullness of God embodied, creator, redeemer, and sustainer.

The heresy behind Colossians can be identified only as reflected in the letter. It had strong affinities with what appeared later as GNOSTICISM, with a mixture of pagan, Jewish, and Christian elements. It assumed a DUALISM of spirit and matter, the former good and the latter worthless or evil. This low view of matter could lead to rigid ASCETICISM or permissiveness. Such dualism posed the problem of how an evil creation could come from the goodness of spirit. The gap was bridged by a theory of a series of aeons or emanations called the pleroma or "fullness," issuing from God and ending with a demiurge (worker) as agent in creation.

The church in Colossae seemingly was founded out of a pagan past (1:21, 27; 2:13) by EPAPHRAS (1:7f.; 4:12f.), as yet not visited by Paul (1:4, 7-9; 2:1). Paul's appeal is that they continue in the tradition already received, that represented by the Christian hymn quoted in 1:15-20.

For Further Study

In the *Mercer Dictionary of the Bible*: CHRISTOLOGY; COLOSSAE; COLOSSIANS, LETTER TO THE; DUALISM; EPISTLE/LETTER; GNOSTICISM; PAUL; PRISON EPISTLES; SALVATION IN THE NT; WOMEN IN THE NT.

In other sources: G. E. Cannon, *The Use of Traditional Materials in Colossians*; E. Lohse, *Colossians and Philemon*, Herm; R. P. Martin, *Colossians: The Church's Lord and the Christian's Liberty*; R. McL. Wilson, *Gnosis and the New Testament*.

Commentary

An Outline

I. Salutation, 1:1-2
II. Thanksgiving and Prayer, 1:3-14
III. Preeminence of Christ, 1:15-23
IV. Paul's Apostolic Ministry, 1:24–2:7

V. Warnings against Entrapments, 2:8-23
VI. Moral and Ethical Admonitions, 3:1–4:1
VII. Closing Appeals and Greetings, 4:2-18

Salutation, 1:1-2

Paul alone in Colossians appears as an *apostle*. It was under this authority that Paul warned his readers against new traditions that threatened the authentic faith of the church, which had been proclaimed by Paul's *beloved fellow servant* Epaphras (v. 7).

TIMOTHY alone is associated with Paul in the salutation, though eight others are named later. Possibly Timothy served as scribe, even sharing in the composition, Paul taking the pen only at 4:18.

Grace . . . and peace was a familiar Christian greeting, modeled on current usage but changing the Greek "greeting" (*charein*) to *grace* (*charis*). *Peace*, like the Hebrew *shalom*, is well-being under the rule of God.

Thanksgiving and Prayer, 1:3-14

1:3-8. Faith, love, hope. This triad, in this order, appears in 1 Thes 1:3 and 5:8, possibly Paul's first letter. To Paul faith was primarily trust. Love (*agape*) is a disposition to relate to others for their good, whatever the cost to self, with no self-serving motive (1 Cor 13:5). *Hope* is eschatological, *laid up for you in heaven* (v. 5; see also 1:27). It sustains and gives meaning to life, overcoming the futility of fate in angel worship.

From Epaphras they had received *the word of the truth, the gospel* (v. 5) and had *truly comprehended the grace of God* (v. 6). The *truth* they received should not be lost to some new tradition presented as *philosophy* (2:8). The gospel derives from *the grace of God*, excluding the need for alleged merits like ascetic practice, angel worship, or worldly regulations (2:6-23).

Paul sees the gospel validated through its worldwide acceptance (not provincial) and its fruitbearing (v. 6; see Gal 5:22-23). It yields a new quality of life (see Matt 7:16-20).

1:9-14. Wisdom and fruitful lives. Along with Paul's confidence in the Colossians is concern that they be *filled with the knowledge (epignosin) of God's will in all spiritual wisdom and understanding* (v. 9). Paul's *epignosis* (thorough knowledge) may be his answer to the *gnosis* (knowledge) sought by the Gnostics, their claim to a higher revealed knowledge of their origin and destiny. Paul stands in the Hebrew tradition of *knowledge* as acquaintance with God (v. 10). Such saving knowledge includes a knowledge of God's will, validated by obedience and fruit, the resulting quality of life. This is not human achievement but the working of God's *glorious power* (v. 11).

The community of the DEAD SEA SCROLLS saw themselves as "the sons of light," as did the later Gnostics; but Paul sees all God's people as children of light. Like a new Exodus, God has *rescued us from the power of darkness and transferred us into the kingdom of his beloved Son* (v. 13). *Redemption* is not paying off God. It is God's act of liberation (*apolytrosis*) by *the forgiveness of sins* (v. 14).

Preeminence of Christ, 1:15-23

1:15-17. Creator of the universe. An early Christian hymn may be preserved in vv. 15-20, even though there is no agreement as to its extent or structure, whether in two strophes or more. Christ is seen as creator of all that is (vv. 15-17), head of the church (vv. 18-20), and redeemer and sustainer of his people (vv. 21-23).

Christ is *the image [eikon] of the invisible God* (v. 15). When we see him, we see "the Father" (John 14:9). "Jesus" means "YHWH Savior," and as "Emmanuel" he is "God with us" (Matt 1:21, 23). New Testament writers would never have said that Jesus is "the second person of the trinity," for this says too little and implies division in deity.

That Christ is *the firstborn of all creation* must be harmonized with the claim that he is *before all things* (v. 17). *Firstborn (prototokos)* indicates not time but primogeniture, the rights of the firstborn.

That *in him all things in heaven and on earth were created* (v. 16) counters the claim that created matter is worthless or evil. It reflects the idea that people are ruled by a hierarchy of spiritual beings, called *thrones or dominions or rulers or powers* (v. 16). Ancient people thought the stars were inhabited by angels or demons and that these determined human fate ("disaster" implies that a star is against us). Christ is creator, but he is not created. He is *before all things* and the power holding together all things (v. 17).

1:18-20. Head of the church. Paul made much of the CHURCH as the body of Christ (1 Cor 12:12-30; Rom 12:1-8; Eph 1:22-23). Against the threat at Colossae, he changed the focus to Christ as the head of this body. He is *the beginning (archē)*, understood absolutely as in John 1:1 or as the originator of the church. He also is *the firstborn [prototokos] from the dead.* As in v. 15, *prototokos* means primogeniture, rights over creation (v. 18).

That all the *fullness (pleroma) of God* dwells in Christ (v. 19) strikes at the heart of the Colossian heresy. *Pleroma* was a term for all the spiritual beings (æons or emanations) supposedly between God and the universe, bridging the gap between spirit and matter. For Paul there is no gap, for in Christ is the fullness of deity, and he is the creator (cf. 2:9).

The "fullness of deity" was pleased not only to dwell in Christ but also *to reconcile to himself all things* (v. 20). Creator and redeemer are the same, and redemption includes all creation (cf. Rom 8:19-23). Rejected is the gnostic idea that spirit and matter are by nature antithetical. Estrangement is moral, and Christ brings about reconciliation by moral means, *making peace through the blood of his cross.* Language here is to be taken seriously, not literally. The cross as timber has no blood, but RECONCILIATION comes through the self-giving of Christ, ultimately in giving his life on the cross. Christ's death becomes effective in our salvation not as an external transaction but only as we are crucified with him (cf. Gal 2:19-21; Rom 6:5-11).

1:21-23. Redeemer and Preserver. The Colossians probably were gentiles (1:27), alienated from God and with a mind-set hostile to God, reflected in their evil works. That was "once," but "now" they have been reconciled to God. God in Christ is the agent in reconciliation, not the problem. Reconciliation has to do with relationship, but salvation in its fuller dimensions intends a new quality of life, holy and blameless and irreproachable. Salvation is not God's unilateral action: it requires the faith that endures (v. 23).

Paul's Apostolic Ministry, 1:24–2:7

1:24-25. The sufferings of Christ. It is a bold claim, yet Paul declared that in his ministry he completed things lacking in the sufferings of Christ. He did so as a part of Christ's *body, that is, the church.* The human body was a primary model for the church to Paul (see 1 Cor 12:12-26; Rom 12:5), one body comprised of many members. Not only does Christ suffer for the church, but it suffers for him. What is done to the church is done to Christ (see Matt 25:40, 45; Acts 9:4). Paul's sufferings included "chains" and more (4:18; 2 Cor 11:23-29).

1:26-29. God's open secret. The *mystery* long hidden but now revealed is summed up as *Christ in you.* As apostle to the gentiles, Paul gave himself to both Jews and gentiles, all alike in sin and called to a new relationship and quality of life in Christ. "You" is plural in v. 27, *Christ in you* all! This eternal purpose of God, overcoming the estrangement between Jews and gentiles as well as that between Jew and gentile and himself, is the revealed *mystery* (Eph 3:9) as well as *the hope of glory.* Life together in Christ is a glorious hope and the only hope offered us by the God of glory.

2:1-7. Faithfulness to heritage. The concern of this unit is that those at Colossae and Laodicea hold fast to the *treasures of wisdom and knowledge* which already they have in Christ, not letting anyone *deceive* them with *plausible arguments,* that is, the art of persuasion. The heresy threatening them made bold claims to something superior, but it was in fact inferior, false, and empty. Although Paul warns his readers of this subtle threat, he affirms them for their *morale and . . . firmness* and encourages them to remain true to their heritage of faith. Here and throughout Colossians, the basic theme is the all-sufficiency of Christ. They need only to hold to and cultivate what already they have been taught.

Warnings against Entrapments, 2:8-23

This unit is the heart of Colossians, exposing the nature of the threatening heresy and pointing to Christ as the *fullness of deity* (v. 9) and as providing for our *fullness in him* (v. 10).

2:8. Captured by human traditions. Paul uses a rare word (*sulagogein*) for capturing and taking booty. This implies the self-serving motive of those who seek to entrap others as well as the fraud suffered by the victims of *human tradition* posing as *philosophy* but in fact only *empty deceit.* Paul's term for this fallacy is *the elemental spirits of the universe.* "Elements" (*stoicheia*) was a term used variously, including what were thought to be the elements of the cosmos (earth, fire, water, air) and the stars thought to be composed of these elements. The stars were thought to be inhabited by angels who controlled the universe and the fates (dis-aster) of humans.

2:9-10. The fullness of deity. Paul takes the gnostic *pleroma* (*fullness*) and applies it to Christ. In him *the whole fullness of deity dwells bodily.* The KJV "Godhead" intended what we mean by "godhood" (NRSV *deity*), but it mistakenly came to stand for "persons of the godhead." The NT knows only one God, and the fullness of deity came bodily into the world in Christ (Jn 1:1, 14).

Fullness also is offered us in Christ. Salvation is seen as becoming fully human: nothing more, nothing less, and nothing other. Christ, who is above *every ruler and authority,* is our sufficiency for our own fulfillment as human beings.

<u>2:11-15. The old and the new.</u> "A circumcision made without hands" (RSV) is the inward "circumcision" of the heart (Rom 2:29). Just as in literal CIRCUMCISION some flesh is removed, so there is *the circumcision of Christ* (i.e., made by Christ) that removes *the body of the flesh* (i.e., sinful nature). Literal circumcision serves here as a paradigm for the cleansing that comes under the lordship of Christ.

Literal BAPTISM also serves as a paradigm for what could be called "a baptism not made with hands." Literal baptism is no more saving than literal circumcision, but each dramatizes something that is saving. "Fullness of life" comes not by religious rites but by the very power that raised Christ from the dead.

New life comes when God forgives us all our trespasses. We are freed from all legalism, whether the cultic laws of Judaism or regulations imposed by *rulers and authorities*. Christ has set aside the record against us with its *legal demands . . . nailing it to the cross* (v. 14). In Christ we are free from the tyranny of rules and from "rulers and authorities" themselves.

<u>2:16-19. Food laws and calendars.</u> God alone is our ultimate judge (1 Cor 4:1-5), and we are judged by his requirements, not those of other people. The Colossians are not to let Gnostics or others judge them by food laws or religious calendars (v. 16). Jesus freed us from calendars (Mark 2:27-28) and kosher laws (Mark 7:15, 19). Such arbitrary rules are but a *shadow*. Christ is the *substance*.

The imperative in v. 18, *Do not let anyone disqualify you*, could be rendered, "do not let anyone award you a prize unjustly." Paul's opponents offer the prize for those who qualify by *self-abasement and worship of angels* instead of *holding fast to the head*, that is, Christ. Such is an empty prize. The true prize is *growth that is from God*, attained only as the body of Christ holds fast to the head.

Dwelling on visions translates difficult syntax. This may be a quotation from the mystery religions, including the Greek *embateuon* ("setting foot upon"; NRSV *dwelling on*), a term used for entering a sanctuary in initiation rites where *visions* were sought (Lohse 1971, 118–20). Paul warns against such *visions* as displacing what God has done in Christ.

<u>2:20-23. Impotence of rules.</u> Since *the elemental spirits of the universe* are but human creations, why be subservient to their rules? We belong not to *the world* but to Christ.

Rules like *Do not handle, Do not taste, Do not touch* relate only to such things as perishable food, not to lasting significance. They are merely human rules. They may have the appearance of wisdom as they impose devotion, self-abasement, and ascetic practice, but they are powerless to check *self-indulgence*.

Moral and Ethical Admonitions, 3:1–4:1

<u>3:1-4. Heavenly vs. earthly claims.</u> That Christians *have been raised with Christ* means that they are under the claim of heaven, the world *above, where Christ is, seated at the right hand of God*, the place of honor and power. Although they have *died* and *been raised*, Christians yet live *on earth*, caught between two claims, those from above taking precedence.

We are to live now a life suited to heaven, not to get there but because already we belong there in Christ. The life above is assured by Christ's present enthronement and by his promised return in glory. Life on earth for those in Christ may have the appearance of dishonor and defeat (e.g., Paul's *chains* [4:18]), but its true honor will be revealed eschatologically when Christ is revealed in his glory.

3:5-11. What to put off. Five *earthly* sins are listed, four as sexual abuses: *fornication, impurity, passion, evil desire.* The fifth is more deadly: *greed (which is idolatry).* The material as such is not evil; it is God's creation. It is materialism that is evil. When it owns us, it becomes a god and we idolaters. The *wrath of God* (v. 6) coming upon this is the outworking of God's moral law (Rom 1:18-32). It is reaping what we sow (Gal 6:7-8).

A second list of five *earthly* things are antisocial vices: *anger, wrath, malice, slander, and abusive language.* Anger in itself is not the problem; it is what we do with it or let it do with us. *Wrath* here is anger become chronic. Malice, slander, and abusive language intend harm to others. In the new life, worldly distinctions are transcended, for in Christ *there is no longer Greek and Jew, circumcised and uncircumcised, barbarian, Scythian, slave and free. Greek* stands for gentile. *Scythian* was a term for that ethnic group as more savage than *barbarian*, a questionable stereotype. This enlarges upon Gal 3:28 but significantly drops "no longer male and female" (see 3:18-19).

3:12-17. What to put on. Five virtues to put on displace the evils to put off. These have to do with conduct serving others, unlike the self-serving vices. Forbearance (RSV) or bearing with one another (NRSV) is holding back from one another when tempted to retaliate. Unlike indulgence, forgiveness is creative. It seeks to free from sin as well as restore relationships.

The main adornment for *God's chosen ones* (God chooses us first) is *love.* This fruit of the Spirit (Gal 5:22), abiding and greatest gift of Cod's grace (1 Cor 13), *binds everything together in perfect harmony.*

The peace of Christ is not the world's "peace" (John 14:27). Augustus Caesar boasted of *Pax Romana*, but the peace of Rome was imposed by military might. *Pax Christi* is inner peace, attained by the cross, not by the sword.

The *word of Christ* is to dwell in each Christian, and all are to *teach and admonish one another in all wisdom.* Nothing here excludes women or laypersons from teaching or admonishing. *Psalms, hymns, and spiritual songs* imply the full range of songs to God, not precise distinctions.

3:18–4:1. Domestic relationships. This is the first appearance in the NT of an early domestic code (also in Eph 5:22–6:9; 1 Tim 2:8-15; 6:1-2; Titus:1-10; 1 Pet 2:13–3:7; see Stagg and Stagg 1978, 187–204).

Wives, be subject to your husbands mistranslates the middle imperative *hypotassesthe.* The text reads, "Wives, subject yourselves." This at least recognizes the right of a wife to order her own life *as is fitting in the Lord.* From the NT as a whole, more is to be said. Codes are historically conditioned, never final or complete. Husbands are to love their wives and not mistreat them; but silence here does not imply that wives are not to love their husbands or may mistreat them.

The code for children and parents rightly implies that parental responsibility requires the child's obedience; but when the code is absolutized, problems arise. The code here does not cover the problems of child abuse, a modern scandal.

Slaves are to give a quality of service that is a credit to them and to Christ, not for self-serving purposes or because the master deserves it. Masters themselves are reminded that they must answer to the master in heaven (see PHILEMON, LETTER TO for another approach to slavery).

Closing Appeals and Greetings, 4:2-18

4:2-4. Prayer. Paul's prayer request was not that the doors of his prison be opened for his release but that *a door for the word* be opened, that he might *declare the mystery of Christ*, the very gospel for which he was in prison. Paul was not imprisoned for preaching Jesus as the Christ, for others did that without arrest. It was because he preached that "in Christ" there was no Jew and Greek that he was evicted from synagogues and Temple and imprisoned. If given an open door, he would preach *clearly* the very gospel for which he suffered chains.

4:5-6. Outsiders. The Colossians are urged to conduct themselves wisely toward outsiders and to make their speech gracious, *seasoned with salt*, appealing as well as informed and honest.

4:7-17. Colleagues. *Tychicus* seemingly was the bearer of the letter, commissioned to add his report to the letter. *Onesimus* is doubtless the runaway slave of Philemon. Once estranged from *Mark* (Acts 15:37-40), Paul now warmly commends him. *Aristarchus, Mark,* and *Jesus Justus* are the only Jews now with Paul, a price paid for his gospel of no distinction between Jew and gentile in Christ. This letter and one *from Laodicea* (probably Philemon) are to be exchanged, with *Archippus* charged to "fulfil the ministry" (RSV) already given him, possibly the release of Onesimus (Knox 1959, chap. 3).

4:18. Paul's autograph. Paul now takes the pen for his autograph. Remembering his *chains*, they should also remember the *mystery of Christ* (4:3) for which he was in chains.

Works Cited

Cannon, George E. 1983. *The Use of Traditional Materials in Colossians.*
Knox, John. 1959. *Philemon among the Letters of Paul.*
Lohse, Eduard. 1971. *Colossians and Philemon.*
Stagg, Evelyn, and Frank Stagg. 1978. *Woman in the World of Jesus.*
Wilson, R. McL. 1968. *Gnosis and the New Testament.*

First Thessalonians

Linda McKinnish Bridges   [MCB 1241-1246]

Introduction

First Thessalonians deserves careful reading. Dwarfed by the giant literary shadows of Romans, Galatians, and the Corinthian letters, 1 Thessalonians has often been overlooked by Pauline scholars. Yet, this small but significant letter offers the reader an opportunity to explore an early sample of Christian literature (certainly the earliest in our CANON), to hear the burning theological and ethical issues of a young, inexperienced Christian community in THESSALONICA, and to see the passion and tender care given to them by their extraordinary leader, the apostle PAUL.

The Writer

That Paul wrote 1 Thessalonians is not contested. The literary style, vocabulary usage, and parallels in Acts point to Paul as the author. *When* he wrote the letter, however, is much more difficult to establish.

Some scholars date the letter around 40 C.E. (Luedemann 1984; Donfried 1985; Richard 1990; Jewett 1986), while others situate the writing around 50 C.E. (Koester 1982; Malherbe 1983, 1987). The reason for lack of consensus is that a detailed itinerary of Paul's missionary activity is impossible to reconstruct from either Luke's story of Paul in MACEDONIA (Acts 17–18) or Paul's own letter to the church in Thessalonica. Neither writer wrote for the sole purpose of relating travel itineraries; therefore, exact dates are conjectures, at best.

Just as the exact date of the writing is difficult to determine, so is the precise setting and surrounding circumstances. Not only are Luke's and Paul's accounts sketchy, sometimes they do not agree. The reader, therefore, must be familiar with both accounts in order to establish background information for the Thessalonian letter.

The Acts Account. How did Paul arrive in Thessalonica? According to the Acts account, Paul was imprisoned in PHILIPPI at the beginning of the mission to Europe (Acts 16:19-24). Paul, along with SILAS and TIMOTHY, then left Philippi, traveled through AMPHIPOLIS and Appolonia and then arrived in Thessalonica. When they arrived, Paul went into the synagogue, as was his custom, and proclaimed Jesus as Messiah (17:3).

How long did Paul stay? Paul stayed in Thessalonica for three Sabbaths (three weeks). As a result, some Jews, a number of gentiles, and many women were converted. Their success angered the Jews, however, and a hostile crowd attacked the home of a new convert, Jason. Jason and other believers were dragged to the city magistrate. Paul, although not present, was charged with treason (17:7). Paul and his colleagues secretly left Thessalonica by night. They traveled to Beroea, where the Thessalonican Jews continued to agitate the crowds. Silas and Timothy remained in Beroea, and Paul went on to ATHENS alone.

When did Paul write the letter? Acts does not give us information about any of Paul's letters. From the Acts account, however, we surmise that Paul wrote a letter after visiting the community of believers in Thessalonica.

The Account from 1 Thessalonians. How did Paul arrive in Thessalonica? Paul does not give details of his initial arrival in Thessalonica. We must learn that information from Acts 17.

How long did Paul stay? In the Acts account, we read that Paul stayed in Thessalonica for three weeks. In Paul's letter, however, the visit appears longer. Again, the details are sketchy. We do know that Paul was in the city long enough to establish his trade of tentmaking and to provide a model of behavior for the Christians (2:9-10). We also know that on several occasions Paul received gifts sent from Philippi by a traveling courier (Phil 4:15). Philippi was about 100 miles distant. The time spent in travel would have taken longer than three weeks (4:15).

When did Paul write the letter? First Thessalonians does not give a date. The letter was written after Timothy reported his visit to Paul. No other churches are mentioned in the letter. We can surmise that Paul wrote 1 Thessalonians shortly after leaving the city of Thessalonica, perhaps in CORINTH in 50 C.E., in the company of Timothy and Silas.

The Letter

Traditionally scholars have viewed 1 Thessalonians according to its thematic structure. The letter has been divided into the categories of thanksgiving, personal remarks, and ethical and doctrinal teaching. Recently, scholars have proposed new readings of 1 Thessalonians, using the exegetical methods of structuralism (Malbon 1983), feminist reading (Gaventa 1990), and Graeco-Roman rhetorical conventions (Wanamaker 1990).

Although various methods are used to outline and interpret the epistle, 1 Thessalonians, nonetheless, remains a letter. This epistle is an authentic piece of correspondence between two parties, Paul and the church at Thessalonica. Unfortunately we only have clear access to one part of the conversation—Paul's. To hear the voice of the other party, the novice Christians in the church at Thessalonica, we must listen carefully.

The Community

Paul's letter was not intended to be a systematic theological treatise. Paul wrote to a community, composed predominantly of gentile believers who were struggling with their new faith (see the description by Blevins 1990, 909, of the setting of the community). Paul does not present dogmatic rules for life; nor does he prescribe a quick fix for their theological anxiety. Rather, in this letter Paul shares himself and pastoral words of comfort with "the beloved ones" in Thessalonica (2:8).

The occasion for the letter comes from the community. Timothy returns to Paul from Thessalonica with a good report and with a list of questions from the community. These questions, either in written or oral form, articulate the basic concerns of the community. The questions also reveal a troubled congregation. Paul writes to comfort them.

As we read Paul addressing the concerns of the Thessalonian church in this intimate letter, we can also hear the anxious voices from the church. The community is experiencing persecution (1 Thes 1:6; 2:14-16). They are concerned about the recent death of church members (4:13-18). They remain confused about the meaning of an incalculable PAROUSIA (5:1). The community in Thessalonica also question Paul's style of leadership (2:1-12). Sexual ethics are also a major concern (4:1-8).

For Further Study

In the *Mercer Dictionary of the Bible*: APOSTLE/APOSTLESHIP; EPISTLE/LETTER; ESCHATOLOGY IN THE NT; PAROUSIA; PAUL; THESSALONIANS, LETTERS TO THE; THESSALONICA.

In other sources: E. Best, *The First and Second Epistles to the Thessalonians*; L. McK. Bridges, "Paul as a Nursing Mother," *Lectionary Homiletics* (Nov 1993); R. Collins, *The Thessalonian Correspondence*; Beverly Gaventa, "The Maternity of Paul," in *The Conversation Continues*, ed. R. Fortna and B. Gaventa; R. Jewett, *The Thessalonian Correspondence: Pauline Rhetoric and Millenarian Piety*; H. Koester, "I Thessalonians—Experiment in Christian Writing," in *Continuity and Discontinuity*, ed. F. Church; A. J. Malherbe, *Paul and the Thessalonians: The Philosophic Tradition of Pastoral Care*; E. S. Malbon, "'No Need to Have Any One Write?' A Structural Exegesis of 1 Thessalonians," *Semeia* 26 (1983): 57–83; I. H. Marshall. *1 and 2 Thessalonians*; L. Morris, *The First and Second Epistles to the Thessalonians*; J. M. Reese, *1 and 2 Thessalonians*; C. Wanamaker, *The Epistles to the Thessalonians: A Commentary on the Greek Text*.

Commentary

An Outline

Greeting the Church, 1:1

Paul begins the letter with the familiar, traditional epistolary greeting (cf. Rom 1:1-7; 1 Cor 1:1-3; 2 Cor 1:1-2; Gal 1:1-4). *Silvanus*, the SILAS of Acts 15:22, and *Timothy*, Paul's missionary colleague, were probably the couriers of the Thessalonian letter. They transported the letter from CORINTH to THESSALONICA.

Paul does not identify himself as servant as he does in the greeting of Romans, or as an apostle as seen in 1 and 2 Corinthians and Galatians. Perhaps Paul's position as leader is not as unstable in the Thessalonian church as it would later become in the other churches. The liturgical prayer, a traditional Pauline greeting, offers *grace . . . and peace* to the church.

Encouraging the Church, 1:2-10

Central to the skill of a good communicator is the ability to make contact with the audience. Paul, an excellent communicator, gains the attention of the listeners by talking directly to them. He praises them and their accomplishments. In this tribute, the themes of the entire epistle are also introduced.

1:2-4. Praise. Paul offers thanks for the believers. The tone of praise is repeated in 2:13-14, 2:20, 3:6-10, and 4:1. A familiar triad—faith, love, and hope—describe the people (1 Thes 5:8; Rom 5:1-5; 1 Cor 13:12-13). The church at Thessalonica is noted for their work that comes from their faith, their labor that proceeds from their love, and their steadfastness that follows their hope (v. 3). Paul also gives thanks because he knows that his friends, "the beloved ones," have been called by God (v. 4). Paul continues to offer tribute for the "beloved ones" throughout the epistle (see 2:19-20; 3:6-10).

The language used in these verses instills community and intimacy. The presence of the second personal pronouns, the use of familial term, "brothers" (ἀδελφοί), translated inclusively as *friends* (NRSV), and the use of the word calling or ELECTION (ἐκλογήν) in v. 4 are used to create intimacy between the speaker and the audience.

1:5-7. Paul's ministry of imitation. Paul encourages the readers to imitate him. At first glance, the injunction sounds self-serving. Paul, however, was not establishing his life as the authoritarian model for morality for the community. Rather, Paul is saying, "imitate me as I imitate Christ." See the further development of the idea of imitation in 1 Thes 2:13-16 and 2 Thes 3:6-9.

Verses 6b-8 clarify the metaphor of imitation. To imitate Paul means to be willing to experience the joy of the Spirit even in times of distress (v. 6b). The persecution may have been emotional or physical suffering, or both. To break from the past, either from the Jewish tradition or gentile cultic worship, required emotional anguish for the neophyte Christians. Persecution may have also been more visible, like political oppression or economic hardship.

Paul's understanding of imitation suggests that believers are to become an example to others as he had been an example to them. As Paul had been instrumental in bringing the Thessalonians to faith, so should the community of faith, in turn, be responsible for spreading the gospel (vv. 7-8).

1:9. Ethics. The community received Paul and his gospel. That reception was manifested in clear and visible ways. The believers left their former way of life; they turned from idols to embrace a new life-style with Christ. Paul clarifies this new ethical behavior in 4:12.

To leave a cultic life-style and embrace the strict, ethical admonitions of Paul was no easy task for the novice, Thessalonian Christian. Religious cults were popular in the city of Thessalonica. Archaeological evidence points to the presence of the cults of Serapis, Dionysus, Cabirus, and Samothrace in Thessalonica. Sexual symbols, mystical rites, and frenzied, orgiastic worship characterized the cults.

1:10. Eschatology. The theme of eschatology is briefly introduced here, foreshadowing further development in 4:13. The community of believers have not only left their former life-styles, they are waiting patiently for the return of Christ.

Notice the didactic use of the relative clauses. The community "waits for God's son *who* is from heaven, *who* was raised from the dead, and *who* is Jesus, our deliverer" (author trans.). With characteristic literary flair, Paul packs a thought unit, using every opportunity to teach the gospel, even through a preponderance of relative clauses.

Serving the Church, 2:1–3:10

Soon after Paul's arrival in Thessalonica he incurred much agony (ἀγῶνι) in opposition (see Acts 17:1-9). Paul had also endured much agony in his previous missionary stop in PHILLIPI (Phil 1:30). Paul ministered in the face of considerable obstacles. His motives for ministry were pure, and the opposition unwarranted.

As a Nursing Mother, 2:1-9

Paul, who is perhaps being maligned by opponents in the church, uses literary energy to explain his innocence. Paul's ministry is not to please people, as he has perhaps been accused. Paul did not minister to the Thessalonians with words of flattery, nor with the motive of greed. Nor did Paul come looking for glory from them or others.

How did Paul come to the people? Although he could have come as a heavy, apostolic tyrant or dictator, "throwing his weight around" in the congregation, he chose to come gently, as a nursing mother, ὡς ἐὰν τροφὸς θάλπῃ τὰ ἐαυτῆς τέκνα (vv. 6-7). This striking contrast of images provides a vivid picture of Paul's relationship with the people. As a mother would nurse her child, giving of her life, sharing her time, being accessible, providing life-sustaining nourishment whenever needed, so does Paul care for the people of Thessalonica. The maternity of Paul challenges the contemporary abuses of pastoral leadership.

As an Encouraging Father, 2:10-16

A second familial metaphor describes how Paul serves the church. Paul responded to them as father, πατήρ (vv. 10-11). Paul's images of pastoral leadership do not come from Roman military structure or the ancient business world, but from the arena of the household. Verse 12, which continues the thought of vv. 10-11, describes the role of the father: to exhort or teach, to encourage or cheer, to witness or affirm. The father in the first-century home was the primary parent responsible for moral guidance. Paul's maternal and paternal images form a unified image that challenges contemporary views of pastoral leadership and power in the church.

Some scholars view vv. 13-16 as an interpolation, added later and not written by Paul. Most argue for the interpolation view because of the anti-semitic tone of the passage. Others argue that although it was written by Paul, vv. 13-16 provide a digression, or interruption of his train of thought.

I suggest, however, that the unit vv. 13-16 is not an interpolation. Rather, these verses are used by Paul to support and expand the familial metaphor given in vv. 10-12. Verses 10-13 illustrate the role of the fatherly pastor. Just as the role of the first-century father was to encourage the children, so Paul encourages the people (v. 13). Paul likewise takes on the role of teacher as he reminds the Thessalonians to imitate him (v. 14). Finally, Paul affirms the congregation by reminding them of his own personal suffering. Paul is fulfilling the role of the traditional Jewish father who brings the memory of past experiences as lesson to be learned for the present (v. 16).

As an Orphan, 2:17–3:10

Paul loves the people of Thessalonica, and he is not ashamed to show his emotion for them. In their absence, he feels like an orphan (ἀπορφανισθέντες), like a child without parents. Again, this potent image reinforces Paul's style of leadership. Paul has not only given these people the gospel, he has given them *himself* (2:8). They have become family to him. The community of believers becomes his *crown of boasting* (2:19-20).

Paul sent Timothy back to the Thessalonians as Paul's official courier (3:2). Paul received a glowing report. Paul is encouraged (3:6).

Praying for the Church, 3:11-13

We already know that Paul prays for this church as seen in 1:2. Verses 11-13 give us some of the content of those prayers.

The verses are linked by verbs found in the optative mood, a grammatical expression for prayer: *may . . . direct* (v. 11), *may . . . make you increase and . . . abound in love* (v. 12). Paul prays so that the church might be blameless and holy (v. 13).

Teaching the Church, 4:1–5:22

Commonly called the paranesis, which means teaching or exhortation, this section deals with ethical behavior in the community. Paul's concern for the ethics of the congregation has already been foreshadowed in 1:9 and reinforced in Paul's prayer in 3:12-13.

Theology and Praxis, 4:1-2

Paul understands that loving God, a horizontal relationship, also means loving the community, a vertical relationship. A sense of urgency is heard in Paul's voice as he begs (ἐρωτῶμεν) the members of the church to have their walk with others parallel their talk about Christ (v. 1). Ethics, for Paul, is not a philosophical abstraction. Rather, Paul summarizes Christian behavior by giving practical guidelines for holy living.

Sexual Ethics, 4:3-8

Paul does not mince words when he says: *Abstain from fornication* (v. 3). In v. 4, Paul exhorts the believer to control one's own "vessel" (σκεῦος). Some English translations, however, render this Greek word as *wife*. For example, the RSV translates v. 4a as, "each one of you know how to take a wife for him." This biased translation limits the exhortation to married men and misses the force of the paragraph. To control one's own sexual urges is the point of this verse. The reason for sexual discipline relates to issues of justice for the entire community, not only within marriage (v. 6). To exploit another person sexually damages both individuals and the life of the community suffers. Paul acknowledges that to live a life with sexual limits is not easy. This is God's way, however, and the HOLY SPIRIT has been given for assistance (vv. 7-8).

Relationships, 4:9-12

Paul begins a new thought unit with the words, *Now concerning*. The new topic continues to highlight the horizontal mandate of the gospel—*love one another* (v. 9). Four verbal infinitives provide the grammatical structure for this section: to love more, to be quiet, to mind your own affairs, and to work with your own hands. Some of Paul's converts may have been refusing to earn their own keep. Some of the church members may have also stopped working thinking that Jesus would return soon. Paul urges them to wait quietly, while working and relating to people.

Return of Christ, 4:13–5:11

A new topic begins in v. 13. Paul addresses directly the questions given to Timothy by the congregation. Their dilemma is this: The church members have had relatives to die since Paul's last visit. They understood that Paul taught the imminent return of Christ, the PAROUSIA. Then their relatives began to die, and the parousia had not yet happened. They are confused. They are also grieving. They grieve over the loss of their loved ones. They also grieve because their teacher is not present with them in their time of mourning.

In response, Paul makes two important points. One, Paul says that those who have died will not be disadvantaged at the parousia (4:13-18). God will take care of them. Reunion with them and union with Christ will occur in the end. Two, the exact time of Jesus' return cannot be determined in advance (5:1-11). Therefore, the Thessalonians should relax and be comforted.

Paul's initial reaction is to comfort his grieving friends (5:11). To do so he recalls a word from the Lord (4:15). He uses powerful, visual images—"the archangel's voice," "a trumpet," "the clouds"—to describe the majestic event that is to come. The most comforting point is found in the tiny Greek word σύν (together with) in v. 17. Paul wants the community to know that we will be all *together with* the Lord (v. 17).

This epistle draws the confused, grieving believers in Thessalonica closer *together with* Paul, their teacher and friend. Paul promises that the return of Christ will bring a grand reunion, where loved ones will be brought *together with* one another (2:17–3:10).

Final Instructions, 5:12-22

Last-minute imperatives of ethical behavior are given in the closing of 1 Thessalonians. Paul earnestly begs that the believers recognize and respect their leaders (vv. 12-13). Paul encourages the community to consider those who are idlers (ἀτάκτους), faint-hearted, and weak with generous and forgiving grace (v. 14). Do not return evil for evil (v. 15).

The imperatives also guide the liturgical life of the congregation. *Rejoice* (v. 16). *Pray* (vv. 17-18). Do not restrain the Holy Spirit (v. 19). Do not despise prophecy (v. 20). *Test everything* (v. 21). Keep away from evil (v. 22).

Blessing the Church, 5:23-28

Using the grammar of prayer, the optative mood, Paul offers a concluding prayer for the Thessalonians. The ethical behavior of the Thessalonians remains a primary focus (see the prayer in 3:11-13). Energy for the task, however, comes not from the believer but from God.

Paul's understanding of apostolic authority surfaces in the conclusion (see 2:1–3:10). Paul not only offers prayers for the people, but he is also eager to receive them (v. 25) The *holy kiss* (φιλήματι ἁγίῳ) became a liturgical gesture in the second or third centuries (v. 26). The letter is to be read aloud in the meetings of the church (v. 27). The ending of the letter echoes the beginning with the word *grace* (χάρις, 1:2 and 5:28).

Works Cited

Blevins, James L. 1990. "Thessalonians, Letters to the," in *MDB*.

Donfried, K. P. 1985. "The Cults of Thessalonica and the Thessalonian Correspondence," *NTS* 31:336–56.

Gaventa, Beverly, 1990. "The Maternity of Paul: An Exegetical Study of Galatians 4:19," in *The Conversation Continues: Studies in Paul and John in Honor of J. Louis Martyn*, ed. Robert Fortna and B. Gaventa.

Jewett, R. 1986. *The Thessalonian Correspondence: Pauline Rhetoric and Millenarian Piety.*

Koester, H. 1982. *Introduction to the New Testament. 2: History and Literature of Early Christianity.*

Luedemann, G. 1984. *Paul, Apostle to the Gentiles: Studies in Chronology.*

Manson, T. W. 1953. "St. Paul in Greece: The Letters to the Thessalonians," *BJRL* 35:428–47.

Malbon, E. 1983. "'No Need to Have Any One Write?' A Structural Exegesis of 1 Thessalonians," *Semeia* 26:57–83.

Malherbe, A. J. 1983. "Exhortation in First Thessalonians," *NovT* 25:238–56. 1987. *Paul and the Thessalonians: The Philosophic Tradition of Pastoral Care.*

Richard, E. 1990. "Contemporary Research on (1 & 2) Thessalonians," *BTB* 20:107–15.

Wanamaker, C. 1990. *The Epistles to the Thessalonians: A Commentary on the Greek Text.*

Second Thessalonians

Linda McKinnish Bridges   [MCB 1247-1251]

Introduction

Although 2 Thessalonians continues the conversation with the church in THESSALO-NICA, this epistle must be read separately. It is not simply the second half of 1 Thessalonians. Let 2 Thessalonians be 2 Thessalonians!

To note the dissimilarities between the two letters helps to separate the readings. Second Thessalonians does not contain the personal warmth and affective language as seen in 1 Thessalonians. Absent in 2 Thessalonians is the frequent use of first- and second-person pronouns. Although a basic epistolary structure remains the same, the syntax and style is more complex in 2 Thessalonians, using more relatival clauses and dependent phrases. Furthermore, while 1 Thessalonians addresses many concerns of the community, 2 Thessalonians focuses on one issue, namely, how to be faithful in persecution.

The Writer

Did PAUL write 2 Thessalonians? Although scholars generally conclude that Paul wrote 1 Thessalonians, consensus has not yet been reached regarding the authorship of 2 Thessalonians. The authorship question, first raised at the turn of the century, still lingers.

Wolfgang Trilling (1981) and others, for example, oppose Pauline authorship on the basis of a study of vocabulary and style. On the other hand, Robert Jewett (1986) and others, argue for Pauline authorship on the basis of vocabulary and style. Both arguments are compelling. Although Pauline authorship was not questioned in the first few centuries of the church, recent linguistic analyses show significant variation in Greek syntax between the two letters. Paul either wrote in a totally new style when he composed the second letter, or another person used Paul's apostolic authority to gain a hearing for 2 Thessalonians.

Questions regarding the author, however, do not diminish the powerful voice of the letter, either for first-century or twentieth-century readers. The writer, whether Paul or another, writes a real letter to real people with real problems. We listen in on the conversation.

The Letter

Traditional, first-century, epistolary conventions are seen in 2 Thessalonians. This carefully constructed letter includes a greeting, body, and closing. Particular attention is given to chap. 2, the central chapter. This crucial section introduces the primary focus of the letter—the community's response to the PAROUSIA of Christ.

Which letter was written first? The question is valid, for canonical sequence has more to do with length of the letters than with chronological concerns. Some scholars, H. Grotius 1679, J. Weiss 1937, T. W. Manson 1953, and others, posit that 2 Thessalonians was actually written first. They assume Paul wrote 2 Thessalonians while in ATHENS. TIMOTHY delivered the letter to the church, as Paul later records in the second letter (1 Thes 3:1-6). First Thessalonians, Paul's second letter, was written from CORINTH and composed after Timothy returned from his previous visit.

Contemporary scholarship remains divided on the issue of the sequence of 1 and 2 Thessalonians. Robert Jewett 1986 presents a cogent argument for canonical sequencing. By contrast, Charles Wanamaker (1990) offers a detailed argument for the reversal.

The question of sequence is valid; the answers, however, remain questionable. For our purposes here, we follow the traditional sequencing and assume that 2 Thessalonians was written after 1 Thessalonians. The second letter continues the conversation with the community. The style of conversation, however, is strikingly dissimilar.

The Community

At least three problems concern this community of believers. One, they are theologically confused (2 Thes 2:2). They think *that the day of the Lord* has already come. Paul describes what will take place before Christ comes to assure them that the parousia, or coming of Christ, has not happened yet.

Two, some members of the community have become social problems and economic burdens for the church. These people, believing that Christ had already come, have become lazy (3:6). They are not working. They depend on others for their economic support.

The third problem, related to the first two, has to do with false teachers in the church. OPPONENTS OF PAUL and his teachings have infiltrated the life of the community (1:4-12). They have introduced faulty theologies and weak ethics. They have also brought suffering and persecution to the members of the community who do not heed their teachings.

Who are these false teachers? We know more about what they said than where they came from. Various options regarding the identity of the opponents have been given, such as gnostic infiltrators, millenarian radicals, or enthusiastic revivalists. We, however, can only guess at their identity and place of origin.

Could it be that these opponents were members from the church in JERUSALEM? The chasm between Paul's ministry and the intended ministry goals of the Jerusalem church was great. The Jerusalem church often sent missionaries to check on Paul's work (Acts 15:22f.; Gal 2:4-10). It is not unlikely that a group of anti-Paul, energetic, Judaizers from Jerusalem also entered Thessalonica causing disruption and distressing the Thessalonican Christians. They contradict Paul's teachings, assuring the neophyte Christians that the *day of the Lord* has already come (2:2).

Furthermore, these opponents oppose Paul's ethical teachings by encouraging the Thessalonican community to relax, not bother with working (3:12). The opponents demand conformity, and the community labors under great pressure and persecution (1:4-12). To this community of new believers in Thessalonica, who have been influenced by these infiltrators, Paul says, "Be faithful, don't give up, hang in there."

For Further Study

In the *Mercer Dictionary of the Bible*: ESCHATOLOGY IN THE NEW TESTAMENT; MAN OF LAWLESSNESS; PAUL; THESSALONIANS, LETTERS TO THE; THESSALONICA.

In other sources: *See also* "1 Thessalonians," above; J. Bailey, "Who Wrote II Thessalonians?" *NTS* 25 (1978–1979): 131–45; E. Krentz, "Traditions Held Fast: Theology and Fidelity in 2 Thessalonians," in *The Thessalonian Correspondence*, ed. R. Collins; M. J. J. Menken, "The Structure of 2 Thessalonians," in *The Thessalonian Correspondence*, ed. R. Collins; R. Russell, "The Idle in 2 Thess. 3:6-12: An Eschatological or a Social Problem," *NTS* 14 (1988): 105–19; D. Schmidt, "The Authenticity of 2 Thessalonians: Linguistic Arguments," *SBLSP* 1983.

Commentary

An Outline

I. Greeting the Church, 1:1-2
II. Thanking the Church, 1:3-12
III. Warning the Church, 2:1-17
  A. The Coming of Christ
     and the Person of Lawlessness, 2:1-12
  B. The Gathering of Christians, 2:13-17

IV. Teaching the Church, 3:1-15
  A. The Prayer for Discipline, 3:1-5
  B. The Discipline in the Community, 3:6-15
V. Blessing the Church, 3:16-18

Greeting the Church, 1:1-2

Note the similarities between the epistolary greeting in 1 and 2 Thessalonians. Three major characters are introduced—PAUL, SILVANUS, and TIMOTHY. Traditionally we focus on the missionary activities of Paul, often to the exclusion of Paul's colleagues. It is important to note, however, that the missionary activity of the early church was not accomplished through the efforts of one, but of many. Paul worked with BARNABAS, JOHN MARK, LYDIA, Phoebe, and a host of others, some of whom are not even mentioned in the letters. Together, they planted churches and nurtured young congregations in the faith.

Thanking the Church, 1:3-12

Paul's letters exhibit liturgical qualities. The depth of emotion is best revealed in the Greek syntax. This section, although containing ten verses in English, is constructed from only two Greek sentences, vv. 3-10 and 11-12. The Greek embedded clauses and phrases give power and personal drama to the moment of thanksgiving.

The thanksgiving section, while liturgical in tone, also has a rhetorical function. The use of second-person pronouns and words of praise urges people to stop and listen to the important points of the presentation. Likewise, the first-century reader hears Paul's affective language and is compelled to listen. While listening to Paul's praise (vv. 3-4), they are also introduced to the main themes of the letter (vv. 5-11).

Two themes are introduced in this section and then further clarified in the body of the letter. First, the theme of *the day of the Lord* is introduced in vv. 5-10 and then discussed in greater detail in 2:1-12. Likewise, the theme of the community is introduced here and is given fuller treatment in the paranetic section of 2:13–3:15.

1:3-4. Praise and prayer. The church is congratulated on their faithful persistence in spite of local opposition. In a spirit of prayer, Paul praises the congregation for their faith in God and love for one another. The Thessalonican church has become a model of faith for other churches (v. 4).

1:5-10. Reversal of fortunes. The *day of the Lord* will bring both reward and punishment. This theology of suffering includes rewards for those who have been faithful and affliction for those who have caused the persecution. This reversal of fortunes, repaying those who caused affliction with affliction, belongs to God's righteous judgment (vv. 5-7). Those who have been faithful, even in persecution, will be able to relax when Jesus returns. To be able to relax at *the day of the Lord* stands in sharp contrast to those who, not knowing God and not obeying the gospel of Christ, will be given punishment. The punishment will be total separation from the face of the Lord and from the glory of his strength (vv. 7-9).

1:11-12. Praise and prayer. The section closes with a prayer (vv. 11-12) just as it began with a spirit of prayer (1:3-4). Attention shifts, however, within the INCLUSIO from the explanation of *the day of the Lord* to the response of the community to Christ's coming. With an understanding of *the day of the Lord*, expressed with apocalyptic images and predicted reversal of fortunes, the community is still faced with the question, "How are we supposed to live in the meantime?" It is this question that lingers in the minds of the young believers. Living in the meantime requires intercessory prayer by Paul and ethical behavior by the Thessalonian Christians (v. 12).

Warning the Church, 2:1-17

The predominant theme of 2 Thessalonians, subtly introduced in the thanksgiving section of chap. 1, is given full treatment in chap. 2. The parousia (παρου-σίας), the coming of the Lord, and our coming together with him (ἐπισυναγω-γῆς) are crucial concerns of the community.

Perhaps the young Christians have been asking particular questions concerning the manifestation of Christ, when and how it might occur. Paul responds by describing not only the details of Christ's coming but also our "assembling" with him.

The Coming of Christ and the Person of Lawlessness, 2:1-12

The believers at Thessalonica were confused, literally "shaken in their mind and continually disturbed" (v. 2, author trans.). Someone, somewhere told the congregation that the parousia had already occurred. It is not clear how they received this information, perhaps by a supposedly spirit-inspired utterance, an oral report, or maybe a letter purported to be written by Paul. By whatever means, the young Christians have been deceived.

The purpose of this section is to prove that *the day of the Lord* positively could not have already arrived. Verses 3-7 detail the events that must precede the Lord's coming, and vv. 8-12 point to the events that have not yet happened.

Paul warns that the day of the Lord will not come unless the *apostasy* comes first and the person of lawlessness, the son of destruction, is revealed. Who is this person of lawlessness? This person represents for both the first and twentieth-century reader the epitome of EVIL. The person of lawlessness opposes God, proclaiming to be God.

By wrapping the abstract concept of evil into human form, the readers can visualize its reality and menace. Many comparable historical figures, like Antiochus Epiphanes, Pompey, Gaius Caesar, probably entered the mind of the first-century reader. The first-century reader, most likely, expected a future historical figure to appear whose power could only be restrained by the preaching of the gospel. Full victory over such a person, which also signals victory over pervasive evil, is only possible in the parousia (v. 8).

What about the people? The person of lawlessness deceives the people. Those who have been deceived, therefore, receive not the love of truth and ultimately perish (vv. 10-11). This rather harsh language describes why some people have chosen to reject the gospel. Perhaps Paul is describing the opponents, those people who saw the radical freedom of Christians as a direct threat to their own religious traditions.

Obviously, *the day of the Lord* has not yet come, Paul asserts. In other words, it is going to become much worse before it becomes better.

The Gathering of Christians, 2:13-17

In tones of worship and praise, Paul gives thanks for God's initiative in calling the young Christians into salvation. The appropriate response to the glory of God in Christ is clear to the young Christians in Thessalonica: *Stand firm and hold fast to the traditions that you were taught by us* (v. 15). Capsuled in elegant, apocalyptic descriptions, complemented by beautiful, liturgical phrases, and supplemented by deep, theological insights stands the core of Paul's thought—ethical behavior. It makes a difference how you live. Talk about the end of time does not make much sense unless one also talks about what the parousia means for the gathered people of God in the present. Paul introduces the concept here of the community's response to the coming of Christ and then gives greater detail in the final chapter.

Teaching the Church, 3:1-15

A small word of transition, *finally* (λοιπόν), marks this new section. This word is used often to signal a change of thought and to mark the beginning of the ethical or paranetic portion of the letter (cf. 1 Thes 4:1; 2 Cor 13:11; Phil 4:2). The chapter begins with praise and prayer and concludes with specific instructions for ethical behavior.

The Prayer for Discipline, 3:1-5

Prayer is crucial for Paul. Prayer is also reciprocal between leader and people. Just as the Thessalonians need prayer, so does Paul. The ultimate goal of righteous living for Paul is not for self-glory. Rather, one is to live righteously so that the gospel of Christ, the word of the Lord, might run on ahead and triumph (v. 1). The progress of the gospel can be encouraged by one's life. Not all people, however, will contribute to the progress. Some are not responsive to the word of God (v. 2).

Paul refers to those people who oppose the progress of the Christian mission as the "out-of-place ones" (ἀτόπων). These opponents are consistent dialogue partner throughout this letter, as well as 1 Thessalonians (see 1 Thes 2:13-16). Paul speaks to them and against them as he communicates to the entire church.

The opponents are also a convenient literary foil to show the young believers how not to act. Paul condemns the behavior of the opponents while at the same time he exhorts the others to obedience.

The Discipline in the Community, 3:6-15

Unlike the paranetic section in 1 Thessalonians that contains many instructions (see 1 Thes 4–5), 2 Thessalonians is concerned with only one issue. It's solitary position makes the single exhortation clear and dramatic: Keep away from every friend who is living in *idleness* (ἀτάκτως) (v. 6).

The word *idleness* (see also 1 Thes 5:14 and 2 Thes 3:6, 7) can denote either undisciplined or disorderly actions or persons, or idle or lazy individuals. In the Thessalonian correspondence, the word seems to denote idle behavior that leads to disorderly lives.

Members of the congregation have not been working. They are living in irresponsible idleness. By depending on the wealthier members of the congregation to provide their economic sustenance, they are creating havoc in the community.

Paul reminds them that he and the ethical tradition that he taught does not advocate laziness (v. 8). His own life is an example. Paul did his missionary work without payment (see 1 Thes 2:9; 1 Cor 9:1-18; 2 Cor 11:7). According to the law of Moses and to traditional religious practices, he could, however, have demanded a salary.

A maxim summarizes Paul's position in v. 10: "If you don't work; you don't eat." The instruction given by Paul is plain and simple. The believer is to work, eat one's own bread, and not meddle in the affairs of others. The church is to take special notice of those who cannot obey this instruction. The church is instructed to isolate the person until the behavior is modified. Ostracizing deviant persons becomes necessary for the preservation of the larger community. Notice, however, that the idle person who is undergoing rehabilitation is still to be considered as friend, not enemy.

Blessing the Church, 3:16-18

Second Thessalonians concludes with a prayer of blessing. Paul notes that he is writing this letter with his *own hand* (v. 17). For some scholars, this is a critical clue that this letter may not have been written by Paul, but rather by someone who needed Paul's authority to gain a hearing in the church. Another position is to see v. 17 as Paul's own personal, written signature to a letter actually written by an AMANUENSIS, or secretary. Paul, or his authority, is an important component of the conversation to the Thessalonians.

As the letter began, so it ends. *Grace* (χάρις), the beginning and ending of the life of an individual believer and the community of faith, also becomes the beginning and ending of a letter written by a faithful follower of the gospel, Paul, to a group of young believers in Thessalonica.

Works Cited

Grotius, H. 1679. *Operum Theologicorum.*

Jewett, R. 1986. *The Thessalonian Correspondence: Pauline Rhetoric and Millenarian Piety.*

Manson, T. W. 1953. "St. Paul in Greece: The Letters to the Thessalonians," *BJRL* 35:428-47.

Trilling, W. 1972. *Untersuchungen zum zweiten Thessalonicherbrief.*

Wanamaker, Charles. 1990. *The Epistles to the Thessalonians: A Commentary on the Greek Text.*

Weiss, J. 1959. *Earliest Christianity: A History of the Period A.D. 30–150.* Vol. 1. Trans. F. C. Grant.

First and Second Timothy and Titus

E. Glenn Hinson [MCB 1253-1262]

Introduction

First and Second Timothy and Titus, referred to since 1703 as the PASTORAL EPISTLES, pose one of the intriguing dilemmas of NT scholarship. Claiming both strong internal and external support as the work of the PAUL, they display enough peculiarities by comparison with other letters bearing his name that many question whether Paul could have written them.

The Problem of Authorship

Five issues have been raised regarding Paul's authorship: (1) Vocabulary, grammar, and style differ from those found in Paul's other letters, especially Romans, 1 and 2 Corinthians, and Galatians. (2) The doctrine of the Pastorals differs from Paul's in some ways. (3) The ecclesiastical organization depicted in them is unlike that existing in Paul's lifetime. (4) The heresy attacked is late. (5) The historical data presented in the letters do not square with the framework of Paul's life sketched in Acts.

Theories about Authorship

Scholars have offered a number of theories about authorship. (1) Some scholars attribute the letters to an admirer of Paul responding to a different set of problems and circumstances, dating them variously as early as 90 to 100 C.E. and as late as 140 to 150 C.E. (against MARCION). (2) Others have developed a "fragments hypothesis." A pious follower of Paul had fragments of letters by Paul which he incorporated into these letters, mostly into 2 Timothy. (3) Still others have argued for the genuineness of 2 Timothy and disputed that of 1 Timothy and Titus.

Paul as Author

Those who sustain Paul's authorship of the Pastoral Epistles make the following responses to the arguments against it. (1) Variations in vocabulary, grammar, and style can be explained by (a) the use of a secretary to whom considerable freedom was given, (b) Paul's aging, (c) natural variations in the vocabulary and style of any writer in different contexts writing to different addressees (individuals in this case), and (d) incorporation of formal elements such as hymns, catalogues of virtues and vices, codes for Christian conduct, and confessions of faith. (2) The doctrine agrees with that of Paul's other letters for the most part. Where it varies, it is not post- but *pre*-Pauline, found in hymns or confessions cited in the letters. (3) The ecclesiastical organization of the Pastorals is that of the twofold office of presbyter-bishops and deacons, as in Philippians, and not the threefold office of IGNATIUS (d. 110–117). The roles of Timothy and TITUS, moreover, do not fit the model of bishops in the second century. (4) The heresy attacked in the Pastorals was not second-century GNOSTICISM or Marcionism but some sort of Judaistic, possibly Essene, aberration. Even if it had a gnostic cast, this does not require a post-Pauline date, for the date of Gnosticism has been moved back to Paul's day. (5) Although the historical setting does not fit the scheme of Acts, Luke did not tell the complete story of Paul's life. There is strong early Christian tradition favoring Paul's release after trial, travels, and reimprisonment. In addition, (6) some have questioned whether early Christians accepted the custom of writing under an assumed name as readily as sometimes assumed by scholars who consider the Pastorals pseudonymous.

Purpose

Those who question whether Paul wrote the Pastorals usually envision them as anti-gnostic or anti-Marcionite. The author used basically the same approach Ignatius, Bishop of Antioch, did in the early second century, that is, strengthening ecclesiastical organization. The names of Paul and his disciples, Timothy and Titus, gave an authoritative ring to the proposal. If there were genuine "fragments" which could be incorporated into the letters, they would add further certification. If the pious forger made up personal reminiscences, he did so deliberately to enhance the Pauline nuances.

Those who interpret the Pastorals as Paul's own must try to interpret them as they project themselves. First Timothy presents itself as the instructions of an old soldier to his young aide-de-camp about mission work—public worship, ministry, behavior in the church, and so on. Second Timothy is much more personal, Paul's last will and testament during his second imprisonment and plea for Timothy to join him. Titus contains directions for a seasoned missionary about his work on the island of Crete. Opponents do not figure very prominently in the letters, but they may have been Judaizers with some gnostic tendencies as in Paul's other writings.

Date

If by Paul, the Pastorals would have to have been written during a period after his release from prison in Rome about 62 C.E. If by some later author, they should not be dated later than the last decade of the first century.

For Further Study

In the *Mercer Dictionary of the Bible*: PASTORAL EPISTLES; CHURCH; PAUL; TIMOTHY; TITUS.

In other sources: W. Barclay, *The Letters to Timothy, Titus, and Philemon*; C. K. Barrett, *The Pastoral Epistles in the New English Bible*; E. G. Hinson, "1–2 Timothy and Titus," *BBC* 11; J. N. D. Kelly, *A Commentary on the Pastoral Epistles*.

Commentary

An Outline
First Timothy

I. Greeting and Affirmation of Apostolate, 1:1-2
II. General Orders to Timothy, 1:3-20
III. Orders Concerning the Churches, 2:1–6:2a

    A. Public Worship, 2:1-15
    B. The Ministry, 3:1-16
    C. Behavior in the Church, 4:1–6:2a
IV. Final Orders to Timothy, 6:2b-19
V. Closing Charge and Salutation, 6:20-21

Greeting and Affirmation of Apostolate, 1:1-2

The letter opens with a strong assertion of apostleship as in Romans and Galatians. Paul addresses Timothy in an intimate way as his legitimate child in faith.

General Orders to Timothy, 1:3-20

A military motif prevails throughout this letter. As a commander to his aide, Paul orders TIMOTHY to stay at his post in EPHESUS and to put a stop to teaching other than Paul did and to wrangling about the Law. The goal is agape-love that comes from a pure heart, good CONSCIENCE, and authentic faith. Some have gone astray by ignoring these and plunging into meaningless speculation, wanting to be teachers of the Law but not understanding what they were doing.

Paul agrees with the Judaizers, or Jewish Gnostics, that the Law is good if properly applied. Its proper use is to show what is wrong, as a catalogue of vices based on the TEN COMMANDMENTS confirms, and not what is right. We learn what is right from the gospel with which Paul was entrusted. The gospel is what reveals God as God truly is.

Frequently a target of attacks from Judaizers, the old apostle cannot help lapsing into a defense (vv. 12-17). Paul is "exhibit A" of the grace of God to which the gospel bears witness. What else could Paul do but give thanks to Christ for appointing him as apostle despite what he had once been—a blasphemer, persecutor, and bad-mouther. He was no better than a pagan. Yet the grace of God overflowed with the faithfulness and love that are in Christ. Yes, Paul has to agree with the saying, *Christ Jesus came into the world to save sinners* (v. 15; cf. Luke 19:10), for he was the prime example. Why? So that Christ might display his incredible patience as an example for future believers.

In typical Pauline fashion these thoughts touch off a doxology (v. 17). Praise of God as the only God may be the apostle's way of negating the emperor cult that burgeoned under Nero.

Paul reinforces his general orders with an appeal to their close ties as father and son in faith (vv. 18-20). Yet the command is clear. Timothy, selected by prophets for the job (cf. Acts 13:1-3), must wage a good battle in Ephesus. He has the qualities Paul wants for the whole community, faith and a good conscience. At least *Hymenaeus and Alexander* have suffered shipwreck in the faith and Paul has *turned them over to Satan*. This phrase probably referred to a formula used in cutting them off from the community (cf. 1 Cor 5:5) with physical illness as a possible consequence.

Orders Concerning the Churches, 2:1–6:2a

Paul next issues more specific orders about the church in Ephesus. He addresses the three major areas of concern for young churches—public worship, the ministry, and behavior of their members.

Public Worship, 2:1-15

Appropriately his directions concerning public worship begin with insistence on prayer for all persons and not just for believers (vv. 1-7). The main point is the universality of the prayer. By contrast with some sects in JUDAISM such as the ESSENES, Christians should entreat God on behalf of the emperor and all persons in authority so that they may live peacefully in their own religious commitment.

Paul predicates this appeal on MONOTHEISM. The one and only God wants all persons to be saved and converted to the truth of Christianity. A snippet from an early Christian hymn or confession of faith buttresses the point. Not only is there one God but also one mediator between God and humankind, the man Christ Jesus, who gave himself as *a ransom* not just for the few but *for all*. The gospel cannot be narrowed to an elect. It is for everyone.

Predictably, mention of the universal gospel touches Paul's defense mechanism. It is to this that God appointed him as preacher and apostle and teacher of the gentiles.

To counter the debates that fractured the assembly, Paul appealed for tranquillity in the conduct of worship (vv. 8-15). *Men should pray* with pure lives and *without anger* or disputes. Early Christians, like both Jews and Gentiles, prayed standing, with eyes open and hands lifted toward heaven. Paul was underscoring character and conduct. They should lift up *holy hands* and leave tempers and taunts behind. We relate to God better with peaceful expressions.

Women, likewise, should do things that would promote harmony in the worship services. One dimension would be to dress modestly. Early Christian women tried to set themselves apart from their contemporaries by simplicity of habit—shunning costly clothing, jewelry, elaborate hair styles (cf. 1 Pet 3:1-6). Instead of majoring in dress, they majored in good deeds.

Another dimension for promotion of harmony would be humility in conduct. Although in the church Paul wanted equality (Gal 3:28), practical realities forced women to accept subordinate roles in public worship (cf. 1 Cor 15:34-35). Context may well have dictated concessions at EPHESUS for the sake of preserving peace.

Paul argues like a RABBI in support of the subordinate role for women. (1) God created man before woman (v. 13; cf. Gen 2:22). (2) The serpent deceived Eve and not Adam (v. 15; cf. Gen 3:1-6). The statement that "woman will be saved through bearing children" (RSV) is difficult, maybe impossible, to interpret. A simple interpretation is probably best, that the gift of women through bearing children offsets her failure if she has other Christian qualities—faith, love, purity, and modesty.

The Ministry, 3:1-16

Paul speaks first about the office of presbyter or bishop. The office (Gk. *episkopos*) may have derived from the "superintendent" (*mebaqqer*) of the ESSENES. The term was used interchangeably with the word presbyter (Titus 3:5-7). From this brief instruction one can surmise that presbyter-BISHOP superintended the churches (v. 5), taught, watched over the charities, and led in public worship. The chief concern in this passage, however, was character and not duties.

The phrase "husband of one wife" (RSV) has been interpreted in several ways: (1) faithful to one wife, (2) monogamous, (3) never remarried even after death of a spouse, (4) never divorced, and (5) necessarily married. The first two are the more likely, although in the NRSV, *married only once*, favors the first, second, and third options.

Paul envisioned the church as an extended family and the presbyter-bishop as the head of it. The bishop needed, therefore, the qualities of a good father. How he presided over his own family would give a good clue to his ability to lead this larger family. In a missionsituation such as Timothy served in Ephesus, moreover, the bishop should not be a newly baptized Christian and should have a good reputation with outsiders. These early communities became victims of Christian failing and the attacks of adversaries in times of persecution. *Devil* here probably means "Satan," however, rather than human adversary.

The office of DEACON (vv. 8-13), unlike that of bishop, probably did not have a direct antecedent in JUDAISM except in the servant model of JESUS. The qualifications listed would indicate that deacons shared leadership in worship, visited the sick and imprisoned, played a leading role in the LORD'S SUPPER or Agape meals, handled money for the poor, and taught. They needed careful scrutiny regarding their ministry. Like bishops, they needed to demonstrate in their families the character and gifts of leaders.

There is much debate concerning the reference to women in v. 11. Does it mean women deacons, wives of deacons, or women in general? The last two interpretations have had few advocates. In favor of women deacons are: (1) the reference to Phoebe as a deacon in Rom 16:1; (2) the absence of "their" which one would expect if Paul meant wives; (3) the nature of the virtues listed; and (4) the use of *likewise* to break the train of thought. In favor of wives of deacons are: (1) the brevity of the statement; (2) the way it is sandwiched between statements about male deacons; (3) the discussion of ministry of women in connection with *widows* in 5:3-16; and (4) the likelihood that a more definite term than *women* would have been used if women deacons were meant. The weight of argument slightly favors women deacons. The qualifications suggest a role similar to that of deacons. Women deacons in the late second century assisted in the baptism of women, visited the sick, discharged a ministry of prayer, and did other diaconal tasks.

Paul interjects another personal note explaining why he was writing (vv. 14-16). If Paul is delayed, Timothy should go right ahead with his task, for he knows very well what to do in the CHURCH.

Mention of the church brings to Paul's mind a hymn about Christ as *the mystery of our religion* (v. 16). The hymn emphasizes the universality of God's saving plan to which the church bears witness.

Behavior in the Church, 4:1–6:2a

At this point Paul turns to a series of miscellaneous orders concerning behavior in the church at Ephesus. He refutes the false ASCETICISM of the Judaizers regarding prohibition of marriage and abstinence from certain foods. He instructs Timothy to avoid debating and instead to focus on his own personal piety, remembering especially the spiritual gift he has received for ministry. He follows this with directives about the proper behavior of groups within the Christian family—older and younger persons, widows, presbyters, slaves, and masters.

Casting his refutation (4:1-5) in the form of a prophecy, Paul cites some specific errors, all of which sound like the kind of teachings which would have originated with the ESSENES. They either spent a lot of time talking about demons or evil spirits or, alternatively, teaching things inspired by them. Having bad consciences as a result, they prohibited marriage and observed certain food laws. Paul rebuts these two practices by citing the OT concept of creation and the Christian concept of thanksgiving. Everything God created is good. Giving thanks further validates it for believers.

By contrast with the false ascetics, Timothy should be a good MINISTER of Christ (4:6-10). For this Paul prescribes three ingredients. First, he should nourish himself on the sound teaching that he received under Paul's tutoring and avoid the speculative interpretations of scriptures the ascetics propounded. In Titus 1:14 Paul called these "Jewish myths" and human concoctions.

Second, Timothy should train himself spiritually. Using an athletic metaphor (cf. 1 Cor 9:24-27; Phil 3:12), the apostle underscores how important this is for a minister. If physical exercise is of great benefit, how much greater must be spiritual exercise, for it bears not merely on the present life but also on the life to come. The promise of ETERNAL LIFE is what Christians strive to attain because they have placed their hope in the living God, the Savior of all persons, as believers amply attest. The main accent falls once again on the universality of God's saving work.

Third, combining command and personal plea, Paul directs Timothy's attention to his spiritual gift as the ground on which he can do what ministry requires (4:11-16). Timothy, now in his thirties, should stop hiding behind the excuse, "I'm too young." He should be an example of believers in all dimensions of Christian life—speech, conduct, love, faith or faithfulness, and sexual purity. A weighty expectation! Until Paul could get there, he should continue with the key duties—reading OT scriptures, preaching, and teaching new converts. The wherewithal for all of this would come from his charisma.

How Timothy received this "spiritual gift" is somewhat unclear. Obviously God gave it, but was Paul (as in 2 Tim 1:6) or the "presbytery" the means? As in 1:18, prophets discerned Timothy's spiritual gifts. It would be unlikely, therefore, that Paul or the presbyters would be required to convey the Spirit he already possessed. Laying on of hands accompanied and confirmed what prophetic utterance indicated, that is, Timothy's God-given capacity for ministry. This aspect Timothy must not forget. The gift of God would assure his progress.

Paul sums up his urgent charge. Timothy must pay heed both to himself and to what he teaches, for the stakes are high. He has responsibility both for his own spiritual welfare and for that of the people who listen to him.

This comment opens the way for a transition to the four groups within the household of faith for whom Timothy is responsible: young and old, widows, presbyters, and slaves. Concerning the first group (5:1-2), the apostle emphasizes the familial approach. Timothy should treat older men and women like fathers and mothers, younger men and women like brothers and sisters. Obviously with the latter he had to be circumspect about sex.

Widows (5:3-16) must have constituted a considerable segment of the Ephesian community and their numbers posed a problem. The main objective of this directive was to enroll on the church's charitable list only those whose needs and manner of life established them as genuinely bereft. Paul lists two basic requirements: (1) need and (2) record of Christian service *before* being widowed.

Regarding need, Timothy should see first whether personal family members, children or grandchildren, could care for the widows, thus relieving the overburdened extended family. An allusion to the fifth commandment undergirds the point. A Christian who does not watch out for members of his or her own family is worse than an unbeliever, for Christian faith makes it a principle (v. 8).

Paul's "real widow" would be truly dependent on God, praying night and day. The early churches, of course, knew some not like that, the kind who abandoned themselves to pleasure and comfort, perhaps even prostitution.

As a safeguard against such self-indulgence, Paul established three practical tests: (1) age over *sixty*, (2) *married only once*, and (3) having good reputation for charitable works. "Wife of one husband" (RSV) probably means a single marriage, but the same possibilities exist here as for presbyters and deacons (3:2, 12; Titus 1:6).

Emphasis on reputation for charity suggests that some widows functioned as deacons. Paul lists four specific items that perhaps hint at duties of women deacons. They reared children, practiced HOSPITALITY, washed the feet of the saints, and relieved the sick. As a catchall, Paul adds, widows should have devoted themselves to every sort of good deed.

In vv. 11-15 Paul explains why younger women should not be enrolled as widows, indicating three sets of problems: (1) sexual passion, (2) idleness, and (3) gossiping. He uses very strong language. Their strong sex drive may cause them to violate their pledge to Christ as their bridegroom, made either when baptized or when enrolled as widows. Moreover, they may become troublemakers within the Christian community. Consequently Paul urges in no uncertain terms the remarriage of young widows. Confronted here with a specific problem, he proposes marriage, child-bearing, and care of a home as the way to safeguard the church's reputation. Paul knew that the mission could not afford scandal.

Once again returning to the problem of overtaxed social aid, Paul urges any faithful woman to take needy widows into her household. Some early manuscripts read "believing man," but wealthy women often headed households (e.g., LYDIA in Acts 16:14, 40).

Elders (5:17-25) should be understood in the non-technical sense of "older men" here to avoid dividing them into two classes. Most leaders, if not all, came from this group. *Honor* would have a dual meaning, both respect and pay, as quotations from the OT would imply. At this early stage pay consisted of gifts of food and necessities rather than MONEY. The older leaders would receive twice the allotment for widows and others on the charitable roll.

Where leaders required discipline, Paul had two bits of advice: (1) Do not accept an accusation against a presbyter unless two or more witnesses confirm it. (2) Reprove the offender publicly, either before the elders or the CONGREGATION. Here Timothy must not let personal bias intrude, a point underlined with an oath.

The best DISCIPLINE is, of course, preventive. Thus Paul counsels Timothy not to baptize or ordain anyone hastily. Laying on of hands accompanied both BAPTISM and ordination. Since Timothy played a key role in choosing people, he must take care lest he be implicated in their offenses. The goodness and wickedness of people are sometimes evident, sometimes not.

Thrown in (v. 23) is a little aside about Timothy's personal health. The ancients ascribed medicinal value to wine.

Slaves (6:1-2a) also constituted an important element of the Christian community. Here Paul distinguished the motives of slaves under pagan and under Christian masters. Slaves should treat pagan masters respectfully to avoid bringing reproach on the name of God and Christian teaching. They should show still greater respect for Christian masters because they are *believers and beloved.* Many slaves must have chafed more under Christian than under pagan owners!

Final Orders to Timothy, 6:2b-19

The apostle shifts from orders concerning behavior in the church to warn about the profit motive in religion (vv. 2b-10), deliver a personal charge to Timothy, and give a special word to the wealthy.

Early Christianity attracted some, like SIMON MAGUS (Acts 8:18-24), who tried to turn it into a profit-making enterprise. Paul suspected that the wranglers at Ephesus were inspired by such motives. They could not square these with the teachings of Jesus. Religion, Paul had to admit, is immensely profitable, but not in the way these people pursued it. Rather, Christians must seek contentment with food and clothing, the necessities. People who crave wealth are headed for destruction, for obsession with money is the root of all evils. That is what has caused many to end up in heartache already.

Timothy (vv. 11-16) should shun this and aim at genuine virtue. In what has the ring of a baptismal or ordination charge Paul challenges his favorite son in faith to keep the pledge he made at baptism, a solemn commitment before God and Jesus Christ. Like a good soldier, Timothy must fight valiantly and discharge the orders given him until Christ returns.

Allusion to the appearance of Christ again touches off a doxology, this time mixing Jewish and Greek elements, probably from an early Christian HYMN. The words throw out a stout challenge to the emperor cult. Christ alone rules, possesses immortality, dwells in unapproachable light, and is thus due honor and dominion.

As for the rich (vv. 17-19), who would have been in a minority in early Christian communities, Timothy must charge them not to trust in their wealth but only in God and to be generous. Paul wants them to consider their wealth a stewardship that would give them a solid foundation in eternity. The Christian's goal is not wealth but "real life."

Closing Charge and Salutation, 6:20-21

Paul ends as he began. Almost plaintively, he commands his sometimes vacillating aide to keep the orders given, that is, the true Christian faith. In sum, avoid silly speculation, so-called knowledge, which has led others astray.

An Outline
Second Timothy

I. Greeting and Affirmation of Apostolate, 1:1-2

II. Recollections and Personal Encouragement, 1:3–2:13

III. Counsels for Timothy, 2:14–4:8

IV. Farewell and Concluding Benedictions, 4:9-22

Written after Paul's reimprisonment in ROME, 2 Timothy is his last will and testament (cf. 4:6-8). It sounds two notes: (1) how much PAUL expects of Timothy and (2) what he hopes Timothy will do as his successor in mission.

Greeting and Affirmation of Apostolate, 1:1-2

This greeting differs only slightly from that in 1 Timothy. As one might expect of someone anticipating his death, Paul throws in a hopeful note. He is *an apostle* through God's will according to *the promise of life* attested in Christ's resurrection.

Recollections and Personal Encouragement, 1:3–2:13

Paul initiates his last will and testament with some remembrances that would offer encouragement to his successor (1:3-5). As in other letters, he begins with a prayer of THANKSGIVING to God, whom he served with the same clarity of purpose as his Jewish forbears did. He prayed night and day for his son in the faith. Remembrance of Timothy's tears at their parting aroused a longing to see him. Paul recalled the sincere faith that both Timothy's Jewish grandmother LOIS and his Christian mother EUNICE had exhibited. So Paul was confident he would find the same in Timothy.

His imprisonment notwithstanding, Paul directed Timothy to have confidence in God (1:6-14). Timothy should *rekindle the gift* God had given as indicated by Paul's *laying on of . . . hands* (cf. 1 Tim 4:14). God did not equip him with a spirit of timidity but of power, love, and self-control. He, therefore, should not hesitate to offer his witness to Christ or to defend Paul. As Christ and Paul had suffered, so too should Timothy suffer for the gospel in the power of God.

Mention of God's power stirs up in Paul's mind a HYMN or confession of faith (1:9-10). The first stanza praises God for God's saving work in Christ, calling humankind on the basis of MERCY rather than merit. The second stanza praises Jesus Christ as the one through whom God carried out the eternal plan. The third stanza declares what Christ did—abolished death and brought life and immortality through the gospel.

The word *gospel* triggers an instinctive apology on the part of the aged apostle (1:11-14). It is to this that God appointed Paul as preacher, apostle, and teacher (cf. 1 Tim 1:11) and it explains his suffering. Yet he has no regrets. He has complete confidence in God, that God will see to it that he keeps his pledge.

Paul appeals to Timothy to look to him as an example of reliable teaching he had heard from him that is grounded in faith and love in Christ. Timothy must guard the truth of the gospel committed to him. Although some have detected in the reference to a deposit a succession theory like that of *1 Clem* 42:2-4; 44:2, the statement here does not have to do with succession of bishops. It is about preservation of truth. The ultimate guardian is the HOLY SPIRIT indwelling us.

Paul recounts briefly his own sad plight (1:15-18). All the Christians from the province of ASIA living in Rome had deserted him, notably *Phygelus and Hermogenes.* Well, there was an exception, *Onesiphorus,* an Ephesian who had sought Paul out and done everything he could to aid him. The prayer for his household would seem to indicate that he may have given his life to help Paul.

Having built a foundation for faithfulness from the example of Timothy's family and himself, Paul comes to the main point. His dear child in faith must be strong and endure suffering (2:1-7). What he had heard from Paul, he must hand on to other faithful persons who will have the ability to teach others. Here again is an embryonic form of succession but of doctrine and not of office.

Paul invokes three images of perseverance: the soldier, the athlete, and the farmer. The soldier models stalwart endurance of hardships, non-entanglement, and desire to please. The athlete image emphasizes the need for *discipline.* The farmer image underlines the importance of hard work. Paul underscores his point with a sort of "Are you listening?"

Ultimately the apostle directs Timothy to the example of Christ (2:8-13). The gospel itself, briefly summarized (cf. Rom 1:3-4), is the reason for faithfulness. It is for the sake of the gospel that Paul suffers imprisonment. Though he is fettered, the word of God is not. The apostle has endured what he has for the sake of those God has chosen to take part in the eternal purpose. Their eternal glory, the antithesis of suffering, is the object of God's plan.

Reflections on God's assurances brings another hymn or confession of faith to mind (2:11-13). The first stanza has an exact parallel in Rom 6:8, suggesting a baptismal context. BAPTISM entails dying and rising with Christ. The second stanza echoes Jesus' words about endurance (Matt 10:22; 24:13; Mark 13:13) and promises participation in Christ's messianic kingdom. The third stanza warns against denial (cf. Matt 10:33). However shaky our faith, God is always faithful.

Counsels for Timothy, 2:14–4:8

Having laid his foundation, Paul turns to more specific directions about the Ephesian problem. His main counsel is to avoid getting entangled in meaningless debates and to discipline those who need it with humility and gentleness. Timothy has to set the example.

By way of contrast with the wranglers Timothy should avoid destructive debating and be a constructive workman (2:14-26). Constant disputation only upsets hearers. Timothy should model constructiveness, steering clear of harmful chatter that spreads through the body like cancer. Prime examples of the type Timothy should shun are *Hymenaeus* (2:17; cf. 1 Tim 1:20) and *Philetus,* who taught that the *resurrection has already taken place.* Some early gnostic groups taught that the resurrection took place in baptism, possibly on the basis of Paul's own teaching (cf. Rom 6:4).

Paul uses two metaphors to draw the line between himself and the wranglers: (1) the solid *foundation* of a strong building (2:19) and (2) the varied utensils in a household (2:20-21). God has established the foundation and inscribed it. God knows his own in an intimate way, and everyone claiming the Lord's name should avoid wrong. Why would any other type be in the church? Because it is a mixed body, like a large household. The key issue is not type of utensil or vessel, but the purity of each.

The apostle once again places the weight of responsibility on Timothy's shoulders (2:22-26). He should flee uncontrolled impulses and aim at the Christian virtues especially suitable in these circumstances, thus putting himself in the company of authentic believers. In handling the disputants he should do two things: (1) stay out of arguments; and (2) treat them with patience and kindliness. The accent falls on gentleness in handling opponents. The aim is to rescue the offenders from the Devil's snare and bring them back to the authentic Christian message.

Paul interjects a kind of apocalyptic warning (3:1-9). Jewish apocalypticists expected dire happenings in the *last days.* To describe these, Paul lists a catalogue of vices similar to the one used in Rom 1:29-31 but not dependent on it. The first two vices—*lovers of [self]* and *lovers of money*—epitomize the whole list. They are arrogant persons who act insensitively toward other persons and toward God. Timothy must shun them.

Paul describes a subtle method of operation. They preyed especially on women burdened by an extreme sense of guilt, always seeking a solution to problems but never able to arrive at the truth. Such charlatans, however, Paul assures Timothy, will not succeed. They will fail like the Egyptian magicians, JANNES AND JAMBRES, who tried their occult powers against MOSES. Everybody will be able to see their counterfeit faith, as they saw the Egyptian magicians' (Exod 8:16-19).

Operating on the assumption that he would have to maximize his plea, Paul invokes again his personal example and Timothy's training (3:10-17). Timothy had shared Paul's missionary labors and knew the price he had paid. He should not be surprised, for the faithful always suffer while the evil imposters get worse and worse. This called for steadfastness. Bedrock for Timothy would be confidence he could place in persons he learned from (his grandmother and mother) and in scriptures.

Scriptures, learned from infancy, furnished the ultimate ASSURANCE. Verse 16 could be translated either "Every scripture is inspired and profitable" or "Every inspired scripture is also profitable" with the latter more likely (ERV, NEB, et al.). The doctrine of inspiration allows room for human agency, but it emphasizes scriptures as the one fully reliable means of REVELATION. They serve, therefore, as the basis of Christian teaching, reproof of SIN, correction, and constructive education in Christian life. Religious leaders like Timothy can count on them.

The apostle buttresses his appeal to example with a solemn exhortation to preach the gospel (4:1-8). With a solemn OATH, he pleads with his sometimes timid colleague to stand fast and do his duty with patience and care. This is urgent because an apocalyptic situation seems at hand when novelty will have more followers than the truth at the time when Paul senses that the end is near. His life about to be poured out on the altar, Paul counts on Timothy.

In this poignant passage the apostle had to reassure himself as much as Timothy. He had *fought the good fight, finished* the race, and *kept the faith* (4:7). Now he could look forward to receiving his eternal reward given to all who have loved Christ's coming.

Farewell and Concluding Benedictions, 4:9-22

The remainder of 2 Timothy consists of personal notices and instructions (vv. 9-18), greetings (vv. 19-21), and a benediction. Scholars who hold the "fragments hypothesis" ascribe all or most of this passage to Paul.

At this point Paul needed Timothy desperately. Demas, his fellow worker during his first imprisonment (Col 4:14; Phlm 24), had deserted him. Crescens and TITUS had taken mission assignments in GALATIA and Dalmatia. LUKE was now the only one with him. Paul, therefore, needed as much help as possible, even John Mark, with whom he must have become reconciled after their rupture (Acts 15:38). MARK would replace TYCHICUS, whom Paul sent to Ephesus with the letter.

Winter approaching (v. 21), Paul wanted Timothy to bring warmer clothing, the heavy blanket-like cloak he had left in Troas with Carpus. He also needed the books, especially the parchments, containing important writings—perhaps parts of the OT, collections of testimonies, and other documents.

Paul could not help inserting a warning about *Alexander the coppersmith*, perhaps the person "turned over to Satan" (1 Tim 1:20) but the name was a common one. Paul was confident God would pay him back, but he knew the danger Alexander posed to Timothy.

After this brief digression the apostle recounts his own sad circumstances. During his first defense, meaning either his first trial or a preliminary hearing in Rome, all deserted him. Yet he would not hold that against them and prayed they not be held accountable in the Judgment. The Lord, God or Christ, stood by him and rescued him from extreme danger. The very thought evokes from Paul a confession of faith and doxology.

The concluding paragraph adds a greeting to long-time missionary associates *Prisca and Aquila* (Acts 18:2, 18; 1 Cor 16:19; Rom 16:3f.) and to Onesiphorus's *household*, a note suggesting Onesiphorus was dead. Paul throws in a couple of other tidbits about mutual acquaintances and passes on some greetings from others.

The fact that he mentions them need not be seen as a conflict with the fact that all deserted him in his first defense (v. 16). These persons did not qualify for a formal defense.

An Outline
Titus

I. Greetings and Affirmation of Apostolate, 1:1-4

II. Instructions for the Community, 1:5–2:15

III. Instructions Regarding the World, 3:1-11

IV. Some Final Instructions, 3:12-14

V. Concluding Salutation and Benediction, 3:15

PAUL did not have as intimate personal ties with TITUS as with TIMOTHY, but he counted heavily on him for effective mission work. Titus had handled the Corinthian problem more effectively than Timothy (2 Cor 8:6; 12:18). At Paul's request (3:12) Titus evidently joined him in ROME. Before writing 2 Timothy Paul sent him to Dalmatia (2 Tim 4:10). From there he went to CRETE.

The letter to Titus has essentially the same objectives as 1 Timothy: to instruct an associate about the ordering of church life and about defense of the mission against agitators. It is both personal and official, intended to be read publicly.

Greetings and Affirmation of Apostolate, 1:1-4

OPPONENTS OF PAUL's mission turned up wherever Paul and his associates worked. Consequently the apostle had constantly to assert his commission. His commission had three aims: to enhance the faith of the elect, to bring them to godly knowledge of the truth, and to share the hope of ETERNAL LIFE. This hope never disappoints because God never lies and has revealed it at the right time through preaching. It is this that God entrusted to Paul.

The greeting to Titus is a bit stiffer than those to Timothy. Titus is an authentic child in a common faith, rather than "beloved" (2 Tim 1:2).

Instructions for the Community, 1:5–2:15

The bulk of the letter gives instructions about the ordering of church life with some warnings about disturbers thrown in. Predictably the qualifications of presbyter-bishops gets attention first (1:5-9). The APOSTLE had left Titus in Crete to set up proper organization and to appoint qualified persons to continue the mission. As in other areas, Paul specified an urban pattern.

Qualifications for presbyter-bishops (NRSV *elders*) correspond closely with that for bishops and deacons in 1 Tim 3. Here too Paul envisioned the church as a family. Success in heading his own household would provide a good clue to management of an extended family. The BISHOP is God's steward. He should be mature, unselfish, and other-directed, able to preach healthy doctrine and refute those who oppose it.

Worthy leadership will be essential in order to counter those who stand opposed to what Paul has taught. Judaistic leanings of the troublemakers are quite clear. Some belonged to the "circumcision party" (cf. Gal 2:12; Col 4:11) and taught Jewish myths. Evidently they also adhered to Jewish dietary laws. They may also have engaged in some kind of magical rites.

Paul had no patience for them because they upset whole families for base motives. The Cretan poet Epimenides characterized them correctly (1:12). Titus must silence them, reprove them sharply, act forcefully to put a stop to them.

Here the apostle offers an antidote to the Cretan troublemakers, exemplary behavior within the Christian community (2:1-10). For this Titus himself offered the key. He had to teach healthy doctrine. Paul directs Titus's attention to four groups—older men, older and younger women, younger men, slaves.

For *older men* (2:1-2) Paul lists essentially the same qualities as he demands of presbyter-bishops and deacons. Christianity does not have two standards of behavior.

For *older women* (2:3-5) he lists qualities similar to those he gives for women deacons or wives of deacons in 1 Tim 3:11. In Crete they would have a special responsibility for the Christian education of younger women, for whom Paul's main concern was strong and stable families. Love of women for husbands and children is the key to the family. As in social codes in other letters of Paul (Col 3:18; Eph 5:22), Paul enjoins wives voluntarily to accept the authority of their husbands lest Christianity's reputation suffer harm in societies that were not yet ready for equality of male and female (Gal 5:28).

For *younger men* (2:6-8) the apostle uses more decisive directions. Titus should set the example of gentlemanly behavior Paul expected. How these individuals behaved would silence the kind of criticism that arose so easily from pagan lips or from the trouble-makers in Crete.

For *slaves* (2:9-10) Paul prescribes acceptance of their status and exemplary service. Christians should not act like typical slaves, talking back and stealing. Rather, they should model reliability so as to make the message of the Savior God noble and attractive to all.

The allusion to God as Savior causes Paul to lapse into a HYMN or confession of faith on God's saving grace as the basis for Christian behavior (2:11-14). GRACE was manifested at a definite moment in history, in the birth of JESUS of Nazareth. It instructs us to lay aside irreligious and worldly behavior, to live godly lives, and to await the consummation of the Christian hope. The signal for the latter will be the return of Christ. Christ came to do two things: liberate us from sin and prepare us to be God's own people. Christ's death furnished the ransom price needed to free us from evil, and it laid a foundation for the church.

At this point (2:15) Paul interjects a general charge to Titus. He must not act indecisively but with full authority, that is, Paul's.

Instructions Regarding the World, 3:1-11

Whereas in chap. 2 Paul gave directions on behavior within the Christian community, in chap. 3 he widens them to the larger world in which Christians live. He wants the Christians of Crete to be model citizens—obedient to their rulers (cf. Rom 13:1-7), honest, and courteous to all (vv. 1-2). They were not always like that (v. 3), but God pulled off a mighty work of recycling.

In support of this plea the apostle cites an early Christian baptismal hymn on regeneration and renewal. Whatever the human situation prior to the Christian era, God decisively changed it in the coming of Christ. Out of goodness and generosity God saved us in one decisive intervention in human history. God acted out of MERCY and not on the basis of our righteousness. We, however, appropriated this mercy through BAPTISM and the gift of the Spirit, which God poured out upon us generously through Jesus Christ. The purpose of the whole divine act is that we may become heirs of eternal life after God has rightwised us. The formula *The saying is sure* (v. 8) looks backward rather than forward.

Concluding the main body of the letter (vv. 8b-11), Paul takes one last shot at the troublemakers. Titus must be insistent on what Paul has said so that believers may apply themselves to good deeds beneficial to humankind. Contrariwise, he must avoid divisive debates deadly for Christian witness. He should shun the factious person after one or two warnings (cf. Matt 18:15-17). If such a person refused to relent, he or she would be self-condemned.

Some Final Instructions, 3:12-14

Paul intersperses in his conclusion some personal notes with his final instructions. When he dispatched *Zenas . . . and Apollos* with the letter, he had evidently not yet decided whether to send *Artemas* and *Tychicus*. He intended to do so soon, however, and to meet Titus in *Nicopolis* where they would *spend the winter*. Zenas and Artemas are not mentioned elsewhere in the NT. Thinking of the needs of these missionary travelers, Paul throws in a final comment about the need for consistent charity, the distinguishing mark of early Christians.

Concluding Salutation and Benediction, 3:15

Paul closes this letter as he did those to Timothy with concluding greetings and a benediction. Probably written earlier, this greeting is more optimistic than 2 Tim 4:9-22.

Philemon

Charles H. Cosgrove   [MCB 1263-1266]

Introduction

Paul writes to PHILEMON on behalf of Philemon's slave ONESIMUS, who has become a convert through Paul's own witness. By comparing the names in Philemon with those in Col 4:7-17, we may conclude that Philemon is a member of a house church at COLOSSAE. While PAUL addresses almost every sentence directly to Philemon, as if the letter were for him alone, he also identifies the church as recipient (along with APPHIA and ARCHIPPUS).

Date and Place of Writing

Although Paul does not state his location at the time of writing, except to indicate that he is in prison (v. 10), he probably writes from EPHESUS around 52–54 C.E. (see Harrison 1950).

The Occasion of the Letter

We know from v. 16 that Onesimus is Philemon's slave. Paul writes in order to persuade Philemon to act graciously toward Onesimus in the wake of some alleged (and unnamed) misdeed by the slave (see v. 18).

Since Paul addresses the letter not only to *Philemon* but *to the church*, he probably intends for it to be read aloud in the assembly. The CONGREGATION is supposed to "overhear" Paul's words to Philemon, which makes the slave-owner accountable not only to Paul but to them as well.

Traditionally it has been assumed that Onesimus is a fugitive slave, and interpreters have reconstructed his story more or less as follows. Once there was a slave named Onesimus who ran away from his master Philemon, and (somehow or other) came in contact with Paul, founder of the CHURCH to which Philemon belongs. Under Paul's influence Onesimus came to faith in the God of Jesus Christ and decided to do the right thing by returning to his master.

The difficulty with this reconstruction is that it fails to provide a plausible explanation of how the runaway slave happens to wind up in Paul's company. It strains credulity to think this is sheer coincidence.

Some have therefore suggested that the fugitive Onesimus grew remorseful and deliberately sought out his master's friend, Paul, in the hopes that Paul might be willing to smooth things over with Philemon. Paul nowhere indicates that Onesimus has had a change of heart about running away.

The suggestion that Onesimus intentionally went to Paul for help is, nevertheless, a step toward a better reconstruction. We should abandon the assumption, nowhere confirmed by the letter itself, that Onesimus is a fugitive slave. It happens that in Roman case law, which was widely respected even outside of ROME, there are precedents establishing the propriety of a slave seeking out a third party, usually an esteemed "friend of the master" (*amicus domini*), in order to resolve a difficulty with a master. If a slave left the household in order to speak with this third party (who may have been in another city), the slave was not considered a runaway.

It is probable that Onesimus, fearing reprisal from his master for some alleged misdeed, sought out Paul as an *amicus domini* who might mediate between him and Philemon. In that case, Paul's letter and his upcoming visit (v. 22) are actions of mediation on behalf of Onesimus.

For Further Study

In the *Mercer Dictionary of the Bible*: ONESIMUS; PAUL; PHILEMON, LETTER TO; PRISON EPISTLES; SLAVERY IN THE NT.

In other sources: J. M. G. Barclay, "Paul, Philemon, and the Dilemma of Christian Slave-Ownership," *NTS* 37 (1991): 161–86; P. N. Harrison, "Onesimus and Philemon," *ATR* 32 (1950): 268–94; John Knox, *Philemon among the Letters of Paul*; L. A. Lewis, "An African-American Appraisal of the Philemon-Paul-Onesimus Triangle," in *Stoney the Road We Trod: African-American Biblical Interpretation*, ed. Cain Hope Felder; J. B. Lightfoot, *St. Paul's Epistles to the Colossians and to Philemon*; E. Lohse, *A Commentary on the Epistles to the Colossians and to Philemon*; N. R. Petersen, *Rediscovering Paul*; B. M. Rapske, "The Prisoner Paul in the Eyes of Onesimus," *NTS* 37 (1991): 187–203.

Commentary

An Outline

I. Opening, 1-3
II. Thanksgiving, 4-7
III. Letter Body: Appeals for Onesimus,
8-22
A. First Appeal: "For Love's Sake," 8-10
B. Second Appeal: For Usefulness' Sake,
11-14

C. Third Appeal: The Rights
of Apostolic Paternity, 15-16
D. The Fourth Appeal: "Receive Him
as Me," 17-20
E. A Statement of Confidence
and Final Instructions, 21-22
IV. Closing, 23-25

Opening, 1-3

Paul, writing from PRISON (cf. vv. 9-10, 13) and naming *Timothy* as coauthor, identifies himself as a *prisoner* (δέσμιος) *of Jesus Christ*. Later in the letter he will voice his wish that Onesimus continue to serve him in the "bonds" (δεσμοῖς) of the gospel (vv. 10-13). The literal chains of Paul symbolize the metaphorical chains that bind Paul as Christ's *prisoner*. Onesimus is also in chains, namely, the metaphorical chains of (literal) slavery to Philemon—and may be clapped into literal chains upon his return. If he has been serving with Paul in the chains of the gospel, he is also, like Paul, Christ's prisoner. Thus at the very beginning of the letter Paul hints that Onesimus shares Paul's status. This hint prepares for v. 17, where Paul says, "Receive him as . . . me" (RSV).

Paul describes Philemon as "our beloved coworker." He next names *Apphia our sister*, and after her *Archippus*, "our comrade in arms." We know practically nothing about these three persons, although ARCHIPPUS appears in Col 4:17. APPHIA might be the wife of Philemon or of Archippus, if she is married to either of them. *Your house* (v. 2), in which the CHURCH meets, may be the house of Philemon or Archippus. The singular *your* would most naturally be taken with the last person named (Archippus), but it could also refer to Philemon as the one most directly addressed throughout the letter.

After naming the recipients Paul gives one of his customary liturgical greetings (v. 3).

Thanksgiving, 4-7

Paul constructs an elaborate epistolary THANKSGIVING in vv. 4-8. In the presence of those gathered to hear the reading of the letter, Paul thanks God for Philemon's many virtues. This is an example of what the Latins called a *captatio benevelentiae*. We might say that Paul "butters up" Philemon before bringing up the matter of Onesimus.

As Petersen (1985, 72) points out, the rhetorical function of the thanksgiving is to inaugurate the basic strategy of persuasion that governs the letter as a whole.

Paul's *I hear* therefore *I . . . appeal* (vv. 5, 9) means "you have refreshed the hearts of the saints with your faith and love, now refresh my heart also" (author trans.; cf. vv. 7 and 20). Philemon is about to learn how he can continue to be his virtuous self and refresh Paul's heart.

Letter Body: Appeals for Onesimus, 8-22

For analysis we can divide the body of the letter into five parts: an opening expression of apostolic authority and general introductory appeal (vv. 8-10), followed by three additional appeals (vv. 11-14, 15-16, and 17-20), a closing statement of confidence (v. 21), and an announcement of an impending visit (v. 22).

First Appeal: For Love's Sake, 8-10

"For love's sake," Paul says, he is appealing rather than commanding, but the command is rhetorically present nonetheless in two ways. First, by calling the content of his appeal "what is necessary," Paul rules out the possibility that Philemon can act honorably without doing what Paul requests. Second, as Petersen (1985, 65) rightly notes, Paul's appeals are a convention used by persons in authority (esp. royalty) to express commands. The language of request functions as a command when the one who requests has the authority to command. Paul includes a reminder of his authority in v. 8 ("Although I have the boldness in Christ to command you," author trans.) and again in v. 9, where he refers to himself by means of a term πρεσβύτης, which carries the general meaning of *old man* and the specialized technical meaning of "ambassador," which best seems to fit here. In 2 Cor 5:20 (cf. Eph 6:20) Paul uses a cognate verbal form to depict himself as God's ambassador. There, too, he describes his ambassadorial mode of discourse as *appeal*.

In v. 10 Paul discloses the purpose of his letter as an appeal for Onesimus. It becomes clear in what follows that Onesimus, whether justly or unjustly by Greco-Roman convention and law, is in trouble with Philemon. Paul does not need to point this out, nor does he anywhere in the letter dispute any complaint that Philemon may have against Onesimus. He tacitly presumes Philemon's interpretation of what has happened, and so his appeal "for my child, whom I have fathered in my chains" (author trans.) sounds initially like an appeal for mercy. The expression "for love's sake" (author trans.) in v. 9 has already prepared Philemon to hear the appeal in this way. Nevertheless, in what follows Paul progressively displaces his argument from love with arguments from usefulness and paternal apostolic rights.

There is, in fact, already a hint of these subsequent arguments when Paul says in v. 10 that he "fathered" Onesimus. This metaphor means that Paul, as apostle, converted Onesimus and now enjoys fatherly apostolic rights over him (cf. 1 Cor 4:14-15; 2 Cor 6:13; 12:14-15). Hence, in calling Onesimus his "child" Paul implicitly lays claim to Onesimus and, in effect, disputes Philemon's prior claims on Onesimus.

Second Appeal: For Usefulness' Sake, 11-14

Having hinted at his rights to Onesimus, Paul goes on in vv. 11-14 to suggest that he might retain the "use" of Onesimus. "Onesimus," a common slave name, means "useful," and it is a synonym of that word (εὔχρηστος) used in v. 11. Onesimus, Paul says, was once *useless* (ἄχρηστον) but now he is *useful* (εὔχρηστον), both to Philemon and to Paul. This is how one talked about slaves in the Greco-Roman world: as property valued for their instrumentality. Since Onesimus suggests servile identity, we should bring this out in English by calling him Useful.

Although Paul calls Useful his child, his argument from usefulness in these verses treats Useful as chattel. Even though Paul has already spoken of himself as a *prisoner*, this does not put him on the same level with Onesimus. Paul's bondage to Christ gives him considerable authority, whereas Useful's status as a slave makes him powerless.

Paul's evaluation of Useful as formerly *useless* probably expresses what he takes to be Philemon's own opinion. We don't know how or for exactly what reasons Philemon may have regarded Useful as a worthless slave. In any case, Paul adopts the perspective of the slave owner. The only question is whether the property called Useful will revert to Philemon or be retained by Paul. The decision is to be made in the interests of usefulness, not those of Useful himself.

Nevertheless, Useful is not merely property to Paul. Paul calls him *my own heart* (lit. "inward parts," the locus of deepest affection). Paul had wished to hold on to his beloved child, so that Useful might "serve" him "in the bonds of the gospel" (v. 13, author trans.). But, he says, "I didn't want to do anything without your opinion" (author trans.). The word "opinion" can mean *consent*. It is not, however, an unambiguous term for consent. By choosing this word rather than, say, "assent" or "agreement," Paul manages to be courteously deferent to Philemon without giving away the right to hold on to Useful. As he goes on to say, the reason he is sending Useful back to Philemon (along with the letter) is so that Philemon can do the right thing ("what is good") voluntarily and not by compulsion. All of this suggests that if Paul did not send Useful back, Philemon would have no choice but to accept the loss of Useful. As it now stands, he can make Paul a gift of Useful.

Third Appeal: The Rights of Apostolic Paternity, 15-16

Paul suggests that divine PROVIDENCE has separated Useful from Philemon for a time. He states the aim of this providence in terms of Philemon's and not Useful's interest. The separation is, "perhaps," so that Philemon *might have him [Useful] back forever, no longer as a slave but more than a slave, a beloved brother . . . both in the flesh and in the Lord.* As a follower of Christ, Onesimus *is* a brother, whether Philemon receives him as such or not. Do Paul's appeals oblige Philemon to give Onesimus his freedom? Paul's suggestion in vv. 15-16 clearly implies this, for brotherhood may exist in the Lord between master and slave, as Paul's letters otherwise suggest, but brotherhood cannot exist in the flesh between master and slave. To put it differently, if Paul had meant to restrict brotherhood to a "purely spiritual" plane, leaving social relations undisturbed, he should have written simply *in the Lord* and not added *in the flesh* as well. So there is scarcely any room to doubt that Paul is appealing for Useful's freedom.

Verse 16 seems therefore to undermine the argument that Paul has been building since v. 10. That argument, at least in part, treated Useful as property and focussed delicately on the question of whose property Useful really is. Verse 16 declares Useful *no longer a slave but . . . a brother*, thus effectively undercutting either Paul's or Philemon's "ownership" of Useful. Useful is no longer to be slave to Paul or Philemon. He is now *brother* to Philemon and, we can add, recalling v. 10, *child* to Paul.

The effect of Paul's rhetoric, however, is in fact to undercut all of Philemon's authority over Useful while maintaining Paul's apostolic fatherly authority over the former slave. Thus Paul comes out ahead, and Useful comes under a new patriarchal authority. Although Philemon gets his property *back forever,* his property is no longer property and he really ought to send Onesimus back to Paul.

Verses 15-16 displace the argument begun in v. 10, which treated Useful as disputed property, with an argument that treats him as a person. This implicit recognition of him as a person scarcely acknowledges that Useful has any rights in Christ. While naming Useful's new status in Christ, Paul does not make it the basis of his mandate that Philemon free Useful. In v. 16 he does not say, for example, that Philemon should receive Useful as a brother *in the Lord* and therefore also *in the flesh*. He leaves it to his hearers to construe the relationship between *in the Lord* and *in the flesh*. Later Christian readers must do the same. We must also confront the fact that in Philemon the mandate for Useful's freedom rests on Paul's authority and not on any stated principle of the gospel. It is the apostle-patriarch Paul who decides Useful's fate, and Philemon is expected to obey not because the gospel requires him to accept Useful as *a beloved brother . . . in the flesh* but because Paul does. Thus Paul acts as a kindly monarch, God's own vice-regent, and Useful is entirely dependent on Paul's paternalistic favor.

By basing Useful's fate on his own decision as father and not directly on the gospel, Paul avoids the general question of Christian slave-ownership. If that question posed a dilemma for Paul, he never treats it as such in this letter.

Fourth Appeal: "Receive Him as Me," 17-20

The fourth appeal contains the first formal imperative in the letter. Referring to the fact that he is Philemon's partner, Paul tells Philemon to receive Useful as if he were Paul himself. Now, in effect, Useful becomes Paul's ambassador and is therefore elevated above Philemon. At the same time all Useful's debts are canceled by Paul's promise (witnessed by an autograph, v. 19) to settle accounts with Philemon. Since Philemon owes Paul his own self, a fact that Paul mentions by saying he's not going to mention it, this settling of accounts really takes place in the letter itself. Paul is calling in part of the debt Philemon owes him, a debt that can, of course, never be fully paid since Philemon owes Paul everything—just as Useful now does. Thus, before any detailed calculation of Useful's debts is made, Useful is in the clear with Philemon, and Philemon and Useful are *both* hopelessly in debt to Paul.

In v. 20 Paul says that he wants to "profit in the Lord" from Philemon, a statement that recalls his "suggestion" that Philemon might grant him the "use" of Useful (vv. 11-14). Then, echoing the language of his opening thanksgiving, Paul urges Philemon to "refresh" his "heart" (again, the word is "inward parts") in Christ.

A Statement of Confidence and Final Instructions, 21-22

If there was ever any doubt that Paul's suggestions through appeal were commands requiring OBEDIENCE, v. 21 dispels it. Paul says that he is confident of Philemon's *obedience* and knows that Philemon will *do even more* than what Paul has requested.

Paul closes the body of the letter with a request that the church *prepare a guest room* for him, informing them that he intends to pay them a visit. He asks for their prayers to help make this possible. An unspoken purpose of these requests is no doubt to back up the letter with a promise of his personal apostolic presence.

Closing, 23-25

Paul concludes the letter with greetings from EPAPHRAS, MARK, Aristarchus, Demas, and LUKE. We may assume that these persons are esteemed by Philemon (and the Colossian church) and that Paul mentions them as further witnesses to Philemon's handling of the case of Useful (vv. 23-24). A liturgical blessing brings the letter to a close (v. 25).

Works Cited

Harrison, P. N. 1950. "Onesimus and Philemon," *ATR* 32:268–94.
Petersen, Norman R. 1985. *Rediscovering Paul: Philemon and the Sociology of Paul's Narrative World.*

Mercer Commentary on the Bible.
Volume 7. *Acts and Pauline Writings.*

Mercer University Press, Macon, Georgia 31210-3960.
Isbn 0-86554-512-X. Catalog and warehouse pick number: MUP/P139.
Text, interior, and cover designs, composition, and layout by Edd Rowell.
Cover illustration (*The Apostle Paul in Prison*) by Rembrandt (see p. ii, above).
Camera-ready pages composed on a Gateway 2000
    via dos WordPerfect 5.1 and WordPerfect for Windows 5.1/5.2
        and printed on a LaserMaster 1000.
Text fonts: TimesNewRomanPS 10/12; ATECH Hebrew and Greek.
Display font: TimesNewRomanPS bf and bi,
    plus University Roman titles (covers and title page).
Printed and bound by McNaughton & Gunn Inc., Saline MI 48176,
    via offset lithography on 50# Natural Offset and perfectbound into 10-pt.
        c1s stock, with 4-color-process illustration and lay-flat lamination.
[March 1997]